DEAD MEN RISEN

DEAD MEN RISEN

AN EPIC STORY OF WAR AND HEROISM IN AFGHANISTAN

TOBY HARNDEN

REGNERY
HISTORY

Cataloging-in-Publication data on file with the Library of Congress

ISBN 978-1-62157-271-8

Published in the United States by
Regnery History
An imprint of Regnery Publishing
A Salem Communications Company
300 New Jersey Avenue NW
Washington, DC 20001
www.RegneryHistory.com

Originally published in 2011 by
Quercus
55 Baker Street 7th Floor
South Block, London W1U 8EW

This is the first Regnery edition, published in 2014

Manufactured in the United States of America

10 9 8 7 6 5 4 3 2 1

Books are available in quantity for promotional or premium use. For information on discounts and terms, please visit our website: www.Regnery.com.

Distributed to the trade by
Perseus Distribution
250 West 57th Street
New York, NY 10107

Lines from "Home Front" from the collection *Laurels and Donkeys* (Clutag Press, 2010) are reprinted by kind permission of Andrew Motion.

Maps © William Donohoe

*In memory of the Welsh Guardsmen and
their comrades who did not return.*

For Cheryl, Tessa, and Miles Harnden

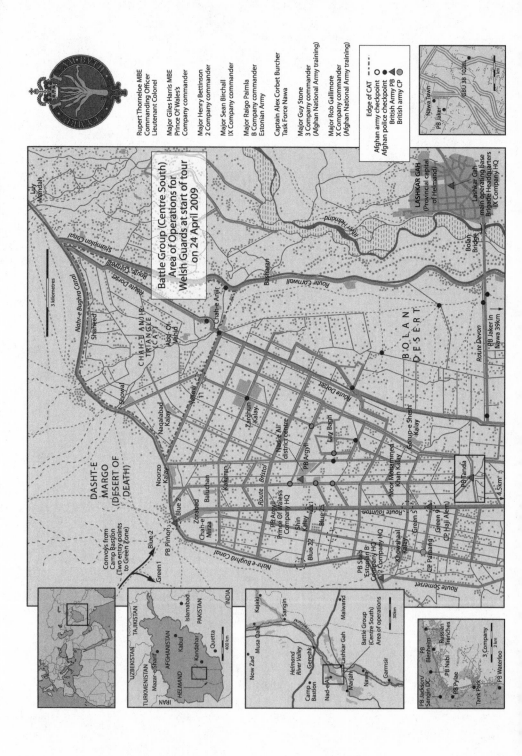

Rupert Thorneloe MBE
Commanding Officer
Lieutenant Colonel

Major Giles Harris MBE
Prince Of Wale's
Company commander

Major Henry Bettinson
2 Company commander

Major Sean Birchall
IX Company commander

Major Raigo Paimla
B Company commander
Estonian Army

Captain Alex Corbet Burcher
Task Force Nawa

Major Guy Stone
3 Company commander
(Afghan National Army training)

Major Rob Gallimore
X Company commander
(Afghan National Army training)

Edge of CAT – – –
Afghan army checkpoint ○
Afghan police checkpoint ●
British Army PB ▲
British army CP ⬤

**Battle Group (Centre South)
Area of Operations for
Welsh Guards at start of tour
on 24 April 2009**

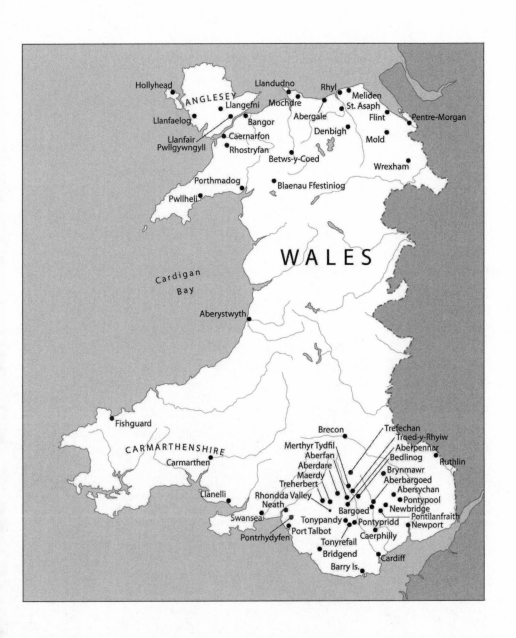

Contents

Author's Note

This book is about what it was like to fight as a Welsh Guardsman in Helmand in 2009. The account will bear little resemblance to what you will have read in the newspapers, heard politicians describe, or tried to glean from the upbeat progress reports of generals. War is chaotic and gruesome, as well as, on occasions, noble and heroic. The reader is not spared that reality.

In his history of the Irish Guards from 1914 to 1918, Rudyard Kipling wrote of the difficulties of retrieving sure facts from "the whirlpool of war." Some things that at first looked straightforward when I was on the ground in Helmand with the Welsh Guards came to appear much more complicated. Areas of near-conviction in my mind became shrouded in uncertainty.

Kipling's two-volume work included the death of his only son John, a lieutenant who perished in September 1915 at Loos, the first battle in which the Welsh Guards fought. "Men grow doubtful or oversure, and, in all good faith, give directly opposed versions," he wrote. Sifting through "the personal prejudices and misunderstandings of men under heavy strain, carrying clouded memories of orders half given or half heard, amid scenes that pass like nightmares" was, he found, a task replete with pitfalls. The more he learned, the more difficult it became to establish what really happened because "the end of laborious enquiry is too often the opening of fresh confusion."

This was my experience over the course of nearly eighteen months spent researching *Dead Men Risen*. During that time I conducted some 246 hours of audio-recorded interviews with more than 260 people, predominantly in Afghanistan, Wales, and England. Many were interviewed several times. A number of further interviews were done on a background basis with no recording. I examined 2,374 military documents made available to me and drew on other sources including letters, diaries, emails, videos, Royal Military Police reports, and the proceedings of coroners' inquests. Acknowledgments of those who assisted me appear after the main text.

As part of the required publishing agreement with the Ministry of Defence (MoD), the manuscript was submitted for review by the army. This resulted in 493 separate questions, suggestions, or requests for changes to be made, followed by protracted discussions that continued even after printing.

The narrator of Robert Louis Stevenson's *Treasure Island* sought to present "the whole particulars" of what happened "from the beginning to the end, keeping nothing back but the bearings of the island." In this case, the "bearings of the island" were those matters that could endanger the operational security of British troops. To protect the safety of those in Afghanistan and for legal reasons, a number of redactions were made at the MoD's request and appear as blacked-out passages. For reasons of personal security or privacy or at their own request, a number of people are identified only by a pseudonym. These appear as: Guardsman Ed Carew, Corporal Chris Fitzgerald, Private Wayne Gorrod, Lieutenant Piers Lowry, Trooper Jeremy Murray, Rifleman Mark Osmond, Serjeant Tom Potter, and Captain Richard Sheehan.

Dead Men Risen should be read with close reference to the maps at the start of the book and the plans of incidents that appear in the Appendix.

Following the Appendix is a list of key personnel, a chronology of events, and a glossary.

At the head of that list is the name of Lieutenant Colonel Rupert Thorneloe, who became my friend in Northern Ireland in the late 1990s, when I was a journalist and he was a military intelligence officer. After I first visited Helmand at the start of 2006, before British troops had begun to arrive, I stopped in Kabul on my way home. I went to the bleak, snow-covered British Cemetery, where crumbling tombstones recalled the men who had fought for Queen and Empire in Afghanistan only to be, in the words of Kipling, "left on Afghanistan's plains" to go to their "Gawd like a soldier." Days earlier in Helmand, an American development official had predicted to me that British troops would "get hit on the roads" while an Afghan warlord told me that some still sought vengeance for the wars of the nineteenth century. Soon, I reflected in print, there would be new memorials for those from another generation of courageous Britons who would be cut down by the Pashtuns. When I went to the cemetery again in early 2010, Rupert Thorneloe's name had just been carved on a marble tablet. By September 2014, a total of 453 British troops had been killed in Afghanistan since 2002.

Nothing in these pages is intended to pass judgment on any of those who fought in Helmand. War is messy and frightening. Rare is the soldier throughout history who ever possessed all the information needed to make the right decision, the optimum plan, or all the equipment desired to carry out that plan. For most troops in Helmand, facing each new day required an act of bravery to function despite the knowledge that it might well be their last. They gave their all and did what they thought was right. When they returned, their loved ones welcomed back a different person.

This is a story of the Welsh Guards, of the British Army, and of Afghanistan. It has been a privilege, as well as a heavy responsibility, to be able to tell it.

Prologue

Sweat streaked the grime on Lieutenant Colonel Rupert Thorneloe's face as he lay flat on his stomach on the dusty track beside the Shamalan Canal. Gently he prodded the baked mud in front of him with a bayonet, checking to see if the Taliban had buried an improvised explosive device (IED) there. In the searing early afternoon heat, the commanding officer of the Welsh Guards was doing the most stomach-churning and thankless task in Afghanistan. One slip and he could be blown to smithereens. Even worse, a failure to find what had caused the beeping on his Vallon metal detector might cause the deaths of others in the long convoy behind him. Thorneloe was meticulous and almost obsessively rigorous in all he did. He checked everything, thought through each eventuality, and left nothing to chance. He was taking a long time to make sure that there was no bomb in this tiny patch of Helmand.

Scouring a road for IEDs was normally the job of the lowliest guardsman, but Thorneloe would never order a man to do something he would not do himself. He drove his men very hard but himself much harder; he believed in leading from the front and by example. Just short of forty, Thorneloe was destined to be a general and perhaps to run the army one day. He had been the defense secretary's military assistant, an influential appointment at the heart of Whitehall, as the government wrestled with how to wage war in Afghanistan. Now he was there, commanding his regiment in battle.

Six days earlier, on June 25, 2009, the Welsh Guards had begun to fight their way up the track beside the Shamalan, designated as Route Cornwall, in an attempt to seal the canal as part of Operation Panther's Claw, or "Panchai Palang" in Pashto. The operation involved more than three thousand troops. Already it was being trumpeted by the beleaguered British government and eager army spokesmen as a decisive offensive that would remove the few remaining Taliban strongholds and make Helmand safe for elections the following month.

Thorneloe had been intensely skeptical about Panther's Claw, fearing it would be yet another big push by yet another brigade that would clear an area the British had too few troops to occupy afterward. He worried that once the headlines proclaiming victory had faded away, the Taliban would return and carry on fighting and intimidating. He knew his battle group of 1,300 men was overstretched and wanted to concentrate them in the parts of Nad-e Ali district that had already been cleared and were now in the balance. Panther's Claw might look impressive on a map back in London, but for Thorneloe it made more strategic sense to deepen the precarious influence of NATO's ISAF (International Security Assistance Force) troops and the Kabul government in territory they already occupied.

He had fretted about the ground beside the Shamalan, on which he was now prostrate, clashing with brigade staff about what he viewed as inadequate reconnaissance. In his ten weeks in Helmand, he had pleaded for more men and more equipment. During the planning of Panther's Claw, he had argued for troops to be dropped close to the canal by helicopter, but it was judged too dangerous. Sure enough, Route Cornwall had proved more isolated and exposed than the planners had assumed. Furthermore, it was crumbling under the weight of vehicles trundling up and down. Two days earlier, a Viking armored track vehicle had toppled into the canal and trapped seven Welsh Guardsmen inside, as their compartment rapidly flooded with water. Two were unconscious and had turned blue by the time the rear door was forced open, but they were resuscitated and survived.

Once the euphoria over the lifesaving heroics had subsided, however, many of the remaining guardsmen were left almost paralyzed with fear. The Vikings, they said, were coffins on tracks. Soldiers were threatening to refuse to get back into one. Young men were vomiting before patrols. Some had been evacuated because of battle shock. Route Cornwall was at the top of an embankment some 2.5 meters above the water and vulnerable to small-arms and rocket-propelled grenade (RPG) fire. Every extra minute that Thorneloe and the other Welsh Guardsmen spent looking for an IED made such an attack more likely. IED blasts had disabled some vehicles; others, driven beyond their limit, had broken down. The narrow track had been repeatedly blocked, stalling convoys and leaving them vulnerable to ambush. Thorneloe knew he simply did not have enough men. More troops would have enabled him to oversee most of the seven kilometers of the canal. With his men spread too thin, the Taliban had been able to slip into the gaps and plant their deadly IEDs. The shallowness of the canal meant that the Taliban, clutching walkie-talkies and even carrying motorcycles, were able to wade across and outflank the Welsh Guards almost at will.

In battle, loss of momentum can be militarily disastrous. Thorneloe wanted to witness the battle on the Shamalan and gird his men for a renewed push up the canal. With helicopters in very short supply—the previous month he had complained to the Brigade that "we all know there are not enough"— Thorneloe knew he would have to travel by vehicle and that it would be dangerous. He had decided to spend the next ten days commanding his men from the front, and to get there he was riding in an eighteen-vehicle logistics convoy. To assess the terrain and stop the growing sense of dread taking root among young guardsmen, he deliberately chose to ride "top cover": standing with his legs inside the Viking and manning a machine gun. In addition, his decision to be a member of the "Barma" team meant that he was in the lead vehicle of the convoy, given the call sign of 32A, and codenamed "Exorcist."

Operation Barma was the name randomly selected by a Ministry of Defense (MoD) computer to describe what Thorneloe was now doing—using a metal detector to search for IEDs and to dig down to check any suspicious areas. The British Army loves to create new words for new situations, and so "to Barma" entered its lexicon. It had become an iconic image of the war in Helmand—the lonely soldier moving ahead, sweeping from side to side, knowing that he might lose his legs or be killed in the next instant. Now that the Taliban were using "low metal content" IEDs, fitted with graphite rather than metal connectors, it didn't even take a mistake to die.

"I'll go top cover," Thorneloe announced on the morning the convoy set off to a surprised Lance Corporal Kingsley Simmons, who was commanding the Barma team that would ride in the lead Viking. Simmons, broad-shouldered and with a ready smile, was a Coldstream Guardsman from Leeds who had volunteered to serve with the Welsh Guards after a divorce and a demotion for going AWOL (absent without leave) left him needing the money. A veteran of one Afghanistan tour and no longer burdened with the reputation for drinking and fighting he'd earned with the Coldstreams, he carried himself with an easy authority that impressed the Welsh Guards. Some were trying to persuade him to join them permanently.

Progress through Helmand was agonizingly slow. In April, when the Welsh Guards had arrived, it was possible to drive around most of the battle group's 160-square-kilometer area of operations in a lightly armored vehicle within a day. Now, with the IED threat increasing exponentially, it could take a dozen hours to move just a few miles—or even days if a vehicle was blown up and stuck. The air conditioning in the Vikings never worked properly, so it was like a sauna for the four who sat inside. They breathed in the white dust, so fine it was like talcum powder, while Thorneloe scanned the fields. This was the Green Zone, the name given to the verdant Helmand River valley crisscrossed with irrigation canals funded by the Americans in the decades between the Second World War and the Soviet invasion of 1979.

From the cab of his supply truck, the sixth vehicle in the convoy, Color Sergeant Dai Matthews was also surveying the landscape. On each side, he could see fields of wheat and maize and the parched brown expanses that marked the recent opium harvest. The Welsh Guards did not touch the illegal crop—they reasoned that the people could not be won over if they lost their livelihood. Matthews was a stocky, graying veteran with a jovial manner who had rejoined the Welsh Guards for the Helmand tour after his South Wales concrete business went bust. Convoys made him nervous. It was not really the IED threat. He had long since ceased to worry about that, knowing that if his vehicle hit one he would be dead. There wasn't even a windscreen in his truck, never mind any armor. What disconcerted him more was that everywhere they went, people stared. It was as if members of an ancient civilization were gazing at spaceships, he thought. He sometimes felt as if he was looking at the Middle Ages. On one occasion, he saw a man in a *kurta*—a traditional knee-length loose shirt—wielding a curved sword. In front of him, a small boy sat in a tin tub brimming with bloody water. His father had been performing a circumcision. The other concern about all those who watched in silence from the roadside was that some were helping the Taliban, using walkie-talkies, smoke signals, or even kites to signal that British troops were approaching.

After dropping off stores at the Yellow 14 compound at the base of the Shamalan Canal, the convoy moved north and was halted by Corporal Kevin Williams, commanding the lead Viking, north of XP (crossing point) 10. Williams had been a central figure in the rescue of the seven Welsh Guardsmen from the canal. Trooper Gaz Owen, his driver, had a sixth sense that the stretch of road ahead was "dodgy." To the left-hand side, there was a typical Afghan brown-mud compound, home to an extended family, surrounded by a low wall. Bushes and overhanging trees provided potential cover for the Taliban and threw shadows onto the track. To the east lay a lush green cornfield shimmering in the hundred-degree heat, and beyond that stretched a line of pomegranate trees.

It was just the kind of place where the Taliban would lay an IED. Corporal Simmons and his Barma team of Trooper Josh Hammond and Guardsmen Joe Penlington, Craig Harrison, and Nathan Chambers jumped out. Thorneloe dropped down from his top cover position onto the road and told Simmons that he wanted to Barma. "Are you sure, sir?" Simmons asked the colonel, who responded with a crisp: "Yep, I'll do it."

Simmons told Penlington to get back into the Viking and take over top cover. That morning, Penlington had been given the option by Simmons of remaining back at the base so that Thorneloe could replace him. The young soldier from Mold in North Wales had decided to give another gunner a chance to stay back, so he challenged Guardsman Joe Lloyd to a game of "rock, paper, scissors." Penlington chose scissors, Lloyd went for rock, so it was Penlington who went out on patrol.

Hammond had started his tour in the company operations room in the sprawling desert base of Camp Bastion in the Dasht-e Margo and had been anxious to get out on the ground. When another trooper, complaining about the weight of kit and a sore knee, made it clear he wanted out of the Vikings,

Hammond, only eighteen, volunteered to take his place. The heavily built Chambers, twenty-four, from Aberpennar, had been due to leave the army on July 4 to become a crane driver. He opted instead to extend his service because he didn't want to let his friends down.

Thorneloe and Hammond took their places in the Barma team as "hedgerow men," out front on the flanks. Harrison and Chambers were behind while Simmons directed from the rear. The idea was for the arcs of each metal detector to overlap so that no patch of ground was missed. The four experienced Barma men had been together several weeks and were well practiced. They had developed a feel for the ground, and when they saw it was baked solid, they knew it unlikely that an IED had been dug in there. With Thorneloe, it was different. Every time his metal detector beeped, he was down on his belt buckle digging to make sure there was nothing there. He was so industrious that he had worn out his mine-prodder and taken Simmons's bayonet instead. The others in the team didn't mind. It was a rule among them that each Barma man should proceed at his own pace, just as a driver or vehicle commander who felt dubious about the route for any reason could halt for the ground ahead to be swept.

During the Barmaing, Corporal Williams relayed to Thorneloe a radio message from further up the canal that army divers had recovered sensitive electronic jamming equipment and weapons from the submerged Viking lost two days before. A relieved Thorneloe received the news with a big smile. "Good stuff!" he said. It took more than an hour to clear the fifty meters or so in front of the lead Viking, as Thorneloe carried out six confirmation digs but found nothing. The road farther ahead was judged to be clear because other armored vehicles had passed through earlier in the day. Neither Williams nor Thorneloe was aware that just over four hours earlier an IED had exploded underneath a Mastiff armored vehicle on this same route.

They were also unaware that after the previous convoy's safe passage, the Taliban had crept up and attached a battery pack to an IED already buried in the road. Whether the slow Barmaing gave the Taliban notice that a convoy was about to roll north and time to arm the device will never be known.

Looking at his breathless, perspiration-stained commanding officer, Simmons asked Thorneloe if he'd like to take a break from top-cover duty. "No, no—I'm fine, I'll jump up," said Thorneloe, who prompted chuckles as he squeezed through Penlington's legs to take up position. Simmons, sitting in the rear left seat next to Chambers, mopped his brow and took a few drags of a cigarette as the Viking moved off. Penlington was between Chambers and Hammond, who was on the front left. Thorneloe was standing between the front two with his knees at their eye level.

Simmons finished his cigarette and told the others to put their helmets back on. At 3:18 p.m., when they'd travelled eight hundred meters or so, there was a massive explosion beneath the Viking. Simmons, who had not yet put his seatbelt on, was thrown into the air, his helmet smashing into the roof. The heavy ceramic plate from his Osprey body armor slid up and crunched into his jaw. Opposite him, Harrison was also smacked in the lip by his plate. Everything happened as if in slow motion. Penlington saw a blinding flash of light as the blast ripped into him, fracturing his back and pelvis. Chambers, next to him, cried out as his right leg was peppered with tiny fragments of shrapnel.

"What the f--- was that?" bellowed Simmons. Then the smell hit his nostrils—fertilizer-based explosive and diesel; dust mixed with blood and scraps of flesh. It was the stench of death.

Cymru Am Byth
("Wales Forever")

*The great thing is that they were all Welshmen. Most came from
the same village. If somebody was left behind wounded everybody
would volunteer to go and get him, even under fire.*

—*Brigadier Sir Alexander Stanier, Bt., DSO, & Bar, MC,
recalling the Welsh Guards at Arras in 1917*[1]

---

*We were pink-faced rugby players from Welsh Wales, the land
of grass-topped mountains, pits and steelworks. Very few of us
had ever been further afield than Porthcawl.... We were WELSH
GUARDSMEN and the Germans will remember us even if
nobody else does. Cymru Am Byth.*

—*Guardsman Bill Williams 36, former miner,
recalling his service in 1939–45*

T he Afghan tribal elders, sitting cross-legged beneath the camouflage net
shielding them from the sun, were unconvinced. They stared impassively
at the Welsh Guards officer before them. "We're glad you've come here,"
said one Afghan with a flowing white beard. "But the trouble is, you won't
stay. You're the note-takers. You come here, you talk and you write in your
notebooks. And then you leave."

Captain Terry Harman, a snowy-haired veteran with a broken nose and
rough-hewn features, was forty-five and looked a decade older. He had
encountered skepticism before. What was unusual was the open hostility of
one of the younger attendees at the *shura*, a consultative council, next to the
Shamalan Canal. Harman had spent the previous week battling up the track

beside the waterway to reach this compound overlooking what had been designated XP-7. He suspected that the dark-bearded man in a black *kurta* had been among the Taliban who had been trying so hard to kill him. "I come from Wales," Harman told him through his Afghan translator, whom he'd nicknamed "Dai." "In Wales, a man is a man when he shakes hands. And the way a man shakes your hand lets you know if he's genuine or not. I believe this is also the Pashtun way."

Harman's goading reference to Pashtun culture infuriated the dark-bearded Afghan, who stood up and began talking rapidly and gesticulating. Harman was a former regimental sergeant major, who had spent twenty-three years in the British Army and risen through the ranks. Five years earlier, he had witnessed similar confrontations in southern Iraq. He needed to defuse the situation and demonstrate that he could be trusted, that he was more than just another note-taker. "I am not English, I am Welsh, and I am certainly not American," he said, in Welsh, to establish the fact that he was different. "I am a man of many talents who can speak many languages. I respect your culture. My life in Wales is similar to yours. My name is Terry Joseph Harman, after my father. My sons are called Kieron Joseph Harman, after myself and my uncle, and Kyle Floyd Harman, after my father. When I go out, my wife checks I am correctly dressed and that I have got money in my pocket. She walks behind me, because I am the man." He was trying to use his Welshness, and a dash of poetic license about the similarities between Celtic and Afghan customs, to establish a bond with the Pashtun elders.

A week later, Harman called for another *shura*. To his surprise, the black-bearded man returned and shook his hand. "I respect you, old man," he said. "I understand what you are trying to say."

Harman had grown up in the old slate-mining village of Talysarm in North Wales. He was raised as a Welsh speaker and did not learn English properly until he joined the army. The family was poor and one of his earliest memories was going to school feeling proud that he had a new pair of shoes and a jumper that his mother had bought him at a jumble sale the previous day. Soon after, a friend came up and told him: "You're wearing my shoes." In 1983, when he was twenty, Harman left his job on a farm and caught the mail train from Bangor to London, bound for the army. It might as well have been a thousand miles away. At Waterloo Station, a tramp came around and the young Welshman fumbled in his wallet for some coins he'd put in a pouch. He had £15 in his pocket, given to him by an aunt. The tramp stole it, and

Harman arrived late at the Pirbright recruiting depot and was sent to the guardroom by an unimpressed training sergeant.

After rising to become a company sergeant major at Sandhurst and then regimental sergeant major of the Welsh Guards, he was commissioned in 2005. Harman was a restless dynamo of a man who did everything with gusto and at maximum speed. He led through sheer force of character and example, giving everything his all. There was something uniquely Welsh about Harman, an emotionalism and kindness that endeared him to the young guardsmen still pining for what the Pontypridd singer Tom Jones immortalized as "the green, green grass of home."

No other Household Division regiment, and very few in the entire army, recruits from so small an area as the Welsh Guards. More than 95 percent of its recruits are drawn from Wales, a third of the size of Helmand yet home to three times as many people. The Scots Guards and the Irish Guards recruit heavily from the North of England, diluting their Celtic nature. Many Welsh Guards recruits come from North Wales and are native speakers of Welsh, a tongue they sometimes use to confuse the enemy (and occasionally their officers), as well as to establish a connection with those suspicious of the English, as in Harman's case. North Walians, often hailing from places like Porthmadog, Llanfaelog, and Blaenau Ffestiniog, are referred to as "Gogs," from the Welsh *gogledd*, meaning "north." There are also jokes about them being "tree frogs" or "cave dwellers" who have accents like Russian porn stars. The Welsh speakers from the north respond that the South Walians are stupid pit ponies or half-breeds from cities like Cardiff and Swansea who can't even speak the language of their forefathers. Banter aside, however, the Welsh Guards are all part of the same brotherhood, whether from Caernarfon, Porthmadog, or the Isle of Anglesey in the north or Llanelli, Bridgend, or the Rhondda Valley in the south. That goes for the few outsiders as well. Even some of the dozen or so Fijians in the regiment have Welsh accents and loyalties to the north or south.

There are so many in the Welsh Guards called Jones, Davies, Williams, Evans, Thomas, Roberts, Parry, Edwards, Morgan, or Griffiths that they have to be identified by their surname and "last two"—the last two digits of their service number. There were twenty-five Welsh guardsmen in Helmand called Jones—a company sergeant major, a sergeant, four lance sergeants, five lance corporals, and fourteen guardsmen. It had always been like this. During the First World War, fifty-six Joneses in the Welsh Guards lost their lives, while thirty-seven Joneses perished in the Second World War. The surname and "last two" are often shortened to just the two numbers—partly for brevity, partly because it allows an easy friendliness across ranks without risking overfamiliarity. Thus, anyone looking for Guardsman Carl Thomas 08 just asks for "Oh Eight," while Sergeant Matthew Davies is known as "Ninety-Six" and Company Quartermaster Sergeant Eifion Griffiths answers to "Fifty." Anyone who has seen the film *Zulu* will remember it: the South Wales Borderers had a similar system.

The numbers are very personal—turning into nicknames and featuring in email addresses and even tattoos. Lance Corporal Jamie Evans 15 is known as "Fift," short for "Fifteen." After he was seriously wounded in Helmand, a Jackal desert patrol vehicle was stenciled with the name "Big Fift" in his honor. But the "last two" monikers can get complicated. An officer calling out for "Fifty-Three" could find Regimental Quartermaster Sergeant Dorian Thomas 53, Lance Sergeant Gareth Jones 53, or Lance Sergeant Gavin Evans 53 responding. A soldier with the misfortune to have "00" at the end of his service number is liable to be called "f--- all" unless, like Sergeant Matt Parry 700 (known as "Seven Hundred"), he might thump you in return. Warrant Officer (Class Two) John Williams rejoined the Welsh Guards in 2009 and was given a new service number ending in sixty-five. He should have been "Williams 65," but he had spent twenty-two years with a different service number, so everyone still calls him "Fifty-Four"; in Welsh Guards documents, there was a compromise with "Williams 65 was 54." Then there are spin-off nicknames. When more than one Williams happened to have the "last two" of "05," each was known by his "last three" to differentiate between them. Ever since then, Sergeant Carl Williams 205 has been dubbed "Peugeot." Lance Sergeant Leon Peek is sometimes called "Eighteen" because half of his right ear was bitten off in a fight, leaving him with an "ear and a half'"—or 18 months. The one nickname you will never find in the Welsh Guards is the one that any Welshman in an English regiment will almost inevitably have to endure—"Taff."

Wales has often lagged behind the rest of Britain economically, and so many Welshmen have joined the Welsh Guards to escape unemployment or dead-end jobs. A desire to avoid working "down the pit" used to be a common reason for joining up. The horrors of war were one thing, but some felt they had experienced worse underground in Wales.

Back in the 1930s, Edward Edwards 14 from Pontrhydyfen enlisted after spending nearly three hours trying to dig out a friend buried alive by rock in a mining accident. "I never forgot his face and vowed I would never work in a mine again," he later remembered. "He was the second man killed that week in the nine-foot area. Willie Rees had been married only six weeks. Thus my mind was made to join the Welsh Guards." Edwards 14 became the regimental sergeant major, the senior noncommissioned officer in the Welsh Guards, in 1958.

John Williams "65 was 54" hailed from Aberfan in South Wales, where, in October 1966, a colliery slag heap collapsed onto homes and a school, killing 116 children and twenty-eight adults. Williams, aged nine, had stayed at home because he was sick. Among those killed were his best friend, his best friend's sister, and several cousins. "It wiped out our generation really," he says. "There was not a great deal going on there anyway with all the pits closing and the village was never the same after that." So in 1975, Williams and two friends from Aberfan went to the recruiting office and joined the Welsh Guards.

Then, as now, some choose the Welsh Guards for fear of ending up in prison. A handful have come close to both, escaping custodial sentences for "grievous bodily harm" and the like after the Welsh courts were content to accept the testimony of their officers that their offenses were out of character. In 2009, this included Lance Sergeant Leon Peek, who proved himself again and again in battle as a ferocious soldier and inspirational leader but was forever in trouble back home. While in Helmand, Peek was facing a court appearance on a charge of wounding after an incident in South Wales two days before he left Britain. It was the seventh time he'd been arrested during his seven years in uniform, this time the result of a drunken brawl during which he'd flung a woman down the stairs in a nightclub after she had jumped on his back.

Bad behavior as a guardsman was not necessarily a bar to later advancement or even promotion to officer. Nicky Mott 84 was twice demoted from lance corporal to guardsman for serious misdeeds, including the notable occasion when he shot at a group of chefs with an air gun. On his wedding day, he donned a lance corporal's uniform even though he had been demoted, as his mother was so proud of him that he couldn't tell her the truth. His brother, Guardsman Johnny Mott 38, who was also frequently in trouble, had to be smuggled out of the Colchester detention center so that he could perform his duties as best man. He had been serving a six-month sentence for fighting in a bar when stationed in Germany, another fact that was unknown to Mrs. Mott. Both Motts, and their better-behaved elder brother Bill Mott 88, rose to regimental sergeant major (though none served in that post within the Welsh Guards, partly, some suspect, because they were Englishmen, from Ellesmere Port). By 2009, Mott 84 was Major Nicky Mott, the quartermaster, in Helmand, and Mott 88 was Garrison Sergeant Major of London District, in charge of all ceremonial matters across the army, including the repatriations and funerals of those killed in action.

The Welsh Guards officers in Helmand were of mostly Anglo-Saxon stock and drawn mainly from England's public schools. Occasionally, the officers' mess is referred to as the "Foreign Legion." Major Alex Corbet Burcher explains: "Some people say that we are all toffs. Fine. But I came from a public school and people that went to public school are my common ground. And therefore I will go to a place where I feel most at home, and the Guards is it."

Yet these well-bred sons of the shires, educated at the Royal Military Academy Sandhurst and before that at Eton, Radley, Oundle, and Charterhouse, usually bonded fairly naturally with men from the Welsh villages. Not without reason, the Guards regiments are regarded as among the last unadulterated relics of the British class system. "Sometimes you hear the boys say: 'Oh, he's not a proper officer because he doesn't speak with that cut-glass English accent,'" says Captain Tom Spencer-Smith, a Welshman who speaks perfect Queen's English and commanded the Reconnaissance Platoon, known as the Recce Platoon, in Helmand. "They are mortified when somebody doesn't speak like that. They think it doesn't count. When I heard that, it was rather touching actually. That is how they expect their officers to be."

In non-Guards regiments, officers are more familiar with their soldiers, sometimes using their first names. Lieutenant Dave Harris, a Prince of Wales's Company platoon commander, remembers Guardsman Craig Jones 23 asking him in a pub in Aldershot after a few beers: "What's your first name? We can't be out on the piss together and I don't know your first name." Before Harris could say anything, Lance Sergeant Milo Bjegovic ended the subject by curtly telling the young guardsman: "His first name is Sir."

Major Alex Corbet Burcher argues that it is the class difference between officers and men that makes things function. "It works well because we are from two totally different worlds which have absolutely no danger whatsoever of threatening each other," he says. "If you try to have an affinity with the Guardsmen and try to pretend you are one of them, they will find it strange, so will you and so will other people. You are effectively just encroaching on their territory." It is a relationship, he believes, that has changed little since the Duke of Wellington's time. "Guys from honourable working-class families join the Army because they like the adventure, or the alternative is crime and a fairly mundane life in Wales. I'd say there were more criminals in Wellington's army, but we are hardly full of saints in the current army. I've been to court a number of times and not for myself."

He feels that Guardsmen probably think officers are clueless because they didn't know what garage music was or couldn't name the Cardiff football team, but that was beside the point. "Secretly, I think, they respect us because when it really matters, we take responsibility for them and look after them." Being a Welsh Guards officer "is my impression of what being a father is like," he reflects. "Love, but in a different way. Which is why, I suppose, you get some commanding officers when they are saying goodbye to their battalions, they start crying."

Guardsman Chris Davis 51, from Bridgend, says: "In the Guards, you kind of expect the officers to be quite posh and well off. But out on operations when they become a little bit more like a friend really you can relax and rip the piss out of them and you don't really notice. The odd one can be a little bit stuck up and puts you off but they're the exceptions." Even a young platoon commander fresh from university, he says, can win respect quickly. "If they're fair about things and switched on without being arrogant with it then the boys will look up to them."

In the Welsh Guards, the gap between the English-born officer class and the Welsh other ranks is bridged by the "Late Entry" officers. They have all progressed through the ranks right up to regimental sergeant major before being commissioned in their forties. In Helmand, these included Major Martyn Miles, the battle group logistics officer, Major Nicky Mott, the quartermaster, and Captain Terry Harman, influence officer with 2 Company. All three had managed to build up an easy rapport on promotion with their new contemporaries, many of whom were twenty years their junior. Miles, aged forty-nine, Mott, aged forty-six, and Harman had close to a century of service between them. Together, they represented the institutional backbone of the Welsh Guards in Helmand.

The Welsh Guards is the most junior of the five Foot Guards regiments. All five share the same structure. There are two ranks unique to the Guards: a private is a guardsman; and a corporal is a lance sergeant, who wears three stripes and eats in the warrant officers' and sergeants' mess. The three most senior Regiments of Foot were born from the English Civil War; they came from both sides of the internecine conflict as part of an effort at national reconciliation. The Scots Guards traces its ancestry to Charles I's Royal Guard, raised in 1642 to suppress the Irish Rebellion. The Coldstream Guards was originally "Monck's Regiment of Foot," founded in 1650 and part of Oliver Cromwell's New Model Army. The Grenadier Guards can date its origins to 1656 when Charles Stuart, who became King Charles II after his Restoration in 1660, inspected four hundred loyal troops near Bruges.[2] The Irish Guards was created by order of Queen Victoria in 1900 during the Boer War "to commemorate the bravery shown by the Irish Regiments during the operations in South Africa," one of the nastier imperial engagements. But the decision also owed something to the need to draw Ireland closer; only a few years later, civil war would split the island.

It wasn't until the outbreak of the First World War that David Lloyd George, chancellor of the Exchequer and a Welshman, suggested raising a Welsh regiment to help provide the troops needed by Lord Kitchener, secretary of state for War. Kitchener himself was highly skeptical. There was a prejudice against the British Army in South Wales mining communities, fueled by nonconformist ministers, after troops had been used to intervene in miners' strikes. The suspicion was mutual. Nonconformist ministers were banned from becoming chaplains in Welsh regiments until Lloyd George's intervention, and the Welsh language was viewed as potentially seditious.

In 1914, Lloyd George, whose first language was Welsh, had confronted Kitchener when he learned that men of the Denbighshire Yeomanry had been forbidden to speak Welsh. Kitchener told Prime Minister Herbert Asquith that "no purely Welsh regiment is to be trusted: they are always wild and insubordinate and ought to be stiffened by a strong infusion of English and Scotch." King George V, however, took a personal interest in the matter of raising a Welsh Regiment of the Foot Guards, and when the monarch suggested this would be a "good thing," Kitchener interpreted the sentiment as a direct order. On February 6, 1915, Kitchener told Major General Sir Francis Lloyd, commanding London Division: "You have got to raise a regiment of Welsh Guards." When General Lloyd expressed concern about the "great many difficulties" of doing this and asked for a timescale, Kitchener responded abruptly: "Immediately." General Lloyd replied: "Very well, sir, they shall go on guard on St. David's Day"—March 1. The Welsh Guards were duly created by royal warrant on February 26 and three days later mounted the King's Guard at Buckingham Palace, just as General Lloyd had promised Kitchener.[3]

In 1915, Welshmen in the ranks of the other four Guards regiments were transferred to the Welsh Guards. After several months of parade ground-training and public duties at Buckingham Palace, the new regiment went to war. On August 17, 1915, its men departed from Waterloo Station bound for Le Havre to join the newly formed Guards Division on the western front. Lieutenant Colonel William Murray Threipland, a Boer War veteran who had transferred from the Grenadier Guards, led the Welsh Guards in action for the first time in the attack on Hill 70 at the Battle of Loos on September 27, 1915. Private R. Smith—the rank of guardsman replaced that of private in 1919—wrote that the duties outside Buckingham Palace had enhanced their fighting skills. "On we went, shells and bullets and shrapnel falling all around us but not a man wavered: you would have thought we were on parade at Wellington barracks."[4]

The Welsh Guards went on to fight in the trenches at the Somme and Ypres. Brigadier Sir Alexander Stanier, who joined the regiment fresh from Eton in 1917 as a second lieutenant, noted that "the Welsh Guards had particularly good trenches, probably because many of them had been miners."[5] Their language was also an advantage, he recalled: "The Germans eventually perfected a listening device on the telephone lines, but the Welsh Guards countered this by speaking in Welsh." (During the Second World War, Welsh speakers were put into Welsh Guards signal companies for the same reason.) By the time the First World War was over, 856 of the 3,853 Welsh Guardsmen who served overseas had been killed, and 1,755 wounded. Only thirteen of the original troops who had set off from Waterloo Station in August 1915 returned to Britain unscathed.

In the Second World War, the regiment had three active battalions and fought across Europe and in North Africa. With an average age of twenty-five by 1943,[6] a large proportion of the Welsh Guardsmen were professional soldiers and many others had served in the police. The 1st and 2nd Battalions both played important roles in delaying the German forces that were sweeping across France in May 1940, enabling nearly 340,000 Allied troops to be evacuated from Dunkirk. The 2nd Battalion defended Boulogne after being ordered to fight "to the last man and the last round," and many of them were left behind as the last vessels sailed. During the Dunkirk evacuation, seventy-two Welsh Guardsmen were killed in action, and 453 were captured. Guardsman Frank Abrams of Penarth recalled the parade-ground discipline amid the sounds of shells exploding and Stuka dive-bombers overhead.[7] "All hell was breaking loose but we were Welsh Guards. We formed up as though on a barrack square. And we marched down the beach."[8]

The regiment's 3rd Battalion was raised in October 1941, at first to supply reinforcements for the rest of the other battalions. In February 1943, it departed for North Africa and sustained heavy losses at Fondouk before moving to Italy, where it fought at Monte Cerasola, Monte Piccolo, and Monte Battaglia. The 1st and 2nd Battalions crossed into France once again in June 1944, landing at Arromanches as part of the Guards Armoured Division. The 1st Battalion was an infantry element, while the 2nd Battalion, rearranged from companies into squadrons, had been retrained for an armored role in Cromwell tanks. Together they formed a Welsh Guards Battle Group and in September 1944 were the first to liberate Brussels, where one Welshman was injured when hit by a wine bottle thrown by an overenthusiastic well-wisher. Both battalions later fought at the Battle of Hechtel, and by the end of the Second World War, the regiment had lost 469 men, with 1,404 wounded.

In 2009, as in 1915, a Welsh Guard's loyalty to his company (about 150 men) was deeply ingrained. The inter-company rugby competition, the "300 Cup" (named after John Williams 300, a former Welsh Guardsman), was especially fierce. The regiment normally had three rifle companies, each with its own distinct identity. Men were once allocated to a company based on height. The Prince of Wales Company had the six-footers, and its guardsmen had been allowed an extra ration of jam because they were believed to require extra sustenance. The cost of the extra jam is said to have been taken from the salaries of the Prince of Wales Company officers. The "Jam Boys," as they have been known ever since, are swaggering, perhaps overconfident, and tend to complain volubly when things get a little difficult. Even today, the Prince of Wales Company likes to take the taller guardsmen. In Helmand, Lance

Corporal Bradley Watkin-Bennett, at six feet, six inches, the tallest man in the battalion, was a Jam Boy.

Traditionally, those under five feet, seven inches, would find themselves in 3 Company. Their nickname "the Little Iron Men" is believed by some to have been earned from an incident near Monte Cassino in 1944, when the Royal Engineers were attempting to set up a floating bridge under fire. According to this tale, men from 3 Company came to the rescue and used their stocky frames to help support the structure and were hailed as "the Little Iron Men" afterwards. Others, however, date the nickname to as early as 1940 with its origin obscure. Although 2 Company has a less defined reputation, it is often the dark horse among the three infantry companies, winning inter-battalion competitions and displaying stoic, but often unsung, heroism in battle. Its motto refers to its "Men of the Island of the Mighty"— Anglesey—and it has always been associated with North Wales.

For the Helmand tour of 2009, there were initially three main companies in the Welsh Guards 1st Battalion. The Welsh Guards had not had a 2nd Battalion since just after the Second World War. Just before the Helmand tour, however, there was suddenly a need for two extra companies. Thorneloe decided that two companies from the old 2nd Battalion would be resurrected, 9 and 10 Companies, and that roman numerals should be used to denote their antiquity. Thus, 1 and 2 Companies of the old 2nd Battalion became IX and X Companies and temporary additions to the 1st Battalion for the duration of the Helmand tour. IX Company was manned at full strength mainly by men on loan from the three existing Welsh Guards companies. X Company comprised just a handful of Welsh Guardsmen among forty British soldiers and fought with the Afghan army to the south of the Welsh Guards Battle Group.

A tremendous spirit of pride emerged within the resurrected IX Company. No one is quite sure who first thought of using the phrase "dead men risen," but Major Sean Birchall, the company commander, was soon using it to refer to his troops. The words evoked IX Company as the reincarnation of the Welsh Guardsmen of the 2nd Battalion who had fought through the *bocage* of Normandy in terrain similar to Helmand as part of the Guards Armoured Division. The official motto of IX Company is "Let him be Strong who would be Respected," but the new version stuck—Lance Corporal Stuart Jones 88 of Denbigh had "Dead Men Risen" and a large "IX" tattooed on his torso.

While he was serving in Bosnia, Birchall's mother had sent him an anthology of First World War poetry. The words "dead men risen" appear to have been taken from the poem "Ypres" by Robert Laurence Binyon, first published in 1917:

> Listen when the bugle's calling Forward!
> They'll be found,
> Dead men, risen in battalions
> From underground.

Ypres 1917 was one of the first battle honors earned by the Welsh Guards. Binyon is best known for his poem "For the Fallen," which contains the passage read out at each repatriation service at Helmand's Camp Bastion, at each funeral in Britain, and then by the regimental sergeant major at the Welsh Guards Memorial Service in Aldershot in November 2009:

> They shall grow not old, as we that are left grow old:
> Age shall not weary them, nor the years condemn.
> At the going down of the sun and in the morning
> We will remember them.

After the end of the First World War, Philip Gibbs, a war correspondent with the *Daily Chronicle*, wrote of the horrors of the conflict that he had neglected to report at the time for fear of falling foul of the censors or damaging morale at home. Gibbs had been at Loos, the first battle the Welsh Guards fought, and wrote of the wounded men left in the swamps of Flanders. A soldier had told him, he recalled, how "as the light of dawn paled over those gray fields of slime he saw blood-stained figures raising themselves out of the pits like dead men risen from their graves."

Beyond his regiment, the Welsh Guardsman feels an affinity with the rest of the Household Division, particularly the four other Foot Guards regiments. "Cut me in two and I'll bleed blue, red, blue," goes an old saying of the guardsman, or "g-man," referring to the colors of the Household Division shoulder flash. The Guards draw their distinctiveness from their perennial role of carrying out public duties, providing the Queen's Guard at Buckingham Palace, St. James's Palace, and the Tower of London. To members of the "red-green machine"—the Parachute Regiment and the Royal Marines—the

Guards regiments are inferior as infantrymen because of all the spit and polish and marching they do. The Guards view themselves as set apart from the rest due to the discipline and precision instilled on the parade ground that prevents sloppiness in any aspect of soldiering. Drill movements are based on how wars were fought in Napoleonic times and so used to have direct military relevance. Nowadays, the Guards ethos is based on doing things properly and not cutting corners, on smartness and attention to detail.

The Guards like to talk of "understated excellence" being their timeless hallmark. "We don't shout about what we do, we just get on with it and people notice that," says Colonel Tom Bonas, regimental adjutant of the Welsh Guards. "It's all about the blue, red, blue," says Guardsman Jesse Jackson from Rhyl. "I've worked with a few different regiments and I've been on courses with other units and even the Parachute Regiment doesn't have the camaraderie and the spirit the Household Division has. I don't know if it's brainwashing or training but I certainly fall for it. I love it. It's the pride factor. I get a kick out of saying I'm a guardsman."

If a job cannot be done by a Welsh Guard, the immediate preference within the regiment is for another Foot Guard. Recalling the camaraderie of the Guards Armoured Division in the Second World War, there were contingents of Coldstream Guards, Scots Guards, and Irish Guards who served with the Welsh Guards in Helmand. When the Welsh Guards were relieved by the Grenadier Guards at the end of their tour, the incoming Grenadiers had an almost instinctive understanding of what their predecessors had been doing, and the transition was seamless. This was a Guards handover on the battlefield. Others have taken place on the parade ground in bearskin caps.

In September 1997, Welsh Guards were flown back from Crossmaglen in South Armagh to carry the coffin of Princess Diana. Major Giles Harris remembers standing on guard beside the coffin of Queen Elizabeth, The Queen Mother, in April 2002. It was 3:00 a.m., and he had been sent back from Bosnia with a contingent of Welsh Guardsmen for the duty. "There were two old girls hoovering around my feet and chatting about having a cuppa afterwards. The Queen Mum was lying a half a foot away from them with the full majesty of British custom around her. It was like a Giles cartoon, it was priceless." A few months after returning from Helmand, the Welsh Guards were Changing the Guard outside Buckingham Palace. Lance Sergeant

Tobie Fasfous from Pencoed liked to describe himself as a "professional bullet dodger and part-time tourist attraction."

Occasionally, the dual role of Sovereign's Bodyguard and infantryman come together. The Prince of Wales is colonel in chief of the Welsh Guards and always has an equerry from the regiment. In 2004, Austen Salusbury, then a captain, was taking over from Captain David Basson as an equerry. Salusbury had just returned from Basra, where he had been second in command of the Prince of Wales Company—a role Basson was taking on. The handover was conducted at Clarence House, the Prince of Wales's residence. It was an incongruous scene: the two officers in immaculate lounge suits sipping tea from porcelain cups with a map of Basra spread out in front of them.

These days, the rivalry between the Guards and the rest of the army rarely extends beyond friendly ribbing. Across the army, the same type of squaddie slang is used, such as: "gleaming" (excellent); "purging" (complaining); "dramas" (problems); "cheeky" (dangerous); "ally" (stylish); and "Gucci" (good quality). In recent years, Americanisms have been added, in particular the use "awesome" (amazing) and "kinetic" (involving military force). "We're scruffy riflemen, they're smart guardsmen from the Household Division," says Lance Corporal Steven Pallett of 4th Battalion Rifles (4 Rifles), who served in the Welsh Guards Battle Group in Helmand. "They're very appearance-orientated. They like short hair, irons, whereas we dress more ally, we look cool, get in the field, get the job done. Which they do too—it's different traditions. We keep on getting picked up for our sideburns but that's rock and roll—they've looked after us." Gone are the days of mass punch-ups in the pubs of Aldershot, Guildford, and Catterick.

Although formed around a battalion (all the Guards regiments are now made up of a single battalion) of about eight hundred men, the Welsh Guards Battle Group swelled to a strength of more than 1,500 in Helmand. From June, there were two companies from 4 Rifles. In addition, cap badges within the Battle Group included the Royal Tank Regiment, Yorkshire Regiment, Royal Marines, Mercian Regiment, Royal Artillery, Royal Engineers, Royal Logistic Corps, and Princess of Wales's Royal Regiment, not to mention the citizen soldiers of the Territorial Army. Private Steve Grimshaw, a truck driver from Sale, near Manchester, rejoined the army for the tour some twenty years after he had left. In the meantime, his Cheshire Regiment had been disbanded. This didn't stop him wearing his old insignia, and he celebrated his forty-fifth birthday, along with the fact that he was the oldest private in the army, under fire on the Shamalan Canal.

In Helmand, the Welsh Guards were also part of an international brotherhood of soldiers. An Estonian company—which included veterans of the Soviet occupation of Afghanistan—was part of the Battle Group. There were U.S. Marines in fire-support teams, and the "Pedro" Black Hawk medical helicopters that swooped in to evacuate wounded Welsh Guards were American. Many nations provided medical treatment at Camp Bastion. When a Welsh Guards officer received a transfusion, the platelets came from an Estonian pharmacist, who maintained its quality had been improved by Baltic beer, and the blood came from a British Army nurse who insisted that it had benefited from her red wine consumption.

At the heart of a Welsh Guardsman's pride in 2009 was his company. That reached out in concentric circles to the Welsh Guards, the Household Division, the British Army, and its NATO allies. Alongside this was a sense of pride in Wales, in Britain, and even, though seldom expressed, in democracy and the Western way of life.

For all this pride, there was also a shadow that had been cast twenty-seven years earlier and had lingered for more than a quarter of the regiment's history. During the Falklands War of 1982, thirty-six Welsh Guardsmen had perished. All but four died onboard the logistic landing ship Royal Fleet Auxiliary *Sir Galahad* when it was bombed by Argentine jets. The Welsh Guards had been embarked in the *Sir Galahad* after being turned back just a few miles into a march over the Sussex Mountains from San Carlos to Goose Green. Carrying one hundred pounds of kit per man in Bergen rucksacks, movement across the boggy moors was slow. Two tractors carrying mortars and .50 Browning machine guns became stuck, and eventually the decision was taken to return to San Carlos. This triggered a chain of events that led to half of the battalion— the Prince of Wales Company, 3 Company, and the mortar platoon, comprising 350 men—embarking in HMS *Fearless* and then the *Sir Galahad*, initially bound for Bluff Cove. In fact, the ship only steamed as far as Fitzroy, where a Rapier detachment and Field Ambulance unit were to be offloaded. There the Welsh Guardsmen were, afloat and undefended, at Fitzroy on the bright, clear morning of June 8, 1982. The two company commanders were awaiting orders as to what to do next, and there was confusion about whether the Welsh Guards should land at Fitzroy and march to Bluff Cove or be taken the eighteen miles there by sea. A plan was made to relay the troops to Bluff Cove by landing craft, but this was delayed when its ramp was damaged, meaning the equipment needed to be lowered down by crane.

There were three Welsh Guardsmen in Helmand who had been onboard the *Sir Galahad* that day—the two Late Entry majors Martyn Miles and Nicky Mott and Warrant Officer (Class Two) John Williams "65 was 54," who rejoined for the Afghanistan tour to be an operations room watchkeeper. Aged fifty-two, Williams was the oldest man in the Welsh Guards Battle Group in Helmand.

Onboard the *Sir Galahad* back in 1982, Lance Sergeant Martyn Miles of 3 Company, from Pontypridd, had been sitting in the galley drinking tea and playing brag when there was a massive bang. He was thrown across the compartment and singed by a huge fireball, landing on the deck as a large metal door fell on top of him and broke his right ankle. It was pitch-black, and smoke was beginning to fill the compartment. Panicking guardsmen ran across the door with Miles trapped underneath. Someone pulled him out, and as a sergeant was carrying him onto the upper deck, he began to realize the scale of what had happened. "There were people with skin literally hanging off their faces and their arms and their legs just black," he remembers. "The smell was horrendous, like burnt ashes nine times over. There were people whose faces had expanded, most of their hair gone, eyebrows gone and skin melted on hands and faces."

Guardsman Simon Weston, the most seriously burned casualty that day to survive, later to achieve fame as a speaker and charity worker, described his "personal Hiroshima" in his autobiography. His skin melting, he thought the ship had been napalmed. He watched men "jerking and writhing to a silent tune of death" and a "human fireball" collapse in front of him, "a disintegrating Guy Fawkes, blistered hands outstretched as he called for his mum" and die. Some friends he recognized by their voices as they pleaded and screamed, some of them begging to be shot. "Even more grotesque, I knew others by the shape of their teeth as the flames pulled back their lips into hideous grins."

Guardsman Nicky Mott 84 of the Prince of Wales Company, who had celebrated his nineteenth birthday on the way down to the Falklands, was just about to step through the door out onto the upper deck when the air-raid warning came. His brother, Lance Sergeant Bill Mott 88, was already in the landing craft. Everything went dark when the bombs hit, and when he clambered outside, the first thing he heard was his brother shouting: "Nicky, Nicky!" At the time, his main concern was that he had lost the magazine for his machine gun. "What's the problem?" he responded, sticking his head out over the side of the ship. Both brothers had survived.

It was a few hours before the extent of the casualties began to sink in. "There was [Guardsman Michael] Dunphy in the mortar platoon who I knew from when we used to go in the Horse and Groom," recalls Nicky Mott. "There was Yorkie [Guardsman Andrew Walker]. He'd just transferred over to the mortar platoon. There was [Guardsman] Neil Hughes, he'd been killed too. The names were trickling through." There were fifty-six killed onboard the *Sir Galahad* that day, thirty-two of them from the Welsh Guards. Around 150 Welsh Guardsmen were injured, many with hideous burns. It was the single biggest loss of life during the conflict and the most significant setback of the successful British campaign to take back the islands. Four other Welsh Guardsmen were killed, three serving with the Special Air Service (SAS).

The last Welsh Guardsman to be killed, on the day hostilities ended, was Lance Corporal Chris Thomas 03, known as "Bowser," a motorcycle dispatch rider who was hit by an Argentine mortar shell. "Bowser used to bring his motorbike into the single accommodation and do oil changes in his room," says Nicky Mott. "He'd go into the Horse and Groom and bring his motorbike in. Nuts. We buried him at Brookwood military cemetery and half of the mourners were Hell's Angels." Shortly after arriving at Camp Bastion in April 2009, a young soldier called Guardsman Philip Allen came to show Major Mott a photograph of his uncle. It was "Bowser" Thomas. "He's from Bournemouth," explains Mott. "He's an Englishman but he joined the Welsh Guards because of Bowser and the Falklands." The few non-Welshmen in the Welsh Guards tended to have a reason to join a regiment that can claim—with more justification than any other—to be a family.

The bravery and stoicism of the Welsh Guards that day is often forgotten. Two decades later, Surgeon Commander Rick Jolly was still moved to tears when he recalled how his Ajax Bay field hospital was beyond capacity, as helicopter after helicopter brought hideously burned men. "All those young Welshmen with burnt skin hanging off them like wet tissue paper—some too badly injured to treat right away; some too lightly injured. The entrance fee to the hospital that night was 10 percent burns, so if you had burns to your face and hands, you didn't get in." The naval surgeon had to go around explaining to the Guardsmen why they could not be treated straight away. Without exception, he remembered, they told him: "Don't worry about me, sir, but please look after my mate over there." And then Jolly would watch them walk away into the night. For nearly two decades, the physical scars sustained onboard the *Sir Galahad* could be seen throughout the regiment. Less obvious were the mental scars, which contributed to a large number of suicides and early deaths due to alcoholism among former Welsh Guardsmen.

For the Welsh Guards, perhaps even harder to deal with than the death, disfigurement, and trauma was the accusation that they had failed to perform and hadn't been fit enough to march from San Carlos to Goose Green. Within the battalion, there were mutterings about officers who had wanted the troops to remain in the *Sir Galahad* rather than landing at Fitzroy and going cross-country to Bluff Cove. "This whole thing was a mess—a mess that got 25 of my mates killed," wrote Lance Corporal Andy Mortimore in a letter home two weeks later.[9] "We were left in daylight for eight hours without air cover!" By a quirk of fate, not one of the Welsh Guards who died in the South Atlantic was an officer, even though many were onboard the *Sir Galahad*. Although the debate within the Welsh Guards about who was responsible had long since faded, the shadow cast by the events that day remained. "The whispers went on for years," says Nicky Mott. "It certainly affected the Regiment. Were we ready? Were we fit enough? We were. It was just the wrong place, the wrong time and it just didn't happen for us. It hurt. It did hurt and it still hurts to this day." Helmand was to give the Welsh Guards the opportunity to exorcise the ghosts of the Falklands.

2

Green Zone

To endeavour to ... control such a people is to court misfortune and calamity. The Afghan will bear poverty, insecurity of life; but he will not tolerate foreign rule.

—**Sir John Lawrence**, *viceroy of India, 1867*[1]

The Dasht-i-Margo, this desert of death, springs to life from centuries of lethargy as these vital streams transform its wastes as if by fairy wand into fields of waving wheat.

—**Paul S. Jones** *(Morrison-Knudsen engineer from Nebraska),* Afghanistan Venture *(1956)*

Wali Mohammed had seen superpowers, their proxies, and their enemies come and go. Each day in 2009, the seventy-one-year-old Helmandi tended to the buildings and grounds where he had worked since he was twenty. The complex at Chah-e Anjir had been established in the 1940s as the headquarters of the Helmand and Arghandab Construction Unit (HACU)—part of the Helmand Valley Authority. It was an oasis of Little America designed to bring civilization to an impoverished corner of Afghanistan. Beside it lay a graveyard of rusting heavy plant machinery, trucks, and earth-movers brought in from places like Carnegie, Illinois, and Mansfield, Louisiana, and abandoned when the Americans departed in 1979.

Among the broken hulks were scattered pieces of machinery made by Ganz-Mavag in Budapest and Stavostroj in Prague, left there since the Russian withdrawal in 1989. Next to the latrines a Soviet army crest had been carved into the wall, while in the entrance was the crest of the Welsh Guards and the words "Prince of Wales's Company, Op Herrick 10." A small stack of booklets left behind by American troops after the 2001 invasion lay in a corner. They were entitled *God's Promises for You* and had a cover featuring soldiers of the U.S. Army's 101st Airborne Division. Daubed on the walls was graffiti in Pashto that read: *"Zindabad Taliban"*—"Long live the Taliban." Littering the area by the "shit pit," for burning excrement, were discarded salary sheets, invoices, and correspondence from American construction workers dating back more than half a century. In the base, the Welsh Guardsmen watched DVDs in their time off that included *Collateral* and *The Departed*, as well as *Charlie Wilson's War*, about the Texas congressman who helped arm the mujahideen resistance in the 1980s.

When the Prince of Wales's Company arrived in Chah-e Anjir ("Well of the Fig Tree" in Persian) in June 2009, they renamed the headquarters PB Shahzad, after the Pashto word for "Prince." Wali Mohammed watched impassively as soldiers posed for Facebook pictures sitting on an old Soviet T62 tank and an armored personnel carrier. He had started work there as a mechanic in 1958 before being sent to Iran to study English and returning as a clerk and then machine-shop manager. After the Americans left, he worked for the Russian invaders. "We were friends with the Americans and friends with the Russians," he said, speaking three months after his latest masters had begun paying him. "It was a desert before the Americans came—they created everything with their bulldozers. I was sad when they went." Next to arrive were the Russians. "There was fighting but they brought tractors, they spent their money and they looked after us. They tried to repair what the Americans had left but there were no spares." In 1994 came the Taliban. "They burnt the bazaar and were very hard on the people. Some of them were from Pakistan. They asked me to continue working so I did. They did not trouble me." Wali Mohammed professed that he was delighted with the Welsh Guards. "The people are very happy with the British because they are working hard to get security here for this place," he beamed. "I hope they will stay, though sometimes I wonder who else will come here before I will die."

By the time the Welsh Guards arrived, Britain's conflict in Helmand had already raged for three years and seemed set to last for many more as the U.S. Marines poured in. Depending on who was doing the counting, Afghanistan had been at war for the seven years since the American invasion after the September 11 attacks of 2001, for thirty years since Soviet tanks rolled in, or for centuries. Long before it was called Afghanistan, it was known as Yaghistan, or "Land of the Unruly." Invaders came, stayed for a while, and eventually left, their legacies crumbling into the dust along with the bones of their dead. The Taliban and most Helmandis expected the British to be no different and, truth be told, neither did the Welsh Guards.

Helmand is the largest of landlocked Afghanistan's thirty-four provinces. It was named after the great Helmand River, which is formed from the melted snow of the Hindu Kush mountain range to the west of Kabul and then flows southwest for 1,400 kilometers before evaporating in marshes and desert lakes at the Iranian border. The Helmand Basin became a trading route between India and Persia as well as a highway of conquest. Alexander the Great arrived in 329 BC after telling his men: "We are dealing with savage beasts, which lapse of time can only tame, when they are caught and caged, because their own nature cannot tame them." His army camped in the fertile valley, filled with orchards and date palm groves, before crossing the Helmand at Gereshk and marching north along the same caravan route to Kabul that the British were to take two thousand years later during the First Afghan War.[2]

The Ghaznavid dynasty, which ruled much of Afghanistan from 962 to 1140, built its winter palace at Lashkar-i-Bazaar, just outside the city of Bost—now the provincial capital Lashkar Gah, which means "army barracks" in Persian. Genghis Khan's Mongol hordes devastated the Helmand Valley and sacked Bost in 1220. Tamerlane the Great, who claimed descent from Genghis Khan, destroyed the Helmand River's irrigation works in 1383.[3] Afghans enjoyed relative calm and prosperity until shipping reduced the need for traders to travel by land through Central Asia. Thereafter it became a backwater with scarce resources and a complex network of tribes.

In the nineteenth century, Afghanistan became a disputed zone in what Rudyard Kipling immortalized as "the Great Game," when Britain and Russia struggled for control of Central Asia. Abdur Rahman, emir of Afghanistan from 1880 to 1901, described his country as like "a grain of wheat between two strong millstones."[4] Anxious to protect India and wary of Russian designs on Iran, Britain sought to maintain Afghanistan as a buffer state, whether through the vigilant non-interference of "Masterly Inactivity" or the interventionist "Forward Policy."

It was close to the banks of the Helmand that two thousand British were decisively defeated by the 25,000-strong forces of Ayub Khan at the Battle of Maiwand on July 27, 1880. Ayub's men, who were lightly equipped and knew the terrain, outflanked and surprised the British, commanded by Brigadier General George Burrows, by fording the Helmand. Like many waterways that looked impassable on a map—as the Welsh Guards were to discover in 2009—the river was not the barrier it seemed.[5] Burrows's heavily laden forces moved in a ponderous column in the searing heat and were short of ammunition and water.

Maiwand was one of the biggest British military disasters of the Victorian era. The tribesmen's encounter with the 66th Regiment (later the Royal Berkshires) there is still commemorated in lore and verse, not least by the Taliban. The fighting was so fierce that Afghans were killed by being grabbed by their beards and pulled onto British bayonets and repulsed by rocks when ammunition ran out.[6] A small group from the 66th retreated to a garden, where they were surrounded before opting to charge out, fighting to the death. Major Hyacinth Lynch, the only officer in the 66th to survive, recalled "the Ghazis advancing with flags and their long knives glistening in the afternoon sun." Some 971 British and Indian troops of the force of 1,500 were killed at Maiwand, their corpses left to the vultures. Another 168 were wounded; Captain John Slade of the Royal Horse Artillery recounted how the gun carriages were "crowded with helpless wounded officers and men suffering the tortures of the damned."[7] Among the wounded—fictionally—was Dr. John Watson, Arthur Conan Doyle's foil for the detective Sherlock Holmes.

The Second Afghan War came to an end in 1880 when Lieutenant General Sir Frederick Roberts gathered 10,000 men who took twenty-three days to march the 334 miles from Kabul to Kandahar, forty-five miles east of Maiwand, and rout Ayub's forces. The British pulled out of Afghanistan the following year amid widespread domestic opposition to the war. The victor, who was to be immortalized as Lord Roberts of Kandahar, remarked: "It may not be very flattering to our *amour propre*, but I feel sure that I am right when I say that the less the Afghans see of us the less they will dislike us."

In 2009, the Welsh Guards Battle Group headquarters was established within the walls of a crumbling British fort at Nad-e Ali, forty miles west of Maiwand. It was a defensive structure that dated back at least to the nineteenth century and the First and Second Afghan Wars, fought from 1838 to 1842 and 1878 to 1880, respectively. A Third Afghan War lasted for a month in 1919 before a lone Royal Air Force plane dropped twenty bombs on Kabul, one of them hitting Emir Abdul Rahman's tomb. "The fort was built when the British were fighting against the Afghan people," said Habibullah Khan, governor of Nad-e Ali district, after a dinner to bid farewell to the Welsh Guards in October 2009. "History repeats itself. British blood has been spilt here again, but this time we are grateful for their sacrifice."

At the very same place, the Russians clashed with Afghan forces in October 1981. Xinua, the Chinese news agency, reported that the Soviets sent reinforcements of nineteen tanks, twenty-one trucks, and four helicopter gunships from Lashkar Gah to relieve its forces in the fort, which was being besieged by the mujahideen. According to the report, likely to have relied on the exaggerations of mujahideen propagandists, the Soviets lost nine tanks as they withdrew, and thirteen guerrillas and twelve others were killed. In 2009, the fort became Forward Operating Base (FOB) Shawqat, named after an Afghan army soldier killed by the Taliban. The most intact of its eight surviving two-story turrets was known as "Salusbury towers" because it was commandeered by Major Austen Salusbury, the Welsh Guards influence officer, as his sleeping quarters until the bats drove him out.

Many of the Taliban fighters that the Welsh Guards fought in 2009 during Britain's fourth Afghan War were the descendants of Ayub Khan's Pashtun tribesmen at Maiwand. In September 2009, the Welsh Guards realized that they were coming under accurate long-range fire from .303 caliber rounds from two separate locations. The Taliban were using the Lee-Enfield, the British Army's standard bolt-action rifle from 1895. During the heyday of the British Empire, millions of Lee-Enfields were distributed to allies. The Lee-Enfield had been phased out in 1957, but more than fifty years later the Afghans were using this great piece of British engineering against the descendants of those who invented it.

Almost since their first recorded appearance in history, the Pashtuns, who make up about half of Afghanistan's population of 28 million, have been portrayed as vengeful warriors. Centuries ago, the Pashtun poet Khushal

Khan-i-Khattack described his own people as "malevolent, ruthless, and contentious."[8] A 1969 handbook for American government personnel described Pashtun society as dominated by "displays of passion, courage, toughness and readiness to do battle." This was personified by "the statuesque tribesman, armed with bandoleer and rifle, whose erect posture and lithe movements dispel any doubt as to his effectiveness in hand-to-hand combat against his enemies." Sir Winston Churchill, who traveled to the North-West Frontier in 1897 as a correspondent for the *Daily Telegraph* with General Sir Bindon Blood's Malakand Field Force, saw the Pashtuns as "savages of the Stone Age" with weapons of the nineteenth century in their hands. "Every man's hand is against the other, and all against the stranger.... To the ferocity of the Zulu are added the craft of the Redskin and the marksmanship of the Boer."

The 1,200-mile Durand Line, drawn up by Sir Henry Mortimer Durand in 1893, divided the lands of the Pashtuns—known as Pathans by the British— in an attempt to assert imperial control. On the Indian side to the east, "assured clans" were co-opted by the British by being given money and rank in the Indian army and used as a proxy force against their Pashtun kinsmen on the Afghan side to the west. Seasonal migration with the harvests, however, continued across this artificial frontier. Today, the Durand Line marks the border between Afghanistan and Pakistan, which came into being in 1947. In the nineteenth century, the boundary was imposed to weaken the Pashtuns. By the twenty-first, it served to strengthen them, giving Taliban fighters, overwhelmingly Pashtun and speaking their own Pashto language, a sanctuary from NATO forces on the eastern side in Pakistan. Some 28 million Pashtuns live in Pakistan, about 15 percent of the population, along with another 2.3 million Pashtun refugees who fled during the Soviet era. Most of the fighters the Welsh Guards faced in 2009 were Pashtun Helmandis, but direction came from Mullah Mohammed Omar and the rest of the Taliban leadership— known as the "Quetta shura"—in Quetta, Pakistan. Resupply lines for ammunition, IEDs, and new fighters extended across the border.

Pashtun culture is regulated by the code of Pashtunwali, which means "the way of the Pashtun," and covers matters of morality and behavior. Six of its main tenets were outlined in the *Op Herrick 10 Operational Guide* issued to all Welsh Guardsmen and other British troops in 2009: *melmastia* (hospitality); *sabat* (loyalty); *ghayrat* (defence of territory); *badal* (justice); *turah* (bravery) and *nanavati* (shelter). The guide omitted the concept of *namus* (honor), while *badal* is perhaps best understood as blood vengeance, which can be pursued through generations or on behalf of a kinsman. A Pashtun folktale about a woman who granted *nanavati* to the killer of her son, even as the killer was pursued by her tribesmen fulfilling their duty of *badal*, captures the essence of Pashtunwali. The code had a direct effect on the way Helmandis viewed civilian casualties caused by British forces, the destruction of property, treatment of women, and searching of compounds. Although Pashtuns have traditionally dominated Afghan government, the principal loyalty of the Pashtun is to his tribe. The largest concentration of Pashtuns in Afghanistan is found in Helmand, where they make up 95 percent of the population.

Afghan engineers rebuilt parts of the old network of canal along the Helmand River starting in 1910 and then established new canals. In the 1930s, the Germans and the Japanese renovated nine miles of a two-hundred-year-old stretch of canal before the outbreak of the Second World War in 1939, when work stopped. After the war, the Americans were seen as the least objectionable of the victorious Allied powers while, with memories of the Great Game still fresh, the British and the Russians were regarded as traditional enemies. Thus, the Helmand Valley Project[9] was established in 1946 by the United States, initially via Import-Export Bank loans and then, from 1960, directly by the United States Agency for International Development (USAID). The project was designed to irrigate 300,000 acres of desert to the west and north of the provincial capital Lashkar Gah and settle up to 20,000 members of nomadic tribes. Lasting until 1979 and costing $136.5 million, it took as its model President Franklin Roosevelt's Tennessee Valley Authority. This series of dams on the Tennessee River helped transform the economy across seven southern states after the Great Depression. The project became a monument to American optimism, good will, and, ultimately, folly.

American self-interest was also involved. This was the Cold War era, and the Soviet Union was extending its influence in northern Afghanistan. The Helmand Valley enterprise gave the United States a foothold in the south. For the project, the Afghan government hired the Morrison-Knudsen company of Boise, Idaho. The largest heavy engineering firm in the United States, Morrison-Knudsen had built the Hoover Dam and the San Francisco Bay Bridge and was soon to construct the North American Space Agency's (NASA) launch complex at Cape Canaveral. It was predicted that the Helmand Valley project would increase agricultural productivity and become a symbol of

Afghan national prestige as well as testament to American ingenuity. It was hoped the project would also return the Helmand Valley to its fabled status as the breadbasket of Afghanistan before the destruction wrought by Genghis Khan and Tamerlane. During a 1951 visit to Chah-e Anjir, the company's cofounder Harry Morrison told his employees: "You people here are pioneers, like in our own early west. You are on the firing line. We can do much to help these backward people."

President Harry Truman told the Tennessee Valley Authority's director that such development projects were an alternative to war. The United States was later to propose dam projects as possible solutions to the Israeli–Palestinian and Kashmir disputes and even the Vietnam War. Visiting the Helmand Valley Project in 1960, the historian Arnold Toynbee was awed by the "high-handed way in which the Americans deal with Nature . . . imposing Man's will on the Helmand River." He concluded: "The new world that they are conjuring up out of the desert at the Helmand River's expense is to be an America-in-Asia." Lashkar Gah was built on the ancient site of Bost as an Afghan-American model town. Houses combined features like the purdah wall, behind which Pashtun women could retire to avoid the gaze of strangers, with American bathrooms and electrical sockets for refrigerators and washing machines. Helmand also experienced an influx of eager American engineers, hydrologists, and technicians. An infrastructure of roads and bridges was built to transport equipment. The annual salaries of Morrison-Knudsen's advisors and personnel alone cost the equivalent of Afghanistan's total exports each year.

Almost from the outset, however, the project was plagued by problems. The original canals were poorly sited and too low, causing fields to flood. A new dam at the mouth of the Nahr-e Bughra Canal raised the water table, and a crust of salt deposits was left on the topsoil. Demolishing the dam would have been an embarrassment for the Afghan monarchy, which had also resisted paying for expensive soil surveys. Morrison-Knudsen, which was seeking a profit rather than a long-term answer, obeyed the client. A 320-foot-high dam at Kajakai and a two-hundred-foot-high dam at Arghandab were supplemented by an elaborate network of smaller dams, sluice gates, drainage channels, ditches, and irrigation canals. Some three hundred miles of concrete-lined canals were created.

There was a persistent weed problem created by flooding, and the salinity of the soil made much of it uncultivable. Around the Shamalan ("North

Wind" in Persian) Canal, waterlogging was so bad that foundations were giving way, and mosques and houses were sinking into the bog. The American solution was to move the farmers from their land, take them to equivalent plots, and level the area with bulldozers. According to a 1983 study by Cynthia Clapp-Wincek of USAID, the farmers refused to budge and "met the bulldozers with rifles." Helmandis who protested that a canal was being run straight through their village were thrown into jail, and construction work sped up. Throughout, there was an insularity to the American approach, Clapp-Wincek noted: "The Americans lived and worked in separate, very American environments, keeping U.S. office hours and observing U.S. holidays ... few Americans spoke any of the local languages."

The project was due to end in 1974, and by this time salvaging it had become what one American observer described as "a gargantuan job with Sisyphean elements."[10] But Henry Kissinger, the U.S. Secretary of State, relented when Sardar Mohammad Daoud, the newly installed president and prime minister after the overthrow of the monarchy in 1973, described the Helmand Valley scheme as an "unfinished symphony" that had to be completed. There was an influx of American soil scientists and some progress was made on the drainage issue but the project's final demise came when the pro-Soviet Khalq party seized power in an April 1978 coup, in which Daoud was assassinated. The last American personnel working in Helmand Valley left in August 1979, four months before the Soviet invasion.

The legacy of the Helmand Valley Project was not just millions of dollars wasted and a blow to American pride. First, it left a complex tribal system in place. In settling central Helmand with just under 5,500 nomadic families from 1953 to 1973 and another 4,000 from 1973 to 1978, the project created an intricate and fragile tribal mosaic. In 1980, the American anthropologist Richard Scott identified twenty-five different tribal groups in the Nad-e Ali district alone. This made it all but impossible for Soviet and later British and American troops to understand the local dynamics. Incomes in the Nad-e Ali and Marjah areas, which became notorious Taliban strongholds, were lower than in other irrigated parts of Helmand. Like the new towns in Britain, everyone in these irrigated areas was originally from somewhere else. The Welsh Guards would joke that they had been posted to the Milton Keynes of Afghanistan.

In 1954, about 1,300 families of nomads and landless farmers were settled in six villages in the Nad-e Ali area and were designated by the letters

A, B, C, D, E, and K for the ease of American contractors. Each one was made up of large sun-dried brick houses and a large central mosque and bazaar area. The local residents gave them Pashto names—Village A became Shin Kalay, "Blue Village"; Village B was Khowshaal Kalay, "Happy Village"; Village C was Luy Bagh, "Big Garden"; Village D was Zarghun Kalay, "Green Village"; Village E was Gorup-e Shesh Kalay, "Group of Six"; and Village K was Naqalabad, "Built by Settlers."[11] All were to become battlegrounds for the Welsh Guards in 2009. The land was poorer than elsewhere, and clumsy attempts at social engineering in the 1970s that involved splitting up tribal and ethnic groups had left the settled families alienated and at a disadvantage when dealing with the government. Suspicion of authority was ingrained.

The Helmand Valley Project created a new landscape that lent itself to armed resistance. Irrigation ditches and dense vegetation provided ideal cover for ambushes of Soviet troops by mujahideen fighters. The Russians chopped down trees to block the canals and laid tens of thousands of landmines in fields and orchards. Soviet mines still occasionally claim the lives of Afghan civilians and British soldiers. Helmand became a stronghold of the Pashtun-dominated mujahideen, with the Soviets unable to hold territory apart from Lashkar Gah and the Kajaki dam. The mujahideen became adept at laying mines too, often stacking three foreign anti-tank mines on top of each other to ensure a catastrophic kill of a vehicle. Tractors were used to transport IEDs across the fields to the roads. Some IEDs were remotely detonated by command wire, others were rigged with batteries connected to wires stretched across the road. The metal tracks of Soviet tanks would complete the circuit and detonate the IED while civilian vehicles with rubber tires would pass safely.[12]

Termed "the Green Zone" by the British when they first arrived in Helmand in 2006, the flat patchwork quilt of irrigation canals, ditches and fields full of crops provided an ideal defensive battleground for the Taliban. Unlike Iraq's Green Zone, the American enclave created in 2003 that insulated coalition forces and their allies from the insurgency raging outside, the Green Zone in Helmand was the Taliban's habitat. The *bocage* hedgerows of Normandy, where the Welsh Guards had fought in 1944, had provided cover and concealment for the Germans while blocking almost all lines of sight for the British. Helmand's Green Zone offered similar advantages to the Taliban. Back then, the Welsh Guards of 1944 who envisioned hedges as waist-high decorative bushes had found dense, impassable hedgerows cultivated since

Norman times on top of mounds of earth and rock. In 2009, the Welsh Guards found the Helmand landscape very different from anything they had seen in Britain. The ditches were wider and deeper than they had expected; in summer the crops were head-high, allowing the enemy to creep up unseen.

The 2009 Operation Herrick guide for troops warned that "drainage ditches can be dug out to create complex trench systems which are covered from view and fire," which "allows Enemy Forces to initiate ambushes from as close as 5 metres away." The Americans had laid down a grid system of roads in the towns and outside them a lattice of narrow, crumbling tracks that greatly aided the Taliban by restricting the movements of military vehicles and channeling them through choke points. The Taliban, on the other hand, enjoyed almost complete freedom of movement. The canals were shallow enough to wade across, while motorbikes were used over the rickety bridges positioned every hundred yards or so. Sluice gates were opened and closed to alter water levels, and sometimes the Taliban flooded fields to impede the route of retreat for Welsh Guards patrols. In some parts of the Green Zone, the grid system created an almost urban environment of narrow alleyways that restricted vehicle movement but allowed numerous routes in and out for those operating on two wheels or on foot. For some, this was reminiscent of Northern Ireland. Brigadier Tim Radford described the terrain as "a cross between the *bocage* and Belfast."

The last and most significant legacy of the Helmand Valley Project was agricultural, though not in the way the idealist American planners of the 1950s had envisaged. Although the conditions for growing wheat, cotton, and corn had not been ideal, the project helped create a near-perfect environment for opium. The poppy thrived in alkaline and saline soils. By 2000, the United Nations estimated that Helmand Valley was producing 39 percent of the world's heroin and that Helmand accounted for more than half the poppy-growing area of Afghanistan. After the Taliban captured Afghanistan's second city of Kandahar in 1994, the one-eyed mullah Omar, its leader, struck a deal with the warlord Rais-e Baghran. In return for Taliban control of Helmand and its massively lucrative poppy trade, Mullah Omar agreed to remove the rival Akhundzadeh warlords from power.

In 2006, Afghanistan yielded the largest opium crop a nation has ever produced, with two-thirds grown in Taliban areas. If Helmand had been a country, it would have been the world's leading opium-producing nation, with the rest of Afghanistan in second place. A 2007 report to the U.S. Congress stated that about 3.1 million Afghans—13 percent of the population—were employed in the narcotics industry. In that year, 45 percent of Afghanistan's Gross Domestic Product (GDP) came from narcotics, exported worldwide, while it was estimated that Afghanistan supplied 90 percent of Britain's heroin.[13] The Taliban even sought to continue the irrigation work that the Helmand Valley Project had started. In 2008, American spy satellites detected large ditches being dug in the deserts of southern Helmand and filled with water in an apparent attempt to create more farmland for poppy growing.[14]

The Taliban were overwhelmingly Pashtun and rose to prominence in part by harnessing Pashtun nationalism. As well as Islamic sharia law, it was inspired by the Pashtunwali code, warlordism, and a distrust of central government. That did not mean they inspired universal support or admiration. For many ordinary Afghans, the young fundamentalist Pashtun students who refused to compromise on their interpretation of Islam were merely the latest in a long line of groups determined to impose their will on the people. Support from the CIA and Pakistan enabled the Islamists to wage jihad against the Soviets and then gain a foothold in Afghan society.

The Soviet withdrawal left a vacuum to be filled. Pakistan, ruled by Sunni Muslims and wary of Shia influence from Iran, continued to fund and support the Islamists. There was heavy investment too from Saudi Arabia, eager to spread the strict Wahhabi version of Sunni Islam. This was done through established *madrassas* (religious colleges), in Afghanistan and along Pakistan's Pashtun tribal frontier, where dispossessed Afghan refugees would be among the pupils. It was these Islamist academies that gave the Taliban their name, from *Talib*, meaning "student who seeks knowledge." Mullah Omar literally wrapped himself in the reputed cloak of the prophet Muhammad, which he had appropriated from the mausoleum of Ahmed Shah Durrani, viewed by many Afghans as the father of the nation. Among those who proclaimed Mullah Omar's legitimacy as self-appointed commander of the faithful was a Saudi jihadist called Osama bin Laden. Advocating a return to pure Islam, the Taliban focused at first on the Pashtun south, co-opting some tribal leaders and militia commanders and coercing or killing others. Many Pashtuns, weary of war and exploitation, embraced the Taliban promises of peace and an end to corruption.

Taliban justice proved brutal but the opposition was divided and isolated. By 2001, the Taliban controlled nearly all of Afghanistan, and the rebel Northern Alliance struggled without meaningful American backing. A fateful strategic alliance between the Taliban and al Qaeda had already been established, providing a safe haven for bin Laden, which he used to plan the September 11 attacks. American forces overthrew the Taliban regime in October 2001, sweeping through the country, with Helmand the last province to fall. Bin Laden, however, escaped to the borderlands of Pakistan, and al Qaeda's leadership continued to function. The Taliban leadership also crossed over into Pakistan to plot and prepare for a return.

The American preoccupation with Saddam Hussein gave the Taliban an opportunity. Lacking sufficient forces in the country, the Americans began to back Afghan warlords, weakening the central government of President Hamid Karzai. For his part, Karzai sought to control the country through patronage and corruption, alienating much of the population. The Taliban's roots in the Pashtun south, particularly in Kandahar and Helmand, meant that it was fertile ground for an insurgency against the Americans and their client Karzai.

While the war in Iraq grew more and more unpopular at home, in late 2005 Tony Blair committed British troops to Helmand for the spring of 2006. Lieutenant Colonel Guy Bartle-Jones, a Welsh Guards officer who had served on the NATO staff in Afghanistan and had attended the Pakistani staff college in Quetta, remembers a United Nations (UN) official and veteran Afghan hand warning him about Helmand. "Why the hell are we going into Helmand?" the UN official asked him. "Do you know what a nasty bit of country it is? It's full of drug smugglers and crime and tribally it's horrible." The view within the government, however, was that Helmand was the place to show what British troops could do. At a Defence Intelligence Staff briefing, Bartle-Jones suggested that a portion of Uruzugan province in which around four hundred Taliban fighters were causing problems might be a better bet for the British. "The line was, 'No, we'll need far fewer troops if we go into Helmand,'" Bartle-Jones remembers. "The assessment was that Uruzugan was too difficult and Helmand was going to be the easier option. How wrong we were." At a subsequent briefing given by a naval commander about requirements for language training, Bartle-Jones, the only officer there who had served in Afghanistan, found himself interrupting. "You do realise we are going down to Helmand and the main language there is Pashto, not Dari?" he said. The embarrassed response from the commander was that he did not. "That's the sort of ignorance there was around at the time," says Bartle-Jones.

The initial deployment was of three thousand troops, less than a third of them infantry and the rest support elements. Following its customary practice of assigning names of operations randomly by an MoD computer, British deployments to Afghanistan were called Operation Herrick, apparently after the seventeenth-century poet Robert Herrick. By the time the Welsh Guards arrived in Helmand, the army was engaged in Herrick 10. General Sir Richard Dannatt, who took over as chief of the general staff in August 2006, remembers an atmosphere in which "we really thought there was a possibility that we could conduct this as a benign reconstruction and development and bring a better life to the people." In military terms, he says, it was "getting on with the build, without any requirement for clear and hold." Looking back, he describes what the British did in 2006 as going into a sleeping lion's cage. "If you left him alone, he's only kipping in the corner. If you gave him a prod with a sharp stick, he'd jump up and attack you. And in a sense that's pretty much what we did in southern Afghanistan and in Helmand."

Sir Sherard Cowper-Coles, special representative of David Miliband, the foreign secretary, while the Welsh Guards were in Helmand, remarks that "good intentions" had prompted Tony Blair to deepen Britain's involvement in Afghanistan in 2006. There was, however, "a certain glibness about Blair and a sort of incurable optimism" that prevented a hardheaded assessment of the realities from the start. Cowper-Coles, who had been British ambassador to Afghanistan from May 2007 until April 2009, suggests that the army, anxious to move on from a bruising experience in southern Iraq, should also take its share of the blame for what happened later. "There was a tremendous desire within the Army to do more and to prove themselves and a laudable enthusiasm to get stuck in—you know, crack on. And all these rather poorly written papers by an enthusiastic military desperate to prove themselves after Basra to keep up with the Americans." The army's very willingness to make do and constantly strive to achieve more with less had sown the seeds of future difficulties. "Part of the problem is a very eager military with a laudable 'can-do' attitude offering politicians over-optimistic advice about what can be done and the resources needed to do it. And politicians not having either the will or the knowledge to question some of the military advice they have received that this is all doable." In addition, he says, there was "a mood in the Foreign Office that you mustn't upset the military."

For the Taliban, the arrival of the British was seen as the return of old adversaries seeking to avenge past defeats at the hands of the great Pashtun warriors of centuries past. "They are our historical enemies," said Maulavi Abdul Aziz Hamdard, a Taliban commander in the Nad-e Ali district, in an interview with the author conducted through an intermediary. "We had very brave ancestors, like Ahmad Shah and Mirwais Nika [an earlier Pashtun king], who defeated our British and Russian enemies. These British now are the same ones whose ancestors were defeated in Afghanistan. They are the grandchildren who have come here to take their revenge, nothing else. They insult our culture and values. Afghans made them feel shame and embarrassment in the past and now the British want to do the same to Afghans."

3

Whitehall Warrior

*Go into it thoroughly, closer scrutiny, think through the
implications, produce some papers, have some inter-departmental
discussions, make contingency plans. We are discussing the
defence of the realm.*

—*The Hon. James Hacker (Ret.) in his diary,*
The Complete Yes Prime Minister *(1989)*

---

*Crystal clear logic and powerful comprehension of complexity often
lead him to a counter-intuitive argument that he has the moral
courage to stay with. This makes him awkward to lead but it is an
essential part of any worthwhile solution.*

—*Group Captain A. J. Dey, report on*
Major Rupert Thorneloe, July 25, 2002

L ittle happened in the Ministry of Defence (MoD) that Rupert Thorneloe
did not know about. As the military assistant to Des Browne, secretary
of state for Defence, most matters of importance crossed the desk of the
lieutenant colonel, newly promoted in June 2008. Thorneloe was usually the
first person to arrive, shortly after 7:00 a.m., and without fail was the last to
leave, often close to midnight. Along with his formidable brain and prodigious
capacity for hard work, he possessed acute political antennae and—just as
useful—charm. He was not the kind of officer who needed to demonstrate
his intellectual superiority or impress someone with his status. He was adept
at reducing a complex issue to its essentials. People listened when he paused
to sum up what he was asking, saying: "So the exam question is...." He was

sought out by those who wanted advice or a sounding board. Thorneloe always made time to talk, which was part of the reason for the hours he kept. All this meant that he could alert Browne to a difficulty that might be developing or tip him off about an admiral, general, or bureaucrat who was a block to progress. Thorneloe remarked with a smile to friends that his habit of watching old videos of the BBC's satirical comedy *Yes Minister* had stood him in good stead. He was a skillful Whitehall warrior who could work the corridors of the MoD's main building with a deft and sometimes cunning touch.

On this particular day in late 2008, the piece of information that Thorneloe had picked up from the office of Sir Bill Jeffrey, the MoD's permanent secretary, was that a fire practice would soon be held. Thorneloe suggested to John McTernan, a Labour Party official acting as a special advisor to Browne, that they escape for a drink. Ten minutes later, the two of them were sitting onboard the *Tattershall Castle*, a 1930s paddle steamer that was now a bar and restaurant moored on the Thames Embankment. Thorneloe, sipping a Diet Coke, explained why he had chosen a military career. They made an unlikely pair: McTernan, a Scot, was instinctively suspicious of the army and the English public school types who populated its senior ranks. Yet the two often had long chats about their respective worlds of the army and politics, and Thorneloe had helped change what McTernan calls his "Leftie political illusions" by persuading him that military values were identical to those of public service. Thorneloe had impressed the Labour Party apparatchik with his willingness to challenge conventional wisdom. The Welsh Guards officer was a skeptic about the value of the British nuclear deterrent, for example, and believed firmly that the Cabinet Office rather than the MoD should pay for it. He had been instrumental in pushing the issue of helicopter shortages in Helmand up the defense agenda and was a firm critic of the civilian effort of Department for International Development (DFID) in Afghanistan. "At times he was frustrated by Gordon Brown's unwillingness to commit more troops to Afghanistan," McTernan recalls.

Thorneloe had recently learned he would be commanding the Welsh Guards in Helmand during the summer "fighting season" of 2009. To command his regiment in action, he told McTernan, would be the ultimate moment of his career. The Welsh Guards' losses onboard the *Sir Galahad* in 1982, he explained, were still painful and a living part of the regiment's history. Afghanistan would be a new chapter.

With a kindly, pockmarked face, broad, open smile, and rather disheveled appearance, Thorneloe was far from the stereotypical aloof Guards officer. Although loyal to a fault, he had a rich appreciation of the absurdity of some official positions, often communicating his feelings with a wry grin. Despite his formidable capacity for work, he always enjoyed a drink. When he was adjutant and in charge of discipline, Lance Sergeant Jiffy Myers was locking up the sergeants' mess bar when he noticed a figure struggling with a one-armed bandit machine. It was 8:00 a.m., and Captain Thorneloe was the last man standing after a rugby night for which the officers had been invited in. The lance sergeant, noticing Thorneloe was trying to insert a pound coin into the reject slot, suggested: "Sir, you're going to have to go to bed." Thorneloe was having none of it. "Just one more pound!" he said. Myers took pity on him and fed the coin into the right slot. Thorneloe didn't win but staggered off to his room contented nevertheless.

Thorneloe was aware of his own foibles and never took himself too seriously. In a rueful letter during his first term at Sandhurst in 1991, he had told his parents: "For the first five weeks, everything is a bit mindless and revolves around room inspections, drill and being impeccably turned out. Unfortunately, if you were to pick the three things I was absolutely not good at, it would probably be those three." Thorneloe was more than six feet, two inches, tall but had a slight stoop that hinted at a touch of shyness behind his intellectual self-confidence. Guardsmen joked that he leant forward because his brain was so large that it weighed his head down, prompting his nickname "The Brain."

While the name Rupert, an education at Radley, and fondness for polo could conjure up an image of a standard-issue toff, those who knew Thorneloe quickly dismissed any such notion. At staff college in 2002, he went out of his way to help foreign students who were struggling with their English. When a friend told him that Rita Restorick, mother of Lance Bombardier Stephen, killed by an IRA sniper in Northern Ireland in 1997, was still anguished about the death of her son, Thorneloe struck up a long-running email correspondence with her. The ordinary guardsmen revered Thorneloe because they knew that their welfare was his top priority. He was a rigorous master, but the heavier burden always fell on those higher up the rank structure—starting with himself—rather than the infantryman at the bottom. One of the few things that would cause Thorneloe to lose his temper was when a careless mistake by an officer had led to a guardsman being messed around.

Thorneloe was brought up in the village of Kirtlington in the green, undulating Oxfordshire countryside, close to Blenheim Palace, birthplace and ancestral home of Sir Winston Churchill. There cannot be anywhere more English in landscape, culture, or history. His father, Major John Thorneloe, a retired Royal Artillery officer who served in Burma, Malaya, and Singapore during the Second World War and later fought in the Korean War, was forty-seven when his eldest son was born. Thorneloe's mother Veronica was twenty-one years younger than her husband. She was the daughter of Commander Christopher Dreyer, who commanded a Motor Torpedo Boat flotilla at Dunkirk and won a DSO and two DSCs while still a lieutenant. It was a traditional and happy upper middle-class upbringing in rural England. The Thorneloe family kept polo ponies at their farm, and Rupert and his younger sister Jessica both became fine polo players. In 1990, at the age of twenty-one, Thorneloe won the *Daily Telegraph* saddle as Best Pony Club Player of the Year and was presented with his prize by the newspaper's editor, Max Hastings, a military historian he admired. The young Thorneloe also worked as a guide at Blenheim Palace, where his mother is still the head guide, and as a groundsman at Kirtlington Park Polo Club.

Thorneloe was attracted to joining the army at least in part because of the opportunities it would provide for playing polo. He was initially drawn to the 5th Royal Inniskilling Dragoon Guards, who had welcomed him on a visit to Tidworth by thrusting a polo stick into his hand. But the regiment was being amalgamated, and he was also being courted by the Life Guards, who had sponsored him at Sandhurst. Much to the chagrin of the Life Guards, Thorneloe was poached by the Welsh Guards, who appealed to his sense of fun, as well as adventure. Major Tony Ballard, infamous for trying (unsuccessfully) to claim insurance for his polo sticks lost aboard the *Sir Galahad* during the Falklands War, spotted him playing polo at Kirtlington. Lieutenant Colonel Reddy Watt, commanding officer of the Welsh Guards and later to become General Sir Redmond Watt, had also noted Thorneloe's polo talents and had him in his sights. Thorneloe was duly invited over for dinner at St. James's Palace, and the evening ended with him being assisted into a taxi, more than a little the worse for wear and having agreed to join the regiment. Thorneloe remarked in a letter to his parents that he had chosen the Welsh Guards because "they seemed to be the nicest Regiment and the most professional of all the ones I had visited." Northern Ireland, where the Welsh Guards were about to deploy, was an attraction because "it will be hard work towards something that I believe in and think worthwhile." He had considered the Royal Artillery, his father's regiment, but felt that the "work hard, play hard lot seem to join good infantry and cavalry regiments."

Almost as soon as Thorneloe was in uniform, however, the "play" element began to recede. His drive and determination to be a professional soldier meant, he soon concluded, that he wouldn't have enough time to pursue polo seriously, so he gave it up and took up sailing as a hobby. As a platoon commander in 2 Company, he displayed a dedication to doing things right and a sense of personal honor. On one occasion, he even reported himself to the Welsh Guards adjutant for a negligent discharge of a blank round. There was no evidence and there were no witnesses, but Thorneloe took some persuading that the matter should be dropped. His room at Ballykelly base in Northern Ireland looked, as one friend remarked, like "the later stages of a jumble sale." He once told his father that the benefit of leaving everything on the floor was that he always knew where to find things. Beneath the mounds of kit and clothes, however, were dog-eared copies of books about Irish history and military strategy. Thorneloe was not the sort of officer who had a pristine and unread copy of Sun Tzu's *The Art of War* placed prominently on a shelf. He also showed himself to be a compassionate officer and a natural problem-solver. A few weeks after he discovered that a guardsman in his platoon had debt problems, the young Welshman found himself on leave, working at a pub just outside Kirtlington, and staying at South Farm with Lieutenant Thorneloe's parents.

Thorneloe became a jungle warfare expert who projected a stoic calmness and cheerfully endured physical hardship. In 1996, he failed by a whisker to become the first officer from his regiment in two decades to pass the SAS selection course, falling just short on the final weapons-handling test. He then served as an intelligence officer in Northern Ireland and was among those who helped lay the groundwork for tracking down and arresting the IRA sniper team that had felled British soldiers, including Lance Bombardier Restorick, each with a single shot. Thorneloe usually traveled on his own in a civilian car with a 9 mm pistol in his coat pocket. He became fascinated with Captain Robert Nairac, another Guards officer who had done the same job two decades earlier and to whom Thorneloe bore a physical resemblance. Nairac was abducted and murdered by the IRA in 1977, and many criticized his *modus operandi* as reckless. Thorneloe, however, chose to focus on his thoughtful and unorthodox approach in understanding the mind of the border

Irish republican. He distributed a paper by Nairac called "Talking to People in South Armagh" to Parachute Regiment officers serving in the area and painstakingly built up diagrams of the connections between IRA families. He worked closely with the Royal Ulster Constabulary Special Branch, often emerging with a valuable morsel of information that had taken a bottle of Black Bush whiskey to tease out of a suspicious policeman.

A man of strong opinions who was not afraid of expressing them trenchantly, Thorneloe was intensely irritated by the soft treatment on television of politicians from Sinn Fein, the IRA's political wing. In a letter in January 1997, he took Jeremy Paxman, the BBC *Newsnight* presenter, to task for being "totally and utterly walked over" by Martin McGuinness, the Sinn Fein leader. "I and many like me sit and watch programmes like yours in first disbelief then anger, as yet again we see terrorists let off the hook by interviewers such as yourselves. It makes a mockery of the principles of a liberal democracy and is a disgraceful insult to the memories of these people's victims." Sinn Fein politicians, he added, "have personally murdered soldiers, policemen and civilians and have organised the murders of thousands more."

Lieutenant Colonel Sandy Malcolm, commanding the Welsh Guards in South Armagh, was instantly impressed by the young brigade intelligence officer. He picked him to become Welsh Guards adjutant, a job given to those set for higher things. Once in the post, Thorneloe displayed formidable attention to detail and an intuitive sense of where a potential difficulty might be emerging. Malcolm, who occasionally had to order his adjutant to leave the office after finding him there late at night, describes Thorneloe as the man who held the battalion together. Trooping the color, however, proved a challenge. Thorneloe's parade-ground skills had not improved over the years, and Bill Mott 88, then the drill sergeant of the Welsh Guards, remarked that it was fortunate that the adjutant would be on a horse for the big day, because at least one of them would know where to put his feet.

Staff college, a crucial career stop for ambitious majors, was much more Thorneloe's forte. His 2002 report from there stated that he had "taken risks, pushed the boundaries and developed himself from a high starting point to an even more rarefied plane." His "crystal clear logic and powerful comprehension of complexity," the report said, would often lead him "to a counter-intuitive argument that he has the moral courage to stay with." Thorneloe was developing into a creative and original military thinker. His next stop was to command 2 Company, which he did with distinction in

Northern Ireland. In 2003, he was chosen to lead a brigade battlefield tour of Monte Cassino in Italy, the devastated town the Welsh Guards had helped hold after it had been all but obliterated by Allied forces in 1944. Many young majors would have regarded such a task as a chore, but Thorneloe reveled in it, bringing in the daughter of a German commander as well as British veterans of the battle to brief members of his brigade. "Rupert Thorneloe gave a really terrific talk in which he set Monte Cassino in the context of the entire Second World War in about 20 minutes," remembers Major General William Cubitt, then in command of the brigade. "He was absolutely fascinated by strategy. He was a major but he conducted the tour as if he was a general."

Thorneloe married Sally Parker on July 24, 2004. They had met in the autumn of 2001 at a mutual friend's birthday party, and he had invited her to go sailing with him in *Valentina*, his thirty-foot Hunter, at the Benbridge Regatta on the Isle of Wight. He managed to run the boat aground that weekend, but this had the happy result that they spent an extra day together. Thorneloe felt a deep sense of personal failure after the breakup of his 1996 marriage to Dr. Francesca de Bono (known as "Ceskie"), whose parents had lived next door in Kirtlington. An academic and the niece of lateral thinker Edward de Bono, she did not enjoy the army or share Thorneloe's eagerness to have children, and the couple had parted amicably. Thorneloe discovered a contentedness with Sally, who was three years his senior, which was to underpin his rapid progression in the army. She embraced service life, giving up her cherished job at the wine merchants Corney & Barrow to move to the 1st Armoured Division base at Herford in Germany. Hannah, born in Germany, was a honeymoon baby; two years later, Sophie was born.

While the hours Thorneloe kept were a source of strain and she worried that he did not see enough of the children, Sally embraced the role of army wife and was devoted to her husband. Thorneloe told his father about one occasion when his long absences were brought up, and he had explained that he had seldom seen his own father because he worked in London during the week or was abroad. "He had a job to do and I've got a job to do," Thorneloe had said, his father recalls. "If there's something to be done, I've got to do it." Although his work habits were modified only slightly, Thorneloe's closest friends noticed the new fulfillment that a happy, secure marriage and fatherhood had brought him.

A few months after Hannah's birth, Thorneloe was deployed to Basra as the 1st Armored Division's Operations Officer, coordinating and planning all British military activities in Southern Iraq. He won plaudits across the army. Major General John Cooper reported that Thorneloe "routinely works 18 to 20 hours per day, seven days a week, managing a vast portfolio ranging from the destruction of chemical munitions, through controlling our daily battle to attack terrorists to the detailed staff work." Thanks to Thorneloe, each unit had always been "in the right place at the right time with everything necessary to succeed." He concluded: "I cannot overstate the contribution he has made to the UK and coalition servicemen and women here, and to helping the people of Iraq take charge of their lives." Thorneloe was awarded the MBE for his work in Iraq. When he drove his wife and parents into Buckingham Palace to receive his medal from the Prince of Wales, wearing a scruffy coat over his uniform, he was directed to the chauffeurs' waiting room. "Actually, I'm the recipient," he replied sheepishly.

After a spell as military assistant to the assistant chief of Defence staff (policy), Thorneloe was promoted to lieutenant colonel at just thirty-eight. Amid stiff competition across all three armed services, he was chosen to work for the Defence secretary, Des Browne. As the lead advisor on Afghanistan in the personal office, Thorneloe planned Browne's visits and was at his side during each one, including Gordon Brown's first trip to Afghanistan as prime minister in December 2007. There, speaking at Camp Bastion, Brown told troops that "to defeat the Taliban and to make sure that we can give strength to the new democracy of Afghanistan is important in defeating terrorism all round the world."

On their return, Thorneloe was part of the small team that drafted Brown's statement to the House of Commons, in which he stated that "we are winning the battle against the insurgency—isolating and eliminating the leadership of the Taliban, not negotiating with them." The following June, Thorneloe wrote Des Browne's "uplift" statement to Parliament, in which he announced a troop-level increase from 7,800 to 8,030 by spring 2009, when the Welsh Guards were due to arrive. In December 2008, this was increased to 8,300—a number that would cause Thorneloe major headaches once he was in Helmand. Des Browne remarked that the Taliban had begun to "reduce their ambition from insurgency to terrorism" by increasingly resorting to IEDs, something that was a "sign of strategic weakness." He maintained that "the green shoots of development and democracy are becoming even more firmly rooted in a security environment that has improved out of all measure since UK forces deployed in southern Afghanistan two years ago."

The language of both Gordon Brown and Des Browne during this period, much of which Thorneloe had drafted, sounded strikingly optimistic at the time and even more so subsequently. Thorneloe was a realist, but he knew that public support was vital to military success. While he would argue his point strenuously behind the scenes, Thorneloe's loyalty meant he kept his doubts to himself outside the walls of the MoD. Though Des Browne lacked defense experience, Thorneloe respected his ability and shared his humanitarian instincts. He also felt that the Defence secretary had been badly treated when Gordon Brown succeeded Tony Blair as prime minister in June 2007 and lumbered him with the additional job of Scottish secretary. Des Browne came to rely heavily on Thorneloe, believing that he had done more than anyone else to "sell" the 2008 uplift to a skeptical Whitehall. Browne also came to value Thorneloe's companionship, remarking that the best part of his day would be when the young lieutenant colonel would stick his head through the door and ask: "Fancy a brew, Sir?" Thorneloe's final report, written by John Hutton, the new Defence secretary, concluded: "He will reach Brigadier and almost certainly beyond."

For all his fascination with the ways of Whitehall and the prestige of working at the highest political levels, Thorneloe could hardly bear to wait to take over his regiment. When he heard the news that he would command the Welsh Guards, who would be deploying to Helmand in April 2009, Thorneloe bounded down to the office of Brigadier Tim Radford to celebrate. Radford, a soft-spoken, cerebral officer, had piercing blue eyes and an understated manner honed during years of operations in Northern Ireland and Iraq. He had been chosen to lead 19th Light Brigade in Helmand, the seventh British brigadier to command Task Force Helmand for a six-month tour. In addition, he would be commander of British forces in Afghanistan, putting him notionally in charge of British troops as far afield as Kabul and Kandahar. Unlike some of his hard-charging predecessors, Radford was a listener rather than a talker. His thoughtful, considered approach, underpinned by great compassion, masked a real determination to seize the initiative in central Helmand, which had been neglected. The brigade was designated the main effort by Regional Command (South), the division which was commanded by Radford's direct boss, Major General Mart de Kruif of the Dutch army.

Thorneloe was to be one of Radford's seven battle group commanders in Helmand, and he didn't stop grinning for days after his new appointment was confirmed. "He was absolutely thrilled," Radford recalls. "For him this was—other than family—the most important thing. To command the Welsh Guards on operations in Afghanistan that summer was right at the peak of what he wanted to achieve and he was just so enormously proud." Radford immediately began deciding how he was going to use his different units in Helmand. Initially, the Welsh Guards were designated as Battle Group (Northwest), based in Musa Qala.

In September 2008, Thorneloe was in the Royal Box at Twickenham for a rugby match to raise money for the Help for Heroes charity. In uniform, Thorneloe was accompanying Des Browne and the Prince of Wales and had invited along his best friend, Tom Gadsby, a former Gurkha Rifles officer. After the match, he pointed out to Gadsby an officer in a wheelchair who was among the troops who had recently returned from Helmand and were being honored. "That's David Richmond, Commanding Officer of the Argyll and Sutherland Highlanders," he said. "He was quite badly wounded in Helmand a few months ago in the place where we're going to be in a year's time. I haven't told Sally." Lieutenant Colonel Richmond had been hit by an AK-47 bullet in Musa Qala in June, shattering his thigh bone and leaving one leg 10 cm shorter than the other.

Barely three weeks after the rugby match, the situation in Helmand changed for the worse when the Taliban launched a major offensive against the provincial capital of Lashkar Gah. Using around 170 fighters in four distinct groupings, on October 11 the Taliban attacked the town from the west, north, and south while placing a blocking force to the east. The plan was to draw British and Afghan troops into close-in fighting that would prevent NATO air power being used for fear of friendly fire casualties. Although the Taliban were comprehensively defeated, with at least sixty-two fighters killed during the four-hour battle, the insurgents had—however briefly—threatened the British headquarters of Task Force Helmand and held a knife to the throat of the provincial government. Central Helmand, where most of the population lived, had been neglected by the recently departed 16th Air Assault Brigade. With only limited resources available, it had concentrated on transporting a new turbine from Kandahar and installing it at the Kajaki Dam. Brigadier Gordon Messenger of 3 Commando Brigade, which had just taken over in Lashkar Gah, decided that British forces needed to be reconfigured. He created a new Battle Group (Center South) in Helmand, based in the Nad-e Ali district, to the west of Lashkar Gah, where the main Taliban thrust had come from in October.

The original British plan in the spring of 2006 had been to focus on the population centers, but the army, encouraged by the Karzai government, had instead got sucked into what became known as the "platoon house strategy." Fixed defensive positions were established in remote locations like Musa Qala, Sangin, Now Zad, and Kajaki, which soon attained mystical status as troops heroically withstood attack.

Messenger concluded that the platoon house strategy had been symptomatic of a flawed British approach. He wanted to return to the original concept of concentrating on the "Afghan Development Zone" in central Helmand, a notional triangle between Lashkar Gah, Gereshk, and Camp Bastion that contained most of the province's population.

In a post-tour interview with the army's Land Warfare Center, Messenger argued that "the centre of Helmand had been under-invested," and his top priority had been to correct that. The "situation that we had inherited [in October 2008] was one where the majority of our combat power was focused on peripheral District Centres … and we had stripped out any combat power we once had in the centre of Helmand." Remedying this had been difficult because there were not enough troops in Helmand, Messenger argued. "We wanted to stabilise Central Helmand as best we could, but there were areas which we could not reach with what we had." He had "no reserve at all during the tour, and could only raise forty soldiers to get out of the Lashkar Gah gates and patrol the area." He had been forced to filch resources from existing battle groups to cobble together the new Battle Group (Center South), but this was still not enough to pacify the area around Nad-e Ali. American military planners were convinced that the British had committed so few troops to Helmand that they were barely treading water.

Colonel Martin Smith, Messenger's deputy and the first commander of Battle Group (Center South), said in his post-tour report that he "probably had only half the number of personnel that you would expect" in his headquarters. "Although we were able to plan and conduct operations, we had little horsepower in influence and intelligence," he said. His task had been to defeat the Taliban in four key villages in the Nad-e Ali area, but: "We did not have a force of sufficient size to clear large areas of ground. Therefore I needed to persuade enemy forces to accept defeat and move out of the area."

Messenger also made the case that the British military effort was misdirected because it had "been focused too much on the kinetic application of violence, and not focused enough on cultural awareness." Referring to the former *EastEnders* actor Ross Kemp, who had appeared in two Sky documentary series reveling in the intense firefights being fought by British troops, he stated: "I still feel that we (as an armed force) think of Afghanistan in Ross Kemp-like terms of rounds flying overhead and getting rounds back, rather than building the trust and allegiance of the population." Even more damningly, he concluded that the British were guilty of what they had often accused the Americans of doing: "our reaction to being fired at is still to react in kind, sometimes disproportionately, alienating sections of the population as a consequence."

In an attempt to ensure continuity from Messenger's 3 Commando Brigade, Radford decided that the new Battle Group (Center South) would be his main effort once he arrived with his brigade in April 2009. Battle Group (Center South)'s job would be to consolidate British control of the Nad-e Ali district, cleared by Messenger's forces in December 2008, and begin winning over the population. It was a task, Radford felt, for a commanding officer who could deal with complexity and nuance, understood the bigger picture and would direct his troops accordingly. Rupert Thorneloe and the Welsh Guards were shifted from Musa Qala to do it.

Radford would have seven Battle Groups in Task Force Helmand as part of his initial total force of around eight thousand, all wearing 19 Brigade's triangular left-shoulder flash depicting a roaring panther. Each battle group was based around a battalion—normally seven hundred men—that was augmented or pared down. The additional companies, vehicle groups, and support elements given to the Welsh Guards eventually swelled its numbers to more than 1,500. The northernmost element would be Battle Group (Northwest) in Musa Qala, led by the 2nd Battalion Royal Regiment of Fusiliers. Some thirty-five kilometers to the southeast, where the Musa Qala and Helmand rivers joined, was to be Battle Group (North), formed around 2nd Battalion Rifles, commanded by Lieutenant Colonel Rob Thomson and including Sangin, where more British troops had been killed than in any other district. Another fifty kilometers southwest along the Helmand was the Danish Battle Group (Center) at Gereshk. About forty kilometers southwest of Gereshk was the Nad-e Ali town, the center of the Nad-e Ali district and earmarked as the headquarters of the new Battle Group (Centre South). For the time being, however, the headquarters would be at Camp Bastion while a new base was created at Nad-e Ali. So Thorneloe would initially be separated from the troops he was commanding. It was a situation inherited from 3 Commando Brigade and a deeply unsatisfactory state of affairs.

In addition, the Black Watch, or 3rd Royal Regiment of Scotland, was designated Regional Battle Group (South), 450-strong, based at Camp Roberts in Kandahar, and used as an all-purpose "flying squad." The Light Dragoons Battle Group, under Lieutenant Colonel Gus Fair, was at first going to be Battle Group (South) based at Garmsir, sixty-five kilometers south of Nad-e Ali. U.S. Marines, however, were arriving in Helmand in their thousands. Based at Camp Leatherneck, right next to Camp Bastion in the Dasht-e Margo, the U.S. Marines were beginning to form a "C" shape around the south, west, and north of British forces. Garmsir was to be handed over to the U.S. Marines, freeing up the Light Dragoons to go into the Taliban-controlled area of Babaji, north of Lashkar Gah, for what was to become Operation Panther's Claw beginning in late June.

The 2 Mercians Battle Group, based at Camp Tombstone next to Camp Bastion, four hundred–strong and commanded by Lieutenant Colonel Simon Banton, was tasked with being the "OMLT"—Operational Mentoring and Liaison Team—working with the Afghan army. OMLT forces would be dispersed in twenty locations throughout Helmand. The Welsh Guards had been told by 19 Brigade that they could only have two infantry companies and that a third would be split up and its core used for OMLT. It was decided that this would be 3 Company. The company's 7 Platoon was sent to 2 Company and its 8 Platoon to the Prince of Wales's Company. Major Guy Stone was to lead a group based in the Sangin district center and four patrol bases, Nabi, Blenheim, Waterloo, and Pylae. The Welsh Guards core of 3 Company comprised three officers, eleven NCOs, and two guardsmen. Drafted into 3 Company for the tour were forty-five soldiers from half a dozen other regiments, swelling the total number to sixty-one men.

The decision to split up 3 Company and detach two of its platoons had initially come as a blow to Stone. It meant being sixty-five kilometers away from the main element of the Welsh Guards under the command of 2 Mercians within the 2 Rifles area of operations, Battle Group (North). This complicated arrangement meant that Stone would technically have four bosses—

Thorneloe, Banton, Thomson, and Lieutenant Colonel Abdul Wadood of the Afghan army. Stone had been three years behind Thorneloe at Radley and was the son of a retired major general. A slightly built officer, his physique suited that of a leader of the Little Iron Men. Engaging and thoughtful, he was known for his formidable attention to detail and capacity for careful planning. He was to complete his tour without losing a single soldier under his command—a remarkable achievement in Sangin, which had attained an iconic status as a killing field for the British Army.

Just weeks before the Welsh Guards were due to deploy with two companies, Thorneloe was told by Radford's staff that he would need a third company after all because of the requirement to protect Lashkar Gah from a growing Taliban threat. It was too late to put Stone's 3 Company back together again—they were deep into their training with 2 Mercians—so a new company had to be formed based on remnants of 3 Company, plus men begged and borrowed from the Prince of Wales's, 2 Company, and the rest of the battalion. Thorneloe, with his keen appreciation of regimental history, came up with the idea of resurrecting the lead company of the old 2nd Battalion of the Welsh Guards, which had been placed in suspended animation in 1947 once demobilization from the Second World War was complete. The old company had been 1 Company of the 2nd Battalion, but 1 Company could not be used because that was the Prince of Wales's Company. In terms of precedence across the regiment, 1 Company, 2nd Battalion, had been ninth, after the three rifle companies of the 1st Battalion and additional companies such as the band and headquarters. Rather than plain 9 Company, Thorneloe decided to use the Roman numerals IX to denote its antiquity and separateness from the 1st Battalion companies. Thus IX Company was born.

There was also a brigade requirement for an additional company to take on the Afghan army training duties under the banner of the 2 Mercians Battle Group. This would require a major leading a group of about twenty-five soldiers fighting deep in southern Helmand alongside an Afghan *kandak*, or battalion of five hundred men, initially within the Light Dragoons Battle Group and later under the command of the U.S. Marine Corps. Having already come up with the concept of IX Company, it naturally followed that this latest creation could be X Company, the old 2 Company, 2nd Battalion, which had as its motto: "I will not return Unavenged."

Even as he was formulating the idea of these new companies, Thorneloe had two officers in mind for leading them. Major Sean Birchall and Major

Rob Gallimore were close friends and contemporaries due to take over as commanders of 2 Company and 3 Company, respectively, during the Helmand tour. New British Army rules, however, dictated that there could be no routine changes in company commanders during an operational deployment. Both Birchall and Gallimore, therefore, were in real danger of not being able to go to Afghanistan.

Sean Birchall had already missed out on going with the Welsh Guards to Iraq in 2004–05 and was showing enormous potential. He was six feet tall, supremely fit, charismatic, and film-star handsome—and keen as mustard to get out to Helmand. Birchall lobbied hard to be plucked from his staff job at the Permanent Joint Headquarters (PJHQ) in Northwood, from where all British military operations are commanded. Thorneloe knew that it was important for Birchall's career that he be given a challenging role in Helmand. Building any sort of cohesion and real combat effectiveness was going to be a tough challenge given the way that IX Company would have to be cobbled together at short notice. Not only had the company not trained together, it did not even meet up for the first time until everyone arrived at Camp Bastion at the start of the tour.

Gallimore, who had been Operations Officer in Iraq, was blond, six feet, four inches tall, and broad-shouldered. He was one of the biggest characters in the Welsh Guards officers' mess. Irrepressible and with an enormous zest for life, he had already served for six months in Helmand in a brigade headquarters in 2007. He had a reputation as a fearless officer with a relish for combat but almost no interest in staff work, small talk, or doing anything, including drinking, in moderation. Another officer described his reports as "A's for operations and C minuses for life in barracks." As X Company commander, Gallimore would have to go to war commanding just two Welsh Guardsmen and another twenty-two soldiers from seventeen different regiments. Mentoring Afghan troops in battle was dangerous and challenging. Thorneloe felt it would be a good fit for the adventurous Gallimore, who got bored easily. He told Gallimore that he thought he was "suited to tearing around with a lot of, shall we say, unpredictable Afghans," adding: "You've always been comfortable in chaos."

The son of a chemical process engineer from Wrexham, Birchall was one of five children and the eldest of three brothers. He had attended St. Peter's Comprehensive near Guildford and then the former Plymouth Polytechnic before joining the army. It was far from a typical Welsh Guards background, though that seemed to matter more to Birchall than it did to anyone else. When asked what school he had gone to, Birchall would reply: "St. Peter's, small school outside Guildford" and then swiftly change the subject. As adjutant, Thorneloe had been instrumental in poaching Birchall, initially committed to the Parachute Regiment, for the Welsh Guards. Birchall was very aware that he did not come from archetypal Guards stock and told his father at one point that he was the only comprehensive-educated officer in the Household Division. Knowing that he was not to the manner born, Birchall was more committed, determined, and serious than almost any of his contemporaries. He looked and acted the part so well and always got so much from his men that he was seen as the epitome of what a modern Welsh Guards officer should be. A slight unease led to the endearing trait of his seeming a touch surprised that he was such a good officer.

His younger brother Paul had become a professional wrestler with World Wrestling Entertainment (WWE) in the United States. He used the name "Paul Birchill" and was known as "the Ripper," sometimes dressing in the ring as a pirate. His signature moves included the Standing Moonsault, the No-Handed Flip Dive, and the Pumphandle Sidewalk Slam. Sean Birchall was reticent about mentioning the career of his brother, who had moved to Kentucky to pursue a life with WWE, fearing it might be looked down on by the Guards. This was not the case, and in the eyes of the ordinary guardsmen it only increased the "street cred" of their company commander. Shortly after arriving in Helmand, a Paul Birchill action doll was produced in the United States; a number of them were duly ordered by members of IX Company.

Sean Birchall had already been tested in combat. During an attachment to U.S. Central Command in Tampa, Florida, in 2006, he traveled to eastern Afghanistan's Ghazni province, on the road from Kabul to Kandahar. In August 2006, he was on a patrol with the U.S. Army's Task Force Paladin, a counter-IED unit, when it was ambushed by the Taliban. The patrol was split, and Birchall found himself as the senior officer in the smaller element, cut off and virtually surrounded. Under fire from machine guns and RPGs, he ordered American troops into firing positions and pushed into a Taliban-held village. His citation for the U.S. Army's Combat Infantry Badge praised his "aggressive actions" and stated that "by moving himself forward into the enemy's field of fire and himself engaging and killing a number of enemy combatants, he motivated his men to fight" at close quarters in the village.

Birchall managed to get himself and his men back to the rest of the patrol without any serious injuries. The firefight had lasted more than four hours.

The mission in Afghanistan was something that Sean Birchall firmly believed in. At a bar in Lexington, Kentucky, after their brother Paul's wedding, Dominic Birchall, the youngest of the three brothers, asked Sean whether he believed British interests were served by fighting the Taliban. Sean, who was just about to deploy to Helmand, put down his beer and said: "Either we do it there or we do it on the streets of England."

Gallimore reveled in his image as a Viking, a fearsome warrior on the battlefield whose carousing off it got him into trouble. But his penchant for enjoying himself to the full masked a sensitivity, as well as a fierce intellect and literary bent. A romantic, he loved the idea of X Company and was soon to be driving across the Helmand Desert wearing U.S. Marine Corps fatigues and hair that was considerably longer than the regulation "high and tight" worn by his American comrades. His style was that of many a Welsh Guards officer from another era—he enjoyed combat and camaraderie but could do without the duller and more mundane aspects of modern army life. He delighted in telling people that he had secured promotion to captain by catching a batsman out off the bowling of the then commanding officer of the Welsh Guards. The quirky randomness of such a decision appealed to him much more than the idea of promotion boards, impressing the right people, and keeping one's nose clean. "I've got a 2:1 from the London School of Economics and I'm in this because it's fun," Gallimore says. "When you take the fun out of it, and ask me to do bone stupid things to humour someone on a Brigade staff whose intellect doesn't actually impress me, I'm not interested."

Birchall had first met Gallimore, six months ahead of him, when he had joined the Welsh Guards a decade earlier. "He wasn't a public schoolboy and he was wonderfully pent up about it," recalls Gallimore. "I was like, 'F---ing hell, mate, relax. We're the Welsh Guards, we're not like that.' I come from a bog in the west of Ireland, my grandfather was in the IRA and I was probably the next most common bloke in the mess. I went to Uppingham, which was described in the *Sloane Ranger's Handbook* [sic] as the place where Northern industrialists send their sons to have their accents surgically removed." This did not stop Gallimore ribbing Birchall. On one occasion, Gallimore, nursing yet another hangover, walked past Birchall's open door in barracks. He spotted his friend, ever fastidious about his kit and equipment, tying bungee cords to the edges of his military poncho. "Sean, if you're going to have to do that please have the decency to close the door," Gallimore grumbled. Birchall was mortified; perhaps the Welsh Guards hadn't changed from the 1930s, when its gentlemen officers would be rebuked by the adjutant if they were caught working in the company office after lunch, he wondered. "Sean thought this was my attitude towards professionalism," laughs Gallimore. "It took him about a year to realise that I was joking."

In the months before IX Company and X Company were dreamt up, Birchall and Gallimore found themselves competing for what might have been just one extra company commander's slot in Helmand. In such a situation it would have been understandable for Birchall, the more career-minded officer, to push himself forward at his rival's expense. But Birchall did not work that way. Despite his eagerness to get to Afghanistan, he would not trample over a friend to achieve it. He told Gallimore: "I'd rather neither of us goes than just one of us." And he meant it.

Once Thorneloe had, characteristically, managed to identify and create slots for each of them, the old sets of IX and X Company colors were retrieved from Welsh Guards Regimental Headquarters and dusted off. The mother of Major Dai Bevan, a friend and contemporary of Gallimore and Birchall, was given the courtesy title of honorary company captain of X Company. Her father, Brigadier James Windsor Lewis, had been wounded and captured at Boulogne in May 1940 while commanding 3 Company of the 2nd Battalion of the Welsh Guards.[1] Gallimore joked that his only reservation about his new role was that Thorneloe had reformed a company that had lain dormant for sixty-two years as a way of getting him out of the battalion.

The preparations for Helmand were relentless but as the commanding officer, there was almost nothing Thorneloe would not sacrifice for his battalion. Company Sergeant Major Andy Campbell, the head rugby coach, had been to him to discuss the Welsh Guards team for the Army Cup semi-finals against the Royal Welsh, the cup holders. At issue was whether a Coldstream Guardsman could be fielded. Campbell had studied the rules, and they stated that a player attached to the battalion could be fielded. Campbell needed the player, so it was decided the Coldstreamer could be attached temporarily for the purposes of the game. Thorneloe gave the OK. "The laws were grey, we saw the gap and we decided to go for it," remembers Campbell. Unfortunately, a clerk at the army's personnel center in Glasgow neglected to stamp the paperwork until the day of the game. The Welsh

Guards had fielded an ineligible player. "Somebody took exception to that," says Campbell. "And they kicked us out of the Army Cup."

It was late February and the Welsh Guards were leaving for war within weeks. Almost any other commanding officer would have let the matter rest, but not Thorneloe. He and Campbell spent hours drinking tea and going over what the grounds for appeal should be. Thorneloe realized that the team had trained hard, and it was an issue of morale not just for the players, but for the whole battalion. On the day of the appeal hearing, Thorneloe missed a brigade planning conference in Northern Ireland so he could drive to Brecon with Campbell to make the case for the Welsh Guards team. "He didn't have to do it," says Campbell. "In a way, it would have been easier for everyone if he hadn't. But he did it and that was a mark of the man." The Welsh Guards won their appeal and were reinstated, but they lost in the final to the Royal Scots Borderers.

4

Fighting Season

[We] are temporary guardians of a large, complex and long term campaign during what will be a critical six-month period in the tactically most significant area of Helmand ... we are extremely short of combat power.

—Lieutenant Colonel Rupert Thorneloe,
Battle Group commander's intent, April 22, 2009

It was our fault, and our very great fault, and not the judgement of Heaven.
We made an Army in our own image, on an island nine by seven,
Which faithfully mirrored its makers' ideals, equipment, and mental attitude—
And so we got our lesson: and we ought to accept it with gratitude.

—**Rudyard Kipling,** *"The Lesson,"* 1901 (regarding the Boer War)

I t was only a thirty-second conversation. "What if the unimaginable happens and you don't come back?" asked Sally Thorneloe. They were in their bedroom in Badajos House, their married quarter in Aldershot, named after Wellington's victory over the French in 1812. They had lived there for the past six months. "Well, it won't," replied her husband. "And if it did, I'd just want you to be happy." Rupert Thorneloe named a couple of schools that might be suitable for their daughters Hannah, four, and Sophie, two, and suggested that the family should live near Calne in Wiltshire, close to Sally's recently widowed father. "But it'll be OK," he reassured her. The day before, his father had filmed him reading Beatrix Potter's classic *Peter Rabbit* and the rather more modern *More Pants* for the girls to watch while he was in Afghanistan. At 2:00 a.m. on Wednesday, April 15, his driver, Lance Corporal Michael Jones 11 from Aberystwyth, was waiting in the staff car outside Badajos House. The couple had been sitting drinking tea in the kitchen for the final hour. Sally told her husband that she loved him very much and that their daughters loved him, too. Then Lieutenant Colonel Thorneloe kissed Sally goodbye and left for war.

Thorneloe had prepared meticulously for Helmand. For weeks he had been returning from Lille Barracks late in the evening and then poring over his computer into the early hours, working out which key personnel should go where and how his troops should be dispersed across the Battle Group's area of operations. Even when the family managed to get away for the weekend, Thorneloe would be sitting in the passenger seat, scribbling away in his notebook in an illegible scrawl.

"Every single night he was planning and plotting and organising and phoning people until he was completely ready and knew he was happy," remembers Sally. "Mentally he'd gone a month before. He was just physically walking around the house."

Thorneloe and his headquarters staff were the last Welsh Guardsmen to fly out. All through the Wednesday, Hannah and Sophie watched the planes overhead and jumped up in the air shouting: "Bye bye, Daddy." Then the telephone rang. "Sal, I'm still here," said Thorneloe. "Can you come and pick me up?" That night they had supper at Sally's father's house in Oxfordshire so that it wasn't too far to drop him back off at RAF Brize Norton later.

On the Thursday came another telephone call. The RAF, apparently without enough planes to fly personnel in and out of Afghanistan, was still unable to find a seat for the commanding officer of the Welsh Guards. By Friday, exasperation was setting in for the officers and their families. "I'm really sorry but the children are completely confused because I keep telling them you're going and you're not, so we'll come and get you but we can't do it again," said Sally. "This is the last time." Thorneloe, who was wearing the same desert combat fatigues he'd donned on Tuesday night, was furious about the delay, which was eating into precious handover time. Mercifully, the RAF TriStar took off on Saturday, taking Thorneloe to Kandahar and then onward by transport plane to Camp Bastion, the desert base where the Welsh Guards Battle Group would be headquartered. The sixty or so men of 3 Company, who were departing a month early, were told they had to fly to Northern Ireland to deploy with the other Afghan army training elements. A day later, they flew back to England. Their plane then had to stop in Muscat due to an equipment problem. All told, it took them six days to get to Afghanistan.

The new Battle Group (Center South) area of operations, bordered by the Nahr-e Bughra Canal to the west, which separated the Green Zone from the Dasht-e Margo, or Desert of Death, contained about 160 square kilometers of inhabited land. In the southwest, the enemy front line was to be kept at bay by three platoons at Checkpoint (CP) Paraang, next to the village of Khowshaal Kalay, CP Haji Alem, and Patrol Base (PB) Tanda. The company headquarters and a fourth platoon were to be housed at PB Silab, where the Green Zone met the desert. The designation of checkpoint was used for the most isolated and Spartan locations. Patrol bases were also very rudimentary compared with the large and relatively well-equipped forward operating bases (FOBs).

Thorneloe allocated these four locations to 2 Company under Major Henry Bettinson. A tall, swarthy man, it was joked that Bettinson might be mistaken for a member of the Taliban if he was captured while unshaven. Educated at Malvern and Oxford Brookes University, the bespectacled Bettinson was described by one senior officer as a "stout yeoman" who was dependable but did not always show the greatest initiative. His elder brother James, five years his senior, had preceded him in the Welsh Guards and died of Creutzfeldt-Jakob disease (CJD) at age twenty-seven. James Bettinson had been prescribed with human growth hormone from the age of nine to seventeen because of his small stature. He grew to over six feet and worked for four years as a fisherman in Australia before joining the army, but the treatment eventually killed him. Fiercely determined to become the first person to survive CJD, James Bettinson lived for fourteen months after diagnosis—rather than the usual six.

Henry Bettinson had married Marlo, an Australian working as a personnel specialist at a London bank, in 2006, and they already had two young children. His grandfather, Second Lieutenant Harold Bettinson of the Machine Gun Corps, had won a Military Cross (MC) on the western front in 1918 when he was nineteen years old. Harold Bettinson was later gassed in Flanders but became a solicitor in the family firm in Birmingham and lived to eighty-seven. His MC citation detailed his "conspicuous gallantry and devotion to duty" in holding up the enemy to help other troops withdraw, displaying "a high example of courage and disregard of danger." There was something of the First World War in Henry Bettinson's style as a company commander. He was stoic and dogged, the kind of officer who could be pointed at the enemy and trusted to get on with things. His earnest, no-nonsense manner endeared him to his guardsmen, who were sometimes suspicious of flashier officers. From the start, Henry Bettinson's 2 Company was given the kind of tough and thankless task that his grandfather might have recognized—out on the edge, face to face with the enemy and starved of resources.

The Prince of Wales's Company was given the role of protecting the district center of Nad-e Ali itself with two platoons and the company headquarters based at PB Argyll, a disused school. Another platoon was based at the more isolated PB Pimon on the northwestern side of the Welsh Guards area of operations, next to the desert and the Taliban-controlled villages of Chah-e Mirza and Zorabad. The company was also responsible for a large area surrounding the district center, including the Taliban-controlled villages of Shin Kalay, Zarghun Kalay, and Chah-e Anjir. They worked alongside two Afghan National Army companies and the Nad-e Ali chief of police; the district center itself was guarded primarily by these Afghan forces.

Unlike 2 Company, which was fighting intense close-range battles along a well-defined front line dividing British-held territory from the Taliban-held south, including Marjah, the Prince of Wales's Company faced a more dispersed and elusive enemy force. Leaving the Afghans to take the lead in the district center itself, the Prince of Wales's Company concentrated on trying to create a buffer zone around the district center. This included countering the Taliban who had infiltrated the area to the north of the district center but also those that operated to the south, behind the front line marked by 2 Company's bases. Using compounds about a kilometer to the north of the district center to lay up overnight, the Taliban would attack the Prince of Wales's Company as they pushed up to engage with the locals. Battles involving the whole company or just a platoon were fought far out in the surrounding towns and villages. Once it became clear how fixed in place 2 Company had become, Gorup-e Shesh Kalay, another Taliban-controlled village, was switched to the Prince of Wales's Company area of operations.

The Prince of Wales's Company was commanded by Major Giles Harris, already marked out as having a strong chance of commanding the Welsh Guards in the future. Graded as one of the top company commanders in Southern Iraq in 2004, when he led 2 Company whilst only an acting major, he had been awarded an MBE for his work in training Iraqi police. It was an experience that was to stand him in good stead in Helmand. A slightly diffident character, Harris's quiet, self-deprecating manner masked a firm ambition and razor-sharp intelligence. He had shown in Iraq that he could wield military force with a rare creative flair. Harris had been educated at Oundle before reading theology at Bristol University, and some teased him behind his back that he had the manner of a country vicar. By his own account, he had joined the army almost by default, having settled on no other career during his school years. An army cadetship paid him through Bristol, meaning that he owed the army five years of service, and he would say that he hadn't thought of any better job options since. One uncle had commanded the Welsh Guards in the 1970s, while another was a Harrier jet pilot in the Falklands War. His father, a Royal Navy jet pilot who rose to commodore, had been a top gun jet-fighter instructor at Miramar naval air station in California and second in command of the destroyer HMS *Bristol* in the Falklands.

Giles Harris's grandfather, Colonel Donald Easten, won an MC as a company commander at the siege of Kohima in northeast India in 1944. Easten, then a captain in the Queen's Own Royal West Kent Regiment, had been part of a small British, Indian, and Gurkha force that held off the Japanese, at one point fighting across the deputy commissioner's tennis court. Before leaving for Helmand, Harris went to visit his grandfather in the Essex village of Wormingford, where they would fish together on the River Stour, overlooking Suffolk. The Welsh Guards officer asked the Second World War veteran if he had any advice about how to lead men in action. "It always seemed to me that the role of the officers was to keep going," replied the ninety-one-year-old. Harris's father's advice, protective and tongue-in-cheek, was that he should "lead from the middle," rather than expose himself to too much risk at the front. Thorneloe rated Harris, who was engaged to Alice Campbell, a London headhunter, as his best company commander and was to give him the opportunities and resources needed to shine.

Drawing all of this together was Battle Group headquarters, led by Major Andrew Speed, a Scots Guards officer who was the battalion's second in command. Captain Ed Launders, the operations officer, had coordinated Iraqi informants in Basra and now had one of the toughest jobs in Afghanistan—coordinating all the moving parts of a huge battle group for Thorneloe. "I soon realised Colonel Rupert was just the most out-of-the-box thinker I've come across not only in my military career but my life," Launders recalls. "If there were five ways of doing things, he'd think of a sixth way and it would be the best. You had to work bloody hard because his philosophy was that if something was the right thing to do and it was somewhere within the realms of human capability to do it, then it should be done and you should stop at nothing until you'd achieved it."

Captain Naim Moukarzel, the signals officer and battle captain, had the unenviable job of attempting to make an inadequate communications system function. The logistics were run by two Falklands veterans, Major Martyn Miles and Major Nicky Mott. Feeding and equipping a battle group of seven companies in an expanding area using a logistics chain that had previously supported only three companies proved an immense challenge. Captain John Bethell, a Cambridge graduate and former Territorial Army officer, was the intelligence officer. From the outset, he was stunned by the low quality of intelligence he received from the Brigade. Thorneloe had assumed command in November 2008, but the core of his staff had been in place a year earlier. It was then that preparations for Helmand began in earnest with an exercise in Belize, for which the Welsh Guards departed the day after they had been on parade in bearskins for the State Opening of Parliament.

Manpower was Thorneloe's biggest headache. When he took command of the Welsh Guards, he calculated that he was understrength for Helmand by seventy-two men. With his customary ingenuity, he set about making up the numbers. John Williams 54, another Falklands veteran, had retired as a warrant officer when the clock struck midnight for the new millennium in 2000. He'd landed a plum job as the beadle (manager) of the Worshipful Society of Apothecaries, a City of London livery company. The same month Thorneloe took over the Welsh Guards, Williams found himself sitting next to the new commanding officer, who was guest of honor at a dinner at the Union Jack Club in London. The two went way back—Williams had been the 3 Company quartermaster sergeant at Ballykelly when Thorneloe was a platoon commander in 1991. With a combination of charm and cunning, Thorneloe reeled Williams in like a fish. First he regaled him with tales of life in the Welsh Guards of 2008 and how everyone was gearing up for the biggest regimental challenge since the Falklands. Then he put out the bait. "There are lots of experienced hands going out to Afghanistan," he said. Eventually, Williams responded: "Oh well, I wish I could go but I'm too old." Thorneloe shot back: "No you're not—there's a procedure in place to come back for the

Helmand tour." A few drinks later, Williams, a grandfather about to celebrate his fifty-second birthday, had agreed to rejoin the Welsh Guards.

Williams woke up the next morning with a hangover and a faint recollection of an animated conversation. Then the telephone rang and it was Captain James Aldridge, the Welsh Guards adjutant, who said: "The Commanding Officer is delighted to have you on board, 54." Williams thought to himself: "F---ing hell. What have I done?"

The procedure Thorneloe had been referring to was Full Time Reserve Service (FTRS), which allowed former soldiers to sign up for a specific period when there was a manpower shortage. The final hurdle was to get the OK from his wife. He'd barely started to outline the situation when she interrupted and told him: "Look, you've been 24 years a soldier. If you want to go, you go. I'm not going to stand in your way." So Warrant Officer (Class Two) John Williams 54 became Williams "65 was 54" and went off to war because he couldn't resist doing it again.

Andrew Morgan Brown 16, who had retired as a color sergeant in 2004, was driving the X1 bus from Llanelli to Caernarfon in April when Thorneloe telephoned him on his mobile phone. As soon as he got to the bus depot, Brown called him back. "Hello, 16," Thorneloe said. "I've got a job for you." Nicknamed "Donk" and a legendary character in the Welsh Guards, Brown had become well known among Llanelli passengers for his habit of departing from the allotted bus route to take friends closer to where they wanted to go, especially those on their way to the British Legion hall. His head shaved, his speech invariably littered with obscene references to self-pleasure, Brown had become a kind of unofficial Welsh Guards mascot by the end of his career. The tales of his exploits were legion and often unrepeatable in polite company. One officer jokes that he had introduced Brown to his mother, who had still not quite recovered from the shock well over a decade later. At a remote watchtower in South Armagh, Brown had become known as the Oscar Schindler of the feline world after rescuing cats that were about to be exterminated and surreptitiously loading them onto helicopters in cardboard boxes. Brown had been a recruiting sergeant in South Wales and was responsible for enlisting at least fifty members of the battalion who served in Helmand. Brown remembers first meeting Thorneloe at Ballykelly in 1991, when the future commanding officer was "a slightly spotty-faced 21-year-old platoon commander and I was a lance sergeant." Thorneloe knew that bringing such a character back into the fold would be a morale booster and a steadying influence, as well as providing an extra NCO.

Now forty-four, Brown had first joined the Welsh Guards just before the Falklands but missed out on the South Atlantic campaign because he was only seventeen. "This is a way of putting that ghost to bed," he said in Helmand. "We've done numerous tours in Northern Ireland since then—I've done five—we've done Bosnia twice, we've been all over the world, performed public duties. I was gutted because I just missed out on my Iraq tour because my 22 years [after age eighteen] was up." Brown's regular career had spanned almost precisely the most uneventful period in the history of the Welsh Guards in terms of combat operations. "In 23 years and 95 days in the Army, I'd never fired a shot in anger till I came out here," Brown admitted. Old soldiers and even some civilians had expressed similar sentiments in 1939 about never having been in action. Hugh Lister, who had been seventeen at the end of the First World War and was thirty-eight at the start of the Second World War, wrote to the regiment requesting an interview: "I just missed the last war, I do not want to miss the next one." He was killed in action in Belgium in 1944.

After the Falklands, Brown remembers, the Welsh Guards were at a low ebb. "I remember getting kicked to f--- quite regularly with a Corporals' Mess wine bottle. A lot of people go on about bullying in the Army now. They should have been in the Welsh Guards in 1982. One morning after having a f---ing wine bottle on my head 10 times, I went on Windsor Castle guard. I did the guard mount but couldn't do the next stag [guard duty] because the f---ing bearskin wouldn't fit on my head because it had swelled so much." He put a lot of this down to the Falklands. "There was a lot of f---ing naughty stuff going on in the battalion. The Falklands did affect people and it did f--- up the battalion for a while." He felt Helmand was a way for the Welsh Guards, at long last, to consign the Falklands to the history books. On a personal level, the Welsh Guards had been his life, and he was a little lonely without them. Returning was like going back to his family; and the fact he'd never made it to the Falklands all those years before had always hung over him. So Color Sergeant Andrew Morgan Brown 16 went to war because he did not want to miss another conflict.

Dai Matthews had been in a state of near-despair when his telephone call from the Welsh Guards came. Also a color sergeant, he'd retired at the age of forty just two years before. A gentle and soft-spoken man, he very rarely had a bad word to say about anyone. During the Iraq tour, he'd been the commanding officer's driver and he'd got to know the Welsh Guards officers well when he'd been the officers' mess sergeant for his final sixteen months in the army. "I'd give them a bollocking so they toed the line," he says, the glint in his eye indicating he'd done no such thing. "Good bunch they are." At first, life outside the army was wonderful. He'd started his own mix-on-site concrete business with his sister in Cowbridge, near Cardiff. The margins were tight but in the first year he took in £280,000, turning a profit of 15 percent after costs and wages. The next year, he was to expand by hiring an additional truck and driver. "It was going great and then Customs and Excise turn up in my bastard yard to check what fuel I was using," he says. "They knew it was red diesel and then they told me they was changing the law." Customs and Excise stopped Matthews using red diesel, for agricultural and building vehicles, and instead made him use the fully taxed white. His fuel bill trebled overnight. Matthews raised his prices, making it harder to undercut his competitors and squeezing his profits. Then the government imposed an additional tax on sand and stone. By Christmas 2008, he was working eighteen-hour days and barely covering his own costs. The business went bust, and he was unemployed just as a worldwide recession was beginning to bite. He was contemplating trying to go to Iraq as a security contractor when his old friend Captain Alun Bowen, who had met his wife at Matthews's wedding, telephoned him. So Color Sergeant Dai Matthews went to war because his other options had run out.

John Williams "65 was 54," Andrew Morgan Brown 16, and Dai Matthews were all told they would be given desk jobs within Camp Bastion or the battalion headquarters. They'd each told their wives they wouldn't be doing anything dangerous. Before long, however, all three were in the thick of the action. Within a few hours of arriving, Brown was in a convoy that had been blown up and found himself firing his rifle at an enemy for the first time. "There was a bit of a buzz in Northern Ireland but this was a whole level up again," he said two months after arriving in Helmand. "This is the real deal. This is war fighting." Matthews spent more time on vehicle convoys than almost anyone else on the Battle Group, leading resupply missions and insisting on sitting in the cab of an unprotected truck. Williams "65 was 54" also went out on convoys and managed to wangle a spell on a mortar line (the position in a base where mortars are fired from), firing ordnance in anger for the first time.

Thorneloe had managed to get an extra ten or so men by persuading veterans to return. Next he turned to the Household Division for help. The Irish Guards obliged with a dozen volunteers, the Coldstream Guards with eight, and the Scots Guards with five. Among the Coldstream volunteers was Lance Corporal Kingsley Simmons, who should have been a lance sergeant but had suddenly found himself a guardsman before regaining his former rank. "I was due to get promoted on the Thursday and instead I got busted on the Tuesday," he says. What he described as "a bit of dramas at home with my mum and my brother" had led to his going AWOL, and his excuse of not having a mobile phone had cut no ice with the Coldstreams. Recently divorced, Simmons had a reputation for fighting and drunkenness that made him a risk as a senior NCO despite his eleven years' experience and leadership qualities. Going to Helmand with the Welsh Guards would be a way of starting with a clean slate; plus he needed to save money to get himself out of the financial hole he was in. Simmons was one of the relatively few British-born black soldiers in the Guards. Since the mid-1980s, when Prince Charles famously decried the lack of black faces during the Trooping of the Color, the Household Division had made major strides in recruiting from ethnic minorities. Times had certainly changed since 1969 when a junior Labour minister reported after a visit: "I was very well received until I raised the matter of the absence of coloured Coldstream Guards. In the Sergeants' Mess I got a most violent reaction. Several of the senior NCO's said that if they had any coloured men in their Regiment they would walk out!" By 2009, racism was all but extinct in the Guards.[1]

While Thorneloe had managed to get another forty men into the Battle Group through the back door, he still had to go to Helmand with thirty-two men below the stipulated "minimum manning strength" for his Battle Group. He later bemoaned in an email to a brigadier at Land Forces headquarters that according to the latest "Theatre Capability Review"—a regular procedure carried out to assess manpower and equipment needs—he should have been given an additional British company of about 125 men in Helmand. The paucity of manpower was to become Thorneloe's most critical concern, particularly when Operation Panther's Claw began to swell the size of the battle space he had to deal with.

As well as planning for Helmand, Thorneloe put a lot of thought into who would remain back in Aldershot to form the Rear Party. Traditionally regarded as a grouping of the sick, the lame, and the lazy, battalion rear parties were becoming increasingly critical to the success of an Afghan tour. The Rear Party had to deal with finding replacements for the battle casualties as well as discipline—going AWOL after the two-week rest and recuperation (R&R) was not uncommon—and care of the families of the dead and wounded. If the Rear Party failed to perform, then problems would develop among the families and the discontent would soon spread to the Battle Group and erode its fighting effectiveness. After a 19 Light Brigade meeting in Northern Ireland, Thorneloe returned to tell his parents that the brigade was expecting between twenty and fifty deaths and many more injuries. Later on, he discussed the prospect of casualties with his wife Sally. "The one thing I want to do is to come home with everybody," he told her. But he was realistic enough to know that this would not be the case. In fact, the Brigade would lose seventy-six soldiers killed in action.

Thorneloe knew there would be Welsh Guards military funerals to be arranged, and probably some of them at the Guards Chapel at Wellington Barracks, near Buckingham Palace. They would be high-profile affairs in which Guards standards would have to be upheld. Thorneloe decided that the two key figures in the Rear Party would be Major Dai Bevan, in command, and Captain Darren Pridmore, the welfare officer. Bevan, an affable Old Etonian who was contemplating leaving the army, had asked to stay behind. His wife Denise, an army education corps officer, was expecting their first child during the tour, and with one failed marriage behind him, Bevan didn't want to risk putting strain on a second. And he had already done a six-month tour with a previous brigade. Pridmore, from Swansea, had also been to Helmand, operating in Nad-e Ali when it was a Taliban stronghold. He had recently become an officer after serving his two-year stint as Regimental Sergeant Major. Beefy and bullet-headed, Pridmore was a man who got things done, and behind the bluff exterior there was a deep reservoir of compassion. "I'm grumpy, bald head, I can take my teeth out to nut you and I was the RSM until last year so everyone associates me with discipline," he says. "Some wives still view me as a bit unapproachable." But a female sergeant who was married to a soldier was brought in to help and that bridged any gap there was.

The fact that both Bevan and Pridmore had served in Afghanistan was important for their credibility with the families. Bevan would spend the whole six months with his mobile phone beside him, even taking it into the hospital when his daughter was born. As the Welsh Guards departed, he began to wonder who might not come back. "I said to my wife, the two people I was most worried about going out to Helmand were Sean Birchall and Rob Gallimore. They were doing two of the hardest jobs. Galli quite likes to be in amongst it and that's where his strengths are. Sean had been plucked straight out of PJHQ. He was relatively untrained in terms of low-level tactics and was commanding a composite company of people he didn't know."

Some of those who were left behind were bitterly disappointed. Regimental Quartermaster Sergeant Dorian Thomas 53, from Pontypridd, was called in to see Thorneloe to be told that he would be in charge of repatriations and funerals. As a former drill sergeant and Sandhurst instructor, he was perfect for the job. Thomas 53 argued that he had missed out on Iraq and needed an operational tour so he could lead young guardsmen with authority and credibility, but Thorneloe's mind was made up. Thorneloe knew Thomas 53 had already proved himself in action when few were given the chance. In 1997, he had been mentioned in dispatches for his gallantry in aiding a Royal Ulster Constabulary officer who had been shot in the thigh by an IRA sniper in South Armagh. Thorneloe also had a plan to get him out to Helmand for the final six weeks or so of the tour. Thorneloe had picked up Thomas 53's underlying empathy: he was more sensitive and emotionally attuned than most NCOs of his vintage. Thomas 53's older brother, also a Welsh Guardsman, had committed suicide in 1995. He had been there when their father had received the knock on the door and had gone with him to identify the body. "Colonel Thorneloe had really thought it through and gave me his reasons, so I just took it on the chin," remembers Thomas 53.

Thorneloe asked Captain Terry Harman, who was initially penciled in for the Rear Party, to give everyone in the battalion a lecture about the wisdom of writing a last letter to a loved one in the event of their being killed in Helmand. It was something that Brigadier Tim Radford had highlighted and was to emphasize when he visited the Welsh Guards. Harman's combination of authority and sensitivity made him the right man for such a task. "This is big boy's stuff," Harman told the guardsmen. "This tour, guys, is a bit more daunting than the last one. If you do not come back, there's a lot of people hurt—you're not, because you're dead—if there's no letter and there's nothing to hang on to. You owe it."

Harman certainly felt he owed it to his own wife, Ceri. In preparation for the tour, he realized, he'd withdrawn from the woman he'd been married to since he was a guardsman and from their children Kieron, Kyle, and Cara.

"I detached myself from my family by stealth," he says. "It was my mechanism of coping and she tolerated that." His last letter to his wife began: "Ceri, I was selfish. I say I love you but have I expressed it enough in life?"

He then wrote a farewell letter to each child, about their individual strengths and weaknesses, what he liked best about them, what he hoped they would develop into. Kieron was told that he would now be the man of the family. "He's 15 and I tried to pack 15 years into a letter that took me four days to write, seven pages," Harman says. "I told him if I died be under no illusions—don't say the Army let me down because it didn't. I know exactly what I'm facing. I want a private funeral with my family. On my gravestone, put the rank because that's what I've achieved in life. Captain Terry Harman, 1st Battalion, Welsh Guards. That means a lot." Harman's own father had left his mother when he was two, and he never saw him again after he left for South Africa when he was ten. In his twenties, Harman tried to find his father and discovered that he had been killed fighting in the Rhodesian army. He eventually located his grave in Warren Hills Cemetery in Zimbabwe. His uncle, a Royal Artillery gunner, had been killed and buried at El Alamein.

As a color sergeant and company sergeant major at Sandhurst, Harman had helped inspire a generation of young officers. Among them was Captain Naim Moukarzel, the Welsh Guards signals officer in Helmand and later the adjutant. "He gave this really inspiring, rousing pitch about what it meant to be a guardsman," recalls Moukarzel, an Old Etonian originally destined for the Irish Guards. "He talked about his life, his background in North Wales, how he joined and what the regiment became to him. He really emphasised the fact that young men can come into the regiment and make something of their lives if the officers advise them properly and put in the effort. I thought: 'Wow.' I was sold on the Welsh Guards."

In al-Amarah in Iraq in 2004–05, Harman was the regimental sergeant major and revered as a man who always gave his all. When the battalion headquarters was being extended, he was there operating a mechanical digger with his sleeves rolled up. As the interrogations officer, he led the questioning of a group of eight hijackers who had been apprehended while wearing policemen's uniforms. Harman played the bad cop, smashing folding chairs on the floor in front of them and screaming like a man possessed. The performance helped elicit full confessions, though it later turned out that each man had given a false name and a bogus story. Harman had an instinctive understanding of the Welsh-speaking guardsmen. He was also a natural charmer, who was a particular hit with Ann Clwyd, the Labour MP and Tony Blair's human rights envoy to Iraq.

Harman might not have admitted it even to himself, but he had something to prove in Helmand. As the former regimental sergeant major, he was the natural choice to become quartermaster of the Welsh Guards in 2010. For a late entry officer, it would have been the pinnacle of his career. Thorneloe, however, had some doubts about Harman's administrative and planning abilities. "Terry's a lovely bloke but it's all done on a wing and a prayer," says Colonel Sandy Malcolm, regimental colonel and a golfing partner of Harman. "He doesn't write very well because his first language is Welsh. Rupert didn't like that."

Thorneloe decided to choose another late entry officer as quartermaster, but Malcolm sensed that he was finding it difficult to inform Harman. "You need to let him know before he goes to Helmand," Malcolm told him. One day, Thorneloe called Harman into his office and said: "Terry, I'm afraid you're not going to be Quartermaster." He told him who the other officer was. "I think he's the better man," Thorneloe said. Harman, a proud Welsh Guardsman, felt humiliated and believed inter-company politics might have been involved. The other officer had spent most of his time in 2 Company, which Thorneloe had started off in as a platoon commander and had subsequently commanded, whereas Harman was a 3 Company man. Ironically, Harman was to become Thorneloe's Mr. Fix-It man in 2 Company out on the front line in Helmand.

At Aldershot, another of Harman's occasional golfing partners was Lieutenant Mark Evison, a young platoon commander destined for the SAS selection course in 2010. In Helmand he was to command 7 Platoon at CP Haji Alem in 2 Company under Major Henry Bettinson. Evison was the kind of junior officer who seemed to have it all. Blond, hazel-eyed, and a talented cellist and pianist, he had won a scholarship to Charterhouse from Dulwich College at the age of fifteen. Before Sandhurst, Evison had been a jackaroo in Australia (his mother's homeland), run a marathon in just over three hours, trekked through northern Spain and the Middle East, and trained for a solo expedition to the South Pole by living in an igloo in Norway. A magnetic personality, he almost invariably had a gorgeous girlfriend on his arm. Evison had a powerful rapport with his soldiers, and they were in awe of the way he carried himself. One of them joked that he had a face that had been "sculpted by angels," and the term stuck. One of his nicknames within 7 Platoon was

"007," though his friends in the officers' mess would quip that it was Evison himself who started that one.

Mark Evison was one of the men Brigadier Radford distinctly remembers from his pre-deployment visit to the Welsh Guards in Aldershot. Sitting just to his right in the front row, Evison was listening especially intently to the brigadier as he held a "fireside chat" in the officers' mess. Radford remembers: "I spoke to them about leadership and the need to be resilient." He offered a quotation from David Kilcullen, the Australian counterinsurgency specialist: "The war in Afghanistan will be won or lost in the next fighting season." Radford says: "It really brought home to them the importance of what they were about to embark on." He gave a similar talk to the warrant officers' and sergeants' mess. "It was about being bold, courageous and daring, but also knowing your limitations. I would be asking the Welsh Guards to do some extraordinary things and told them that the least likely people would surprise them—in both a good and a bad way. At that stage, I don't think they really understood the extent of it, what it's like to see people blown up in front of you. I tried to get them mentally prepared."

There was banter among the platoon commanders about what might happen in Helmand, and Evison was quickest with the black humor, asking at one point: "Do you reckon there'll be wheelchair access at the Christmas Ball?" But Evison wasn't joking when he told his friends that he had been having vivid dreams about getting shot in the neck. In a diary entry of April 15, written at Kandahar air base just after he arrived in Afghanistan, Evison wrote: "Anticipation, excitement, fear—all words which could be used to describe what one should be feeling right now but the only one that I really feel is uncertainty.... The only other feeling is that of an emptiness for those that I have left behind."

The next stop was Helmand's Camp Bastion. A sprawling, dusty cantonment in the Dasht-e Margo, Camp Bastion was the largest overseas British Army base since the Second World War. When Tony Blair visited shortly after it was first established in 2006, he described it as "this extraordinary camp that's been created here, literally in the middle of nowhere." It was a "piece of desert ... where the future in the early 21st century of the world community is ready to be played." Bastion expanded enormously in the three years afterwards but always seemed remote from the action in the Green Zone. Most of its inhabitants never ventured beyond the camp perimeter and its desert location made it safe from attack. "Bastion is a bizarre place," Evison wrote in his diary as he prepared to move out to the front line. There was a "feeling of complete isolation within the base ... so powerful that it does not feel like we are in a war zone and only a few km's [sic] outside of the walls are people who would want to do you harm." He added: "On top of this the food is fantastic—there is a pizza hut and an internet suite which is faster than those at home."

Lieutenant Chris Fenton, commanding 1 Platoon, and Lieutenant Dave Harris, commanding 2 Platoon, both of the Prince of Wales's Company, and Evison had a meal from the Pizza Hut trailer, sitting outside on the pub-style benches beneath an open-sided tent. Harris was Evison's best friend in the army. They had been through everything together, from night exercises in the Brecon Beacons to nights out in the West End. Both were fancy free after breaking up with long-term girlfriends the previous year. They made quite a pair when out on the town: Harris, endearingly vain, dark-haired, and brown-eyed, with the smoldering looks of a department store catalogue model; Evison, fair-haired, a few inches shorter at almost five feet, eight inches, and utterly charming with a constant smile on his face. "He was a good wingman," recalls Harris.

Evison would give Harris good-natured stick for being a grammar school boy. Harris, who had a master's in intelligence and international security from King's College London, would shoot back: "All those thousands of pounds for public school and you got yourself into a Poly?" Evison had never been academic—he failed his A-levels and had to retake a year at Oxford Brookes University, the former Oxford Polytechnic, after scraping in to read land economy. Just before leaving for Helmand, Harris and another young officer sneaked into Evison's room and moved all his pictures so they were slightly off-center and mixed his shoes up, leaving them in odd pairs. "His room was always immaculate and he was completely anal about his kit," says Harris. "It just absolutely rinsed him. He came back and it really stressed him out." Evison was a natural charmer, and Harris jokes that at least three women thought they were his girlfriend when he left for Helmand.

On April 16, Evison wrote in his diary that while out on the Camp Bastion shooting ranges he had bumped into an old school friend who was just completing his six-month tour. "When he asked where I was heading and he found out it was Nad-e Ali he took a small step back and wished me all the best." Evison was already bored with Bastion and wanted "to get stuck in and see for myself what it is like." But he wondered how he would perform under fire. "How will I react with my first contact? Will I freeze or hopefully prove my worth. At the moment it is a waiting game and until that moment comes I can only speculate."

Camp Bastion felt like a rear echelon base, and there was no danger there. But the young platoon commanders were given frequent reminders of what they were about to face when Chinook and Pedro CASEVAC helicopters would land with their cargo of the dead and wounded. Every time there was a casualty, "Operation Minimize" would be declared, and all the telephones and internet terminals switched off so bad news could not be relayed home until the next of kin had been informed. After their Pizza Hut meal, the three young officers went on their separate ways knowing they might not see each other for another six months—or perhaps ever again. Not since their great-grandfathers' generation had the dangers of being a platoon commander in the British Army been so acute. As they bade farewell, Harris shook Evison's hand and said: "Goodbye, mate. Don't do anything silly." As Harris walked away, Evison came back and gave him a hug. It struck Harris as out of character for his normally happy-go-lucky friend.

Others also seemed to be behaving a little differently. Lance Sergeant Tobie Fasfous, a mortar-fire controller who was going to be in a mortar platoon attached to a Light Dragoons company serving as part of the Danish Battle Group (Center), was distinctly uneasy. Fasfous had been brought up in Dubai, and his late father was a Lebanese Christian. But he became an avid Welshman—even developing a pronounced accent—after he moved at the age of nineteen to Pencoed, just outside Bridgend, in South Wales. With no family connection to Wales, he ended up there because a Dubai friend's parents had a house there where they could stay rent-free. Fasfous initially wanted to join the Royal Navy but didn't meet the two-year UK residency qualification. While he was waiting for the two years to be up and working as a taxi dispatcher, he met Welsh Guardsmen in pubs in Pencoed and eventually found his way down to the army careers office. Fasfous was six feet tall and pushing seventeen stone (235 pounds), with a large personality to match. He qualified as a sniper and during the Iraq tour was an invaluable asset because he spoke fluent Arabic. The Iraqis never knew this, so Fasfous would stand at the back during meetings picking up the asides and nuances that were not being translated. His fellow mortarmen had been sent to Helmand in 2008, but, to his frustration, Fasfous missed out because he was being treated for an old knee injury.

Fasfous had worked hard to get fit and lose weight for the 2009 tour, but as the date of departure approached, he seemed increasingly jittery. In late March, he was told his departure date was being brought forward. "Tobie Fasfous is really looking forward to the imminent barrage of incoming for the next six months (can you sense the sarcasm?)" he posted on Facebook—prompting such responses from friends as "Please come back alive! Xx," "keep your head down fat boy," "STAY SAFE!" and "Give 'em some stick mate!" When he telephoned his mother Anne to tell her he was going earlier than expected, there were tears streaming down his face. The day before he left, he told Kelly Gore, his girlfriend of nine months whom he had moved in with in October, that he wanted to be cremated and that "Sloop John B" by the Beach Boys should be played at the funeral. An avid rugby fan, he stipulated that all mourners should wear Welsh rugby shirts, with the caveat that shirts of Ospreys, rivals of his beloved Cardiff Blues, should be banned from the chapel. As he cuddled his girlfriend before he left, he told her: "Stop crying now because I want to remember you smiling." She replied: "You'd better come back because you've got that new motorbike to take me out on."[2]

Fasfous would normally telephone his mother once every week or two. "This time, he rang nonstop," she remembers. "He rang on the way up to Brize Norton. He rang me from Brize Norton before they flew out. He rang me as soon as they arrived in Kandahar. It was as if he felt he had to speak to me as many times as he could." On April 11, he posted: "Tobie Fasfous is in sunny afghanistan and not looking forward to the storm after the calm" on Facebook. Six days later it was: "Tobie Fasfous is fed up of sweating in this shit hole dusty bug infested country," drawing retorts from Welshmen of "you cant talk about cardiff like that tobe" and "thought you'd left ENGLAND m8!! Lol, u an all the boys take care mucka x." When Fasfous got to FOB Keenan in the Upper Gereshk Valley, computer access was limited, but one Sunday lunchtime he telephoned his mother. "Hello, it's me," he said. Anne Fasfous was relieved to hear from him and that he seemed to have relaxed. "He was complaining about the conditions and the usual stuff but it was a really, really normal conversation. There was no sign he was concerned about being in danger or anything. I'd had an uneasy feeling about him being out there the whole time, but after speaking to him I felt so much better."

5

The Afghan Factor

Well, that is how it is supposed to be, and then of course
you add the Afghan factor.

—*Major Sean Birchall, IX Company commander,*
1st Battalion Welsh Guards, May 8, 2009

"It's great to be an Afghan man," he affirmed. "You wear a
beard and carry a gun. You don't pay too much attention to
what the government says."

—*James A. Michener,* Caravans *(1963)*

T he Welsh Guards had barely arrived in Helmand before IX Company
found itself carrying out the regiment's first company-sized offensive
operation since the Falklands War. Located in Lashkar Gah alongside
the brigade headquarters, Major Sean Birchall and his men had been
expecting to carry out base protection duties and light patrolling in the
relatively benign environment of the provincial capital. IX Company would
be separated from the rest of the Welsh Guards Battle Group, which would
have its headquarters in Camp Bastion initially and, from June, at FOB
Shawqat in Nad-e Ali town.

Lashkar Gah base was very comfortable by Helmand standards—it
housed a large number of civilian officials and contractors whose terms of

service dictated they could not be subjected to the conditions most soldiers experienced. There was a volleyball court, a wooden pavilion jokingly known as "the bus stop," Premier League football on widescreen televisions, and gourmet food with three types of ice cream on offer for lunch and dinner. Soldiers arriving from remote patrol bases would sample the facilities, gaze at the sunbathing females (mainly foreign office staff), and refer to the place as "Lash Vegas." It certainly wasn't a bad place to be. IX Company, Birchall joked, would be "commuting to war." This was to be IX Company's home for six months, and their Afghan tour looked likely to be uneventful. They had not had time to train together or even get to know each other properly, so they were being given the least onerous task of the five Welsh Guards companies in Helmand. That, at least, was the plan.

Barely two weeks had passed before Company Sergeant Major Andy Campbell was remarking: "The first casualty of war is always the plan." Or as Major Birchall put it in an email to friends, there was "how it is supposed to be, and then of course you add the Afghan factor." With twenty-one years in the army, Campbell, from Pontypridd, was the archetypal Company Sergeant Major. The Welsh Guards rugby coach and a former stalwart of the front row of the scrum, he was stocky, powerfully built, and capable of delivering a tongue-lashing that a young guardsman would never forget. At the same time, he had the jokey, teasing manner of the parade-ground instructor that made guardsmen laugh as well as keep them on their toes. With his wife, Catrina, and two children back home in Aldershot, IX Company was to become his surrogate family. An intelligent man, Campbell was also a military history buff. Apart from a rugby match, there was nothing he would enjoy more than a battlefield tour of Hechtel or Arras.

When word of the reforming of IX Company slipped out, Campbell was determined the job of company sergeant major should be his. Not only was it a chance to escape Battle Group headquarters, it was a part of regimental history. Campbell had known Sean Birchall, his new company commander, since the major had joined the Welsh Guards a decade earlier. They had worked together in Bosnia when Birchall was the battalion signals officer and had impressed Campbell with his enthusiasm and insistence on doing everything the right way.

Thorneloe's pairing of Birchall and Campbell in IX Company was inspired. Campbell took the role of bad cop, laying down the law and imposing standards to help bring the company together. Birchall was the good cop. If there was screaming and shouting to be done, that was Campbell's role. Birchall would then come in and smooth things over. It suited their respective personalities, and it was an approach they had discussed. They shared an office, and Campbell was consulted on virtually every decision that Birchall made.

IX Company was a mixed collection of men and Birchall and Campbell shared a determination to mould it into an effective fighting unit. He and Birchall decided that they would talk about the Second World War forebears of the current IX Company and make the disparate collection of soldiers feel part of something unique.[1] When IX Company soldiers went on R&R later in the tour, some returned with "IX" tattoos on their biceps and shoulders. "The company commander said we were dead men risen and the boys latched onto that," remembers Sergeant Jack Owen 75, from St. Asaph in North Wales. "It was like we'd been reborn all of a sudden, out of nothing. The whole 'IX' Roman numerals thing helped massively. I've never been in a company where there's been such a fierce *esprit de corps* and pride so quickly."

No one was prouder of IX Company than Birchall, who was said to be contemplating a "IX" tattoo himself. "We are a band of disparate men, having been brought together just before we deployed to Afghanistan, but are now a consolidated unit who work as a unified team," he wrote in an email to friends. It was, he added, "a team which I consider it a privilege to command." IX Company had the lowest number of "non-battle" injuries such as sprains and sickness—often a barometer of morale—in the Battle Group. When Captain Deiniol Morgan, the battalion chaplain, arrived to visit one day, Birchall greeted him with the words: "Oh, Padre, it's nice to see you but everything's all right here." Morgan complimented him on his non-battle injury figures, which had been noted with approval by Thorneloe. "Well, there you go, Padre," Birchall said, smiling broadly. "The morale is good in my company."

Rupert Thorneloe and the Welsh Guards took over Battle Group (Center South) from Lieutenant Colonel Doug Chalmers and his 2nd Battalion, Princess of Wales's Royal Regiment (2 PWRR) on April 24, 2009. Three days later, Operation Zafar (Pashto for "Victory") was launched. The Battle Group area was, in army parlance, "immature," in that it had previously been virtually empty of British troops and was being held by only a very small force. Chalmers had two British companies and one Estonian, about 450 men, having taken over from just a single company of 150 Royal Marines in October 2008.

Thorneloe had three below-strength British companies and one Estonian company, about 550 men, but the Battle Group (Center South) area of operations was due to expand, and more bases had just been set up. In June, just before Operation Panther's Claw, Thorneloe would get two more British companies from 4 Rifles, and his total force would swell to over 1,500. Thorneloe and Chalmers had been discussing the Nad-e Ali district for months and had met back in February when Thorneloe flew over for a pre-tour familiarization visit. The two colonels—both on the army's fast track to general—were very much on the same wavelength.

Chalmers, a slim, dark-haired, and erudite officer, was later to write a paper about preparing for battle group operations in Helmand entitled "Lots of Physics, Not Enough Psychology." In it, he wrote that in Battle Group (Center South) he had found that "fighting at arm's reach with long range fires did not win us respect" from Afghans. "More often, it lost us consent as the locals were understandably scared of our firepower and irritated by the occasional collateral damage. Restricting our use of overwhelming firepower meant that we took more risks. But it worked." Chalmers had never been heard to shout, projecting a sense of easy calm and lack of ego.

Thorneloe was more intense but had a similarly thoughtful manner. The two young colonels immediately clicked. They both tended to think several layers more deeply than many of their contemporaries and viewed their task in Helmand as part of a continuum, rather than a stand-alone six-month opportunity for heroics and dramatic impact. An interesting point of connection for them was that the Welsh Guards had taken over from the PWRR's 1st Battalion in al-Amarah in Iraq's Maysan province in October 2004. The PWRR's six months had seen some of the most intense fighting since the Korean War, and they were rewarded with an astonishing tally of gallantry medals, including Private Johnson Beharry's Victoria Cross, the first awarded to a living soldier of the British Army since 1966. The Welsh Guards, under Lieutenant Colonel Ben Bathurst, took a different approach, concentrating much more on engaging the local population, marginalizing the Shia militias, pacifying the area, and suffering no serious casualties.

In Iraq, the two battle groups were dealing with different situations and the PWRR's firefights arguably laid the foundations for what the Welsh Guards achieved. But the PWRR's relish for combat versus the lighter hand of the Welsh Guards was a matter of wide debate. "Rupert and I discussed it," remembers Chalmers. "You could argue the Welsh Guards' approach was better." Thorneloe and Chalmers were of a very similar mindset. They talked at length about the villages of Basharan and Chah-e Anjir, key strategic locations held by the Taliban. "We were in each other's minds," says Chalmers. "He wanted to secure the population and then expand the bubble out, at the centre of which would be normal Afghan governance. We both agreed it was slow expansion and don't take anything you can't pin because it's all about proving to the Afghans we're going to stay."

During April 2009, as Chalmers prepared for Thorneloe's arrival, there were indications that the Taliban could be preparing for a reprise of their October offensive against Lashkar Gah. Intelligence reports contained details of hundreds of Taliban fighters preparing to surge towards the provincial capital from Babaji and the Chah-e Anjir Triangle (known as the CAT) to the northwest and from Marjah across the Bolan Desert to the southwest. There were also reports of rocket attacks against the Brigade base being planned by the Taliban's Quetta shura. Brigadier Tim Radford's staff officers were already formulating the concept of Operation Panther's Claw, designed to clear Babaji and the CAT in order to deepen the protection around the provincial capital. It was tentatively planned for the summer.

A threat to Lashkar Gah had to be taken seriously, for political as well as military reasons. Governor Gulab Mangal, the Helmand provincial governor, had been agitating for months for additional Afghan army forces to be sent to Helmand. His position was precarious, and while a Taliban attack on Lashkar Gah was unlikely to succeed in capturing the town, it could disrupt it and make Mangal seem weak. The governor's compound was within the range of Taliban rockets fired from the Bolan Bridge across the Helmand, which connects Lashkar Gah to the Bolan Desert to the west. President Hamid Karzai eventually responded by dispatching two Afghan army kandaks to the south. Mangal, in turn, was pressuring Brigadier General Muhayadin Ghori, the Afghan army commander in southern Afghanistan, to confront the Taliban and protect Lashkar Gah.

As well as the delicate Afghan political situation, Radford was conscious that the impending influx of U.S. Marines would change the equation in Helmand. If the British did not act, then the incoming Americans certainly would. "It was important to protect the populated ground that successive British brigades had fought so hard for," says Radford. "And it was important strategically at that stage to retain British influence in the provincial capital, especially with the governor."

Another senior officer reinforced this view that if the U.S. Marines had arrived in Lashkar Gah with large numbers of helicopters, there was the prospect of "strategic embarrassment" for Britain. "The message the British therefore wanted to send to the Afghans was, 'Don't worry about the central belt where the people are because that's British.' Parochial, I know, but seriously important in the great scheme of things. It could have gone completely pear-shaped. The Americans were coming in. The governor's position was looking quite dodgy. And so we needed a bit of a victory." The British needed to show they had the will to fight and to secure Lashkar Gah without American help. The generals back home, the senior officer added, feared "another Basra"—a humiliation for British forces who pulled out of the city in southern Iraq and then faced accusations that they had to be bailed out by the Americans because they were not prepared to fight. "The U.S. Marines could have gone to Lashkar Gah, put lots of helicopters beside the provincial governor and said 'Hey, we're here.' Strategic failure."

Radford calculated that an operation to clear and then hold the village of Basharan would also be a valuable "shaping" or preparatory move for Operation Panther's Claw. If British and Afghan forces were occupying Basharan then they could cut off Taliban fighters fleeing south from Babaji.

The plan for Operation Zafar was drawn up in just over two days— "absolutely back-of-a-fag-packet stuff," according to Lieutenant Colonel Jasper de Quincy Adams, a brigade staff officer responsible for development of the Afghan police. It was an Afghan army operation, but the plan bore the heavy imprint of Lieutenant Colonel Simon Banton, the brigade's Afghan army training commander. The original intention was to push up from the Bolan Bridge, clearing north step by step before taking Basharan. But it soon became clear that the routes north were saturated with IEDs, so movement would be too slow. Instead, it was decided that the Afghan and British forces would go west into the desert and then loop north of Basharan and push the Taliban south back towards Lashkar Gah.

The Taliban knew that an operation was being launched, but the British hoped that tactical surprise would be achieved by the unconventional route of the attack. The Light Dragoons were to establish a block between Marjah and Lashkar Gah to prevent any attacks on Lashkar Gah from Marjah, to the southwest. "There were also highly effective U.S. Special Forces operations taking places around Marjah," says Radford. IX Company was to secure along the canal to the east of Basharan, while 2 Mercians would accompany the Afghan forces and clear the village itself, supported by the Royal Gurkha Rifles troops and aging Scimitar tanks—the army had first used them in the Falklands—operated by the Light Dragoons.

Thorneloe was concerned about the haste with which the plan for Operation Zafar had been put together, but Chalmers advised him: "Roll with it and just grab it while you can—because this momentum is rare." Birchall had reservations about the Afghan motivation for the offensive and the competence of the Afghan army and police. "When they come up with a hare-brained scheme to attack the enemy and retake ground well and truly under the control of the Taliban, you tend to get a little concerned," he wrote later. "Especially when all their plans revolve around your Company being the point of the spear they want to throw at the enemy." But Birchall also knew that this was a significant moment for IX Company. It was the kind of opportunity he had pushed so hard to get to Helmand for—to lead his company in combat. But there was some levity in the situation, not just in the short notice to get prepared, but also the contrast between IX Company's comfortable billets and the dangers they were about to face. "Once we finished the Lash Vegas volleyball competition and unloaded all the lobster and sirloin steak, we then started battle prep for Op Zafar," Campbell joked in a briefing after the tour.

IX Company's departure to rendezvous in the desert with a squadron of Scimitars was delayed for several hours because Prime Minister Gordon Brown was visiting Lashkar Gah, and, Birchall remarked, "required a warm fuzzy feeling of security, cue the Welsh Guards." The photo op over, IX Company set off in Land Rovers and WMIKs (Weapons Mount Installation Kit—a Land Rover fitted with a .50 caliber machine gun or grenade machine gun). The Light Dragoons were delayed because a Scimitar detonated an old Soviet mine. The combined force was soon moving north through the desert and then west through the Green Zone to what later became known as Checkpoint North—a large compound two kilometers northeast of Basharan. The Taliban, realizing what was afoot, were ready with a reception committee.

"We were feeling slightly exposed," remembers Owen 75, who commanded a WMIK. "There were rounds winging past our heads plus we couldn't see anything because of the dust being kicked up by the vehicles in front." Birchall noted in his group email that probably 99 percent of IX

Company had never been under fire. "Half didn't know whether to return fire or not. The other half were just in awe of the situation and reached for the most important thing, their cameras. Oh, the YouTube generation, alive and well in the Welsh Guards." Birchall was pleased, however, that the initial hesitation lasted only a couple of seconds before the "killer instinct" set in and they returned fire. Birchall headed to the front of the convoy to see what was going on. As he stuck his head out from behind a Scimitar to look for the Taliban, bullets whistled a few inches past his head. "For f---'s sake, that was too close!" he exclaimed.

IX Company pushed forward towards CP North, passing the bombed-out compounds hit by Russian forces in the 1980s. The fear of hitting IEDs or more Soviet mines was intense. Soldiers would joke darkly about WMIKs having about the same amount of protection as a baked-beans can against an IED. "By getting in behind the Taliban it went massively kinetic, very quickly," remembers de Quincy Adams, from the Queen's Dragoon Guards, a Welsh cavalry regiment. "The first day's fighting was tooth-and-nail stuff ... and a hell of a lot of the enemy got killed." He estimated that between seventy and 150 Taliban were caught between the forces approaching from the north and Lashkar Gah to the south. Most were killed, and the remainder fled into Babaji.

During the first night, three five-hundred-pound bombs were dropped on Taliban-occupied compounds by American aircraft at the request of Joint Tactical Attack Controllers (JTACs) from the Royal Artillery, out on the ground. An investigation later found that one of these bombs killed two Afghan civilians and wounded two others, as well as injuring three insurgents. A week later, a IX Company intelligence report concluded that this had resulted in a belief that British forces were killing, rather than protecting, the population: "LNs [local nationals'] perception is that fellow LNs being killed instead of INS [insurgents]—this was due to incidents on Day 1 of Op ZAFAR."

Night was falling by the time Birchall and his men arrived at CP North and dismounted under fire to link up with Lieutenant Colonel Banton and his OMLT Battle Group staff, which had established a small headquarters there. The plan was already under strain. Afghan army and police had encountered many more Taliban than had been expected, and their progress had been slow. Eight British trainers for the Afghan army were holed up at Objective Worcester (a compound on a hill nine hundred meters away) along with a force of Afghan army and were in danger of being overrun. They were virtually surrounded and running out of ammunition. "It looked at one stage that we were going to have to do a night assault to get them out of the crap," recalls Campbell. "But luckily enough, as it got dark the insurgents melted away." Objective Worcester, a fortification dating back to the earlier Afghan wars, was known as "British hill" by the locals. From it could be seen an old Russian position, protected by a minefield, and an ancient fort dating back to Alexander the Great.

Banton ordered Birchall to head with his fifty or so men to a compound three hundred meters away that was occupied by thirty Afghan police. It was not a welcome prospect—moving across an open area at night with the Taliban nearby plus heavily armed and doubtless jittery Afghan police ahead of them. Using night-vision goggles and infrared headlights, the IX Company men along with their twelve Land Rovers and WMIKs arrived at the compound without coming under fire from their Afghan allies.

Perhaps fortunately, the Afghan police had been too busy passing around opium joints to keep a proper watch. Birchall noted that the Afghan police's usual night routine when within a hundred or so meters of the enemy was to "get stoned and go to sleep maintaining a single sentry (looking in the wrong direction)." Birchall's opinion of the Afghan police was such that he was seriously concerned for his men's safety from within the compound as well as outside it. He estimated that 70 percent of the police (who, unlike the Afghan army, were locally recruited) were in cahoots with the Taliban—"the ANP [Afghan National Police] is a treacherous organisation at best and downright sympathetic to the Taliban at worst."

In order to get the stoned Afghan police out of the way, he told the colonel in charge that they were "true heroes and warriors" who deserved a proper night's sleep after the day's fighting, "allowing my men the honour of providing security all night." They had to remain in their enclosed portion of the compound, however, or the Welsh Guards might mistake them for the Taliban and shoot them. Birchall wrote in his email that "we didn't hear a peep out of them for the rest of the night."

With the Afghan police out of the way, Birchall readied for a Taliban enemy counterattack, only to realize that the compound was also occupied by a herd of cows. He came face to face with one of the beasts as he was looking through his night-vision goggles. And a large and unruly guard dog had been let loose in the compound by one of the Afghan police. Birchall wrote: "So now we have an enemy looking to attack us, an ANP force drugged up and heavily armed and probably on the other side, cows bumping into us and our vehicles [and] also a (probably) rabid dog of an impressive size running loose. It never rains it just pours!" That night, no one in IX Company slept as Birchall ordered a 100 percent guard around the compound. Apache helicopters and F-16 jets were stationed overhead, providing a real-time video downlink to enable Birchall to monitor the surrounding battlefield.

At first light, IX Company headed out to relieve Objective Worcester. Progress was frustratingly slow as the counter-IED team made the route safe. With Welsh Guardsmen providing the protection, the engineers used Vallon metal detectors to sweep every inch of the ground the troops and vehicles would pass over. Nothing was found, but it took almost three hours to clear the nine hundred meters they had to go. The Afghan troops and their British mentors were exhausted after fending off Taliban attacks through the night but now had the task of going into Basharan itself. Characteristically, the Taliban had disappeared with the intention of returning another day rather than standing and fighting against a superior force.

Birchall's next task was to continue searching the compounds around Basharan, heading north for 1,000 meters and then swinging around to the east. After just 150 meters, the engineers found an IED that took an hour to isolate and detonate. From his WMIK, Owen 75 looked down at the pressure-plate IED and thought: "That could have been me, gone." Then, thirty meters farther along, there was another one. The IEDs were dealt with but IX Company was now two and a half hours behind schedule. The dense vegetation made the ground unsuitable for the vehicles so Birchall's men had to continue on foot. The vehicles were sent back to Objective Worcester along with the bomb-disposal teams that were needed elsewhere. As IX Company walked two kilometers east, scouring the ground for IEDs with Vallons as they went, the Scimitars to the north were firing directly over their heads in support of the Afghan army to the south.

When they got two hundred meters from the compounds they had to search, Birchall sent a dozen men forward. "Suddenly, we came under very effective enemy fire from one of the buildings within the compound," Birchall wrote in his email. "There were only two things you can do in a situation like this, turn and run or face up to it and fight." He chose the latter option, with the first group firing into the Taliban-occupied compound while the second group, followed by Birchall's small command team, ran into another compound. Birchall was right in the thick of it, firing his rifle over the top of the compound wall and then breaking off to call in air support over the radio before returning to the fray. Soon there were two Apaches overhead, but they were required for another task—a common, and frustrating, occurrence in Helmand. To his chagrin, Birchall was ordered to withdraw, which he did under heavy fire as IX Company responded with its machine guns and covered the retreat with smoke grenades.

That night, IX Company defended Objective Worcester, while the Scimitars to the north lit up the sky with brightly colored tracer rounds, used to indicate where the Taliban forces were. Birchall watched with approval as a Javelin anti-tank missile, capable of locking onto a human heat source, was used to deadly effect. He wrote: "The lone enemy sniper that was harassing our people and couldn't be hit with a machine-gun found about 3.5 kilogrammes of high explosive landing on his head; a sniper no more and at a mere £80k, quite a bargain." On their walkie-talkies, the Taliban referred to Javelin operators as "dragons."

According to the Operation Zafar plan, IX Company's final task was to return to Lashkar Gah and escort a logistics patrol back up to the Basharan area, delivering materials to build patrol bases at Objective Worcester, CP North, and another objective named Checkpoint South. Back at Lashkar Gah, however, the plan was being modified. The Afghan troops had failed to take CP South and appeared unlikely to be able to hold CP North. After a conference call with Thorneloe, it was decided that IX Company should occupy CP North and provide protection so that the patrol base at Objective Worcester could be built safely. Birchall had a thirty-six-hour breathing space to prepare sixty men and his dozen vehicles for a week at CP North. As each man needed at least six liters of water per day, that meant transporting more than 2,500 bottles, along with ammunition and 420 ration packs, in cramped vehicles.

When Operation Zafar was concluded, Brigadier Radford, accompanied by General Muhayadin, flew into Basharan in his Sea King helicopter to be briefed by Banton and Birchall. As the helicopter was coming in to land and thirty meters from the ground, the Taliban opened fire. Four bullets penetrated the fuselage and ricocheted inside as Muhayadin shouted: "Taliban! Taliban!" One of the rounds went right between Radford and his bodyguard, Sergeant Terry Ferguson of the Royal Military Police, missing each of them by less than an inch, and then bounced off the floor. A lance corporal sitting opposite was grazed by shrapnel. The pilot banked the Sea King away and then lifted it up, aborting the landing and heading to Camp Bastion instead. "This sort of thing happened to lots of people," reflects Radford. "But for me, as the commander, it was important to be on the front line."

IX Company set about fortifying Checkpoint North and making it habitable. Birchall was disgusted with the Afghan army, stating later: "I have no idea what they actually did apart from loot the compound and eat the livestock left behind. They really are animals and next to useless as soldiers." The Afghan troops had defecated all over the compound and, more seriously, appeared to have no control over when or at whom they opened fire. "Every time we came under enemy fire, they would blast off hundreds of rounds in every direction, often aimed at anyone outside of the compound who was still around." CP North was reasonably secure, with ten-foot-high walls a meter thick and with only one entrance. Birchall's men used picks and shovels to knock holes in the walls to create sangars for the .50 caliber machine guns, taken off the WMIKs. At the far end of the front courtyard, an entrance opened up to an orchard of mulberry trees with a stream of milky green water flowing through it—perfect for washing, keeping water bottles cool, and jumping into after firefights with the Taliban.

Outside the compound, a mound of stone and gravel blocked the arcs of fire from one of the sangars, so Birchall led a team in Land Rovers and WMIKs to clear it with shovels. After a few minutes of digging, something whooshed overhead. "What the hell is that?" wondered Campbell. Then there was a loud bang. "I know what that was," he thought. "That was an RPG."

The crack of small-arms fire followed, but as the guardsmen began to withdraw to the base, Birchall stood up at the front and returned fire with his SA-80. "Come on, let's get some rounds down!" he shouted. His retreating men turned around and joined him, aiming their weapons at the muzzle flashes they could see from the Taliban compounds. Birchall reveled in being in a firefight. "You've got to love this stuff," he enthused afterwards once he and his men were safely back inside Checkpoint North.

A few days after Checkpoint North was established, a sentry spotted men moving between compounds and intercepted walkie-talkie chatter indicating that a Taliban attack was imminent. At the same time, a farmer and his four sons aged between ten and three had just arrived outside the base and were about to begin plowing. "When the civilians move, we will start firing," a

Taliban commander was heard to order. As the Welsh and Irish Guards took up their firing positions around the base, they called out to the father to get back in the car and drive away, but he could not understand their English. After half a minute of shouting and gesticulating by the soldiers, the Taliban opened fire, and the British troops responded. Lance Sergeant Matt Turrall, twenty-eight, an Irish Guardsman from Sale, watched as the farmer and his sons were caught in the crossfire. "We had our heavy machine guns firing and I was up on the steps from the sangar looking over," he recalls. "I was trying to get the boys just to stop firing. But obviously the ones that were far away from me couldn't hear because they were using their .50 cals." The father was crawling towards a ditch while trying to pull his sons into his body to protect them from the bullets. Turrall, who had an eighteen-month-old son and another baby on the way, was horrified. "I just thought of my little boy straightaway," he recalls. "My grandad [sic] died a few years ago and he was like a father figure to me, so the old man with his kids was just like my own family. I didn't want to see them get killed."

Turrall got on the radio and told Captain Tim Evans, who was commanding Checkpoint North that day: "I'm going out to get these kids." He did not wait for the reply but jumped down from the sangar and ordered two young guardsmen to come with him. When they got to the gate, there were AK-47 rounds hitting either side of the doorway. Turrall stepped out but the two guardsmen would not go with him. "We can't go out, we're getting fired on," one of them shouted. Turrall, one of the strongest NCOs in IX Company, ordered them: "Get the f--- out! Follow me! Let's go!" But the guardsmen stayed where they were. Turrall remembers seeing two heads peering tentatively out of the doorway as he ran forward, crouched down to fire at the Taliban positions, and then ran forward again. "They didn't give me no covering fire, they just left me on my own," he says. "They came to the gate with me fine, but then as soon as the rounds came in that's when both stopped." One of the guardsmen shouted: "Matt, come back, come back!"

About forty meters outside the base—halfway to the five civilians cowering beside their bullet-riddled car—he reached the stream that flowed out from Checkpoint North. Turrall called out to Guardsman Bridgman, manning one of the sangars, telling him to direct the father and his sons towards him so he didn't have to run out into the open. But they wouldn't move. An interpreter was sent down to the gap where the stream flowed out.

The interpreter started shouting out in Pashto but turned back when he heard the whiz of bullets.

Ordering Bridgman to give him covering fire with his GPMG, Turrall went forward along the ditch, thigh-deep in water and firing as he went, until he got to about six meters away from the father and his sons. He then ran out and grabbed one of the boys and pulled him back into the stream. The father and his other sons followed, crawling. Turrall picked up the bawling youngest boy, held him in front of his body, and pointed back to the base. Bullets continued to whistle past them as Turrall guided them all back along the ditch and then, still under fire, pushed and pulled them into the base. One of the sons had been cut in the back by a piece of shrapnel that had bounced off a tree, but—miraculously—they were otherwise unharmed. As the medic gave them water and sweets, Turrall returned to the firefight. He never saw the father or his sons again.

Afterwards, Turrall confronted the two guardsmen who had refused to follow him. "I gave them a f---ing mouthful," he recalls. "I suppose it was their lives on the line as well and they probably didn't think of it like I did. They were just in their own little world." Turrall says he had acted instinctively. "It wasn't till I got back and was having a fag and a brew with the boys that I realised what I had done. You don't think about what you are doing—you just go off and do it. When it comes to kids, I'm quite soft." Recommending him for a gallantry award, Thorneloe wrote that what Turrall had done had a strategic as well as a moral dimension: "His act that day physically proved that we are here to protect the Afghan people." Turrall's actions would lead to him being awarded the MC.

At Checkpoint North, a daily routine of "movement to contact"— patrolling out and being engaged by the Taliban—developed. These patrols were maintaining a buffer zone and keeping the enemy front line well away from Objective Worcester, which had been renamed Tapa Paraang, and Basharan. On day six at CP North, Birchall was expecting to leave the position and hand it over to the Afghan army. It seemed, however, that he had done his job a little too well and that his assessment of the Afghan army's capacity to hold CP North was shared by Thorneloe and the brigade. Just as worrying as the Afghan army's capacity was its commitment. "The ANA remain reluctant stakeholders in this project, refusing to share the CP North commitment or to conduct significant patrol activity around BASHARAN," Thorneloe reported to Brigade on May 8. It was decided that IX Company would continue to occupy CP North with two dozen or so men. This was enough to protect the position but not much else. Thorneloe warned in the same report that he had "concerns about the IX Company Platoon's ability to withstand a determined, large scale assault on CP North," adding that "what this really needs is more manpower, to allow patrolling in depth to disrupt the FLET [Forward Line of Enemy Troops]."

The troops in Checkpoint North recognized the limitations of what they could do. "You couldn't really push out anywhere without getting contacted," remembers Sergeant Owen 75. "So you were basically stuck there defending the place." Birchall reckoned he needed another dozen men to assault the compounds that were being occupied by the Taliban. Campbell believed CP North ought to have been occupied by a hundred-man company rather than a twenty-four-man platoon. "Every sub unit in Helmand is fixed in its current location, the cupboard is barer than Old Mother Hubbard's!" wrote Birchall. "So we hold our position and put up with this daily activity."

British maps give compounds a number, and around Checkpoint North it was established that five compounds were the chief hostile firing points, with Compound 21 the Taliban's favorite. "Compound 21 is just the other side of the canal road, which is 150 metres away at most," explained Campbell later in the tour. "We've smashed it with HMG, GMG, we've dropped 105 mm on it. And they still come back. We've actually gone over and cleared it on foot. It's a hell of a mess, it's basically just knocked-down buildings but they just keep coming back, infiltrating back into it. And hitting us again. How they are getting in there, we don't know." One strong possibility was that the Taliban were using tunnels, possibly part of the ancient *karez* system of irrigation that dates back hundreds or even thousands of years. The option of simply destroying the compound was never seriously contemplated. "The idea would be great, yeah, just absolutely level Compound 21," said Campbell. "But one, it's slightly too close to us anyway, so if we dropped big munitions we'd be in danger of getting hit ourselves. And two, you don't want to level somebody's house because they are going to be moving back in at some stage hopefully."

Just over a month later, General Stanley McChrystal took over NATO forces in Afghanistan and told his staff: "I want you all to stop dropping compounds."[2] The Welsh Guards and the rest of the Brigade were already practicing "tactical patience"—or what would become known as "courageous restraint." This meant taking on risk not just to save civilian lives, but also to minimize damage to compounds and other infrastructure. Soon, the concept would become central to a new counterinsurgency approach laid down from NATO headquarters in Kabul.

Operation Zafar and the subsequent establishment of Checkpoint North had bonded IX Company together. Thorneloe was pleased with how Operation Zafar had gone and had been mightily impressed by Birchall, though he fretted about spreading his resources too thin. "We would not have chosen to conduct the operation now (the hold will extend us) or in the manner the Afghans did it, but there is a real prospect that it will represent a net gain for our ability to provide security to LKG [Lashkar Gah]," he reported to the brigade on May 1. Chalmers, the outgoing PWRR Battle Group commander, was full of admiration for the way in which IX Company had been brought together. "Sean Birchall did an outstanding job of corralling the bits," he says. "On a big ANA-led operation, it's quite tough to have your voice heard and try to manipulate—because you are not the primary dog—and therefore get what you want out of it and not get too sucked into the deep fighting but sucked in enough to have kudos. He trod that line very well." Thorneloe was also struck by how well Birchall, who was due to take command of 2 Company once the tour was over, had performed leading IX Company in action.

Basharan had been taken much earlier than Thorneloe had anticipated, but he was determined to protect and consolidate it now that the Taliban had been evicted. In the village was a school that had been built in 2004 with American money but had never opened because the Taliban had seized control. It was a classic example of misconceived Western strategy—the school was provided before security had been achieved. One of the daughters of the headmaster of the school described to a guardsman how her father had been disemboweled by the Taliban in front of his family in 2008. His brother, a headmaster in the Babaji area, had apparently suffered a similar fate. Their crimes had been collaborating with American forces and wanting to educate girls. As a father of two daughters, Thorneloe was greatly affected by the story of the Basharan headmaster. Now that IX Company was providing the security, Birchall was anxious to reopen the school. With an eye to the future development of Afghan security forces, brigade staff officers wanted to turn the school into a police training center, but Birchall argued strenuously against this and prevailed. After a series of shuras in Basharan, Birchall set up a program for local workers to renovate the school and also made plans for wells and a hydroelectric turbine. The village, he and Thorneloe decided, could be a shining example to Afghans of what British troops could deliver.

6

Barma Inshallah

Go as a pilgrim and seek out danger
far from the comfort
and the well lit avenues of life.

—*James Elroy Flecker,* Hassan *(1922)*

The Americans and the British have the money and the technology
and the resources. The power of the Taliban does not compare but
they are from the people and they know this land.

—*Abdul Salam Zaeef, former Taliban minister, 2010*

The mission for the few dozen members of Task Force Nawa was simple—survive. Or as Major Andrew Speed, the Battle Group second in command, put it, they had to "keep Nawa on a steady glide path downwards without the glider hitting the ground" before 1,500 U.S. Marines arrived to relieve them in June.

Captain Alex Corbet Burcher commanded the force from PB Jaker, a two-story roofless building that was one of Helmand's most isolated outposts. Known in the Welsh Guards as "CB," he was the son of a former Royal Artillery officer and Dee Dee Wilde, a founder of the dance group Pan's People that appeared on *Top of the Pops* in the 1960s and 1970s. His parents founded a dance and rehearsal studio in Fulham, and he had grown up meeting show business royalty: Tina Turner, Martin Sheen, the Spice Girls, and Take That. During a tour in Basra, Corbet Burcher's men were impressed when Kylie Minogue sent a signed photograph to them all wishing them good fortune. As well as Iraq, Corbet Burcher had served in Helmand as an Afghan army trainer and was taken with the romance of life in the army. Thorneloe rated him highly and was eager to give him an opportunity to command a company early, just as Major Giles Harris had done in Iraq with 2 Company. But Corbet Burcher's theatrical leanings, the family dance studio, and thoughts about marriage to his girlfriend Amy, a London barrister, meant that he was contemplating a return to civilian life and applying to drama school.

Corbet Burcher's deputy was Company Sergeant Major Lee Scholes, a blunt, thickset man from Anglesey who was due to become the drill sergeant of the Welsh Guards. The Taliban front line was five hundred meters away when they arrived, and Scholes led patrols to keep the enemy at bay. Mortars at PB Jaker were lined up on known Taliban positions before a patrol went out. If the Taliban opened fire, their positions could be mortared within seconds, allowing the British to retreat back to the base. One day, Scholes was among ten British troops and fifteen Afghan soldiers pinned down in a ditch with Taliban fire coming in from three sides. Before leaving PB Jaker, Scholes had often joked to Color Sergeant Mark Roberts 99, a mortar-fire controller known as "Nerf," that he could have his motorbike if he was killed. That day, as the patrol came under fire from the Taliban and Roberts 99 launched his mortars, Scholes radioed back: "The bike's in the Support Company shed back in Aldershot." Minutes later, Scholes was telling him where the keys were. Finally, as the Taliban continued to pursue the patrol, he told Roberts 99, who was getting the message that his friend was out there fighting for his life, where he could find the vehicle documents.

Scholes and his men crawled through an opium field and crept along irrigation ditches in three feet of water while the Afghan soldiers sauntered back alongside them, apparently oblivious to the bullets flying past them. Scholes watched the Afghan troops and thought: "They have a different concept of life than us. They walk about as if nothing is ever going to go wrong." It took eight strafing runs from an A-10 Thunderbolt ground-attack jet flown by the U.S. Air Force to help the patrol get back in. Within a quarter of an hour of the patrol reaching safety, the Taliban launched a ninety-minute RPG and machine gun attack on PB Jaker. Scholes, still out of breath and sitting down with just a towel around his waist as the adrenalin subsided, had to grab his sodden combat fatigues and body armor, pick up his rifle, and help defend the base into the night.

With such a tiny band of men at PB Jaker, it was in constant danger of what Scholes described as "the Rorke's Drift scenario": the 1879 battle during the Anglo-Zulu War in which 139 British soldiers successfully defended their garrison against more than four thousand Zulus.[1]

At times there were just a dozen British troops left in PB Jaker. "If the Taliban had been cunning enough to have done a diversionary attack on the ground against the boys and a major attack against the base itself when we had the minimum left behind then that would have been a problem," says Scholes. "If they had realised what we had left at our location sometimes then maybe they'd have tried it." With Lashkar Gah the closest base, any reinforcements that arrived would be too late for anything other than body retrieval.

Corbet Burcher never had any more than forty-three British troops at the base, just fifteen of them Welsh Guardsmen, including a mortar section. Not all were directly under his command—Major Rob Gallimore's X Company and a British police mentoring team operated separately alongside more than two hundred Afghan troops and policemen.

The base was often attacked two or three times a day and was under particular threat from Taliban rockets. It was right next to a mobile phone mast. The Taliban sometimes disabled it to prevent local people informing on them, but the mast provided an ideal aiming point. One rocket would land one hundred meters away and then another fifty meters away. The next one would overshoot, and then everyone would take cover as the fourth rocket headed straight for PB Jaker. One rocket landed a few meters away from Lance Corporal Jon Edwards 97 as he was having a shower. He escaped unscathed, his life saved by a Hesco barrier (a fabric-lined wire-mesh container filled with earth to make a blast wall). An Afghan soldier was not so lucky; he was blown to pieces by a rocket that landed right at the entrance. PB Jaker was some ten kilometers east of Marjah, the Taliban's biggest stronghold in Helmand. It was believed that the Taliban sent fighters from Marjah to be "blooded" at Nawa before they were dispatched north to where more British troops were concentrated.

The Taliban would often use up to thirty fighters to launch simultaneous attacks against PB Jaker and a nearby police checkpoint. One Afghan police checkpoint just north of PB Jaker was overrun by the Taliban several times.

There was little doubt that it was the Taliban who held sway in Nawa district. In May, three Afghan policemen in Nawa defected to the Taliban, taking with them three PKM machine guns later used in an attack. The Taliban used coercion and brutality to enforce their authority, but they also tried to win the consent of locals just as NATO troops did. Intelligence sources reported that a Taliban "commission" in Nawa was functioning as a court, enforcing a ceasefire during the wheat harvest and holding shuras with local elders. The paucity of British troops in the area meant that the Taliban had free rein to do this. There were signs that the Taliban was stepping up its efforts before the US Marines arrived. At a Taliban shura on June 2, Haji Malauwi Zahir Sahib, a local Taliban leader, conferred with about seventy of his fighters about attacks on PB Jaker and police stations.

The size of Corbet Burcher's force meant that he often had little choice but to resort to artillery and air power to prevent a patrol becoming surrounded. Inevitably, this increased the risk of civilian casualties. Early in May, three civilians were killed when Corbet Burcher ordered a mortar to be fired on a ten-figure grid square from which rockets were being fired by a Taliban team. "It's every commander's dilemma," he says. "Do you not do anything and not fire and then have your own get injured or do you do something? You try to work these things out on a second-by-second basis."

At 8:00 a.m. on May 19, Corbet Burcher led a patrol of thirteen British troops and a similar number of Afghan police out to the area near a cemetery to the southeast of PB Jaker. Local Afghans employed there on work projects by the British had reported harassment by Taliban fighters who gathered at the cemetery. Nearly an hour into the patrol, an Afghan warned the troops that the Taliban were in two compounds nearby. The patrol split up, with Corbet Burcher and six of his men occupying a compound and the five other British troops taking up a position overlooking it. A hand-launched Desert Hawk 3 surveillance drone sent aloft from PB Jaker observed four men moving into another compound, and five minutes later the Taliban attacked from the cemetery using rifles, machine guns, and RPGs.

The patrol was split up and pinned down. The intercepted walkie-talkie messages indicated that the enemy were very close to Corbet Burcher's position and were preparing to reinforce their numbers with fresh fighters arriving in two minibuses. Corbet Burcher was accompanied by a JTAC, who was codenamed Widow 16. The JTAC was a young captain who had only recently qualified and had yet to call in an air strike. About fifteen minutes after the attack had started, two French air force Mirage jets, codenamed Rage 31 and Rage 32, arrived. Widow 16 requested they engage the Taliban firing points with guns but was told the aircraft did not have any. With both parts of the patrol still pinned down, a Quick Reaction Force (QRF) was sent from PB Jaker but was then attacked and forced to retreat into a compound. At 10:20 a.m., Corbet Burcher was told that an Apache helicopter was fifteen minutes away—but he decided he couldn't wait that long.

Corbet Burcher was reluctant to use mortars. He knew that several buildings close to Compound 29, where most of the Taliban fire was coming from, were Afghan homes and a stray mortar shell might cause civilian casualties. A laser-guided bomb would be more accurate. At 10:35 a.m., Widow 16 directed the pilot of Rage 31 as he dropped a five-hundred-pound GBU-12 bomb onto Compound 29, the main Taliban firing point, scoring a direct hit. The enemy fire stopped and the patrol and the QRF were able to withdraw to PB Jaker under the watchful eye of the Apache.

An hour after the patrol arrived back in PB Jaker, a local Afghan called Abdul Hamid and a friend appeared at the gate with a wheelbarrow full of human remains and asked to speak to the officer in charge. As Corbet Burcher walked out to meet him, Hamid ripped open his shirt. In that split second, Corbet Burcher thought he was going to be killed by a suicide bomb. As he braced himself for Hamid's body to explode, he thought to himself: "Oh my word. I can't believe I've been so stupid." It was one of the oldest tricks in the book to entice someone of senior rank out into the open to kill him. But the explosion didn't come. Corbet Burcher opened his eyes and realized that Hamid was tearing at his clothes in anguish. "I just started saying sorry in as many languages as I could," he recalls.

The bomb, Hamid said, had killed his nephew Shah Sanam, Sanam's wives, Shareen and Spino, three sons, Nik, Agha, and Saied, and two daughters, Gulali and Lali. Hamid also complained that two *jeribs*—two-fifths of a hectare—of wheat had been destroyed. The Afghan foreman of one of the British work programs later reported that the Taliban had been in Compound 29 just before the bomb dropped, but they had fled after listening in to messages on the radios of the Afghan soldiers and police. They were more than one hundred meters away when the bomb had destroyed the compound. A few days after the incident, Major Rob Gallimore, the X Company commander, was being briefed by Widow 16 when he noticed that the young captain was shifting his map slightly every couple of seconds and fiddling obsessively with his hair. These were, Gallimore concluded, classic signs of battle stress. Widow 16's actions during the incident had been investigated, and this had added to the pressure he was under.

Later in the tour, Gallimore discovered clear evidence that the Taliban were trying to trick the British into killing civilians so that the deaths could be exploited for propaganda purposes. He and his men were attacked near the village of Mian Poshteh from several firing points next to an isolated compound believed to have been abandoned. Gallimore was about to call in GMLRS rockets (Guided Multiple-Launch Rocket System—an artillery weapon based at Camp Bastion) onto the compound when something made him hesitate. "This is too obvious," he thought. "Let's clear the compound the old-fashioned way." When they got to the compound, the soldiers found cartridge cases beneath the palm trees surrounding it but no indication that the Taliban had been firing from inside the compound. In the center of the building, Gallimore found locked doors. Inside the room was a family of twelve Afghans bound and tied together.

Civilian deaths could be disastrous in terms of relations with locals, but it depended on the area and whose family had been killed. When a stray American artillery round landed on a compound, killing a farmer's wife and two of his daughters, Gallimore braced himself for a distressing scene as the farmer approached with a wheelbarrow. The farmer was indeed angry, and he demanded money. Further discussions revealed, however, that it was not the loss of three female members of his family that he required compensation for. In the explosion, he explained, his motorbike had been badly damaged and several goats killed.

Like Birchall and Scholes, Gallimore was discovering differences between the British and Afghan armies. On one operation Gallimore, wearing body armor and helmet, squeezed himself into the back of a Ford Ranger beside Lieutenant Colonel Abdul Hai, the Afghan army commander he was mentoring. Hai, a graduate of the American staff college at Fort Leavenworth, Kansas, and fluent in English, looked at him and sighed. "Rob, Rob, Rob, you are always worrying about these IEDs going off," he said. "With your armour plating, ballistic matting and body armour you worry: 'Will I lose a leg? Will I lose an arm? Will I die? Will I still look pretty for the girls?'" He smiled. "In a Ford Ranger, there is no doubt whatsoever that we are all dead, and if that is God's will then so be it. So take off your silly armour and helmets and let us advance towards the Taliban, air conditioning on and Afghan music blaring." A little farther down the road, Ali, Hai's loyal bodyguard and driver, spotted and defused an IED ahead of them. Hai turned to Gallimore and said: "There, Rob. We need no protection. I have Ali."

The Afghan army method of searching for IEDs was dubbed "Barma inshallah" (*inshallah* being the Arabic word for "God willing") by Gallimore's men. British troops would dream up tongue-in-cheek names for the different methods, mostly common sense, of being cautious about the roads they travelled on or the fields they traversed. One was "Toyota Barma"—making sure that Afghan civilian vehicles had been observed driving the road ahead. Another was "farmer Barma"—an Afghan farmer would lead the way, drawing on his intimate knowledge of his own land. When troops were traveling in heavily protected vehicles such as Mastiffs and Ridgebacks the temptation was to use "armor Barma." This would involve driving over vulnerable routes rather than getting out and Barmaing, safe in the knowledge that an IED blast was highly unlikely to penetrate the vehicle. This might save lives, though the occupants of a stricken vehicle were always likely to come under small-arms attack. Tactically, however, it was disastrous because a vehicle recovery could take hours.

During the Soviet occupation, the mujahideen would tie a branch to the tail of a donkey as they approached a suspected minefield and pushed the beast ahead to clear a path. Life in Helmand was dangerous for donkeys. In 2009, they would often wander over IEDs and be blown up. Occasionally, the Taliban used donkey-borne IEDs, tethering a beast to a tree with containers strapped to its back linked to a command wire set up to be triggered by a military vehicle.

Gallimore found that some Afghan soldiers had an almost uncanny knack of recognizing a change in the ground that indicated an IED had been dug in. British soldiers found it extraordinarily difficult to spot IEDs. The Taliban would spread leaves or sweep dust over the place where they put a device. Sometimes they would urinate on the ground so the surface would bake hard in the sun and appear undisturbed. "The ANA can just read it," said Gallimore. "It's like a sixth sense." Warrior Shaffi, one of the Afghan soldiers he worked with, found thirty-seven IEDs in six months. On one occasion, Gallimore was leading a patrol along a tree line after a Taliban attack when Shaffi shouted: "Stop!" Sure enough, half a meter in front of the X Company commander was a pressure-pad IED that would have blown him to pieces if he'd taken another step. Gallimore hugged him.

The Afghan army certainly had its own way of dealing with IEDs. Up in Sangin, an Afghan company commander decided he would prefer not to wait five hours for a British counter-IED team to cordon off a device and defuse it. Major Guy Stone watched in horror as the officer poured petrol on the IED and tossed a lighted cigarette on it. Stone also found that the Afghan army's fire discipline with mortars left a lot to be desired. "They tended to fire almost anywhere that they could hear the enemy firing from," he remembers. The Afghan army in Sangin was battle-weary and viewed the area, in Stone's words, as "the South Armagh of Afghanistan—a tough, grim place to be." Stone's 3 Company were the tenth set of mentors the unit had worked with. As with elsewhere in Helmand, very few of the Afghan army in Sangin were Pashtuns—about 95 percent of them were Tajiks from north of Kabul. "That was a problem in that there was an intellectual and cultural superiority that came across very strongly to us," says Stone. "Colonel Wadood, who was my right-hand man, wouldn't accept much that the governor of Sangin said because he saw him as a peasant farmer, despite the fact that he was sort of working for him. It was very unhealthy."

Stone's eventual view of the Afghan troops he fought alongside, however, was that their long operational experience and bravery saved British lives. Lieutenant Colonel Wadood, the Moscow-trained kandak commander he mentored, had been fighting in Sangin for three years and in Afghanistan for thirty. "In the early weeks, it was the Afghan army who mentored us. We became a potent joint force against the Taliban, combining British discipline, weapons and technological superiority with Afghan knowledge of the enemy and sixth sense of knowing when something was not right." Stone's company sergeant major was Brian Baldwin, a tough, no-nonsense Welsh Guards rugby player from Pontypridd. He mentored Regimental Sergeant Major Mohammed, his Afghan counterpart. Mohammed would sit on the banks of the Helmand reading Shakespeare, in English, in the evenings and was particularly fascinated by *Hamlet*.

The problem with the Afghan police tended to be the opposite to that of the outsider Afghan soldiers. The police were from the area they operated in and therefore tied up with local tribes, feuds, and rivalries. There was evidence that in Nad-e Ali the police were deliberately kept weak by members of the provincial government who were involved in the drugs trade. In the village of Shin Kalay, the local police chief was using his men to exact revenge on the family of a Taliban commander who had seized some of his land. There were also regular incidents of police from the village taxing locals for transit or confiscating goods such as food or ice.

The police were often at odds with the Afghan army. On May 12, an Afghan army truck speeding through the Nad-e Ali bazaar sparked a confrontation with the police that soon escalated into gunfire. Four Afghan soldiers were killed and one wounded. The four dead each died in the arms of Prince of Wales's Company medics who had tried desperately to keep them alive in PB Argyll until the medical helicopters arrived. For some of the medics, it was their first experience of dealing with a casualty in combat. The helicopters took away only the wounded, leaving the bodies lying in the heat under tarpaulins between two ISO freight containers until the Afghan army arranged for their own vehicles to take them away. A policeman and a local caught in the crossfire were also wounded. Thorneloe reported to the brigade that the incident was "symptomatic of very deep distrust" between Afghan army and police. "I believe it is rooted in money—potentially connected with the security provided to the bazaar."

The outbreak of fratricidal violence was an extremely complex incident for Major Giles Harris of the Prince of Wales's Company to control and created a day of mayhem and horror for his men. It also hampered Thorneloe's attempts to reverse the positioning of Afghan forces so that the police moved in from the periphery and the army moved out of the villages. The lack of legitimacy the police had in many villages was also a problem. "In Basharan, they were stealing from everyone," remembers Captain Mike Brigham, an Afghan army trainer. "They were going to local nationals and taking their food. They were conspiring with the Taliban forces." On June 28, eight Afghan police were murdered at their checkpoint in nearby Mukhtar in a Taliban attack that was believed to have been carried out with the assistance of the policemen's cook.

Birchall had been scathing about the quality of the Afghan soldiers, but Gallimore found that they sometimes got results when the rule-bound British might not. X Company had been trying without success to set an ambush at a Taliban staging post where it was known the fighters would gather before an attack. Every time the trap was set, the Taliban would fail to turn up. In a country where people watching seems to be the national sport, there were eyes everywhere and it was clear that locals in the fields were tipping off the Taliban that British and Afghan troops were lying in wait. This was often done by mobile phone, but British intelligence officers believed that other methods included flying kites (an irony, since the Taliban had banned kite-flying when they were in power), smoke signals from fires, and flashes of light from mirrors in the sun. Once, the Welsh Guards found a small boy in a field who had several pounds' worth of Afghanis in his pocket and was clutching a car wing mirror. In Northern Ireland, lookouts for the IRA were known as "dickers," and the term had been revived in Afghanistan.

Gallimore was about to abandon the idea of laying ambushes in a particular position when Lieutenant Azidullah insisted they try one more time. He was sure they would fail yet again but decided to humor the Afghan officer. To his astonishment, the plan worked like clockwork. A booby trap was set up, a Taliban IED team, arrived and Gallimore's men blew them up while the Afghan troops opened fire, killing the survivors. Afterwards, Gallimore slapped the lieutenant on the back and said: "Azidullah, that's mega. How come it didn't work before?" Azidullah smiled. It turned out that the Afghan soldiers, without the British even noticing, had gathered all the local Afghans together, confiscated their mobile phones, and locked them in the mosque. Gallimore felt himself start to panic. Treating the local people with respect was a key tenet of the British approach. "Azidullah, what are you doing? What if someone finds out?" Azidullah smiled again. "But no one is going to find out," he replied. The villagers appeared not to mind. After the successful ambush, they filed out of the mosque, thanking the Afghan soldiers as they were politely given back their mobile phones along with an apology for the inconvenience.

The Afghan troops were less polite after two of their number were killed in an area called Majitech. Colonel Hai, the Leavenworth graduate, called a shura in the village and invited the elders in to discuss the matter. "They came in expecting all the usual chai and shoot the shit and work things out," says Gallimore. Instead, Hai tried a different approach. Ripping away the canopy shading the elders from the sun in the fifty-degree heat (122-degree heat Farenheit) as his men outside cocked their weapons, he told them in Pashto that he was going to deliver a new truth. "There are no longer three ways," he said. "You think there is the Taliban way, our way, or the way of waiting and seeing which direction things go before deciding. Now, there is no third way. You are either with us or you are with the Taliban." He then made them sit in the sun for the next six hours. After that, there were no more Taliban attacks on British or Afghan troops in Majitech.

Children were used by the Taliban as more than just dickers. Sometimes they were an unwitting part of an IED ambush. On May 8, Company Sergeant Major Baldwin of 3 Company was at the rear of a foot patrol in Sangin when he saw a small boy standing by the road. He was passing an area known as the Tank Park, where the Soviet forces had abandoned their tanks in 1989. He remembers seeing the boy wave to the driver of a Snatch Land Rover in the patrol just before a huge explosion. Baldwin was blown off his feet and landed about ten meters from where he had been standing. Then the Taliban opened fire.

"I was badly winded and couldn't breathe, my rifle was broken and I was in the middle of an ambush and couldn't fire any rounds," Baldwin says. "I got to my senses and went to drag the kid out of the way. My first reaction was that he had died. Luckily, he just had a graze on his back from a piece of shrapnel." At nearby FOB Jackson, the Last Post was being sounded during a memorial service for a soldier who had been killed. The memorial service had to be cut short so that the QRF could be sent out to help rescue the patrol.

Major Guy Stone was struggling to establish radio contact with his company headquarters in the Sangin district center when he realized he had been separated from Lieutenant Colonel Wadood. "He was standing in the centre of the road without a weapon," Stone remembers. "He never carried one, as a testament to his invincibility. He was smoking a long Russian cigarette as bullets winged around him and he directed his warriors into positions of cover." Afterwards, it was concluded that the Taliban had used the unwitting child as a marker to be lined up with the last vehicle in the patrol, at which point the IED was detonated by command wire. Wadood explained to Stone that he was unafraid of death, telling him: "You must have faith and believe in fate. If you are going to go, you are going to go." It was a maxim that Stone and 3 Company drew on many times in the coming months as they negotiated the carpet of IEDs laid around Sangin.

While Gallimore soon found himself enjoying the unique style of the Afghan army approach, he was shaken by the events that took place later in the tour when a six-man Taliban IED team was captured by the Afghan army near the village of Mian Poshteh. The six were caught in the act of digging IEDs into the road as the Afghan army approached. The Afghan sergeant major took charge as they were arrested, their hands were tied behind their backs, and they were put into the ANA vehicles for the drive back to base.

After a two-hour drive through the desert, Gallimore asked the sergeant major for the prisoners so they could be tested for explosive residue, charged, and processed. "What prisoners?" the sergeant major replied. When an impatient Gallimore explained that he meant the prisoners that he had seen the sergeant major and his troops arrest, he got more stonewalling. "I don't know what you are talking about, Major," the sergeant major insisted. The day before, the kandak had lost three soldiers in an IED strike. It turned out that on the way back to Nawa, the Afghan soldiers had stopped by the road, dragged the Taliban prisoners out, and delivered justice. Several of the soldiers described how three of the prisoners were strangled to death as their comrades watched. The remaining three, they said, were shot in both kneecaps and ordered to crawl back to their villages to tell people what would happen to them if they laid IEDs. The sergeant major later insisted that the prisoners had been released because he had decided they were innocent civilians. When his men were interviewed, they too stuck to the story. But neither Colonel Hai, Gallimore, nor the U.S. Marines believed him. On a previous occasion, Gallimore had stopped the sergeant major from summarily executing a Taliban prisoner. Another time, he had to be dissuaded from hacking an arm off of a dead enemy fighter. The incident was investigated by Colonel Hai, who reported his suspicions and his findings to Brigadier General Muhayadin Ghori. Afterwards, Gallimore sat with his head in his hands asking himself: "What has happened to my moral compass?" He had found himself justifying the turn of events in his own mind as an example of "the Afghan way." It was, after all, their country, and this was the way justice had been meted out for centuries. But that did not make it right.[2] More than eighteen months after the incident, Gallimore was interviewed about it by the Royal Military Police, who concluded that all the correct procedures had been followed and no further action was necessary.

When the Americans finally relieved Task Force Nawa, it really was like the Cavalry arriving. One night in June, 1st Battalion, 5th Marines flew three hundred men into PB Jaker in eight CH-53 Sea Stallion heavy-lift transport helicopters. The next morning, a fifty-strong vehicle convoy arrived with the rest of the battalion and its equipment. Suddenly, 1,500 U.S. Marines with a staggering array of equipment had replaced forty British soldiers. "I would have paid good money to have been a fly on the nearest tree of the insurgents' dicking screen that night," laughed Corbet Burcher. "It would have been

'Holy shit—can you see what I can see?'" Within hours of the U.S. Marines landing, Nawa fell silent and the attacks on PB Jaker ceased. U.S. Marines later stopped vehicles full of fighting-age men leaving the area. In one car there was a letter from a local Taliban leader instructing insurgents to regroup in Marjah.

Under the U.S. Marines, Nawa was to become the showpiece district in Helmand, an area held up by the Pentagon as a shining example of what the right number of troops and resources could achieve in Afghanistan.

As Scholes and his fellow mortarmen arrived at PB Jaker, Lance Sergeant Tobie Fasfous and 3 Section of the Welsh Guards mortar platoon were settling into a routine at FOB Keenan, near Gereshk. Fasfous was on a fitness binge, running around the base in his off hours and losing nearly two stone (thirty pounds) in the mounting heat. He shared a bed space at FOB Keenan with Lance Sergeant Richie Cunningham from Merthyr Tydfil, whom he'd known for eight years. They slept on camp beds placed between Hesco barriers with a plywood screen to separate the two halves of the space. Cunningham had once mentioned to Fasfous that his seven-year-old daughter, Emily, collected glass snowstorm ornaments. Six months later, Fasfous had returned from Dubai with one of the ornaments as a present. "That's the type of guy he was, just a big friendly guy," said Cunningham. Both men were mortar-fire controllers; they would take turns to go out on patrol while the other stayed behind to command the mortar line. The two would remain in contact by radio throughout the patrol so that the one outside the base could call in fire to a precise grid reference if need be.

On Tuesday, April 28, it was Fasfous's turn to go out on a patrol of eight British soldiers training an Afghan army platoon. They had been out for about two hours and were returning to the base when they approached Salamaka Bridge, a vulnerable point across the canal. The route was being cleared by Corporal Les Binns, the Barmaman, walking ahead of Captain Johnny Arkell, the Light Dragoons patrol commander. Popal Shah, the interpreter, was behind Arkell while Fasfous was about five meters to his left. Suddenly there was a massive explosion. "The demons in my head say that one of us, Fas or me or the terp, stepped on the pressure pad and then boom," Arkell says. "There was a big old ringing in my ears and as the dust cleared I looked to my left and there was Fas, who really wasn't in a frightfully good state. I had a bloody big hole in my leg and my arm." Fasfous was obviously dead, killed instantly as the bottom half of his body was devastated. He and Shah, who was decapitated, had taken most of the force of the explosion. Arkell felt a sense of despair. He'd gotten to know Fasfous well during the previous three weeks both on patrol and playing poker at the base. "He was a good, punchy Welsh Guardsman, all over his game, a fantastic soldier." The consensus within the platoon was that Shah, who had been told repeatedly to keep to the path, had stepped outside the Barmaed lane. Two other interpreters with the Welsh Guards were later killed after stepping on IEDs. It took 3 Company in Sangin some thirty hours to recover the body of one of them after he was blown fifty meters away into a river.

Back in FOB Keenan, Cunningham knew something was badly wrong because Fasfous's radio had cut out. Fifteen minutes later, after they had seen the Chinook carrying the casualties fly over the base towards Bastion, the Light Dragoons base commander came down to the mortar line to tell the Welsh Guardsmen that Fasfous had been killed. He was the first member of 19th Light Brigade to die in Helmand and the first Welsh Guardsman to be killed in action since the Falklands War.

In Pencoed, Kelly Gore was driving home from work when she got a call from a neighbor who said: "Kell, there's an Army guy waiting at my house for you. He's been here since 1 pm." It was 4:00 p.m., and she began to panic as she pulled up outside the house.[3] She took one look at the two grim-faced officers dressed in suits and collapsed on the ground. Once she had composed herself and let the notification officers in, she agreed to telephone Fasfous's mother in Dubai. It was 8:30 p.m. in the United Arab Emirates when the telephone rang in Anne Fasfous's house. "It's Tobie," said Kelly, before bursting into tears again.

Around the same time, Cunningham and the rest of the eighty soldiers at FOB Keenan not on duty were conducting a memorial service for their comrade. At the end of it, the Welsh Guards fired eleven illumination mortar rounds into the air, lighting up the night sky. Afterwards, they put up a memorial to Fasfous with a simple wooden cross and a Welsh flag. On top of the cross was placed a Cuban cigar—the mortar platoon had each bought one to smoke at the end of the tour. Cunningham went to sleep that night without his friend snoring on the other side of the plywood partition. The following morning he and another Welsh Guardsman gathered up his photographs of Kelly and his mother, his clothes, and his iPod and packed them in a cardboard box ready to put on the next convoy to Camp Bastion for an onward flight to Britain.

The news of Fasfous's death was a dreadful blow. He had been a big man with a large presence, and he had been in the battalion for nearly ten years. Everyone knew him. As soon as Fasfous was pronounced dead, Operation Minimize went into force, meaning that all telephones and internet terminals for the troops were turned off so that the news could not filter back to Britain before the next of kin were informed. Once the bad news had been relayed, Minimize was lifted and Kelly Gore and Anne Fasfous were given a twenty-four-hour grace period to grieve privately before the death was made public. During this time, however, the news spread fast via email and Facebook. It was late at night by the time it was confirmed in Helmand that the next of kin had been informed, so the decision was taken at some patrol bases to wait until the morning to tell the other Welsh Guardsmen they had lost a comrade. This meant that some of those coming off duty at night and logging on to the internet were in for a shock. At PB Argyll, Lance Corporal Jamie Evans 15, from Cardiff—"Fift"—logged on to Facebook at 3:00 a.m. to find that a member of the Rear Party in Aldershot had posted "R.I.P. Tobie" on Facebook. "I was just devastated," said Evans 15, who had ridden motorbikes with Fasfous and traveled with him to Dubai for a holiday. "It clicked straight away. I then had to wait until 7 am to tell the platoon sergeant what I'd found out. About 20 minutes later we were all on parade to be told officially what had happened to Tobie. He'd just bloody ordered a brand-new Yamaha R1 from Bridgend and was looking forward to riding it." After this, everyone would be woken up if necessary to be told before they could find out from the United Kingdom.

On the Sunday night, all off-duty British personnel at Camp Bastion gathered for a vigil service at dusk, forming a square as Captain Deiniol Morgan, the chaplain, read a passage from Scripture and led prayers for Fasfous, his family, and the regiment. Captain Tom Anderson, his platoon commander in Iraq, praised Fasfous as a "knowledgeable, confident, reliable and exact" mortarman. "We have all looked into ourselves and started to grieve, whether in quiet moments or with tears, with friends or alone," he told those assembled. "When we send him home, we must turn our faces back to the task." Anderson, a wiry, ginger-haired officer, was now Thorneloe's brigade liaison officer in Lashkar Gah. After the service, a bugler sounded the Last Post, and a minute's silence was ended by a salute from a Royal Artillery gun.

Just after midnight, six of Fasfous's closest friends shouldered his flag-draped coffin and carried it at a slow march towards a pool of light at the open ramp door of a C17 transport plane. Marching behind the coffin were Captain Anderson and Company Sergeant Major Scholes from PB Jaker, a close friend of Fasfous who had shared his passion for motorbikes. Flanking the ramp door were two ranks of Welsh Guardsmen at attention. Scholes put out his arm to steady the coffin as the six bearers walked up the ramp and into the belly of the plane. There, with the plane's engines running, Chaplain Morgan read the Lord's Prayer and the words of St. Paul's Letter to the Philippians: "Our true home is in Heaven and from there we await the Savior Christ our Lord." It was the first of many repatriation ceremonies, each one codenamed Operation Pabbay, after an uninhabited island in the Outer Hebrides, to be carried out by 19 Brigade.

The next morning, Kelly Gore and Anne Fasfous were waiting at RAF Lyneham as the body of Lance Sergeant Fasfous was repatriated. As the ramp door opened, six Welsh Guardsmen, all of whom had known Fasfous, marched onto the C17 and picked up his coffin. Fasfous, even though he had lost two stone (thirty pounds), was a big man, and the coffin was lined with lead. The six had difficulty lifting him—one was later treated for a back injury—and eight men were used for future repatriations. They also struggled to curb their emotions as the reality that their friend was dead finally began to sink in. With the Fasfous family watching, they carried the coffin to a waiting hearse, lowered it inside, and then marched off the runway. Once they were out of sight behind an aircraft hangar, they leant against a wall and wept.

The next leg of Fasfous's final journey took him through Wootton Bassett, the Wiltshire market town five miles from Lyneham, that since 2007 had been silently marking the return of the country's fallen. What began with a spontaneous salute by two members of the town's Royal British Legion branch had grown into a national phenomenon, with traffic coming to a standstill and hundreds thronging the streets to pay their respects. A bell tolled as Fasfous's cortege stopped, and the undertaker, walking ahead, turned and stopped before the Wootton Bassett War Memorial and removed his top hat. Several coachloads of veterans from the Welsh Guards Association were in attendance and bowed their heads along with the mayor, councilors, shopkeepers, mothers, schoolchildren, and leather-clad bikers. Once through Wootton Bassett, the hearse was escorted by police outriders to the morgue at the John Radcliffe Hospital in Oxford where post-mortems on all dead servicemen are carried out.

There had never been a funeral quite like it in Pencoed, a drab former mining town on the edge of Bridgend. Captain Pete Robinson, a South Walian former regimental sergeant major with a clipped mustache and upright manner, went to the funeral directors to check that all was in order with the body before the viewing. He drove past it twice before he realized that it was in a lock-up garage at the back of a derelict church. "On the right-hand side was a white stand-up fridge, you could get three bodies in there. Along the walls were shelves of coffins ready to go. At the top left-hand corner, you had this little space with a piece of carpet on floor, a bit of a curtain, two trestles and a chair. That was where you visited the body."

Before the funeral, a small team of Welsh Guardsmen dressed the coffin, placing a Union Flag on top along with Fasfous's forage cap, medals, belt, and a wreath. "Standing in a garage with a friend of mine in there was so peculiar," said Robinson. "I couldn't get my head around it at all."

Fasfous's body had been badly damaged in the IED blast, but Kelly Gore insisted she wanted to see him. It was probably a mistake—almost the only thing that resembled him was his hair. "They'd put so much make-up on to cover his injuries it didn't look like him at all," she later recalled. "The only thing that made me smile a little was the fact he had no gel in his hair. He never left the house without gel so I thought: 'He'd be going nuts!'"

Salem Chapel, designed to hold 550, was packed to the rafters: a dilapidated traditional Welsh chapel with two aisles and a gallery looking down on the main congregation. Most of the male mourners were dressed, as Fasfous had decreed, in rugby shirts. Among the exceptions were those in uniform and Guards officers immaculately turned out in dark suits and black ties. Fasfous's friends decided it would be best for a serving guardsman, rather than Colonel Tom Bonas, the regimental adjutant, to deliver the oration. The job was given to Sergeant Jimmy Broe, a mortarman who was about to leave the army. Although a fine soldier, Broe was known as something of a "drama merchant." He was not the person the Welsh Guards hierarchy would have chosen to represent the regiment at the first funeral in twenty-seven years for one of its soldiers killed in action.

There was a sense of apprehension among the officers as Broe, dressed in a pink rugby shirt, flipped open a notebook and began to deliver the eulogy as if briefing a group of guardsmen. They need not have worried. Broe, visibly emotional, paid a heartfelt tribute to his friend as not only "the utmost professional," but a man who was loved by his Welsh brothers in arms. "Everybody looked up to him and everybody wanted to be like him. He was completely dependable. If he was ever given a task, you could sleep safe at night knowing it was done to the best standard." There were chuckles as Broe recounted how an officer had once told him that Fasfous "was an officer's worst nightmare—a soldier with brains who was possibly more intelligent than you." Fasfous, he said, was unflappable. "When things were going wrong and things start to go into a tailspin and the wheels come off, he would stand there, a massive smile and a big grin on his face, and say: 'What can you do about it, Bud? Let the wheels come off and then we'll see if we can put it back together.'" He added: "He remained 100 percent adamant that what was happening in Afghanistan was a 100 percent just cause."

7

Flashman's Fort

He cares deeply about his men and takes great trouble to ensure that they never want for anything.... His men are fortunate to have him as a commander and he should have confidence in himself for Op HERRICK.

—**Major Guy Stone,** *report on Lieutenant Mark Evison,*
March 12, 2009

The platoon had long ceased to question any direction he took; they knew he would be right as infallibly as sun after darkness or fatigue after a long march.

—**Norman Mailer,** The Naked and the Dead *(1948)*

aji Alem Fort was one of the most isolated bases in Afghanistan. Next to an irrigation canal and surrounded by poppy and maize fields and a few mud compounds, it looked towards the badlands of Taliban-controlled Marjah some sixteen kilometers to the southwest. To the arriving Welsh Guardsmen, it seemed like a scene from *A Thousand and One Nights.* CP Haji Alem was modeled on the small British forts established in Afghanistan in the nineteenth century. It had battlements and its baked-mud walls were over a meter thick, meaning it could withstand anything the Taliban might throw at it. The fort took its name from the local drug baron who had built it. He had been well compensated for leasing it to the British

Army and would occasionally turn up, wearing a flowing white robe, to cast a proprietorial eye over his personal citadel.

Lieutenant Mark Evison was immediately struck by the romance of the place, calling it "Flashman's Fort." It was his own outpost of empire—just like Piper's Fort, the beleaguered Afghan garrison that was defended by George MacDonald Fraser's Lieutenant Harry Flashman. The bully of Rugby School in *Tom Brown's Schooldays*, Flashman was recreated by Fraser as an anti-hero of the Victorian army whose combination of abject cowardice and good fortune stood him in good stead in an era of adventurism and the Great Game.

CP Haji Alem, Evison noted in his diary, was "very defendable—four turrets on each corner give excellent views to all compass points." Commanding such a place was everything a young platoon commander dreamed about in Helmand. He was entranced by Afghanistan. One of the few downsides of CP Haji Alem, he remarked to a guardsman, was that its walls were so high that he was unable to see how beautiful the Afghan landscape was. Evison was in command of 7 Platoon, which had been switched from Major Guy Stone's 3 Company to Major Henry Bettinson's 2 Company for the tour. 7 Platoon had not been split up like other 3 Company platoons that had been detached. As such, it had a strong sense of its "Little Iron Men" identity, though they proudly wore their maroon 2 Company T-shirts, ordering more of them than 4 and 6 Platoons combined.

Just as Evison arrived, there were reports of Taliban and even al Qaeda fighters traveling from Pakistan to Helmand to help with the poppy harvest. Some madrassas in Pakistan closed to facilitate this. The fighters were paid up to $30 per day or a group share of a quarter of the harvest. During the harvest, the Taliban in Helmand were under orders from the Quetta shura headquarters, issued on April 6, not to engage the British and to focus their energies on the poppy fields instead. It was clear, however, that the Taliban were reinforcing and reorganizing in preparation for resumed hostilities after the harvest. According to intelligence reports, about ten al Qaeda fighters— seven Pakistanis and three Arabs—had moved into Marjah from Pakistan in March 2009 at the direction of the Quetta shura.

Iran, as well as al Qaeda, was helping the Taliban bolster their presence and capabilities in the Nad-e Ali district. In mid-April, it was reported that the Taliban commander Mullah ▮▮▮▮▮ had arranged for a large shipment of weapons and explosives from Iran, which had consistently been supporting the insurgency. The shipment was believed to include mortars, AK-47s, RPG launchers, and ██████████ for IEDs. At the end of April, a number of sources indicated that 250 Taliban fighters were transferred from central Helmand to Marjah, Nad-e Ali, and Chah-e Anjir.

At the start of May, ████████████████████████████ IEDs, all apparently of Iranian origin, were moved into Helmand. They were given to Mullah Malik, the insurgent governor of Marjah, with an instruction from the Iranian Security Service that there was a bounty of $800 payable to any fighter who killed a British or American soldier with one of these devices. A Brigade intelligence report assessed that "the supply of weapons, ammunition and devices from Iran is considered to be relatively common and demonstrates a degree of influence and support to the insurgency from Iranian organisations." In an important success for the brigade, Mullah Malik was killed in a strike by U.S. Special Forces on May 14 as he and his men were forming up to mount an attack on Lashkar Gah.

After the poppy harvest ended in early May, many of the Pakistani fighters remained to do battle with the British and raise money for the Taliban by transporting narcotics. Just as the British were beginning to concentrate their resources in central Helmand, so too were the Taliban. Central Helmand, and the Nad-e Ali district in particular, was to be the main battleground.

Haji Alem fort was square, with each wall fifty meters long. The towers—seven meters high and reached by rickety wooden ladders—did indeed give ideal firing arcs in all directions. Around the inner perimeter were fifteen roofless rooms that made ideal sleeping quarters when camouflage canopies were rigged up. Haji Alem had been seized during Operation Tor Paraang just a fortnight before the Welsh Guards got there, but apart from putting in a few sandbags to plug gaps in the outer wall, there was little extra that needed to be done to make it fit for purpose. The fort itself was impressively defended.

The problem was that it was located in the wrong place. The original plan had been to put the patrol base a few hundred meters north at the Green 5 crossroads. This key junction, next to the settlement of Noor Mohammed Khan Kalay, had been regularly seeded with IEDs; an IED factory had recently been discovered nearby. But the inhabitants of the cluster of thirty-three compounds to the southeast, known as the Green 5 triangle (and occasionally by a morbid guardsman as the "triangle of death"), had protested that situating a base there would put civilians at risk. Instead, the triangle's residents urged, the base should be set up further to the south at Haji Alem and Green 9 where, as it happened, their tribal rivals lived. Discussions with the elders of the Green 5 triangle elicited promises that they would not allow the Taliban to place IEDs there, and they agreed it was in their own interests to keep the crossroads safe and clear. There was, moreover, no building there nearly as militarily attractive as the Haji Alem fort. 3 Commando Brigade agreed to set up a base there.

Almost at once, the Welsh Guards realized that the promises of the elders had been worthless. Green 5 became a magnet for IEDs. It soon required a convoy of 256 men with ten Scimitars, five Jackals, and three Mastiffs, taking a day in the process, to resupply CP Haji Alem—under RPG and small-arms fire while detecting and defusing IEDs.

Rupert Thorneloe had described 2 Company's area as the "hard shoulder" of the Battle Group's territory. It comprised PB Silab to the west, CP Paraang in the centre and CP Haji Alem to the east. This defensive line was intended to maintain a static Taliban front line to the south, providing a protective barrier so that governance could be developed to the north. For the Taliban, a fixed front line gave them areas where they could establish IED factories and "bed-down locations" (places to sleep before mounting attacks) in relative safety, though there was always the risk of a special forces attack. In reality, the Welsh Guards were to discover, almost anywhere beyond a thousand-meter radius of a patrol base was a sanctuary for the Taliban.

One of the results of Operation Tor Paraang was that CP Haji Alem was further south than PB Silab and CP Paraang, jutting out beyond the natural defensive line. CP Haji Alem was two kilometers east of Paraang, which was 2.2 kilometers southeast of the company headquarters at PB Silab. The Green 5 junction was to the north of Haji Alem. Since any resupply convoy had to pass through the junction, if the Taliban should take control of it, Haji Alem would be cut off and behind enemy lines.

Another problem was that a patrol going out or returning was very limited in its route. One option was for the patrol to wade through the irrigation canal, a time-consuming and therefore dangerous prospect. The other was to cross a small but very visible infantry footbridge installed by the Royal Engineers over the canal about fifteen meters from the base entrance. Holes were later blasted in the rear wall, but at first there was only one way in and one way out of Haji Alem.

Bettinson also had to deal with a manpower shortage that bordered on a crisis. He arrived at Camp Bastion to be told by Thorneloe he now had to man four locations—PB Silab, CP Paraang, CP Haji Alem, and PB Tanda—rather than the two he had planned for and would be given no extra troops.

PB Tanda was located at a five-way junction between Marjah, ten kilometers to its west, and Lashkar Gah, twelve kilometers to its northeast. It was deep in no man's land, surrounded by an enemy that could move at will and had virtually no population to influence. Four months earlier, Lieutenant Colonel Chalmers, Thorneloe's predecessor, had argued vigorously with the staff of 3 Commando Brigade against it being established. The notion that PB Tanda could act as a forward buffer between Marjah, assessed by the brigade to be an insurgent "safe-haven, C2 [command and control] node and facilitation hub," was always unrealistic. It would probably have needed a full company of 180 men to have created much of an effect there, but the Welsh Guards were able to devote just two dozen. The only way to man the four bases—far from an ideal solution—was to break the platoons up into smaller units.

Lieutenant Owen James, a politics, philosophy, and economics graduate of Jesus College, Oxford, and his 6 Platoon were sent to take over CP Paraang. James, one of just a handful of Welsh officers in the Welsh Guards, was already marked out as destined for great things. Paraang, every bit as vulnerable as CP Haji Alem and much less fortified, was located on the southern edge of the inaptly named Khowshaal Kalay, or "Happy Village."

Thorneloe reported to the brigade that "the locals [in Khowshaal Kalay] are scared." The walls of CP Paraang were so thin that bullets sometimes came through them and so low that the Welsh Guardsmen had to crouch down to avoid being hit in the head by a lucky shot. A few days after James arrived, Abdul Haq, one of the four Afghan policemen stationed there, walked from the Paraang base into Khowshaal Kalay to get a cup of tea at the village shop beside the Green 4 junction. Two Taliban on a motorcycle, presumably tipped off by a villager, arrived shortly afterwards and shot him dead, also killing the shopkeeper's teenage son, Rhaz Mohamed. Thorneloe noted that Haq was "a 19-year-old from LKG [Lashkar Gah]—a good man, but clearly unwise on this occasion." It was also reported the same day that a forty-year-old villager had been beheaded by the Taliban.

After the incident, the remaining three Afghan policemen at PB Paraang disappeared for several days before returning with a dozen reinforcements. Among the new arrivals was a fresh-faced fifteen-year-old wearing a loose-fitting uniform. "We were naïve," remembers Owen James. "They were a

dodgy bunch and there was this young kid but we didn't think much of it."
A few days later, the youth approached one of the snipers and admired his
sunglasses. He then pointed first at the sunglasses and then at himself, as if
to say: "You give me the sunglasses and you can have me." The sniper shook
his head in disgust and walked off. It had become clear that the youth was a
catamite, a sexual plaything brought along by the policemen for their
gratification.

There were further problems with the policemen when they began to steal
water and food from the Welsh Guards as they slept. One night, Terry
Harman decided he had had enough when the policemen lit a large fire—
silhouetting the sangars—and sat around it laughing and singing. Harman
stormed over to take them to task. James listened as the former regimental
sergeant major bellowed: "Right! Put the fire out and keep quiet!" There was
a pause and then another order from Harman as he discovered a policeman
and the catamite under a blanket in the corner. "And stop making love!"
roared Harman. All the policemen had deserted the base by dawn the next
day, telling the interpreter that they were scared and not being paid enough
by the police chief in Nad-e Ali. "It was quite amusing but also rather
disturbing," says James.

In late 2009, a study into homosexuality and pedophilia in Afghan
society was commissioned by American and British forces in Helmand. It
examined the high cost of marriage within Pashtun tribes and the tradition
in which adolescent boys are cherished for their beauty and apprenticed to
men to learn a trade. "Homosexuality is strictly prohibited in Islam, but
cultural interpretations of Islamic teaching prevalent in Pashtun areas of
southern Afghanistan tacitly condone it in comparison to heterosexual
relationships," the study stated, citing an old Afghan saying that "women are
for children, boys are for pleasure." The report noted that for a man to have
sex with a boy was considered a "foible," whereas intercourse with an
"ineligible woman" could cause "issues of revenge and honour killings."
Lieutenant Colonel de Quincy Adams, the brigade staff officer responsible
for Afghan police development, says: "There are cultural issues about the
whole Pashtun people when it comes to homosexuality. There are myriad
reasons for that but some young men have probably only seen a handful of
female faces in their entire life. The whole thing is weird and f---ing difficult
to understand."

PB Tanda and its 4 Platoon force were commanded by Lieutenant Charles Fraser-Sampson, a former Buckinghamshire prep school teacher. Thorneloe had already secured agreement from the brigade that PB Tanda would be closed in late May—shutting it down was a major operation that required planning. But even that would not ease the manpower situation because a group of five Mastiffs was being allocated to 2 Company. These were essential assets given the increasing IED threat (Mastiffs and Ridgebacks were the only vehicles with sufficient armor to prevent serious casualties from an IED in nearly all cases), but they had to be manned by the Welsh Guards. Thorneloe decided that the nucleus of those at PB Tanda would become the Mastiff platoon once the patrol base had closed and that Fraser-Sampson would lead it.

Thorneloe was very concerned about the situation in Nad-e Ali South, the 2 Company area. "Our additional platoons have in practice been swallowed up by the post TOR PARAANG laydown," he pointed out to the Brigade. "Our ability to project beyond GDAs [Ground Dominating Area patrols] is currently minimal." Thorneloe realized that GDAs, often called "presence patrols" in Northern Ireland, were of little value in Helmand, where the new counterinsurgency strategy was all about engaging with the people. Patrolling simply to deter the enemy and—in theory—to reassure the population was pointless. And when things went wrong, such patrols could be deeply counterproductive.

Almost as soon as he arrived at CP Haji Alem with 7 Platoon, Evison was laid low with "D&V"—diarrhea and vomiting, a constant problem in Helmand. In his place, Lieutenant Piers Lowry, Bettinson's logistics officer, was sent down to the base. Lowry, a strapping, blond-haired cavalry officer who hailed from the Scottish Borders, was eager to take on the challenge. "Haji Alem was what I expected Helmand to be like, what you'd seen in pictures," Lowry remembers. "It was like your own little world as platoon commander down there. You were master of your own destiny."

Lowry took 7 Platoon out on their first patrol in the searing early afternoon heat with several guardsmen who had just spent five hours "on stag" manning the sangars. CP Haji Alem's interpreter and contingent of Afghan soldiers had not yet arrived at the base, so there were no means of talking to any locals or monitoring the Taliban's walkie-talkies. The patrol had barely got 150 meters from the base when Guardsman Thomas James from Bridgnorth, Shropshire, one of those who had been on sangar duty, collapsed with heat exhaustion. As they began to withdraw, the Taliban opened fire from a woodline and some compounds two hundred meters away. Most of the guardsmen hesitated. It was their first contact, and some later said they were concerned there might be civilians in the fields. But Lowry, who had already been in a contact near PB Silab, and another soldier returned fire. Barely ten minutes after the firefight was over and they had got back to the base, an old Afghan man arrived with his son, aged about thirty, who had been shot in the abdomen and was bleeding profusely. Guardsman Jon Caswell, trained as a medic, set about treating him and kept the casualty alive until the Pedro—an American Blackhawk MERT (Medical Emergency Response Team) helicopter—could arrive to evacuate him. That evening, the wounded Afghan died at Camp Bastion. "Colonel Rupert was furious," says Bettinson. "It was not so great in terms of trying to win over the people, you know—'We're ISAF and we're here to protect you. Sorry, we shot your son.'"

When Evison returned to CP Haji Alem on April 26 after his brief sickness, he received a warm welcome from 7 Platoon. "It is good being back," he wrote in his diary. "The Platoon cheered me when I turned up and so for some strange reason I think they must have missed me." He too was dismayed by what had happened under Lowry in his absence, writing in the diary that their objective had been to search known Taliban compounds to the southwest, an area where "one would not venture to with soldiers who have not been out on the ground and do not know the combat indicators." He wondered whether Lowry's actions had been due to a desire to say he had fought in Afghanistan and fired back at the enemy or perhaps even sheer incompetence. He had moved across raised open ground with well-known firing points across a nearby poppy field. Whatever the reason, Evison felt Lowry had risked a lot more than he knew.

One of the first things Evison did was to tell the platoon that they would not patrol in the way they had with his stand-in. "When we went out with Lowry, we just walked," says Langley. "But when we went out with Mr. Evison it was tactical movement staying in cover the whole time rather than just going trudging along the roadway." Lowry later reflected that his actions on the patrol had been wrong, but he had been sent by 2 Company to an unfamiliar area at no notice, with soldiers he did not know. "I was naïve but I learnt from my mistakes," he says.

Evison was well aware of the difficulties he was facing at CP Haji Alem. His original platoon of twenty-eight men was now down to twenty-two, and he was deeply concerned about equipment and supplies. Writing in his diary at PB Silab en route to CP Haji Alem, he had complained that he would be without sufficient "radios, water, food and medical equipment" at his patrol base. "This with manpower is what these missions lack. It is disgraceful to send a platoon into a very dangerous area with two weeks water and food and one team medics pack. Injuries will be sustained which I will not be able to treat and deaths could occur which could have been stopped." He concluded: "We are walking on a tightrope and from what it seems here are likely to fall unless drastic measures are undertaken."

At his level, Thorneloe was also beating the drum about lack of resources. CP Paraang, CP Haji Alem, and PB Tanda were under persistent attack from a group of Pakistani fighters "who commute from Marjah," he reported to the brigade on May 1. It was imperative for the Welsh Guards to be able "to get much further onto the front foot to disrupt and deter this activity in depth." He was immensely frustrated with the situation, concluding: "I cannot do this myself." He informed Brigade that he was seeking assistance from Task Force 31—American Special Forces. Their "attitude and effect on the ground have really impressed me" during their operations in Marjah (technically within the Welsh Guards' area of operations), he reported. Thorneloe also highlighted the "extremely ropey communications" he had with 2 Company in PB Silab.

To ease the pressure on Bettinson and help 2 Company make greater inroads into engaging with the locals, Thorneloe dispatched Captain Terry Harman, the forty-five-year-old former regimental sergeant major, down to 2 Company. He was to act as influence officer, with a brief to engage with Afghans in Khowshaal Kalay and around Green 5. Thorneloe calculated that Harman's avuncular style—he had been a color sergeant at Sandhurst when Bettinson was a cadet—would also help steady the young platoon commanders like Evison, James, and Fraser-Sampson. Every day they were facing several attacks on their bases, as well as Taliban ambushes whenever they ventured out.

On May 8, Thorneloe told the brigade that the Welsh Guards could conduct only "limited BG [Battle Group] level activity" during the following month because "we are not resourced to conduct it at present." It would be impossible to meet any additional commitments placed on the Welsh Guards because "currently we have nothing left." He could do little more than hold the line, he argued, with the implication that the central mission of winning over the people would have to wait. He also bemoaned the size and number of stabilization teams available within the brigade. "I believe they are force multipliers and that we should have generated more than we did."

Thorneloe's unvarnished appraisals were causing considerable angst within the brigade staff, who had to manage limited resources across the whole brigade area. There had been an early clash over Thorneloe's fierce disagreement with the brigade plan to detach most of his mortar sections and lend them to other battle groups. Some staff officers viewed his weekly reports—which had a wide distribution—as direct criticisms not only of them, but of the whole system. No other commanding officer complained in writing about PJHQ's requirements being "confused." Few would have engaged with U.S. Special Forces on their own initiative and reported back blithely to brigade, as Thorneloe had done on May 1, that Task Force 31 had "kindly agreed to come and discuss how they could help." With the Americans pouring troops and state-of-the-art kit into Helmand and the British anxious to prove they were in control of the province, such a move was fraught with delicate national sensitivities. No one appreciated this more than Thorneloe, but he was determined to get what he needed for his battle group. Before he left for Helmand, he gave Dai Bevan, the Rear Party commander, the mobile phone number of a senior aide to the Defence secretary. It was, he said, a "silver bullet" to be used if ever there was a crisis and all else had failed.

The Brigade staff suspected—correctly—that Thorneloe was working back channels in the MoD and PJHQ. His view was that if the Welsh Guards Battle Group was the brigade's main effort then it was being resourced far too thinly. "There were frustrations for him at times," remembers Major Ed Launders, the ops officer, "because he saw things that he felt could be achieved if people worked a bit harder. In fighting for resources, he didn't necessarily make friends along the way." The Welsh Guards officers referred to their Battle Group (Center South), without irony, as "Battle Group (Center of the Universe)." Thorneloe's relentless pushing for more resources prompted a group of brigade staff officers to talk sarcastically of "Battle Group (Special Needs)." Everyone knew Thorneloe was on the army's fast track, but a few felt that his time in the Defence secretary's office had made him too big for his boots and that he should stop trying to do the jobs of those above him. He was not, one staff officer remarked acidly, a general yet.

Despite the complaints in his diary, Evison relished being in CP Haji Alem. He noted that morale at the base would swing one way and then another, but he himself remained stoic and was even ebullient at times. At the end of one diary entry, he wrote: "Life here is great." Owen James spent a couple of hours with him on the way to Paraang when a logistics convoy dropped off batteries and water. "He was pretty chuffed with where he was and the set-up he had," James recalls. "He was showing me where he was living and his bed space then he started taking the piss out of me and saying he'd heard Paraang was a complete dump and there was no protection there." When Bettinson visited, he too was struck by how proud Evison was of CP Haji Alem.

Evison's grandfather had been a missionary in China, and before leaving for Afghanistan, Evison had been busy typing up his grandfather's diary from 1937. This had prompted him to keep his own account of life in Helmand, and he would often be seen sitting away in a corner writing in pencil. His leather-bound Aspinal of London journal had been a Christmas present from a girlfriend and was inscribed: "To continue your grandfather's tradition...." Evison's connection with Wales was little more than long walks in the Brecon Beacons with his mother. But he was a perfect fit for the regiment—he loved singing, rugby, and socializing, and he related to the emotionalism and expressiveness of the Welsh. He relished living in the field but was immaculately smart and well organized in barracks. His mother, Margaret, was a clinical psychologist and his father, David, a sculptor; he was drawn to people and creative. His parents had separated when he was eleven and his sister Lizzy was thirteen. David Evison later based himself in Berlin but saw his children weekly throughout their teens and spent holidays with them.

Few young officers had Evison's ability to relate so intimately to the guardsmen while at the same time maintaining their unstinting respect. This quality, along with his supreme fitness and zest for everything he did, meant that he was rated by Thorneloe as the top platoon commander in the Welsh Guards. His most recent report had described him being "set apart from his contemporaries because he combines real talent with great humility and charm." Just before leaving for Afghanistan, Evison had had a long discussion with his mother, who worked in cancer care, in her garden about death and dying. He anticipated he would lose one or more members of his platoon and wanted to prepare himself. The one thing they did not discuss was the possibility that he might be one of those who did not come back.

Batteries were a major problem at CP Haji Alem. Thorneloe was livid that he had not been provided with enough chargers for the VHF Bowman radios to be distributed to outposts like CP Haji Alem and CP Paraang. He fulminated in a weekly report that he had been ordered by Land Command to leave one battery charger back in Aldershot where "it is sitting there gathering dust." This meant that 2 Company convoys had to move along IED-seeded roads twice a week purely to resupply batteries. Even with the resupplies, when patrols were not out there was only enough battery power for 6 and 7 Platoons to be able to turn their radios on every two hours to establish communications.

Supplying CP Haji Alem was so hazardous that ammunition, water, rations, and medical supplies had to be given priority. There were no satellite phone chargers there, and the mail delivery was forever being delayed. Evison and his men could not telephone home and felt isolated from the outside world.

After a week of this, the guardsmen began tearing apart the base Land Rover, which was fitted with radios and used as a makeshift operations room. Soon, the vehicle's battery had been jerry-rigged to charge up the satellite phone. Later, the oil was siphoned off to fuel a new generator and the guardsmen charged up their iPods and DVD players with it. Finally, Lance Sergeant Leon Peek, the acting platoon sergeant, then tore the bonnet off the Land Rover and used his skills as a former bricklayer to construct a barbecue.

Peek was a born fighter. That was how he had survived in the former mining village of Tonyrefail in the Rhondda Valley. He had lost part of his ear when it was bitten off in a fight when he was fifteen, a year before joining the army. "This big geezer called Dai Pitbull was beating my mother up, punching the shit out of her," Peek remembers. "We were all on the piss. I ran in, hit him and he hit me back. I rugby-tackled him and started giving him a proper shoeing and he bit my ear off. I managed to get up and I just kicked the shit out of his face while he was down." Afterwards, Peek picked up the piece of his ear and tried without success to get it stitched back on. "Blood everywhere. Just one of them days. I've always been a bit of a scrapper. I think that's why the Army has suited me."

He was fiercely proud of being a Welshman and a soldier, and his ambition was to join the SAS. Peek had "Made in Wales" tattooed around his belly button. On his back, he had pledged lifelong allegiance to 3 Company with the words "Little Iron Man Till I Die" etched into his skin. The eldest of four boys, Peek had grown up on Tonyrefail's notorious Springfield estate, which has since been bulldozed. Raised primarily by his mother, with help from his nan and grandfather, a former miner, he had witnessed his father beating up his mother when he was a young boy. His father still lived in Tonyrefail but hadn't spoken to his eldest son in more than five years. "He's got hepatitis," said Peek. "He's probably smacked out of his face because he injects f---ing heroin. He's got one eye because he got smashed in the face with a glass bottle. To be honest with you, he's a waste of oxygen."

Married for a year, Peek had met his wife, Karly, outside the Talbot Arms pub when she pulled up in her black Vauxhall Corsa and had a man land on her hood. The man had been flung out of the pub by Peek, who had gained the upper hand in a fight. "It was love at first sight," Peek jokes. Two years later, he crashed the Corsa, writing it off.

Peek's most recent conviction had been for being drunk and disorderly and resisting arrest after he had punched a policeman. The policeman had allegedly intervened in an argument and thumped Peek's wife, cutting her head open, after she told him: "F--- off, you prick—it's nothing to do with you." Peek, who received a £475 fine, recalls: "I didn't get done for assault because the copper hit my wife first and it was on CCTV." He marked their wedding anniversary shortly after arriving in CP Haji Alem, celebrating the occasion with a boil-in-the-bag compo meal of chicken, sausage, and beans.

Peek, an emotional, fiery Welshman, was counterbalanced by Evison, the cultured, public school–educated Guards officer. While Evison wondered in his diary why he seemed "to be the only one here who believes that war might not be the answer to this particular problem," Peek was eager to kill at close quarters. The fact that he never managed to get close enough to a Taliban fighter to bayonet one of them was a source of regret. "It's like a fight when someone wants to kick the shit out of you and you want to kick the shit out of them. And you have a knife—you've got the upper hand. You have to be willing to put that bayonet in a place where it's not going to be pretty for him. Unfortunately, they'd always melted away by the time we fixed bayonets and got there. To be honest, it would have been nice to have at least had the one."[1]

Despite Evison's relative youth at age twenty-six, the young guardsmen saw him as something of a father figure. "Mr. Evison would sit down and go through it with you, he saw his men as human beings instead of pieces of meat," remembers Peek. "He listened to what you'd got to say instead of coming in with a pip on his chest and thinking he owned the gaff." Evison felt slightly surprised at the way the platoon looked up to him and even confided in him about difficulties with girlfriends and fears about dying. His toughest task was to break the news to the platoon that Lance Sergeant Tobie Fasfous had been killed up near Gereshk. After a discussion with Peek, it was decided that Peek would first tell Lance Corporal Damien Crombie, one of Fasfous's closest friends. "He was like brothers with Tobie, shared the same house and everything," says Peek, who had also known Fasfous well. "I'd already had my cry and then I told Mr Evison I'd tell him. I just went in and said: "Crom, Tobie's f---ing dead. Sorry, mate."" Evison wrote in his diary that Crombie "has taken the news badly and will need to be monitored closely over the next few days to make sure he is OK."

Evison worried about the spirits of his guardsmen at the remote outpost. "The biggest fear I have whilst in the fort for six months is keeping the morale up of the men," he wrote in his diary. "Currently we have a satellite phone but as it stands, no way of charging it. On top of that, the CLP [Combat Logistics Patrol] that arrived today did so without the post which was expected." In his diary, Evison wrote: "The loos are fairly basic with just a hole in the ground for pissing and an ammo tin for turds which must be burnt by the unfortunate individual who fills it up."

When the mail did eventually arrive, Peek was in raptures about the tins of custard and pair of false breasts his nan had sent him. Meanwhile, Evison delighted in the pickled onions, foie gras, and a cigar dispatched to him by family friends, the d'Ambrumenils. A girlfriend had sent him heel balm. From his father, he received a book about the cathedrals of England packaged up along with some Chinese tea and a bamboo mug with his name on it. The parcel amused him and he joked that some wonderful flying buttresses was just the thing he needed to take his mind off being shot at; "random to the last item!" he wrote in his diary. Despite the class gap between them, Evison and Peek were close and relied upon each other. Although three years younger than Evison, Peek had been under fire in Iraq in 2004 and knew more about basic soldiering than his commander.

Evison fretted about letting Peek and the others down. On May 1, the young officer described in his diary his first experience of being shot at. He outlined how his patrol came under fire, fought back, and then searched two compounds that had been used as firing points by the Taliban before returning to CP Haji Alem via the infantry footbridge. "I managed to push my lead section over the bridge but as I did so we came under accurate small arms fire from 4 or 5 firing points.... The radios were down and so I had no comms with either PB Silab or the [mortar] gun line [at PB Silab]. I therefore had to use my own fire, a Javelin, GMG [grenade machine gun] and sniper pair. Two Javelin missiles were fired onto a firing point which eliminated one threat."

This meant that he and seven of his men were stranded on the wrong side of the canal. "We had to make the decision just to go for it. With a rapid fire from the Platoon we sprinted down the bank, through the canal, back up the friendly bank and then tried to push back into the checkpoint. More luck than anything else saw the platoon safely back behind sturdy walls, laughing at the contact we had just been in." He reflected on the responsibility he had for the lives of his men. "For me it is still the fear of making a wrong decision which sits heavily on my mind ... I fear that we will not always be as lucky as we were today. At least today I proved to myself that I will not freeze the next time I get shot at. I do not expect this to be in the distant future."

Like Major Sean Birchall over at IX Company, he was unimpressed by the military skills of the Afghan soldiers. "The ANA are an interesting bunch," he wrote in his diary. "They earn $200 a month, compared to what they could do if they farmed poppies, $4000 a month. Many of them fight for blood feuds with the Taleban who have killed various family members. All they want to do is kill Taleban." The guardsmen were alarmed that the Afghan soldiers did not take cover when they were fired at and instead stood in the open and fired wildly. During an ambush, one of them fired an RPG at a cow but, to the amusement of the guardsmen, missed by some distance.

In these early encounters with the enemy, Evison had certainly proved himself to Peek. "We were in a lot of firefights together and he was as cool as f--- in every one of them," Peek remembers. Although Evison had an easy rapport with his soldiers, they were in awe of the way he carried himself. They would—and did—follow him anywhere.

Evison worked hard at creating opportunities for fun in the evening and chances to take his men's minds off the prospect of death. On one patrol, Peek negotiated the purchase of a turkey from a local man for the inflated price of $25—about a month's wages for an Afghan laborer. The platoon named the turkey Terry and began trying to fatten it up with compo rations, which the bird proved reluctant to eat. After fighting in the sweltering heat during the day, the evenings were spent taking part in improvised television game shows. In *Squaddie's Got Talent*, platoon members were called upon to perform, with Evison playing the role of judge Simon Cowell. Guardsman Gareth Lucas, from Merthyr Vale, snorted Tabasco sauce, chilli powder, and coffee through his nose. His encore of downing a liter of water and then consuming a raw onion was recorded for posterity and posted on YouTube.

Guardsman Adam Kastein, a sniper, ended up naked after his portrayal of a Pontypridd stripper while Guardsman James, recovered from his heat injury, performed a karaoke version of *Aladdin*'s "A Whole New World." Another guardsman juggled hand grenades. At the end of one round, Evison decreed that the winner was Gunner Steve Gadsby, a hefty, blunt-speaking Royal Artillery soldier from Lincolnshire. His special talent was drinking the urine of his platoon mates. "I got spammed last minute and I didn't have anything prepped so I drank six people's piss," he remembers. "All in all, it was just under a litre of piss." Gadsby was defeated in the semifinals by the projectile-vomiting Lucas.

On other evenings, Evison was Noel Edmonds, conducting games of *Deal or No Deal*. Proceeds from this—each win or loss was faithfully recorded in a platoon notebook—were to go towards a night out in Blackpool at the end of the tour. Money was also raised from a kangaroo court that sat periodically. The maximum fine was $300 to Guardsman Luke Langley. "He got his hand covered in shit when he was burning the shit pit so he took a buckshee shower," explained Peek. Not even Evison could escape the sanctions of this people's court. He was fined $100 for allowing his magazine to fall off his rifle during a patrol. Evison had grown a scrubby beard especially for his appearance as Noel Edmonds. He shaved off the beard but left a mustache, prompting fits of laughter amongst the guardsmen when he described to them how he had found himself stroking it in the middle of a Taliban ambush.

Terry the turkey did not get much fatter, but his days were numbered nevertheless. "You could see the boys were getting hungry because they started throwing stones at the f---ing thing," remembers Peek. Evison decided that Terry should be shot, preferably in the head to avoid a bullet contaminating its flesh. Soldiers took turns with a 9 mm pistol, but after ten rounds fired the turkey had suffered just a graze on the neck. At this point, Guardsman Joe Korosaya, a powerfully built Fijian who played prop for the Welsh Guards rugby team, charged at the turkey with a machete and hacked its head off. Korosaya was softly spoken and had a gentleness that belied his size. Like many Fijians, he was deeply religious and believed that God would dictate what happened to him in Helmand.

Evison wrote in his diary that the heat was "something I have never experienced in my life." Temperatures were now reaching 42° C (107° F). "The sun here is just so powerful. By 09.00 the sun is already fairly high in the sky and the power is staggering. The hottest part between 11.00 and 14.00 and then it suddenly drops and is relatively cool by 17.00.... Added to the proximity of the walls within the fort and we have a living oven. There is no respite and it seems the shade makes no difference."

He had a nagging feeling that it was the Taliban who held all the cards, and he did not quite know what the purpose was of 7 Platoon being at CP Haji Alem. "The most frustrating thing is that they take us on, on their terms," he wrote in his diary. "They are very accomplished at moving into firing positions using good cover and it is almost impossible to identify the firing points." The Taliban would fire through "murder holes" in compound walls, which gave them cover and also made it harder for British troops to see the muzzle flashes that would give away their position. Without knowing where the Taliban firing points were, Evison wrote, "I cannot make decisions and am fairly useless."

Evison was also concerned about the difficulties of returning to CP Haji Alem after a patrol. "There is a canal directly outside which although it gives good cover is terribly exposed on both banks and can be covered by at least three or four firing points." In his training, the importance of not setting patterns when patrolling had been drilled into him, but in this situation it was virtually impossible not to do so.

Most seriously, Evison felt he had little sense from Bettinson, his company commander, of what 7 Platoon should be trying to achieve at CP Haji Alem. This uncertainty spread to the platoon. "The patrols were basically to go and have a look at compounds," says Guardsman Caswell, brought up in Coventry, but from a Welsh-speaking family. "To me, I couldn't understand why we were going. We'd get spanked every time. It seemed to us the main objective was to go out and get shot at." There was an eerie sense of calm before the Taliban would attack. "You'd just see all the farmers disappearing up the fields. You're just waiting for it then. There was a point just before contact and it was if the birds had stopped singing and everything had just become this dead silence and you just knew." Peek says that he understood the platoon's role to be to defend CP Haji Alem but "we were f---ing bored basically ... we wanted to go out and take on the enemy. I know we're supposed to be out here for hearts and minds and stuff but if there are no known civvies in that area and we know there's Taliban there, why not have a crack at them?"

The arrival of the generator and the mail was a mixed blessing. It meant that the complications of life back home crept into the mind and it was a struggle to relate to those left behind in Britain. Peek's wife would sometimes hear gunfire erupt in the background when he telephoned home, and the call could often end abruptly with his saying: "Got to go!" She might not hear from him for several days after that and would panic that he might have been killed. Evison felt guilty that he might have frightened his mother by being too honest about what was happening at CP Haji Alem. In his final diary entry on May 7, he wrote: "Spoke to mum this morning. I hope I have not scared her too much.... Don't think I should have mentioned the ambush a few days ago—it is hard as the two worlds are so far apart." He had also reflected that he would not see any girls for four months and that there were always complications on that score. "But if life was easy then it would be easily boring."

Without a fellow officer to confide in, Evison felt somewhat marooned at Haji Alem despite the camaraderie he had built up with his men. It was a classic case of the loneliness of command, with Evison having no peer to unload on, mentally or emotionally. His diary was part of his way of dealing with this. Captain Terry Harman sensed the isolation Evison was experiencing and arranged to travel from Paraang to Haji Alem on May 9 to see his young Aldershot golf partner. "Listen, I'm coming down tomorrow," Harman said over the radio. "Make sure I have good bed and breakfast—remember, I'm an old man. Give me a nice mattress and look after me." Evison laughed: "I'll put your poncho on the outside of the CP and not the inside. See you tomorrow." Harman replied: "No problem. Make sure you're a better host than you are at playing golf."

8

Life Is Fragile

Many thanks for that little book of poems. It IS a great joy having it out here ... I got hit in the face by a small piece of shrapnel this morning, but it was a spent piece, and did not even cut me. One becomes a great fatalist out here.

—*Second Lieutenant Christopher Tennant, Welsh Guards, in a letter of September 2, 1917, found on his body the day after he was killed in action at Ypres*

My first contact ... I was pinned down and when a round splashed approximately two metres away, my heart was racing....

—*Lieutenant Mark Evison, Welsh Guards, in his diary for May 1–2, 2009, returned with his personal effects after he was mortally wounded in Helmand a week later*

North of CP Haji Alem in the Prince of Wales's Company area of operations, Mark Evison's friend and fellow lieutenant Dave Harris was also operating in hostile territory. PB Pimon, on the edge of the desert, was surrounded by the Taliban-controlled villages of Chah-e Mirza, Zorabad, and Kakaran. The poppy harvest was still under way, and Harris found the lack of attacks on his 2 Platoon almost eerie. A few days into May, Evison told Lance Sergeant Peek that he was worried about Harris, even though the Taliban seemed to be lying low in the area around PB Pimon. It felt odd, he said, that Harris was just a few miles away but he would probably not speak to his friend for six months. He remarked that Harris had seemed apprehensive at Camp Bastion, and he wished he could phone him to cheer him up by chatting about what they would do in London when they got back.

On May 6, Harris had his first contact. Intelligence had indicated that the Taliban were preparing an ambush close to Zorabad involving machine guns and 82 mm mortars. Harris decided to push through the village to disrupt the enemy. He split his platoon into two sections, with his section moving through the center and Sergeant Matthew Parry 700's section on the western edge. Parry 700, from Cardiff, was a classic Welsh Guards NCO— dour, brusque, and a little intimidating. Tattooed on the inside of his right forearm was: "Guardsmen Don't Die They Reorg in Hell." Harris knew he was just the sort of man you wanted on your side in a fight.

As Dave Harris and his men reached the northern edge of the village, his section came under accurate fire from the Taliban and took cover. Using hand signals and moving rapidly from block to block into the village from the west, Parry 700 sensed he had an opportunity to outflank the enemy. The Taliban did not normally engage until its fighters were sure where each British unit was. This time, they appeared unaware that Harris's men had split into two sections. Parry 700 reached a corner and gestured to Lance Corporal Bradley Watkin-Bennett, carrying a GPMG, to stop. The sergeant could hear gunfire about thirty meters away. He peered around the corner and saw three Taliban, rifles on their shoulders, firing at Harris's section to the east from the alleyway. "This is it," he thought, and signaled to Watkin-Bennett that he had located the enemy and was going to open fire. Parry 700 stepped into the alleyway and fired five shots into the group of Taliban, hitting one of them several times in the leg and side. Blood sprayed up the wall beside the fighter as he slumped to the ground. Then Parry 700 heard what soldiers refer to as the "dead man's click." His rifle had jammed. "Shit," he thought, and flung himself across the alleyway into a ditch. "Stoppage!" he shouted. Watkin-Bennett, behind Parry 700, waited for the sergeant to get out of the way and then fired one hundred rounds up the alleyway, hitting at least one of the Taliban, who had turned with his AK-47 and was firing straight at the Welsh Guardsmen. By the time the smoke and dust had cleared, the bodies had been dragged away. "It was either he killed me or I killed him," remembers Watkin-Bennett, an Englishman from Derby whose father was Welsh and had served in the Welsh Guards. "So I gave him the good news."

That night, Harris reflected on the exhilaration of what had happened. "The whole experience was absolutely awesome," he wrote in his diary. "During the actual contact the guys were laughing and smiling, enjoying it."

Around the same time, Major Giles Harris returned from a full-scale company operation without sustaining a casualty, despite an audacious close-range attack from the Taliban. He stood underneath a solar shower and thought: "Bloody hell, Giles. You've just commanded a rifle company in combat." He felt he was the luckiest man in the world, having experienced the excitement that every boy raised on Action Men and *Commando* comics dreamed of. Then, a nearby guardsman pressed the "Play" button on his iPod, and the words "My life is brilliant, my love is pure" wafted out. It was the singer James Blunt. To Harris, Blunt was better known as James Blount, an old Bristol University friend and former Life Guards officer. The commander of the Prince of Wales's Company reflected on the millions of pounds his friend had made from that song "You're Beautiful" and swiftly reappraised the extent of his luck.

Down in Haji Alem, Peek had also felt fortunate to lead men in action and felt the high of bringing everyone back unharmed. "If no one gets hurt, it's fun," he says, looking back. "The Taliban will usually win the first two or three minutes but when you step back and assess the situation, that's when you start winning and you smash the f---er. Once you've taken control, that's when you enjoy it." Both Peek and Evison already knew, however, that in war people got hurt. A fortnight before Fasfous was killed, Evison had been talking to him in Camp Bastion. "Life is fragile and out here it feels like it can be removed in an instant," his diary says, "It almost makes life even more valuable...."

Just after 8:00 a.m. on May 9, Evison led fifteen of his men plus four Afghan soldiers and an interpreter out of the main gate of CP Haji Alem. He had briefed the patrol that he wanted to investigate three compounds to the northwest that the Taliban had been using to attack the base. The patrol was split into two sections, one led by Peek and the other by Lance Corporal Thomas "Tinny" Hiscock, from Merthyr Bedlinog. Evison's plan was to follow a square route. They would head directly west across the infantry footbridge, past three compounds flanked by wheat and poppy fields, and then halt Peek's section at Compound 29. Peek's section would then provide covering fire for Hiscock's section, accompanied by Evison, to turn north to search Compound 1, which had been used as a Taliban firing point, and two more suspected Taliban compounds beyond. Once this had been done, they would return by heading east and then south along the canal and back into the fort. Most of the compounds in the area were empty, though some had been occupied temporarily during the poppy harvest.

The chain of command above 7 Platoon was complicated, and made even more so by radio difficulties in the area. Evison would report directly to Major Henry Bettinson in the 2 Company ops room in PB Silab. Above Bettinson was Thorneloe in the Battle Group ops room in Camp Bastion. Thorneloe reported to brigade headquarters at Lashkar Gah, which had to request air support or medical helicopters from Kandahar, though the helicopters were likely to take off from Bastion.

Half an hour after setting off, Hiscock's section—accompanied by Evison—moved from Compound 29 along an irrigation ditch, which was waist-high and filled with knee-deep stinking water. They were preparing to go forward to Compound 1 while Peek's section, in an irrigation ditch beside Compound 29 some thirty meters away, took up position ready to provide covering fire. "The enemy are making their weapons ready," Evison said over the platoon radio—known as the Personal Role Radio (PRR)—relaying a message the interpreter had heard on the Taliban walkie-talkies. Three minutes later, Evison warned: "They're about to open fire." Almost immediately afterwards, at 8:32 a.m., Peek's section came under attack from compounds to the south and southeast. "Sir, push into Compound 1. You're in perfect view of the enemy," Peek shouted as the bullets came in.

Korosaya, the barrel-chested Fijian, in Hiscock's section, saw a Taliban fighter wearing a black *dishdasha* robe firing from three hundred meters away and emptied four magazines as he shot back. There was confusion as to where the Taliban were firing from. "They're firing in that direction over there," shouted Lance Bombardier Andrew Spooner. "That f---ing wall. Where's that coming from? Are they in that compound?" Part of the platoon's two-man Fire Support Team (FST), Spooner's job was to call in mortar and artillery fire, but the antenna had snapped off his fire-control radio, and it had stopped working (see incident map in Appendix).

Evison first tried retreating to Compound 29, but the weight of fire coming in made this too dangerous. Instead, he ordered the section to carry on along the ditch and take refuge in Compound 1. They made it there safely as heavy fire started from the west. Hiscock ordered his men into firing positions around the edge of the compound. Korosaya found himself on the east side, lying on a four-foot-high platform piled with dried cow dung, firing at a Taliban fighter as he popped up every few seconds from an irrigation ditch 250 meters away. Lance Corporal Shane Evans 74 from Meliden, Guardsman Leighton Tucker from Llanelli, and Guardsman Thomas James began firing at the Taliban from the south wall of the compound. Guardsman Adam Hobbs found a "mouse hole"—a small aperture—on the west side that allowed him to lay down machine gun fire. Hobbs, from Cardiff, was nicknamed Amy Winehouse because of the tattoos that covered his upper body and neck. Before the tour he had gone AWOL and been recaptured by the military police after jumping into a river in an attempt to elude them. Out in Helmand, he was already proving his mettle under fire. Afghan soldiers with the section were at the compound doorway on the west side, firing RPGs at the Taliban.

Peek felt the adrenaline pumping but told himself this was nothing new—he'd been in more than two dozen contacts close to CP Haji Alem already. "We've got our baselines now and we'll fight them," he told himself. "It's all under control. It's hunky-dory." Then gunfire started to come in from three compounds to the north and northeast—followed shortly thereafter by the sangars at CP Haji Alem blazing away at them with GPMGs. Peek's heart began to beat faster. This was something new from the Taliban—they were mounting a coordinated attack from three sides with multiple firing points between two hundred and five hundred meters away. The enemy was close and about to surround the Welsh Guardsmen. CP Haji Alem fort was also under attack. This was not going to be easy.

In Compound 1, Evison struggled to get a proper signal on his Bowman, his best means of communicating properly with Peek. After several minutes of frustration, he ran over to the doorway on the east side of the compound, peered out, and shouted to Peek: "Can you see the enemy?" Bullets were kicking up dust just a meter from his feet. Bowman radios were notoriously unreliable in Helmand's Green Zone because of the heat, humidity, and thick vegetation. In addition, the electronic jamming equipment carried on all patrols interfered with Bowmans, and thick compound walls absorbed radio signals. Communications are a perennial problem in battle. Gunfire has a deafening effect, and when troops take cover, their radio antennae often become horizontal rather than vertical, hampering the signal. Guardsmen, however, tended to blame the equipment in their hands rather than the laws of physics, talking of "Bowman moments," when the radio would not work at the worst possible time. The familiar joke that Bowman stood for "Better Off with Map and Nokia" was beginning to wear thin. In Helmand, the inadequacy of radios was a matter of life and death rather than a subject of wry amusement. As well as trying to get his Bowman working, Evison wanted to get a sense of where the Taliban firing points were. He knew that by moving into the doorway he would put himself at risk, but communications and situational awareness were essential.

There had not yet been any fire from the east, but Evans 74 saw that Evison was exposed to the fields through the doorway. "Sir, push into the compound!" he shouted. Seconds later, at 8:40 a.m., Evison stepped back inside the compound and turned around. As he did so, a volley of five bullets came through the doorway. One of them hit the back plate of his body armor. Another missed the plate by half an inch, ripping into his back just below the right shoulder and exiting underneath his right collarbone. "I've been shot," Evison said, staggering sideways. Evans 74, about four meters behind Evison, saw him stumble and hold up his left hand, which was covered in blood. "Get into the f---ing room!" Evans 74 shouted. Evison staggered into a small room on the north side of the compound. He began putting on his own bandage and appeared to have been only slightly wounded. He had bloodied his left hand as he clutched his shoulder, and Evans 74 thought he had been shot in the wrist. Picking up Evison's Bowman, Tucker managed to get a signal straightaway and reported to PB Silab that there was a casualty.

Just as Peek heard Hiscock shouting out: "Man down! Man down!" over the radio from Compound 1, the Taliban began firing from Compounds 24 and 26 to the east, directly in front of CP Haji Alem and right on the patrol's escape route back. Now rounds were coming in from at least a dozen firing points from four sides. More than fifty Taliban fighters were out on the ground surrounding the wounded Evison and his nineteen men in a 360-degree ambush. At 8:51 a.m., CP Paraang was attacked with small-arms fire, causing Lieutenant James's 6 Platoon to "stand to" and defend the base, thereby stopping him from sending out a patrol to assist Evison. Seven minutes later, PB Silab was attacked with small-arms fire, RPGs, and mortars. Taliban forces were coordinating attacks at three locations simultaneously, aiming to isolate 7 Platoon and prevent any reinforcements being sent to CP Haji Alem. No cavalry would be coming to the rescue.

In Compound 1, Taliban bullets were coming in through the two doors and ricocheting around the inside. Evans 74 ran over to Guardsman James, who was firing out to the west. "Man down! Man down! You're the only team medic," he said. James asked who it was. "It's the boss," said Evans 74. One in four Welsh Guardsmen was a team medic, with training in treating combat casualties. It was the first time James had dealt with a casualty, and he had not yet been issued with his team medic's pouch, which contained HemCon (hemorrhage control) or QuikClot bandages.

Evison was still lucid when James got to him. "Is the HLS [Helicopter Landing Site] secured?" Evison asked him. "Where's Lance Sergeant Peek's section? Make sure he has taken over command." James told Evison that everything was being taken care of. He was getting paler, and it was clear he was already losing a lot of blood. James took the lieutenant's body armor and helmet off and put a First Field Dressing onto what he thought was the entry wound. Evison's pulse was slowing and he began to drift into unconsciousness. James punched Evison's chest to keep his heart beating and the lieutenant opened his eyes.

The PRR radios had gone down, so the details of the casualty had to be shouted back to Peek. "You need a Shocker callsign [Black Hawk] because that's the helicopter that's going to land for us," Spooner yelled over the gunfire to Peek. At 8:46 a.m., Peek sent the initial "nine-liner" casualty report, listing Evison as "Category C"—a relatively low priority of "walking wounded" who needed to be evacuated within four hours. In fact, the bullet had severed Evison's subclavian artery, and he was losing blood rapidly. A less athletic man would have deteriorated much faster; Evison's supreme fitness compensated for the desperate distress his body was in.

Seven minutes later, the nine-liner was received at brigade headquarters after being passed up via the Battle Group ops room in Camp Bastion. Within three minutes, Evans 74 realized that Evison had been hit in the chest and relayed the message to Peek, who radioed that the casualty was "Category B," the highest priority. (Category A is a non-combat medical emergency. Under the British system, both Category A and B casualties should be treated within two hours.) Amid the chaos and with the radios functioning only intermittently, it was a message that either failed to get through or was not passed up the chain of command, which went from the company ops room in PB Silab to the Battle Group ops room in Camp Bastion and then to the brigade.

Some fifty meters away, in the irrigation ditch beside Compound 29, Corporal Ben Lacy was hesitating. "Medic!" shouted Evans 74 from Compound 1. "We're losing him!" But gunfire was coming in from every direction, and the open ground between the ditch where the medic was and the doorway where Evison had been shot was dangerously exposed. Peek threw a phosphorus grenade to create a smokescreen, but it failed to function. "I'm not running over there," said Lacy, who reasoned that it made more sense for the casualty to be brought to him as that was the route back to the base. In the heat of the moment, the other soldiers began to lose their tempers. "Get in that f---ing compound or I'll fill you in," shouted one. Gunner Steve Gadsby told him: "Stop f---ing messing around and get over there!" Fists were raised, and Lacy got up, crawled along an irrigation ditch, and then scuttled across the road towards Compound 1. He zigzagged wildly, his medical bags bouncing off his hips, while Gadsby and the others provided covering fire. Rounds hit the ground around his feet and the compound wall behind him as he ran. The smoke grenades thrown to give him cover failed to activate as Lacy, just as army medics did every day in Helmand, risked his own life by running through enemy fire to treat a casualty.

Guardsman Andrew Richards 85, from Trefechan in Merthyr Tydfil, was carrying a folded stretcher and needed to follow Lacy to get it into Compound 1. Taliban fire was still coming in. "F--- it, I'm going," said Richards 85 and ran to Compound 1. Gadsby and Guardsman Luke Langley provided covering fire with light machine guns, but both weapons jammed, leaving Richards 85 to cover the last few yards with no protection at all.

Gunner Gadsby was the other man, along with Spooner, in the Fire Support Team. A brigade-level heavyweight boxer with seven years in the army, he was not a man to mess with. He was stuck at the level of private because of repeated disciplinary problems and had been employed back in barracks in Northern Ireland as a sergeants' mess waiter. "I've been a bad lad for most of my time and pretty much ruined my own career," Gadsby reflected later. "I've gone AWOL a few times—not for long—disobeying orders, just things like that. I've been arrested for fighting, I got arrested for ABH [Actual Bodily Harm] and then got let off because the bloke dropped the charges. You get arrested fighting in town and then in the morning an ex-squaddie who's on duty just gives you a fine and says: "Don't do it again.""

When Lacy got there, Evison was pale and staring straight ahead. He applied a HemCon to the exit wound, about the size of a fifty-pence piece, on Evison's chest, believing that it was where the bullet had entered. "OK, he's as stable as he's going to be at the moment," said Lacy. "We've got to get him to the PB." Lacy asked if there was an exit wound, and James replied that he had not found one. They rolled Evison over and could see a lot of blood on his back but nothing else. "Is there an exit wound?" Evison asked. "I can't see one," said James. Evison replied: "Well, that could be a good thing."

Peek's mind was racing. The equivalent of a corporal, he was now doing the job of a platoon commander as well as a platoon sergeant. They were 450 meters away from the base, and he had to come up with a plan to get Evison back to safety.

Ideally, they should clear a landing site so the medical helicopter could touch down as close as possible to Compound 1. But the Taliban fire was so intense that this would be very hard to do without sustaining another casualty; the small size of his patrol severely limited his ability to protect a clearance team. British Chinooks, moreover, were reluctant to land under fire, and there was no sign yet of air or artillery support. The best of a bad set of options was to get back to CP Haji Alem. Peek had watched admiringly as Evison had conducted three withdrawals to the base under fire and decided to do exactly what he thought the lieutenant would have done in the same situation. Evison was the priority, and he had to get him back as quickly as possible.

Peek made his decision and shouted orders to Hiscock: "Right—what's going to happen. Once you've got the casualty on the stretcher, we're going to give you covering fire and you're going to f---ing take him as fast as you can to the PB." Peek's plan was for Evison to be evacuated from Compound 1 across the fifty meters of open ground to the irrigation ditch beside the main track into CP Haji Alem. The casualty had no body armor or helmet on and would be protected by a box of men firing out from each side. Then Evison would be carried 350 meters east along the irrigation ditch. Fire from the sangars had driven the Taliban from Compound 24, so Peek told Hiscock that Evison should be taken there; the north side of the compound was rubble so it should be relatively easy to get inside safely. From Compound 24, Peek directed, they should run across the canal and over the final fifty meters of open ground into the fort. As all this was happening, the rest of Hiscock's men would retreat from Compound 1, moving through Peek's section and leaving Peek to bring up the rear. Those who had not gone into the fort with

Evison would all regroup in Compound 24 for Peek to give quick battle orders to get them all back. The Welsh Guardsmen were returning so much fire that Peek was concerned about them running out of bullets. He ordered them to conserve ammunition as much as they could. "I'm not going back into that base until I make sure every one of my men is in there safe," Peek told himself. "Even if I die doing it."

Gadsby ran from Peek's group over to Compound 1 to help out. His light machine gun had jammed so he helped Korosaya lift Evison onto the stretcher. "Give me a smoke will you?" Evison asked. Korosaya lit a cigarette and put it in his platoon commander's mouth.

Someone in Peek's section shouted: "Get AH [attack helicopter—Apache]! Ask for mortars!" But Peek was also having trouble with his Bowman. It seemed that every message he gave had to be repeated two or three times before it was understood. He requested an Apache, mortars, and artillery to suppress the Taliban firing points. The Apache—codenamed Ugly 51— arrived at 9:00 a.m., eight minutes after it had been called for. Peek felt a wave of relief. "Apache will give cover—leg it!" he shouted. But the pilot would not open fire because it was unclear over exactly where the enemy firing points were, and there was a danger of killing civilians. The pilot asked for green mini-flares to be fired onto the Taliban positions, but Peek had none left.

With the patrol split, there was also a danger of hitting friendly forces. At one point, the ops room in PB Silab had marked up Compound 1 as an enemy firing point, as it dealt with four contacts simultaneously. With the FST radio broken, the Bowman next to useless and the situation very confused, it was simply too risky to fire mortars from PB Silab or artillery from Camp Bastion.

Peek was desperate. There could be few things more demoralizing than being in mortal danger with an Apache flying overhead but failing to open fire on the Taliban. "The only way I'm getting out of here is using my men and we're going to have to fight our f---ing way through," he told himself. Over the PRR, he summarized the situation: "Boys, we've got one casualty, no fast air, no helicopters, no Mastiffs and no gun," he said. "We're in the shit and we've got to get out of here on our own."

Back in the Silab ops room, about four kilometers away, Bettinson felt helpless as he tried to monitor the situation. "I was trying to establish a picture and one second I could hear Peek, the next second he'd just disappear and then he'd come back mid-sentence," he recalls. "I'd say: 'No, say again, say again.' And he'd just very slowly repeat the message. He was fighting for his life, short of breath and very, very calm."

Langley, with Peek's section, was concerned about how close the Taliban were getting. The AK-47 rounds were not making their normal crack and thump. Instead the bullets were giving a zoof-zoof sound as they came in from the poppy field next to him. That meant they were very near indeed. Taliban fighters were creeping through the poppy field and must have been within fifty meters. The interpreter's walkie-talkie scanner was receiving stronger and stronger signals, indicating the Taliban were closing in. "The poppy was so high we couldn't see from the prone position or kneeling. So me and Gadsby were standing up, putting a burst of rounds down and then getting down again. Every time I stood up, I thought I was going to die."

In the Battle Group ops room at Camp Bastion, there was still confusion about how badly wounded Evison was and how he should be evacuated. Peek's change from Category C had not come through, but a medical liaison warrant officer, hearing it was a chest wound, declared that it had to be treated as a Category B. At 9:07 a.m., the brigade staff in Lashkar Gah still had him listed as a Category C when they authorized a medical helicopter. There had been another casualty in Helmand that morning, and medical helicopter resources were scarce. Initially, the decision was to send a Chinook to PB Argyll in the Nad-e Ali town—which made little sense because there was no way of getting Evison there, even within the stipulated four hours for a Category C. A Chinook was too big to land inside CP Haji Alem, and the presence of so many Taliban close to the base meant it would be impossible to prepare a safe landing site outside the fort.

Back at Compound 1 just after 9:00 a.m., Evison was lifted up on the stretcher by Gadsby, Korosaya, Hobbs, and Richards 85 and taken over to the irrigation ditch near Compound 29. Those who had not yet seen Evison still thought his wound was minor. "What's this stretcher for?" joked Spooner. "You've been shot in the hand. What a woman!" Then he saw blood covering Evison's chest where his shirt had been cut open and shut his mouth. Spooner moved down the irrigation ditch that ran parallel on the southern side of the road, giving covering fire down towards the Taliban positions to the south. Evison was only conscious intermittently but still asking for updates on the helicopter landing site and where the fire was coming from. "Has the bleeding stopped yet?" he asked. "Yeah, it's all stopped," the medic answered. A few minutes later Evison said: "I can feel blood running down my back." There were attempts at banter to buoy Evison's spirits and keep him conscious. "You lucky sod, sir," one guardsman told Evison. "You've only been here a month and you're getting to go home already."

Spooner had turned on a "head cam" video camera, which he had fitted to his helmet after it had been lent to him by Lacy seconds before Evison was shot. The jerky footage, showing the chaos and confusion of battle, was later handed over to the Royal Military Police by Lacy's mother. The video shows the men moving down the ditch, wheezing and swearing, as Taliban fire comes in.

Progress along the ditch was slow—the water was waist-high and the stretcher had to be held up above the water. Weapons kept jamming, and every time there was a stoppage everyone had to halt. Langley's light machine gun was useless, so he had borrowed Peek's rifle for a while and then taken Evison's from the interpreter. Soldiers took it in turns to lug Evison's body armor and helmet. The stretcher proved too difficult to maneuver as the ditch got narrower, so it was abandoned. Korosaya heaved Evison onto his back in a fireman's lift and powered his way through the waist-deep water for more than two hundred meters down the ditch, with Gadsby beside him, before charging into Compound 24. By this time, Evison's eyesight was failing. "Who is this?" he asked Korosaya. "I can't see properly."

Now it was Hiscock who was reluctant to step through the Compound 1 doorway, where Evison had been hit. "Tinny, f---ing come out!" Peek screamed. Hiscock called back: "I'm not coming out until I've got a f---ing Apache above my head." Peek steeled himself to run out to Compound 1 to bring back Hiscock's section. "We've got nothing," he said over the PRR radio. "I'm going to give you rapid fire and then you get out of there." If they didn't move soon, they were going to be cut off and in danger of being overrun. Rounds were still thumping into the doorway where Evison had been shot, splintering the frame. Hiscock tried to persuade one of the Afghan soldiers, a former mujahid who had fought against the Russians, to go through the door first, but he refused. There was nothing else for it, Hiscock decided. He took a deep breath and ran out shouting: "Follow me!" Peek cheered inside when he saw his lance corporal and his remaining men running towards him.

After his Herculean effort getting Evison into Compound 24, Korosaya collapsed with exhaustion. Without hesitating, Gadsby picked Evison up, slung him over his shoulder, and ran out into the open towards CP Haji Alem. Rather than take the safer route of jumping down into the canal, he opted to run straight across the infantry footbridge. It would be quicker, he decided, and if he was hit crossing the canal, then Evison would drown. The bridge was now at the center of a two-way shooting gallery as the Taliban fired into it from Compound 8 to the north and Compound 17 to the south. Normally, soldiers crossing the flimsy bridge had to proceed gingerly, holding on to the rails on each side. Gadsby took it at a sprint, landing on the bridge and then bouncing forward as if he'd hit a diving board. Bullets whistled past his head, dinged off the bridge, and kicked up mud from the canal bank as he carried his platoon commander the final fifty meters. He kept on running right up to the CP Haji Alem gate where a stretcher was waiting. "I'm f---ing licked," he thought. It was 9:14 a.m.

At around this time, the brigade staff at Lashkar Gah finally learned that Evison was in fact a Category B. The Chinook authorized at 9:09 am was canceled and a pair of American Pedro Black Hawks tasked instead at 9:25 a.m. A medical helicopter cannot land before a casualty is ready to be loaded because waiting on the ground may enable the Taliban to reorganize and attempt to shoot it down as it took off. But the switch meant that the helicopter was not ready even after the Welsh Guardsmen had spent thirty-three minutes battling to get Evison back. More precious minutes were slipping away. A statement to the Royal Military Police by an Army Air Corps captain who was the ops officer of 662 Squadron of Apaches underlined the confusion that led to the delay in Evison being evacuated. "Initially [the casualty] was assessed to be a CAT C by the troops on the ground. Only later was the casualty reassessed to a CAT B," he said. "One IRT [medical Immediate Response Team—Chinook] asset was stepped up to do the extraction, but it was established later that it couldn't land at the Fort because the ground had not been swept for mines/IEDs. A separate CASEVAC [casualty evacuation] asset was then launched iot [in order to] land where it was needed." Weeks earlier, Bettinson had established that a Chinook could not land in CP Haji Alem. As soon as Evison was wounded, Bettinson had stated that he needed a Black Hawk. "You don't normally specify what you want," he says. "We specified a Black Hawk because we knew it was the only helicopter that could physically land inside CP Haji Alem."

Evison was placed on the ground just inside the main part of the base and was initially treated by Caswell, who had been stood down from his position on one of the sangars, where he had been firing a grenade machine gun at the Taliban. By the time Lacy got back a few minutes later, Evison was becoming listless, but he sat up with a jolt when Lacy stuck an IV line into his left shinbone. "What the f--- are you doing to me?" he cried out. Lacy and Caswell rolled him over and discovered the entry wound. "Sir, you're going to be all right," Caswell told him. "It's gone in and it's come out. You're going to be f---ing sound." Korosaya was standing over Evison holding the drip as the lieutenant was given some morphine and another cigarette. "Cas, what the f---'s going on with that bleeding?" Evison asked Caswell. Lacy applied a HemCon bandage, and guardsmen gathered around trying to keep the platoon commander conscious. "Sir, you're all right!" shouted one guardsman. "Keep talking! Keep talking!" Another said: "Sir, you're going to be in the pub in a couple of days." Another asked: "Where are you from?" No response. "You can go fishing when you go home, sir," said another. Evison mumbled: "Yeah, I like fishing." A third told him: "I can't wait for that piss-up in Blackpool." Evison smiled faintly. Caswell cradled his head and comforted him. "I'm going down," Evison rasped, slipping into unconsciousness. "No, you're not going down," wailed Caswell. "Sir! You're not!" Evison was carried into a side room.

In the PB Silab ops room, Bettinson had finally managed to get through to Thorneloe up at the Battle Group headquarters in Bastion. "Who are you going to send down there, to replace Mark?" asked Thorneloe, who, typically, was thinking several steps ahead of everyone else. "Christ, I'm still trying to get the boys off the ground here," thought Bettinson.

As Gadsby reached the base, Peek, Hiscock, and the remaining Welsh Guardsmen at Compound 28 made a mad dash under fire across a wheat field to Compound 24. Rounds slammed into the mud walls. "Right, now I need to come up with a plan to get across this canal," Peek told himself as he got there and caught his breath. The next part of his plan was to throw smoke grenades from Compound 24 and the CP Haji Alem sangars to prevent the Taliban getting a clear shot at the troops retreating the final fifty meters. With Taliban fire intensifying by the minute, Peek divided his men into pairs and ordered them to run across the road, down into the canal, and up the other side towards safety. The pairs began to head off. Some ran down one bank, across the canal, and up again in one concerted effort, while others took it in two stages, pausing in the canal before the second push. Guardsman Mark Edwards 27, from Pentre-Morgan in Carmarthenshire, was one of the first to get back into the base. He ran straight up to one of the sangars and threw smoke grenades down to help the others.

None of the rest of the section attempted to repeat what Gadsby had done and take the short cut across the footbridge. Guardsman Stuart Gizzie, from Rhyl in North Wales, an avid weightlifter and one of the fittest men in the platoon, was carrying his thirty-three-kilogram kit, an LMG, and Evison's rucksack, the weight slowing him down as he staggered up the far bank of the canal. Suddenly his feet were taken away from him by what felt like a sledgehammer blow. A bullet fired from Compound 17 had gone straight through his right ankle and embedded itself in his left calf. Gizzie dropped back to the edge of the canal, blood welling out of the top of his boot. It was 9:28 a.m.

A minute later, two Pedro Black Hawks took off from Camp Bastion. By then Evison had been experiencing massive bleeding for forty-nine minutes. It had taken twenty-nine minutes for a helicopter to be authorized and, once the switch had been made from Chinook to Black Hawk, a further twenty minutes for an aircraft to take off. This helicopter delay was the longest experienced by the Welsh Guards throughout their tour. It was the first major casualty evacuation the Battle Group had been faced with, and the wounded man had been the commander at one of the most isolated checkpoints in the area of operations. Communications were appalling, the patrol was split, and there had been confusion over the casualty category. Almost every possible "possible" had been thrown into the mix.

As Langley plunged into the canal, he heard Crombie shout: "Man down, man down!" Gizzie was screaming: "Go on Lang, get across." Langley landed beside him and asked: "Who's been shot, mate?" Gizzie replied. "I have." Langley giggled at the matter-of-factness of the response. "Leave me here," Gizzie told him. But Langley wasn't going anywhere without Gizzie, who nearly passed out from the pain as he pulled off his boot. Langley slammed a field dressing onto Gizzie's ankle as blood spurted from the wound. "There was rounds splashing all around us in the canal," Langley recalls. "It was like *Saving Private Ryan.*"

Inside CP Haji Alem, Gadsby, who had been lying on the ground, breathless and wheezing, was approached by an Afghan soldier who was saying "British" and pointing at the gate. "What's this plonker on about?" Gadsby thought to himself before twigging that another soldier had been hit. Barely pausing to think about it, Gadsby ran out of the gate and back across the open ground to the canal. As more bullets flew past his head, he thought to himself: "F--- me, this is quite f---ing stupid." The pain in Gizzie's right ankle was so excruciating he hadn't yet realized he'd also been hit in his left leg. "You're going to hop like f--- now," Gadsby told him as he and Langley grabbed Gizzie from either side. "You Taliban c---s!" Gizzie screamed as Langley and Gadsby dragged him into the base.

True to his vow, Peek was now the last man left outside CP Haji Alem. After Gizzie had been dragged in, the fire had reached a crescendo as several dozen Taliban aimed up and down the shooting gallery. The lance sergeant was down to his thirteenth and final thirty-round magazine and was stuck in an irrigation ditch on the wrong side of the canal. Mud hit him in the face from the bullets landing around him, but fire from the Welsh Guardsmen inside CP Haji Alem was petering out as more guns jammed. "I need rapid fire and smoke from the sangars!" Peek shouted out to Crombie. "We can't— all the guns have gone down," Crombie replied. Virtually every weapon had been firing constantly for more than an hour. The four GPMGs on the sangars had fired more than 20,000 rounds and the GMGs nearly four hundred grenades. Langley had fired more than eight hundred rounds from his LMG. Together, the fifteen in the patrol had probably fired more than 10,000 rounds plus whatever the four Afghan soldiers had let loose. The only thing Crombie had left available was a 66 mm M72 Light Anti-Tank Weapon (LAW)—a shoulder-launched missile known in the army as the 66. Taliban messages on their walkie-talkies indicated that two fighters had been killed by a 66 fired from Haji Alem a few minutes earlier—and that a determined attack on the base itself was being prepared. As Peek made his final dash to the base, Crombie stepped out and fired another 66, slamming it into Compound 17 to the south. Everyone was back. It was 9:39 a.m.

Once safely inside CP Haji Alem, Peek was incredulous that the Pedros had not yet arrived. The guardsmen were panicking and feeling abandoned. In the small side room, Evison was losing consciousness. "Sir, you're all right!" shouted one guardsman. "Keep talking! Keep talking!" Another said: "Sir, you're going to be in the pub in a couple of days." Evison had lost his sight completely. "Cas, Cas, is that you?" he asked Caswell, his voice husky. "Where are the boys?" Caswell and the medic slapped him to keep him awake, but life seemed to be ebbing out of him. His lips were chapped, and there was white foam coming from his mouth. He was given water from a bottle top and lapped it up but then regurgitated it seconds later. Then he stopped breathing. The medic started chest compressions while Guardsman Dominic Austin, from Ammanford in Carmarthenshire, gave him mouth-to-mouth resuscitation, prompting Evison to splutter and retch. "He's breathing again, he's breathing again!" someone shouted. Peek screamed at Spooner, who was manning the VHF radio in the Land Rover "ops room," that he would thump him if the helicopter didn't come soon. "He's dying!" he shouted. "We need that f---ing MERT [Medical Emergency Response Team helicopter]. We need it in here."

Spooner kept getting contradictory messages on the radio: the helicopter had been diverted to another casualty; a Chinook had been sent by mistake and then turned back; the helicopter had to refuel; the crews were changing over. At 9:42 a.m., Caswell ran over to Spooner, fixed his eyes with unnerving intensity, and said: "They're giving him life support now. The helo has to get here." Evison stopped breathing three times and was resuscitated twice.

The Pedro made a "hot landing"—under Taliban fire—at 9:47 a.m. while another Black Hawk hovered firing 30 mm rounds into enemy positions. "Good luck!" Evans 72 shouted as Evison was carried onto the helicopter. The Pedro lifted off after just thirty-three seconds on the ground, with Evison and Gizzie onboard. It took another fourteen minutes to get back to Camp Bastion. By the time Evison was inside the operating theater in the Bastion hospital, codenamed "Nightingale," it was 10:03 a.m. This was twenty-three minutes outside the "golden hour" within which the American military aims to get troops to a medical facility but inside the two hours laid down by the British for a Category B casualty.

Four hours later in Dulwich, South London, Margaret Evison had just returned home after buying a newspaper and some groceries. It was 10:30 a.m. on a beautiful day, and she was feeling very cheerful after going to a good party the night before. Two days earlier, she had enjoyed her first proper conversation with her only son since he had arrived in Afghanistan. He had been in good spirits, regaling her with tales of life at CP Haji Alem. As she got out of her car, Mrs. Evison saw a man in a suit outside talking to the father of a next-door neighbor, an ex-military man. He seemed to be waiting for something, and she thought he might be an estate agent. "Can I help?" she asked him. "I'm Major Brian Ransom from the Royal Artillery," he replied. "Oh, I've got a son in the Army," Mrs. Evison said. "I know," Ransom responded. "Can we go inside and talk?" As they walked up the path together, she said: "I hope there is nothing wrong, is there?"

After Ransom had left, Mrs. Evison went out and gardened for the rest of the day. It was what she always did when she wanted to take her mind off things, and it somehow made her feel closer to her son, who had a green thumb himself. It was the same elegant garden, with its cherry tree, roses, and box hedges, that Mark Evison had asked about in his last letter to her; the place where they had sat down together and talked about death. For the first few hours, she did not know where he had been injured, just that he was very seriously ill. That afternoon she was told he had been shot in the shoulder and was priority one to be flown home. An eternal optimist, she told herself that he had two lungs, two arms, and two shoulders. He had hiked around the world and had lots of rugby injuries. He would be all right. That night she slept well. The next morning, however, she had an uneasy feeling. He had been on priority one to come home, but he was not back yet. She was out in the garden and said to her next-door neighbor: "You know, I think he is fighting for his life."

At 11:00 p.m. local time, Evison's blood pressure dropped and he suffered seizures. At 3:55 a.m. local time, shortly after Evison's mother had gone to bed in Dulwich, his pupils became fixed and dilated, and a CT scan indicated that he was effectively brain-dead. He had lost half his blood before he even reached Camp Bastion; the brain had been starved of too much oxygen to recover. The word was spread among the Welsh Guardsmen that Evison was being flown home to die with his family.

When Lieutenant James Harvie—IX Company's forward air controller— first heard that his friend had been shot in the shoulder, he penned a note teasing him about his poor "skills and drills" and expressing the hope that he would make it back out for the end of the tour. After his rapid overnight deterioration, Harvie hurriedly retrieved his letter and instead wrote one of condolence to Mrs. Evison. Thorneloe spoke to Dave Harris at PB Pimon by satellite phone. There was no helicopter available to take him to Bastion to bid farewell to his friend. Thorneloe expressed his sympathy. "Would you like me to do anything?" the commanding officer asked. Harris responded: "Would you shake his hand for me, sir?" That evening Parry 700 took Harris aside. He could see that his platoon commander was agitated and flustered. "Sir," he said, "I know he was your mate but you just need to go away and calm yourself down. You need to focus because the men are looking to you and there will be hard times ahead. I'm saying this not as your platoon sergeant, I'm saying this as a mate. Have an hour or two to yourself. And if you need to talk, I'm here for you."

Thorneloe and many other Welsh Guards officers were able to spend a few minutes alone with Evison before he was flown back to Britain. He was surrounded by tubes and had bandages on his shoulder but looked otherwise as if he was sleeping peacefully. Major Andrew Speed, the Battle Group second in command, remembers being with four other Welsh Guards officers sitting in silence in the waiting room before Captain Deiniol Morgan, the Welsh Guards chaplain, took them in one by one. "I stood by Mark's bed and it was almost impossible to hold back the emotions. The padre asked me if I would like to say something and all I could choke out was a request for him to say a prayer on my behalf. To see this talented and vibrant young man lying there and knowing that he was never going to recover was heartbreaking."

Back at Selly Oak Hospital in Birmingham, army nurses washed Evison's hair and shaved his face in preparation for the arrival of his parents, his sister Lizzy, and a small number of his closest friends. Mrs. Evison noticed the suntan marks on her son's feet where he had been wearing flip-flops inside the base, and that he still sweated. Evison's treatment book from Camp Bastion recorded details of the more than thirty pints of blood and a similar amount of plasma and platelets he'd been given. In it, Padre Eddie Wynn, an army chaplain, wrote of the privilege it had been to sit with him during his final hours. "Your family loves you and I know that you will rest in peace in God's loving arms." At 10:23 a.m. on May 12, Margaret and David Evison turned off their son's life-support machine.

In his tribute to Evison, Thorneloe declared: "He was a natural leader— tactically astute, clear sighted and cool and decisive under pressure. I suspect that his life, tragically cut short, would have gone on to shape history."

Sitting looking out on her garden six months later, Evison's mother lamented that she had not been able to bring her son home. "I would have liked him to just be here," she said, fresh tears flowing. "If he'd been in his bed for a hundred years, it would have been nice having him here. But, you know, it wasn't possible." Margaret Evison's persistent questioning of whether her son's life could have been saved was to win her the ear of journalists, generals, and politicians, including two prime ministers.

If everything had gone smoothly and a helicopter had arrived at 9:14 a.m., he would have been in Camp Bastion more than half an hour earlier. Lieutenant Colonel Adam Brooks, who operated on Evison at Bastion, said in a statement that the chances of surviving the gunshot wound "should it have occurred on the doorstep of almost any hospital in the UK would be negligible." He concluded that it was "unproven and conjecture" that surgical intervention half an hour earlier "would have altered the outcome" and his belief was that the helicopter delay had a "minimal impact" on Evison's condition.

According to medical evidence, the severing of a subclavian artery causes massive bleeding and cannot be stopped except by a surgical clamp applied in an operating theater. It therefore made no difference, the MoD argued, that James had no HemCon or QuikClot bandages and that Lacy was delayed in reaching Compound 1. At an inquest held in Sutton Coldfield in July 2010, Aidan Cotter, the coroner, stated that "neither the Army nor the inquest has been able to explain" the helicopter delay but decided this was a moot issue because, in his opinion, Evison would probably have died anyway. He concluded that he was entirely satisfied that the initial wrong categorization of Evison's wound did not contribute to his death and found that there was no neglect in any medical attention.

Margaret Evison found it hard to accept that the unexplained helicopter delay was moot. If her son had arrived back at Bastion still conscious and talking, rather than in a state of full cardiac arrest, she reasoned, then surely he might have lived? No one could provide a definitive answer. In any event, the issue of the helicopter delay needed to be addressed because even if it had not led to Evison's death, if it happened again it could mean another soldier dying.

Before the tour was over, another Welsh Guards platoon commander would be wounded millimeters away from his subclavian artery and survive. 3 Company's Lance Sergeant Gethyn Rowlands 39, from Llangefni on the Isle of Anglesey, was shot in the shoulder in Sangin. He was standing behind a wall returning Taliban fire when an Afghan soldier he was helping train was shot through the bicep. and a 2 Mercians private was hit in the center of the breastplate of his body armor. The patrol was fixed behind the wall, and almost any movement was at a soldier's peril because the ground had not been Barmaed. Rowlands 39 heard a cry from the 2 Mercians sergeant next to him when a bullet ripped through his tunic and grazed his arm. As he turned to look, Rowlands 39 felt a sharp pain in his shoulder and was thrown to the ground. A bullet had grazed his throat and gone through his shoulder, but hit only soft tissue.

The initial plan was to get Rowlands 39 back to the patrol base six meters away, but the Pedro opted to land outside. He refused morphine because he did not want to slow down the withdrawal. As he was being moved to the helicopter landing site, a Taliban commander ordered a fresh attack, noting that there was a wounded British soldier who could be finished off. With no weapon to defend himself, Rowlands 39 felt utterly vulnerable. The Pedro was able to land, however, and Rowlands 39 was on the operating table in Camp Bastion within forty minutes, less than half the time it took to get Evison there. Rowlands 39 was one of the very few soldiers in Helmand to suffer a gunshot wound and not be evacuated back to Britain. After a few weeks' recuperating in Camp Bastion, he returned to duty. Rowlands 39 had left the army in 2004. But he was bored with plastering and always regretted missing out on Iraq, so he rejoined the Welsh Guards just so he could go out to Helmand. "I needed to go out and prove something to myself," he says. "And I did that."

The experience of being wounded, along with the drugs that were administered afterwards, could be disorientating as well as petrifying. A guardsman in the Battle Group who was wounded later in the tour described how he had rolled down a slope towards an irrigation ditch after he was shot in the arm. "My body's supposed to take over," he thought, waiting in vain for the pain to subside. "But it's not. This is f---ing shit." He didn't want to look at his wound because he was afraid of how bad it might be. When a tourniquet was put on his arm by the platoon medic, he panicked and, under the influence of morphine, thought that this would mean he would lose the limb. As soon as the medic turned away, he undid the tourniquet thinking that would save his arm. The blood rushed from his wound, intensifying the agony.

The medic gave him Entonox, often administered to pregnant women, the pain disappeared, but he was gripped with renewed fear. "I'm going to die here," he thought. "They're coming over the hills to get us." Then the fear subsided, and he felt a rush of happiness that he was leaving the battlefield and would soon be back in Britain. "I'll be shagging my girlfriend next week," he called out at one point. "That's 30 grand insurance for me," he said a few moments later. But as he was put onto the Pedro, he seemed to have second thoughts, grabbing hold of a senior NCO and refusing to let go. "I don't want to leave!" he screamed. The NCO pulled his hands off his trouser leg and pushed the stretcher onto the helicopter.

Once onboard the Chinook, the guardsman was overcome with relief and burst into tears. An American medic leant over him, and the guardsman recognized his aftershave. It was the first clean thing he had smelt in days. "Is that Hugo Boss?" he asked. The medic replied, laughing as he produced a large needle filled with Ketamine: "What? Are you gay?" Ketamine, nicknamed "Special K" by medics, is sometimes used as a recreational drug or even in date rape. Once it was injected, the guardsman felt swept away by a dreamy, almost hallucinogenic, feeling as the pain evaporated and was replaced by a sensation of intense euphoria.

Evison's death taught the Welsh Guards some painful lessons. In his incident report, endorsed by Thorneloe and the brigade, Bettinson concluded that the Taliban front line at CP Haji Alem was "all around and not just to the south as previously thought." With an "intelligent and patient" enemy, there was a need either to base more troops at Haji Alem or pre-position an attack helicopter or surveillance overhead before a patrol went out. Everyone knew that the British did not have enough aviation resources to do this.

In addition, the situation with communications was "unsustainable," Bettinson stated, making it difficult to provide direction at company level and—crucially—to call in artillery, mortars, and air power to kill the Taliban. It was decided that patrols could no longer go out without "satisfactory communications" on the brigade strike net (the radio net used by the FST) being established. Thorneloe later reported to the brigade that Bowman radios were "insufficiently robust and heat resistant for this theatre."

Within two hours of Evison being evacuated from CP Haji Alem, Sergeant Steve Young, a fully qualified platoon sergeant, had arrived at the base. Peek had performed superbly and with great courage and was recommended for an MC. To have had a nineteen-man patrol commanded in action by the equivalent of a corporal, however, was courting disaster. Patrolling was limited to within three hundred meters of Haji Alem fort—Evison had been shot 450 meters away—and Thorneloe ordered that nighttime patrols be launched to put the Taliban at a disadvantage because they lacked night vision. The sophisticated and complex ambush laid by the Taliban on May 9 had almost certainly been put in place in darkness the previous night. Bettinson summarized his report by stating that CP Haji Alem "would benefit from an increase in combat power and improved communications."

Evison's death was a hammer blow to the members of 7 Platoon, who had made such superhuman efforts to get him back to the base alive. "Everybody gelled that day and everybody did their job," says Caswell. "But it was all for nothing. To get him back when he was still conscious and then have to wait for the equivalent of a Number 37 bus was just shit." It was pitch-black when they were gathered together and given the news by Lieutenant Lowry, who had returned as temporary platoon commander. There was silence, a few sobs, and then the men, with barely a word exchanged, set about gathering materials from around the fort to construct a memorial. It was as if everyone instinctively knew what to do. As they were arranging the clay bricks and putting the finishing touches to a rough wooden cross, tracer rounds began to fly overhead. The Taliban were attacking.

Peek and his men pulled on their body armor, grabbed their rifles and manned the sangars and battlements. "Every man went up on the wall and fired their weapon," said Peek. "We went nuts. I was on the GPMG and must have gone through six boxes of ammunition." There were roars of "If you want to fight, we'll fight you" and "This one's for Mr. Evison." When the guns were finally quiet, Peek lay down on his camp bed, stared up at the stars, and wept.

9

Mystery Junction

*Wherever we arrived, they disappeared, whenever we left, they
arrived—they were everywhere and nowhere, they had no tangible
centre which could be attacked.*

Napoleonic officer, *on fighting Spanish guerrillas during the
Peninsular War, 1810*[1]

---

*A scrimmage in a Border Station—
A canter down some dark defile
Two thousand pounds of education
Drops to a ten-rupee jezail.*

Rudyard Kipling, *"Arithmetic on the Frontier" (1886)*

Under cover of darkness, Captain Tom Anderson and seven Welsh
Guardsmen lifted out sandbags from a hole blasted through the east
wall of CP Haji Alem and slipped out. It was shortly before 9:00 p.m.
on May 26, two weeks after Lieutenant Mark Evison had died at Selly Oak
Hospital. Anderson, the brigade liaison officer, had been sent down to CP
Haji Alem to replace Evison as platoon commander, and now he was acting
on Lieutenant Colonel Rupert Thorneloe's order that he should own the night.
The eight men dropped silently into the canal and waded across it towards
Compound 24. This was the same bullet-pocked building that many of them
had gathered in just before making the final fifty-yard dash across the canal
on the day that Evison was mortally wounded. Getting 7 Platoon back out

on the ground after Evison's death had been a challenge for Anderson, who already had one Helmand tour under his belt as a mortars officer. Anderson felt that his men had begun to view the terrain around CP Haji Alem with a kind of mystical foreboding. In their minds, he thought, it was like those ancient maps on which unknown regions of ocean would be marked with the words: "Here Be Monsters."

The night patrol's destination was to be Compound 8, the structure directly to the north of CP Haji Alem from which the Taliban had fired down the canal as Gizzie and the others ran across. Further north still was the Green 5 junction that the Taliban had saturated with IEDs, isolating CP Haji Alem. Anderson's plan was to set up a covert observation post overlooking Green 5 and lie in wait for an IED team to appear. At Haji Alem, a team armed with a Javelin anti-tank missile was positioned in the northeast turret, ready to kill any Taliban who ventured onto Green 5. Stopping the Taliban laying IEDS there had become a top priority for the Battle Group—and the men of 7 Platoon were eager to avenge Evison's death.

At 9:22 p.m., as Anderson and his night patrol reached Compound 24, Lance Bombardier Andrew Spooner was up on the northeast turret looking towards Green 5 some 1,200 meters away through his "Sophie sight" thermal binoculars. He saw two men moving around and immediately alerted Gunner Steve Gadsby and Guardsman Stuart Jones 08, the Javelin operator. They watched as a vehicle with headlights off drove in from the west and appeared to stop at Green 5. Two men got out and walked into a tree line to the east, moving torches from left to right as they went. "This is dodgy," thought Spooner, who alerted Sergeant Dean Morgan 10 from Swansea (see Appendix).

Morgan, manning the Land Rover "ops room," reported to Major Henry Bettinson up at PB Silab that this was outside the normal pattern of life at Green 5 and that his assessment was that these men were digging in an IED, attaching a command wire, and then running it into the tree line. Bettinson responded that this showed hostile intent. Anderson listened in on the radio as the discussion took place. He was still in Compound 24 and could not see Green 5, but it sounded as if the perfect opportunity had presented itself and had to be seized quickly. Morgan told Jones 08 to get onto the turret firing platform in CP Haji Alem and instructed Spooner to guide him to the target. "This is the IED team," thought Spooner. "We've caught these bastards this time."

At 9:44 p.m., Jones 08 watched through his CLU (Command Launch Unit) infrared sight as the vehicle then moved east into the Green 5 triangle.

After a minute, the vehicle reappeared, and Jones 08 launched his Javelin, a "fire and forget" missile. Five seconds later, the missile, containing two HE (high-explosive) shaped charges, scored a direct hit on the vehicle, which burst into flames. Guardsman Caswell watched the Javelin launch and said to himself: "Goodnight Vienna." As Jones 08 confirmed the successful strike, he counted six men running towards the flames. Shortly afterwards, a Desert Hawk surveillance drone was launched from PB Silab to gather images so that a damage assessment could be done. The images from the drone showed nothing at Green 5 but identified a hot spot in a field some 350 meters to the northwest of the junction.

The next morning, it became clear that Spooner and Jones 08 had not been watching an IED team at Green 5 but farmers in the fields behind the junction in the same line of sight. The Javelin CLU had no range finder, contributing to the error. A local farmer called Zahir Khan had been killed, and his father Haji Alludud and other family members drove to Nad-e Ali with parts of the tractor to see Habibullah Khan, the district governor. An American F-18 Hornet with an "Epic 01" callsign overflew the area and saw a large patch of burnt wheat where the drone had identified the hotspot and a badly damaged tractor nearby. Zahir Khan's funeral was taking place in the graveyard next to PB Silab the following day. When Captain Terry Harman went to speak to the gravediggers to suggest a shura to discuss the previous night's events, he received such a hostile reception that Bettinson feared he was going to be dragged off. Eight elders, however, agreed to return to the base for a shura after the funeral meal, which the Welsh Guards paid for.

Addressing the elders, Bettinson apologized profusely but would not say that such an incident would never happen again. "I'll do everything I can, but you need to help me by telling me when you are working your crops," he said. That night, the Welsh Guards broadcast a similar message across the fields. "It was not a great day for the Battle Group," reflected Bettinson, looking back on the incident. "It was just a f---ing horrendous mistake." Five days afterwards, the brigade issued a press release stating that an "investigation has commenced into claims that an Afghan civilian was killed" near CP Haji Alem.

Thorneloe was deeply dismayed, reporting back to the brigade that "on this occasion we got it badly wrong" and that local Afghans were "understandably upset and angry" about what had happened. "We have reviewed our procedures and I am confident we will not make the same mistake again." Weeks later, he told Captain Alex Bourne, the liaison officer with the Estonian company, of his distress about the incident. "A man's gone out to farm a field in the middle of the night and we've engaged him with a devastating weapon that's killed him," he said. "A man from a good family is now dead as a result of our being gung-ho."

But Thorneloe pushed hard to defend his men, recommending to the brigade that no further investigation was needed into what had been "a tragic but honest mistake." He highlighted his own part in what had happened by stating that as a result of the "extreme" threat from Green 5, "I have directed Mongoose 20 to routinely mount operations to catch the IED teams in the act and prevent them from being able to lay more IEDs." His men at CP Haji Alem acted "under the honest belief that they were engaging a target in the act of laying an IED." Firing a Javelin to hit an IED team was "necessary in order to prevent this act being committed (and hopefully deter subsequent hostile acts), lawful … and proportionate."

The brigade legal advisor backed Thorneloe up, but Brigadier Tim Radford overruled him, ordering that a Royal Military Police investigation be carried out. Several of those involved in the incident were interviewed under caution, but no charges were brought. Once the investigation was completed, the brigade was in a position to pay Zahir Khan's family $7,000 compensation, which it did in June. Identifying Taliban IED teams at night was a constant problem for the Welsh Guards. Farmers would often dig at night to irrigate their fields. To do so in the daytime might meant incurring a tax from the Taliban, as well as having to endure the ferocious heat.

Major Giles Harris's Prince of Wales's Company was also finding out that civilian casualties were a fact of war. On the morning of May 9, less than half an hour after Mark Evison arrived in the operating theatre at Camp Bastion, Harris and his men came under fire north of the town of Nad-e Ali. It was the company's first major operation and was designed to gather intelligence from a known Taliban area. Lieutenant Chris Fenton's 1 Platoon was hit from the front as they reached a prominent crossroads.

Fenton, viewed as one of the most able Welsh Guards platoon commanders, was a Durham University graduate with something Victorian about his manner. He had grown a bushy moustache during the tour and sometimes wore a bandanna in combat. He was unruffled when his Viking was blown up while he was riding top cover during the operation to close PB

Tanda. Almost carefree under fire, Fenton would not have looked out of place fighting on the North-West Frontier more than a century earlier.

As Harris and his command group pulled up alongside in Vikings so that Fenton's platoon could get into cover and organize a withdrawal, he saw guardsmen frantically waving at him to get his head down. Suddenly, gunfire was flying over his head. What he couldn't see was Taliban fighters holding AK-47s over a compound wall about ten meters to his right, behind trees, firing blind onto the Vikings. It was Harris's first contact in Helmand, and most of his men had never been under fire before. Fenton's platoon withdrew under the covering fire of the Vikings, and guardsmen then cleared the compound from which the Taliban had been firing. The enemy, however, had already slipped away along an irrigation ditch that ran out of sight away to the east.

Giles Harris felt disbelief that there had been no casualties, mixed with the delight of having survived and also a heavy weight of responsibility. His whole company was out on the ground, along with the Viking troop, and they had been attacked by an enemy fearless enough to open fire from almost point-blank range. They headed back south to the Blue 16 junction, close to PB Argyll, and were then attacked again, both from the rear and ahead. Bullets were hitting the ground just feet away from Harris as he crawled behind a mound. At this stage, he was aware of a wall of fire being unleashed by Welsh Guardsmen behind him to his left. Everyone was firing at a wood line from where the enemy had been seen. "The weight of fire was incredibly intense," recalls Harris. "A combination of nerves from the close contact only 30 minutes before and the exhilaration for many of firing their weapon in anger for the first time in their careers combined to create a disproportionate response."

In a maize field between the Welsh Guards and the Taliban was an elderly farmer named Gul Mohammed. As Giles Harris's men withdrew under the cover of artillery fire called in to smoke off the area, a bullet sliced into his face, taking part of his jaw off. In all likelihood, it was a bullet fired by a Welsh Guardsman.

A few hundred meters away, Harris saw Mohammed, who had been picked up by the Afghan police and was sitting in the back of a 4×4 truck. The Welsh Guards had halted after reports of a civilian casualty, and Harris had stopped the truck to see what the injuries were. The bottom half of the old man's face, attached by a few threads, was hanging down on his chest.

"I'll never forget the look he gave me," Harris says. "He stared right through me. He was about 80 and his jaw was just two bits of skin. There was blood pouring down the front of his dishdasha and his family were putting rugs around him. His eyes trapped me. I was clearly the commander. Poor guy— just farming and caught between two fighting forces."

Mohammed died of a heart attack before he could be operated on. The incident caused Harris to rethink how he conducted large operations. "I never conducted a company-size patrol in that way again. I learnt to use an alternate axis to draw fighters away from where we were going so we could engage locals in peace and quiet. I avoided regrouping troops at key junctions—I assumed we would be outflanked and hit more than once. We learnt to control our fire until we could see exactly where locals and the enemy were." More importantly, he decided that he would only conduct an operation when he was certain that the benefit gained would outweigh the potential costs.

Thorneloe accepted that mistakes would be made. Indeed, he almost lost his own life because of one. In May, Thorneloe, Jim Haggerty, the British stability advisor, Major Giles Harris, and the Afghan army kandak commander for Nad-e Ali were in PB Argyll when a shot very nearby startled them. Harris swung around and saw the junior brigade legal advisor, a captain who was accompanying him for the day, standing there, his eyes bulging in shock. Unused to handling a rifle, he had pulled the trigger without realizing there was a bullet in the chamber and had accidentally fired a shot. "He was about a metre away from me with his rifle on his hip like one of those prison guards in American films," Harris recalls. "His finger was on the trigger and the rifle was at a 45-degree angle over Colonel Rupert's head about two metres away from him. It was one of those very British moments. Everybody pretended not to notice because they didn't want to embarrass him. No one was angry about the fact that he'd nearly slotted the Commanding Officer."

Harris walked over, quietly took the captain's rifle from him, and suggested he report to the ops officer and tell him what had happened. Afterwards, Harris joked with Thorneloe that perhaps he should have played it differently. "Would it have been better if I'd just gone over and punched his lights out, then walked back and winked at the kandak commander? I'd have been a legend!" Thorneloe, who had previously discussed with Harris the Afghan commander's fondness for bravado, laughed and said: "Actually, the British approach is probably better."

Any negligent discharge of a weapon was a disciplinary offense, not least because it could have tragic results. A Welsh Guards officer visiting FOB Keenan shortly after Lance Sergeant Fasfous had been killed was loading his rifle before a patrol when he accidentally fired a shot. An hour later, an Afghan man called Jabar, aged about sixty-five, was brought to the base with a bullet wound to his neck that had paralyzed him. He had been on his knees praying in a field when he had been shot. He identified himself as a migrant worker who had come to the area for the poppy harvest. He said he had a wife but did not want her to be told what had happened because he would be ashamed if she saw him incapacitated. Jabar was evacuated to Camp Bastion hospital but later died. A police investigation into his death was carried out, but it was unclear who fired the shot that killed him. A soldier on the patrol had fired warning shots at a suspected Taliban dicker, and it is possible that either one of those bullets or the negligent discharge by the officer could have killed Jabar.

The Green 5 incident had dealt another blow to 7 Platoon's morale. Harman remembers visiting CP Haji Alem and seeing Welsh Guardsmen peering out of the square holes where their bed spaces were. They appeared to have lost their color. "There the boys were in their little holes with these long stares, like *Harry Potter* characters," Harman recalls. When gunfire erupted outside, Lance Corporal Hiscock flinched and ducked behind the Land Rover even though there was no possibility of a bullet hitting him. "This is tough for these boys, tough," Harman thought.

Harman was concerned that 7 Platoon had let their fear conquer them. They were not venturing out as often or as far from the base as he believed they needed to. One night, he told Anderson that he was going to go out of CP Haji Alem and show the platoon that the Taliban could be taken on. "I'm going to walk across the road and draw fire from the Taliban, so make sure the men are up on the parapets with their weapons," he said. Harman would be taking four Afghan soldiers with him, including a sergeant who had been a mujahidin fighter against the Russians, and Dai, the interpreter.

At 7:30 a.m. the next day, the six men walked west across the infantry footbridge and set out on exactly the route Evison and his men had taken the day he was mortally wounded. "You can come and talk or you can come and fight," Dai shouted in Pashto through a loudhailer. "The old man is not afraid. He is ready to fight." They walked on straight ahead until they got to Compound 29, where Peek had halted and turned north toward Compound

1, where Evison had been shot. When he got there, Harman could see his dead friend's blood, baked dry in the sun, where it had soaked into the ground. Around the doorway were strike marks where the bullets had hit it. His Bowman radio did not work in the compound, so he was incommunicado. "This is not a good day for dying," he told Dai. "But we need to show the enemy we want to fight."

Two hours later the Taliban had not fired a shot, despite the constant, goading messages being broadcast by Dai. It was unprecedented for a patrol to head that far west and not come under attack. Harman's actions were so brazen and provocative that the Taliban probably feared an elaborate trap. Harman and the five Afghans retraced their route, pulling back to the base with considerably more ease than Peek and his men had managed on May 9. As they got to the front gate of the base, a single shot rang out, way above Harman's head. "You foolish boy, Terry," he thought to himself.

After that, 7 Platoon did more patrolling, and the paralyzing effect of Evison's death began to wear off. "The boys all thought I was f---ing nuts and maybe I was," says Harman. "The night before, I had tried to justify to myself why I might be killed in the morning. There were young soldiers who didn't want to go out on patrol but they had to. They needed a bit of leadership." Harman would take similar risks again.[2]

Thorneloe believed 2 Company was ███████████████████, and he discussed this with Colonel Sandy Malcolm, the regimental lieutenant colonel, who was back in Britain. Malcolm, a serving officer in a training post and approaching retirement, had commanded the Welsh Guards a decade earlier and made Thorneloe his adjutant. Now, Malcolm's part-time role with the Welsh Guards was to act as a source of counsel for Thorneloe and as a link to the wider regimental family beyond the operational battalion. "I know he was ████████████████████████████ and he was going to ██ ████████████████," says Malcolm. "Rupert thought that ██████ ██████████████████████████ PB [Haji Alem]." Both Thorneloe and Malcolm saw themselves as 2 Company men and perhaps instinctively felt that it should be the premier company in the battalion."

7 Platoon scored some successes against the Taliban, but even these came with a price in terms of winning over the local population. One evening, Guardsman Langley was looking through the monocle night-sight fitted on his helmet when he spotted an infrared torch at Compound 8, the Taliban firing point that Anderson and his team had been heading for on the night

Zahir Khan was killed at Green 5. Once Anderson had given the OK, GPMGs opened fire from the two turrets on the south of CP Haji Alem, and a Javelin was launched into the compound. "The tracer was going everywhere and we just wasted whoever was in there," recalls Langley. "We just smashed them." As well as killing the Taliban, however, the Javelin had set the wheat fields around Compound 8 alight. It was a scene that reminded Langley of the opening sequence to Francis Ford Coppola's *Apocalypse Now* and its soundtrack by The Doors. "I just had that tune and the words "this is the end" going through my head again and again." The difficulty with this was that the local elders were constantly complaining at shuras about their fields being burned—the poppy and wheat harvests were their livelihood.

In late May, Afghan elders in Nad-e Ali held a shura with Taliban commanders in the area to request a four-week ceasefire because ordnance had already burnt their wheat in four different places. The Taliban agreed to a two-week ceasefire in the immediate area of the Welsh Guards' patrol bases. This gave the insurgents a breathing space they needed to carry out a resupply of ammunition as well as an important local propaganda victory—they liaised with the elders, just as the Welsh Guards were doing, and gained additional kudos from taking action to prevent crops being damaged.

Over at Paraang, Lieutenant Owen James's 6 Platoon made more progress in dealing with the locals in Khowshaal Kalay. Harman earned the soubriquet "Old Man of Paraang" after Thorneloe suggested he grow a gray, whiskery beard, and he soon built a rapport with several figures, including a shopkeeper. Thorneloe worried that excessive force would only alienate the population. "I can unleash fury, Terry," he said one day. "But what would that achieve?" Locals were employed to rebuild a damaged bridge, and Harman slowly began to build up confidential sources about where IEDs were laid and the placement of stones as signals to the locals about where devices had been dug in.

Influence operations were also being conducted by the Taliban. A local man was beheaded for talking to a Welsh Guards platoon, and it was clear that people in Khowshaal Kalay were very frightened. "It all flipped overnight," recalls Harman. "Intelligence stopped, the man in the shop wouldn't speak to me and the people just changed. We'd got to the stage where people would recognise me and they'd come and talk to the Old Man. But the Taliban had come in behind us and warned people. The Taliban will only allow you to move where they want you to move. They are local people. A lot of intimidation was going on in front of us and behind us."

The Taliban had long followed the traditional Afghan practice of using *shabnamah*, or night letters, to send messages to the people, often threatening them with reprisals for cooperating with NATO forces. At the suggestion of a guardsman, Lieutenant Owen James used his 6 Platoon to leave night letters for the Taliban in compounds used as firing positions near CP Paraang. Each Welsh Guards night letter was decorated with the Ever-Open Eye symbol designed by Lieutenant Rex Whistler for the Guards Armoured Division in the Second World War. Messages in Pashto included: "We are always watching you"; "Your cause is lost"; and "We shall return."

James found that if the Welsh Guards patrolled south of CP Paraang, even by a few meters, they would immediately come under attack. On May 29, James, accompanied by Harman, took a twelve-man patrol to the south as part of the preparation for a shura and immediately heard on the walkie-talkie scanner that the Taliban had seen them and were moving into position. "The people had all left the fields, we'd heard the Taliban and the Icom and we were just waiting for them to attack," remembers Harman. "Then they hit us and it was bad." The patrol was caught in a 270-degree ambush, pinned down in the field with bullets passing so close no one dared lift their head. As soon as CP Paraang started to engage the Taliban firing points with machine guns and Javelin missiles, James's patrol sought cover behind a wall.

Lance Corporal Gareth "Gatch" Davies 16, from Treherbert, was just about to jump over the wall when he was hit. The bullet passed through his left forearm, shattered the bone, and exited just above his tattoo of Chinese characters for Strength, Honor, and Courage. Davies 16, no longer able to use his SA-80 rifle, slapped a field dressing onto his wound and proceeded to fire his 9 mm pistol with his right hand, giving covering fire so his men could get into an irrigation ditch. The nearest Taliban were about fifty meters away, firing across a road and over the ditch. Davies 16 crawled forward to brief James on where the fire was coming from, enabling him to call in mortar fire from PB Silab as the patrol withdrew.

The patrol needed to move five hundred meters up the ditch to a point where they could be met by a Quick Reaction Force (QRF) of three Jackals. Blood was still pouring out of Davies 16's forearm, but he refused morphine. "If I took it, the boys would have to carry me and there was so much heavy fire I didn't want anyone standing up," he recalls. The wounded lance corporal, who lost nearly six pints of blood, was pushed to the front so that everyone could proceed at his pace. As Harman crawled along the ditch, he was aware that accurate fire came in every time he edged forward. "Every time I move, the f---ing weeds in this ditch are moving," thought Harman. "And every time the f---ing weeds move there are f---ing rounds coming in because the f---ing Taliban can see where I am."

Before the tour, Harman had never fired his rifle in action in a twenty-five-year military career. He had come under fire once, on Lenadoon Avenue in West Belfast in 1986; he did not count the shots way over his head in al-Amarah, Iraq, in 2004. Harman had done almost everything it was possible to do in the army, apart from being in battle.

Now he was fighting for his life. "I thought I was going to die that day," he says. "Suddenly, your wife is irrelevant, your children are irrelevant and you're just surviving in the moment. The guys you are with are your family and when they get hurt, you get hurt." As they crawled up the ditch, Davies 16 said to Harman: "Sir, I'm f---ing dying here." Harman pushed aside his own fear and told him: "Just keep going, Gatch. You are not going to f---ing die."

James fired smoke grenades to reveal the patrol's position to Lance Sergeant Gavin Evans 53, leading the QRF. The suppressing fire from Paraang onto two of the three Taliban positions had to cease for Evans 53 to lead his three Jackals through the friendly arcs of fire. As he did so, with Evans 53 manning the GPMG on his Jackal, named "Celtic Dragon," the Taliban turned its fire on the vehicles as they drove in to rescue the patrol. The fire continued as Davies 16, now beginning to lose consciousness, was loaded onto the back of "Celtic Dragon." Evans 53, a fiery redhead from Maerdy in the Rhondda Valley, spoke quickly at the best of times. Now he was barking out orders nineteen to the dozen, his voice getting higher and higher. "Get him in the vehicle!" he shouted again and again, pausing intermittently to fire bursts of machine gun fire at the Taliban.

Rather than the Jackals driving back at speed, Evans 53 and James coordinated a fighting withdrawal. This meant those on foot could move back behind the Jackals and allowed troops at Paraang to continue suppressing the enemy positions once the vehicles had passed safely through their arcs of fire. "It was a bit like the end of *Black Hawk Down* as we ran alongside the Jackals using them as cover to get back into the checkpoint," recalls James. Minutes later, an American Black Hawk landed at Paraang to take Davies 16 back to Camp Bastion. From there he would be evacuated back to Britain.

"That was difficult," reflects Harman. "People say the Welsh Guards is a family regiment, which it is. But you take it down to the level of the guardsman, he's part of a gang, his identity is his small group of people. When you take him out of that identity, he's vulnerable. So seeing one of your guys going, like Corporal Gatch in the chopper, that's it. You've lost him and now he's on his own." Davies 16 would soon be home in Treherbert.[3]

The death of the farmer at Green 5, common though such things are in war, happened just as the issue of civilian casualties was rising to the top of the Afghanistan agenda. The day before Evison's life-support machine was switched off, General David McKiernan, commander of NATO's International Security Assistance Force (ISAF), was sacked by Robert Gates, the Pentagon chief. McKiernan, who had been in post for eleven months, was viewed as too conventional in his thinking and accused of conducting the Afghan campaign as a contest against the Taliban rather than a battle for the people. Hamid Karzai, the Afghan president, had lambasted McKiernan for American airstrikes in the Farah province that he claimed had cost the lives of 130 Afghan civilians.

His replacement was to be General Stanley McChrystal, a legendary special forces officer and former head of the Joint Special Operations Command in Iraq. McChrystal had dismantled al Qaeda in Iraq's car-bomb network by conducting nightly raids that killed the enemy on an industrial scale, but he brought to the Afghanistan conflict an almost messianic belief that raising enemy body counts and defeating insurgents in tactical battles were not enough. Only "a holistic counter-insurgency campaign," he said in testimony to the Senate on June 2, could deliver success. "Our willingness to operate in ways that minimise casualties or damage, even when doing so makes our task more difficult, is essential to our credibility." He added that "the perception caused by civilian casualties is one of the most dangerous things we face in Afghanistan, particularly with the Pashtun people ... we've got to recognise that that is a way to lose their faith and lose their support, and that would be strategically decisive against us."

This philosophy was very much in keeping with Thorneloe's views about the way Battle Group (Center South) should operate—and, indeed, Brigadier Radford's approach across the whole brigade. Thorneloe had told his company commanders that "killing 20 Taliban cannot bring us victory but killing one local national can bring us defeat." The other area in which Thorneloe was in complete accord with McChrystal was on the issue of resources. McChrystal would soon be pouring manpower and equipment into southern Afghanistan, including Helmand. In his commander's initial assessment of August 30, McChrystal would write: "Our campaign in Afghanistan has been historically under-resourced and remains so today.... Resources will not win this war, but under-resourcing could lose it."

The Taliban knew that the British were under-resourced in Helmand and that their vehicles were vulnerable. The network of roads in the Green Zone meant that they were confined to predictable routes. Added to this, aviation resources were so scarce that virtually all movements were taking place by road.

The only land route into CP Haji Alem was via the Green 5 junction. With depressing predictability, the resupply convoys were unable to get through because the lead vehicle would hit an IED. Bettinson had repeatedly requested that resupplies of CP Haji Alem be conducted by air, to no avail. "I ask that air resup [resupply] via Sea King [helicopter] with a long (five-meter) strop be given close consideration by JHF for the next resup in 10 days time," he wrote in a report of May 16. "Particularly when SHOCKER/PEDRO [medical evacuation helicopters] actually land inside CP HAM. I do not have the resources to picket a separate route in and out of HAM." Thorneloe took up the issue with brigade, but nothing to do with helicopters was easy. "We remain extremely eager for JHF-A [Joint Helicopter Force–Afghanistan] to begin resupply into these bases twice a month each at night by under slung load—we have been discussing this with them for some time," he wrote in a weekly report of June 19, adding: "This concept will save lives and PM [protected mobility] vehicles." Eventually, JHF-A acquiesced, just as 2 Company was leaving the area.

Exploiting this situation, the Taliban devoted more and more effort to placing IEDs that would disable vehicles and perhaps kill their occupants. At the same time, increasing the IED threat would separate the Welsh Guards from the Afghan locals by making every interaction with them fraught with danger. In addition, the success of the IED would create an environment in which mistakes like the one at Green 5 would be more likely, again undermining relations between the Welsh Guards and the locals. Intelligence reports indicated that Mullah Taleb, the Taliban's deputy shadow governor, had visited Nad-e Ali town in the middle of March. He informed fighters that the Taliban had learned lessons about fighting the British by conventional means and in the future would focus on IEDs.

Virtually every resupply convoy that had attempted to cross Green 5 had been either blown up or bogged down for hours as devices were defused. On May 15, Thorneloe had experienced first-hand just how severe the IED problem at Green 5 was becoming. Concerned about morale in 7 Platoon after Evison's death, he had traveled down there by convoy to deliver a pep talk. As he viewed the new memorial—a wooden cross with a sign mourning "The Boss"—the base came under attack, and an RPG whooshed overhead. "F---!" exclaimed Thorneloe, before resorting to a cricketing term to note that it was the first time he had been under fire: "I've broken my duck." While this was happening, the Taliban had moved into Green 5 and activated several IEDs in preparation for the convoy's return. On the way back, Guardsmen James Barber, Carl Thomas 08, and Jonathan Screen were part of the Barma team clearing the road up to the bridge. As they walked over it, there were two explosions behind them that sounded like mortars landing, followed by a much louder bang. The force of the blasts threw the three guardsmen forward, with Thomas 08 suffering bruising and cuts to his neck as they jumped into an irrigation ditch to take cover.

The three had just had an incredible escape from a daisy-chain IED. As they had been Barmaing the road, a Taliban fighter had been lying in wait about seven meters away holding two metal connectors ready to initiate a command-wire IED on the bridge. It was a "low metal content" IED—one of a new type of device using components such as graphite and carbon to prevent them being detected by the Vallon metal detectors wielded by the Barma team. The Taliban fighter had held the connectors together when the Mastiff vehicle at the head of the convoy was just about to reach the bridge. The command wire had triggered three devices—a main one that blew the wheels off the Mastiff and ripped off its bar armor and two smaller ones designed to kill the Barma team. Fortunately, the two smaller devices had failed to activate properly. When an SV (Support Vehicle) recovery truck arrived to haul the stricken Mastiff away, part of the bridge collapsed, trapping the Mastiff and the truck. Thorneloe was stranded overnight with the rest of the convoy at Green 5.

Four days later, another Mastiff was destroyed at Green 5 by a command-wire-initiated IED that was also suspected to be a low-metal-content device. Minutes after the blast, the translator heard a Taliban commander on his walkie-talkie ordering: "Attack the tanks with rockets." For the next five hours, the convoy and the bomb-disposal team clearing the area came under fierce attack. One IED was found by the counter-IED team, and another was set off by a Taliban lying in wait nearby but failed to blow up because the command wire failed. The translator picked up the Taliban commander reporting: "Artillery fuse was not correct. Get another fuse and it will be ready." Before he had time to mend the fuse, the team had located a compound that the Taliban was firing from and dropped a five-hundred-pound bomb on it.

On May 24, two days before the Javelin killed the farmer Zahir Khan at Green 5, Bettinson mounted a nighttime resupply of CP Haji Alem. It was the fifth time he had attempted to get a convoy across Green 5, and on each occasion the convoy had taken hours to cross the junction because IEDs had exploded or been found. This time, Bettinson mounted a major clearance operation with a specialist counter-IED team. They stopped at Green 5 and Staff Sergeant Kim Hughes, commanding the counter-IED team, got to work. "All the counter-IED teams had been through the area but none of them could crack Green 5," says Bettinson. "Staff Sergeant Hughes [later awarded the George Cross] spent six hours on Green 5, trying to isolate it, looking for command wires. Where we'd lost the previous Mastiff vehicles, you could visibly see the ground was a lot softer. He went over that area on three separate occasions, with his dedicated team, didn't pick anything up and after the third go he was happy—the area had been isolated, there was no risk. Then Charles Fraser-Sampson drove over it in the lead vehicle. Bang. Here we f---ing go again." The Taliban had perfected low-metal-content devices that could defeat even one of Britain's top bomb-disposal experts.

This was the second time that Lieutenant Fraser-Sampson had been blown up in a Mastiff. "There's the explosion," he recalls, "then everything just seems to go quiet for what seems like an eternity but must be literally a tenth of a second. Then you hear all the earth and stuff raining down on the vehicle. The warning lights and alarms are screaming at you from the dash and there's lots of smoke billowing in from the air vents and the acrid smell of explosives. Then everyone's shouting to check everyone's OK." Immediately after the explosion, he had to get out of the vehicle and lead a Barma team across the bridge, even though he knew there was a danger of more low-metal-content devices ahead. Thorneloe, who had already seen Fraser-Sampson in action the first time he had been blown up, was in awe of his bravery and wanted to recommend him for a gallantry award. "You've got to write him up for the Military Cross," he told Bettinson. "What he's doing is the same as going over the top of trenches in the First World War."

As with Fenton, there was something of another era about Fraser-Sampson—and not just because he was by now sporting a neat mustache. His clipped vowels, perfect manners, and unruffled demeanor gave him the air of a young Edwardian gentleman, though he had an earthy sense of humor and could on occasion swear as well as any junior guardsman. Company Sergeant Major Martin Topps describes him as "phenomenally, frighteningly calm." Fraser-Sampson was a teacher at The Davenies School, a preparatory school for boys in Beaconsfield, Buckinghamshire, in his gap year and went back again after completing his degree in public policy, government, and management at Birmingham University. He then opted for the army because he wanted to be a platoon commander on operations—this was 2006 and combat was pretty much guaranteed for an infantry officer. "I went for the Welsh Guards because I wanted to join a regiment with a strong identity and there's not too many of them about any more," he said. Fraser-Sampson, later selected to become an equerry to the Prince of Wales, had a strong sense of honor and of the moral burden on officers. On two occasions later in the tour, he was to spare his men the gruesome task of collecting body parts by doing it himself, and on many others he led them under fire along IED-seeded roads, urging them on as fear threatened to paralyze them. By the end of their six months in Helmand—most of it spent commanding 2 Company's Mastiff Group—Fraser-Sampson and his driver, Guardsman Richard Hill of Prestatyn, had been blown up five times.

In many respects, Fraser-Sampson was lucky. The brand-new twenty-six-ton Mastiff Mark 2 vehicles he was commanding had V-shaped hulls to divert the force of an explosion and blast-attenuating seats. By the end of 2009, no British soldier had been killed in a Mastiff. Even though he and Hill did not wear helmets (because they found them uncomfortable in conjunction with the radio headsets they also wore) or seat belts (for fear of getting trapped), they emerged from each blast no worse than dazed.

On one occasion, Captain Richard Sheehan, an Apache pilot, spent four hours hovering over Green 5 protecting the Welsh Guards. "They had an IED north of Green 5 by 500 metres," he wrote in his diary. "They must have moved 100 metres in an hour and a half. Literally, guys on their belt buckles clearing, prodding and Barmaing the route. It must be horrendous." Sheehan had to fly back to Camp Bastion because he was running out of fuel.

"Hopefully we prevented something/anything," he wrote. "They ended up making it out without further incident. You can tell from observing the triangle that it's full of bad people."

IED strikes soon became so routine that Lieutenant Trystan Richards, son of Rod Richards, former Conservative MP for North West Clwyd, neglected to report over the radio that his Mastiff had been hit. Thorneloe was with Giles Harris at Khowshaal Kalay during a joint 2 Company and Prince of Wales's Company operation to secure the village for Governor Habibullah Khan's first shura there, when they heard a loud bang. "Was that an IED?" Thorneloe asked. "No, sir," Harris replied. "We'd have heard a radio report." It later emerged that Richards's vehicle had been hit by a command-wire IED but was only lightly damaged and had continued to be driven. "You should really send an initial contact report but I was on the top cover and with all the dust and all the mayhem and all the noise I must have just forgotten," says Richards.

For those in the Viking and Jackal vehicles, the experience of getting blown up was altogether more serious. The Swedish-built Viking was a tracked, all-terrain amphibious vehicle designed for off-road maneuvering. It had two cabs linked together—the infantry dismounts or Barma team would travel in the rear cab—and could drive across fields and canals or even down a canal if it was wide enough. When confined to the roads, however, it was highly vulnerable to IEDs, and its width meant that a mistake by a driver or the earth giving way could lead to a Viking toppling over into a canal.

The Royal Marines Viking Group had spent nearly five months operating with the previous battle group, initially as part of the surge force into the area that had carved out the new Battle Group (Center South). Increasingly, however, they had come to be used in convoys or, as marines liked to grumble, a taxi service. In the context of a counterinsurgency campaign, the use of tracked vehicles across agricultural fields could easily lose the consent of the people. "We could tear around the place," said Sergeant Simon Culkin, a plain-speaking Yorkshireman in the Viking Group. "The thing that crippled us was keeping us to the roads. Give us the free rein to plough through fields and you can pay compensation afterwards. But no, they didn't want to do that, they wanted to keep the farmers and everybody onside. Which you can understand, but doing that to us was like tearing a dog's teeth out." Vikings were fast attracting the reputation among the Welsh Guards of being a "coffin on tracks" or the "new Snatch." Snatch was the much-maligned Snatch Land

Rover that provided virtually no protection against IEDs; thirty-eight British troops had been killed in them in Iraq and Afghanistan.

In the Vikings, the seats most dreaded were in the front cab, where many troops had died, often through massive blood loss after traumatic amputations caused by a blast ripping through the underside. Two months before the Welsh Guards arrived, an armor mine-blast protection plate was added underneath the Viking front cabs, making the difference between injury and death.

Jackals were also all-terrain vehicles, used for long-range reconnaissance and rapid assault. The Brigade Reconnaissance Force, or BRF, which operated mainly in the desert and acted as a highly mobile additional company for brigade tasks, usually moved in Jackals.

The difficulty was that movement in the Green Zone was necessarily along crumbling dirt roads that were ideal for laying IEDs, and the army did not have enough Mastiff vehicles or their smaller variant, the Ridgeback, for the task. As the IED threat increased exponentially, the obvious solution would have been to switch the bulk of movement to the air. In South Armagh, all troop movement and resupply had been carried out by helicopter since the early 1980s because of the Provisional IRA's success in planting IEDs. Towards the end of the troubles, each movement involved at least three helicopters at a time to provide mutual protection in case of missile attack. In Helmand in 2009, however, there was a chronic shortage of helicopters, exacerbated by the inability of the Lynx to fly in daylight hours because of the heat. For the Welsh Guards, there were often no good options—if troops were to move, it had to be by road and it could not always be done in Mastiffs.

Sangin had effectively become a large minefield: 1,200 IEDs had been located and marked on maps by the British. Three Company, based there, did not have any Mastiffs and had to make do with Snatches. "We asked plenty of times for a change of vehicle," says Company Sergeant Major Brian Baldwin. "Were we a low priority? I don't know. But to ask an individual to go on patrol in a Snatch was quite a task for me to motivate them and say: 'You'll be okay.' None of us liked it." The IED threat was so high that 3 Company used the Snatches as "mules" to transport food, water, and ammunition with everyone but the driver on foot. This meant, however, that a patrol that would have taken three hours in a vehicle would take ten to fifteen hours as the Snatches rolled slowly along the road at walking pace while every inch of ground was Barmaed.

Thorneloe was acutely aware of the vulnerabilities of Vikings and Jackals. In May, he had grabbed a coffee in Camp Bastion with Lieutenant Colonel Gareth Bex, who was in Helmand on a familiarization visit before deploying as commanding officer of the 11th Explosive Ordnance Disposal Regiment. Bex was an old friend of Thorneloe's from their South Armagh days more than a decade earlier. They discussed the rising IED threat, Barma drills and the difficulties in detection as well as the relative levels of protection afforded to troops in Vikings, Jackals, Mastiffs, and Ridgebacks. Bex recalls: "We also talked about counter-insurgency and the requirement to take greater risks by getting in amongst the populace and the fact that you can't win hearts and minds through six inches of ballistic glass."

In September 2008, Bex reflected on the conversation and how the IED threat had developed. The IED was the perfect weapon for the Taliban because none of the roads in the Green Zone was tarmacked and devices could be dug in so quickly. "They seed IEDs like vegetables and then basically just have the arming wires covered over or hidden under a stone, or marked in some fairly unobtrusive way," he said. "All they have to do is come up with a battery pack, plug the leads in and it's ready to go. So they're pre-dug-in, pre-prepared." A battery pack would provide power to the device for a few hours before it had to be replaced.

The Taliban had tried radio-controlled IEDs (RCIEDs) and realized they didn't work because of the effectiveness of the British electronic jamming equipment, so they continued to use RCIEDs against the Afghan police and Afghan army but dropped a level in sophistication in order to beat British forces. "They've upped their complexity in tactic by reducing the complexity of the device that they employ," said Bex. "People say it's not very sophisticated over here, but in terms of the tactics and methods of employment, it's incredibly sophisticated. It reminds me of the more capable Provisional IRA scenarios where you weren't impressed necessarily by the bomb but by how the ambush was set up and the thought that was put into it."

More broadly, the Taliban had learnt how to use IEDs "like a proper military force" against the British. "They lay defensive minefields of IEDs to delay, harass, block, fix us, channel us—all the classic military terms." The British had yet to find a way of attacking the networks of bomb makers, as had been done successfully in Northern Ireland and, eventually, under McChrystal, in Iraq. Instead, there had been a tendency to focus on the devices themselves. "If you just concentrate on defeating the device, which to be honest is exactly what we've done for the last three years, I would equate it with 'mowing the lawn.'" The term "mowing the lawn" was used by Brigadier John Lorimer, brigade commander in Helmand in 2007, to describe the futility of operations being repeated again and again because the Taliban were killed but the ground was never held for any length of time.

"If you just continue to deal with the device, find the devices, neutralise the devices, then we will be beaten," said Bex. "Beaten in terms of counter-insurgency because we are fixed by the devices, we can't go out and patrol and we can't integrate with the local population, which is what we need to do." The Taliban realized, moreover, that IEDs could sap the will of the British. "They've got time on their hands and know full well the devastating psycho-logical effect that IEDs have on our will back in [the] UK," said Bex. "It's death by a thousand cuts."

Thorneloe was anxious to relieve pressure on the Nad-e Ali town as well as laying the foundations for seizing control of Chah-e Anjir later in the tour. To this end, he directed Major Giles Harris to take Zarghun Kalay, between the two towns. The village had been originally cleared by the Royal Marines as part of Operation Sond Chara in November 2008. One soldier died, and several marines were injured on the operation. Afterwards, a lone Afghan police station had been left in the village at the Yellow 23 crossroads, split between a destroyed school and a small compound opposite it. The police station was constantly being attacked and the village was a key route for the Taliban coming from Chah-e Mirza, Zorabad, Naqalabad, and Showal. To the west and north was Taliban territory, with regular reports of fighters on motorbikes and conducting their own vehicle checkpoints. To the north was Yellow 11, known as "Mystery Junction," a gateway to the Taliban-held CAT and Chah-e Anjir.

Zarghun Kalay was important for the Welsh Guards because it was a large population centre with a beleaguered police presence and under Taliban influence just a few kilometers from the Nad-e Ali district center. It was also a key thoroughfare for locals and enemy fighters. Controlling it would alleviate pressure on the district center. Most critically, seizing Zarghun Kalay would put psychological pressure on the Taliban in the CAT and confront them with a threat on their doorstep whilst giving the Welsh Guards a foothold to push northeast into Chah-e Anjir later on. Major Giles Harris deliberately avoided Zarghun Kalay early in the tour because he wanted to prevent it being IEDed. Once he went there, he decided, he was going to stay.

For Operation Tor Hajdaar, beginning on June 1, Harris was to use his Prince of Wales's Company plus 2 Company's Fire Support Group—FSG-2, a troop of Scimitars from the Light Dragoons, and a Gurkha police mentoring team. The plan was based on the deception of inserting Lieutenant Dave Harris's 2 Platoon into the police station just before last light to start painting the buildings and fixing the well. The Taliban, viewing the scene from Mystery Junction, were apparently fooled into thinking the Welsh Guards were lending temporary assistance to the police and then would leave.

Just before first light on June 2, Major Giles Harris brought an "armored screen" of Scimitars and Jackals from Nad-e Ali to the north of Zarghun Kalay along with Major Austen Salusbury, the influence officer, whose job was to persuade the owner of the compound at Yellow 17, just south of Mystery Junction, to rent out his home. Once the screen was in place, Lieutenant Dave Harris's 2 Platoon and Lieutenant Chris Fenton's 1 Platoon moved north towards Yellow 17. The Taliban, not anticipating that the Welsh Guards would head up towards Mystery Junction, were caught flat-footed. Six months earlier, the Royal Marines had found themselves fighting through the village after approaching across open ground in daylight from the south. This time, the Welsh Guards were not fired upon until they broke through the outskirts of the village to the north. It took Salusbury three hours and a fistful of dollars to persuade Khuday Noor, the compound owner, to part with his building.

Once that was done, the Welsh Guards set about establishing what was to become CP Khuday Noor. The CP was immediately attacked with RPGs and small arms, and one Light Dragoon was hit in the shoulder. "It was a bit of a bunfight getting in but there was plenty of firepower on our side," remembers Fenton, who became the new sheriff of Zarghun Kalay. For the next month, he and his men came under almost constant attack from Mystery Junction as they convened daily shuras in the village and probed north to gain intelligence in preparation for the taking of Chah-e Anjir.

On June 19, Fenton's 1 Platoon pushed north to carry out a reconnaissance of two canal crossings that would be used in the operation to take Chah-e Anjir. Lance Corporal Rhodri Lodwick, from Llanelli, was the GPMG gunner for his multiple. As they were about to return, it became clear from the Taliban walkie-talkie chatter that the enemy was trying to outflank the Welsh Guards on both sides and cut them off. As they sought cover in a deep irrigation ditch, they immediately came under heavy and accurate Taliban fire from several positions. They were effectively surrounded and pinned down. Suddenly, Lodwick clambered to the top of the ditch in full view of the Taliban and began firing. This gave the others the chance to begin extracting back towards CP Khuday Noor. As the rest of the section moved along the ditch, Lodwick bounced along the edge, switching his aim to different Taliban positions and screaming instructions to the others. On the walkie-talkies, the Taliban could be heard panicking and refusing to obey their commander's orders to fight. Lodwick was the last man back into the base. After firing more than a thousand rounds, he collapsed with exhaustion as he got there.

Giles Harris couldn't quite believe what Lodwick had done. "He was a sullen and fairly negative influence at times," he says. "I remember him once saying in front of his guardsmen: "I just want to smash the Taliban," which was unhelpful. His opinion of the chain of command and our direction was always pretty clear!" As he wrote up a citation for Lodwick to receive a gallantry award, Harris couldn't help but think of Private Alfred Hook, who won a Victoria Cross at Rorke's Drift. Described in the film *Zulu* as "a thief, a coward and an insubordinate barrack-room lawyer," Hook fought with astonishing heroism as the Zulus attacked the hospital in the British outpost. "I was recommending someone who had actually been pretty disruptive," says Harris. "But you can't deny a man his bravery and skill and he had shown both."

The Taliban never managed to get back into Zarghun Kalay, and a new buffer zone had been achieved. "It was a real result," remembers Major Giles Harris. "We had taken just one casualty, kept the fighting out of Zarghun Kalay itself and set up a foothold for the next phase—Panther's Claw."

10

Low Metal Content

*God! They should have hanged the politicians who sent young boys
into battle without the means to fight. Give credit to the Welsh
Guards, it is one thing to fight with proper equipment, but to fight
and not to run without equipment is quite a different kettle of fish.*

—*Lance Corporal Eric Coles, 1st Battalion Welsh Guards,
from Pontypool, writing to his father after being evacuated
from Dunkirk in May 1940*

---

*You hallucinate. You look ahead a few paces and wonder
what your legs will resemble if there is more to the earth in that
spot than silicates and nitrogen. Will the pain be unbearable?
Will you scream or fall silent?*

—*Tim O'Brien, in his Vietnam memoir* If I Die in a
Combat Zone *(1973)*

Before getting on a convoy from PB Silab back to Camp Bastion on June
2, Thorneloe announced quietly that he was going to start doing what
was now the most perilous job in Helmand. "I'm going to Barma," he
told Charles Fraser-Sampson. "Are you sure, sir?" the startled young officer
responded. "Yep," said Thorneloe, picking up a Vallon. He was given a quick
refresher lesson about the procedures before getting to work on the Green 1
junction. Thorneloe was rather slow, and there was a degree of bemusement
from the guardsmen as he picked up washers and spent cartridge cases from
the ground, investigating every beep. The guardsmen had begun to fear they
were viewed as expendable IED fodder, and he was countering this, making
the statement that he would deliberately expose himself to the same risks. "It

was massive," says Fraser-Sampson. "To lead from the front as an officer is always the best way, and this was the Commanding Officer being prepared to get down on his belt buckle and sift through the dirt. It was good to see."

On the trip back to Bastion, Fraser-Sampson's Mastiff, with Bettinson riding in the back, hit a device as the convoy crossed the desert. Mercifully, it was traveling so fast that the damage was minor and no one was hurt. Two days later, Sergeant Aare Viirmaa, a member of the Battle Group's Estonian company, lost both his legs a few kilometers north of PB Silab as he stepped through a compound entrance that had just been Barmaed.

Thorneloe continued to Barma and rode in the lead vehicle of a convoy whenever he could. The psychological effect of IEDs on the Welsh Guardsmen was potentially devastating, and he wanted to mitigate it by his example. "It is absolutely terrifying," said Fraser-Sampson, who would occasionally Barma. "It is just the most awful feeling in the world thinking that every step you take could be your last, or you might miss the device and someone else will be killed. You're almost wishing for the Vallon not to detect anything because when it does start beeping you know then you've got to get down and start confirming. The whole time, you're thinking: 'I didn't join the Army to do this, I'm not an expert, I don't know how to deal with these devices.' And when you see what an IED does to somebody, all you can think about is: 'Jesus, that might be me.'"

After Barmaing over a device that subsequently blew up under a Mastiff, Guardsman Barber had to do the same thing again to secure the area around the damaged vehicle. "I was shitting myself because I didn't want to Barma ever again," he recalls. "I Barmaed up the road thinking 'Oh f---' with every little beep, but I managed to do it. Barmaing was f---ing horrendous." In his diary, Lieutenant Dave Harris wrote of clearing compounds in the pitch-black when he knew there was a strong possibility the Taliban had booby-trapped doorways and laid IEDs all around. "I have just grown to accept that everything is fate and not worry." Black humour also helped the Welsh Guards deal with the petrifying task of searching for IEDs. Down in PB Jaker, the guardsmen played Op Herrickopoly on a makeshift board in which "Any Chance—Op Barma" had been substituted for the "Chance" squares in Monopoly. When at all possible, guardsmen would move along the irrigation ditches, sometimes chest-high in water, to avoid walking on tracks and fields; whatever the Taliban's skills, they had yet to develop an underwater IED.

The Viking crews were also in the front line of the IED threat. At 5:42 p.m. on May 14, Marine Jason Mackie had been killed when a massive IED detonated underneath his Viking. It was the lead Viking of four returning to Lashkar Gah from Objective Worcester, soon to be renamed Tapa Paraang, which Major Sean Birchall's IX Company had taken over during Operation Zafar in April. The marines in the Viking Group had been supporting a counter-IED team and had spent most of the day waiting around doing very little. "We were all starving and were heading back to scran at Lash," said Marine Matthew Vowles, a cousin of Corporal Hiscock and also from Bedlinog. Marine Tristan Sykes, driving the front Viking beside Mackie, who was commanding the vehicle, had decided to head back to Lashkar Gah across an open gravel track rather than along the narrow, canalized roads they had used on their way out.

Captain Gez Kearse, the Viking troop commander, later concluded in a report that "the extended period of waiting for the entire day and the incorrect knowledge of how to task assets appropriately probably contributed to a degree of frustration in the minds of the VIKING operators and contributed to the choice of a known and previously used route." The gravel-track route had previously been guarded by Scimitars from the Queen's Royal Lancers, but these had since been withdrawn, enabling the Taliban to put in IEDs. "This is a common scenario and is a result of deliberate operations taking ground for which insufficient resources exist to hold," wrote Major Rich Hopkins, the Royal Marine officer commanding the Viking Group, in his incident report. This created space behind the British front line that the Taliban could exploit to plant IEDs, further isolating patrol bases. Overextending, Hopkins argued, meant that previously secure areas had "become porous" and previously safe routes were now vulnerable.

The IED that killed Mackie had a main charge up of up to one hundred kilograms of explosives packed into a five-gallon yellow plastic tub and was triggered by a pressure plate. The resulting blast was massive, breaking the Viking in two and catapulting Mackie, and the metal turret mount he was behind, more than thirty meters away. Mackie's left leg was sliced off, and he received major wounds to his torso, killing him instantly. A track girder weighing 250 kilos was blown one hundred meters. Sykes was knocked unconscious and suffered critical injuries, including severe facial wounds, a fractured spine, punctured lung, broken hip, and shattered left foot.

The IED was part of a carefully planned ambush, with the blast followed at once by RPG and small-arms fire from compounds a hundred meters to the north. Despite the gunfire, Warrant Officer (Class Two) Matt Tomlinson, the Viking Group's company sergeant major, jumped down from his vehicle, the second in the convoy, and ran towards the front cab of Mackie's Viking. It had been blown twenty meters in front of the rear cab, from which Guardsman Ed Carew from Aberdare and another Welsh Guardsman from the Recce Platoon were emerging. So many metal fragments had been scattered across the ground that Barmaing was pointless.

Tomlinson was joined by Lance Corporal Michael Stoker of the Queen's Royal Hussars. Stoker had run from the third Viking, as they got to the burning front cab, which had both doors and most of the roof blown off. Sykes was on the ground groaning faintly and partially covered by a mine-blast protection plate that had been blown off the underside of the cab. Taliban fire was coming in, and ammunition was exploding in the fire. After treating Sykes, Tomlinson ran forward thirty meters to find Mackie dead and trapped in his turret mount. With bullets hitting the sand around his feet, Tomlinson pulled Mackie's body clear and then ran back to organize the evacuation of Sykes.

Carew helped Tomlinson carry parts of Mackie's body and put them in a bivouac sack. Marine Vowles was manning a light machine gun on the third Viking when he heard over the radio that his friend had been killed. "I just went crazy," he recalls. "I went through all my ammo—2,500 rounds. Enemy rounds were coming in from everywhere, bouncing off my turret, but after I heard they'd got Jason I didn't care." Tomlinson, who had won a CGC serving with the U.S. Marines in Fallujah in 2004, was later awarded an MC.

Company Sergeant Major Andy Campbell was there when Carew and the other Welsh Guardsman who had been in the back of the Viking returned to Lashkar Gah that evening. "They were in a hell of a state," he remembers. "They'd been in the vehicle that got hit, then once it happened they got ambushed big time and they had to do a fighting withdrawal to get out of there while carrying bits of dead marine. Their faces were blank, as if there was nobody at home. The boys were TRiMing [Trauma and Risk Management] them. All the emotions were there—anger, embarrassment, fear, crying, everything." Afterwards, Birchall reported that he was "concerned by the two Welsh Guardsmen who were actually in the vehicle when the IED detonated and personally dealt with the recovery of the two casualties," adding that they were receiving trauma counseling and "any concerning results will be passed on to the relevant personnel." For Carew in particular, the nightmarish experience was to have a lasting effect.

Mackie, aged twenty-one, grew up in Zimbabwe but moved with his family to Britain in 2002 after President Robert Mugabe's regime seized their farm; he was buried in Bampton, Oxfordshire, on June 4, 2009. His brother, Second Lieutenant Richard Mackie, also a Royal Marine, delivered the eulogy, and Marine Vowles was among those who carried his coffin, draped with the Union Flag. Hopkins says that many of his marines were "pretty emotional" about Mackie's death because there had seemed no point in their being out the day he was killed. "We went out on thousands of patrols where something like that might have happened, and on the way back we probably thought: 'We didn't really do much today did we?' but that was never an issue when nobody got killed."

Eight days later, the Viking Group suffered another bitter blow when Lance Corporal Rob Richards was mortally wounded by a low-metal-content IED during Operation Tor Kali, the closure of PB Tanda, which had been ordered by Brigadier Tim Radford after discussion with Thorneloe. Like CP Haji Alem, PB Tanda was in the wrong place and had achieved little if any effect. Hopkins wrote that it was "isolated and only able to influence a few hundred metres of the ground surrounding its perimeter" and had been opposed from the outset by the PWRR during 3 Commando Brigade's time. "EF [Enemy Forces] have enjoyed complete FoM [Freedom of Movement] around the base and were able to lay multiple devices along all the trafficable approach routes," he continued. "The moves in and out have therefore been particularly hazardous, time and resource consuming."

Two months earlier, during a resupply of PB Tanda, a Viking that was the fourth vehicle in a huge convoy had hit an IED. The front cab was destroyed and the two men in it very seriously injured. At the time, there was mystification about how a pressure pad device could have detonated when the route had been cleared by a specialist bomb-disposal team with metal-detecting equipment and three other vehicles, including one Viking, had already passed over it. The possibility most favored after the incident investigation was that the Viking had strayed off the cleared route; this was strenuously denied by the marines. Since then, another resupply of PB Tanda had taken place without incident, and the baffling IED strike back in February was largely forgotten.

Hopkins, however, remained concerned and requested that Mastiffs be used. This was never seriously considered because Mastiffs were in short supply, and it was assumed that vehicles behind a specialist IED clearance team were safe. In hindsight, the clues were there—as well as the PB Tanda resupply in February, the May 15 daisy-chain explosion involving Guardsmen Barber, Thomas 08, and Screen had happened after all three had Barmaed over the area. Both times, however, the Battle Group concluded that its own troops had made a mistake. In fact, the Taliban had circumvented bomb-detection techniques by modifying their devices.

More than fifty vehicles were involved in the PB Tanda move, rolling from the south of the Bolan Desert. The route had been declared safe by the counter-IED team after a painstaking clearance in which several devices had been discovered.

Richards had just swapped places with Lance Corporal Stoker, who eight days earlier had helped save the life of Marine Sykes, moving from the driver's seat to the commander's position, where Mackie had also been. About three hundred meters away from the base, just fifty meters short of the crater marking where the IED had hit the Viking in February, the road exploded. "I saw the dust cloud starting and then something coming out of the dust and landing further away," recalls Sergeant Culkin, the 3 Troop Sergeant. "I thought it was a section of bar armour or a piece of track or something but it turned out to be Rob."

The blast blew Richards several meters into the air. His helmet came off, and he landed on his head, causing a catastrophic brain hemorrhage. The Viking was thrown onto its left side, trapping Stoker in the driver's seat underneath a pile of dislodged kit. Burning fuel dripped down onto him, setting fire to his uniform and burning 30 percent of his body. "Get me out! Get me out!" he screamed as his comrades desperately cut off his body armor and poured water over him. Stoker managed to crawl out despite a broken pelvis. "I'm going to go into shock soon," he said, and passed out. He eventually made a full recovery.

Five days after Richards was blown out of his Viking, he died of his wounds at Selly Oak Hospital. A Welsh speaker from Betws-y-Coed, North Wales, he was known as "Rob the Gob" or "Rob the Body" by his fellow marines. Their tributes to him mentioned prowess with women, capacity for alcohol, prodigious strength, and love of amusing underpants. A vastly experienced Viking operator who was completing his third tour of Afghanistan, he was described by Tomlinson as "the Einstein of Viking" and someone who had regarded Helmand as his backyard. "You could see how content he was when out on the ground, during the winter period stomping around in his black Wellington boots looking like Rommel … his choice of phys rig was basically chav; regardless of his fellow marines digging out blind to look like an extra from *Top Gun*, Rob would be comfortable in a large pair of shell-suit-type shorts and T-shirt."

As Richards lay on his deathbed, the explosion at Green 5 underneath Fraser-Sampson's Mastiff confirmed that the Taliban were using low metal content devices. The stubborn faith in the omniscience of the specialist bomb-disposal teams suddenly evaporated. "The engineer team didn't pick it up because it was low metal content, the CVRTs [Scimitars] missed it because they've got a wider axle and the first Viking didn't detonate it because it was so deep but crushed the ground enough that the one behind it set it off," says Hopkins. "That's the most plausible explanation."

The Taliban had watched large convoys travel down to Tanda four times and observed exactly what the bomb-disposal teams had done. The enemy had ███ ███████████████████████████████████ made the British more vulnerable to small-arms and RPG ambush. Low-metal-content devices could kill them outright and bog convoys down for half a day or more.

"The route to Tanda was always mined," says Culkin. "Whenever we did this move down, it was a deliberate clearance and you were talking six or eight plus IEDs that were found. God knows how many weren't found, because you were only clearing a channel big enough to use. This time it was like an IED come-on. The Taliban were thinking: 'We'll give them the ones that we want them to find at the levels of metals that we know they can detect.' Then, bang, they put this completely different low metal content one in." Thorneloe saw this as extremely ominous. "It seems to us that our reliance on ███████████ in the measure/counter measure business of IED/C-IED has become a vulnerability," he reported to the brigade, adding that there was a need to enhance "our technical ability ███████████████ ███████████ IEDs."

In a report, Hopkins concluded that the Richards incident marked "the confirmation of a new threat in the Nad-e Ali AO." He argued that it was time to stop using Vikings on predictable routes. "All movement on high risk routes should be conducted in mine proof platforms [Mastiffs or Ridgebacks] and no other platform should transit the safe lane unless such a platform has led through initially," even if a counter-IED team had done a clearance. The threat from low-metal-content devices was so great, he wrote, that perhaps it was time to consider Vikings being "withdrawn from the AO [Welsh Guards area of operations]" if they could not operate off the roads.

The other aspect of the death of Richards that rankled was that PB Tanda should never have been set up in the first place. "As in other areas of the Nad-e Ali AO the need for CLPs [combat logistics patrols] to PBs on the edge or beyond the ISAF bubble has dictated battle tempo and placed men at considerable risk equal to combat operations but with less tangible gain," Hopkins wrote. "The pattern of taking ground and placing fixed bases at stretch and with insufficient forces to dominate the surrounding ground and approach routes should be re-considered at a higher level." This pattern, however, was the way the British had been operating in Helmand since 2006.

Thorneloe was equally outspoken on the subject of low-metal-content IEDs, bemoaning in a June 13 report his belief that the brigade's weapons intelligence section was not only "agnostic as to whether Low Metal Content IED threat actually exists," but also recommended that Barma and IED search methods needed no modification. "We believe that the weight of evidence for Low Metal Content is now overwhelming—there is a clear need to adapt procedures to do something about them. In our view existing TTPs [Tactics, Techniques, and Procedures] and equipment are not adequate. To say nothing of the human casualties we are currently losing 1 × PM [Protected Mobility] vehicle per week. This is not sustainable." The brigade was aware of the limitations of Vallons, and intense pressure was being put on the frustratingly slow procurement system back in Britain to put in an Urgent Operational Requirement (UOR) order for devices fitted with ███████████████ .

Since the start of May, Thorneloe outlined, Battle Group (Center South) had sustained two deaths, six wounded, and five vehicles disabled on ground that had just been cleared moments before by Barma or specialist counter-IED. The numbers were questionable, since Marine Mackie had been killed on ground that had not been Barmaed, but the force of his point was hard to refute. There was no typical device that was being used—tinfoil pressure plates, palm oil containers, command wire with kite string, and military mines were all found—but it was increasingly clear that low-metal-content

IEDs were becoming the Taliban's weapon of choice in the area. While some existing counter-IED drills such as ██████████████████████████ █ could help mitigate the threat, he argued that a "more coherent response" was required, probably at brigade-level, and there should be "rapid work to roll out new kit and TTPs." It was self-evident that the Vallon was no longer an effective tool against IEDs. There were plans to ████████████████████ ████████████████████████████ but the army still did not have any in service a year after the Welsh Guards left Helmand.

The Americans were concerned about the lack of British counter-IED capability. In February 2010, Robert Gates, the Pentagon secretary, told reporters that he had offered to supply equipment to Britain and other countries. "I told our allies that the United States will be able to offer them more intelligence, training and equipment including jammers, route clearance robots, surveillance systems and ground-penetrating radar [GPR]." Such overtures, which were not always accepted, cemented the reputation among American troops of the British forces being "the borrowers." Some NATO countries moved swiftly to buy off-the-shelf kit to combat low-metal-content IEDs. The Australian army bought a number of handheld detectors that incorporated GPR.

The fact that the Battle Group was no longer certain that the counter-IED teams would find all the devices gnawed away at the confidence of the troops. Major Andrew Speed, commanding the closure of PB Tanda, recalls being in a Viking that was the next vehicle to drive down the "cleared lane" after Richards's Viking had been destroyed. Major Martyn Miles, the Battle Group logistics officer and a survivor of the bombing of the *Sir Galahad* in the Falklands War, was sitting opposite him. Miles was as apprehensive as Speed was, but there was no need for any words. He caught Speed's eye and gave him a look that said: "Whatever will be, will be."

Jackal patrol vehicles were becoming every bit as vulnerable as Vikings. FSG-2, the fire support group for 2 Company, was right on the front line. Of platoon strength, the FSG's role was to provide additional firepower using their highly mobile Jackals. The vehicles, however, offered almost no protection against IEDs. On May 29, three FSG-2 Jackals, commanded by Lance Sergeant Gavin Evans 53, were returning to PB Silab from CP Paraang. They were still celebrating their rescue, a few hours earlier, of Lance Corporal Davies 16 and his patrol when the "Celtic Crusader" Jackal was hit by an IED. Guardsman Adam Mortimer-Rees, from Caerphilly, was wounded by shrapnel to his left leg when a command-wire device detonated underneath "Celtic Crusader." Lance Sergeant Dai Lewis 29, from Port Talbot, suffered loss of hearing from the blast and was treated back in Britain. Lewis 29, outside center for the Welsh Guards rugby team, had earned the nickname "Dai Barma" because of his proficiency with and enthusiasm for wielding a Vallon. In the space of a few weeks, he had detected five IEDs. The device that hit his vehicle was an improvised Claymore mine angled to fire upwards. It was too small to do much damage to a vehicle and seemed designed to kill someone, which it just failed to do. 2 Company's Jackals were in almost constant use, and FSG-2 felt the odds were tilting against them. "We were going from tasking to tasking being used and abused," said Lance Corporal Geraint Hillard, from Cardiff. "It was just a matter of time before it came round to your Jackal."

Hillard and his best friend, Drummer Dale Leach from Barry Island, had already had a couple of close escapes. One night they had been out in a night overwatch position taking turns to keep lookout. Guardsman Luke David 30, from Pontypool, was on duty while Leach and Hillard, who had taken their helmets and body armor off, watched a DVD. Suddenly they came under accurate fire from a tree line and rolled under the Jackals to take cover. David 30 did the same and was lying with his head next to a tire when a bullet went in and burst it. "They're coming in too f---ing close," shouted David 30. "Dave, shut up and go and get us a can of Coke," Hillard shouted. "F--- off!" came the reply as the rounds continued to ping off the Jackals, and David 30 buried his head in his rucksack.

On another occasion, a command-wire IED had blown up just seven meters away from Hillard, Lance Sergeant Lewis 29, and Lance Corporal Cai Davies 95, from Bargoed in South Wales. The Taliban fighter lying in wait hesitated for just a moment, and the device went off between the three Welsh Guardsmen. "We were running through the cloud of dust in stitches laughing," recalls Hillard. "We knew we'd nearly just died but we were safe."

At 5:15 am on June 12, three Jackals, with four Welsh Guardsmen in each, left 2 Company's PB Silab base. The first task of the dozen men from the FSG-2 was to Barma the Green 1 junction, three hundred meters from PB Silab, in preparation for a resupply convoy coming in from Camp Bastion. Their second task was to then take an overwatch position in the desert looking down on the junction. From there, they were to provide cover for a foot patrol of Welsh Guards and Afghan army searching Compounds 29, 31, 34, and

36. These were to the southwest of Green 1 and believed to be possible points from which the Taliban were initiating command-wire IEDs. The three Jackals moved behind Compound 1 and stopped for Color Sergeant Jonathan J. J. Jenkinson, from Shrewsbury, to give them their orders. He told them that Evans 53's "Celtic Dragon" and Lance Corporal Davies 95's "Celtic Fury" should take position looking to the southwest while his "Celtic Crusader" would stay to the rear and face north (see incident map in Appendix).

Evans 53 and Davies 95 were close friends. "Me and him are quite the same characters," says Evans 53. "We're quite hot-headed." In Davies 95's vehicle were Leach, manning the grenade machine gun, and Hillard, who normally commanded a vehicle but had jumped on as a Barma man because he did not want to miss a patrol. The dozen men, mostly South Walians, were part of a particularly close-knit platoon. Most of the names could have come from a list read out by a mine foreman or a Welsh Guards sergeant major nine decades earlier: Evans 53, Davies 95, Jones 78, Jones 14, Jones 09, Griffiths 21, Lewis 88, Thomas 58. Three of them played in the backs for the Welsh Guards rugby team—Lewis 29, who had already been evacuated back to Britain with loss of hearing, Lance Corporal Phil Lewis 88 from Maesteg, and Davies 95.

Before the tour, FSG-2 had competed for the Leuchars Cup, a contest to find out which was the best platoon in the Welsh Guards, they emerged the clear winners after being physically tested on the assault course and shooting range as well as quizzed on cultural awareness and Pashto. They had also been tested with a practical exercise using real-life amputees as actors. The scenario was that of a vehicle straying onto a minefield and being blown up, causing traumatic amputations and other injuries. Guardsmen had to clear a safe lane using Vallons and then treat the casualties. Hillard, the platoon medic, had performed so well that he was asked to provide instruction to the rest of the platoon—which he then did with aplomb.

Evans 53 was looking over at Davies 95's "Celtic Fury" as they moved off and stopped short of what they considered to be the vulnerable area they needed to Barma. It was 6:49 a.m. "95's vehicle had just about come to a stop and he was turning around," Evans 53 remembers. "Then it went booph. He just blew up. There was smoke and you could see bits of the Jackal flying everywhere. The thing that still upsets me is I could see the three of them in the air—95, Hillard and Leach." At PB Silab, nearly a kilometer away, Guardsman James Francis, a mortarman from Cardiff, heard the explosion and saw a huge cloud of smoke rising from Green 1. "F--- knows how anyone could survive that," he thought.

Davies 95 landed on his head ten meters away, got up and dusted himself off, apparently unharmed. Hillard hit the grenade machine gun as he left the vehicle, shattering his right foot, rupturing his spleen, and breaking his pelvis and back. The ballistic plate in his body armor was ripped out and propelled upwards, smashing his teeth and nearly severing his tongue. Leach landed beside Hillard, thirty meters in front of the Jackal. Leach had also hit the GMG, which had sliced off his left leg at the knee. His ballistic plate had broken his left eye socket, and he suffered a broken back and shattered right hip. Guardsman Kyren Thomas 58, the driver, from Swansea, was the only one who had remained in the Jackal—the steering wheel had held him in place. Without thinking about the grave danger of more IEDs, he jumped out of the vehicle, ran over to Leach and Hillard, and began applying a tourniquet to the bloody stump where Leach's left leg—which had landed a further fifteen meters away—had been.

As this was happening, Evans 53 jumped out of his vehicle, grabbed a Vallon, and began to Barma towards the casualties with Lance Corporal Ted Jones 09, from Wrexham, carrying a stretcher, behind him. Evans 53 wanted the information for the nine-liner casualty report as soon as possible, but he couldn't get Davies 95, clearly in shock, to make any sense. "What's the situation?" shouted Evans 53. "Just f---ing get over here, just f---ing get over here," screamed Davies 95. "Shut your f---ing trap," Evans 53 ordered his friend. "I'm coming for you. I just f---ing need the information about the casualties." Davies 95 composed himself and gave the lance sergeant the details he needed to pass to Jenkinson, who was on the radio to PB Silab from his Jackal nearby.

As they neared the casualties, Evans 53 turned around and told Jones 09 to stop. "If something does go, both of us are going to get it. Dress back, wait till I prove a safe route and then you come through." When he got to the casualties, Leach was unconscious and Hillard just murmuring. Jones 09 applied another tourniquet to Leach's stump, which was still bleeding heavily. Leach was then taken back to Evans 53's Jackal on a stretcher while Hillard— whose injuries did not appear to be nearly as severe as they were—was lifted onto a poncho and taken to join him. "95 was still bumping his gums—that's how he is," recalls Evans 53. "He was all over the shop." As they were taking Hillard back, Evans 53 told Davies 95 to give Hillard, who was in severe pain,

Prince of Wales's Company wading through an irrigation ditch. *Welsh Guards*

Rupert Thorneloe with his daughters Hannah, left, and Sophie. *Sally Thorneloe*

Three Company in a Sangin poppy field. *Welsh Guards*

Lance Sergeant Tobie Fasfous. *Anne Fasfous*

Captain Terry Harman, known as the "Old Man of Paraang," conducts a shura. The identity of the translator is concealed. *Captain Terry Harman*

Memorial at CP Haji Alem. *Welsh Guards*

Above: Lieutenant Mark Evison at CP Haji Alem. His diary is on the bottom shelf to the right. *Welsh Guards*

Below: Guardsman Joe Korosaya, after Lieutenant Mark Evison was wounded on May 9. *Welsh Guards*

Above: Major Sean Birchall talks to local children in Basharan, where he reopened the school. *Welsh Guards*

Below: Lance Sergeant Gethyn Rowlands 39 waits to be medevaced by a Pedro after being shot in the shoulder. The Afghan soldier to the right had been shot in the bicep. *Private Matt Boffy*

Above: Lieutenant Colonel Rupert Thorneloe, stranded at Green 5 after an IED strike. *Colonel Rupert Frere, MoD*

Below: Part of the Recce Platoon two days before their Viking rolled into the Shamalan Canal. Standing, L–R: Barber; Young; Thomas 08; Evans 88; Kastein; Guest; Raymond Hill. Crouching, L–R: Biggs; Cometson; Spencer-Smith. All but Guest and Spencer-Smith went into the canal. *Welsh Guards*

Above: Guardsman Jon Caswell snapped at XP-7. When guardsmen heard him fire a shot in a darkened room, they feared he had killed himself. *Sergeant Dan Bardsley, MoD*

Below: Thorneloe's body is repatriated at RAF Lyneham in Britain after being flown from Helmand. Garrison Sergeant Major Bill Mott 88 steadies the coffin. *MoD*

Above: Guardsman James Francis, a mortarman, reloads his SA-80 on a compound roof near XP-7 during Panther's Claw. Comrades from 2 Company were pinned down in a nearby field by Taliban fire. *Sergeant Dan Bardsley, MoD*

Left: Lieutenant Colonel Charlie Antelme addresses the Prince of Wales's Company at Chah-e Anjir: "You should feel ten feet tall." *Toby Harnden*

Below: Lance Corporal Dane Elson (L) and Lance Sergeant Dan Collins on the eve of Panther's Claw. Elson was to be killed by an IED days later. Collins suffered from PTSD and took his own life on New Year's Day 2012. A copy of this photograph was found in Collins's car after his death. *Lance Sergeant Dan Collins*

Above: Lieutenant Piers Lowry is casevaced by a U.S. Pedro Black Hawk, after being wounded at XP-7 beside the Shamalan Canal on June 29. *Sergeant Dan Bardsley, MoD*

Below: A Prince of Wales's Company mural at PB Shahzad in Chah-e Anjir, the former headquarters of American workers in the 1950s and Russians in the 1980s. *Toby Harnden*

some morphine. Still dazed, Davies 95 plunged the syringe in but got it the wrong way around and stuck it in his own hand. "You're not going to believe this," said Davies 95. "I've just self-administered."

Meanwhile, Jenkinson was desperately trying to get a medical helicopter to come in. An emergency helicopter landing site had been Barmaed but the danger of more IEDs was so high that Jenkinson requested a helicopter with a winch. The minutes were ticking away as the message came back that no winch was available. Evans 53 had never witnessed the mild-mannered Jenkinson so much as raise his voice before. "There was lots of umming and aahing about whether they were going to put a winch in or not. JJ was going f---ing bonkers. I've never seen him lose it like that. In the end he just said: "Get this f---ing chopper in!"" An American Black Hawk came in and landed at 7:33 a.m., lifting Hillard and Leach off to Camp Bastion forty-four minutes after they had been blown up.

Just as the noise of the helicopter had died down, small-arms fire began to come in from Compound 14 and a tree line. The remaining ten Welsh Guardsmen with the Jackals immediately began returning fire. Lance Sergeant Gavin Jones 14, from Llanfairpwllgwyngyll on the Isle of Anglesey, called in mortar fire from PB Silab. Guardsman Francis was one of those launching the mortars. "We got an immediate fire mission and we were firing mortars all around the boys with the Jackals so the Taliban didn't have a chance to close in on them," he remembers. Jones 09, a trained sniper, picked off two Taliban fighters with his L96 rifle. The Welsh Guards patrol that was near Green 1 also opened fire. Even Davies 95, much calmer since he had given himself morphine, got in on the act, manning a GPMG from the top of a Jackal. Evans 53 looked through a sniper-spotting scope to see the Taliban dragging off their dead and retreating to the southwest of Green 1, where they regrouped and continued to fire from Compounds 24, 26, 27, and 29. Jenkinson had been refused permission to destroy the wrecked Jackal with a five-hundred-pound bomb, and his men had to Barma the area to retrieve the GMG, blown thirty meters from the stricken Jackal, pistols, and SA-80 rifles, which in any case had been bent so badly they could never be fired again.

By 8:45 a.m., the firing had stopped, and Jenkinson called Evans 53 over. "Now look, you're not going to like this," he said. "But you need to go and get his leg." Evans 53 played for time: "What do you mean? I don't know where it is." Jenkinson, however, would not be moved. "You'll have to go look for it," he replied, and walked away. "I'd made the decision that I wasn't leaving the leg there," Jenkinson recalls. "I just didn't want the Taliban going up there and retrieving a part of one our lads." Evans 53 picked up his Vallon, and he and Lance Sergeant Simon Jones 78, from Brecon, with Lance Corporal Lewis 88 began to Barma the area.

Eventually they found the leg, which had landed about forty meters behind the Jackal, the opposite direction from which Leach had been catapulted out. The boot was still on the leg, as well as some singed parts of Leach's combat trousers. "I could see all the hairs on the leg," recalls Evans 53. "It was f---ing horrific." Just as he was moving forward, his Vallon started beeping, almost certainly indicating an IED. He froze and gestured to Jones 78 to go around the other way. "He works on a farm and he's used to killing animals so he weren't so queasy with it," says Evans 53. He threw Jones 78 a poncho to put the leg in. As Jones 78 picked the leg up, the ankle turned and the foot moved.

When they got back to PB Silab, most of the men broke down. "The thing with the boys was they were really close and all good mates," says Evans 53. "I've never seen grown men cry like that. It was quite moving. But the first thing we said to them was they'd got to crack on and go and secure Green 1. Fair play to the boys, they literally dried their eyes and went back out." That night, Bettinson ended his situation report defiantly with 2 Company's motto, stating: "We remain the Men of the Island of the Mighty."

A few days later, Davies 95 complained of persistent headaches and was taken to Camp Bastion to be examined by a doctor. He was diagnosed with bleeding on the brain and evacuated back to Britain but was playing rugby again for the Welsh Guards before the year was out. When the platoon had arrived back at PB Silab, Leach's leg was handed to Company Sergeant Major Topps. "It was probably the most surreal moment of the tour for me," he remembers. "I put it in surgical bags and then in a box and stored it in the refrigeration container we had down there." In the end, the leg was incinerated. After the incident, FSG-2, now down by four men and a Jackal, was disbanded and its members distributed elsewhere throughout the Battle Group.

The day before Leach and Hillard were blown up, Harman had received a telephone call from his interpreter, Dai, who had spoken to "Hamid," an intelligence source he had cultivated. "Hamid tells me the Taliban are planting 14 to 15 IEDs all around the crossing," Dai said. It turned out that the crossing that Hamid was talking about was Green 1. Harman, who was at CP Haji Alem, called up the PB Silab ops room and passed on the information.

"I don't know whether the intelligence is correct or exactly where the IEDs might be," he said. "But be extra vigilant and make sure you tell all the patrols this." At 11:00 p.m., he says he spoke to Lieutenant Lowry, the 2 Company logistics officer, on the radio to reinforce the need to disseminate the intelligence to the troops going out because he knew that a resupply convoy was coming in through Green 1. "Make sure that all the information I've given out today is passed on," he said. According to Harman, Lowry responded: "Yeah, yeah, not a problem."

Harman gives an account of confronting Lowry the next morning after he heard Jenkinson on the radio describing how his men had Barmaed across an IED minefield to retrieve Leach's leg. Harman says he got straight on to the 2 Company ops room and demanded: "Get me the logistics officer now" and that when Lowry came onto the radio, he said to him: "Answer this question or I'll be up there. Did you tell the f---ing patrol this morning all the callsigns what I passed on last night?" Harman remembers Lowry replying: "No, because they'd already gone out this morning." Harman says he was incandescent, responded "Fine!" and slammed the radio down before going up to one of the turrets at CP Haji Alem, where he sat down and wept.

"That f---ing broke me," he recalls. "You can never say that the incident wouldn't have happened, but who knows? If the information had been passed down, perhaps Jenkinson would have been more cautious. But the fact is, it wasn't passed down." Lowry disputes Harman's account and denies that such a conversation took place. "We were very aware that IEDs were all over the area," Lowry says. "We had been struck there a number of times before and I absolutely did not 'forget' to tell the patrol. Even if I had, they would have acted no differently as the IED threat was always very high, as it was throughout the tour."

When Thorneloe had visited CP Haji Alem, he had heard complaints about a lack of supplies that echoed those in Evison's diary. The difficulties in resupplying the base had not been anticipated when the location was chosen, and when the Welsh Guards took over CP Haji Alem, there were only about two weeks' worth of water and rations. As the temperatures soared and summer approached, each man required a minimum of six liters of water a day and ideally should have drunk seven or eight. After Evison's death, 7 Platoon went down to three days of rations and two days of water. Soldiers were then limited to three liters a day, and showers were banned. On the day the next resupply convoy was due to come in, the water ran out. Soldiers commandeered cartons of orange juice that Afghan soldiers had been secreting away.

Then the resupply convoy got hit by an IED and couldn't get through for several hours. "We were in a firefight for four hours and we didn't have water," says Sergeant Steve Young, who had taken over as platoon sergeant. "There was literally boys with their lips stuck to their teeth." Lance Sergeant Peek remembers the convoy finally arriving: "The boys were like a tramp on chips, climbing on the back of the SVs [Support Vehicles], smashing bottles of water out." After this, a huge resupply convoy was laid on and enough water and rations for several months delivered. But the fact that 7 Platoon had been required to fight without water raised another question mark about 2 Company in Thorneloe's mind.

Bettinson felt he was being undermined by some of his officers, who had been bad-mouthing him on a radio net being listened in on by guardsmen. He also had growing concerns about the abilities of Lowry, who had argued vociferously that he should have taken over 7 Platoon. Bettinson and some others felt Lowry was ill-suited to the coordination role of company logistics officer. "When there was an incident going on and he was in the ops room, he was great, he was all over it," says Topps. "But when there wasn't a patrol out, you couldn't get him in there. You couldn't get him to go through the planning. He was a massive character, you could have great banter with him, but he didn't like doing the staff work side of things. He just thought it was all about the fight at the time. He was a bit of a cowboy."

Harman had another confrontation with Lowry over a plan to resupply CP Haji Alem with three Jackals at night—a mission that Harman felt was plainly suicidal. The issue, Harman says, was dumped on the lap of Henry Bettinson. "Henry was having to do the company logistics officers job as well as his own, and when that happens, something's going to get missed. And that was rations, because there was no proper planning by Lowry. The Commanding Officer was irritated at 2 Company because we lacked a bit of traction and everything was being laid at Henry's feet."

As well as putting Harman into 2 Company, Thorneloe had sent down Regimental Sergeant Major Mike Monaghan, the most senior enlisted man in the regiment, to help steady the ship. Monaghan, from Newport, was the archetypal Welsh Guardsman. He was six feet five inches tall, broad-shouldered and with red hair, and had an instant aura of authority, rarely needing to raise his voice—a disapproving look was usually enough to propel an errant guardsman back into line. Like Thorneloe, he was softly spoken and rather understated. Despite all entreaties, Monaghan had declined the offer of a commission and was due to leave the Welsh Guards in 2010 and move to Spain with his wife to start afresh.

The tenseness of the situation was exacerbated by the appalling communications between Thorneloe's headquarters at Camp Bastion and PB Silab. Evening conference calls, when each company commander was supposed to be on the net, were painful affairs, as Bettinson could often hear nothing other than broken sentences and white noise. He would spend hours after the conference ended trying to reach Battle Group headquarters via satellite phone in order to get a brief from Captain Ed Launders, the Battle Group ops officer, on what had been discussed. "In the worst case, it took me four hours after the conference to find out what was going on," says Bettinson. It was clear to those on the conference calls that Thorneloe was growing impatient with 2 Company.

During the June 12 incident in which Leach and Hillard were blown up, Bettinson found himself typing out a message to Thorneloe that began: "Dear Colonel, this is just shit. We're in a contact and I cannot f---ing speak to you. This is unsustainable for six months." Then he deleted it and wrote out a standard contact report.

Bettinson felt 2 Company was fighting on its own and the Battle Group was struggling to support him due to lack of resources and long lines of communications both within the company's area and between PB Silab and Camp Bastion. At the nightly brigade conferences in Lashkar Gah, each battle group would show one PowerPoint slide to illustrate the incidents that day. Battle Group (Center South) often had to show two slides because it could not cram all the incidents onto one. Almost invariably, the vast majority of these incidents involved 2 Company. During the first ten weeks of the tour, 2 Company had just five days when it wasn't attacked by the Taliban. As on the day that Evison had been shot, coordinated attacks against more than one base simultaneously were often carried out from multiple firing points against each base.

Thorneloe was every bit as frustrated as Bettinson. "Currently I can neither command nor control 2 Company effectively because I cannot talk to them," he had reported to the brigade on May 22. These were lonely weeks for Bettinson, who had no peers to talk to at PB Silab and precious little chance of communicating meaningfully with anyone outside the base. "I befriended a couple of swallows," he recalls, laughing. "Until they started waking me up and then I'd throw an old Croc sandal at them and then they soon moved out."

████████████████ Thorneloe wanted ██████ 2 Company. After considering various options, including removing Lowry from his post, he came up with the idea of ████████████████████████████████ ████████████████████████████████████. He discussed the possibility with Brigadier Radford who, like Thorneloe, had been hugely impressed with Birchall's dynamism and charisma in bringing IX Company together and leading them from the front on Operation Zafar. Birchall was due to take over 2 Company at the end of the tour, ████████████████████████ ████████████████████████████. Radford told Thorneloe that it was the battle group commander's call as to how to proceed. This was war. Tough decisions needed to be made. The discussions were sensitive and conducted with great secrecy, but Thorneloe's confidences to a select few indicated that his mind was almost made up. Thorneloe discreetly told ████████████████ ██████████. It seemed that the best moment ████████████████████ would be in late June, when ████████████████████████████ and be in the vanguard of the push up the Shamalan Canal by the Welsh Guards during Operation Panther's Claw.

11

Heaven in Helmand

*On either side of the life-sustaining canal is a row of beautiful
mulberry trees, their leaves now opening forth with the warmth of
spring. Wheat fields are taking on green and vigorous life, as are
small patches of clover and alfalfa.*

—*Paul S. Jones,* Afghanistan Venture *(1956)*
(about the Shamalan Canal)

---

*Near the end of life in my own body
I slept in a grove of mulberry trees,
with a mattress of soft sandstone
and warm breeze for my blanket.*

—*Andrew Motion,* "Home Front" *(2009)*
(opening section based on Rupert Thorneloe)

D-Day was approaching, and Rupert Thorneloe was like a man with the weight of the world on his shoulders. He would be hunched over his laptop at 2:00 a.m., a can of Diet Coke and tin of Café Crème cigarillos beside him, surrounded by maps and papers. Pinned up on his noticeboard were family photographs and drawings by his daughters Hannah and Sophie. D-Day was June 25, when the Battle Group would begin its part in Operation Panther's Claw, the largest British operation since its forces arrived in Helmand three years earlier.

The aim of Panther's Claw was to isolate the Taliban-controlled area of Babaji to the west of the Shamalan Canal and clear it of approximately 350 enemy fighters who had been using the area as a base for threatening Lashkar

Gah. Once this had been done, Brigadier Tim Radford envisaged, reconstruction projects could be set up, schools reopened, and a road built across the area. Thousands of Afghans would come under the writ of the Afghan central government, and the two key centers of Lashkar Gah, the political capital, and Gereshk, the economic capital, would be linked up.

Babaji was one of four major uncleared areas in central Helmand that were Taliban safe havens. The lower Helmand River area around Garmsir was already in the sights of the recently arrived U.S. Marines, with whom Major Rob Gallimore's X Company was now operating. Ridding the CAT, the triangle north of Nad-e Ali town, of the 150 Taliban who were believed to be operating there was initially to be an objective of Panther's Claw. The toughest nut of all would be Marjah, home of approximately one thousand Taliban; it had already been decided that this would have to be left until after Radford's brigade had departed in October 2009. The brigade assessed Babaji to be a potential base for a massing of Taliban forces to mount a determined attack on Lashkar Gah. On one recent occasion, Governor Mangal had stood in Lashkar Gah with Colonel Greville Bibby, Radford's deputy, and watched as enemy fighters, who had moved south from Babaji with impunity, fired mortars towards them across the River Helmand from the Bolan Desert.

Until July 2008, the Babaji area had been relatively benign because of a deal struck between the British and Haji Kaduz, a local warlord and former Taliban commander, in which he was paid to keep the insurgents out. When the Kabul government withdrew the money, however, Kaduz returned to his former pastimes of murder, drug smuggling, extortion, and kidnapping to pay his men. The people of Babaji turned back to the Taliban to seek protection from Kaduz, allowing their fighters to establish what the Brigade described as a "key INS C2 [insurgent command and control], facilitation, funding and logistic node."

The CAT was also a problem not only for Lashkar Gah, but also for Nad-e Ali. Thorneloe was skeptical about the importance to the Taliban of Babaji, viewing it as essentially an insurgent transit area whose significance was being overblown by the brigade staff. He was keen to clear the CAT, not least to relieve the pressure on Nad-e Ali town and the surrounding villages where the Welsh Guards were fighting, but only if he was given more troops to do so.

According to the brigade's plan, the Welsh Guards would have two central tasks in Panther's Claw: to clear the Taliban haven of the CAT and to provide a "seal" along the Shamalan Canal. By taking control of the canal, the Welsh Guards would provide the anvil against which the hammer of the Light Dragoons Battle Group, pushing in from the east, would crush the Taliban. It was envisaged that the two tasks would be completed sequentially with the Welsh Guards moving from west to east across the CAT. Initially, Naqalabad Kalay and Showal, the seat of Taliban governance, where the movement's white flag flew from a crane, would be cleared. This would be followed by Abd-ol Vahid Kalay and Chah-e Anjir, from which the Welsh Guards would advance to the Shamalan Canal.

But Thorneloe was troubled by the whole concept of Panther's Claw. He viewed it as yet another sweep across Helmand by yet another brigade that would seize ground that the British lacked the forces to hold. He had barely sufficient troops to control his existing area of operations, and Panther's Claw would enlarge Battle Group (Center South), further extending his men. The focus of his efforts, he felt, should be to deepen the Battle Group's influence in the Nad-e Ali district. During the six weeks planned for the operation, moreover, the Welsh Guards Battle Group would not be Brigadier Tim Radford's main effort. Instead, the Light Dragoons would get first call on the very limited helicopter and surveillance resources.

Thorneloe was incensed about helicopters. He knew from his time in the Ministry of Defence that there were too few British helicopters in Helmand, but what infuriated him most was the mismanagement of the few precious air assets that were available. This was, in his view, just as likely to lead to deaths and catastrophic injuries among his troops as the emergence of low-metal-content IEDs. "I have tried to avoid griping about helicopters—we all know we don't have enough," he wrote in his weekly report to brigade on June 5. "But the new Ring Route system for managing them is very clearly not fit for purpose."

He compared the situation in Helmand with the one in Basra in 2006 when he was on the divisional staff and therefore personally able to influence how air assets were used. Then, he pointed out, there were fewer helicopters to support eleven thousand troops—over two thousand more than in Helmand—"and yet we seemed much better off because the SH [support helicopters] was managed in a more sympathetic and efficient manner." Spelling out the risk to life and limb for his soldiers, he concluded: "We cannot not move people, so this month we have conducted a great deal of administrative movement by road. This increases the IED threat and our exposure to it.... The current level of SH support is unsustainable." The brigade staff insisted that the problem lay with Regional Command (South), the divisional headquarters in Kandahar, and that daily protestations about the helicopter situation were being made.

When Hillard and Leach were critically injured on June 12, Thorneloe was even angrier. He told the brigade: "I know it is being worked by your staff—but I cannot report any improvement, in fact I think it has got worse." In the past month, he stated, the number of helicopter flights available to the Welsh Guards had fallen by 60 percent. Because soldiers were now going on R&R, this meant that the amount of road movement he was forced to carry out in an extraordinarily high-risk environment had increased by 75 percent. "The new system cripples our ability to conduct operations and exposes us to a very high IED threat."

Thorneloe was an avid reader of military history, and one of the well-thumbed books on his shelves at home was Norman Dixon's seminal *On the Psychology of Military Incompetence*. In Helmand, he felt, his men were falling victim to a classic case of what Dixon had been writing about.

The debacle over helicopter management on the day Evison died had brought the issue into sharp relief. Thorneloe noted that helicopters were based at Kandahar airfield (KAF), resulting in "a significant number of precious hours ... being chewed up by helis commuting from KAF to Helmand." Instead, he argued, they should be moved to Camp Bastion. About 90 percent of the aviation worked for the brigade, so it made much more sense for the brigade to manage the system, especially when it was "appallingly badly managed at present" by Regional Command (South). The brigade had been making a similar case. When helicopters for resupply were canceled, Thorneloe lamented, he was forever being told this was "because of operations." He mocked the obtuseness of this, pointing out that the cancelations meant that he had to cancel his own operations to free up vehicles for resupply on the ground. "We cannot responsibly continue like this," he thundered. "Quite apart from the effect on operations, the chain of command looks like an ass."

As casualties mounted, manpower became more and more of an issue for the Welsh Guards. The lack of helicopters meant that everyone going on R&R had to be moved by road. It was impossible to predict how long a convoy might take, so men had to depart for Camp Bastion early in case there were IED delays. If a soldier was at CP Haji Alem or Paraang, then they were pulled out several days before they were due to fly from Bastion. On the way back, it could take them several days to get from Bastion to the patrol base. "It was such a drain on resources," recalls Company Sergeant Major Martin Topps of 2 Company. "At one point, I had 35 people [out of 125] away. They were either in Bastion waiting to go or they were in Bastion waiting to come back." Getting the transport to get them back and forth would become an operation in itself.

Two weeks of R&R during a six-month tour had become standard for deployments to Northern Ireland, when transport back to mainland Britain was straightforward. Changing the system was judged to be an unacceptable downgrading of conditions of army service. "Rightly or wrongly, we've always had R&R at some point in the six-month tour," says General Sir Richard Dannatt, Chief of the General Staff and the Army's head. "It's an inconvenience. What this says to me is we shouldn't be deploying at 100 percent strength, and then sending a portion on R & R, so having to operate with 85 percent. We should deploy at 115 percent, so that once R&R kicks in you are at 100 percent."

The broader issue was whether it made sense for an entire brigade to be rotated in and out twice each year. U.S. Marines served a seven-month tour without R&R, while the U.S. Army ran a system of yearlong tours with a single two-week break. Yet the routine of six-month "summer tours" and "winters tours" in Helmand had permeated the British Army. In 2007, Sir Sherard Cowper-Coles, then British ambassador to Afghanistan, had argued vigorously that the brigade commander and his staff should serve longer so that they could pace themselves and there would be greater continuity. "Getting to know the physical and human terrain takes time in a complicated counter-insurgency," he says. Lieutenant General Sir Nick Houghton, chief of joint operations at PGHQ in Northwood, also made this case. But the army hierarchy at the MoD prevailed, arguing that breaking up brigades would undermine the command structure. To the frustration of Cowper-Coles, the system of six-month tours continued "for reasons to do with the Army, not to do with the wider British interest."

Thorneloe had not deployed with even 100 percent of his force, never mind the 115 percent Dannatt thought optimal. He was down one company of 125 men to begin with. Within the companies he did have, he was thirty-two men short. By June, he was fighting a bureaucratic battle to secure an additional three multiples (thirty-six men) promised by the Irish Guards.

These would replace the dozen due to return to the United Kingdom in July, so they could get time at home before coming back to Helmand with their own battalion in 2010. This was being blocked, however, by Land Forces headquarters in Britain. In an email to a brigadier at the headquarters, Thorneloe apologized "for breaking through the chain of command ... but I have done all I can on this through official channels to no avail." He wrote that "given the casualties we have had and the fact we came out below MMS [Minimum Manning Strength] anyway I am desperate for these 3 multiples to deploy ... we are under real pressure and these 3 multiples would make a huge difference." The reason being cited by the brigadier's staff, he said, was "political headroom"—the government's cap of 8,300 on troops in Helmand. Thorneloe protested: "I really do not think that the political intent re headroom will be served by not allowing these guys to deploy. That is about not taking on additional tasklines (which exposes us to strategic risk)."

Thorneloe was fully prepared to take the issue right to the top of the Ministry of Defence, he said. "If it would help I am very happy to engage with old contacts in S of S's [Secretary of State's] office on this." In the end, his machinations were to be of no avail. The extra three Irish Guards multiples were blocked from deploying, and the gap left had to be filled by Battle Casualty Replacements. "All the guys were ready to go and it was stopped I think two days before," says Captain Tim Evans, who commanded the twelve Irish Guards who went home in July. "They had done all their training. But there was a government quota on the number of troops that were allowed."

As well as fighting the Taliban—and lobbying for greater manpower, improvements in helicopter tasking, and new IED countermeasures—being in command of a regiment's single battalion meant that more mundane business had to be attended to. Never a man to do anything by halves, Thorneloe was waging a fierce rearguard—and, again, ultimately unsuccessful—campaign to reverse a decision to move the Welsh Guards from Aldershot to Hounslow in 2011.

To add to his frustrations, Thorneloe's headquarters were still in Camp Bastion, outside the Battle Group (Center South) area of operations, meaning that he was separated from all his fighting men as well as from the Nad-e Ali district governor and officials he needed to work with. With the full backing of the brigade, he had pushed relentlessly for the establishment of his new headquarters in Nad-e Ali town at FOB Shawqat, named after the first Afghan soldier to be killed in Battle Group (Center South). In barely two months, the Royal Engineers had built a new FOB, often under fire, and a date for the move had now been fixed for June 24, the eve of Panther's Claw. In the meantime, going out on the ground for long periods was the only way Thorneloe could command properly. His trips around his area of operations also gave him a chance, however fleeting, to escape the grinding resource issues. Ironically, one of his chief bugbears—the inadequacy of communications—meant that being away from headquarters was even more of a relief.

In May, after being out visiting his men for seven days, Thorneloe reported back to brigade that the trip had been "extremely useful and great fun," though with difficult communications, probably two days too long away from his headquarters. He added: "I am sorry that this letter is a day late— during my visit to 2 Company I was involved in a multiple IED strike which led to a 20-hour cordon operation." This was a reference to his being stranded at Green 5 on May 15. Just after the daisy-chain IED went off, he sat down against a wall with notebook on his knee and his SA-80 rifle and a bottle of water—purified at Camp Bastion—by his side. He was photographed looking as if he didn't have a care in the world. The picture was published shortly afterwards on the cover of the *Leek*, the monthly regimental newsletter. His daughter Hannah later described it as showing "Daddy having a picnic." Thorneloe remarked ruefully to Major Henry Bettinson: "I can't believe that the one photograph they've taken of me is sitting down."

Few could accuse Thorneloe of sitting down on the job, literally or metaphorically. During the Green 5 cordon operation, Lieutenant Charles Fraser-Sampson had briefed a group of guardsmen who had been lying on their stomachs in the dark, looking through the Viper night-sights on their SA-80 rifles at potential Taliban positions. Fraser-Sampson ended his instructions about where the men should move with a curt: "Come on, get up and move." It was only when the guardsmen got up that Fraser-Sampson realized that his commanding officer had been among them, helping provide cordon protection just like an ordinary infantryman.

The IED threat was growing every day, and Thorneloe was worried about the psychological effect this was having on his men. Some might have been skeptical about the prevalence of low-metal-content devices, but the Barma men were in no doubt about the dangers they faced as they took their pigeon steps along the dirt roads. A great believer in the moral component of leadership, Thorneloe decided that he would expose himself to the same risks as his men. He took to riding in the front right-hand seat of the Viking, right over the point in the track where an IED might be detonated. It had become known as the "death seat" because of the number of troops killed while sitting in that spot. Major Rich Hopkins, who commanded the Viking Group at the start of the tour, reflects: "It was a strong shout for him to do that."

The rising casualty rate was something that Thorneloe felt deeply. "Life here is not for the faint hearted," he wrote in the email to the brigadier at land headquarters. "The boys are doing a cracking job and are revelling in the challenge of being on the main effort and in the centre of it all during the Fighting Season. But it has not been without its tragedies."

Thorneloe had come to regard his Estonian company with particular affection. With a professional armed force of just over two thousand, the tiny Baltic nation had committed a significant proportion of them to Afghanistan in 2009, and one of the two companies in the country was under his command. The Estonian A Company, which had taken over from B Company in May, were true warriors. Operating out of PB Pimon, on the northwest edge of the Battle Group area of operations, they were given the tough villages of Zorabad and Chah-e Mirza to control, but their Pasi armored personnel carriers were much in demand for route clearances and convoy escort duties. Having worked closely with the Americans in Iraq, the Estonians were puzzled by the lack of resources in a British battle group, but eventually accepted that items like grenade machine guns were so scarce among the other companies that none could be lent. Thorneloe patrolled with the Estonians and admired their fighting spirit. Before the tour, he had traveled to Tallinn, the Estonian capital, to inspect the Baltic troops who would be under his command. Theirs was a martial culture forged through the domination of the big powers. The grandfathers of some of the troops had been members of the Waffen-SS during the occupation of Estonia by Nazi Germany from 1941 to 1944. A few members of A Company had fought in the Soviet army in Afghanistan following the Russian invasion of 1979. Now they found themselves alongside Afghan soldiers who had fought against them in the mujahideen.

When the Estonians arrived at PB Pimon in mid-May, they were so eager to get into action that they had refused a familiarization patrol with Lieutenant Dave Harris's 2 Platoon. Instead, they wanted to mount a night mission into Zorabad immediately. Captain Alex Bourne, the Battle Group liaison officer, warned Major Tarvo Luga of A Company that this would be suicidal, but he would not budge. Bourne was reduced to stopping the mission by arranging for his corporal to interrupt him talking to Luga with a bogus report that Patrol Minimize (a ban on patrols going out because there were no medical helicopters available) was in force.

The next day, an Estonian patrol did go out into Zorabad. Within fifteen minutes, Lance Corporal Toomas Mikk had been shot five times in the head, abdomen, legs, and arm with an RPK machine gun. "They'd just crashed out of the gate, the Estonian second-in-command wasn't in the ops room because he was manning a machine gun in a sangar and it all started to go to rat shit," recalls Bourne. "That was the big wake-up call. I remember the young bayonets coming back in and they had a look of complete shock and horror and I suspect a certain amount of guilt. From that moment on they were very cautious and totally professional." Mikk was treated at Selly Oak before being flown back to Estonia. Miraculously, he survived. That night, Luga reported ruefully to Thorneloe that the Taliban were "cunning, daring and are not seemingly concerned by the larger force now operating" from PB Pimon and that "significant planning and preparation" would be needed for future patrols. "It is to be a long and interesting summer," he predicted.

On June 15, just over a week after Sergeant Aare Viirmaa had lost both his legs in a compound entrance near PB Pimon, the Estonians were conducting an operation to clear Zorabad village and establish a platoon house there. They had occupied a compound next to Route Taunton, which ran parallel to the main canal through the village, and were conducting a handover from Second Platoon to First Platoon. Master Sergeant Allain Tikko, leader of First Platoon's Section One, crossed the road and looked around the corner of the compound, turning back to brief Corporal Marek Piirimägi. At that moment, a Taliban fighter fired an RPG from more than two hundred meters away that hit Tikko, killing him instantly and seriously wounding Piirimägi and two others. Tikko was a much-loved veteran of Iraq, Kosovo, and a previous Afghanistan tour. "Usually, if someone gets wounded or killed, everybody says that he's the best," says Lieutenant Madis Koosa, First Platoon commander. "But Tikko actually was the best."

As a mark of respect for their dead comrade, Tikko's platoon later took his helmet into the desert and blew it up. Tikko, thirty years old, had been an avid chess player and was studying law in his spare time. Back in Estonia, every military fatality was a major national event. On their return, Tikko's comrades presented his girlfriend and their three-year-old daughter with the onyx chess set he had bought at the Afghan market in Camp Bastion and his law notebooks.

One of the soldiers who treated those wounded by the RPG that killed Tikko was later evacuated after he went into battle shock under fire. In the main, however, the Estonians were remarkably stoic and continued driving around in the lightly armored Pasis. Bourne says that Thorneloe admired the straightforwardness of the Estonians.

"When he gave [Major] Tarvo Luga something to do, Tarvo would say: 'I can do that, that and that but I can't do that—and this is why.' Colonel Rupert would say: 'Fine.' It was quite a lot easier than, dare I say it, dealing with British company commanders who are fighting for their reports and competing with their fellow company commanders in the battalion. They don't let their commanding officer know as much as they perhaps should do because they don't want to be seen as the weak link."

This was a syndrome that some senior British diplomats believed went right to the top of the army and was part of the reason why the Helmand mission had been underequipped and undermanned for the previous three years. Six brigades had already arrived and left after six-month tours. Some diplomats felt that successive brigade commanders had told the generals above them what they wanted to hear, and the generals, also eager to gain plaudits and promotion, had done the same with the government. Thorneloe had viewed the development of the Helmand campaign from the very top of the MoD. Whether or not he shared the opinions of these diplomats, he had decided he was not going to sugarcoat things to please the brigade.

Thorneloe would telephone his wife Sally every three or four days and occasionally mention that he would be leaving Camp Bastion. "He would say: 'I'm going out on my travels tomorrow, Sal,'" she recalls. "I never knew where they were and he never said. Or he'd say: 'I saw so-and-so's husband today.'" During one call, he mentioned that he had spent an evening with Major Sean Birchall. They had marveled at the clarity of the stars in the Afghan sky before sleeping beneath them. "Oh Sal," Thorneloe said. "I slept in a mulberry grove. And it was so beautiful. It was a little like waking in the Garden of Gethsemane. I fell asleep listening to Pachelbel's Canon on my iPod." Sally Thorneloe thought that her husband, who often sounded stressed and very tired when he spoke to her, seemed calmed by the memory of that night. "I found it comforting that he was there in Helmand but he had found this little piece of Heaven."

He neglected to tell her that Checkpoint North was situated one hundred meters from the Taliban front line and had been attacked that same day. IX Company was now split between those at Checkpoint North and those at Lashkar Gah, where the Quick Reaction Force and patrolling force for the provincial capital were located. It was the routine that Birchall, who would rotate people out of Checkpoint North every two weeks, had referred to as "commuting to war"—the creature comforts of Lashkar Gah combined with the full-on action up in Checkpoint North. "We get the best of both worlds— we get a break and a scrap," said Sergeant Owen 75. "You get two weeks of comfort, decent food and a bed and then after getting bored of the people here in Lash who don't go out of camp picking faults with you, you get out on ground again and get involved in crap basically because it was there for us." Birchall told friends that he wanted to change personnel around "to ensure that all get a chance at having fun and games in Basharan." He was delighted at their thirst for action. "I am not joking; the men actually had to pull straws when we had to leave half behind. The losers had to go back to Lashkar Gah. After all that is exactly what we all joined the Army to do!"

Life was good in Checkpoint North. Trees were cut down to improve the arcs of fire and the holes in the compound walls filled with sandbags. Part of the stream was dammed off to create a bathing pool. A mini-gym was set up, and there were boxing matches and press-up competitions between the Irish Guards and the Welsh Guards, as well as "Olympic" swimming races in the stream. Fire pits were dug and a brick stove made. Soldiers would risk getting fired at by the Taliban to run outside and catch passing chickens for an evening barbecue. Chips were fried up in ammunition tins using a basket constructed from Hesco wire. The chips would be served with a "Mick Dip" made from mayonnaise filched from the Lashkar Gah cookhouse mixed with curry powder from the ration packs.

The threat to the east, however, was being ratcheted up. On June 16, Birchall was leading three Jackals southeast along the canal road between Checkpoint North and Checkpoint South when an RPG was fired at the middle vehicle from 250 meters away, exploding on the bank just in front of it. Fortuitously, Company Sergeant Major Andy Campbell, in the rear vehicle manning a .50 caliber gun, was looking at a line of hedges to the east just as the RPG was fired. The rocket moved so slowly he could see it sailing through the air towards the convoy. "I just malleted the hedgeline with the .50 cal," recalls Campbell. "Lewis 65, my vehicle commander, put a box and a half of

GPMG into it as well, so the balance of probability is that we got whoever fired the thing. Then we just put our foot down and got the hell out of there because we were being hit by small-arms fire as well."

That night, Birchall hailed his company sergeant major's "heroic actions" during the attack and stated that the increase in Taliban attention on the road had become "my No. 1 concern." Birchall was buoyed, however, by the progress he was making with the setting up of the school in Basharan, where 150 locals had attended a shura earlier that day. But he noted that one elder had made the case against British forces and the Afghan government because "they had failed to provide anything of benefit" for villagers. "He emphasised that when they were under TB [Taliban] control, things were bad and nothing was provided but at least they had security. Now, there is fighting but still nothing has been done." Afghans were paid to work on the Basharan school and another in nearby Muktah. Birchall also set up local work projects to repair roads, build a footbridge, and install a generator and electric pump. As well as providing jobs, they showed that life could improve without the Taliban.

At 6:05 a.m. the next day, June 17, Captain Mike Brigham, a 2 Mercians reservist mentoring Afghan soldiers, left Checkpoint South with seven British troops and seventeen Afghans. An hour and a half into the patrol, they were ambushed by the Taliban. A section of Afghan troops were cut off from their mentors and pinned down. Their commander, a captain who had already been identified as a weak officer, had gone into battle shock and was cowering on the ground. None of the Afghan soldiers was shooting back and the Taliban fire was intensifying. It was a 270-degree ambush. Fearing they might all be killed, Brigham ran two hundred meters across an open field towards them, firing his SA-80 as he went, in an attempt to stir the Afghan troops into action. Taliban bullets were flying past him, and he could hear Sergeant Marc Giles, his platoon sergeant, shouting at him over the radio: "Boss, you're a f---ing madman." Only one of the Afghans began firing—a sergeant named Ohlab. Brigham, half-Iranian and with a flair for languages, had learnt Dari in Helmand and become particularly close to his Afghan soldiers. A few weeks earlier, he had been about to shave after coming back off patrol, still loaded down by kit. "I had my hands full and Ohlab thought I was struggling," Brigham remembers. "He came over and says: 'It's OK, I'll shave you' in his best Dari. So he shaved me. The boys all thought it was hilarious." After that, Ohlab had become Brigham's right-hand man.

As he reached the Afghan position, Brigham slapped Ohlab on the shoulder to thank him for providing covering fire. At that moment, Ohlab was hit. "The bullet went through his hand and he seemed to shake it as if he'd touched something hot. But it was the round travelling up his arm to his elbow," recalls Brigham. "It then went from his elbow into his chest, right through the other side of his chest and out the other side through his forearm. I put my hands on either side of his chest and he'd gone. He was dead instantly." Brigham called in air support, and the jet overhead counted forty-three Taliban fighters firing on the twenty-four British and Afghan troops who were still alive. Several Taliban were firing from two compounds about 120 meters away. One bullet went through Brigham's rucksack, another knocked an Afghan soldier's helmet off. Brigham knew that he had to get a bomb dropped beside those compounds.

It was what the army terms a "danger close" situation, when friendly troops are very near to an enemy position being attacked. The compound was so close that there was a real possibility that they might be killed when the bomb hit the compound. "This is drop a bomb or die," thought Brigham, working out the grid coordinates of the position between the two compounds. "I want the biggest bomb you've got and I want it on this grid," he told the U.S. Air Force pilot of the B-1 bomber overhead before telling all the Afghans to get flat on their faces. Seconds later, the aircraft dropped a two-thousand-pound GBU-31 right on the spot that Brigham wanted. The walls the Taliban had been firing from were blown to pieces, showering pieces of earth and baked clay onto Brigham's back. At the time, it was the closest to friendly troops that a bomb had been dropped during three years of operations in Helmand.

The bomb gave Brigham and his Afghan charges the opportunity to pull out of the enemy's killing zone. As they did so, the B-1 dropped a five-hundred-pound GBU-38 air-burst bomb that took out some of the remaining Taliban positions. Video footage later showed that at least fourteen Taliban were killed. Brigham ran eighty meters with Ohlab's body and then gave it to Giles to evacuate so he could return to corralling the Afghan soldiers. By this time, the Afghan commander was praying, firing his rifle in the wrong direction, and at one point even pointing his weapon at some of the British mentors. Brigham kicked him and dragged him as he urged the other Afghan troops to follow his withdrawal route. Giles, under fire and shooting his SA-80 back towards the Taliban, then ran three hundred meters with Ohlab's body up to a compound beside the canal road, where a Welsh Guards Mastiff had come to pick up the casualty.

Before loading the body onto the vehicle, they had to clear a path to the Mastiff. And as four of the Afghan soldiers were Barmaing, Giles suddenly had a feeling that something was not right. At that moment, one of the Afghan Barma men stepped onto an IED and was blown twelve meters into the air. The force of the blast sent Giles slamming into a compound wall ten meters behind him. Shards of flesh and bone rained down on Brigham as he watched Giles fly back. He was convinced the sergeant was dead. "F--- off, boss, I'm all right," Giles replied when Brigham shouted at him. They then began organizing the removal of Ohlab's body and the parts of the soldier who had stepped on the IED.

Of the nine British troops who had gone out, only one returned without a piece of his equipment being hit by a bullet. One round had struck the sight of an SA-80 rifle as the soldier looked through it, and others had bullet holes in their trouser legs. The medical helicopter was canceled after it was determined that both Afghan soldiers were dead, causing an uproar among their comrades. "They were left out in the sun like they were pieces of meat," remembers Brigham. "It was terrible." Eventually, the Afghan soldiers drove the bodies to Lashkar Gah themselves. The message that Afghan dead would not be afforded the same respect as that given to British dead was a deeply damaging one. "Rebuilding the relationship with the Afghan National Army after that was the hardest challenge of my tour," reflects Brigham.

Up in Sangin, Major Guy Stone faced similar problems. When an Afghan soldier was blown up by an IED and died after being brought back to the base, Stone radioed for a helicopter, expecting it to arrive within thirty minutes as it would for a British casualty. "There was a delay, and a delay, and a delay, and then it came through, 'Well, actually, no we can't. We'll try and get you one there by tomorrow,'" he recalls. "It was just horrendous. With the Muslim custom being to get people buried within 24 hours, this was not sitting pretty. We were also in 50 degrees of heat [122 degrees Fahrenheit], so there were health and safety and environmental issues to consider." Stone was told by the Joint Helicopter Force (Afghanistan) in Kandahar that Afghans were "priority two." It took seven hours to get a helicopter there, and the issue was pushed by the brigade staff right up to the divisional headquarters of Regional Command (South). "We had to be pretty blunt about it," Stone says.

"We said: 'Look, if this was a Brit, you'd be here now. We've got to treat the Afghans the same because that goes to the core of everything.' The damage that could have been done to our relationship with them was incalculable. We lived, ate and fought together. It was desperate to categorise the dead by nationality."

On June 18, the day after Ohlab was killed, Brigham managed to persuade the Afghan soldiers to patrol with him to the east of the canal road once again. They came under Taliban fire but discovered a number of IED components in a compound that was clearly being used as a bomb factory. Among the components were graphite rods, which were often used in low-metal-content IEDs as the electrical connectors instead of saw blades. That night, Birchall reported back to the Battle Group that it was "increasingly evident" that the Taliban were "intent on preventing our incursion to the east of the canal line." He added that the following day he would be hosting three majors from the Grenadier Guards who were conducting an advance visit to prepare for their deployment to Battle Group (Center South) as company commanders in October. Birchall promised he would give them "the chance to see what life outside a FOB will be like for their men." He relished any opportunity to show off what IX Company had done.

IX Company had received three Jackals and four Mastiffs at the beginning of June. This was a significant boost in terms of mobility and protection because until then Birchall's men had been making do with Snatch Land Rovers and WMIKs—death traps if they hit an IED. At the start of the tour, IX Company had been traveling up the canal road in these unprotected vehicles, journeys that Company Sergeant Major Campbell described as "bum clenchers." The Welsh Guards now had better vehicles, but the IED threat was much greater and the Taliban were able to watch IX Company's patrolling patterns and make their calculations. Across Helmand, the Taliban knew how vulnerable the Jackal vehicle was. After the Hillard and Leach incident a week earlier, the Welsh Guards were under no illusions about the Jackal either.

Birchall set off first thing the following morning, taking the Grenadier Guards officers to see the Basharan school and then to Checkpoint North, where he briefed them on enemy activity in the area. He explained to Major Alex Cartwright, due to take over from him as company commander a little over three months later, why he preferred travel by Jackal. "His personal preference was to be the Jackal commander because he wasn't covered in armour and it allows him situational awareness," remembers Cartwright. "That's how he wanted to do it to be the best company commander possible."

The plan was to travel back to Lashkar Gah via Checkpoint South because a number of Brigham's men needed to have "TRiM" interviews following the traumatic events of two days earlier when they had picked up body parts under fire and come close to being killed. There was also electronic jamming kit to be delivered, and it was an opportunity to show the Grenadier Guards officers more of the area they would be taking over. When Birchall arrived at the base, Lance Sergeant Matt Turrall greeted the company commander. Birchall's face was covered in yellow dust apart from the eyes, where he'd taken off his protective sunglasses. Turrall and another lance sergeant made a joke about the image-conscious major looking like "a bit of a prat." Birchall laughed good-naturedly. "I'm fighting a war, boys," he said. "Don't worry about me, worry about yourselves."

Lance Corporal Jamie Evans 15—"Fift," the friend of Tobie Fasfous who had found out about his death on Facebook—and Lance Sergeant Pete Duffy had driven to Checkpoint North together. Duffy, the vehicle commander, and Evans 15, the driver, were sitting outside the ops room feeding Shit Lips, a mangy mongrel adopted by the Welsh Guards as the base dog, when Birchall came striding out. "Right, Fift," he said. "I'm jumping in with you." Duffy, bumped out of his commander's place, shrugged and said that he would ride with Campbell. The three-vehicle convoy moved off for what was expected to be a simple two-kilometer journey down the straight road to Checkpoint South. There was one known vulnerable point halfway down that could not be seen from either base and was flanked by compounds that had been temporarily occupied by families harvesting poppy and wheat but were now empty. It was at this point that the Afghan soldier had stepped on an IED two days earlier and been blown to pieces.

Leading the way was a Mastiff. In the right-hand seat was Lance Sergeant "Pistol" Pete Owen 39, from Llanelli, the patrol commander and also on Barma duty. In the back of the Mastiff were the three Grenadier majors and two more Barma men, Guardsmen Jason Roberts 34, a native Welsh speaker from Caernarvon, and Chris Davies 35, from Holyhead. The fourth member of the Barma team was supposed to be a brigade education officer, traveling as a rear passenger in Birchall's Jackal. As the patrol was leaving, however, there had been confusion over how many Vallon metal detectors there were. The Afghan soldiers at Checkpoint North had borrowed one, and Lieutenant

Tim Evans, an Irish Guards officer commanding the base, rushed off to see if he could retrieve it. By the time he got back, just after 10:30 a.m., the patrol was already moving off.

It was only when vehicles halted two hundred meters short of the vulnerable point that Owen 39 realized they only had three Vallons. The Barma drill involved ███████████████ to ensure that ███████████████ ████████████████████████. Once they had left the base, however, Owen 39 had little choice but to make do with three. "35 was on the right-hand side of the vehicle, 34 was on the left and I was in the centre covering the overlap myself with the Vallon," recalls Owen 39. "We came to the crater that killed the ANA soldier, we Barmaed over that and then we came to a speed-bump-type thing. 35 and 34, they couldn't see anything. We pushed over and we still didn't detect anything on the Vallons." Roberts 34 was normally a driver. "When I woke up that morning, I thought: 'I've got a bad feeling that something bad is going to happen today.' It was really my first time proper doing Barma." The three edged forward, moving more slowly than normal because Roberts 34 was inexperienced. "There was ████████ ████████████████████████ the Taliban will ████████████████ just to f--- you up," he says.

Once the three Barma men had cleared the vulnerable point and were in view of Checkpoint South, the Mastiff started driving towards them to pick them up. The Mastiff went over the speed bump, and Birchall's lead Jackal, some forty meters behind the Mastiff, moved off too. It was quiet, and there was no one moving in the field. Evans 15, driving the Jackal, had no thoughts about the danger of IEDs because he'd seen the Barma team search the route. As he steered the Jackal around the crater where the Afghan soldier had been blown up, he turned to Birchall and said: "Look at that, that's where he must have been killed." Birchall, manning the GPMG, looked down to his left and exclaimed: "Bloody hell, that was a big one!" At that moment, at 10:55 a.m., the road underneath them erupted (see incident map in Appendix).

In the Jackal behind, Campbell, riding top cover, swiveled his heavy machine gun forward to see a huge cloud of dust. The sound of the explosion rattled his eardrums a split second later. At first he thought it was an RPG because this was the same place where he'd been attacked with one three days before. As the dust cleared, he realized the blast had been too loud for an RPG and that he had seen two objects being flung high into the air. He quickly scanned the mangled Jackal, squatting upright but oddly askew beside the shallow canal which, a mile further south, flowed into the River Helmand. A brief silence descended before the grim realization hit Campbell like a punch in the stomach—those two objects in the air had been Welsh Guardsmen.

12

Big Hand, Small Map

Will you please send me another Daily Telegraph *map of the Northern section of France?*

Letter to his mother from Second Lieutenant Arthur Gibbs of the Welsh Guards, *on the western front, January 18, 1916*

So I unrolled the fifteen-foot map I carried. It was on heavy parchment and showed the Helmand Valley from Girishk to below Shamalon, with river, maps and existing canals plainly indicated ...

Paul S. Jones, Afghanistan Venture *(1956)*

The moments immediately after the explosion were the same as any other in Helmand—confusion, panic, and a gut-wrenching feeling of helplessness. Then a frenzy of activity kicked in, and the next hour seemed to last a few minutes. There was no time for fear.

Company Sergeant Major Andy Campbell jumped out of his Jackal and ran toward Major Sean Birchall's wrecked vehicle. Up on top cover, Guardsman Reece Edwards 90, one of two brothers from Colwyn Bay in the Welsh Guards, was knocked out for a few seconds after hitting his head on his machine gun and came to as the dust cleared. He looked down at where Birchall and Lance Corporal Jamie Evans 15 had been and saw that their seats were empty. He felt spooked and briefly alone before he heard the frantic screams of the education officer, who was also dazed but otherwise unhurt.

Edwards 90 jumped down to see where his vehicle commander and driver had gone. "There's two in the river!" he shouted as Owen 39, followed by Davies 35 and Roberts 34, ran toward him. Down in the canal, about fifteen meters from the damaged Jackal, Evans 15 was bobbing in the water, shouting: "Help me!" Birchall was a couple of meters away, face down and motionless, a pinkish mist tainting the blue-green color of the canal. Both men had been blown more than ten meters in the air and landed straight in the water. Evans 15's friends would later joke about his doing several somersaults and making a perfect entry into the canal. He could not recall anything about the blast itself but remembers waking up under water feeling winded and wondering where he was. His left leg had been badly damaged, his femur broken when he hit the Jackal steering wheel as he was blown out. There was also shrapnel in his hand, elbow, and backside.

Birchall's injuries were caused mainly by the blast itself, which was right underneath his left-hand seat. He also hit his GPMG, later recovered from the canal, as he was ejected from the Jackal. Owen 39 slid down the steep 2.5-meter embankment from the road to the canal and plunged waist-deep into the water to get Birchall. Davies 35, clambering down behind him to reach Evans 15, screamed: "Medic! Medic!" Owen 39 dragged the broad-shouldered, hulking figure of Birchall to the side, pulling off his helmet. His Osprey body armor had been shredded and fell away in Owen 39's hands.

As he arrived and launched himself down the embankment, Campbell could hear Evans 15 screaming in agony while Davies 35 dragged him from the canal. "He's OK," Campbell thought. "Or alive, anyway." Birchall was also alive, but barely conscious. "His legs were just f---ing jelly," remembers Campbell. "From the middle of them down they were just shattered and flopping around." He was groaning. Campbell checked his pulse. Among those who had run over from the Mastiff was Corporal Darren Dunn of 3 Yorks, who had been traveling on the patrol as part of the TRiM counseling team.

When Dunn got there, Campbell was leaning over his company commander and saying in a soft Welsh lilt: "You can't leave me. I can't do this by myself." Dunn could not believe that a hard-bitten, bullet-headed Company Sergeant Major renowned for the sardonic tongue-lashings he delivered to his troops was speaking this way. "I broke down," says Dunn. "I just sat on the bank and couldn't do anything."

Birchall was six feet tall and solid muscle. Wearing full kit and sodden with water, his pulverized legs slippery with blood, it proved impossible to manhandle him up the bank. Dunn recovered enough to run over to the Jackal and grab a wire towrope that was then looped around Birchall's waist. Private Colin Walstow, the medic, wrapped bandages around his legs and applied HemCon bandages. Roberts 34 climbed up the bank to fetch a stretcher. By this time Evans 15, who had suffered a shattered leg and arm and shrapnel wounds to the buttocks, had been pumped full of so much morphine he was laughing deliriously.

Just before Birchall was hauled up the earth bank, Campbell told him: "Don't you dare die on me. I need you." Then he gripped his hand and said: "If you can hear me, squeeze my hand." Campbell recalls: "At the time, I thought he had squeezed back. But the more I think about it now, I believe it was wishful thinking. To be honest, I hope he didn't squeeze because if he did he must have been in agony."

When Birchall reached the top of the bank, he had stopped breathing and the color had drained from his face. By this time, the Quick Reaction Force (QRF), commanded by Lieutenant Tim Evans, arrived in a Mastiff. The education officer was almost hysterical. "I was in the f---ing back! I was in the f---ing back!" he blurted out when Lieutenant Evans asked him what was happening. Turrall, also in the QRF, jumped out of the Mastiff and saw Birchall. He thought back to conversations he had had with the major up at Checkpoint North about how his son Charlie was having difficulties walking. "Oh, he's like his son," thought Turrall. "He's going to walk like his son." Above mid-thigh, Birchall seemed intact. "He's going to make it," the Irish Guardsman reasoned.

Campbell, however, was beginning to fear the worst. The major had stopped groaning, and the company sergeant major could no longer find signs of life. "He hasn't got a pulse," he told Walstow. The medic checked and told Campbell he had found one. Then the pulse went. He gave Birchall chest compressions to restart his heart, but it was too late. "He's gone," someone said as Birchall was lifted into the Mastiff.

On the short journey back to Checkpoint North, Turrall manned the GPMG on the Mastiff and looked down at Birchall, lying at his feet. Walstow was still trying to revive him, but it was clear he was dead. There was silence in the Mastiff. Turrall felt angry and powerless. Up at Checkpoint North, Birchall's body was put under a poncho and carried down to the helicopter landing site ready for the Pedro helicopter. Evans 15, who had been brought up in the QRF Mastiff while Birchall was still being dragged up the embankment, kept on asking: "Is everyone all right?" and was told that they were and he should think about all the pretty nurses in Camp Bastion. As Lieutenant Evans was talking, Evans 15, high on morphine, said: "Hang on. I recognise your voice. Who are you?"

In the Battle Group ops room in Camp Bastion, it was still unclear who was injured. Major Andrew Speed, the Battle Group second in command, was pulled aside by Rupert Thorneloe. "Do you know who the casualties are?" Thorneloe asked. Speed replied that he didn't. "Sean Birchall has been killed," Thorneloe said. "I want you to pack your kit. You're going to take over IX Company."

Sitting on his Bergen rucksack waiting for a Chinook to take him to Lashkar Gah, Speed opened his army-issue spiral notebook and jotted down bullet points for what he wanted to say to IX Company. "Terrible day," he scribbled at the top. Birchall stood out because of his "enthusiasm and drive." He was "inspirational" and had "taken you guys to places none of us anticipated." It was a "horrendous loss for the Welsh Guards" but it was imperative for IX Company to pick themselves up and continue under his temporary leadership until a new company commander was appointed. "Ultimate professional would respect and demand that we carry on in his footsteps—I will not be able to replace a uniquely talented officer but I will try to emulate."

Down in the IX Company operations room in Lashkar Gah, Second Lieutenant Tom Thompson, who had just arrived in Helmand and was standing in as Birchall's deputy, suddenly found himself the acting company commander. As news spread of the death of Birchall—a hugely popular and well-known figure around the base—staff from the brigade began to filter in. Major Mark Jenkins, the brigade liaison officer, who had been commanding the Prince of Wales's Company at the end of the 1990s when Birchall joined as a platoon commander, slipped into the back of the room. "I'm not here to do anything, I'll just sit in the corner," he told Thompson. Jenkins remembers: "Every man jack in the whole world suddenly came along to try and take over so I just growled at anyone who tried to interfere while Tom got his plan together."

Thompson wasn't the only Welsh Guardsman with some unusual pressure from above. As well as his own troops, Campbell had Major Cartwright and two other Grenadier company commanders out on the road. But the three majors immediately deferred to him, letting him take charge of the incident and direct them. "You could say it is a company sergeant major's nightmare to have three majors, all thinking they were born and brought up to command, out there involved," reflects Cartwright. "But there was no grey area. He was in command and we were all very much working to him."

Shortly after the Pedro took off for Camp Bastion at 11:39 a.m. with Birchall's body and the wounded onboard, the Taliban opened fire with AK-47s and PKM machine guns from the compounds and tree lines to the east. Campbell ducked behind a low wall, popping up periodically to return fire. "I'm getting too old for this," thought the company sergeant major, who had turned thirty-eight two days earlier. An RPG flew over the top of him as the Welsh Guards returned fire from the heavy machine gun mounted on the Mastiff and Roberts 34 jumped up on the .50 caliber gun on Campbell's Jackal. The .50 cal was jammed. "It's not working!" cried out Roberts 34 as bullets whizzed past his head. "It f---ing does work!" a guardsman on the road shouted back, climbing up to take over. Roberts 34, who was already experiencing a wave of guilt about having Barmaed over an IED, was almost relieved when the other guardsman couldn't clear the stoppage either. The Taliban fire was accurate, taking lumps out of the red-baked clay wall as Campbell, drenched with sweat and his combats stained with Birchall's blood, flattened his face into the dirt. "I was getting lower and lower as the bullets came closer and closer," he remembers. "It was close enough to make me start digging in with my teeth."

When Captain Mike Brigham heard the "Contact IED, wait out" message on the radio net, he quickly gathered a team together to go out and Barma a clear route up to the convoy. As he moved his Vallon from left to right across the road, he spotted two Taliban, one carrying an RPG and the other a rifle, emerging from the side of a compound eighty meters away. They had not seen him and were clearly moving north to attack the Welsh Guardsmen still on the road. Brigham brought his SA-80 rifle to his shoulder and shot them both dead.

An American MQ-9 Reaper drone, controlled by a "pilot" using a joystick at Nellis Air Force Base just outside Las Vegas, Nevada, was beaming back video footage of the scene to the IX Company ops room. Within a few minutes, Campbell heard what soldiers consider the most wonderful sound in Helmand—he dull "woomph" of an Apache helicopter—and looked up to see a dot in the sky getting bigger. "Thank f--- for that," he thought. "This is going to end soon." The Taliban referred to Apaches as "mosquitoes" and usually fled when they approached. There was a boom as the helicopter launched a Hellfire missile and a rattle as it strafed the tree line with its 30 mm cannon. Then silence.

It became clear that the Jackal, which had lost both its front wheels, could not be towed back to Checkpoint North by a Mastiff, so Campbell set about organizing, removing everything from the vehicle that might be of any use to the Taliban—weapons, ammunition, radio equipment, even food and water. He ordered the bloodstained maps to be burned and even took off a Welsh flag that had been flying from the vehicle—there was no way he was leaving that as a trophy for the enemy. When Brigham got to the scene, Campbell had everything under control. He even reminded Brigham that he had yet to radio in his contact report after killing the two Taliban and then handed him the electronic jamming equipment that Birchall had been due to deliver to him.

Brigham was awed by Campbell, describing him as "the beating heart of IX Company and the iron man that day." He had admired the double act Birchall and Campbell had established as they shaped IX Company into a fighting unit. It suddenly struck him that Campbell had lost not just his company commander, but his friend and companion. "Sergeant Major, are you all right?" he asked. Campbell looked at him, his eyes wide open in a blank stare. "Sir, I am f---ing gutted," he responded. "But my job is to get these boys back and to deliver the equipment that you need to do your job. Thank you very much. You are the first person who has asked me. Now please get your kit and get the f--- back on with your mission."

Once everyone was back at Checkpoint North, Campbell addressed his soldiers. "Right," he said. "It's happened, it's over and we've got to crack on. We've got men in the company now that are injured and men that we've got to get back from here alive. We can't switch off. It's unfortunate, but shit happens. We all knew in the back of our minds that it could happen. It has. Unfortunately it's taken away the boss, but that's life. He wouldn't want us to sit worrying about it. We've got to get on with it."

It was, Campbell says, not an occasion for grand words. "Guardsmen need it broken down. I come from the same background as them. I'm from the same Welsh villages. They take in more from the way I speak, in their language, littered with profanities and whatever, than an eloquent speech." They were barely halfway through their six-month tour, he reflects. "The world can't stop for one man, however important and good a man he was."

It was not until several hours after Birchall's death that Campbell returned to the office that he had shared with him. He was surprised but curiously comforted to see Major Speed sitting in the company commander's seat having just taken over IX Company. Major Jenkins had had the foresight to remove all Birchall's personal effects and pack them into a box to be sent home to his widow. Campbell had spent most of each day with Birchall and had known him since the officer had joined the army nine years earlier. "I couldn't have faced seeing the pictures of his wife and son and the little kid's handprints on the wall. On the other hand, it was strange. It was as if he'd never been there."

That evening, Colonel Greville Bibby, deputy commander of the brigade and a former commanding officer of the Coldstream Guards, arrived at IX Company clutching something in a carrier bag. He ushered Speed and Campbell into their office and beckoned Thompson to come in too. Alcohol was banned at Lashkar Gah, but this was no time for protocol, even for the Guards. Pulling a bottle of Johnnie Walker Red Label out of the bag, Bibby cracked it open, poured generous measures into four plastic cups, and offered a toast. "To the memory of Major Sean Birchall," he said. Bibby was a sunny character and almost invariably smiling. His presence that evening helped lift some of the gloom.

Major Rob Gallimore, now based at FOB Delhi near Garmsir, sixty-five kilometers south of Nad-e Ali, had just got back in after an operation when he saw a lieutenant colonel striding over to him. "Rob, I've got some bad news," the colonel said. "I'm afraid the OC [Officer Commanding] 2 Company, Welsh Guards has been killed. I'm very sorry." It was like a kick in the stomach for Gallimore. Henry Bettinson had two young children, just as Gallimore had, and they had been platoon commanders together. He went and sat in a corner and wept. Just as he began to pull himself together, the lieutenant colonel came running back. "I can't believe I've done this," he said. "It's OC IX Company who's been killed." Sean Birchall was a closer friend than Bettinson, but Gallimore found that his tears were spent. "It was weird," he recalls. "The one that should have hit me much harder didn't at first." That evening, Gallimore sat listening to "Brothers in Arms," the Dire Straits song, on his iPod and thinking about the time he had spent with Birchall.

Some thirty kilometers to the south, Captain Alex Corbet Burcher was standing beside the burns pit at PB Jaker when he received a satellite telephone call from Thorneloe. He and his sixty men were just about to hand over their Nawa area of operations to more than one thousand U.S. Marines. It was an insecure line, and Thorneloe, a stickler for operational security, was so cryptic that it took Corbet Burcher a few minutes to fathom what his commanding officer was saying. "Nine no longer," Thorneloe told him. "I think you're the right man to take over." Eventually, the penny dropped. "Right, sir," said Corbet Burcher. "Bloody hell!" he thought. A few days later he was in Lashkar Gah assuming command of IX Company from Speed.

Taking over from a dead man was an unnerving experience. "I didn't want to sleep in his bed, which they had reserved for me," remembers Corbet Burcher. "I refused to. It's just not good karma." When anyone in the company questioned something Corbet Burcher wanted by saying "Major Birchall wouldn't have done that," Campbell came down hard. "He's dead," he would say. "He isn't here any more so it doesn't matter whether he would have done that or not, Major CB is here now and he's the boss."

As soon as Birchall had been formally pronounced dead at Camp Bastion's Hospital at 12:03 p.m., Captain James Aldridge, the adjutant, telephoned Major Dai Bevan, commanding the Rear Party in Aldershot, to break the news. It was shortly after 8:30 a.m. in Britain. Bevan's job then was to arrange for two casualty notification officers to inform Birchall's widow Jo and to select a visiting officer, who would from that point on be the army's link with the Birchall family through the repatriation, funeral, and beyond. The visiting officer's job could last many months as he helped sort through financial matters, moving out of married quarters, and even future schooling for children.

The notification officers' job was grim but straightforward. They were to knock on Jo Birchall's door and tell her that her husband had been killed in an IED blast near Lashkar Gah and that a visiting officer would be coming to see her very shortly. Normally the visiting officer would be in a car outside the house waiting for the notification officers to emerge, usually after a few minutes, to give him a quick brief about how the next of kin had taken the news.

The Welsh Guards would take great care in matching the visiting officer with the next of kin in terms of background and rank. "This does sound really snobbish and classist but we didn't want a 55-year-old Territorial Army signalman from Croydon," explains Bevan. "Knowing Jo as a 33-year-old public school girl, I wanted someone who could speak her language, someone from the Household Division." The man chosen was Captain Tariro Mundawarara, a Zimbabwean-born Life Guards officer whom Bevan had instructed at Sandhurst. But it took several hours to get Mundawarara cleared as available by his unit, fully briefed, and outside Jo Birchall's house.

By the early afternoon, everything was in place and the two notification officers knocked on the door of Sean and Jo Birchall's married quarters in Putney. There was no reply. All the next of kin in Afghanistan had been briefed by the Welsh Guards to let the battalion welfare office know if they were going to be away from home for an extended period. As the hours came and went, it became clear that Jo Birchall had neglected to do so. These were anxious hours for Bevan because news of Birchall's death was all around the base at Lashkar Gah. Although Operation Minimize meant that all internet terminals and telephones available for the troops to call home were disabled, brigade staff were still communicating with the MoD and various army headquarters in Britain. In addition, there were journalists at Lashkar Gah and Camp Bastion eager to report such a high-profile casualty—only one British company commander had been killed before in Helmand. There was a very real danger that the news would leak out and Jo Birchall would find out about her husband's death from some well-meaning acquaintance anxious to offer condolences.

Bevan eventually telephoned Major Ed Mellish, a Welsh Guards officer who was particularly close friends with the Birchalls, and was told he thought she had gone to spend the weekend with her parents in Essex. It was late afternoon before Mundawarara and the visiting officers were dispatched there. In the meantime, it was decided that Sean Birchall's parents should be informed in case their daughter-in-law could not be found in Essex.

Just after 4:00 p.m., Maureen Birchall looked out of her window in Cranleigh, Surrey, and noticed two smartly dressed men studying the house names along the street. Mrs. Birchall and her husband Brian had brought up five children. Sean had been their second and was the oldest of three boys. Mrs. Birchall thought the men were probably Jehovah's Witnesses and went upstairs. When the knock on the door came, she nearly didn't answer. She opened the door, and one of the men introduced himself as an army major and asked if she knew where Jo Birchall was. Even as she told them that Jo was with her parents, Maureen Birchall had only the faintest inkling of what might be coming. "It isn't bad news, is it?" she asked. "I'm afraid it is," the major replied. Once she had asked them into the house and been told that her son had been killed, Maureen Birchall's first instinct was to offer the men a cup of tea. "How terrible for you to have to come here and do this job," she told them. The major responded gently: "No, we'll make the tea, Mrs. Birchall." As soon as the kettle started boiling, she found herself wishing she'd asked for something stronger.

Maureen's husband Brian was due back any time after spending the day at their eldest child Claire's house in nearby Guildford, doing some work in the garage with a percussion drill he had hired. The two officers drove her over to the house. Brian Birchall heard his name being called by his wife and walked around to the side of the house. "I saw Maureen and these two chaps and I knew within a millionth of a second exactly what had happened," he remembers. The major asked: "Can we go into the house?" Mr. Birchall replied: "We don't need to." He knew his son Sean was dead. The Birchalls waited in the house to tell Claire, who arrived back within twenty minutes after taking her kitten to the vet, and her sister Katherine, the youngest of the five children, another half an hour later (the two sisters lived together). They telephoned their sons—Dominic in Birmingham and Paul, the professional wrestler, in Kentucky.

"Jo still didn't know so I told everyone: 'We've got to keep this to ourselves,'" recalls Mr. Birchall. "I was so numbed that I had two more holes to drill and went back out to the garage to finish them off before we all drove home."

It wasn't until after 7:30 p.m. that Jo Birchall was finally informed. After receiving confirmation that she knew, the Birchalls sent out an email to all their friends telling them that Sean had been killed in Afghanistan. "We are so proud of him," it ended. The following morning, as Brian Birchall drove back from Birmingham after picking up Dominic, it was broadcast on the radio that a soldier in the Welsh Guards had been killed and the family had been informed. "On the Sunday, it was breaking news on Sky, the BBC and everywhere there was Sean's picture and name," he recalls. "Then the world knew."

Informing the next of kin of a death or injury is one of the trickiest and most unpredictable jobs in the army. After the *Sir Galahad* was hit in 1982, scores of families of Welsh Guards had to be told. On the married quarters patch in Pirbright, wives watched from the windows as men in Welsh Guards uniform approached down the streets, passing some houses and knocking on the doors of others. Some fainted with relief when their door was missed. Sue Miles, the wife of Major Martyn Miles, was pregnant with their first child. When she heard the knock on the door and saw the uniforms, she collapsed in the hall. Mercifully, Miles had only been slightly injured, but the shock meant that she nearly miscarried.

Notes taken at the time give a hint of how difficult were some of the visits carried out by Captain Lewis Evans in South Wales. After seeing Gillian Parsons, the mother of the late Guardsman Colin Parsons, in Cardiff it was recorded: "Captain Evans stated that when he left Mrs. Parsons she was very hysterical and still refused to believe it." Evans found that anger, as well as disbelief, was a common reaction. In Port Talbot, he informed the parents of Guardsman James Weaver that their son had been killed. Notes from the visit summarized: "Capt. Evans stated that there was a lot of bitterness when he left. Matters were not made easier by the fact that about 10 to 15 relatives were present."

After Captain Pete Robinson told Sue Mellars, the mother of Drummer Dale Leach, that he had been very seriously injured, she telephoned her ex-husband Lincoln, a shaven-headed, heavily set builder. The situation was already tense because Leach's sixteen-year-old brother had gone into a rage and started throwing things around the house. When Lincoln Leach arrived, he put his nose right up against Robinson's and asked him: "What have you done to my f---ing son?" Robinson, who knew Leach had lost his leg but was unable to tell him that until it was formally confirmed, thought: "I've got to be careful here. He's going to drop the head on me." Robinson escaped unscathed and later saw the family at Selly Oak Hospital once Leach had been flown back. Spotting Robinson, Mrs. Mellars ran over, hugged him, and said: "Thank you very much for coming to the house. I'm sorry about what happened." Robinson, who had never expected or thought he was owed an apology, felt tears welling in his eyes. Lincoln Leach later helped raise thousands of pounds for the Welsh Guards Afghanistan Appeal.

It was never determined whether the IED that killed Birchall, buried in the road next to the speed bump, was a low-metal-content device, but Brigham's discovery of the graphite components nearby the day before suggested that it was. The battery pack for the IED, which should have been picked up by the Vallon, had somehow been missed. There were questions

about why only three men had been Barmaing and why Birchall and Evans
15 had not been wearing seatbelts. Like most British soldiers in Helmand,
they had found the seatbelts too restrictive when used with body armor to be
worthwhile.

In hindsight, IX Company had been setting patterns by routinely sending
a resupply convoy down to Checkpoint South shortly after one had arrived
at Checkpoint North. This would have given the Taliban time to arm the IED
by connecting the battery pack just before the Mastiff and two Jackals set
off. The incident also appeared to show a new step in Taliban sophistication—
the pressure plate that set the IED off was placed towards the center of the
road. This meant that the IED-proof Mastiff's wheels passed outside the plate
while the more vulnerable Jackal, with a narrower wheelbase, went right over
it.

After Birchall's death, Corporal Dunn, who had rushed to the canal and
watched Birchall die, put in his notice to leave the army and said that he could
not face patrolling. "I haven't gone out on the ground again," he said just
before the end of the tour. "I refused. I joined the Army to go to war. And I
volunteered to come out to Helmand because I wanted to experience
something I never had before. Be careful what you wish for." He had had
trouble sleeping because he kept replaying the experience of watching Birchall
die and questioning each element of that day. "Even though you can't change
what has already happened, you are still sitting there thinking about whether
we could have done anything different to change the situation and how it
ended up." His mind had become trapped in a loop of circular thinking that
offered no resolution. "There's a lot of variables that could maybe have altered
the outcome. But you can't change it, so there is no point. Everybody at that
moment in time thought they were doing the best thing. There's no blame for
it."

But Guardsman Roberts 34, the Barma man who had stepped on top of
the IED and had not detected the battery pack, could not help blaming
himself. "I missed it, I don't know how," he said eight months after Birchall's
death. "I always start thinking about: 'If I wouldn't have missed that, he'd
still be alive.' Everyone tells me: 'It's not your fault' but I still feel f---ing upset.
I think: 'If I'd just done this, or that, I could have changed it.' I just wish I
could change it but at the end of the day I can't, so I've just got to live with
that." He underwent several TRiM sessions and felt that they were helpful.
"They tell you to talk about that incident, and go through it from when you

woke up all the way to after the incident. They get you to say how you're feeling, how you're eating. And then they come back and see you six weeks later."

Rupert Thorneloe was deeply affected by Birchall's death. In a report to brigade the next day, he expressed his dismay that it was "only by luck that OC IX Company's widow found out about her husband's death from the Chain of Command" because the news had first spread through Lashkar Gah base seven or eight hours before. "This—clearly—is what we must avoid at all costs. I believe we need a fundamental rethink about our processes to control access to this information before Kinforming [informing of next of kin] has taken place."

Professionally, Birchall's death meant that Thorneloe had to abandon his preferred solution for ███████████████. The Welsh Guards had lost a man who might well have been their commanding officer in six or seven years' time. Thorneloe also bore the heavy personal burden of any commander who loses men in war. He had schemed and pulled strings to get Birchall out of his job at PJHQ back into the battalion and selected him to take over IX Company. As the parent of young children himself, Thorneloe was hit hard by the fact that Birchall had left behind not only a widow, but also an eighteen-month-old son who would never know his father. "God, the battalion will need to look after Charlie," he told his wife Sally, when he telephoned her to say that he was all right after news that a Welsh Guardsman had been killed. "Look, Rupe," she replied. "We ought to just wait until everybody is back and see how many children there are and then something can be done about it."

Sally Thorneloe remembers her husband as being in "quite a dark place" that night. "He was so shocked Sean had been killed. He was very, very shaken and sounded terrible on the phone, almost speechless. He couldn't believe it."

By this time, it had become clear that the brigade was determined to launch Operation Panther's Claw and that Thorneloe would have to put his deep misgivings aside. Large swaths of central Helmand had been divided into "operations boxes" designated by the brigade staff as "Chaucer," "Tennyson," "Tolstoy," "Dickens," "Sartre," "Orwell," and—for the more modern-minded—"Rowling." The air space above the Welsh Guards Battle Group area had been carved up into sections dubbed "Ship," "Scot," "Snarl," "Seedler," "Smart," and "Savoy." The key "ops box" was Tennyson, which stretched from Spin Masjid in the east to the Shamalan Canal in the west. Though there were contingencies for stopping short of the canal, the brigade plan was for the Light Dragoons to meet the Welsh Guards at the waterway.

To Thorneloe's frustration, for the next six weeks the Welsh Guards would no longer be on the main effort. No longer Battle Group (Center-of-the-Universe), the brigade staff officers denied almost every request Thorneloe made for additional resources. The email response to Captain Ed Launders, Thorneloe's ops officer, when the Battle Group asked for an additional company was: "No.... Why would you get one?" A request for a vehicle logistics group to resupply his new areas was met with: "No.... There are other BGs [Battle Groups] on this op as well you know."

One evening in early June, Thorneloe had sat with Captain Alex Bourne, the liaison officer with the Estonians, at PB Pimon. Bourne, an affable and discrete officer who had already served tough operational tours in Iraq and Helmand, found himself being used as a sounding board for his Commanding Officer. They were the only two British officers in Pimon that night, and Bourne was surprised that Thorneloe was in the mood to let off a bit of steam. They discussed at length Thorneloe's worries about Panther's Claw. At that stage, Thorneloe still held out hope it would not go ahead. "I fear this is becoming the typical Herrick thing where every tour there's a big operation, you lose several people doing it and it does a certain amount of good but not really anything long-lasting," Bourne recalls him saying, "I don't think we've got enough to do the job." Thorneloe added: "If at the end of the day I get told to do it, I'll do it. But sadly people are going to die and I'm not sure it's going to be that beneficial." Thorneloe vented his deep frustration over the lack of helicopter availability. "He was depressed by the whole thing," says Bourne. "It was winding him up."

Thorneloe was very anxious to move his Battle Group headquarters to FOB Shawqat, not least because of what he viewed as an unhealthy culture at Camp Bastion. "His view was there were lots of people in theatre in Helmand but not a lot of people actively patrolling and having an effect," says Bourne. "Sometimes there would be dozens of people playing football outside Colonel Rupert's room. It seemed like there were five people doing two people's jobs. Colonel Rupert said it was a complete disgrace that there were people sitting around doing sod all when there were guardsmen on stag in the sangar, then out on patrol, then sleeping for two hours and then doing the same all over again."

Captain Scott Broughton, a Welsh Guardsman serving as a liaison officer with the BRF [Brigade Reconnaissance Force], also discussed the plan with Thorneloe. "He had a number of issues but his main concern was the lack of helicopters," Broughton remembers. "If you're moving troops around in an area that's IEDed then you need to do it with helicopters. If you haven't got helicopters, you're driving. If you're driving, you're going to hit IEDs."

As June 25 approached Thorneloe, against all evidence, seemed to believe that the brigade staff might see reason and shelve the operation. "He really dragged his heels over the whole Panther's Claw land-grab stuff, which he thought just wouldn't be able to be sustained," remembers Major Mark Jenkins, his brigade liaison officer. Jenkins, an urbane and cultured officer, had left the Welsh Guards in 2001 after serving as adjutant, aide-de-camp to General Lord Guthrie when he was chief of the general staff, and Prince of Wales's Company commander. During his eight years outside the army, he had taught religion and philosophy at Oundle and King's School, Canterbury, as well as studying in Russia. He had decided to rejoin the army temporarily for the Helmand tour before returning to civilian life to take up a post as an advisor to Prince Ghazi bin Muhummad of Jordan. As someone who had been slightly senior to Thorneloe—he was a near contemporary of Brigadier Radford—and was essentially outside the army system, he was a natural person for Thorneloe to unburden himself to. As Thorneloe's eyes and ears at Brigade, Jenkins had sight of the wider picture as well as an outsider's perspective on operations. When Jenkins was a battle captain in the Battle Group ops room at the start of the tour, Thorneloe had often confided in him about his frustrations and dilemmas. Whenever Thorneloe visited Lashkar Gah, there were long conversations in which the pair tried to put the world to rights.

Captain James Jeffrey, a Queen's Royal Lancers officer working as a tactical air controller in Battle Group headquarters, believed that Thorneloe earned a reputation in the brigade as being difficult because he was unafraid of telling things as he saw them and was above toeing the party line. "This found its culmination with Panther's Claw," he remembers. "Panther's Claw was the Brigade's baby, their ready-made, large-scale operation that was 'on the shelf' before deployment and good to go once we were in Afghan. They did not enjoy hearing it criticised." Jeffrey agreed with Thorneloe that what was needed was consolidation in the Nad-e Ali district through small, battle-group-level operations. "We didn't need a macro-level, grand Brigade operation that was basically your good, old-fashioned assault in the style of the history books. Everything about it, such as the Chinook insertion, smacked of sexy planning, in order to allow Brigade to have its moment of glory, its big opportunity to flex its muscles. But Thorneloe favoured the less dramatic type of business."

Just before Operation Panther's Claw was due to start, Thorneloe met Brigadier Radford for a long and frank one-to-one discussion. Thorneloe had concluded he did not have enough men to carry out the brigade plan of clearing the CAT and putting in a block on the Shamalan Canal. He feared that clearing the CAT would be illusory because he did not have enough troops to hold Showal, Naqalabad Kalay, Abd-ol Vahid Kalay, and Chah-e Anjir. The Taliban would simply infiltrate the "cleared" areas behind the Welsh Guards as they advanced to the canal. Radford's argument was that it was tough but it could be done, and clearing the CAT would make establishing the block on the canal easier because it would greatly reduce the opportunities for the Taliban to attack from the west. "It is vitally important to the operational design of Panther's Claw that you do this," Radford said. But Thorneloe would not budge. "With the resources I have got, I cannot do it," he replied.

It was a tense moment. Radford asked Thorneloe to leave his office for a cigar while the brigadier considered how to resolve the impasse. Thorneloe had left it very late in the day to take this stance. Radford knew that some on the brigade staff would contend that he should just give Thorneloe an order and be done with it. If Radford took this route and Thorneloe still insisted he could not carry out the mission, then the brigadier would have no option but to fire Thorneloe and elevate Major Andrew Speed in his place.

Radford called Thorneloe back in and told him that he would agree to postpone the clearance of the CAT until after October, when the next brigade came in. In hindsight, Radford says he was "really pleased" that Thorneloe had the "enormous moral courage" to resist the pressure to just salute and get on with it. "It was disappointing for a lot of people who had put a lot of effort into it," says Radford. "But for me what was more important was that I brought people with me in this very, very complicated and dangerous operation." The sole job of the Welsh Guards would be to put in a block on the Shamalan Canal. "I can do that," Thorneloe said, smiling, as he left. "Thank you, sir. You're a gentleman." Thorneloe had got what he wanted from the meeting. It was more than he might have expected. Afterwards,

Thorneloe told Jenkins that the plan had been changed. "Are you happy with what you've got?" Jenkins asked him. "Well, it's doable," Thorneloe replied.

Though he had not expressed them to Radford, however, Thorneloe also had deep concerns about the finer points of the task of blocking the Shamalan. It was uncharted territory where British troops had not been before, and detail was sparse. He told Jenkins he had proposed a *coup de main* operation to the brigade staff in which the Welsh Guards would be inserted onto the canal by helicopter, but he had been told by the RAF that the presence of pylons made this impossible. Thorneloe felt there was not a firm grip on the practicalities of putting in the block along the Shamalan Canal. He told Jenkins that he feared this was a classic example of the "big hand, small map" syndrome in which a lack of command of detail is covered up by a lot of hand-waving during briefings.

With the tension subsiding, Thorneloe and Jenkins laughed at the suggestion of a re-creation in Helmand of the *Blackadder* episode set in Elizabethan England in which the protagonist is about to explore the "Sea of Certain Death." Just before Blackadder embarks on his journey, Lord Melchett, one of the Queen's courtiers, hands him a scroll of parchment and says: "The foremost cartographers of the land have prepared this for you. It is a map of the area that you'll be traversing." When Blackadder unrolls it, he finds the map is completely blank. Lord Melchett adds: "They'd be very grateful if you could just fill it in as you go along. Bye-bye." Thorneloe had a deep respect for Radford, whom he viewed as a man of integrity as well as considerable military acumen. He knew too that Radford felt the loss of every soldier in his brigade as intensely as the Welsh Guards mourned the deaths of Fasfous, Evison, and Birchall. His beef was with certain brigade staff officers.

Crucially, Thorneloe felt there had not been a proper terrain analysis of the state of the road alongside the canal and its suitability for heavy vehicle movement. The thirty-one-page Panther's Claw "mission pack" issued by the brigade contained virtually no information about the Shamalan. Harman remembers Thorneloe telling him of his concerns one night at CP Paraang. "He didn't believe in the plan for the canal," Harman says.

13

On the Canal

How can we take this pass which is so narrow? It is reported that the enemy are at the exit in great numbers. Will not the horses have to go in single file and the soldiers likewise?

Counsel of Thutmose III's officers, *on the eve of the Battle of Armageddon, 1479 BC*

Oh Gods! From the venom of the Cobra, the teeth of the Tiger, and the vengeance of the Afghan—deliver us.

Old Hindu saying[1]

Down in Khowshaal Kalay, Captain Terry Harman called a small shura. The "Old Man of Paraang," he told the village elders, was leaving. "I am travelling to Kabul on your behalf," he said. "I need to speak to the governor to get more electricity, more money, and in my absence this young man will act on my behalf." He gestured towards Captain Harry Parker of B Company, 4 Rifles, who was taking over from him as influence officer. The elders, sitting cross-legged under a camouflage net sheltering them from the fierce midday sun, looked skeptically at the white-haired Welsh Guards officer. They had already seen Americans, Russians, and the Taliban arrive, promise to stay, and then leave. It came as little surprise that the British were no different. "When are you going to be back, old man?" one of the elders asked. "I don't know," replied Harman, aware of the piercing gazes he was being fixed with. "That was hard because they had trusted me and I knew I was never going to go back there," he explains. "I let the people down." Harman and the rest of 2 Company were departing because they were needed to spearhead the advance up the Shamalan Canal.

This was June 22, 2009, the day that Major Neil Bellamy's B Company took over from 2 Company in PB Silab, CP Paraang, and CP Haji Alem. Major Mark Gidlow-Jackson's R Company, also from 4 Rifles, had already relieved Major Giles Harris's Prince of Wales's Company in Nad-e Ali. Even a six-month tour was barely enough to build meaningful relationships in Helmand, but two of the three Welsh Guards companies in Thorneloe's Battle Group were shifting areas after only ten weeks. B Company and R Company were part of the election support force dispatched to Helmand to bolster troop numbers for the August 20 presidential elections. Operation Panther's Claw had been "sold" by the brigade partly on the basis that it would provide security for the elections, which it was hoped would provide a boost to the shaky legitimacy of the Afghan government.

The arrival of 4,500 U.S. Marines in Helmand—half the size of the entire British force—was affecting the political as well as the strategic equation. "It was really important that we got control of the situation as the Americans came in," explains Brigadier Radford. Brigadier General Larry Nicholson, the new U.S. Marine commander in Helmand, was, he says, keen to launch a major operation to take Marjah, the most significant Taliban stronghold in Helmand, and then move southeast to Garmsir.

Nicholson agreed with Radford that clearing the Helmand River valley south of Lashkar Gah was a more urgent priority than dealing with Marjah. He and Radford's staff, five of whom were seconded to Nicholson's headquarters, then synchronized Panther's Claw with the U.S. Marines. The British operation would happen at the same time as Operation Khanjar (Pashto for "Strike of the Sword") in which the Americans would sweep the Taliban away from Nawa, Garmsir, and the surrounding areas. Khanjar, launched on July 2 with four thousand U.S. Marines and four hundred Afghan troops, was to be the biggest offensive airlift by the U.S. Marines since Vietnam. Radford was concerned that he had relatively limited support from above, particularly in terms of provision of Afghan forces. The situation was complicated by the fact that Major General de Kruif, his divisional commander at Regional Command (South) in Kandahar, went home on routine leave just after Panther's Claw began. To Radford's relief, however, de Kruif's American deputy Brigadier General Mick Nicholson was able to give the British additional resources just at the moment when it was most crucial.

Radford concedes that with Panther's Claw "if you were to do this mathematically we didn't have nearly enough resources" but believes he had created conditions in which the Taliban felt isolated. He also had the "top cover" of the operation being endorsed by Air Marshal Sir Jock Stirrup, the chief of the Defence staff, and Gordon Brown, the prime minister. "It was important to do something that summer because there was a degree of stalemate in the campaign and we needed to kick-start it again," Radford says.

Two of the four aims of the Brigade media plan, issued two weeks beforehand, were to "deliver positive media coverage of a successful op" and to "protect the reputation of the British Military." The others were to maintain operational security and emphasize the role of Afghan security forces.

The preparations for Panther's Claw tested the Welsh Guards Battle Group's logistical limits. It required reshuffling the area of operations like a pack of cards to get the right elements in place by D-Day—June 25. One Battle Group movement of 2 Company involved ninety-six vehicles navigating high-risk routes in and out of the Green Zone. As well as the reliefs in place of the Prince of Wales's Company and 2 Company by 4 Rifles, the Battle Group headquarters had to move from Camp Bastion to FOB Shawqat. Big resupplies were sent into CPs Paraang and Haji Alem while PB Jaker was handed over to the U.S. Marines. Ever on the hunt for additional manpower, Thorneloe had spotted Normandy Company, Territorial Army reservists from 4 Mercians, languishing on perimeter security duties at Camp Bastion. Through a characteristically persistent campaign of cajoling and maneuvering the brigade staff, he managed to get sixty-five men from Normandy Company into the Battle Group to reinforce IX Company.

For the brigade, Panther's Claw began just before midnight on June 19 when 350 Black Watch troops from the Royal Regiment of Scotland were landed by ten Chinooks—six of them American—at Luy Mandah at the top of the Shamalan Canal. Luy Mandah, site of a drugs bazaar where the Taliban operated with impunity, had become totemic to the local insurgency. The task for the Welsh Guards, starting six days later, was to advance seven kilometers up the canal from its base at Yellow 14 to link up with the Black Watch. The bridge across the canal there was designated XP-1, while Yellow 14 was XP-14. In between them, there were twelve other crossing points that were to be either destroyed or held so that no enemy forces could flee from Babaji to the east or infiltrate from the CAT to the west. The Black Watch were to clear down as far as XP-3, and the Welsh Guards were to clear up from Yellow 14 to meet them. The brigade plan was to drive the Taliban out of Babaji so that stabilization and development projects could offer choices to the people there and a chance to align themselves with the Afghan government.

Thorneloe's plan was for the Prince of Wales's Company to break into the town of Chah-e Anjir and then push east to establish a foothold on the south of the canal. This would facilitate a "forward passage of lines," with 2 Company passing through to advance up the canal road—Route Cornwall. Major Giles Harris, commanding the Prince of Wales's Company, was told to seize XPs 13 to 10—blocking 13 and 12, destroying 10, and holding 11— as a precursor to the 2 Company advance up the canal to seize XPs 9 to 4. The Prince of Wales's Company was to end up taking over XP-9 because 2 Company was too stretched.

The brigade plan was for the Shamalan Canal to form the western side of a triangle bordered by the Nahr-e Bughra Canal to the north and the River Helmand to the south. Inside it, the brigade staff briefed, would be a "gated community" from which insurgents would have been driven out.

Now that he did not have to clear the CAT, Thorneloe calculated that he would take over Chah-e Anjir, a Taliban stronghold where a valiant band of Afghan police had been holding out. Chah-e Anjir was on the southeast corner of the CAT, some 1.5 kilometers due west of XP-11. It would give the Welsh Guards some protection on the west flank during the advance up the Shamalan by hindering Taliban forces attacking from the CAT. The brigade staff were concentrating on Panther's Claw to the east of the Shamalan Canal and had relatively little interest in Chah-e Anjir. But Thorneloe had long had his eye on it as a way of establishing a line of security north of the Nad-e Ali town that would protect the district center. There had also been indications that locals in Chah-e Anjir, who remembered the Americans of the Helmand and Arghandab Construction Unit (HACU), would welcome British troops. Thorneloe decided, therefore, that the Prince of Wales's Company should occupy Chah-e Anjir as well as seize XPs 13 to 10. Implicit in Thorneloe's plan was that Harris should leave enough forces in Chah-e Anjir to keep the Taliban at bay so that the town could be properly held later on.

The day before D-Day, Bettinson was making his final battle preparations at FOB Shawqat when he was alerted that two vehicles from a logistics convoy had been attacked at the nearby Blue 25 junction. The whereabouts of the convoy personnel were unknown. Bettinson and a small team jumped on three Vikings and headed out to Blue 25. There they found one truck on fire and another abandoned after driving off the road and into a shallow canal. The Royal Logistic Corps personnel, some of them female, had fled from the vehicles and were hiding behind a wall. "They were all pretty shaken up and the girls were very teary," remembers Bettinson. After evacuating the convoy personnel, the Taliban attacked again from two flanks as Bettinson ran between the two vehicles, rescuing electronic jamming kit and other sensitive equipment. There were no casualties apart from a large number of ration packs—and a "comfort box" of Thorneloe's, containing items that had been sent out by his wife Sally. When Bettinson returned to Shawqat he had to break the bad news to Thorneloe: "I'm sorry, sir," he said. "It's gone up in flames."

With 2 Company now in Shawqat, Thorneloe learnt more about the exploits of Harman at Paraang and CP Haji Alem. There had been strain between the two men after Thorneloe had told Harman he would not become quartermaster. It was a decision that was too late to alter, even if Thorneloe had wanted to. But there were indications he was beginning to reassess Harman's worth. "You know, maybe I misjudged Terry," he told one officer.

Shortly after Bettinson departed on Panther's Claw, Thorneloe discussed the forthcoming operation with Tom Coghlan, Kabul correspondent for the *Times*, in his new home of FOB Shawqat. Thorneloe was sitting by the crumbling walls of Nad-e Ali's nineteenth-century British fort reading a yachting magazine by the light of a red-tinted head torch as Coghlan approached. Thorneloe had swapped his comfortable Portakabin at Camp Bastion for one of a row of camp beds underneath a poncho. Food was from ration packs, and when he wanted to take a shower, he had to fill a bag with water from a jerry can and then hoist it up by a string. Lavatory facilities were even more basic—a "desert rose" urinal or a "wag bag" for defecating in that then had to be placed on a large pile to be burned.

Despite his outspoken internal opposition to many aspects of Panther's Claw and his near-despair at the under-resourcing of Battle Group (Center South), Thorneloe was the soul of discretion in the interview. The Taliban were light and quick on their feet, but they were having trouble with their logistics, he said, and their only option was to outlast NATO forces. "Their campaign is a delaying operation. Their military professionalism is a myth. They make mistakes."

When asked about resourcing, Thorneloe said that "the training and kit are outstanding." In narrow terms, he was being honest—his main criticism was not the poor quality of kit (with the exception of the Bowman radios) but the lack of it and, in the case of helicopters, abysmal management of scarce resources. "The mission itself is one that people do believe in," he emphasized. Again, this was true. Thorneloe himself believed that the NATO mission in Afghanistan was both morally just and in Britain's interests; indeed, it was this belief that fuelled his anger at the way the campaign was being waged.

There was no doubting, either, Thorneloe's pride in commanding the Welsh Guards in battle. "After 9/11, this war has real resonance and it is the top end of soldiering, a real test," he said. "We are conscious in the Welsh Guards that we are writing regimental history here." It was also clear that he had been deeply affected by the losses of Fasfous, Evison, and Birchall, as well as those in the Battle Group from outside the regiment. "We are a one-battalion regiment," he said. "Everyone knows everyone. It is a big hit to lose someone, but there is an absolute understanding that the mission is vital, and that those we've lost wouldn't have wanted to be elsewhere—and they would want us to see it through."

At 9:20 a.m. on June 25, 117 men from Major Giles Harris's Prince of Wales's Company headed northeast from Shawqat and drove straight into the town of Chah-e Anjir without a shot being fired. As the convoy of nine Vikings, four Jackals, and six other vehicles arrived, it was greeted by Mirza Khan, the local police chief, a hard man of few words whose dark eyes stared out from behind a heavy beard. Khan, who always wore two bandoliers of ammunition across his broad chest, had held the line in Chah-e Anjir. American police mentoring teams and Estonian troops had briefly occupied the town before, but Harris had slipped in three weeks earlier to tell him that the British were going to come again, and this time they would stay. The pre-operation visit had been unannounced, but rather than the typical shambolic and drugged-up Afghan police unit Harris had expected, Khan and his minions were alert, in uniform, and resolute in their determination to oppose the Taliban. Thorneloe had proposed that Harris make the visit—it would exert psychological pressure on the Taliban and let the people of Chah-e Anjir know that they would soon have a choice to make (see Operation Panther's Claw map in Appendix).

It had been a curiously nineteenth-century scene as the understated British major embraced Khan, who had all the charisma and trappings of a tribal warlord. "We'll fight together!" Khan declared. Telegraphing their intentions had certainly carried some risk, but when the Prince of Wales's Company arrived, it was in such force that the Taliban had little option but to watch and wait to see what their next move would be. The sudden advance of the Welsh Guards into the heart of the town had completely surprised the enemy. As Harris climbed down from his Viking, the police chief came out, hugged him, and said: "You've come! You've come!" Essentially, Harris had managed to steal Chah-e Anjir from under the noses of the Taliban. In the future, British officers would talk of the counterinsurgency stages of "clear, hold, build" being modified to "steal, hold, build" by incorporating a deception plan at the outset.

Harris's men were now inside the old headquarters of HACU, which would become their company patrol base. Just before Panther's Claw, Thorneloe had told Harris that he considered taking Chah-e Anjir to be much more important than what he had been ordered to do on the Shamalan. "By the way, Giles," he said. "Although Brigade doesn't see it as a priority, I do. I want you to build a patrol base in Chah-e Anjir and hold the town." The base was later named Shahzad—Pashto for "Prince"—after the suggestion of Glendower was vetoed on the ground that while undeniably Welsh it would have no resonance for Afghans and could not be translated into Pashto.

It was now dusk, and Chah-e Anjir was eerily quiet. The Prince of Wales's Company had yet to complete the main part of their mission, the seizing of XP-11 and XP-14 on the canal. Although they had got into the old HACU headquarters without being attacked, there was no guarantee of getting out again safely. The Taliban would routinely attack the HACU headquarters from directly outside the gate and had free run of the town itself. One option was to use the road to the south of Chah-e Anjir and loop east and then north up the canal, but Harris felt this would be too predictable and would alert the Taliban of the British intention to take control of the Shamalan. Instead he decided to head directly east to the canal, patroling through the streets of Chah-e Anjir itself and then across the fields with Vikings for protection. "They're coming from behind us," a Taliban commander said on his walkie-talkie. "We're facing the wrong way. We need to change our positions." The deception had worked.

"It's the most wonderful thing to hear your enemy talking on the radio like that," says Harris. "It was one of those rare moments when you felt you were the cavalry coming over the horizon." One Platoon captured XP-14 without a shot being fired. Two Platoon's advance to Crossing Point 11 was more complicated. Sergeant Matt Parry 700 and his men were stranded in an irrigation ditch overnight as Taliban from no more than one hundred meters distant blazed away at them with RPGs, AK-47s, and machine guns. At last, American jets came in to drop three five-hundred-pound bombs on compounds the Taliban were using, enabling Parry 700's men to advance to XP-11.

Perhaps the biggest risk Giles Harris took that night was to leave Dave Harris and just a handful of men occupying the HACU headquarters. If the Taliban had decided to mass and attack the Welsh Guards there, it would have been a bloody fight. But Giles Harris had calculated correctly that the Taliban would be preoccupied with defending the canal.

Harris's next move was to fan out from the heart of Chah-e Anjir into the town and secure it using the elite "Tiger Team," drawn from the Afghan army and police, to fan out into Chah-e Anjir alongside a stabilization team. They told the townspeople that the Welsh Guards were there to stay and they began drawing up a list of projects that the British could fund and facilitate.

With the Prince of Wales's Company holding two key positions at the base of the canal, the stage was now set for 2 Company to advance up the Shamalan. It was a move that was akin to sticking a dagger seven kilometers long right into Taliban territory. The first Welsh Guards actions of Panther's Claw, the taking of Chah-e Anjir, Yellow 14, and XP-11, had been relatively straightforward. As soon as 2 Company set off north at 6:33 a.m., however, it became apparent that Thorneloe's concerns about the Shamalan Canal had been justified. He had been right to question the quality of the terrain analysis, which had been performed almost exclusively from aerial photography.

The plan had been for eight Scimitars from the Light Dragoons to provide flank protection for the main 2 Company advance along Route Cornwall, the track running along the west side of the canal, by fanning out to the west. The Scimitars would then move up beside the main 2 Company force, comprising Mastiffs and Vikings along with guardsmen Barmaing and moving on foot. The problem was that the track was too narrow to fit two vehicles side by side. An irrigation ditch and compounds right next to it meant the Scimitars could not shadow the advance. Instead, they would have to take their place in a single-file snaking convoy up the track.

It was also apparent that the canal track was much higher and more exposed—2.5 meters above water level—than had been anticipated. This meant that there was a perilous drop into the canal from a track that was barely four meters wide in places. There was precious little room for error—Mastiff vehicles were 3.2 meters wide and Vikings measured 2.2 meters. "The canal filled us with dread," remembers Major Charlie Burbridge, commanding the Royal Tank Regiment's Egypt Squadron of Vikings. "The track itself was no different than Yorkshire, frankly, but we knew that if we came off it then we were in an armoured vehicle in water and those two don't mix. That was the thing that scared us." The men of Egypt Squadron—known to the Welsh Guards as "the Tankies"—were soon to have their fears realized.

Moving up Route Cornwall, two Mastiffs were in front, followed by two Vikings, the Scimitars, and then more Vikings behind. At the head of the column were seven Barma men. Two Company was going to have to proceed up the canal like a collection of waddling ducks, presenting a mouth-watering target from either side. Another surprise was that the water was not three meters deep, but half that. This meant that a man six feet tall could wade across, and two could carry a motorbike—the preferred means of travel for Taliban fighters. The brigade's notion of a "gated community," a concept introduced in Iraq by General David Petraeus, was therefore problematic from the outset. Although some perception of a security bubble could be created, it would be temporary at best and there could be no "seal" on the canal. It also proved at that stage difficult to monitor the population with biometric testing, planned as part of a "human terrain-mapping" process.

For Terry Harman, who took his place right at the front of the 2 Company advance in a five-man team protecting the Barma men, the canal instantly presented a nightmarish vision. "When I think of a canal, I think of the Basingstoke Canal or the Brookwood Canal," says Harman. "Lovely barges. But it was nothing like that. Was it f---. It was open either side and raised up. I felt lonely and I felt vulnerable. I looked around me and there were boys far younger than me very scared. And I was scared too."

There at the bottom of the route up the canal was an old man sitting by a woodpile. "Don't go up there," he told Harman through Dai the interpreter. "You may die today. The Taliban are waiting up the road to ambush you." Minutes later, an RPG whooshed overhead and small-arms fire began to come in. "Once we got onto the canal, we were at the point of no return," recalls Harman. "We had to go forward."

It soon became apparent that the Taliban attacking them from either side had superior military tactics to those around CP Paraang and CP Haji Alem. These appeared to be foreign fighters with battlefield experience. They would hit the Welsh Guards, then peel off, get into cars or motorbikes, and attack again further up. Groups of fighters were being dropped off strategically, and those wounded were being picked up fast and driven off. "Rules of Engagement" meant that the Apaches could not engage once a wounded man was put in a car—and the Taliban knew this. Just as he had at CP Haji Alem, Harman moved out into the open in order to draw fire from the Taliban. He was concerned that guardsmen were hanging back and 2 Company was losing momentum. "My attitude was, I'm 45, I've lived half my life and it's been a good life," remembers Harman. "For a 19-year-old, maybe he was thinking he'd hardly lived his life so why run after this maniacal old guy?"

At one point, Harman shouted to Fraser-Sampson: "Engage, now!" and ran forward. As the Taliban opened fire and he flung himself into a ditch, he heard a voice behind him saying: "Sir, I'm with you." It was Lance Corporal Phil Lewis 88, who had Barmaed towards Leach's leg back at Green 1 a fortnight earlier. A powerfully built battalion rugby player, Lewis 88 stuck with Harman all the way up the canal that day. They reached one compound and hit the ground, laughing from a combination of fear and adrenaline, as bullets flew through the doorway. "The rugby season starts shortly doesn't it?" Harman asked the corporal while they took cover. "As soon as this tour's over, sir," Lewis 88 replied. Trapped in the compound for thirty minutes, the pair discussed rugby, golf, and their children before debating how long the canal was and whether they would survive until nightfall.

Seven hours into the battle, a young guardsman turned to Harman as they sheltered by a compound wall. He was weeping. "I'm burned out, sir," he said. "I can't do this any more." Harman ushered him into a Viking and told him not to worry and that he had done his bit. "That boy had done a lot," recalls Harman. "He has got issues now because for him that was the one that broke him. It wasn't the incident the day before or four days before or two weeks before but the accumulation. That one was the last straw. There was no shame in it. Everyone had their limit."

For Guardsman Caswell, the team medic with 7 Platoon who had treated Lieutenant Evison back at Haji Alem, emerging onto the canal was like being plunged into the heart of a battle in which the enemy had all the advantages. Led by Captain Anderson as they emerged from their Viking to patrol eight hundred meters up to XP-7, the platoon's relief at being out of the cauldron of the vehicle soon evaporated when the Taliban opened fire. "We were being hit from about 200 metres away and the Taliban were just leapfrogging from compound to compound. There were two RPGs fired at us from either side of the canal simultaneously. We'd been attacked every day at Haji Alem but I'd never experienced anything like this. People call the Taliban ragheads and stuff but they are good at what they do. They knew our Rules of Engagement and everything and that we couldn't shoot them if they didn't have a weapon." As the fire intensified, Caswell ran out of the killing zone where the Taliban bullets were landing but dropped his SA-80 and had to run back and get it. As he hid in an irrigation ditch, a Predator drone launched a Hellfire missile at the compound the Taliban were using, and there was a brief respite that allowed the platoon to get into XP-7.

Guardsman Chris Davis 51, a new addition to 7 Platoon, was in the back of a Viking that moved off the road and crashed through walls and over trees as the Taliban attacked. The vehicle stopped short of a group of four compounds, and the guardsmen in the rear cab jumped out. As Davis 51 and his comrades lined up beside a compound wall, they were told they were "going in red"—storming the buildings with bayonets fixed, guns blazing, and grenades being thrown into each room before entry. "Fix bayonets!" came the order from Anderson, which was passed down the line. "That really gets your heart racing," remembers Davis 51. "You know you're going into a building and you've no way of knowing what's going to be behind that door." He was detailed to clear the second compound with another guardsman. "Grenade!" he shouted as the man ahead of him booted down the door. They both ran into the room, spraying it with bullets. There was no one there. "They'd scarpered," says Davis 51. "They'd seen the Vikings coming across the fields and knew it was time to leave or they were going to get it." It was the same in all four compounds. Company Sergeant Major Martin Topps was concerned about fire discipline. There were bullets going everywhere. "Lads, this isn't a turkey shoot!" he shouted. A few seconds later another door was kicked down, and there was a loud squawking and a flurry of feathers as several turkeys panicked. The guardsmen burst out laughing and, almost in unison, shouted at Topps: "It is a turkey shoot!"

Guardsman James Francis, the Silab mortarman, Guardsman Simeon Howells, and Guardsman Luke Langley, found themselves cut off from 7 Platoon comrades, who were lying flat on their faces in a field with bullets whistling over their heads. The three guardsmen were among those who clambered onto a roof and laid down a relentless weight of fire onto the Taliban fighters who were attacking the guardsmen in the field from a nearby tree line. Pausing to put another magazine into his SA-80, Francis remembers thinking: "Our boys are stuck in the field. We need to give them a chance to get out."

The only mercy of the initial advance was that no IEDs exploded on the west side of the canal, though the counter-IED team identified and either removed or detonated several. The Taliban appeared to have miscalculated, expecting the Black Watch to move south down the east side of the canal, and had therefore laid more live IEDs there. They had not anticipated the Welsh Guards moving north up the west side. In addition, a deception operation by the BRF around the Nahr-e Bughra Canal to the north of Chah-e Anjir drew some of the Taliban in the CAT away from the Shamalan.

As the Barma team advanced under sporadic fire, the Welsh Guards responded with rifles and machine guns while an Apache helicopter strafed Taliban positions. Adding to the cacophony, the Taliban exploded IEDs on the east side of the canal. It was like a scene from the western front, with the Welsh Guards moving slowly, ducking, flinching, and sometimes crawling as ordnance exploded all around and AK-47s cracked in the distance, sending bullets towards them. As ever, the radios didn't work, Bettinson recalls. "Comms were fantastically crap and the only way I could coordinate things was walking up and down and briefing individual commanders face to face. This was highly repetitive and obviously you were always running the risk of someone trying to catch you with a bit of 7.62."

That night, 2 Company halted at a compound beside XP-7. The sky was illuminated by flares and red tracer bullets arcing in the sky. In the distance was the crump of GMLRS rockets, precision-fired from Camp Bastion, and the sputter of 30 mm rounds from Apaches. Occasionally, a few moments of relative calm would descend, only to be quickly shattered by the whoosh of a Taliban RPG or the crack of AK-47 rounds.

The next day, the IEDs started blowing up. Two Company found itself fixed at XP-7 with lines of supply stretched and communication back to brigade and Battle Group patchy at best. Some vehicles were struck or broken down and had to be towed or pushed to the side. There were only a few places where vehicles could turn, but they needed to go back to pick up more men and supplies. Some crossings had been "denied"—blown up, simply dismantled or covered with razor wire—but it was already apparent that there were too few men to guard the route. The Taliban were coming in behind the Welsh Guards, stealing the razor wire and wading or using improvised rafts to get across the canal. Back in brigade headquarters, Thorneloe remarked ruefully to Major Mark Jenkins that he knew all was not well. "The Taliban is standing back there watching us all trundle up the Shamalan Canal and they are not attacking us seriously because they think there is some f---ing master plan, some trick," Jenkins recalls him saying. "But there isn't."

Some of the Brigade staff officers blamed Thorneloe for his battle group's slow progress. The plan to proceed up the canal so methodically and predictably was his, they argued. More creative officers might have largely kept off Route Cornwall, moving up to the crossing points by probing from the west. Of course, they said, clearing the CAT first would have made taking the canal easier.

In Battle Group headquarters, Captain Jeffers, the tactical air controller, watched a video downlink from a drone that showed real-time images of people traversing the canal at an unidentified crossing point. "After all the effort, the companies sweating away and pushing through up the track and yet there it was, literally in black and white through the downlink that the canal hadn't been secured. I did not know whether to laugh or cry at that image. I am sure that in the Brigade planning room, talk of 'securing the flank' sounded right and proper. It's what we have been doing for time immemorial. But it could not be done on the ground with the numbers available."

The Recce Platoon had occupied compounds beside XPs 8 and 9 in an attempt to control the canal behind the main advance. Considered the elite platoon in the battalion, it had been attached principally to 2 Company throughout but had often been split up for different tasks. Its snipers had been used in Paraang and CP Haji Alem, teams had laid ambushes at Green 5 and some had been assigned to Vikings. To the disappointment of its commander,

Captain Tom Spencer-Smith, a softly spoken officer who was himself a trained sniper, the Recce Platoon had never been used in its primary role—moving ahead into enemy territory in front of the main force.

On the night of June 28, the order came through for the Recce Platoon to move up to XP-7 and then after a short pause onward to XP-4. It was a chance to operate ahead, just as they had been trained to do. The difficulty was the additional amount of kit they were carrying, including sniper rifles, tripods, Javelin missiles, electronic jamming kit, radios, Bergen rucksacks, rations, water, and ammunition. This amounted to more than ninety kilograms per person, more than the body weight of an average soldier, and meant that the kit at least would have to be moved by vehicle.

The number of IEDs found by the counter-IED team and the number of Taliban attacks meant that 2 Company was already a day behind Thorneloe's schedule. There was intense pressure from both brigade and Battle Group to step up the pace of the advance, but Bettinson would not rush the counter-IED team. Attempting to force them to move faster, he feared, would cause them to miss an IED, which would then detonate. He would then probably be dealing with a casualty extraction probably under enemy fire, because the Taliban were closely monitoring every movement, preparing to flood the area with fighters once the Welsh Guards were fixed. Two Company moved six kilometers from XP-10 to XP-1, compared with the 1.75 kilometers of the Prince of Wales's Company advance, which stopped at XP-10. The dangers of using white light at night meant that the counter-IED team searched only in daylight hours, usually in the searing heat. "We could not go any faster without increasing the risk," remembers Bettinson. "And it was an incredibly risky operation anyway."

A Viking troop was assigned to take the Recce Platoon forward, but the vehicles sent up to get them were delayed. When they arrived at XP-9 at 4:00 a.m. on June 29, it turned out that several Vikings were loaded with other supplies, and there were only two available to take the fifteen men and all their kit from the Recce Platoon. Lieutenant Piers Lowry was in charge of the move. The Tankies manning the Vikings had been driving almost continuously for more than a day and some had not slept for three days. Spencer-Smith and Color Sergeant Shane Pullen, his second in command, protested vehemently that it was not safe to overload the vehicles. Several of the Welsh Guardsmen wanted to walk the few hundred meters from XP-9 to XP-7. Lieutenant Terry Newton, a wiry Ulsterman commanding the Viking troop, wanted to do the move in two trips, but there was pressure from 2 Company headquarters to move up in one go; Newton reluctantly acquiesced.

There were snorts of disbelief from the Welsh Guardsmen as they looked at the space they had to cram into. Spencer-Smith, Pullen, and five others were in the second Viking. The remaining eight somehow had to squeeze into the third. Looking into the vehicle, Guardsman Carl Thomas 08 was at the far back on the left, next to Guardsman Mark Biggs, from Pontypool, and then Guardsman James Barber. Thomas 08 and Barber had both had a close call when the daisy-chain IED had exploded next to them after they had Barmaed over it at Green 5.

Next to Barber, by the door, was Sergeant Steve Young, who had taken over from Leon Peek at CP Haji Alem on the day Lieutenant Mark Evison had been mortally wounded. A full sergeant at just twenty-six, Young, from Tonypandy, was viewed as a bright prospect, perhaps even a potential regimental sergeant major. He had nearly missed Panther's Claw after being stung in the eye during a patrol between Paraang and CP Haji Alem. After his eye became inflamed and started producing cheesy deposits, he had been flown to Camp Bastion. Once there, a maggot was extracted from his eye, where a botfly had deposited larvae. Young, a section commander, was keen to return to duty and take part in the operation. Opposite him was Lance Corporal Dean Cometson, from Caerphilly, his second in command. Both Barber and Cometson had recently married and were expecting their first children, respectively. Their laps were piled with Bergens, Javelin tubes, and electronic jamming packs. On top of these lay Lance Corporal Ray Hill, from Swansea, and Lance Corporal Gareth Evans 88, from Newport. "Are you shitting me?" Young had said to Hill as the corporal crawled in over the kit and then lay on his back with his face a few inches from the roof. The last man due into the vehicle was Guardsman Adam Kastein, a rail-thin sniper who had performed as a Pontypridd stripper back in the CP Haji Alem *Squaddie's Got Talent* contest. "I'm not going in there," he said. "I'm claustrophobic. I'll sit on top of the vehicle."

As the Viking moved off just after 4:30 a.m., Kastein was sitting on the roof with his legs dangling through the top cover hatch. "Imagine if the f---ing thing rolled now," said Young. There was some nervous laughter.

In the Viking behind, Trooper Gaz Owen had the same thought. He and the other Viking drivers had been at the wheel almost non-stop for twenty-nine hours, ferrying people up and down the canal, over to Chah-e Anjir, and down to Shawqat. Once this short journey to XP-7 was completed, they had been promised some rest. Up ahead was a slight curve in the road and a Viking parked hard up against a compound wall. The gap between the parked vehicle and the edge of the canal was little more than the width of a Viking. "It would be very easy to roll down there if you weren't switched on," Owen said through his headset to Corporal Kev Williams, commander of his Viking. Just as he finished speaking, now more than two minutes after setting off, he saw the ground underneath the rear cab of the Viking in front of him begin to crumble. The rear cab, top-heavy with extra bar armor to defend against RPGs as well as all the men and kit loaded in, started to topple over. The driver tried to steer back, in but it was too late.

Inside the rear cab, Hill felt a lurch, and the Viking hit what he thought was a pothole. The vehicle tilted but he expected it to move back and right itself within a second or so. Cometson, facing away from the canal, felt himself go back as the Viking tilted. He looked at Young and said: "F---!" as he realized the vehicle was toppling over. A split second later, Young tumbled towards him, his head hitting Cometson's chest. On top, Kastein and Trooper Martin Morrin, the Viking commander, realized the vehicle was rolling and jumped off into the canal. The front cab of the Viking slid towards the canal but got stuck on part of a sluice gate. The rear cab rolled over completely and landed on its roof at an angle in the water. Inside, everything went dark, and there was screaming and shouting as men were pinned down by kit and struggled to free themselves. Thomas 08 had been knocked out by an electronic jamming pack, and Barber was smashed in the face by a machine gun. Hill shouted: "Calm down! Calm down!" but the pandemonium only intensified as the realization hit that the Viking was in the water.

Cometson could only move his right arm and was stuck completely upside down. He felt moisture on the top of his head and thought he'd been injured and it was bleeding. The moisture started to rise, and he thought: "F---, that's a lot of blood" before he quickly concluded that there was too much of it for blood and it had to be water. The water rose over Cometson's eyes, nose, and then his mouth. All the screaming had stopped, and there were just muffled sounds and movements as if under water in a swimming pool. Cometson reached into the pouch in his body armor, pulled out a photograph of his wife, Arianna, and an ultrasound picture of his unborn daughter, and clutched them to his chest. He felt lethargic and proceeded to pass out.

Young had ended up with his face down in the bottom corner of the rear cab. He was panicking and pushing pieces of kit away as the water came in. He tried to feel for the door handle, but there were too many obstacles in the way. "I can't die this way," he said to himself as the water came over his head, and he thought of his mother and his girlfriend Emma. For some reason, he counted the number of gulping breaths he took, each one filling his lungs with water. The first gulp created a cold, burning sensation in his lungs. The water was filled with brake fluid and diesel, and some in the cab had urinated and soiled themselves. By the fourth gulp, the burning had subsided and his breathing felt almost natural.

Just as the thrashing around subsided, Young felt a hand touch his arm and then grab his hand. Cometson had felt alone as death approached. Young didn't know whose hand was clutching his, but at least during his last moments he would experience the comfort of holding one of his comrades as he died too.

Barber felt the grip of the hand he had grabbed go limp and fall away. "He's gone," he thought. He felt a stab of sorrow and then calm. His body relaxed, the pain from his face and back evaporated, even the weight of the equipment seemed to disappear. "This is it," he said to himself, thinking of his wife and his unborn son. "I'm going to miss him being born." He wondered if he had sorted things out at home. "Is all my insurance done? All the bills paid?" Then the thoughts ebbed away and he felt light-headed. There was a sparking sensation in his eyes.

Suddenly there was noise again as the door sprang open. Barber's drift into unconsciousness was halted as light flooded in and arms plunged into the water, pulling kit out of the way and grabbing at the seven trapped inside. Williams, commander of the Viking forty meters behind, had seen the vehicle go in, told Owen to drive up to it, jumped off, and slid down the bank. By the time he reached under the water and pulled the door handle open, the seven had been trapped inside for at least two minutes. The first thing he saw was kit everywhere—electronic jamming packs, rucksacks, rifles, helmets—which he just pulled out and threw into the canal. The first man he grabbed was Cometson, who came to retching and vomiting on the canal bank. Ten seconds after Williams got there, more soldiers began to arrive. Soon there were nearly a dozen, pulling people out and forming a chain up the bank to the medics.

Young had come to when the door came open. It felt like dawn breaking. But his arm was stuck, and Williams couldn't pull him out. Hill and Evans 88, who had both managed to pull their heads out of the water and reach the air pocket in the three-quarters-filled rear cab, were clambering over him, pushing his head back under water. "Leave him, he's gone," Young heard someone say. Hill was in severe shock. "What happened? Where's my weapon?" he was saying. Three men were now out and on the bank. Next to come was Barber, grabbed by Guardsman Carew, one of the two Welsh Guardsmen who had been so traumatized by picking up body parts under fire when Marine Jason Mackie had been killed back in May. Young, normally unflappable, was freaking out, fearing he might drown every time his head was plunged back in the water as Williams and Spencer-Smith tried to free him. Trooper Tom "Mo" Morris, his nails red raw, unhooked Young's body armor and helped haul him out as Young screamed: "Get me f---ing out of here! Get me out of here!"

The scene on the bank was chaotic. Several Welsh Guardsmen were in shock at seeing their friends drown, and some were weeping. Others were angry, jumping to the conclusion that the driver of the submerged Viking had fallen asleep or lost concentration. As Trooper Owen, driver of the Viking behind, ran back to get a stretcher from his vehicle, a young guardsman confronted him. "Where the f---'s the driver?" he said. "I'm going to kill him!" Owen, a burly, heavily tattooed Brummie, was having none of it. "You know, you aren't helping anyone so just f--- off," he said, brushing past him.

Amid all the confusion and shouting, Williams was trying to establish whether there was still anyone left in the Viking. The move had been so disorganized that no one knew who or how many men had been in each vehicle. "They're all out," one guardsman said. But Williams wasn't satisfied, grabbed a torch from him, and went into the cab. Holding the torch in his mouth, he used his hand to feel around and put his head underneath the water to try to see. Others were behind him as he shouted: "F---ing hell, I've got one here." It was Biggs. Williams pulled him out and continued to feel around until he found Thomas 08, who was caught up in a rifle sling. Once he was out, Williams did a final check that there was no one left. When Biggs came out, his pallor was a blue-gray, his tongue distended, and his eyes dry and staring straight ahead. After thirty seconds of CPR, he coughed and vomited. He was alive and being comforted by Carew. Shortly afterwards, Biggs went into acute shock, his whole body shaking.

Initially, few thought that Thomas 08 would make it. His eyes had rolled back, his tongue was so distended it was touching his earlobe, and he was completely blue. Guardsman Chris Davis 51, one of those helping on the bank, looked at him and thought: "Shit, we've lost another boy." Captain Spencer-Smith, exhausted from pulling men out of the Viking and certain that two or more of his guardsmen were dead, sat on the bank and wept. It took Williams and two medics several minutes to revive Thomas 08, and he began coughing up blood. Carew had fetched a neck brace for Cometson, who had cadged a cigarette and began puffing away. It was the first time he had ever smoked.

The casualties still had to be taken in another Viking to complete the three-hundred-meter journey to XP-7, where the medical helicopter would fly in. It took a lot of persuasion to get them back into a vehicle exactly the same as the one that had nearly been their watery grave a few minutes earlier. The Tankies agreed that the back door could stay open, but when the Viking set off at speed, the fear of another roll into the canal took hold of those in the rear cab. Young grabbed the legs of the top gunner and screamed: "F---ing slow down! Stop! Stop!" Hill was suffering a panic attack, gasping for breath. The Viking stopped a hundred meters short of XP-7. "I've got to get out," said Hill, climbing down through the open door. Hill and Young then walked the last hundred meters. They no longer cared about the possibility of getting shot or blown up by an IED. All they wanted to do was ensure they did not go back into that canal.

As the Pedro Black Hawks arrived overhead at 6:07 a.m., the Taliban attacked. One Black Hawk landed under AK-47 and RPK fire while the other, supported by an Apache, opened up on the Taliban positions. The Taliban appeared to have been taken by surprise when the Viking went into the canal. Many of those helping in the rescue had thrown off their body armor and helmets as they went into the water, and if the Taliban had opened fire, they could have killed up to a dozen men and probably ensured five of the seven inside the Viking would have drowned.

There were eight Recce Platoon casualties from the incident plus two Tankies, and 2 Company was fixed at XP-7 for another day. It was the last straw for Bettinson, who decided that he wanted Lowry transferred outside 2 Company. A few days earlier at Camp Bastion, just before Operation Panther's Claw began, Bettinson had had a long talk with Thorneloe about who might replace Lowry. "We went through the entire officers' mess as to how we could skin this particular cat, maybe send him to a different job and get someone loaned to us," Bettinson recalls. "But then we didn't want to dump a bad egg on another battle group." Bettinson had reluctantly agreed to keep Lowry and try to make things work, but the Viking incident had changed his mind.

Bettinson says he had instructed Lowry the night before not to browbeat the Tankies into using their Vikings to transport the Recce Platoon if the vehicles were overloaded or the drivers needed rest. Confronted by Bettinson, Lowry said he had not forced the Tankies to do anything. "I was only a lieutenant, not a field marshal," Lowry says, looking back. "I asked the troop commander if he could do the move in one go and he said that he could. Afterwards, he told me that he was happy that it was just an accident. Somebody's trying to cover up their own failings."

Bettinson says that his snap conclusion was that Lowry had ignored him and this had contributed to the subsequent events. "We'd had a civilian shot down at CP Haji Alem, we'd had traumatic amputations and other injuries after possible G2 [intelligence] not being passed on, now I had boys in the f---ing water, two unconscious, another five petrified and lost classified kit. I'd got to the stage where I'd decided he'd got to go." Bettinson was going to inform Thorneloe of his decision two days later when the commanding officer was due to visit 2 Company on the canal. In fact, Lowry had been cleared by the Military Police of any wrongdoing in the killing of the civilians at Haji Alem. His friends said that there were many frictions within the command group of 2 Company and that some were trying to make Lowry a scapegoat.

Towards midday, after the ten casualties had been evacuated by the Pedro, Lowry was at XP-7 washing his feet in a stream beside Guardsman Caswell, the 7 Platoon team medic who had treated the mortally wounded Evison at Haji Alem. Caswell's second child was about to be born, and he had been denied a request to fly home for the birth because he could not be spared during Panther's Claw. "Ah, Caswell, so you're going to enjoy your paternity leave are you?" Lowry teased. A downcast Caswell replied: "Sir, you know I'm not getting it." Lowry chuckled as Caswell grimaced. It was all good-natured banter.

Five minutes later, Lowry was beside a Panther command vehicle, parked on a mound because it was the only place where the Bowman radio worked. Caswell and Guardsman Luke Langley, who had also been down in CP Haji Alem with Lowry, were nearby. "He was stood on the road having a fag,"

Langley remembers. As he looked up at Lowry, the Taliban opened fire. Lowry heard the crack and a thump of a shot but ignored it—on the Canal, there were warning shots being fired all the time. Then there was a second crack and thump, considerably closer. Before he could take cover, there was a burst of three or four rounds, and Lowry felt an excruciating pain in his knee. "F---, I've been shot!" he shouted. "Medic! Medic!"

He was dragged behind a compound for Corporal Jamie Craig to treat him as a full-scale firefight with the Taliban raged.

The lieutenant was loaded into a Viking and driven down to the helicopter landing site. Bullets bounced off the side of the vehicle as he was driven down to where the Pedro was about to land. As the Black Hawk disappeared into the distance, Caswell giggled to himself. Lowry thought he'd had the last laugh when he was ribbing him about his lack of paternity leave, and minutes later he'd been shot. "I thought that was quite fitting to be honest. F---ing suicide Lowry! Mad bastard but a good bloke."

The next thing Lowry remembers is waking up to an attractive Canadian nurse bending over him and Sergeant Steve Young, and half a dozen other Welsh Guardsmen, all in wheelchairs, sitting around staring at him. It was the Recce Platoon members who had been hauled out of the submerged Viking a few hours before Lowry had been shot. "They were all crowded around me, poking me, trying to get me because they wanted to play basically," says Lowry. "They'd been there for a while and they were bored."

In the early hours of the following morning, as he lay in the Camp Bastion hospital a few beds from Lowry, Sergeant Steve Young wrote a poem about being trapped inside the Viking. It began:

> Metal grinding, metal twisting,
> Carnage within the metal box,
> Seven souls trapped in the darkness,
> Screams and wails, a doomed man's last effort,
> Held down, helpless, the water starts to come,
> It trickles down my face. At first denial,
> Then panic, terror, as the water claims me,
> Fear floods my body, as does the water,
> I feel the cool water enter my being,
> Fingers probe at my arm, searching,
> A hand grasps mine, calmness comes.

The poem ended with a tribute to those who had saved him:

> Our gratitude to you cannot be measured,
> Thank you my brothers.

14

Top Cover

L ieutenant Colonel Rupert Thorneloe was struggling to find the right words. Sitting in his cubicle beside the new operations room in Shawqat, he scrunched up yet another piece of paper and tossed it toward the bin. Fighting was continuing on the Shamalan Canal, but even in the heat of battle this was something he wanted to get right. He was agonizing over the letter of condolence to Major Sean Birchall's widow Joanna, in which he wanted to tell her of the role he had played leading IX Company, the difference he had made in Afghanistan, and the way in which her husband had died. Thorneloe was meticulous about condolence letters and determined to avoid the usual clichés and empty phrases. He knew that Jo Birchall would cling to the contents of the letter for many months and possibly years.

Thorneloe had decided that the next morning, Wednesday, July 1, he would travel on a supply convoy to visit 2 Company on the Shamalan Canal. He had despaired over the Viking roll incident and felt intensely concerned that 2 Company appeared to have ground to a halt at XP-7. To add to his frustration, the electronic jamming packs that Corporal Kev Williams had thrown out of the Viking as he began to get the seven Welsh Guards out were still missing. During the evening conference call, Thorneloe had made clear to Major Henry Bettinson his displeasure that the jamming equipment remained unaccounted for. If any of it fell into Taliban hands, they could give the enemy invaluable knowledge about the British jamming frequencies being used to counter radio-controlled IEDs.

The previous night, Thorneloe had smoked a Villiger cigar with Major Charlie Burbridge, commanding the Tankies, and discussed the events of the day. Thorneloe had been awed by accounts of the heroics of Williams. "I need to speak to Corporal Williams because he is an absolute hero," he said. "He deserves a medal." Burbridge, who had been up on the canal, told Thorneloe that he thought 2 Company were isolated and having a rough time and would probably be boosted by seeing their Commanding Officer. "Henry [Bettinson] in particular would benefit from an arm around his shoulder," he added. Thorneloe had already concluded that it was essential he visit his men. "I'll come up with you the day after tomorrow," he said. Thorneloe knew that young guardsmen were overwhelmed with fear at the prospect of traveling in Vikings and that the Shamalan Canal was already taking on an aura of almost mystical foreboding. Seeing their commanding officer traveling up the canal in a Viking—the supposed "coffin on tracks"—would provide a steadying reassurance.

The day before he left for the canal, Thorneloe had asked for Williams to be sent to meet him at the Shawqat operations room. He shook the corporal's hand and said: "Thank you very much for saving the lives of my men." He then added, deadpan: "However, on your little rescue mission you managed to lose six ECM packs, two LAWs [Light Anti-Tank Weapons— Javelins], four rifles and a couple of pistols." Williams responded that saving the kit hadn't been his priority at the time. "Yes, of course," Thorneloe responded, smiling. "I wasn't suggesting otherwise. You did the right thing— men before the kit."

Thorneloe needed to talk through the Panther's Claw plan with Speed, his second in command, who had just returned from IX Company after his spell in charge following Birchall's death. The two men sat down on some empty Javelin missile tubes. Thorneloe was intending to be out on the ground with the Welsh Guards for ten days, and, with communications expected to be as poor as always, Speed would have to hold the fort in the ops room. When the discussion turned to his journey the next morning, Thorneloe said: "I'm going to travel in the lead vehicle and I'm going to do the Barmaing."

The resupply convoy was just the sort of dangerous "administrative move" that Thorneloe had railed against in his report to the brigade a few weeks earlier. It is doubtful whether Thorneloe would have traveled to XP-7 in a helicopter even if one had become miraculously available on the day. But if British helicopters had not been such rare commodities in Helmand, then resupplies would have been conducted by air rather than road. In any case, the question was academic—the only way any Welsh Guardsman, from lieutenant colonel downward, would be getting on a helicopter during Panther's Claw would be if he was wounded, or dead, and was being evacuated to Camp Bastion. There was no option other than to go with the convoy if Thorneloe wanted to get to the Shamalan Canal. Making a virtue of necessity, he reasoned that it gave him a chance to examine the ground his men were fighting on and to be seen to be experiencing what they were. The convoy would also pass through the new Shahzad base, and it was a good opportunity to be briefed by Giles Harris on events in Chah-e Anjir.

Some had questioned Thorneloe's practice of Barmaing, which carried the additional risk of putting him in the lead vehicle, always the most vulnerable in a convoy. "We'd had a conversation about it," said Regimental Sergeant Major Mike Monaghan, who raised the issue the day before the convoy left. "I wasn't happy." Thorneloe dismissed Monaghan's concerns about his Barmaing at the front of the convoy, insisting he would face the same dangers as his men. Monaghan was uneasy. "You need to be careful, sir," he said. "At the end of the day, you are the Commanding Officer. I don't think you really need to be doing that." Monaghan would normally have gone with Thorneloe but had to stay behind to coordinate the influx of men and equipment to FOB Shawqat. Major John Oldroyd, the Royal Artillery battery commander, was also due to accompany Thorneloe, but he had been standing in for Speed and needed to hand over to him properly. Thorneloe, therefore, would be traveling without any of his senior staff.

That day, Thorneloe had stopped to talk to Color Sergeant Jenkinson, the FSG-2 commander who had ordered that Leach's leg be retrieved. In a freak accident, Jenkinson had been hit in the back by a Desert Hawk drone a few days earlier as it came in to land at PB Silab. He had tried to carry on but by this point could barely move. Jenkinson was related to Lance Bombardier Stephen Restorick, the soldier killed in Northern Ireland whose mother Thorneloe had corresponded with. "The Commanding Officer said how much he was looking forward to going on leave and seeing his wife and daughters," Jenkinson recalls. "He also mentioned how tired he was." Before he turned in, Thorneloe sat in the ops room with Williams "65 was 54," the Falklands veteran he had persuaded to return at the Union Jack Club dinner. "I'm off up the canal, 54," he said. "I'm going to see the boys."

The next morning, Thorneloe was delighted to find out that Williams would be the commander of the lead Viking. While they were waiting to leave, the two men chatted again, and Thorneloe realized that Williams was the same Trooper Kevin Williams who had killed an Iraqi in a controversial incident in southern Iraq in 2003. Williams and another soldier had given chase to Hassan Abbad Said after he and five other Iraqis were stopped with a handcart filled with munitions. Said was cornered in a courtyard, and Williams shot him dead when he thought he was about to grab the other soldier's weapon. Even though Williams had been cleared of any misconduct by two senior army officers, the government decided to pursue him through the civilian courts, and he became the first soldier since 1993 to be charged with murder while on duty.

Williams's case became a *cause célèbre* in the army because it was seen as indicative of a Labour government that sent soldiers to do dangerous things but did not understand the nature of warfare. The charge was eventually dropped when the judge said that the case could be seen as "a betrayal of soldiers who risk their lives for their country and who are expected to make difficult decisions in split seconds." Williams, from Burnley in Lancashire, who had spent eighteen months in military custody, quietly got on with his life and his career. He was extremely fit, unfailingly polite, and due to be promoted to sergeant. Remarkably, he displayed no trace of rancor despite the way he had been treated. "Bloody hell, I'm surprised you're still in the Army," Thorneloe said to him. Williams surmised that Thorneloe disagreed with the murder charge, and they had an amiable chat about what had happened. He remembers Thorneloe telling him that the casualties from the Viking roll were "doing all right, recovering in Bastion with their legs up, chilling out."

Sergeant Paul Howard, commanding the Viking troop that day, was also unhappy about Thorneloe traveling in the lead vehicle. While the death of Lance Corporal Rob Richards had shown that no Viking in a convoy was safe, it was indisputable that the front vehicle was at the greatest risk. "Sir, we don't really want you going in the front vehicle," Howard said. But Thorneloe was adamant. "I'll go in the front vehicle," he replied. The night before, Burbridge had suggested Thorneloe travel in the right-hand seat of the front cab—no longer the "death seat" since the extra armor had been added. Again, Thorneloe would not be budged. He wanted to get out and Barma and see the ground.

Before jumping into the back of the Viking, Thorneloe chatted to Color Sergeant Dai Matthews, the former officers' mess manager who had rejoined for the tour because his concrete business had gone bust. "Could you give this to the Adjutant?" he asked Matthews, commanding the resupply vehicle in the convoy. It was the letter Thorneloe had written to Jo Birchall. Eventually, Thorneloe had found the words to write to Jo Birchall. Before he turned in for a few hours' sleep, he finished the letter, several pages long and written in his own hand, and slipped it into an envelope. "His character was defined by his tremendous and infectious enthusiasm—I do not think he had a negative bone in his body," he had written. "Like many others I find it impossible to imagine that this irrepressibly warm, energetic and positive man can no longer be with us. He really was an inspiration to those of us who were lucky enough to have known him. The unselfish and positive manner in which he led his life could not contrast more starkly with the nihilistic cruelty of the people who took it from him."

Shortly after 9:00 a.m., the eighteen-vehicle convoy—ten Vikings, seven SV trucks, and a Panther—rumbled out of FOB Shawqat and headed north from Nad-e Ali up toward Chah-e Anjir. Matthews was commanding the convoy, though Howard was in charge of the Vikings. Onboard the trucks were ammunition, equipment spares, diesel fuel, mail, rations, and twenty thousand liters of water, as the mission was to resupply 2 Company and various other positions en route. Thorneloe stood in the top cover position manning a light machine gun with the rest of the Barma team, Lance Corporal Kingsley Simmons, Trooper Josh Hammond, and Guardsmen Joe Penlington, Craig Harrison, and Nathan Chambers, sitting at his feet.

By midday, the convoy had dropped stores off at Yellow 14 and doubled back to the new PB Shahzad in the town of Chah-e Anjir. Thorneloe was welcomed to the former Helmand and Arghandab Construction Unit premises by Major Giles Harris, whose Jam Boys along with the Royal Engineers had now fortified the buildings with sandbags, razor wire, and Hesco barriers. Those manning the convoy grabbed a quick nap and posed for group photos beside the old T62 tank and armored personnel carrier left behind by the Russians two decades earlier. Harris showed Thorneloe into a large dusty room with huge windowsills and lime-green walls. Thorneloe, whose new accommodation at Shawqat was decidedly Spartan, declared enviously that it was "the best office in Helmand." Only a few weeks earlier it had been full of human excrement after being used as a latrine by the Afghan police. Under the brigade's concept of "expeditionary COIN" (counterinsurgency), the Prince of Wales's Company was to receive very limited stores and equipment until it was confirmed the company would be staying at the base. Harris decided to use local Afghans to help the Welsh Guards clear up the base. It was an unconventional move that carried obvious security risks, but he calculated that allowing the Afghans in would spread the message that they had considerable firepower available. It was also the only way he could get the locals, who were too scared or distrustful to hold a shura in the town, to engage with the Welsh Guards.

On the old American pine desk sat a hand-sewn leather cricket ball that Harris's fiancée Alice had sent him as a reminder of summer back home. Beside the ball was a dried opium bulb and the twin metal pressure plates from an IED that Harris was using as a letter rack. Just outside was the former HACU rose garden, which Harris was soon to restore to something of its former glory, directing it to be cleared as a living legacy of the last "good times." It was cleared by local Afghans and saved one morning by Harris himself when he rushed out to stop a Royal Engineers tractor driving over it. The long-abandoned American tennis court had already been designated the Helicopter Landing Site—its white lines still visible from the air. The planned reappearance of the rose garden particularly delighted Wali Mohammed, the old caretaker who had faithfully guarded the headquarters building and its trove of maps and survey documents through the town's American, Russian, and Taliban periods before the Welsh Guards arrived.

Poring over a map, the two officers discussed what could be done to turn the former lawless and Taliban-influenced town into the kind of "ink spot" that could spread the influence of the British—and, ultimately, the Afghan government—into the surrounding area. The Afghan police reported that they had suffered dozens of casualties a month; they had held out but had been afraid to walk the bazaar. Locals said that the Taliban had walked freely through the town, gathering at the mosques in the evening.

The ink-spot counterinsurgency strategy was first developed by the British in Malaya and used by the Americans in Vietnam. It was based on the idea of an occupying force establishing a set of small, safe areas and then pushing out from each one to extend control until they join up, just as ink spots would coalesce on blotting paper. Turning Chah-e Anjir around, Thorneloe believed, could be the most significant success notched up by the Welsh Guards.

It was evident, though unspoken, that Thorneloe regarded what could be done with the town as more significant and enduring than anything achieved by Panther's Claw. Summarizing their discussion, Thorneloe said: "Giles, you need to do three things. I want you to establish a ring of steel and then push battle group influence into the area. And I want you to do stuff. Don't look over your shoulder and worry and wait for everyone else. Just get on with it, use your gut instinct and if it doesn't work it doesn't matter because you can try something different." Thorneloe's point about influence was a subtle acknowledgment of the reality that there were so few British resources to go around and it took so long to get them that local solutions had to be the way. He wanted Harris to get things moving rather than to wait, very possibly in vain, for the Provincial Reconstruction Team in Lashkar Gah to help. It was a reflection, Harris says, of "our overall inability as a troop-contributing nation to flex resources fast to areas recently cleared." Over the following months, Harris took the "do-stuff" order to heart, putting the townspeople to work, establishing an Afghan town council, and mentoring the Afghan police and army—while fighting the Taliban relentlessly at the same time.

Their discussion over, Thorneloe, with a big grin on his face, shook Harris's hand. "You're doing a great job, Giles," he said. "Good stuff." Before he left, Thorneloe spent a couple of minutes talking to Company Quartermaster Sergeant Eifion Griffiths 50, from Rhostryfan in North Wales. Griffiths 50 was eager to go to Brunei as a jungle warfare instructor, and Thorneloe, typically, had been lobbying on his behalf even in Helmand. "We're trying our best for your posting, 50," he said. "We should have an answer soon."

Giles Harris watched Thorneloe climb onto what he thought was the third Viking in the convoy. In fact, Thorneloe resumed his spot in the rear cab of the Viking that was to lead the convoy and stood up in the hatch so he could look out and train the general-purpose machine gun onto the convoy's flanks. "I've often wondered," Harris says, "whether if I'd seen him get into the front vehicle, I'd have stepped forward and said: 'Sir, come on—back you go.'"

The convoy stopped at Yellow 14, where Thorneloe got a brief from Lieutenant Chris Fenton. Thorneloe, his face covered in dust from riding top cover, talked to Fenton about how pleased he was to be able to get out of Battle Group headquarters. Before they moved off up Route Cornwall, Sergeant Howard received a ground brief about the situation there. At 10:54 a.m. that day—barely three hours earlier—a Mastiff that was fourth in a convoy from the Prince of Wales's Company had hit an IED close to XP-10. It was the fifth IED to hit the Welsh Guards beside the Shamalan in three days.

The convoy headed up Route Cornwall. Progress was slow due to the weight of the stores, the narrow, crumbling track and the need to scan the route for any sign that an IED had been dug in. Just north of XP-10, the convoy rumbled past the crater where the Mastiff had struck an IED that morning. A few minutes after 2:00 p.m., Trooper Owen, driving Exorcist, called for the convoy to halt so that the portion of the track ahead could be Barmaed. It took more than fifty minutes to Barma the three hundred meters or so ahead as Thorneloe diligently checked every spot where his Vallon had beeped. With a degree of impatience among the Tankies setting in, the convoy resumed its journey. Moments later, at 3:18 p.m., as XP-9 came into view, there was a huge explosion underneath Exorcist's rear cab. The spot where the IED detonated had been driven over and Barmaed three hours earlier as well as being transited several other times during the previous two days. It appeared that the Taliban had placed low-metal-content IEDs along Route Cornwall, enabling fighters to slip in and quickly connect battery packs as a convoy approached (see incident map in Appendix).

The aftermath of the explosion underneath the Viking was sheer chaos. "F---ing hell!" Williams, riding top cover in the front cab, screamed over the radio net. The blast lifted the rear cab into the air, pushing the front cab forward before it was dumped back down on the track. Williams's head was struck by a large piece of a light machine gun that had been blown to bits behind him. Trooper Owen was blown upwards from the driver's seat. His head hit the roof of the front cab, and his face smashed into the steering wheel on the way down.

The windscreen was a maze of cracks and Owen couldn't see anything because of the dust, but he registered that the Viking was still rolling forwards. Remembering that they were right beside the canal, he slammed his foot on the brake, fell back into his seat, and passed out. As the rear cab filled with dust and debris, Simmons felt for the door handle and found it. The door was buckled but sprang open with a swift kick.

Williams leapt out of his top cover position, leaned down into the driver's hatch, and began shaking Owen, who woke up. "Check your f---ing legs!" Williams shouted. "No, I don't want to," replied Owen. "You do it." He could feel nothing below his waist and feared that his legs were gone. Williams shook him again and slapped his face, telling him once more: "Check them!" Owen crouched forward and felt down. "Yeah they are there, but I think I broke something," he said.

The corporal turned around and jumped from the roof of the front cab onto the rear. It was clear at once that Thorneloe was very gravely wounded. The explosion had ripped open the floor of the rear cab, slicing him virtually in half. The top portion of his body had been thrown forward and was leaning at a forty-five-degree angle up against the toolbox, a long container welded to the vehicle roof that the troopers sometimes referred to as "the coffin." His helmet had been knocked askew on his head and his body armor pushed up to his nose. The toolbox had blown open, and a cable inside it had sprung out and wrapped around Thorneloe.

"He appeared to have both legs missing," remembers Williams. "And as I was going towards him, he followed me with his eyes, which said to me: 'This guy is still conscious and responsive.'" Thorneloe was mumbling and seemed to be trying to say something as Williams got to him. "Don't talk, save your energy," Williams said as he pulled out a tourniquet and began to put it on where the colonel's left leg had been. "You'll be fine, don't talk, you're OK." Owen could hear Williams talking via the vehicle intercom. "I'm not listening to this," Owen thought, struggling to get his headset off. He couldn't unhook the Bowman cable from the radio, so he ripped it off. He had no desire to hear a man dying.

Williams needed another tourniquet and shouted to a soldier on the road below. When he turned around, Thorneloe's eyes had rolled back, and blood was coming from his mouth. He had lost consciousness. Williams checked his pulse and confirmed that he was dead.

The corporal is still haunted by the moments that Thorneloe remained alive after the blast. "There is absolutely no doubt in my mind that he didn't have a clue what had happened," he says. "The pure force of the trauma that affected him and the massive blood loss, he wouldn't have felt it. The nerve endings would have been severed so quickly there would have been no pain whatsoever. It would have been just like getting a huge bang to the head and laying back wondering what it was." His main regret is that he dissuaded Thorneloe from speaking. "If I could turn back time, I'd have definitely let him say something because I now know they were going to be his last words."

The light flooded in as the door of the rear cab swung open and Simmons saw Harrison, sitting opposite, covered in dust, blinking, and paralyzed by shock. "Get out!" Simmons shouted at him, and then turned to Chambers, who had suffered shrapnel wounds to his left leg. Both guardsmen climbed through the door and out onto the road, where Chambers pulled out his field dressing to staunch the flow of blood from his leg.

Penlington was in a bad way. He had been thrown into the center of the cab and was lying face up, moaning: "My back, my back." Flesh had been ripped off his left arm, and his left leg was bleeding and broken in so many places that Simmons could not get a proper grip on it. Not wanting to drag Penlington out for fear of damaging his back further, Simmons called Harrison back in to help him, and the two men lifted Penlington up and out. Corporal Trev Hopkins, a Tankie, was applying a tourniquet as a medic ran over and gave Penlington a shot of morphine. Owen had been helped out of the front cab by Corporal Lee Scott, commander of the "Elephant" Viking that was fourth in the convoy, and was sitting against a wall. When he heard Williams say that Thorneloe was dead, he felt a sharp stab of anger and flung his helmet and headset away.

Back in the rear cab, Simmons—who now knew that Thorneloe had been killed—was looking for Trooper Hammond. Fumbling through the dust and the darkness, he saw a hand that he thought was reaching out for him. When he grabbed it to pull Hammond out, however, he realized it was not attached to an arm and quickly flung it to one side. His hopes of finding Hammond alive quickly fading, Simmons got out of the Viking and ran around to the side, where he could kneel down and see where the explosion had torn through the bottom of the vehicle, leaving a gaping hole. "It looked like a jelly that hadn't set had been turned upside down," he says. "It was just flesh and mush and bits of body armour and combats." A few minutes earlier, Hammond had been sitting in the back chatting about how he was looking forward to his nineteenth birthday and getting back home on leave, then he'd been eviscerated in a split second.

Hopkins ran back to get body bags and nearly came to blows with a medic who, in all the pandemonium, thought he was asking him for a cigarette. The corporal crawled under the Viking and located Hammond's torso, missing an arm and both legs. He took a pistol, which was still strapped to the top of Hammond's hip, and then put the remains he could find in a body bag.

Color Sergeant Dai Matthews had returned to the road after he'd supervised the Barmaing of a landing site for the medical helicopter to land. He had been too far back in the convoy to gauge properly what had happened. At first, he was relieved to see Chambers and Penlington being stretchered away followed by three of the walking wounded. "Fantastic," he thought. "They're alive and they've got all their limbs, no one's been badly hurt." It was then he was told that two had been killed in the blast and two body bags were needed. Matthews gathered his resupply group men together and told them: "Look, the Tankies have had an IED strike and two of their boys are dead. I don't want to do it but someone needs to get the bodies and it's better that we do it because we don't know them well." As he walked over to the Viking, a Tankie approached him and said: "Dai, your Commanding Officer is on top of that vehicle." Matthews, who had known Thorneloe for nearly twenty years, assumed that the colonel was taking charge of the incident scene from the Viking roof. It was only when he saw Hopkins and another soldier lifting the lifeless torso down that he realized what had happened. "That's my colonel!" Matthews cried out. "Be careful with him!" Tears streamed down his face as the color sergeant helped get the corpse down and zip it into the body bag.

Captain Richard Sheehan, hovering overhead in his Apache, could see the devastation caused to the Viking. He had been introduced to Thorneloe a few weeks earlier in the Battle Group ops room, and the Welsh Guards commanding officer had made a point of thanking him for the sterling work of the Apache crews. There had been chatter on a Taliban walkie-talkie frequency about a suicide bomber being prepared to attack the now static convoy. As usual, however, the presence of an Apache meant that the Taliban lay low and kept their distance. In his diary, Sheehan recorded that Thorneloe had been killed. "He was on top cover. Should he have been there? ... F---ing IEDs. They're now using very low metal content so the metal detectors aren't finding them."

Simmons stumbled into an irrigation ditch as he walked towards the landing site that Matthews had cleared for the medical Chinook to land. What had just happened only began to register fully as, soaking wet, badly bruised, and his left ear still tingling, he sat on the helicopter for the fifteen-minute flight—fast, low, and rolling from left to right to present a harder target for the Taliban—to Camp Bastion. The two body bags were lying at his feet ,and he could see Penlington, naked after his uniform had been cut off him, shaking as the medics worked on him. He didn't know if he was going to make it.

Also sitting in the Chinook, dazed and in shock, was Owen. He knew that Thorneloe was in one of the body bags, and he was trying to work out who was in the second. Penlington, the soldier shaking as the medics treated him, looked exactly like Hammond. But Owen remembered that Hammond had lots of tattoos, a tribal sleeve on his arm and across his chest and his initials on the back of his neck behind his ear. This soldier had no tattoos. As the Chinook touched down, he kept going over and over in his mind: "Did I do enough? Did I do enough?" At Camp Bastion there were three ambulances waiting—one for Penlington, one for Simmons and the other less seriously injured, and one for the dead. As Simmons looked around to check that all his men were off the helicopter, he saw a group of medics taking the body bags away. "I don't know if they dropped the body or the body bag ripped open but the Commanding Officer's torso just rolled out and hit the floor." One of the medics tried to shield Simmons and push him away. "Don't look at it," he told him. "Don't look at it."

In the Battle Group ops room, there was confusion as the zap numbers— the identifying codes for the casualties—came over. Guardsman Harrison was initially reported as dead and one of his best friends woken up to be given the news; then it was established that Trooper Hammond was the fatality. Zap numbers, made up of the first two letters of the surname and the last four digits of the service number, are used to avoid the full name of a casualty being passed over an insecure radio net and are not instantly recognizable to most. Mistakes with them were common, and every time one was broadcast it triggered a morbid guessing game.

When Thorneloe's zap number came over the radio, several in the ops room wondered whether it had been a Thomas who had died, just as the name Evans had first leapt to mind when Lieutenant Mark Evison had been wounded. But Captain James Aldridge knew it was Thorneloe as soon as Captain Naim Moukarzel, the battle captain, gave him the zap number to check. No one in the ops room recognized it. As adjutant, Aldridge regularly filled in forms that included Thorneloe's service number. "Tango Hotel Five Four Seven Two," he repeated to Moukarzel as the zap number was read out to him. "God, that's him." Everyone stared at the video feed from a Hermes 450 drone, known as "Green Eyes," which showed the damaged Viking sitting askew on Route Cornwall and figures scurrying around it.

A short distance from the ops room, Major Andrew Speed, the second in command, was standing with the Regimental Sergeant Major and Major Martyn Miles discussing how to organize the new base. He turned and saw Captain Ed Launders, the ops officer, striding grim-faced towards him. Once he'd been given the news that he was now commanding the Battle Group, Speed spent ten seconds summarizing the discussion about base arrangements before following Launders back to the ops room. There was still a major incident to manage and troops out on the canal in considerable danger. Another IED had been found, and there were messages from the Taliban walkie-talkies indicating an attack might be imminent.

Burbridge remembers a sense of shock and suspended animation for no more than three minutes before the regular tempo of managing an incident resumed. He looked over at Moukarzel, who was giving orders and speaking on the radio as if nothing had happened, except that tears were rolling down his cheeks.

While arrangements were still being made to tow away the stricken Viking, a message came in that a drone had detected three men farther up the canal who appeared to be digging on Route Cornwall. The intelligence assessment was that there were very few civilians near the canal now that Panther's Claw was underway. It was almost certainly an IED being laid. An air controller announced that there was a fast jet on station that could take out the three men in seconds. Everyone looked to Speed, who was now commanding the Battle Group. "What are they doing?" he asked. "Digging," came the reply. "No, what are they doing? What are they digging?" The air controller conceded that he didn't know. "Right, we are not doing that," said Speed. "I am not just killing people." Whatever appetite there had been for a swift act of revenge evaporated, and everyone continued to concentrate on how to get the Viking off the canal.

Up at XP-7, Bettinson heard the blast and within minutes received a radio message from the Battle Group ops room stating: "Mongoose Two Zero Alpha [Bettinson's callsign] will proceed south and lead the convoy up to XP-7." Bettinson immediately felt something wasn't right. It was unusual to get such a specific order from Battle Group headquarters, and he had not heard Thorneloe's voice on the radio net. On the way down to where the Viking had been blown up, another IED was discovered. When Bettinson got to the incident scene, the casualties and bodies had been evacuated. "I'm sorry," a Royal Engineer major said to him. "Your boss has got it." By the time the damaged Viking had been dragged up to XP-7, the identity of the casualties had still not been given over the radio net. "Where's the Commanding Officer?" asked Harman. Bettinson steered him to one side and said: "Terry, the big man's gone."

Bettinson gathered his company around to deliver the news. There were sobs as he told how he had been a potential officer visiting the Welsh Guards when he had first met Thorneloe in 1993. "I have a hunch that the last commanding officer to die in battle was Colonel H Jones in 1982," he said, before concluding: "Tonight, we mourn. Tomorrow, the sun comes up and we're working." Up in Sangin, Major Guy Stone was calling 3 Company together. He had followed the Viking IED incident on the brigade's J-CHAT instant message system and then been informed by secure email that Thorneloe had been killed. After group prayers and recollections, Stone spoke to each of his Welsh Guardsmen individually. Their emotions ranged from intense anger to stolid shrugs. Color Sergeant Justin Hooson, a towering triathlete from Llantwit Major, had known Thorneloe for fifteen years and wanted to head straight out to exact bloody retribution on the Taliban. Guardsman Karl Evans 28, a thickset North Walian from Wrexham, known as "Twent," was calm and philosophical. "That's very sad, sir," he said. "But at the end of the day, it is no sadder than any other guardsman dying."

After addressing 2 Company, Harman told Bettinson: "Right, I'll take care of cleaning out the vehicle." The area around the Viking was sealed off in a corner of the compound by positioning Mastiffs around it. Then the three officers at XP-7 set about the grimmest of tasks—separating and cataloguing the body parts, weapons, ammunition, clothing, and personal effects of the two men killed and the four wounded. The procedure was that everything should be sent back to Camp Bastion. It was pitch-black, so Bettinson, Harman, and Fraser-Sampson wore head torches. "It was something that had to be done," says Fraser-Sampson. "We didn't want the boys to see it. It was down to us as the officers to do it. It was my first experience of death up close. I went in and grabbed a belt of ammunition. As soon as I picked it up, there was just a load of bloody flesh on it."

Harman climbed right inside, passing out Thorneloe's pistol, pieces of uniform, and body parts. "There were fingers, two feet, a rib," he remembers. "In addition, there was the Commanding Officer's right leg, which had been ripped off by the bottom of the vehicle as it was peeled back like a bean can. I've smelt death before and I've seen people get injured but I still have nightmares about what was behind that door." Each item was logged in an inventory and placed in a box—someone had forgotten to bring body bags up to XP-7. "We did it out of respect for the Commanding Officer, his family and his children. But it still hurts me."[1]

Bettinson told Harman he would take personal care of Thorneloe's lieutenant colonel's rank slide, worn on the front of his body armor, his telescopic pointer for PowerPoint presentations, and his head torch. He didn't want anyone further up the army chain to have the chance of stealing these things. A childhood friend of Bettinson's had known the family of Lieutenant Colonel David Blair, the commanding officer of the Queen's Own Highlanders blown up by the IRA outside Warrenpoint in 1979.[2] Bettinson had been appalled to hear that there had been virtually nothing left of Blair's body, and so a new rank slide had been put into the coffin. With this in mind, he decided to deliver the items personally to Sally Thorneloe. That night, the last thing Bettinson had to do was to go into Thorneloe's briefcase to retrieve his next set of orders for Panther's Claw.

Further down the Shamalan Canal, Lieutenant Chris Fenton listened in to the Taliban walkie-talkie chatter as they boasted about their handiwork. "We could hear them insurgents laughing and celebrating and congratulating each other on a job well done," he remembers. "It turned my stomach."

The fighting continued around XP-7, and there were no helicopters made available to collect the body parts despite Harman's entreaties. At the best of times, helicopters were a scarce commodity. With Panther's Claw raging, collecting dead bodies—or parts of them—was at the bottom of the priority list. Harman wrestled with the dilemma of what to do. He could bury the body parts, but eventually the Welsh Guards would have to leave XP-7. Burning them was an option, but that would be seen by the guardsmen, and the psychological effect could be devastating. In any case, Harman reasoned, it was important for any family to have the remains of their loved one returned to them. Concerned about decomposition, Harman decided he needed to keep the parts as clean as possible before they were collected. "So each night I took the body parts down to the canal and washed them, quietly and discreetly with nobody there," he says. "The third night, I couldn't do it."

Harman still struggles with what he felt he had to do. "I still find it difficult to cope with. When anyone asks me about the Commanding Officer, that's all I can see. I knew him for more than 15 years, but that's all I can see." On the fourth day, the body parts were collected when a Royal Military Policeman arrived on a convoy from Shawqat. "Are we not better than this?" Harman asked him, weeping, when he handed over the boxes. All the human remains recovered from the Viking were taken to Camp Bastion and then repatriated to Britain. At the John Radcliffe Hospital in Oxford, DNA tests were carried out as part of the post mortems so that each piece could be reunited with the correct body before burial.

Around the same time that Bettinson, Harman, and Fraser-Sampson were cleaning out the Viking, Aldridge and Major Nicky Mott walked into the morgue at Camp Bastion—known as "Rose Cottage"—to identify the main part of Thorneloe's body. Apart from a small nick on his chin, Thorneloe's face was intact and he seemed at peace. A little later, there was a knock on Aldridge's door. He looked up to see Color Sergeant Dai Matthews with an envelope in his hand. "Sir," he said, his voice almost a whisper. "This is the Commanding Officer's letter of condolence to Mrs. Birchall. He asked me to make sure that you got it."

15

Regret to Inform

DEEPLY REGRET TO INFORM YOU YOUR SON DAVID
REPORTED KILLED IN ITALY. DATE UNKNOWN.
WILL CABLE FURTHER NEWS IMMEDIATELY RECEIVED.
BANKIER. COMMANDING WELSH GUARDS.

*Telegram of February 25, 1944, to Ian Elliot reporting the death of
his son, Captain David Elliot, killed while leading a
bayonet charge at Monte Cerasola nine days earlier*

We are sad to report that there has been a fatal incident involving a
member of 1WG. NOK have been informed. Details will be
published shortly.

*Text message of July 1, 2009, sent via mobile phones to relatives of
Welsh Guards serving in Helmand regarding the death of Lieutenant
Colonel Rupert Thorneloe earlier that day*

F or Major Tom Charles, the three-hundred-meter walk along Knollys
Road in the garrison town of Aldershot felt like several miles. The
Welsh Guards officer had been in some tight spots as a company
commander in Afghanistan, but this was the most terrifying thing he had
ever done. By the time he and the female army captain with him reached
Badajos House, the residence assigned to the commanding officer of the
Welsh Guards, his mouth was dry and his legs were shaking. He paused, took
a deep breath, and rang the doorbell.

Inside the house, Sally Thorneloe was relaxing and catching up on some
emails after putting her daughters Hannah, four, and Sophie, two, to bed. A
couple of hours earlier she had been out jogging with Catrina Campbell,

whose husband Andy was out in Helmand as IX Company's sergeant major. They were laughing as they got back. "Rupe won't believe I've been for a two-mile run," Sally said. "You'll have to tell him so there's an independent witness." The wives who lived on the married quarters patch in Aldershot, just around the corner from the Welsh Guards base at Lille Barracks, had increasingly leant on each other as the casualties in Helmand had mounted. The Welsh Guards welfare office, just around the corner, had become a regular meeting point. Sally had been around there for a cup of tea that afternoon. The doorbell rang and she saw figures in green through the glass. It was a little late, she thought, for the welfare office staff to call.

Tom Charles waited as he heard footsteps in the hallway and the front door opened. He had only met Rupert Thorneloe's wife once, about 10 years earlier when the couple had first been courting. Now, his was about to become the last face she ever saw when she was a happy person. "Hello," she said, smiling. "Are you Sally Thorneloe?" he asked. He knew who she was, but military protocol dictated that the casualty notification officer had to establish that he was speaking to the next of kin. "Yes," she replied, her hand moving to her mouth as she realized what two officers in uniform standing on her doorstep meant. "Can we come in?" asked Charles. "No," she replied. Her head was spinning. She wanted to stop everything right now and rewind, back to when she went for a run and could talk to Catrina Campbell about their husbands out in Afghanistan together. Back to earlier in the day when she had recorded an interview for the Aldershot Army Show about what it was like to be the commanding officer's wife and how the families were coping with news of deaths and injuries. If she didn't let these two officers into her house, then she would never be told what she was about to hear. She would have a husband, and her daughters would have a father, and he would be coming home for R&R in just over a fortnight. Charles repeated the question twice, and then Sally Thorneloe, her life disintegrating, stepped aside to let him and the captain into the house. "Rupert was killed in a bomb blast this morning just before midday," he said.

Standing in the driveway of Badajos House, Tom Charles used his mobile phone to break the news to Rupert Thorneloe's parents and then Sally Thorneloe's father and sister. Then he called Major Dai Bevan, commanding the Rear Party, to let him know that the next of kin had been informed. For the previous nine hours, the knowledge that Thorneloe was dead had been eating away at Bevan. He knew that Sally Thorneloe was going about her everyday life, but the piece of information he possessed meant that the future she was counting on was never going to happen. It was a similar feeling to the one he had experienced in Helmand when he was a staff officer responsible for ISTAR—Intelligence, Surveillance, Target Acquisition, and Reconnaissance. Then, he would be looking down at an insurgent captured on live-streaming video from a drone—dubbed "Kill TV" by troops—knowing that his life would end in thirty seconds. As an American jet locked onto the target and released a bomb, there would be a countdown of twenty seconds, ten seconds, five seconds. At that point, the insurgent's death was inevitable because the bomb was on its way. Just before Charles had begun his walk up Knollys Road, he had telephoned Bevan to say that he had located the house, and he was going in. It was as if the jet had released its bomb.

Once Sally Thorneloe had been informed, it was the job of Color Sergeant Jiffy Myers to send a text message to all the families of the Welsh Guardsmen in Helmand. Before doing so, he had to make sure that the relatives of the person who had been killed were removed from the distribution list. He searched down the list of names, found Sally Thorneloe's, and pressed delete. He found himself choking with grief as he thought of the young officer he had helped with the one-armed bandit machine and of Sally, the coffee-morning stalwart and happy visitor to the welfare office. A few seconds later, wives, mothers, fathers, and girlfriends in Aldershot, throughout Wales and further afield received a text message that said: "We are sad to report that there has been a fatal incident involving a member of 1WG. NOK have been informed. Details will be published shortly." Each time such a message arrived—almost always in the late evening—the reactions of each recipient would be similar. Initially, there was a stab of sadness that someone had been killed. Then would come relief that the person who was dead was not their own loved one. Almost invariably, that was followed by a wave of guilt about feeling relief that someone else's husband or son or boyfriend was dead. Then the telephones would start ringing as everyone tried to find out who it was.

While Tom Charles was telephoning everyone, Colonel Tom Bonas, the regimental adjutant, and Captain Darren Pridmore, the welfare officer, arrived at the house. They had been in a car three hundred meters away waiting for Charles to complete his task. For weeks, Sally Thorneloe would never be alone—Charles had called friends who were already on their way—but she felt as if she was in a bubble. People were asking her questions but she couldn't decide anything, not even whether she wanted tea, coffee, or a glass of water. Everyone else seemed to be running around, but she was just sitting there feeling numb and sick and worrying about her daughters asleep upstairs. She had only recently spoken to her husband and could not believe what was happening. Maybe, she thought, they had got the wrong person. When Tom Charles got up to leave, she found herself wanting him to stay. "I suppose it felt like the end of the beginning," she recalls.

Bonas had known it was very bad news as soon as he heard Bevan's voice. He was sitting in his oak-paneled office at the Welsh Guards Regimental Headquarters in Wellington Barracks when the phone rang. Bonas, who had retired from the army in 2007 after thirty-four years, was in charge of all non-operational aspects of the regiment. A courtly, punctilious man who was the epitome of a Guards officer, he had commanded Support Company during the Falklands War. Many of his men had died onboard the *Sir Galahad*. Bonas had also commanded a battalion, though not the Welsh Guards, and one of his informal roles had been to offer counsel to Thorneloe. Bevan did not even have to tell Bonas who had been killed. "It's not, is it?" Bonas asked, somehow sensing what had happened. "Yes," Bevan replied. Months later, Bonas could not recall the moment without his voice cracking and tears welling in his eyes.

The next morning, a family friend took Hannah Thorneloe to school, her last day before the summer holidays, but her mother picked her up as normal. As Sally Thorneloe got out of the car, she saw the wife of another Welsh Guards officer approaching. The news was not yet public, but clearly she knew what had happened and wanted to offer her sympathy. "I remember just running away from her, I didn't want anyone to touch me or come near me or hug me or be nice to me. I didn't want anyone near me. I couldn't face it. I just wanted to be on my own."

Once safely back home, Sally Thorneloe, with an army padre in the room, sat Hannah down on the sofa. "You know there are a lot of people here." Hannah nodded. "Yes," she said. Her mother continued: "Well something very, very sad has happened, Hannah. Your Daddy is in Afghanistan." Again, Hannah nodded and said that she knew this. Sally Thorneloe said: "Daddy can't come back now because Daddy has died." Hannah looked at her. "What, never?" she asked. Her mother said: "No, he can't ever come back." Hannah looked a bit confused and gave her mother a hug. Then she asked if she could do some coloring. Sally Thorneloe explains: "They are very in the moment, little people. Whatever happens immediately happens and then their brain flicks on to something else."

Thorneloe was the second battalion commander in the ninety-four-year history of the Welsh Guards to be killed in action. The first was Lieutenant Colonel John E. Fass, aged thirty-three, who was struck by a shell on June 30, 1944 at Cheux in Normandy, sixty-five years and a day before Thorneloe. Johnny Fass, like Thorneloe, had recently moved from the rarefied atmosphere of a higher headquarters to the sharp end of the war. As an intelligence officer on the staff of General Dwight Eisenhower's Supreme Allied Command, he had been intimately involved in the planning of the Normandy invasion and on occasion briefed Prime Minister Winston Churchill. On June 29, 1944, eleven days after landing in Normandy with the Welsh Guards, Fass assumed command of the 1st Battalion when Lieutenant Colonel George Browning and three other officers were wounded by a German shell.

The following evening, Fass was visited by Lieutenant Colonel J. O. E. Vandeleur, a close friend who was commanding the 3rd Battalion of the Irish Guards. Fass was celebrating because he had just received a telegram from his wife saying that she had given birth to Michael, their third child and first son, eight days earlier. The two battalion commanders sat in a slit trench with Fass's soldier servant, Guardsman Davies, drinking mugs of tea with whisky in them, and Fass asked Vandeleur to be Michael's godfather. Moments after Vandeleur had said goodbye to them, a shell landed in the trench, wounding Davies and sending a fragment into Fass's head, killing him instantly. The commanding officer's body was wrapped in blankets and buried in a temporary grave in an orchard and later interred at St. Manvieu War Cemetery. Fass had been a watercolorist and, like Thorneloe, an accomplished rider who chose the Welsh Guards after first considering the Inniskilling Dragoon Guards. Vandeleur, always known as "Joe," from his initials, became a brigadier and was played by Michael Caine in the 1977 film *A Bridge Too Far*.

It was another week before Fass's widow, Elizabeth, received word of her husband's death. She was still recovering from childbirth in Sonning, Berkshire. The telegram was sent to Johnny Fass's parents, Sir Ernest and Lady Fass. The news was then delivered by Elizabeth's own parents, Lieutenant Colonel Henry and Mrs. Lucy Verey, who caught the bus from nearby Twyford. Elizabeth Fass wrote to her brother Michael, who was serving in Italy, telling him of her grief and the comfort that her three children, Serena, six, Virginia, two, and baby Michael, brought her. "I look at them thinking what they have lost. Johnny adored them and was so proud of them. He was so thrilled too to have a son. He was such an exciting and glamorous father ... for myself it just seems the end of everything ... He planned the whole invasion and then when it was ready said he must go and take part in it. The guardsmen thought the world of him and when he got command said apparently he was where he belonged and would lead them to success." She added that "pride is about the only thing that helps to keep me going." In a letter to a Fass family friend, Browning, recovering from his wounds in hospital in Penarth, wrote: "<u>Blast</u> it!! I am so damned angry, but being quite helpless what is the use? ... It was damned good of Johnny to break away from his staff job." Following Fass's death, the Welsh Guards contacted firms with which he still had unpaid bills and asked them to waive the debt. The Welsh Guards did the same thing for men killed in action in 2009 and met with a positive response from nearly every creditor.

Thorneloe's death was the first time that the human cost of the war in Afghanistan was brought home personally to politicians and civil servants in the Ministry of Defence. Every loss was grievous, but suddenly someone they had known intimately was dead. The news there broke five hours before Sally Thorneloe was informed. Lieutenant Colonel Chris Ghika of the Irish Guards was a close friend of Thorneloe who had worked closely with him when they were both military assistants in the MoD. He was talking to Commodore Clive Johnstone, principal staff officer to Stirrup, the chief of the Defence staff, when Lieutenant Colonel Simon Gilderson, military assistant to General Sir Richard Dannatt, chief of the general staff, approached them. "I've got something to tell you," he said. The three of them went to a corner of the office, and Gilderson, who had already told Dannatt, said: "It's bad. It looks as if Rupert Thorneloe's been killed." Johnstone went straight in to tell Stirrup. "It was the first time that the losses personally touched the higher echelons of defence, those who had committed us to war in Afghanistan," remembers Ghika. "Rupert was genuinely liked by people across the MoD, so the shock was very broad. Especially for some of the civil servants, it brought the conflict into stark relief." Thorneloe was the 171st British soldier to die in Afghanistan. By the time he was buried two weeks later, another fourteen had been killed.

At brigade headquarters in Helmand, thoughts turned swiftly to who should succeed Thorneloe. This was the first time in twenty-seven years that a British Army battalion commander had been killed in action, and Panther's Claw was about to reach its critical phase. Still dealing with the personal loss of one of his commanding officers and a man he had known for a dozen years, Brigadier Tim Radford needed to make some quick decisions. He had to think not just about the Battle Group, but about the Welsh Guards as a regiment.

An obvious choice to command the Battle Group was Lieutenant Colonel Rupert Jones of 4 Rifles. Jones had two companies in the Welsh Guards Battle Group but was stuck in Camp Bastion without any troops to command. To his immense frustration, his battalion had been split up and given to other battle groups. At the time, there were more of his riflemen out on the ground in the Welsh Guards Battle Group than there were guardsmen. Jones was the son of Lieutenant Colonel H Jones VC, the last battalion commander to have died in battle, and the possibility of his taking over from Thorneloe was soon in the newspapers. Radford also considered Lieutenant Colonel Simon Banton, the OMLT commander, and Lieutenant Colonel Jasper de Quincy Adams, the brigade staff officer in charge of Afghan police reform. All three men had intimate knowledge of the Battle Group (Center South) area of operations.

By that evening, however, Radford had decided that it had to be a Welsh Guardsman who would take over and, most importantly, be able to take the battalion home in October. It would take some time for that officer to be chosen, fully briefed, and flown out to Helmand, so in the meantime there needed to be an interim leader. Radford quickly settled on the PWRR's Lieutenant Colonel Doug Chalmers, the man who had helped create Battle Group (Center South) and with whom Radford had served during the Iraq invasion of 2003. He would become the temporary Battle Group commander. Chalmers knew the Welsh Guards because he had spent several days handing over to them in April, and he was very familiar with the terrain they were operating in. He also had established relationships with Habibullah Khan, the Nad-e Ali governor, and Afghan army, and police commanders. Chalmers's 2 PWRR battalion, based in Cyprus, was currently the reserve for Afghanistan. Crucially, he had a deft touch and nothing to prove as a battle group commander. The Welsh Guards would need to be steadied, but an outsider eager to stamp his authority could be disastrous for morale. It was a delicate task, and Radford was sure that Chalmers was the man who could fill the void until a Welsh Guards officer could be brought in as Thorneloe's permanent replacement.

"An unbelievably sad day," Radford recorded in his diary that evening. "Doug knows the area well and will slot in. He will do the job brilliantly.... The

Welsh Guards have been resolute.... The force field is still intact—just." As had been the case when Sean Birchall had been killed, Radford wrote that "news has now spread to other parts of the army about Rupert's death" before Sally Thorneloe had been informed. "I just wish people would resist the temptation to spread rumours," he noted. Radford was struck by the news that day that the next of kin of all servicemen and women killed in action since the Second World War would be eligible for a commemorative emblem called the Elizabeth Cross. It was the first time that a reigning monarch had given their name to a new award since King George VI instituted the George Cross in 1940. "The irony of the announcement today of the Elizabeth Cross is not lost on us," Radford wrote.

The next morning, Chalmers greeted Air Marshal Sir Stuart Peach, chief of Joint Operations and the commander of all deployed troops, as he arrived in Cyprus for a long-arranged visit. Peach was grim-faced and abruptly asked Chalmers: "Do we have any one-on-one time?" Once in Chalmers's office, Peach asked the nonplussed colonel to sit down. "Rupert Thorneloe's been killed," he said. "I want you to get on the next available plane and take over." Some twenty-one hours later, Chalmers was on a flight to Bahrain, where he was put on a British government VIP jet and flown to Kandahar. After being issued with weapons and body armor, he was taken by helicopter to Lashkar Gah to meet Radford before assuming command.

In the meantime, Radford had visited FOB Shawqat to brief the Welsh Guards about his decision to put Chalmers in command. As he was taking off in his Sea King, the Taliban opened fire. Luckily, their aim was poor. Otherwise, having just lost their first battalion commander since 1982, the British Army might have had its first brigade commander to be killed in action since 1945. Radford, recalling that he had also had a close call in Basharan in May, wrote in his diary: "Visited Welsh Guards. They were shocked but steady.... Six rounds fired again at the helicopter. Missed again. Seven lives left." One thing that Radford and Chalmers agreed on from the outset was that he would command Battle Group (Center South) but not the 1st Battalion, Welsh Guards. It was a subtle distinction but one that sent a clear message to the guardsmen that one of their own would soon be on his way.

Inside the Welsh Guards Regimental Headquarters in Wellington Barracks, there were two imperatives. Thorneloe's death was a shattering blow, but there was a high-profile funeral to arrange and a successor to appoint. Bonas took charge of the funeral and the repatriation as well as fielding calls from Buckingham Palace, Downing Street, the MoD, and retired Welsh Guardsmen offering condolences and support. It fell to Colonel Sandy Malcolm, the regimental lieutenant colonel, to coordinate the selection of the new commanding officer.[1] It was the first time since 1944 that a Welsh Guards battalion commander had been killed in action, and Thorneloe's death had turned regimental plans upside down. Normally, a commanding officer is earmarked about two years in advance. Chalmers was in place, so that gave some breathing space, but the new man would need to be in Helmand before the end of the month.

Malcolm telephoned four Welsh Guards officers to tell them that they were contenders to replace Thorneloe and that they should prepare themselves for Afghanistan. Three were lieutenant colonels. Alex Macintosh was a staff officer at PJHQ closely involved with running the Helmand campaign. Guy Bartle-Jones had served in Afghanistan as a company commander with the Coldstream Guards and had recently completed a staff job at NATO's headquarters in Kabul. Dino Bossi, newly promoted, had been a Welsh Guards company commander in Iraq and had just started at the army's personnel headquarters in Glasgow. But it was a fourth candidate who had sprung to Radford's mind within a couple of hours of Thorneloe's death and was immediately the heir apparent in the eyes of Malcolm.

Major Charlie Antelme was a swashbuckling, charismatic officer who had seen more combat in the previous eight years than virtually any other officer in the British Army. He had already been identified as the likely next commanding officer of the Welsh Guards, but he had not yet been promoted and still had to complete the required staff job. With his piercing blue eyes, dark hair, and prominent cheekbones, Antelme had a long-established reputation as a lady-killer and enjoyed to the full what he would describe only half-jokingly as his "James Bond lifestyle." He had spent less than a year in an anti-terrorism staff job at the MoD in which he focused on combating al Qaeda in Afghanistan, Pakistan, and the Horn of Africa. It was the first time he had been behind a desk in his 15-year Army career, a setting and role which was in stark contrast to Antelme's front line experiences across the world, much of that in Iraq. Antelme had been awarded the DSO, a rare honor for a major, for his leadership and bravery in Iraq at a time when al Qaeda's suicide-bomb network had threatened to tip the country into all-out civil war. The citation has never been released, but it was reported in the press that the award was for leading an attack on an al Qaeda safe house in Iraq in 2007, armed only with a pistol after his rifle had jammed. After the September 11 attacks of 2001, Antelme took part in operations in Iraq and Afghanistan while on secondment from the Welsh Guards. Importantly, however, he had returned to his parent regiment to command 3 Company in southern Iraq in 2004–05, when he was rated the best British company commander in the country. After the PWRR in their Warrior armored fighting vehicles had fought the Mahdi Army of Shia militiamen to a standstill in Al Amarah, Antelme had entered the town in Snatch vehicles with 3 Company. Regimental Sergeant Major Mike Monaghan had been his company sergeant major while Lance Sergeant Leon Peek was then a young guardsman. At the time, Antelme remarked that the Welsh Guards, after a number of tours in South Armagh, had again found themselves operating in the badlands. "People respect the tough guy with the gun," he said. "It's gangland. It's the Wild West. It's people breaking out of jail. They fish in the river using hand grenades." The Welsh Guards would later find, however, that Helmand's Green Zone would make these badlands seem almost benign.

Antelme had always wanted to be a soldier. The dueling scar on his cheek had been inflicted with a pitchfork wielded as a pretend bayonet by his brother Mark when they were playing a game of Falklands War when he was twelve. His other early passion was acting, and he played Henry V at the age of thirteen. After studying English at Exeter University, he spent a year at LAMDA—the London Academy of Music and Dramatic Art—and very nearly became an actor. "David Niven was my great hero," he remembers. "I thought it would be fun living that Hollywood lifestyle, sharing a flat with Errol Flynn and roistering it up." He was, however, more strongly drawn to the romance of the army, and adventure was in his blood.

Antelme was descended from a prominent family of Mauritian sugar planters, who had produced a first minister, Sir Celicourt Antelme, and one of Napoleon's battalion commanders. His great-grandmother was a Polish princess who battled for the emancipation of Islamic women and was forced to leave Egypt in the 1920s after her alleged part in an assassination plot against the Khedive. He was also related to Major France Antelme, a Franco-Mauritian who worked for Special Operations Executive (SOE) and was executed by the Germans at the Gross-Rosen concentration camp in Poland in 1944. France Antelme had been recruited by the SOE in Durban in November 1941 while he was serving with the South African artillery. His first assignment was to gather intelligence in Vichy-held Madagascar before the Allied landings of May 1942. He was captured by the Gestapo near Chartres after parachuting into occupied France in February 1944, after his radio operator Noor Inayat Khan, an Indian princess, had been compromised. France Antelme's body was never found, and his posthumous awards included the OBE, the Croix de Guerre, and the Légion d'Honneur. Several of Antelme's cousins fought in the Rhodesia Light Infantry against Robert Mugabe's forces, including one who was killed and one who was wounded. Two great-uncles served with the South African Division through Africa and into Italy, Marcus Kane Berman making a notable escape as a prisoner of war.

After much soul-searching, Antelme plumped for the army rather than acting. "I kept on getting cast as a soldier and I decided that pretending to do stuff wasn't going to be as much fun as actually doing it," he says. Before he went to Sandhurst, he spent a year traveling. Initially, he worked his way around America, stacking shelves in supermarkets and even ending up going on a crack raid with the Detroit police. It was the first time he had donned body armor. He also retraced part of the journey across Europe of Patrick Leigh Fermor, the soldier and scholar. Sleeping rough and making money by selling his watercolors, Antelme trekked from Moldova to Rotterdam.[2]

After passing out of Sandhurst, Antelme became an instant star in the Welsh Guards. As a platoon commander in South Armagh, he was part of a triumvirate with Jimmy Stenner and Giles Harris. Stenner was to join the SAS and won a Military Cross in Iraq in 2003 before being killed in a road accident in Baghdad. Antelme and Giles Harris became firm friends. Over the years, they would meet up after operational tours to spend their hard-earned savings on longboard surfing around the world with other members of the Welsh Guards Surf Club. Antelme tired of life in the peacetime army, however, and resigned his commission in 1998 with the intention of breaking into journalism or the film industry. He also had plans to marry an actress who, he says, then "ran off with her leading man."

Antelme secured a job as a location manager with Merchant and Ivory, doing everything from scouting out locations at stately homes to getting up at 5:00 a.m. to put signs on lampposts to direct the crews and arranging for the Portaloos to be delivered. But some aspects of the film industry began to make him think again. Working on a film called *The Golden Bowl*, an adaptation of the Henry James novel, he found himself sitting in a room with a very prominent actress waiting for the lighting to be arranged. For an hour, she sat there in silence without deigning to acknowledge even his existence. Antelme found himself thinking that this wasn't the kind of thing that would happen in the army, where a general would strike up a conversation with the lowliest of soldiers and there was a sense that everyone was on the same team. He also began to think about the values of honor and service.

Watching news reports of the war in Kosovo from a hotel room, Antelme decided to rejoin the army and resume his career. When he told Ismail Merchant: "I'm sorry, I've got to leave, the Queen needs me," Merchant replied with a smile: "This queen needs you!" He was gracious about his assistant location manager's ambitions and gave him a £500 leaving bonus, which Antelme spent on a shotgun. The Welsh Guards eagerly welcomed Antelme back into the fold, and before long he would find himself on the front lines of what the Americans had declared to be the "war on terror." Garrison Sergeant Major Bill Mott remarks that Antelme's dramatic bent was far from wasted when he returned because there is a strong element of theatre in military command. "He wanted to become an actor," says Mott. "Then he came back and became one."

One of the biggest admirers of Antelme's determined aggression and fighting prowess was General Stanley McChrystal, who had taken command of all NATO forces in Afghanistan two weeks before Thorneloe was killed. McChrystal had overseen the dismantling of al Qaeda in Iraq and helped stave off defeat there in 2007, and had worked closely with Antelme, who was one of a number of British soldiers sent to Iraq to operate with the Americans. McChrystal later described Antelme as possessing "a burn-in-your-gut passion to accomplish the mission" in Iraq but also a sophisticated understanding of the al Qaeda IED networks throughout the country. "Charlie could sit down with you and he could describe exactly how what he was doing fitted into the bigger picture and the effect he was trying to achieve." McChrystal describes the period as a successful attempt to halt the "slaughter of Iraqis on a grand scale" that al Qaeda was orchestrating. "There were days with 14 car bombs, each of which were killing in the double digits." Antelme's leadership, he said, was "instrumental" in preventing al Qaeda from taking control of a large swathe of Iraq. "Charlie. What a hero."

The new commanding officer of the Welsh Guards, however, was not going to be chosen either by Stanley McChrystal or Sandy Malcolm. It was a decision to be taken by an army personnel board in Glasgow. Fortuitously, a board had recently sat and graded all potential battalion commanders in the army. Antelme had been right at the top and way above his three Welsh Guards competitors. Before he left for Afghanistan, Thorneloe had told Malcolm that he believed Antelme was the man who should succeed him. Antelme, however, was still a major, and his lack of staff experience was leading some to be uncertain about his broader credentials. The question he was getting from General Dannatt's office, Malcolm remembers, was: "He may be the right man for the next two months, Sandy, but is he the right man for two years' time?"

In the wings, the Welsh Guards had the powerful lobby group of its regimental council, made up of four retired generals—General Lord Guthrie, Lieutenant General Sir Christopher Drewry, Lieutenant General Sir Redmond Watt, and Major General Peter Leuchars. All had signed off on Malcolm's recommendation that Antelme was the man the Welsh Guards wanted. Guthrie, CGS from 1994 to 1997 and then CDS until 2001, knew and admired Antelme. Malcolm says that Guthrie "wanted to wade in and say to CGS: 'Keep out of regimental business, this is our man,'" but Dannatt was persuaded before it came to that.

The bodies of Lieutenant Colonel Rupert Thorneloe and Trooper Joshua Hammond were repatriated at RAF Lyneham on July 8. Thorneloe had been two decades older and ten ranks more senior, but the two soldiers were treated equally in death. This was not modern egalitarianism but a long-established practice.[3]

It was, however, the first repatriation ceremony that Dannatt had attended—recognition that the death of a commanding officer was a rare tragedy. As they waited for the C-17 aircraft to arrive, Thorneloe's mother Veronica, who had just downed two glasses of brandy, was talking to Dannatt when she suddenly found herself saying: "I'm frightfully sorry" and repositioning his epaulettes because they weren't buttoned up properly. Also attending the ceremony was Major General Bill Cubitt, who commanded the Household Division and had been a forceful advocate for Antelme taking over in Helmand. The two generals discretely discussed the matter, and Dannatt gave his final agreement that Antelme would get the nod.

Placing his hand on Thorneloe's coffin as it was carried down the ramp in the driving rain was Garrison Sergeant Major Bill Mott, in charge of all ceremonial matters in the army. Bill Mott was the older brother of Major Nicky Mott, quartermaster of the Welsh Guards and the man who had identified Thorneloe's body, packed up all his kit, and watched as the coffin was put on the C-17 at Camp Bastion. "Nicky was repatriating him from the Afghanistan end," says Bill Mott. "I'm at the other end at Lyneham. Two brothers that have grown up together, that love each other, that were on the *Sir Galahad* together, and there we are repatriating our Commanding Officer, who was also a friend."

Just as Sally Thorneloe had not been alone since the casualty notification had taken place, at least one person had been with her husband's body at all times. Even through the night at Camp Bastion there was a rota of warrant officers keeping vigil. At Wootton Bassett, the Thorneloe and Hammond families were discreetly ushered into a solicitors' office for them to watch the hearses drive through the town, where hundreds had gathered to pay their respects. Down in the street afterwards, they could see Dannatt shaking hands with members of the public and thanking them for their tribute to the fallen.

It was not until the Iraq War that ceremonies took place to mark the repatriation of British troops killed in action. While the Americans had long since brought their dead home, the British practice had always been to bury them temporarily close to where they fell and then properly in a designated grave later.[4] The poet Rupert Brooke memorably described the practice of placing a grave in "some corner of a foreign field that is forever England."

This began to change after the Falklands War. Then, families were given the option of the bodies of their loved ones being disinterred and shipped back to Britain. Many, including the widow of Lieutenant Colonel H. Jones, opted to leave graves undisturbed. Most of the bodies of the Welsh Guardsmen who died onboard the *Sir Galahad* were never recovered from the ship, which became a war grave. Ann Green, the mother of Guardsman Paul Green, whose body sank with the ship, moved from Rhyl in North Wales to the Falklands to be close to her son. The bodies that were brought back were unloaded in shipping containers at a military port near Southampton and driven away without ceremony in privately hired hearses.

From 2003, a repatriation ceremony, designed by Bill Mott, was held for all servicemen brought back to British soil. The ceremony had distinct echoes of that held for American servicemen at Dover Air Force Base in Delaware. Burial ceremonies for British soldiers also began to take on an American flavor—right down to the folding of the Union Flag into a triangle and its presentation to the next of kin; this had long been done with the Stars and Stripes in the United States.

For Sandy Malcolm, the Mott brothers were not only part of the living history of the regiment, but also an invaluable conduit for assessing how the guardsmen were reacting to Thorneloe's death. "The old chins of the Welshmen can wobble like mad," explains Malcolm. "When they're on a low, they're really morose and their shoulders hunch. On a high they're fantastic and I felt they needed to be on a high. I'd heard from Garrison Sergeant Major Mott that his brother Nicky had said chins were down." The "high" that Malcolm was planning on delivering was the appointment of Antelme, whose warrior pedigree would give him instant credibility. In the meantime, he was relying on the likes of Major Nicky Mott and Major Martyn Miles, both of whom had also been in the RFA *Sir Galahad* on June 8, 1982, the darkest day in the history of the Welsh Guards, to steady the battalion at a critical moment.

The day before the repatriation, Malcolm sent an email to Nicky Mott and Miles. The first of July, he wrote, "will undoubtedly rate as one of the most difficult days in our short Regimental history" of ninety-four years. "The loss of any Welsh Guardsman is bad news, but the loss of a Commanding Officer on operations is magnified many times over. What cannot be allowed to happen, and I know that you will understand this all too clearly, is for all Colonel Rupert's good work over the past 6 months to be allowed to falter or at worse come to naught." Thorneloe, he said, had "always had the greatest respect for you both as well as placing huge trust and faith in your abilities. Now with his death, it is for me to articulate to you both that you have my total support in everything you are doing to maintain the morale and ethos of the Battalion in these very difficult circumstances." Mott and Miles, he directed, were to use their "robust and vital leadership" to bolster the Welsh Guards not only in the coming days, but also in the months ahead "when the realisation of what the Battalion has suffered will become more apparent." He concluded: "Colonel Rupert will be replaced, yet he will never be forgotten and I ask you both to continue to ensure where you can that the resolve of the Battalion is strengthened."

In Battle Group headquarters at FOB Shawqat, the staff had lost not only their commanding officer, but a man they had lived and worked with. At the start of every evening conference call with the companies, Speed would always end his opening preamble with "The Commanding Officer is present" or, if he was out on the ground, "The Commanding Officer is not present." On the night of July 1, he scored through the mention of the commanding officer's whereabouts on the index card he used and omitted the sentence. Everyone was gathered for the call, which was conducted so smoothly that a Royal Engineer officer who had been away from the ops room all day and had not learned of Thorneloe's death did not find out until afterwards. When the call was over, Speed held back the Welsh Guards members of the staff and told them that the coming days would be crucial in the history of the regiment.

Speed had only just returned from commanding IX Company after Birchall's death. Less than two weeks earlier, he had been taken aside by Brigadier Radford, who had looked him in the eye and asked: "Are you up for this?" Speed knew that Radford would again want an answer to the same question, this time from the entire Battle Group staff. "We are Colonel Rupert's immediate legacy," Speed said. "Our actions must cement that legacy." Thorneloe had prided himself on the quality of the Battle Group staff he had brought together, shaped, and tested. Major Mark Gidlow-Jackson, who was commanding R Company of 4 Rifles, which was based in Shawqat, feels that the fact that the headquarters staff barely missed a beat after their commanding officer's death was a testament to Thorneloe. "They were massively upset but amazingly stoical about it. It was a hell of a hit to take but they just dug in and got on with it."

Captain Jeffrey, the tactical air controller, had been sitting outside his tent talking to Speed when the subject of Thorneloe's death came up. Speed related what he had heard relayed from Corporal Williams about the immediate aftermath. "I found that image of his final moments so utterly tragic it is hard to express," recalls Jeffrey, who was becoming deeply disillusioned about the war in Afghanistan. "All that talent, all that goodness, reduced to such a warped, f---ed up last few moments of him clinging onto life. You want an image of what has gone wrong in Afghanistan and there you have it." For Jeffrey, a cavalry officer, the stoicism of the Welsh Guards in the aftermath of such an horrific event was initially impressive. "But after a few days and as time wore on, I started to wonder that it was almost too calm and disciplined. It seemed to mirror what I felt was applicable to the whole British enterprise in Afghan in a way. Everyone was maintaining that good old traditional British stiff upper lip about what was going on in the face of what was arguably a f---ing disaster. On the one hand it was commendable, but at the same time I almost wanted to grab people by the shoulders and say 'Can you not see what is going on here, this is ridiculous!'"

Two days after Malcolm's email to Major Nicky Mott and Major Martyn Miles, the military secretary's Command Board in Glasgow held an extraordinary meeting and formally selected Acting Lieutenant Colonel Charles Kane Antelme, DSO, to be the new commanding officer of the Welsh Guards. Malcolm broke the news to him while they were standing at the urinals in Wellington Barracks just after Sean Birchall's funeral service.

That evening, Antelme's girlfriend, Margaret Grimsley, a glamorous brunette from South Carolina, returned home to find their house full of desert combat uniforms. "I'm leaving next week," he said. Margaret, fourteen years younger than her boyfriend, was from a military family and had worked in the Pentagon for Donald Rumsfeld. Major General William Grimsley, who, as a U.S. Army colonel, had led troops into Baghdad in 2003, had been the matchmaker who had introduced his niece to Antelme. For their second date, Margaret had accompanied Antelme to Windsor Castle, where he was presented with his DSO by the Queen. Over the next five months, they were almost inseparable. "We'd meet for drinks after work most nights," she remembers. "I'd virtually forgotten he was in the Army because of our life in London."

Antelme had left despondent females behind as he departed for an operational tour on more occasions than he chose to remember. As Margaret drove him to Brize Norton, however, he felt that this time might be different. Just before he left, Margaret took out a copy of Psalm 23—"the Lord is my Shepherd"—that a commander he had served under in Iraq had given Antelme to carry with him in Helmand. "I love you," she wrote on the back.

16

Men of Harlech

Men of Harlech stop your dreaming,
Can't you see their spear points gleaming,
See their warrior pennants streaming,
To this battlefield.

The opening verse of "Men of Harlech,"
regimental song of the Welsh Guard[1]

The battle must be fought to the bitter end at all costs....
Commanders and senior officers should die with their troops.
The honour of the British Empire and the British Army is at stake.

Letter from Winston Churchill to General Sir Archibald Wavell,
February 10, 1942

After slipping out of the Wellington Barracks reception following Major Sean Birchall's funeral, a Welsh Guards officer dressed in an immaculate Savile Row suit and wearing a regimental tie strode purposefully along Birdcage Walk towards the Palace of Westminster. Several weeks earlier, the officer had spoken at length to Thorneloe about the under-resourcing of British operations in Helmand. Now, he had an appointment at the House of Commons. He had been asked to provide a confidential briefing to an advisor to David Cameron, the then Leader of the Opposition, about the reality of what was happening in Helmand. Thorneloe's death had been front-page news in Britain and, along with the other Panther's Claw casualties, had triggered a political furor. It had been twenty-seven years since a battalion commander had been killed in action, and only seven had died on active service since the Second World War.[2] Thorneloe was the first battalion commander in the American or British forces to have been killed in action on the ground in Afghanistan.

Once the pleasantries were over, the Conservative Party official was straight down to business. He wanted to know whether Prime Minister Gordon Brown's protestations that British commanders had everything they needed were justified. The officer recounted his conversation with Thorneloe, who had been emphatic that the lack of helicopters and the poor aviation-management system was costing the lives of soldiers and undermining everything the British were trying to achieve in Helmand. When the officer had finished his account of Thorneloe's views, the official shook his head in disbelief and said he needed to be absolutely clear about what had to be done. He wanted to get to the crux of the helicopter issue by asking three questions. "First, did Rupert Thorneloe say there were not enough helicopters? And second, is it correct that more helicopters are in fact needed? Finally, and most crucially, would more of our troops be alive today if we had more helicopters in Helmand?" The officer paused and thought carefully. There was no doubt about his response to the first two questions, he said. But the third question was problematic because more helicopters meant a greater risk of one being shot down, perhaps killing as many as twenty troops. On balance, though, movements by road had led to more deaths than even that hypothetical worst-case scenario. "The answer to all three of your questions," the officer said, "is yes."

Six days later, on July 15, Cameron leaned against his dispatch box in the Commons chamber as Brown, perched opposite, scowled at him. "Let me ask some specific questions about helicopters and Afghanistan," the Tory leader said. "Is not the basic problem this: the number of helicopters in Afghanistan is simply insufficient?" Cameron pummeled Brown, noting that as chancellor of the Exchequer he had reduced the military helicopter budget by £1.4 billion in 2004. He quoted General Lord Guthrie as saying that "of course they need more helicopters" and that more helicopters would have made it "likely that fewer soldiers would have been killed by roadside bombs." Brown, glowering back at Cameron, was at his least convincing. It was the case that "our military commanders will always want more equipment," he said, and that "while the loss of life is tragic and sad, it is not to do with helicopters."

That week, Brown had telephoned Brigadier Tim Radford in Lashkar Gah to discuss Panther's Claw and subsequent operations in Helmand. In the Commons, Brown stated: "I have talked to Tim Radford, the brigadier on the ground, and he has assured me that his troops have the equipment that they need." Radford declines to discuss any details of his discussions with Brown. The consistent advice, however, that the prime minister was receiving from General Dannatt and other senior military figures was not quite as Brown had described it. While the Army felt it had enough resources to conduct the operation—otherwise, Radford would not have launched it— Brown was being told that more troops and more helicopters were needed if the gains from Panther's Claw were not to be in vain. To many in the army, Brown was lying by omission and misrepresenting the views of the military commanders waging the war in Helmand.

The combination of a vulnerable and uncertain prime minister and the death in action of the first commanding officer since the Falklands War was too much for the press to resist. For much of July, the issues of helicopters and Afghanistan dominated the headlines and news bulletins.

In Helmand, the situation with helicopters was as bad as ever because what helicopters there were had been allocated to Panther's Claw. Chalmers found himself facing the same dilemma as Thorneloe. "Taking command, I drove because I could not get a helicopter," he remembers. "I'm not sure that was very clever. But I had to get forward." On July 17, he reported to brigade that "aviation has been erratic," just as it had been the previous week. This meant that soldiers going on R&R had to be driven to Camp Bastion in seven Mastiffs. "As a result we conducted an unnecessary road move but perhaps more importantly reduced our ability to project our presence around NDA [Nad-e Ali]. It is hard to stay on the front foot when so much of our ground force is forced to pick up tasks that should be met by SH [support helicopters]." Largely missing from the debate in Britain about helicopters was Chalmers's point that the lack of them was preventing the core mission being carried out. Thorneloe's fears that Panther's Claw would make it harder to deepen security in the Nad-e Ali district were being realized.

Towards the end of July, the Afghan army made the decision to withdraw its men from PB Pimon and CPs Paraang and Haji Alem. On July 31, Chalmers lamented that this was because of the continued cancelation of helicopter resupplies, which the Afghan army viewed as a failure "to deliver on our repeated promises." Chalmers had been unable to supply the Afghan troops with the bread, meat, oil, and wood they needed. "It is deeply regrettable but they do have a point," Chalmers concluded. "We have failed to supply them in these isolated, high threat areas." The result was that there would soon be no Afghan army or police in the five bases that made up the outer ring of Battle Group (Center South)—a calamity in terms of the central strategic aim of building Afghan capacity to provide security.

The contrast with American forces could not have been starker. By now attached to the 2nd Battalion, 8th Regiment of the U.S. Marines, Major Rob Gallimore was astonished when the Americans sent in Black Hawks under fire carrying underslung loads of frozen water for the Afghan army. Every time an Afghan soldier or policeman was wounded or killed, a Black Hawk would fly in to evacuate them just as if he were an American. Part of the British helicopter problem was that because airframes were so limited in number and so precious, there was little appetite for incurring any significant risk in using them. After Thorneloe's death, there was a sense in Whitehall that the loss of a single Chinook might be enough to prompt a major reassessment of government policy in Helmand. The result was an almost paralyzing lack of political and military confidence.

The day before prime minister's questions, extracts from Lieutenant Mark Evison's diary, highlighting equipment shortages and a lack of manpower, had been published in the *Daily Telegraph* at the instigation of his mother. Her actions in going public prompted dismay at the MoD and within the Welsh Guards regimental hierarchy, where it was felt that a platoon commander did not always understand the bigger picture. Several of the younger officers who had been close to Evison felt that his writings had been a private way of venting his frustrations and he would have been mortified to have them plastered all over the newspapers. References to different girlfriends in the diaries prompted much heartache. Others, however, argued that the diary was a raw account of the realities of Helmand and that the public needed to know the ground truth of what was happening there. Whatever the pros and cons, publication of the diary propelled Margaret Evison into a position of some influence. Eventually, she would put the leather-bound diary on display in the Tewkesbury Museum and pass the headcam footage of her son's death to Channel 4 for broadcast on the evening news.

After appearing on *Newsnight* just after the diary extracts were published, Mrs. Evison was invited to 10 Downing Street to meet Prime Minister Brown. "I had three-quarters of an hour with him," she remembers. "It was supposed to be half an hour but he kept the Chancellor waiting for 15 minutes. I didn't want to go in there as a cross mum or weeping mum. I wanted to engage him in stuff that was useful." There were big issues she wanted to highlight. "One was that an army's job is to fight. But if the army is not properly equipped and the government hasn't given them what they need, should the men be sent out? That was a fundamental dilemma that every officer out there had to deal with. And Gordon Brown listened to that very carefully. And I said there was another issue, which was that it appeared the brigadiers and the people at the top were saying there was enough equipment. The army are great ones for saying we will make do." At a Downing Street reception for the Mark Evison Foundation six months later, Brown said to her: "Margaret, I've got to tell you how much I enjoyed our talk and, yes, it did make a difference."

Both Guthrie and Dannatt feel that the summer and the impact of Panther's Claw and Sangin marked a watershed for Brown. Guthrie says: "I think he had a mistaken idea that the Army had voted Tory, which is not true. He had a prejudice and maybe still has. He may feel uncomfortable with the Army. The Services have been underfunded for a long time, and when he was Chancellor he was very unsympathetic as far as the defence budget was concerned." The root of the problem may have been Brown's rivalry with Tony Blair, whose idea the initial deployment to Helmand had been. "When I was CDS, sometimes just because Blair wanted to do something, Brown wanted to stop him, the relationship was so bad." For the army, the result had been disastrous. "I'm absolutely certain that if there'd been better investment in some helicopters and some vehicles, we'd have more soldiers alive today." Since the summer of 2009, things had improved. "He took more of an interest, actually chairing defence committees and trying to coordinate Whitehall. He did most of the things that he was being implored to do. He ordered more helicopters, though they won't arrive for ages."

Dannatt retired in August 2009 after he was blocked by Brown from becoming CDS, and Air Chief Marshal Sir Jock Stirrup's tenure was extended instead. But despite Labour's intense irritation with Dannatt's public criticism of the government, he believes the weight of criticism in the wake of Thorneloe's death did have an effect. "I don't think I personally managed to get through to Gordon Brown until my last month as Chief of the General Staff. I had three discussions with him in the course of a few weeks, which was three more than I'd had the whole of the previous year. His whole attitude changed and he became rather more convincing about the importance of

Afghanistan. I think he had to frankly." Dannatt also blames the other service chiefs, Admiral Sir Jonathon Band and Air Chief Marshal Sir Glenn Torpy, and Stirrup for a "real reluctance to commit resources" to army helicopters and vehicles. This was motivated, he says, by the narrow interests of the Royal Navy and RAF, who wanted procurement money to go into long-term projects for aircraft carriers and jets that had no relevance to Afghanistan or Iraq. He says he found himself in a minority of one on the helicopter issue. "To be honest, it didn't move Jock Stirrup in the slightest. It didn't interest Jonathon Band in the slightest. Glenn Torpy saw it as being another way of taking resources away from his fast jets. And Gordon Brown didn't understand."

When Thorneloe was killed, there were just ten of the RAF's forty Chinooks in Afghanistan, along with five aging Sea Kings. Eight Chinooks had been grounded in Britain since 2001 due to a software problem. Chinooks were the workhorses used to move troops and supplies around Helmand, but with one acting as a medical helicopter, two being serviced, and one in reserve, there were usually no more than six available for "heavy-lift" duties at any one time. Dannatt was also frustrated by the lack of a light utility helicopter in Afghanistan because the Lynx could not operate in daytime in the high temperatures of summer. He says that new T800 engines for the existing Lynx helicopters, enabling them to operate properly in Helmand, could have been bought and fitted by the start of 2008, but he was blocked on the issue, and the order was delayed and then almost canceled. "I got as close to resigning over that one as I got to anything," says Dannatt. The importance of the Lynx, he emphasizes, is that they were the type of aircraft that provided the "oil that keeps the dynamic of the battlefield moving, particularly in terms of moving commanders and command groups to be able to influence operations at a time when it was necessary." He says: "When I was commanding the Green Howards [1989–91] I jumped on the back of a Lynx and was gone. When I was commanding 4th Armoured Brigade in Bosnia [1994–05], I jumped on the back of a Lynx." Thorneloe, of course, did not have that option. There is every chance that he might have opted to go on the convoy on July 1 even had there been a Lynx available because he wanted to see the ground and spend time with his guardsmen. On the other hand, if there had been Chinooks available to move routine stores there might have been no need for a convoy and certainly no requirement for so many along the Shamalan that they were setting patterns and inviting an IED strike. Dannatt also bemoans the Brown-ordered cut in the helicopter budget in 2004 that Cameron had highlighted at Prime Minister's Questions. "What could we have done more with a billion and a half, in the rotary wing programme? The answer is quite a lot." This was, he adds, "controversial but it is germane to Rupert Thorneloe."

As Thorneloe's body was being repatriated from Helmand, the Welsh Guards and Bridgend suffered another fatality—Lance Corporal Dane Elson. In his last telephone call to his mother Debra, he had told her that no one felt safe now that the commanding officer had been killed. "It's going to be hairy, Mum, and there are going to be more people killed," he said, telling her that he was just about to depart on Panther's Claw. She replied: "Just take care and make sure you're not one of them." He said: "Don't worry, I will." When the Welsh Guards had been back in Aldershot, Elson had occasionally shared lifts back to South Wales with Lance Sergeant Tobie Fasfous and Lance Corporal Jamie Evans 15, now in a hospital bed in Selly Oak. He and Fasfous drank in the same pubs in Pencoed and Bridgend, where Elson would tease Fasfous's girlfriend Kelly Gore by saying to her: "Why are you going out with that fat f---ing Arab?" Elson's funeral service was to be held in the same Salem Chapel where mourners had bidden farewell to Fasfous.

Elson was part of FSG-3, given the callsign Cobra 24, commanded by Captain Phil Durham and attached to B Company of the 2 Mercians, part of the Light Dragoons Battle Group. The Light Dragoons were the brigade's Main Effort for Panther's Claw, tasked with clearing from east to west from Malgir and through Babaji with the eventual aim of reaching the block established by the Welsh Guards on the Shamalan Canal. Spirits were high as they received their battle orders at FOB Price on July 1. FSG-3, which had already established itself in the role of the jokers of the company, staged a naked conga for the rest of the company.

Shortly afterwards, the news of Thorneloe's death came through. Durham was too choked up to inform his men, so Lieutenant Colonel Gus Fair, who had worked with Thorneloe in the MoD and been an ally and a fellow skeptic during the planning phase of Panther's Claw, undertook the task. Durham had been a close friend of Mark Evison, but he found that his commanding officer's death affected him much more because the Welsh Guards had lost their figurehead and focal point. Once the shock had worn off, his mind started racing. "That means Speedy is now Commanding Officer. Is Speedy going to stay? Just imagine them in the ops room, that Falklands moment."

Durham and his men were going to be moving long distances on foot, clearing compounds as they went. Even before they set off, he realized that the weight they would be carrying in temperatures exceeding 50°C (122° F) would be crippling. He weighed his kit and found that it came in at fifty-five kilograms. This included a rifle, helmet, body armor, five liters of water, six magazines, and a bandolier of 7.62 mm bullets, medical kits, radio and spare batteries, eight maps, two high-explosive grenades, two smoke grenades, mini-flares, a torch, battle orders, and a notebook. In his rucksack he had his personal kit for four weeks—a pair of socks, T-shirt, toothbrush, and toothpaste. Some of his men were carrying sixty kilograms, and there was electronic jamming equipment as well. "We were pukka tooled up," Durham recalls. "The temperature had just jumped an extra 5 to 10 degrees [Celsius] and it went from hot to just stupidly hot. We were still in the mentality that we can fight all day with breaks and it proved not to be the case. We could work the first few hours in the morning and last couple of hours in the evening and that was it. Any other time, we just had to survive in the heat."

The men knew they would not all survive the next few days. The night before heading out, the Light Dragoons chaplain offered blessings and a prayer that began: "Be with us Almighty God as we go forth into battle.... " Guardsman Etika Macedru, a Fijian, sang "I Know the Lord Will Make a Way" and taught some of the Welsh Guardsmen the words. Lance Sergeant Dewi Ahearne, from Aberbargoed, accompanied by Drummer Sam Potts, from Ruthlin on the penny whistle, sang "Working Man," about a miner:

> It's a working man I am and I've been down underground
> And I swear by God if I ever see the sun
> Over any length of time, I can hold it in my mind
> Then I will never again go down underground.[3]

Major Stewart Hill, commander of B Company of 2 Mercians, delivered an eve of battle speech in which he quoted Field Marshal Viscount Montgomery of Alamein about the need for decision in action and calmness in crisis. "Is it to be the insurgents' summer or will it belong to us?" he asked. "Of course, it's going to be ours."[4]

B Company came under fire before it had covered 150 meters of the push west during Panther's Claw and was attacked relentlessly throughout the day by local Taliban reinforced with foreign fighters. A brigade post-operation report stated that, contrary to intelligence assessments beforehand, there "were a large number of INS [insurgents], determined and motivated to resist [friendly forces'] advance. They had not buckled under the advance of two battle-groups, were not deterred by the presence of armor, AH [attack helicopter] and aviation, and continued to fight despite heavy losses." By the end of the afternoon, the company had progressed a few hundred meters when a Spartan troop carrier was hit by an RPG that detonated a box of 40 mm grenades inside the vehicle. Private Robbie Laws, only eighteen, was killed, and Lieutenant Guy Disney, beside him, was heard over the radio saying: "I need a heli. I think I have lost my leg." Disney's right foot and lower leg were hanging off, attached only by skin and sinew, and three others had also been wounded. Durham and his men raced across a bridge over an irrigation ditch to assist in the casualty evacuation. There was a very high threat of IEDs and the bridge—an obvious place for a device—had been Barmaed. In all, the bridge must have been crossed more than fifty times by at least a dozen soldiers, including Lieutenant Colonel Fair who manned a stretcher to carry one of the wounded onto the medical Chinook.

A couple of minutes after the Chinook had lifted off, Lance Corporal David "Duke" Dennis stepped on the bridge and an IED exploded beneath him. It was a scene of carnage. Durham saw Dennis's rucksack get blown more than fifteen meters in the air. Major Stewart Hill was in a desperate state, with a gooseneck radio antenna embedded in his head. Company Sergeant Major Paul Muckle had lost most of his hearing and was in battle shock, wide-eyed and falling over repeatedly as he tried to give orders. Lance Sergeant Dan Collins, from Cardigan, was one of the first to find Dennis, about thirty meters away, lying face-down in an irrigation ditch. He was alive but unconscious and had lost both legs and his left arm. Collins, who minutes earlier had carried the body of Laws to the Chinook, gave Dennis chest compressions while the medics fought to save him, tying tourniquets onto the stumps where his limbs had been and injecting fluids straight into his sternum. "As I was doing compressions, I looked at Duke's face and I could see his eyes opening. I don't think he knew anything about what was going on but it was like he was looking at me." When the Pedro arrived, Muckle refused to be evacuated, saying: "I want to stay with my Company," and had to be pushed onto the helicopter by Fair. Dennis remained alive for more than ten minutes but was pronounced dead as the Pedro flew back to Camp Bastion.

Also onboard with Muckle and Dennis were several heat casualties and Major Hill, who had suffered serious brain injuries but survived. Durham was told by Fair to take over command of the company, which now had to retreat two hundred meters to secure a compound where they could stay overnight. "In an hour we'd gone from doing awesomely well, getting into fights, winning them, advancing, finding IEDs, to literally just chaos," says Durham.

The next day, the company was attacked again as it crossed the bridge. By 5:30 p.m., they had fought forward another six hundred meters, blowing through compound walls as they went. Apache helicopters fired Hellfire missiles and 30 mm cannon rounds into Taliban positions, but the enemy would not give up. Durham and the company command team halted in a compound to deal with yet more heat casualties. He called on two Barma men from FSG-3 to help clear the track leading to the next compounds. Elson and Guardsman Gareth Bisp, from Cardiff, came forward and sat down against a compound wall in an area that had already been Barmaed. Minutes later, Durham ordered them to begin clearing the track. As Elson got up, an IED detonated. Bisp looked back to where he and Elson had been sitting and saw a crater and pieces of a rifle and body armor.

Three soldiers around Elson had been wounded, including a forward air controller who had been flown in the previous evening to replace an SAS man who had been wounded that day. "Bisp, Dane, are you all right?" Collins shouted over the radio. Bisp responded but there was silence from Elson. "Dane! Dane! Dane! Can you hear us? If you can hear, do anything, just click and blow, just do anything!" Collins screamed. Bisp spotted an object in a field about twenty meters away, beckoned a medic to come with him, and then Barmaed over to it. Just like Dennis the day before, Elson had been catastrophically wounded, losing both his legs and an arm, but mercifully he had been killed outright. Lance Sergeant Chris Scarf, from Aberdare, a second row in the army rugby team, saw Elson's body and returned to the rest of FSG-3 to tell them: "Dane's gone. He wouldn't have felt a thing."

Captain Richard Sheehan, whose Apache had accompanied the Chinook that took away Elson's body, reflected on the day's carnage in his diary: "The IRT picked up at least 30 British casualties from Panchai Palang. Three KIA, at least one double amputee and one that lost a leg to an RPG. The only thing you'll read about is the three KIA. The IRT is just picking up bits of people and I've no idea how many the Pedro's picked up." He later observed: "More blood is used in Bastion than in the whole of the UK and more life-saving trauma equipment is used in Bastion than in the whole of Birmingham. The casualties must be at Falklands or World War Two levels."

Major Andrew Speed broke the news of Elson's death to those Welsh Guards at Camp Bastion in the early hours of the next morning just after Thorneloe's body had been loaded onto the C-17 bound for RAF Lyneham. Standing beside the runway, he was aware that some heads were dropping, and the impact of the deaths was weighing heavily on guardsmen's shoulders. "Every one of these deaths is a tragedy and every one hurts," he told them. "Some of you have seen and experienced things that have been shocking. But we must continue to be strong." He praised their bravery and resilience and reminded them that there were still three months of the tour to complete. "We will persevere and we will prevail because you are Welsh Guardsmen."

The escalating casualties through June and July created a sense of barely suppressed hysteria among the families. Those who lived in Wales or elsewhere tended to suffer alone, whereas for the wives living on the patch in Aldershot, the shared fear of a husband being killed or maimed meant that they banded together. Aldershot is a garrison town, and there is no escape from the army. Streets lined with married quarters are named after the battles of Arnhem, Cassino, and Anzio. There is even an enclave called Goose Green Park that is dedicated to the Falklands, where people live in McKay Close and H. Jones Crescent—named after the two posthumous VC recipients—South Atlantic Drive and San Carlos Approach. Several of the Welsh Guards officers' wives lived in Blenheim Park. The Welsh Guards welfare office organized coffee mornings and weekend trips for the children. There were briefings at which it was said gently that wives should avoid mentioning problems with the dishwasher or the bad behavior of the children when a husband called back during a lull in Panther's Claw. "We spent every waking hour with each other," remembers Major Rob Gallimore's wife Rebecca. "We'd move the kids from one house to the next. After Rupert's death, some people were very tearful and very, very nervous all the time."

Major Dai Bevan, commanding the Rear Party and overseeing all the casualty notifications, and his pregnant wife Denise also lived in Blenheim Park. Some wives came to regard him with trepidation, even though he had made it clear he would never be the one to deliver the bad news. One morning, Marlo Bettinson, the Australian wife of Major Henry Bettinson, heard the doorbell ring and was overcome by a sense of dread that this was to be the tidings of her husband's death. Scooping up her two children, she ran into a bedroom, closed the door, and refused to answer. The person on the doorstep turned out to be Bevan, in his pajamas, who was just being neighborly. After that, it was agreed that no one would go to anyone else's front door. Instead, everyone would knock quietly at the side door or window, so there was no danger of the person inside collapsing in hysterics.

It was the same in Wales. In St. Athyn one morning in July, Ceri Harman was getting changed when she heard a knock on the door and saw an unfamiliar car outside. Her heart began pounding, and she was saying "Oh my God" over and over again to herself as she walked down the stairs. She opened the door and saw a friend who looked at the expression on her face and immediately asked: "What's the matter?" Ceri Harman, an army wife for some twenty-three years, replied: "Nothing, I'm just so glad it's you."

Rebecca Gallimore had never relished the idea of being an institutionalized army wife but found it a comfort to be on the Married Quarters patch in Aldershot with people who instinctively understood. "It was a place where you didn't have to explain, where everybody knew exactly what was going on, how you were feeling, and didn't have to ask you questions." It became harder to relate to friends who had no connection with the army, some of whom seemed oblivious to what was happening with the Welsh Guards in Afghanistan despite the saturation media coverage. Rebecca Gallimore found herself wanting to scream: "This is my world. I don't understand how you've missed this."

The growing casualties were also having an effect on the Rear Party. Bevan would hand the folded Union Flag to the next of kin once it was taken off the coffin just before cremation or burial. Usually, he would say: "On behalf of the Welsh Guards and a very grateful nation" as he did so and then step back as they clasped it to their chest while the coffin disappeared behind a curtain or into the ground. Sean Birchall, however, had been a very close friend, and he found he did not need to say anything to Jo Birchall because she knew what he felt and what the moment signified. What he found hardest was that she smiled as he walked towards her with the flag. After the funeral, he pulled his car over in a lay-by, got out, and vomited. Bevan spent the whole tour receiving telephone calls very early in the morning from Captain James

Aldridge, the adjutant, giving him bad news about the dead or wounded. His voice would then be the one that everyone in the Welsh Guards dreaded as he telephoned those who needed to know what had happened. "I had no influence over what was happening so I was in a completely reactive role," he remembers. "You felt as though you were just being punched and you had your hands tied behind your back and there was nothing you could really do about it."

While the dead had to be buried, the wounded also had to be attended to. Often sedated in Helmand, they would wake up in a hospital bed at Selly Oak not knowing where they were. Drummer Dale Leach initially thought he was on R&R and then felt the tubes up his nose and through a hole in his throat and ripped them out. It was days before his mother told him he had lost his leg. His friend Lance Corporal Geraint Hillard felt so spaced out from morphine that he wouldn't accept anything he was told. "My mum told me that Michael Jackson had died. I didn't believe her so she had to tell me again a couple of days later."

Guardsman Carl Thomas 08, the last man to be pulled out of the Viking and revived on the canal bank, was in a coma for two weeks at Selly Oak. Like Leach, he had had a tracheotomy and was fitted with a catheter. To communicate, he had to write on a piece of paper. His dreams were so violent that he had to be secured to his hospital bed. "One dream was I was on the bed, and a helicopter came in and dropped bodies on me and they were operating on them. Another one was we were in Afghan and I had the microchip on my head and a little kid slit my throat and I couldn't breathe." Whether it was a dream or memory – he couldn't recall anything from two days before the Viking went into the canal—when he slept he would hear voices shouting and the sound of vehicles arriving. When he was well enough to sit up and read, Thomas 08 was shown a booklet that had been beside his bed at Camp Bastion. It was full of messages from Welsh Guardsmen wishing him well. Among them was a scrawled note that said: "Once you're better, we'll go for a pint." It was from his friend Lance Corporal Dane Elson.

Guardsman James Barber dreamt of being in the Viking again as it rolled and rolled without stopping. When he was released from hospital, he collapsed at home. "I'd had a little argument with my missus and was walking down the stairs. All of a sudden, I just went light-headed, couldn't breathe, stumbled down the stairs, fell onto the floor. She was shouting at me. Everything went all tingly and all heavy and I could taste the water and see all the images again." Sergeant Steve Young, whose hand Barber had clutched underwater as they slipped into unconsciousness, was only slightly injured. After being treated for fluid on his lungs and taking R&R in Wales, he returned to Camp Bastion, where he told the physio he didn't want any more treatment because it was time for him to get back with his men. "I wanted a helicopter but obviously there weren't any so the only way I could get back to the boys was in a Mastiff. I'd been having panic attacks and didn't like enclosed spaces so I had to grit my teeth to get on the back." He tried putting a seatbelt on but couldn't bear to be strapped down.

An hour and a half later, close to XP-1 at the top of the canal, the Mastiff hit an IED. "It lifted about 10 foot in the air, blew the wheels off, blew all the bar armour right off and I was thrown upwards and forwards." In the darkness, Lance Corporal Kingsley Simmons, sitting next to him, felt liquid and started shouting: "There's blood everywhere." It turned out that a crate of water had exploded. Young was writhing in pain, shouting: "F---ing hell, my back, my back." A Coldstream Guardsman tried to give him morphine, but the first time the needle hit the bone and the second syringe wouldn't function. Young, in agony, lost his temper and punched him in the face. Young had a burst fracture of the vertebrae and spent four months in a spinal bed. If he had been wearing a seatbelt, he would have escaped uninjured. "I feel really bad for smacking the lad who was trying to calm me down and help me," he says.

Once discharged from Selly Oak, the wounded received treatment at Headley Court in Surrey, the military rehabilitation center. The facility looks like a country house from the outside. Inside, amputees walk along the corridors with their aluminum artificial legs, and there are wheelchair races on the wards. Although most of the residents have lost limbs, their sense of humor remains, with injuries being compared and leg amputations judged only minor if they are below the knee. Guardsman Joe Penlington, only eighteen, was the worst injured of anyone from the Battle Group. He spent seventy-two hours in surgery in the three months after he had been injured in the blast that killed Thorneloe and Hammond. He did not walk for eighteen months, and in June 2011 he opted to have his left leg amputated.

Regimental Quartermaster Sergeant Dorian Thomas 53, in charge of the repatriations and funerals, had wept for each of the men who had been killed. But he found Thorneloe's death particularly hard because he was making the arrangements for the man who had given him that job.

Thorneloe's coffin left Lyneham and passed through Wootton Bassett and all the other villages where people also turned out to pay their respects. After the coroner released the body, it was transferred to Kenyon's Funeral Directors, which had a contract with the MoD for all repatriated remains, to prepare it for burial.

Thomas 53's job was to ensure that Thorneloe would be wearing Service Dress with all the correct insignia and medals. The Afghanistan Campaign Medal, due to be presented to each Welsh Guardsman by Prince Charles and other dignitaries at a parade after the tour was over, was awarded automatically on death. It was the same procedure for every Welsh Guards fatality. Thomas 53 had to retrieve Thorneloe's kit—no easy task, because his personal organization was notoriously shambolic. Every officer's kit was difficult, with the single exception of Mark Evison's. "Every single thing in his room was just immaculate," recalls the former Sandhurst color sergeant. "From his civilian clothes, all clean, to his military clothing, all clean, to his drawers, all tidy and everything folded and in piles." Bevan had asked Antelme—then a fellow major—to travel down to south London with him to check Evison's uniform before his funeral in the Guards Chapel. "This was when Charlie was still Charlie," Bevan remembers. "The traffic was appalling. It took us three hours to get there and three hours to get back. It was a fairly grim chapel of rest and Mark looked heavily made up. Our uniform is not super-complex but we wanted to make sure everything was right."

Thomas 53 bulled Thorneloe's boots, shined his medals, and polished the peak of his cap. He ironed his uniform and the Union Flag that was to be placed on his coffin. In Thomas 53's eyes, Thorneloe was his commanding officer until the moment the Union Flag was taken off the coffin just before burial. The casket was opened for viewing by the family, and so much of his business was done alone with the body lying there in repose. Every time he had to use a pin to hold something down, he said: "Excuse me, sir." When speaking about the body, he referred to it as "my Commanding Officer." He found that seeing the body, which he did in the case of Birchall and Thorneloe but was not possible in the case of most IED victims, was a comfort, as it had been after his brother had killed himself. "With my brother, I always remember going to him six or seven times, asking him questions. And what a good job they'd done of making him look normal, really. And the same can be said for those from Helmand that I was lucky enough to get to view and pay my last respects properly."

Before the funeral, Thomas 53 and a small team "dressed" the coffin, aligning the Union Flag so that it was perfectly straight. "I didn't want the stripe to be off," he remembers. "I didn't want it to be wavy. So I took it off and put it on, took it off and put it on. Until it was right." No one would see the brass plaque on the coffin because it would be under the flag, but it was polished until it was gleaming. Thomas 53 also had the job of gathering all the personal effects of the deceased from the barracks and unpacking the items that had been sent back from Camp Bastion by Major Nicky Mott. He would then catalog everything in a single inventory and pack it up in large boxes for the next of kin. He struggled to control his emotions as he dealt with Thorneloe's effects and came across a little tile made by a child with the words "I love you Daddy" on the back.[5]

There was one difference between Thorneloe's funeral and that of the other Welsh Guardsmen. When leaving the battalion, each commanding officer would be bidden farewell by the Welsh Guards with the officers jovially pulling his staff car out of the barrack gates as the guardsmen cheered. Thomas 53 felt that Thorneloe should be given a proper barracks send-off, because even in death he was still a commanding officer relinquishing the reins. Most of the Welsh Guardsmen were in battle in Helmand, but he could rely on the other Foot Guards regiments to turn out in force. On July 16, the day of the funeral, the rear gates of Lille barracks were opened and a hearse with Thorneloe's flag-draped coffin inside it drove in and stopped outside the commanding officer's office in the Headquarters Company block. With Garrison Sergeant Major Bill Mott calling time, the eight members of the bearer party, Thomas 53 among them, then took their positions either side of the hearse and marched alongside it as it was driven through the barracks and out of the front gate. Coldstream, Irish, and Welsh Guardsmen lined the road, their heads bowed when the hearse passed.

With police outriders halting traffic and clearing the forty-mile route, the cortege drove from Aldershot into central London and the Guards Chapel. The funeral was a very English as well as a Welsh affair. The music included "I Vow to Thee My Country" and "Onward, Christian Soldiers" and the hymns were "Cwm Rhondda," "Jerusalem," and "Make Me a Channel of Your Peace," the anthem of the Royal British Legion. Among the hundreds of mourners were Prince Charles and a host of generals including Guthrie and Dannatt. There were also three of Labour's defense secretaries in attendance— Des Browne and John Hutton, both of whom Thorneloe had worked for, and

Bob Ainsworth, who had taken over from Hutton the previous month. Most rousing of all was the rendition of "Men of Harlech," the regimental song of the Welsh Guards, which concludes: "Welshmen will not yield." In 1982, "Men of Harlech" had been sung in the lifeboats as hideously wounded Welsh Guardsmen were evacuated from the *Sir Galahad*.

In his eulogy, Tom Gadsby, best man at both of Thorneloe's weddings, spoke of how his friends had marveled that "such a consummate professional could move through his career so flawlessly whilst looking like a badly packed kitbag." It was, he added, "a wonderful antidote to those who dress the part but fail to launch." Thorneloe had stood out among his fellow officers "as being gentle and thoughtful, making time to listen to others and understand a particular problem." There was laughter as Gadsby gave an example of Thorneloe's understated manner and calm. During a sailing trip, Gadsby had managed an accidental gibe, swinging the boat sharply over and nearly casting Thorneloe overboard. Clinging tightly to the side of the boat and largely submerged, Thorneloe had said, very politely: "Would you mind bringing her back on course please?" His wife Sally, he said, had completed him and become his cornerstone. "I don't think any of us have ever seen him happier than in recent years, as the family man, with Sally, or catching bubbles in the garden with his beloved girls Hannah and Sophie, happy at home entertaining friends, sitting in companionable silence by the fire."

Browne, whom Thorneloe had greatly respected, had also been asked by the family to speak. In the midst of the furor over the lack of helicopters and Labour's mismanaging of defense, Browne's words struck a note of self-justification, perhaps even a touch of guilt. "I have a letter he wrote to me at Christmas," he said. "I shall treasure it for the rest of my life—that is if I don't wear it out before then. It is a source of great solace to me because that letter shows that the strength and depths of what I felt for this man were reciprocated by him." In his response to that letter five months earlier, Browne had written to Thorneloe: "I am grateful to you for reassuring me that what I was trying to do was getting through to those who mattered most and that, for me, was always the service personnel on the ground." After Thorneloe's death, Browne released the letter to his family. In twelve years of government—eight of them at war—Labour had already had six defense secretaries. Dannatt says: "What was really depressing with the sequence of defence secretaries that we had was they got it but they could get no traction in the Government. John Hutton was hardly allowed to speak to Gordon Brown and Des Browne was much the same."

Colonel Sandy Malcolm, speaking for the regiment, highlighted the national significance of Thorneloe's death, how a previously private figure had become known throughout Britain "and through him and the other recent casualties we have got a glimpse of what the fighting in Afghanistan is really like and more importantly what kind of men are fighting on our behalf."

The original Guards Chapel had been bombed during a service in June 1944. Malcolm reminded everyone crammed into the postwar chapel of the men under Thorneloe's command who could not be in attendance. "It is late afternoon in Afghanistan and the sun will soon set and Welshmen will stand-to across the Helmand valley," he said. One of the mourners in the chapel provided a living link with the events of June 1944. Serena Fass, aged seventy-one, was the eldest daughter of Lieutenant Colonel Johnny Fass, the only other Welsh Guards commanding officer to have been killed in action, and could remember, as a girl of six, being told the dreadful news.

After the funeral, Thorneloe's coffin was driven to the village of Buckland, Oxfordshire, for burial in the family plot in the graveyard of the twelfth-century church of St. Mary the Virgin. Thomas 53 and the other seven members of the bearer party undressed the coffin—removing Thorneloe's sword, cap, belt, and medals and folding the Union Flag into a triangle—before lowering it into the ground. As the firing party fired three volleys into the air, Warrant Officer (Class Two) Terry Fade, who was just about to fly out to Helmand, watched Thorneloe's father, impeccably dressed with a bowler hat and umbrella, standing to attention in the driving rain. Fade, who was also in the bearer party, had known Thorneloe for more than a decade and sailed with him in the late 1990s. The sight of Major Thorneloe, a traditional officer of the old school witnessing the burial of his remaining son with such dignity, prompted the tears to well up in Fade's eyes. To maintain his composure, he looked beyond the churchyard into a deciduous wood and thought about how his own father taught him the names of the trees. "Oak, elm, sycamore, horse chestnut," he said to himself, repeating the names of the trees to take his mind away from the heartrending sight of the Thorneloe family beside the grave.

In a long handwritten letter to Thorneloe's parents after the funeral, Prince Charles wrote: "For us, the service and Rupert's tragically curtailed life represented the best of Britain.... How blessed this country still is that such special people as your son choose the path of service and sacrifice." He continued: "We can only stand in awe as they pass by to 'greater glory.' But, oh, the anguish and misery on their departure and the dreadful burden of grief on their loved ones.... You made us so incredibly proud of being British last Thursday. Your son's death has reminded us of those special personal qualities that will always matter whatever age we live in."

If Thorneloe's funeral had been a largely traditional English occasion with the stiff upper lip very much in evidence, then Lance Corporal Dane Elson's send-off was an altogether more Welsh affair. The Welsh funerals were so emotional that the bearer party would retreat outside the chapel during the service because the sobbing and wailing from the packed congregation was likely to be too much for them.

Although he was born to English parents and spent most of his life in England, Elson had a red dragon and "Cymru Am Byth" tattooed on his right shoulder and proudly proclaimed his Welshness. Elson had been the kind of teenager who might have ended up in prison rather than on parade outside Buckingham Palace and leading men in battle. His parents split up acrimoniously when he was just two, and he lived with his mother until he was six and then with his father. Before joining the army when he was sixteen, he was packed off to live with grandparents in Devon and finish the last eighteen months of his schooling there. Described by his mother Debra Morris as "a bit of a bugger" and his father Stuart Elson as "full of devilment," the tales of his childhood escapades were legion. On one occasion, he was sent out of a school lesson and the door handle came away in his hand. Rather than put it back, he took it with him and went home, leaving the teacher and thirty children locked in the classroom. His parents or grandparents would be summoned to see the headmaster because Elson had been caught jumping on the roof of a teacher's car or urinating on an old lady's dog or throwing a javelin into someone's garden. Once in the army, however, he thrived. He drank until he was paralytic and smoked like the proverbial chimney, but was so naturally fit he would be able to run or play rugby the next morning without any trouble—though he did have a penchant for fainting on parade.

When army duties allowed, Elson played rugby for the South Wales Police, along with his father, who was a constable in nearby Barry. For the funeral, large numbers of mourners turned out in the pink rugby shirts of the South Wales team. Delivering the eulogy, Police Constable Stuart Elson, dressed in his best uniform, began: "Dane Falcon Stuart Elson. Born 28 September 1986. Killed in Action 5 July 2009. An impressive name for an impressive man." He had been called Dane after a character in the 1980s television drama *The Thorn Birds* and Falcon after the explorer Robert Falcon Scott. "I don't know if we should be at war in Afghanistan but what I do know, as a police officer even in the quiet backwater of Barry, I see some information which shows that we need to take some kind of action to stop the terror that would surely come our way. Dane was part of that action and he has paid the ultimate price." Just as at Thorneloe's funeral, the hymns "Cwm Rhondda" and "Men of Harlech" were sung. The proudest moment of his life, Elson's father said, was seeing his son march past the Queen and give an "eyes, right" as "Men of Harlech" was played. He knew, he said, that in the case of his son "the blood that he spilt on the battlefields of Afghanistan he would have considered to be Welsh." As Elson's coffin was lowered into the ground, Thomas 53 introduced a variation to the normal procedure at the request of the family. Removing the Union Flag from the casket, he replaced it with the flag of Wales.

17

Battle Shock

Guardsman S ... suddenly leapt out of his slit trench and ran towards the enemy, unarmed ... I was able to listen in to all this on my own wireless set which suddenly became monopolised by the Commanding Officer shouting, "Kill him! Kill him! Kill him!"

Lieutenant Philip Brutton of the Welsh Guards,
recalling an incident in February 1945

He just took his body armour and helmet off, dropped his weapon and walked away.... It was absolutely mad. I had to give the order to shoot him if he turned left or right towards the Taliban.

Captain Mike Brigham, *attached to the Welsh Guards Battle Group, recalling an incident in May 2009*

After Rupert Thorneloe's death, Major Giles Harris decided it was time to take the fight to the Taliban. The Welsh Guards had linked up with the Black Watch and were now establishing long-term positions overlooking key crossing points (XPs) up and down the Shamalan Canal. The Prince of Wales's Company were the custodians of the lower portion of the canal from Yellow 14 up to XP-8. The task for 2 Company was to control from XP-7 up to XP-1 at Luy Mandah, next to the new PB Wahid, which the Black Watch had set up and now handed over to them. Taking the canal had been a slow, bloody grind, while the Taliban attacked from both sides, bogging down and halting the canalized convoys through the use of IEDs. The enemy had dictated the pace of the battle.

The Welsh Guards were now entering a new phase of holding fixed positions on the canal while expanding British influence in Chah-e Anjir to the west. Giles Harris was determined to seize the next opportunity to go on the offensive and show the Taliban that his Jam Boys were going to be more than sitting targets. He had discussed his aim with Captain Duncan Campbell, a Royal Artillery officer attached as the FST commander. The two had met in 2008 while they were both on courses at Larkhill and had hit it off at once. Campbell was a powerfully built Yorkshireman who oozed machismo and was eager to try SAS selection. A reconnaissance specialist, he had served in Helmand before and had a manner as direct as Harris's was subtle. Campbell had played in a heavy metal band and appeared on the cover of *Men's Health* magazine with the combined services water polo team. Harris, in contrast, spoke quietly and had a thoughtful, understated manner, though no one who knew him well doubted the steel underneath.

Giles Harris did not have to wait long for the chance to put the Taliban on the back foot. He was with Lieutenant Dave Harris's 2 Platoon as they established a patrol base in a compound at XP-9 when a firefight broke out to the south of them just as last light was approaching. A multiple of ten men from 1 Platoon was moving north up the canal from XP-11 to bring water and other supplies to 2 Platoon. As they moved across open ground, they were silhouetted against the canal. The Taliban opened fire from several compounds to the west, pinning down half a dozen men commanded by Lance Sergeant Barry Canavan, from Merthyr Tydfil.

The enemy controlled much of Route Dorset, the road beyond the compounds to the west that ran from Chah-e Anjir to XP-1, where it intersected the canal. Again and again, fighters were coming in from Route Dorset to mount attacks on the Prince of Wales's Company positions both in Chah-e Anjir and on Route Cornwall.

With Canavan's men located two hundred meters to the south of XP-9 and receiving fire from the compounds three hundred meters to their west, Giles Harris realized he had a chance to turn the tables on the Taliban. A quick survey of the ground showed there was a tree line to the north of the compounds that would give cover from the enemy's view, enabling an assault team to sneak up to beside where the Taliban were firing from. Troops moving along the tree line would have their right flank vulnerable across the open fields, but this was an acceptable risk.

Giles Harris looked at Campbell, who could see what he was thinking. "Yep—go for it," Campbell said. Harris hastily assembled a crew of twelve men to take on the Taliban. There were jokes later about it being the Welsh Guards version of *The Dirty Dozen*, the 1967 film about a band of miscreants assembled for a secret mission before D-Day. Among this dozen were Campbell, Company Sergeant Major Jeff Jones 27, an interpreter, and several NCOs. It was a top-heavy team. "Right, QBOs, figures one," ordered Harris, meaning that he would outline his intentions in Quick Battle Orders in a minute, or as soon as everyone could assemble. He outlined the plan to move west along the tree line onto the Taliban's left flank. With Canavan's men providing fire support, the "dirty dozen" would then turn south and attack the line of five compounds.

"Right, follow me!" ordered Giles Harris. "Let's go!" Spotting Guardsman Ropate Waqanisaravi, one of 2 Platoon's Fijians, manning a GPMG on the roof of XP-9, Harris shouted out to him: "Cover our arses on the right!"

As he moved west along the tree line, Harris looked behind and felt a momentary sense of relief that his men were indeed following. "This is proper bloody scary," he thought. "These men were being shot at and now some lunatic officer has rounded them up and ordered them to go up a tree line towards the enemy." He felt a sudden hammer blow of responsibility. "Holy shit," he thought. "What if we get opened up on from a flank, what am I going to do? Is this crazy? This has got to go right." They ran three hundred meters, stopping every fifty meters or so to catch their breath and scan their arcs to the right across the open fields. In less than five minutes they were at the northernmost compound.

Giles Harris could now see that the fire was coming from the southernmost three compounds. He set about coordinating air and ground forces so that Canavan's men would fire into the Taliban positions and a jet would be engaging just as the dirty dozen stormed through the compounds. There was no margin for error—a mistake could have him and his men cut down by friendly fire. To complicate the situation, he couldn't get radio contact with Canavan's men; he had to relay all his messages to them via Dave Harris at XP-9. "I'm a compound and a half from the enemy," he thought. "We can still bug out and abandon this now." But he knew that everything was in place—there was an American F-15 jet overhead, he had all the supporting fire he needed, and the Taliban were running out of options.

There was a chance of Afghan civilians being stuck in the compounds or even being held as human shields by the Taliban, so Giles Harris decided to burst into the buildings without firing until they could see an enemy fighter. He also wanted to preserve the element of surprise. He wanted to get as close as possible to the Taliban firing points without being seen or heard. The F-15 swooped down low over the Taliban firing positions. Canavan's men opened up as the dirty dozen scuttled across open ground into the first compound, which was surrounded by an orchard. They could see tracer fire thumping into the compound walls no more than forty meters away and let off a green mini-flare to indicate their position to Canavan's men and the F-15. "Move as if you're in the jungle," Harris told two of his lance sergeants.

Danger lurked everywhere. There were clumps of trees between and behind the compounds and narrow paths leading away to low walls and alleyways. Harris's instruction clicked. His men darted this way and that, swinging their rifles from side to side in case of a close-in ambush. They charged into the back of the second compound, bathed in darkness, and realized that there was Taliban fire coming from the third one.

Now came the moment infantry officers dream of, the line in the sand that a commander draws, letting every soldier under his command know that the assault is truly for real and they are upon the enemy. But Giles Harris, anxious about keeping quiet for the final few yards, fluffed it. "Duncan, I think it's probably time we put the old bayonetos on," he suggested. This was not the way his Sandhurst color sergeant had taught him to deliver the ultimate order in battle. Campbell looked at the company commander with amused astonishment. "*Bayonetos?* What the *f---* is he talking about?" he thought, before barking: "Fix bayonets!" at the Welsh Guards behind them. "Yes, I suppose it's more like that," muttered a sheepish Harris. A few steps later, Harris abandoned the stealth he had employed up to that point, ordering Lance Corporal Mark Owen 84, from Caernarfon, to open fire with his GPMG. Owen 84 laid down a wall of lead to the rear of the compounds, hoping to scythe down any Taliban trying to escape.

The interpreter, monitoring the Taliban walkie-talkies, reported panicked messages of "They're moving forward" and "They're coming towards us." The dozen moved into the third compound and the fourth, each time marking their advance with a green mini-flare to prevent friendly fire. There were warm cartridge cases on the ground but no sign of the enemy. The Taliban were still firing from the final compound as the Welsh Guardsmen fired another mini-flare and Giles Harris led his men, bayonets fixed, into the building. By the time they burst in, it was empty apart from several puppies scampering around in a corner. On the ground were hundreds more cartridge cases, two pairs of flip-flops, and two ladders leading to firing points on the roof. The Taliban had slipped away.

Giles Harris wanted the compound secured quickly, then to withdraw before being attacked. If they came under fire and then had to pull out, then the moral victory they'd gained by pushing the Taliban back might be lost. Company Sergeant Major Jones 27, from Brynmawr in South Wales, set about getting men into defensive positions on the roof. First up there was Owen 84, a native Welsh speaker. "Thank f--- we've stopped," he said, wheezing, in Welsh. Lance Sergeant Luke Rowlands 99, from Llangefni, a fellow North Walian and also from a Welsh-speaking family, responded in his native tongue: "Yeah, I think I'm going to die." The conversation in Welsh continued, to the exclusion of the South Walians, who all spoke only English. "Pass me some link will you?" said Owen 84. "And have you got a bottle of water?" Suddenly, the unmistakable voice of the sergeant major sounded from below. "Stop speaking f---ing Welsh!" boomed Jones 27. "We can't understand a f---ing word!"

After twenty minutes in the compound, Giles Harris and his men slowly patrolled back to XP-9 in what Campbell describes as "a two-fingered salute to the Taliban," sending the message that the Welsh Guards could take a Taliban compound at will. The action had energized the Prince of Wales's Company. "It was the first time we'd actually gone forward under contact," remembers Owen 84. "Basically, every time we got into contact we used to stop and smash them from where we were. But we were chasing them this time." Yet there was frustration that the Taliban were so elusive. "They'd just done a runner," recalls Lance Corporal Alex Safee, from Llanelli. "It was gutting because we'd worked f---ing hard to get down there, smashing through five compounds, and they just disappeared at the last moment. It's like fighting a ghost. They're f---ing clever at what they do, I'll give them that."

For the Welsh Guardsmen defending their beleaguered positions at crossing points along the Shamalan Canal, the last light before dusk signaled danger. Almost invariably, the Taliban would mount their final attack of the day, known to the Welsh Guards as the "tea-time TIC"—Troops in Contact. "It's coming up to half five now," said Lieutenant Dave Harris on July 9, the day when the new base XP-9 was being fortified. "Reckon they're going to have another go again?"

Half an hour earlier, Private John Brackpool, from the Princess of Wales's Royal Regiment, had reported for his duty on one of the two lookout positions. He was due to go on the rear position facing west but told Guardsman Michael Muia that he would take the front position, built by the Royal Engineers that day. It was a longer walk, and Brackpool was always eager to please. The position, facing west over the canal and looking out to XPs 8 and 9, was rudimentary—sandbags piled three high on top of the highest roof in the compound. More sandbags were due to be delivered to XP-9 the next day. The building they had occupied was far from ideal because it did not provide views up and down the canal. A solution to this would have been to build Hesco structures in front of it, but it was not known how long they would be on the canal, and the last thing the Welsh Guards wanted to do was to vacate a fortified position that the Taliban could then use. So for the time being, any structure they built had to be easy to dismantle.

Brackpool, aged twenty-seven, from Crawley, Sussex, had left the army after two tours of Kosovo but went to Iraq as a reservist with the Royal Anglians and then decided to go to Helmand to earn some extra money. He had an eight-year-old child from a previous relationship and was planning to propose to his girlfriend. He had arrived with the Welsh Guards as a battle casualty replacement just a few weeks earlier. While waiting at Camp Bastion to link up with the Welsh Guards, Brackpool had become friendly with Lance Sergeant Milo Bjegovic, from Barry Island, who was also joining the Battle Group late. After the two of them had attended a repatriation ceremony and listened to the eulogies, Brackpool said to him: "I wonder what is going to happen if I die?" Bjegovic asked what he meant. "Well, you've all got mates and they know you and they'd have something to say about you but no one knows anything about me," he replied. Bjegovic told him not to worry. "You're not going to die," he said. "And if you do, I'll say something about you."

Once he joined 2 Platoon, Brackpool fit in well, taking part in the ribbing that any Englishman would receive. "PWRR—pride of the South, mate," he'd say when asked about his regiment. He proved to be somewhat accident-prone, prompting everyone to collapse with laughter when he fell through the straw roof of a room in a compound and couldn't get out. "Get in 'ere, get in 'ere," he shouted as the Welsh Guardsmen left him in there for a few minutes.

Going straight from civilian life to fighting in Helmand was difficult for him. "We just had the hardest day in the history of my life," he wrote in a letter to his girlfriend. "I've never struggled and been in so much pain. The patrol we did was so long and I had so much weight on my back. I just felt like breaking down and giving up. But just thinking about you and coming home to you kept me going to the end."[1]

Brackpool climbed up the ladder to the rooftop lookout position and got down on his stomach behind the GPMG. He was briefed by Guardsman Sherwin Chance, a cheery Grenadian, to stay low behind the sandbags and to be careful because he had just seen a motorbike, often an indication of Taliban activity. Earlier that day, Dave Harris had been concerned about accurate Taliban fire coming into the compound. Three times there had been what seemed to be high-velocity rounds zinging close to the engineers as they built the new lookout position. At one stage, Dave Harris had gone out of the compound to aim some rounds at the far bank of the canal to deter whoever was firing. Over the previous three days, the importance of soldiers keeping their heads down had been a persistent refrain from the platoon commander and NCOs. It had, however, been a struggle to get them to take notice.

At 5:31 p.m., Guardsman Craig Jones 23, an eighteen-year-old from Mostyn in North Wales, shouted up to Brackpool to ask him what they should cook for dinner once his duty was finished. Brackpool lifted his head up to look down at him and said: "Yep, OK, no worries. I'm off in a quarter of an hour." As he did so, there was a short burst of machine gun fire and the sound of one high-velocity round.

Jones 23 saw Brackpool's helmet fly off, his shoulders fall back on the sandbags, and blood start gushing from the back of his head and down the baked-clay wall of the building. "Man down! Man down!" screamed Jones 23. Sergeant Matthew Davies 96, from Cardiff, pulled on his body armor and helmet and scrambled up the ladder to Brackpool. As Davies 96 got there, it was as if Brackpool was slumped in an armchair with his mouth open. His eyes were wide open, but he was clearly not conscious, and there was a single bullet hole in the center of his forehead. Davies 96 put his hand on the back of Brackpool's head in a vain attempt to staunch the pulsating flow of blood and dragged him off the roof. "When I move my hand away now, there's going to be a lot of blood," he warned the men behind him on the ladder. Taliban fire was still coming in from the other side of the canal to the east. As Brackpool was passed down the ladder, Davies 96 took his hand off his head and blood splattered all over the men below. Owen 84 climbed up, took Brackpool's place behind the GPMG and began firing across the canal.

Lance Corporal Phil Pimlott and Guardsman Martin Fatchu, the platoon medics, put field dressings and Hemcon bandages onto Brackpool's head, but they knew they were fighting a losing battle. The rest of the platoon were still returning fire across the canal, and Safee stepped out of the compound to send a shoulder-launched 66 mm missile into the suspected firing point. As the missile whooshed from the tube, there was another shout of "Man down!" Dave Harris rushed over to see Jones 23 curled up in a corner saying: "He's been shot in the head, he's been shot in the head" over and over again.

Jones 23, a cocky, voluble character, had gone into battle shock. Harris tried to no avail to calm him down and then decided he needed to be taken out of the way before he affected the other young guardsmen. Davies 96 came to help, but the two men could not uncoil Jones 23. It was as if he had rigor mortis. The lieutenant and the sergeant picked him up and carried him, still curled in a ball, into the makeshift ops room. Harris then played the role of soothing good cop while Davies 96 played the bad cop, telling him: "Get a grip of yourself!" Neither approach worked. Jones 23 was weeping, punching himself in the head, and screaming: "He's dead, he's dead."

Brackpool still had a pulse when the MERT Chinook landed at 6:17 p.m. Guardsman Karl Henneberry, from Swansea, was told to grab the kit of Brackpool and Jones 23 and take it to the helicopter landing site. As Brackpool was taken to the Chinook, Jones 23, still curled in a ball, was carried behind him and put on the helicopter as well. Less than fifteen minutes later, Brackpool was pronounced dead on arrival at Camp Bastion Hospital. Jones 23 remained at Bastion for observation and trauma counseling and did not return to the platoon.

"Right, we need to clean this place up," said Dave Harris, grabbing a shovel and scraping up the blood-sodden dust where Brackpool had been treated. Davies 96 went up to the lookout position and took down sandbags that were also soaked in blood. As Owen 84 got down from the roof after being relieved on the GPMG, he realized he was shaking and out of breath. He punched a wall in anger and asked Bjegovic to wipe the blood off his face. Owen 84's shorts were bloodstained, but Bjegovic couldn't see blood anywhere else. But Owen 84 kept insisting: "Get the blood off me, get it off my face," so Bjegovic wetted a towel and began to wipe his face with it anyway.

Once the cleaning up had been done, the platoon gathered to remember Brackpool. Fatchu led the prayer. The Ghanaian had begun training to be a priest at a Roman Catholic seminary before leaving to take a degree in population studies at the University of Cape Coast. "Father, help us to remember that everything happens for a reason and You decided that it was time for John to depart this world," he said. He prayed that the platoon would accept what had happened, continue fighting for each other, and not allow Brackpool's death to demoralize them. Before he finished, he said a few words about the Taliban fighter who had killed their friend. "Father, we pray that You forgive him and help him realise that what he has done is wrong."

That evening, Bjegovic sat down to compose a eulogy to his dead comrade. "Private Brackpool had settled in well, making many new friends in 2 Platoon," he wrote. "There were plenty of times where Bracks would make us all burst out in to tears of laughter."

The next day, a Taliban commander was heard on his walkie-talkie announcing that a sniper using a German rifle had carried out the attack. "The Hunter has taken one of their heads off," he boasted. Accurate fire continued to hit XP-9 from the east. On one occasion, a bullet smashed through a sniper scope on the parapet next to the sentry, and the walls behind the sentry positions showed the strike marks of other near-misses. In his diary, Dave Harris lamented that he "had hoped to bring everyone back safely, but it was not to be." The horrific images of Brackpool's death were etched on his mind. "All of us asked ourselves, did we do enough? Could we have done things differently?"

South of XP-9, Lieutenant Trystan Richards and his FSG-1 were occupying Compound 34, the building right next to where Thorneloe and Hammond had been killed on July 1. Their task was to "straighten the canal" by plugging the surveillance gaps between XP-11 and XP-9 to stop the Taliban slipping in to place IEDs. They arrived there five days after the deaths of Thorneloe and Hammond, when the Prince of Wales's Company took responsibility for the canal up to XP-8. In the subsequent two months, only one IED exploded within the Prince of Wales's Company area. This was due in large part to the almost obsessive desire of Richards to deny the Taliban the opportunity to get an IED onto the canal track.

Putting FSG-1 on the canal meant that Giles Harris lost another of his platoons from Chah-e Anjir, but there were so many convoys up and down the Shamalan that it was imperative to be able to dominate the ground.

During the planning for Panther's Claw, one of the crucial early tasks identified was to establish a detailed "dead-spot matrix" to show which bits of Route Cornwall were overseen by the Welsh Guards from the XPs and which "dead spots" would need additional surveillance assets such as drones, jets, and satellites from the brigade. Once Panther's Claw began, however, it became clear that the brigade's entire surveillance capability was needed in the Babaji area, designated as the Main Effort. The Welsh Guards had to use their own manpower for the task. Even then, not all the canal track could be observed. Between XP-9 and XP-7, there was a point that could be seen at dawn and dusk, but in the middle of the day the heat haze was so intense that movement could not always be detected. Giles Harris and Henry Bettinson tried to cover the spot with their Desert Hawk drones, but the range was such that the drone could only be overhead for about fifteen minutes. "We had so few people and so much to do that as ever it was left to the Barma men to get out and clear the ground for the convoys," remembers Giles Harris.

Before Major Charlie Burbridge's Egypt Squadron had left for Helmand, the Tankies who would be manning the Vikings had made up T-shirts depicting a longboat against a sunset and the words: "If you can read this … I've been blown out of my turret and I've lost my body armour." It was part black humor and part psychological preparation for what they knew was ahead. Even after Thorneloe's death, Vikings continued to be driven at the front of convoys. On July 6, Lance Corporal Sami Boyd was commanding a Viking leading two Mastiffs clearing a route through near XP-1 at night for Jackals from the BRF to move into Babaji. A Brimstone counter-IED team had Barmaed a vulnerable point near the Luy Mandah bazaar but failed to detect a low-metal-content IED. The device overturned both cabs of Boyd's Viking; he was flung from his turret, broke his neck, and ruptured his spleen when he landed, but survived.

The commander of a Foden recovery vehicle broke his ankles and damaged his spine when his vehicle hit an IED. The Viking troop accompanying the Foden were stuck overnight beside the canal that ran along the southern edge of the CAT. As the sun went down, the Taliban attacked. Lance Corporal Bradley Watkin-Bennett knelt down with a 66 on his shoulder as a Tankie on Viking top cover indicated where the gunfire was coming from. Watkin-Bennett fired the 66, scoring a direct hit, and the Taliban attack ceased. Shortly after dawn broke, Trooper Neil Collins was manning a GPMG on his Viking when he saw something flying towards him. He had no time to duck. It was an RPG that landed three meters away, slamming into a compound wall and sending a blast wave that knocked Collins's head back and sucked it forward, smashing his nose onto the GPMG. The ballistic glasses Collins was wearing saved his eyes, and he staggered into the compound, blood pouring from his face. The fighting was so intense that the MERT Chinook could not land for ten hours. There was another IED strike on the way back to FOB Shawqat, and by the time the Vikings rolled back in they had spent more than two days on a journey that should have taken about three hours.

On July 10, Corporal Lee Scott was commanding his Viking, codenamed Elephant, leading a convoy from FOB Shawqat to resupply the Prince of Wales's Company at Chah-e Anjir. Scott, an inspirational figure, had a reputation for being lucky. Before the tour, he had booked a holiday to Disneyland Paris with his wife and two children, but the money was not debited from his account. When he got to the EuroStar terminal there were no tickets for them, but he told the agent that he'd booked and managed to blag their way onto the train to enjoy a free holiday. The number of food and gift parcels he received from his wife Nikki was the envy of many in the troop.

The convoy stopped at what Scott considered a vulnerable point after he said that there was "a funny smell in the air" and the road ahead needed to be Barmaed. After the Barmaing, further reassurance was given by the sight of a Toyota pickup driving up the road. It appeared, however, that the Taliban were now not only using low-metal-content IEDs but were also constructing weight-sensitive pressure plates that would function only if driven over by a heavy military vehicle.

As the convoy moved back off, Scott was blown out of his turret and landed facedown in the water in an irrigation ditch forty meters away. He had sustained massive leg injuries and was unconscious. A firefight was raging as the Taliban attacked the halted convoy while Scott's comrades tried to staunch the bleeding from his legs and give him CPR. Trooper Rob Saddington remembers seeing hand prints of Scott's seven-month-old daughter Brooke tattooed on his stomach and telling him: "You're doing well, you're going to be OK." Another Tankie urged Scott: "Think of your wife and kids." After ten minutes, the medic looked up at Sergeant Paul Howard and shook his head. "Look, please just carry on," pleaded Howard, a close friend of Scott. The medic did CPR for another five minutes, but Scott was clearly dead and Howard reluctantly called a halt. "Right, let's make him decent," he told his men. The Tankies put his top back on, buttoned it up, and straightened out his uniform as best they could. Howard used a rag and some bottles of water to wash the blood off Scott's face.

As the Tankies lifted Scott into a body bag, Howard told them: "Right guys, you need to say your goodbyes." Five or six men were kneeling beside Scott as they spoke to him. "You were a legend," said one. "Top bloke, we'll miss you," said another. Howard looked at his friend and said to himself: "You've done enough. You can be proud of yourself. You were the best troop corporal anybody could have had." As he zipped up the body bag, he added: "Goodnight."

A rucksack that Scott had kept at his feet in the turret had been blown out and the contents scattered in a cornfield. Captain Dan Shepherd, a bomb-disposal officer dispatched to the scene, told the Tankies that they had been through enough and his men would gather up Scott's possessions. Among the things they found in the field was a scorched photograph of his five-year-old son Kai. The cause of Scott's death was recorded by a coroner as "drowning associated with blast injuries."

Trooper Karl Rowe, known as "Paddle," had been driving the vehicle and was in such a state he seemed unlikely to live. He was unconscious with multiple wounds. His intestines were spilling out of his stomach. Trooper Jeremy Murray was just eighteen and the youngest member of the squadron. Before flying to Helmand he had never been abroad before. He was in the Barma team that had just cleared the road and been in the rear cab of Scott's vehicle when the IED had exploded. Murray had already seen the attempts to treat Scott and went into battle shock when he saw Rowe. "I didn't know what to do," he remembers. "I dropped my helmet, I had my gun in my hand but it wasn't in the correct position. I just broke down and was coughing because of all the dust from inside the vehicle when we got blown up." Others remember Murray having a blank look and wandering around as if he was lost. He was put onto the MERT Chinook along with Rowe and Scott's body. Rowe had initially been placed to one side because it was believed he was dead. He had suffered abdominal wounds, multiple broken bones, and a head wound. On the helicopter, he twice went into cardiac arrest. Remarkably, he survived.

Almost as soon as the Chinook had left, Sergeant Dean Morgan 10 spotted the telltale edges of a pressure plate in the road ahead. There were IEDs ahead, and the convoy had nowhere to go. Minutes later, the Taliban opened fire from compounds to the north, the beginning of eight hours of sporadic firefights during which French Mirage jets, a Tornado, and Apaches pounded the Taliban positions as the Tankies and Welsh Guards fired fourteen thousand rounds from their GPMGs.

Trooper Mo Morris had begun the day still bemoaning the loss of his iPod and a copy of *The Hobbit*, both ruined when he had jumped in the canal to help the Recce Platoon men trapped in the submerged Viking. After the IED blast, Morgan 10 had told him no one had been hurt. Morris was way back towards the rear of the convoy in his "Elastoplast" Viking that carried medical supplies. But then Sergeant Howard, tears streaming down his face, pulled the Tankies aside to tell them that "we've lost Scotty." Morris, a burly, shaven-headed man, wept for the first and only time of the tour. He had been through Iraq with Scott. They'd argued and fought with each other at first before becoming firm friends. "This is crap," he said to himself. "I can't do this any more. I hate this f---ing country." He got up on his Viking and onto his .50 caliber gun to fire back at the Taliban.

The enemy was concentrated in one compound, and Taliban walkie-talkie messages were heard indicating they were trapped there. After several strafing runs from the jets the fire had still not subsided, Lieutenant Terry Newton, the troop commander, requested that a five-hundred-pound bomb be dropped. To the frustration of Morris and the other Tankies, permission was denied. Once again, he thought with frustration, the British were unable to kill the men who were trying to kill them for fear of civilian casualties. He trained his gun onto the edge of the compound, vowing to shoot the next Taliban who poked his head around the corner. His finger was quivering over the trigger when he saw a movement from a spot where gunfire had been coming moments earlier. For some reason, he hesitated and then watched as a woman dressed all in black and carrying a child walked out of the compound and across the field. He looked over at Howard, who had also been about to fire. "Thank f--- for that!" Morris said. The decision not to bomb the compound had been the right one.

Much more precise than a five-hundred-pound bomb was the L96 sniper rifle in the arms of Morgan 10, crouched in the top cover position of the rear cab of a Viking. He spotted a figure crouching down and moving away from the other side of the compound towards a small orchard. Looking through the sight, Morgan 10 could see he was carrying a weapon and was close to a low wall. Morgan 10 fired one round and missed. The fighter stopped and turned around. Morgan 10 didn't have time to fix him in the sight but did a small, almost instinctive, adjustment and fired again. The bullet ripped into his chest. "I can't tell you if he was dead or not but he hit the f---ing deck and I didn't see him get back up again," he remembers.

Trooper Murray, casevaced back to Bastion with battle shock, had been a close friend of Trooper Josh Hammond. After Hammond was killed along with Rupert Thorneloe, Murray and some other Tankies had been sent to the vehicle "graveyard" at Camp Bastion to collect some radios. While they were there, they looked behind the black sheets put up to hide the carcasses of vehicles hit by IEDs. Murray went in and found the rear cab that Hammond and Thorneloe had died in. "It was like somebody just punched it from underneath and bent all the metal up inside," he remembers. The young trooper spent the next six weeks in Bastion and was sent to see a psychologist and Captain Deiniol Morgan, the Welsh Guards chaplain. "The psychologist asked me about my family and growing up and stuff and then about Hammy and what happened when the IED hit Scotty's wagon. I'm not really into God and wouldn't normally go and see the padre, but he was better. He made everything sound so much clearer. He'd been out on the ground as well so he knew what it was like."

Later in the tour, Murray began going on patrols again as a Viking driver. "Since I got home," he says, "I keep seeing random images, really fast, when I'm dropping off to sleep. It's like the inside of a vehicle. Everything's a mess. Everything's dark."

A native Welsh speaker from Aberystwyth, Chaplain Morgan had been at Checkpoint North when the body of Major Sean Birchall was brought back and had visited CP Haji Alem after the death of Lieutenant Mark Evison, when Lance Sergeant Leon Peek had tried unsuccessfully to persuade him to man a GPMG. He had spent time discussing faith with Rupert Thorneloe, a Roman Catholic who had become a more active Christian since his second marriage in 2004. Morgan was painfully thin by the end of the tour and had been deeply affected by what he had seen and heard. He found dealing with those who had battle shock harder than memorial services and repatriations. "There's something awful about seeing a great young guy for a time quite literally a gibbering wreck," he says. "It's like a freezing panic. You ask a question of somebody who is in that condition and the answer bears absolutely no relationship to the question. There's very little you can do but hold their hand saying you will be OK and you're safe."

When Captain Terry Harman saw Morgan at Camp Bastion, he was struck by how much weight he had lost and how emotionally drained he seemed. "Can we have a chat please?" Harman asked him in Welsh, before pouring his heart out about what had happened to him. When he had finished, Morgan said: "I'll have a chat with you as well then," and proceeded to do the same.

Relatively few Welsh Guardsmen were religious, but a number became more godly during the tour. One guardsman who narrowly escaped death was quietly baptized by Morgan at Camp Bastion after telling him that "it all makes sense now." Guardsman Simeon Howells, a Javelin operator with 2 Company, was a practicing Christian. He says: "I prayed a lot and I do believe I had God on my side out there. In fact, in my heart there's no doubt about that." One night at CP Paraang, Howells felt his Javelin tube lurch to one side. A bullet, fired by the Taliban fighter from the murder hole Howells had been observing, had gone straight through the CLU sight. About fifteen minutes later, Howells fired a missile into the murder hole, killing the fighter. "I prayed pretty hard that night," he says. "Well, it was more thanking than praying." By the end of the tour, he had killed thirteen Taliban.

For every death or serious injury there were several stories of a miraculous near-miss. Down near Garmsir, FSG-3 experienced four in one day. A bullet ricocheted off the ground and hit the helmet of Lance Sergeant Lee Davies 84, from Newbridge in South Wales. "F---ing hell, I've just been shot!" he shouted. Guardsman Nathan Wyer, from Fishguard on the southwest coast of Wales, had the top of his GPMG shot off. Lance Sergeant Ahearne, the "Working Man" singer, was knocked off his feet by a round that whistled past his shoulder. That afternoon, Lance Sergeant Collins was kneeling in an irrigation ditch. He had just posed for a photograph with Sergeant Grant Lewis 34 when the FSG came under fire again. Collins felt a thumping blow to the base of his spine. "I've been shot in the back," he said. Lewis 34 told him to stop joking. "Seriously, Grant, I've been shot in the back." Collins was writhing in pain as Lewis 34 crawled over to him. The sergeant found a large hole in the bottom of Collins's rucksack and gingerly put his hand inside his friend's body armor. "Oh God," he said as he felt wet stickiness. When Lewis 34 checked his hand, he could see no blood. It was sweat. Collins had a large purple bruise on his back but was otherwise unharmed.

At XP-6 on the Shamalan Canal, five members of the Recce Platoon were pinned down. The Taliban were firing from several positions, the closest just

35 meters away, and neither of the two Bowman radios would work. Sergeant Jay Gordon, the battalion physical training instructor, decided to go to XP-7 to gather reinforcements, and Sergeant "Moose" Millar, a Parachute Regiment reservist and sniper, volunteered to go with him. As they ran across the open ground, a bullet hit Millar's helmet, bowling him over. He got up, carried on running, and minutes later he and Gordon returned with a signaler and several Welsh Guardsmen who enabled everyone to withdraw safely.

Further down the canal, at Compound 34, Guardsman Mark Hopkinson of the Prince of Wales's Company's FSG-1, from Shrewsbury, was manning a heavy machine gun on a Jackal being used as a stationary lookout position. Shortly after taking over the duty, he bent down to pick up a bottle of water. As he did so, an RPG flew right over him and hit the Jackal, blowing up a fuel tank. Hopkinson's helmet was blown off, and he suffered a perforated eardrum and burns to an arm, but he crawled away. He managed to get into the compound, under fire from the Taliban, and arrived at the feet of Lieutenant Trystan Richards. "Help me, sir, help me," he said. Hopkinson would have been killed had he not stooped down. The Jackal and everything in it, valued at about £1.5 million, was destroyed. Munitions from the Jackal set a pile of hay alight inside Compound 34. Hopkinson's friends in the FSG teased him that he had been reaching into the ration box of Guardsman Tyrone Evans 35, from Swansea, to steal some food when the RPG hit. It was proof, they maintained, that crime did indeed pay. Evans 35, known as "Curly" because he was completely bald, thought Hopkinson was still in the burning Jackal. He ran out to put the fire out with an extinguisher until Richards screamed at him that Hopkinson was safe and the vehicle was in danger of exploding. Lance Sergeant Douglas Bick, from Pontllanfraith, near Caerphilly and nicknamed "Caveman," used his prodigious strength to knock down a bricked-up doorway to allow the guardsmen to run into the next compound and flee the flames.

Such near-misses fed superstition among the Welsh Guardsmen. Sergeant Parry 700 would not patrol without wearing the "lucky underpants" that had also kept him safe in Iraq. Around his neck, along with his dog tags, Major Giles Harris wore a signet ring, given to him by his fiancée Alice. It became his charm as he reflected on the appropriateness of her family's motto engraved on it: "*fac et spera*," Latin for "do and hope." On the day his body armor stopped a bullet, Lance Sergeant Dan Collins was unshaven. After that, he never shaved before going out on patrol, adding that to his ritual of listening to Linkin Park on his iPod before going out. Like many others, Collins wore a wooden cross underneath his body armor, one of hundreds blessed in Bangor Cathedral before the tour and distributed by the chaplain.

At XP-7, Harman and the other 2 Company men there did their best to make the austere compound as homely as possible. The Royal Engineers obliged by digging a hole and diverting a stream into it to create a plunge pool that offered a welcome relief after a firefight in the insufferable heat. In the evenings there were games of cards and even Mexican, Indian, and Italian theme nights when culinary creativity was at a premium as ethnic cuisine was concocted almost entirely from ration packs. Pizza was made using flour, bicarbonate of soda and water for the dough, with a topping of tomato powder in water for the sauce, with cheese, hot dog sausages, Spam, and beans added. Someone constructed a sofa made from Hesco wire, and the sound commander speaker, used for broadcasting messages to the locals, was hooked up to an iPod so that house music could be played. Harman preferred Welsh music, lying on his camp bed listening to stirring versions of Cwm Rhondda or the North Walian opera singer Bryn Terfel.

For some, however, life on the canal was proving too much. On June 29, Guardsman Jon Caswell, who had treated his mortally wounded platoon commander down at CP Haji Alem, broke down as he manned a stag position beside the canal close to XP-7. That day, he had witnessed Lieutenant Lowry being shot shortly before being sent out to the position, made up of two Hesco barriers. Caswell said it wasn't safe and that four Hescos were needed but he was ordered to take up his post. "I had a meltdown," he remembers. "I pulled my helmet off and booted it across the road. I wanted out." He was led back into XP-7 and taken to his room to calm down. A request for him to be evacuated due to battle shock was refused—there were casualties across Helmand and there were no helicopters to spare.

The next day, Captain Tom Anderson heard a shot from Caswell's room. He took a deep breath and ran over. As he pushed the iron door open, he steadied himself for the worst. Mercifully, Caswell had not blown his own head off but, in a desperate state, had fired a shot into the wall. "Caswell was weeping, uncontrollably, huge gulps of air, head buried in his hands and his whole body shaking," Anderson later wrote in his diary. "I knelt beside him and cradled his head in my arms for about 10 minutes, just telling him it'd be OK." Next to Caswell was a suicide note written on a cardboard flap ripped off a ration box. He had scrawled a few words to his wife Beccy before changing his mind about killing himself. "I'd reached the lowest point," Caswell recalls. "I was thinking that if I died, what would my two kids have? A beret, a buff belt and some medals."

When Anderson told Bettinson what had happened, Harman interjected: "Does Caswell speak Welsh?" Anderson said that he did and Harman headed to the room. The figure Harman found sobbing and rocking back and forth in the dark reminded him of Gollum from *The Lord of the Rings*. "I can't do it any more," Caswell said. "I just want to get out of here." Harman talked to him in Welsh for nearly three hours, explaining that he was a Welsh Guardsman and needed to contribute to the team. He persuaded Caswell to reintegrate by making tea for the platoon and manning the radio. That evening, Anderson wrote in his diary: "He is terrified of being killed and I think we may find that he is the first of many to be demonstrating a degree of battle shock. 'PTSD' is not the word for the utter incapacitation that Caswell has experienced, and I don't know if he will ever be the same again." The next day, Caswell was taken in a Viking back to Camp Bastion for psychiatric evaluation. Later that week, he telephoned his wife Beccy in Aldershot as she was going into labor. "I'm sorry," she said. "I'm trying to hold on for you but I can't." He arrived in Britain shortly after the birth.

On another occasion, Harman was under fire from the Taliban beside the Shamalan Canal when he shouted "Come on, let's go" to the group of Welsh Guardsmen, led by an NCO, behind him. He ran forward and was pinned down in a ditch, alone, for fifteen minutes until suppressing fire from Fraser-Sampson enabled him to pull back. "Where have you f---ing been?" Harman shouted at the NCO, who had been taking cover by a compound wall with his men and had not moved since being given the order to follow. "It's too dangerous," the NCO replied. Harman raised his SA-80 rifle, put it to the NCO's head, cocked it, and told him to fight. "I nearly snapped that day," he admits. He then dragged the NCO along the ground out into the open, where the Taliban were still firing, putting him in a position where he had little choice but to engage the enemy. Back in Aldershot after the tour, Harman saw the NCO at Lille Barracks and returned his salute. "You're lucky," he thought. "I would have wasted you. Coward. 100 percent."[2]

Guardsman Ed Carew of the Recce Platoon had been badly shaken by witnessing the death of Marine Jason Mackie and the mortal wounding of Lance Corporal Rob Richards back in May. He reached his limit when he took part in the rescue of those trapped in the Viking that rolled into the canal on June 29. That day he had helped pull Guardsman James Barber out of the vehicle and assisted with resuscitating Guardsman Mark Biggs, who had drowned but was brought back to life. Days beforehand, Sergeant Steve Young remembers, there had been a firefight in which his section was taking cover behind a mound alongside the canal road as intense Taliban fire came in. Suddenly, Carew stood up. "He walked onto the road and fired on automatic, Rambo style," says Young. "He was screaming his head off, changed magazines and used all his ammunition up. Then he just walked back, sat down and lit a fag. He had really gone in the head." Just after the Viking incident, Young and the others were evacuated, and Carew was among the remnants of the Recce Platoon who took refuge in a mosque. Sergeant Steve Peters remembers Carew sitting in the corner with his knees up to his chin, repeating: "Get me out of here, get me out of here," over and over again to himself. Carew was evacuated to Camp Bastion and after several weeks there sent back to Britain for treatment at the MoD mental health unit in Parklands Hospital in Basingstoke. He was later discharged from the Army.

The most extreme example of erratic behavior by a soldier had come back in May. Towards the end of a patrol near the Nad-e Ali town, Private Wayne Gorrod, a reservist in Captain Mike Brigham's OMLT unit, suddenly ripped off his body armor and helmet, flung his arms in the air, and walked off. Brigham asked Sergeant Marc Giles what was going on and was told: "Boss, I have no idea." The rest of the patrol shouted at him to come back and then began chasing him. As they did so, the Taliban attacked the patrol from each flank. Brigham now had to make one of the toughest decisions a soldier could ever face. Gorrod showed no sign of turning back and was liable to be killed or, worse still, captured. Images of Gorrod in an orange jumpsuit being beheaded on video flashed through Brigham's mind. Under interrogation, moreover, Gorrod could well reveal details about British and Afghan troops that could put many lives in danger. "We are going to have to stop him no matter what it costs," Brigham thought. He summoned the QRF from PB Argyll and then gave Giles the order over the radio to shoot one of his own men. "If he goes left or he goes right, you have to take the shot," Brigham said. "You can aim for his legs but you need to stop him."

Giles responded as if it was a run-of-the-mill order. "Yes, boss," he said. Giles had Gorrod, who was still heading up the road, in his sights as the QRF arrived. The lead Viking drove up the road after him. When it drew level with Gorrod, Captain Gez Kearse of the Queen's Royal Hussars jumped off and rugby-tackled him. Back at PB Argyll, Brigham asked Gorrod what he had been thinking. "I just don't want to do it any more," Gorrod replied. Army psychologists could find nothing wrong with Gorrod, so legal proceedings were activated with a view to his being tried at court-martial on charges of cowardice in the face of the enemy. The army later decided, however, that pursuing such a case would not be in the service's wider interest, and Gorrod was administratively discharged instead.[3]

During the First World War, battalions would usually spend a week in the front line before moving back to the support lines, the reserve lines, and then a period week out of the lines altogether. In Helmand, an infantryman would spend up to six months in the front line with only a two-week break for R&R in the middle. Time on R&R was frequently neither restful nor recuperative. Major Rob Gallimore hit the bottle while he was back home, did not sleep for forty-eight hours. and then collapsed. Another officer dropped into Regimental Headquarters and held forth to Tom Bonas for nearly three hours about what was happening in Afghanistan. There were feelings of guilt about being at home while comrades were fighting and resentment from wives who realized that their husband's mind was still in Helmand. Being home led to heightened fears about going back and a build-up to a second farewell to loved ones.

Lance Sergeant Leon Peek's wife Karly laid on a house party for him when he returned for R&R in July. Peek couldn't take it. "I had just got out of killing people, people trying to kill me, and I'm sat there in my living room," he remembers. "I had to get out of there. I had to slip off in my car for a couple of hours. I sat down and had a chat on the beach with my wife and had a cry." For his second week, Peek and his wife went to Benidorm. He had his wallet stolen while he was there and couldn't stop thinking about how all the British holidaymakers didn't have a clue about the war.

Back in Aldershot, there were Welsh Guardsmen who had just completed basic training at Catterick and were waiting until they turned eighteen before they were eligible to be sent to Afghanistan. Among their duties was to be part of the firing party at the Welsh Guards funerals. Guardsman James Edwards 93, from Llandudno, fired a volley of three shots in the St. Mary the Virgin graveyard and then bowed his head as Lieutenant Colonel Rupert Thorneloe was laid to rest. As he was standing there, he found himself wondering how the Taliban had managed to get to the commanding officer. Shortly afterwards, he was on firing party duty again at Private John

Brackpool's funeral in Crawley and pondering what it would feel like to be shot in the head. Just over a week later, Edwards 93—nicknamed "Slug" because, he says, "I'm so f---ing slow"—found himself as a battle casualty replacement in Brackpool's 2 Platoon.

One afternoon, Edwards 93 was on sentry duty at the Red Five position outside Chah-e Anjir when he saw some movement in the undergrowth about twenty meters away. As he turned, bullets came flying in, bursting the sandbag in front of his face and slamming into the wall behind him. He shouted out and flung himself onto the ground. Guardsman Karl Henneberry, who had witnessed Brackpool getting shot and had carried his kit and that of Jones 23 to the helicopter, had just come off duty. He saw Edwards 93 go down and thought he was dead. It was as if what had happened to Brackpool was happening again before his eyes. "I cracked then," he remembers. "It was too much of a close call. I couldn't do any more. I was crying. I just wanted to open my eyes again and feel I was back home." Edwards 93 was unhurt, but the incident, on top of the constant patroling and hearing walkie-talkie messages about the Taliban watching, had ground Henneberry down. "I felt rage, I felt like chucking all my f---ing grenades I had on me, just launching them over and saying: 'Get away.' I'd just had enough."

Henneberry was transferred to clerical duties back at PB Shahzad for the remainder of the tour. "I really wanted to go on patrol but something was just saying: 'F---, no.' We were coming close to the end but the ops room wanted so much more out of us. I can understand, we were trying to make that f---ing place better. But, they just constantly wanted more and more and I couldn't do no more. I was bust." Henneberry's friends in 2 Platoon accepted that he had genuinely reached his limit. He had fought bravely for more than four months, seen IEDs blow up vehicles, a friend die before his eyes, and been shot at dozens of times. He was still pitching in by typing up orders and doing whatever he could around the PB. No one suggested there was any dishonor in that.

18

One Shot, Two Kills

The best man of all without a shadow of a doubt is the hunter.
A person who does his patrol for the sheer love of hunting, the finest
game in the world, MAN. The game which has a brain capable to
hit back and become the hunter instead of the hunted.

Lance Corporal Eric Coles, *sniper with*
1st Battalion Welsh Guards in France, 1944–45

You can kill ten of my men for every one I kill of yours,
but even at those odds, you will lose and I will win.[1]

Ho Chi Minh *to a French official, 1946*

The feeling of déjà vu was something that Major Henry Bettinson could have done without. He was in a convoy moving south towards XP-7 when he heard the sound that had become all the more sickening because of its familiarity. There was a pause and then the inevitable report over the radio: "Contact IED!" Bettinson was heading for a rendezvous with Lieutenant Colonel Charlie Antelme, his new commanding officer. "F---!" he thought, as he jumped out of his Mastiff and ran forward to the front of the convoy. His boots pounded the canal track, which could very well have harbored IEDs, as he quickly assessed the situation. Antelme was probably still almost a kilometer away and the explosion seemed much closer, Bettinson calculated. The cloud of dust was just subsiding as he reached the front

Mastiff in the convoy—the days of Vikings on Route Cornwall were over. His Barma team was in disarray after being blown off their feet, but they were staggering back up and realizing with relief that there were still five of them and each had two legs. They had Barmaed over a low-metal-content IED that had been detonated by the Mastiff behind them. The vehicle had lost a wheel and some bar armor, but there were no casualties.

Once the stricken Mastiff was out of the way, the convoy continued to XP-7, where Antelme had arrived after being brought up from Chah-e Anjir by the Prince of Wales's Company. Traveling with him was Major Ben Ramsay, who had just arrived as the new Battle Group plans officer and relief company commander for when Giles Harris and Bettinson were on R&R. "F--- me, this is the Wild West!" Ramsay said, greeting Bettinson with a hug. Bettinson welcomed Antelme and guided him up Route Cornwall towards his Mastiff. There was a thick fog blanketing the canal that night, and movements in the dark were very risky because there was even less chance than usual of spotting a Taliban fighter creeping up to the road to connect an IED to a battery pack. As the two men walked, Bettinson could not stop himself thinking: "I do not need another IED now. We can't have two commanding officers die on the f---ing canal."

Ramsay, who had commanded the Prince of Wales's Company before Giles Harris, had spent four years of his childhood in Afghanistan when his father, a British diplomat, was stationed in Kabul. A genial, balding officer, he had been due to take up a staff job in Kabul but was asked by Thorneloe to take a planning post at Battle Group headquarters after Sean Birchall was killed. Ramsay was penciled in to become battalion second in command when Andrew Speed left at the end of the tour. Thorneloe had calculated that having a tested company commander on hand would give him additional options should he decide to shift officers within the Battle Group.

Standing in for Bettinson in August, Ramsay managed to pull off something that had previously eluded the Welsh Guards—killing a Taliban team in the act of laying an IED. His plan was a deception that involved sending Mastiffs down Route Cornwall and simulating a breakdown. As the "recovery" of the Mastiffs was taking place, he inserted a sniper team. Sure enough, an IED team soon arrived and began to attach battery packs to catch the Welsh Guardsmen after their withdrawal. Lance Sergeant Lynn Williams 57, from Cardiff, crawled across Route Cornwall with his .338 sniper rifle and watched for ninety minutes before three silhouettes appeared. The figures moved back and forth from the trees to the track, lying flat for up to ten minutes as they armed IEDs. After reporting the movement back to Ramsay, he was given the authorization to fire. The next time one of the figures stood up, Williams 57 fired a single shot, hitting him in the chest and killing him instantly.

"Sniping is the way forward," says Ramsay. "The deception was the oldest trick in the book but it worked. It was raw courage for the sniper team to get themselves into position where they could shoot that guy."

Despite all his combat experience in Iraq and Afghanistan, Antelme admits he felt nervous when he took command. "I was told not to take any risks, and on my first day in theatre Henry says: 'Of course, you'll want to be in the first wagon to show the blokes.' Giles took me on the ground and I was in the first wagon. Trying to get me killed early doors!" Antelme was awed by Thorneloe's courage in Barmaing the most dangerous routes in Helmand but had decided he would not follow suit. "Perhaps that's cowardly but I came to the conclusion that whilst not flinching from danger I was more useful to the battalion at this stage alive," he says.

Antelme took over the battalion as soon as he arrived in Helmand on July 22 but did not assume command of the Battle Group for another two weeks. In the meantime, he was able to spend a week on the ground visiting each company and then several days working alongside Chalmers, who had two years of battalion command under his belt and knew the area of operations intimately. Chalmers had turned out to be the perfect choice as interim commander. Major Andrew Speed and others in the Battle Group headquarters had feared that a temporary replacement might arrive like a bull in a china shop and seek to impose his personality. But Chalmers, who instinctively understood Thorneloe's approach from their discussions since February and the handover in April, had changed almost nothing. Ed Launders, the ops officer, newly promoted to major, found him to be "charm on legs." Chalmers had bridged the gap and been a soothing influence on the Battle Group. Now it was Antelme's task to stiffen the backbone of the Welsh Guards and take them through the potent challenges that remained in the final two months of the tour.

Shortly after taking over, Antelme reflected on how his strengths could be used to build on those of his predecessor. "Rupert has set up a very efficient, thoughtful Battle Group that reflects his personality—incredibly thoughtful, cerebral, and likes to write a lot and really think about things," he said. "Now the Battle Group will reflect my personality a bit more, which is perhaps more intuitive, knowing my mind in a slightly different way, which is not a bad combination. If you've got the thoughtfulness and rigour there already, you can afford to be a little more instinctive on top of it." For Thorneloe, there had been a long, deliberate build-up to Helmand, whereas Antelme had been thrown in at the deep end. "Rupert preparing to come out here would have read everything and really thought long and hard about the problem," said Antelme. "My advantage is that having been fighting counter-insurgency on the practical end for the last eight years I've got a feel for it as well but in a different way. In a sense, Rupert's work was done because the most difficult part is taking the battalion through the training and building the machine."

Antelme was well known in the battalion because he had commanded 3 Company in Iraq as recently as 2005, and his combat experience was unrivaled. His biggest advantage in taking over was that he had instant credibility with his men. The Antelme legend was such that one officer said, only half in jest, that he was slightly surprised that the new commanding officer had not arrived by parachuting onto Route Cornwall in a ninja suit.

Addressing each company in turn, Antelme told his new charges that the reputation of the Welsh Guards was riding extremely high. The job they were doing was, in his view, essential because al Qaeda had been defeated in Iraq and had chosen Afghanistan as the next battleground between Islamism and the West. He peppered his talks with references to his combat experience after the September 11 attacks and cautioned against counting down the days to the end of the tour. "Listen, it's not over until the very end," Ramsay recalls him saying. "I lost a couple of guys in Iraq. We need to keep on fighting to the very end." Ramsay says that Antelme's insistence that he had never done anything as brave as the Welsh Guards were doing every day in Helmand was an astute way of bonding with them. "The blokes would go: "Yeah, you're f---ing nuts, you've done loads of hardcore ops, you got a DSO, of course you have!" But he still made them feel good about themselves. It was an interesting dynamic to watch." Antelme also spoke about coping with death. "We will remember our mates but we're here to do the job first," he said. "There'll be time for beers and tears when we get back." It was perfectly normal, he told the guardsmen, to feel stress. "Talking to your mates and being honest with each other is the best way to deal with all that sort of stuff."

Antelme also emphasized battlefield discipline, keeping weapons clean, shaving, and all "the Guards standards that through history have been our strength." Back in June, Thorneloe had been concerned about the sloppy appearance of some of the Welsh Guardsmen, telling Giles Harris at one point: "Let's not look like a defeated army." This was a criticism that had been leveled at the British by senior American officers in Iraq. Antelme was dismayed that the U.S. Marines tended to look smarter and more orderly than his Welsh Guardsmen. His view was that the soldier who was unshaven one day would have a dirty weapon the next—a potentially fatal lapse. General Cubitt, commanding the Household Division, was concerned that this part of the Guards ethos was being eroded. "I know the Eighth Army was very proud of its scruffy appearance in the North African desert, but I don't think the Americans are very impressed by seeing scruffy British soldiers," he says. "That doesn't help us strategically. I don't think the Afghans are particularly impressed by seeing a load of ruffians turning up either."

For all his broader experience, Antelme was a great believer in the traditional Guards ethos and was serious when he said he would enforce it. Sergeant Matt Parry 700 and others from the Prince of Wales's Company found this out to their cost in September when they arrived in FOB Shawqat and were spotted by Regimental Sergeant Major Monaghan. "Right. On parade!" Monaghan shouted as they jumped down from their Mastiffs. Just over an hour earlier, the men had been on their stomachs in the dust searching for IEDs. Unfortunately several of them had neglected to shave that morning or had allowed their sideburns to creep below halfway down their ears—and Antelme had issued a warning about slipping standards just two days earlier. A furious Antelme came out of the ops room and addressed the troops after Monaghan had inspected them. He couldn't believe his instructions had been ignored. "I've seen more Taliban killed than you lot put together and I still manage to shave every morning and trim my sideburns," he told them.

"We were in three ranks, being inspected from f---ing top to toe as though we were going on Queen's Guard outside Buckingham Palace," recalls Parry 700. "Then we got a f---ing good bollocking. I had my balls f---ing chewed big time because I was platoon sergeant." Afterwards, Parry 700 and the other offenders were ordered to report to the adjutant for disciplinary action. Giles Harris and Company Sergeant Major Jones 27 also faced the wrath of Antelme and Monaghan. Looking back, Parry 700 had no complaints about what happened. "We were in combat, searching for IEDs and finding them. One of the lads picked up for being unshaven had got up at 4 am and was shaving in the pitch black. He couldn't find a mirror so he was shaving in a

DVD and he missed a couple of bits. But it's still the Household Division and we are Welsh Guardsmen. We need to keep on top of our standards. It's what makes us a bit different from the rest. The bullshit makes you do your job better."

This was the Guards way. In his diary, Mark Evison had grumbled that "the problem with the Guards is that even when deployed they are still a stickler for rules." He recounted how Major Andrew Speed had picked up 7 Platoon for wearing non-issue sunglasses and cutting down the brims of their desert hats. Evison recorded that Speed had walked off muttering: "Platoon commanders these days." Evison wrote in his diary: "It seems that they are more interested in how we look rather than the fact that as a battalion we are soon to be facing the fiercest fighting probably since the Second World War." Speed was unrepentant when the diary was published after Evison's death. "The ethos of the Guards is smart and soldierly, no matter what the conditions and no matter what everyone else is doing around you," he says. "He failed to grasp that point."

Even in the Guards, however, protocol and procedures were sometimes waived. Almost all of the PBs and the FOBs had stray dogs that were treated as pets by the guardsmen. FOB Shawqat was no exception. An ailing, timid mongrel known as Trevor had been an inhabitant of the ruined fort when the Welsh Guards took it over. Major Martyn Miles viewed the dog as a health hazard and was anxious to have him shot. Miles knew that Trevor was being fed and was constantly on the lookout for the guardsmen responsible. As he was leaving Shawqat at the end of the tour, Speed, a dog lover, let slip that he had been feeding Trevor leftover steaks from the field kitchen. In Iraq, both Miles and Terry Harman, then the regimental sergeant major, had been avid opponents of dogs on the base. Harman, whose sheep farming background made him unsentimental about dogs, would wander around with a shotgun dispatching strays. At one point he could not get access to a lair underneath the guardroom where a litter of puppies were living, so he shoved the shotgun down a hole and blasted away. The floorboards later had to be taken up to get rid of the smell of dead animals. Speed's view was that for a guardsman to be able to make a fuss over a dog after coming back from a firefight was a reminder of home and a more civilized world.

Antelme concluded his talk to the companies by saying that he expected the Welsh Guards "to step up to the plate, to patrol hard, to take the fight to the enemy and use courageous restraint." The term "courageous restraint" soon became a buzz phrase in the Welsh Guards and later throughout the British Army. By it, Antelme meant that he expected his men to use proportionality when exercising lethal force and to take on personal risk in order to spare civilian casualties. This was Antelme's interpretation of his mentor General McChrystal's directive, issued on July 6, which stated that tactical victories secured at the expense of civilian casualties would become strategic defeat. "I recognise that the carefully controlled and disciplined employment of force entails risks to our troops—and we must work to mitigate that risk wherever possible," McChrystal wrote. "But excessive use of force resulting in an alienated population will produce far greater risks."

McChrystal later paid tribute to Antelme's understanding of what he meant. Both men knew how to kill people but they also knew that killing could sometimes be an impediment to victory. "Charlie got it absolutely right with courageous restraint," McChrystal says. "You don't need to be secured away from the people. You need to be secured by the people so that, as you win their support, it's in their interests to secure you, to report IEDs. But it does take courageous restraint, it takes them understanding that you're willing to take some risk to not put them at risk." Heavy armor and overwhelming force would provide short-term protection at a long-term price. "If we respond with overwhelming fire to limited small arms fire from a compound we do protect ourselves but we destroy their livelihood and potentially the people. When we run around in armoured vehicles or personal armour we often send an unintended message that we're more important than the people."

The Welsh Guards embraced the concept of courageous restraint at every level. In the early years of British involvement in Helmand, Fire Support Team (FST) commanders would judge the success of their tour on how much ordnance they had dropped. By late 2009, the culture had changed so that it was "not all about how much you drop, it's about the difference that you can make," according to Captain Duncan Campbell, FST commander with the Prince of Wales's Company. There were, however, skeptics. "General McChrystal is being a bit of a tree hugger in my view," said Staff Sergeant Dave Cooper, a JTAC with the Royal Artillery, in September. "The enemy are killing our blokes on a shoestring budget with pressure-plate IEDs and we've got millions and millions of pounds of technology in the sky but we're not using it." Neither McChrystal nor Antelme was much used to being described as a tree hugger.

Right across Helmand, the IED threat was showing no signs of subsiding. On July 20, a platoon from R Company of 4 Rifles accompanying a Viking troop from FOB Shawqat to PB Pimon had found an IED on the road. After registering beeps on the Vallon, the troops dug down and discovered a red drum with white wires protruding from it, with a battery pack wrapped in plastic set off the side of the road. Captain Dan Shepherd, the bomb-disposal officer who had helped gather up Corporal Scott's belongings a few days earlier, was playing scrabble in FOB Shawqat when he was scrambled to deal with the IED. Shepherd detected another device in front of the one that had been detected. After dealing with the first IED, he continued his "long walk" to the device in the red container. Despite the risk of small-arms fire from the Taliban, Shepherd chose not to wear his protective bomb-disposal suit, partly because of the sweltering heat and partly because it would restrict his movement. In any case, the suit would not withstand an IED explosion. Lying flat on his stomach, Shepherd ████████████████████████ then got up to deal with the IED itself. He brushed ███████████████████████ with a Vallon before kneeling down to █████████████████████. At 2:43 p.m., Captain Tom Cairncross of R Company was looking through his binoculars at Shepherd when the IED detonated. "He was just atomised," Cairncross recalls. "There was almost nothing left of him. His helmet was split in two." A few seconds before the blast, it had been stated on the radio that there would be a controlled explosion in five minutes. "That was no controlled explosion," said Rifleman Mark Osmond, a sniper, to a colleague. For a couple of seconds, he thought the sounds he was hearing was the Barma team cheering. In fact, it was soldiers screaming as small pieces of Shepherd rained down from the dust cloud.

Shepherd's assistant, a corporal, had been ten meters behind him and went into battle shock. A medic ran forward but Sergeant Paul Howard, the Viking troop sergeant who had been a close friend of Corporal Scott, told him: "F--- off, you don't need to see this! Get away! Get away!" The medic replied that he wanted to help. "There's no one to help," said Howard. "Leave!" Howard handed Shepherd's mangled helmet to Lieutenant Terry Newton, his troop commander, and said: "I'll do this, boss." He then retrieved what remains of Shepherd he could find. The Vikings had no air conditioning, never mind refrigeration facilities. This meant that the stench of death never quite left a Viking that had been used to carry body parts. For this reason, Howard would always put the human remains in his vehicle, used to carry food and ammunition, so that no one in his troop would have to deal with the smell.

Less than three hours after Shepherd was killed, another IED exploded nearby, killing one Afghan child and critically wounding another. Dogs and the occasional donkey would also quite frequently set off IEDs. In Nawa, a camel met its end when it stepped on an IED.

It will never be known how the IED that killed Shepherd was detonated, but many of the Taliban's devices were highly unstable. Dealing with them was like playing Russian roulette. It was common for Taliban laying or taking out IEDs to be blown up by an "own goal." The Taliban often moved IEDs to different locations as they altered their defensive lines or reacted to the routes the Welsh Guards were taking. On one celebrated occasion, a Predator drone controller in Nevada was watching an insurgent dig up an IED while his accomplice waited nearby on a motorcycle. The Predator controller was poised to kill both men with a Hellfire missile as soon as the IED had been retrieved and was on the back of the motorcycle. █████████████████ ████████████████████████. As the insurgent lifted up the IED, probably less than a minute before the Hellfire would have been launched, the device detonated, killing both men. They died oblivious to the fact that their demise was assured anyway and that they were saving the American taxpayer the $70,000 it cost to purchase a Hellfire.

Shepherd had cleared more than fifty IEDs in Helmand, including thirteen at the drugs bazaar at Luy Mandah, close to XP-1, in the space of thirty-six hours. He was later awarded the George Medal for his bravery. Another bomb-disposal technician who worked with the Welsh Guards was Sergeant Olaf Schmid. He was with FSG-3 when Lance Corporal Dane Elson was killed and spent day after day clearing the route ahead through Babaji, locating IEDs and then defusing them or blowing them up. A notoriously shambolic figure, after a week out on the ground Schmid's trousers were ripped from top to bottom. "Oz was defusing bombs with his balls hanging out," recalls Captain Phil Durham. "When he got pulled out to go off somewhere else, he came up to our boys and said: 'Hoofing platoon!' I was like: 'Cheers, thank you very much.' That was the last time we saw him." Schmid was to be killed in October, shortly after the Welsh Guards returned to Britain, after dealing with sixty-four IEDs, including seven that were connected in a daisy chain. He was awarded a posthumous George Cross.

On July 22, as Antelme arrived in Helmand, Lieutenant Charles Fraser-Sampson was leading a convoy from XP-1 to XP-7 to deliver batteries for their radios. Once out of sight of XP-1—some twenty meters short of XP-4—Fraser-Sampson, in the front Mastiff, stopped the convoy and ordered the five-man Barma team to get out. Guardsman Christopher King, a Coldstream Guardsman who had volunteered for the tour, was the lead Barma man. Minutes earlier, King, who came from Barnstaple and had been a gamekeeper before he joined the army, had been sitting in the Mastiff putting on an exaggerated North Devon accent. Fraser-Sampson watched as King, five meters ahead, concentrated on the ground in front of him, taking pigeon steps and sweeping 180 degrees in front as he went. As he completed a sweep, he looked to his front, as if he had seen something. At 10:29 a.m. he stepped on top of an IED—almost certainly yet another low metal content device—and the ground erupted beneath him. Fraser-Sampson felt a pressure wave buffet his Mastiff vehicle and debris rain down on the roof. At first he thought the vehicle had hit a device, but as the rest of the Barma team came running back to jump on the vehicle, he saw a large crater behind them. "Is everyone OK?" Fraser-Sampson shouted after they were in the back of the Mastiff. "We're fine," said someone. But Fraser-Sampson had already seen half a set of Osprey body armor in the crater. "Let's do a head count," he said. There were four people. "F---, we're missing one," said Fraser-Sampson. "Who are we missing?" The four Barma men looked at each other and said almost simultaneously: "King!"

Fraser-Sampson then had to get the Barma team out and lead them forward to look for King. As they began, Guardsman Ben Hellyn, another Coldstreamer and close friend of King's, broke down and went into battle shock. He was put back into the Mastiff and given water and cigarettes. As they edged forward, fear gripped the rest of the Barma men. Guardsman Sam Williams 07, from Abersychan, began wobbling and hardly moving his Vallon; it was clear he could no longer function properly. Guardsman David Griffiths 21, from Neath, who the previous month had witnessed Drummer Dale Leach lose his leg, was manning the GPMG on top of the Mastiff. Seeing what was happening as Fraser-Sampson cajoled and encouraged his men, Griffiths 21 shouted down: "Sir, do you want me to take over from Williams?" It was one of the bravest acts Fraser-Sampson had witnessed during the tour. Griffiths 21 jumped down, went to the front, and began Barmaing.

The Barma team detected two other suspected IEDs, which turned out to be false alarms, and soon they began to find body parts on the road. Pieces of flesh were hanging from the trees. Fraser-Sampson saw King's body lying faceup in a dry irrigation ditch and ordered the Barma team back into the Mastiff, saying he would recover the corpse himself. There were no body bags with the convoy, so Lance Corporal Craig Green 08 moved forward with a sleeping bag as Fraser-Sampson tried to lift King's body. "His head was intact but he had a horrible look on his face," Fraser-Sampson recalls. "I was trying to pluck up the courage just to touch him and I knew it wasn't going to be nice. Eventually I did and the body was still warm. It was a struggle to lift him because he was quite a tall lad, over six foot, and even just a torso weighs an absolute ton." Fraser-Sampson was struggling, so Green 08 and Griffiths 21 came to help out their platoon commander. "We all got on him, put him in the sleeping bag and we closed his eyes and zipped him up," says Fraser-Sampson. As King's body was being taken back to FOB Wahid in a Mastiff, Fraser-Sampson led the rest of the convoy down to XP-7 to deliver the batteries.

Operation Panther's Claw was concluded on July 27. The number of IEDs laid by the Taliban meant that the Light Dragoons Battle Group's progress from east to west toward the Shamalan Canal had been much slower than planned. When the BRF was sent south from Luy Mandah along the east side of the canal, it was unable to link up with the Light Dragoons as intended. "At first, Brigade wanted us to do an air assault operation," recalls Scott Broughton, the BRF liaison officer. "That wasn't sustainable because after about four or five days you become stranded and there weren't enough helicopters to lift you in and out. Driving down from Luy Mandah, there weren't enough counter-IED teams so that was out." This meant there was a bubble of uncleared territory inside what the brigade had intended to be a "gated community." Just before the end of the operation, the brigade reported to Regional Command (South) that there were "increasing indications of a residual INS [insurgent] presence amongst the population" with Taliban fighters "watching and waiting." In the last week of July, three IEDs exploded deep inside the "cleared" area of Babaji, a potent sign of continued Taliban capacity.

As ever in Helmand, there was what General Dannatt called a "revolving door effect" as the enemy shifted elsewhere and mounted attacks in places left vulnerable. "We push there, so they pushed here." This was what happened in the Wishtan area of Sangin, from where Radford had to pull out troops he needed for Panther's Claw. "In the summer of 2008, we had about 200 soldiers holding it. In 2009, it went down at its worst to about 30. Well, that was not unnoticed by the Taliban. The 2 Rifles company that was in the Wishtan area took a tremendous number of casualties." This was a classic problem associated with undermanning a counterinsurgency campaign. "It was stripping out an area that we had previously cleared and had been holding so that we could no longer hold it securely," says Dannatt. Taliban fighters who left Babaji regrouped in Marjah and to the east of Lashkar Gah. Having caused major jitters in Downing Street as casualties swelled in early July, Operation Panther's Claw had seized the imagination of the British press, which had eagerly declared it a success. In a report at the end of July, Major Ollie Kingsbury, Radford's chief of staff, remarked ruefully: "The slightly embarrassing UK media coverage has declared the battle for Helmand won: this is very far from the truth, and long-term continued effort will be required."

Antelme had decided with Chalmers that after Panther's Claw the most immediate priority was to rationalize the southern boundary of the area of operations, which had been a headache from the start. The position of the base at CP Haji Alem, where Lieutenant Mark Evison had been mortally wounded, had been a costly mistake. The Green 5 junction had become almost impassable because of IEDs, making the base a logistical nightmare to resupply. The triangle area of Noor Mohammed Khan Kalay was an insurgent stronghold, and most of the local population had fled because of fighting and Taliban intimidation.

Linked to the problem of Green 5 was the village of Gorup-e Shesh Kalay to the east. A long-established narcotics hub, Gorup-e Shesh Kalay had also become a base for up to forty Taliban fighters under the command of Haji Talib Aka, a "high-value target" codenamed "Titusville." Relations between the villagers and the Taliban had been generally good, though there had been some tension recently because the insurgents had been demanding food. Haji Talib Aka was believed to be coordinating insurgent groupings at Green 5 and further west in Khowshaal Kalay, as well as overseeing IED factories supplying low-metal-content devices. He was also believed to have led attacks to the north around the villages of Luy Bagh and Zarghun Kalay. Antelme calculated that by moving the CP Haji Alem base 1,200 meters north to Green 5 and establishing a new patrol base at Gorup-e Shesh Kalay, he would create a fixed boundary to the south that would be both more defendable and more in keeping with McChrystal's directive that NATO troops should be where the people are. Brigadier Tim Radford had also stated that he was concerned about "the impunity with which INS [insurgents] are able to intimidate and attack inside the areas we nominally control."

The move of the CP Haji Alem base beginning on August 7 was named, appropriately enough, Operation Tor Duraahi, or "Black Junction" in Pashto. Antelme's plan was to use such overwhelming force that the Taliban would flee rather than fight, and local Afghans would be reassured that the British meant business. The Estonian company would clear Route Taunton, the main road from FOB Shawqat, and then remain in place securing the area for R Company to move through them and halt just before Green 5, codenamed "Llanelli." Vikings and Scimitars would then break off and clear the triangle, codenamed "Merthyr," while B Company to the west would move in from CP Paraang, codenamed "Holyhead," to provide support. As if to emphasize that he was now the commander of the Battle Group and not just the Welsh Guards, Antelme's forces for the operation consisted almost entirely of 4 Rifles, Estonians, and Afghan troops.

As soon as the operation began, Antelme experienced what he would refer to as "the treacle effect"—the laboriously slow process of encountering and clearing IEDs. It was what the military theorist Carl von Clausewitz referred to as "friction," noting: "Everything in war is very simple, but the simplest thing is difficult." There were seven IEDs found at Green 5 alone, and both R and B companies were harassed with small-arms and RPG fire. R Company managed to kill three Taliban as they cleared the triangle. Rifleman Mark Osmond, a sniper, recalls what he describes as "the slowest bayonet charge in history" after Major Mark Gidlow-Jackson, the R Company commander, ordered "fix swords," using the Rifles term for bayonets. The advance took place behind a Barma team clearing the way. As they approached the compounds where the Taliban had been firing from, two fighters ran out. One of them had the misfortune to run into the sights of Serjeant Tom Potter, one of the best snipers in the army, who blasted a hole in him, knocking over Gidlow-Jackson with the muzzle blast. "F---er!" exclaimed Company Serjeant Major Paul Bosley. "You stole my kill. I was just about to shoot him." Frustration reigned, however, when a Predator observed a group of Taliban laying an IED and tracked them to a small outbuilding only for the drone controller to be unable to get into the right position for an attack.

Given McChrystal's focus on avoiding civilian casualties, not to mention the human tragedy, it was unfortunate that a 105 mm illumination shell fired from PB Silab hit a girl of fourteen called Gulalay, killing her. All the correct safety checks were made before the shell was fired at 11:40 p.m. over the triangle to light up an area of threat, but by incredible bad luck Gulalay had been working in a field exactly where it fell. Bos Mohammed, her father, was given an initial compensation payment of $300. Once the triangle was cleared, the Taliban, as Antelme had calculated they would, withdrew towards Gorup-e Shesh Kalay. "I knew from my previous life that you need to be very patient and you need to be determined to get through treacle," Antelme reflects. "It's just what happens when you're doing military operations. But I was surprised just how slow everything was. We stayed for four or five days out in the field, however, and we got it done. No one got hurt and the reason was because we'd gone really big."

With Haji Talib Aka and his men still regrouping, Antelme's next push was to capture Gorup-e Shesh Kalay in Operation Tor Shadey, beginning just two days after Tor Duraahi had been completed. "We do not want to fight for the town ... a perception of overwhelming force ... will give the INS [insurgents] every opportunity to clear out," Antelme reported to the brigade. "A non-violent solution will make the turning of the citizens of GEK an easier prospect. We will be, of course, prepared to fight." Intelligence indicated that the Taliban commander was anticipating an attack but had positioned his forces in the expectation that it would come from the west and the new base at Green 5. To fuel this expectation, Antelme set up a feint from B Company in the west with foot patrols out in force between Green 5 and Gorup-e Shesh Kalay, which was codenamed "Bodmin." In the meantime, the IED threat was so great that the American counter-IED unit Task Force Thor was used. The array of equipment available to Task Force Thor was enough to make any British commander envious. They had MRAPs (Mine-Resistant Ambush Protected vehicles), Buffalos, with steel wheels and rollers that allowed the vehicle to drive over and detonate IEDs, and Huskies, fitted with metal detectors and a long arm with a camera and remote control claw.

Once the route was cleared, the Estonian A Company moved towards Gorup-e Shesh Kalay. Part of R Company was inserted by Chinook into the Bolan Desert to the west of the village, with the riflemen under fire almost as soon as they hit the Landing Zone. Not enough Chinooks were available, however, so vehicles from IX Company and the Prince of Wales's Company had to be brought in to get everyone in place. The rest of R Company, accompanied by Afghan army and police, moved on foot to Gorup-e Shesh Kalay from the east. B Company's feint was successful, and as the attack came in from the north and west, Haji Talib Aka and his fighters pulled out of Gorup-e Shesh Kalay in order to survive and fight another day. An Apache helicopter accounted for three insurgents with its 30 mm cannon, but there was what a post-operational report described as "another frustratingly indecisive moment" when a Reaper drone detected a Taliban IED team "but failed to do anything about it." A Hermes 450 "green eyes" drone also observed a group of men digging in an IED but could not pursue them because it was moved to another location in Helmand where British troops were under attack.

Most of the villagers had fled, probably along with the Taliban, as the operation started, but they began to drift back once it was clear that the insurgents had gone and the British were using a compound to set up a permanent patrol base, named PB Shamal Storrai—"North Star" in Pashto. Habibullah Khan, the Nad-e Ali district governor, was brought in to conduct a shura. That night, Antelme and Major Mark Gidlow-Jackson, commanding R Company, crossed a field to look at the new base location before returning to the temporary Battle Group headquarters set up for the operation. The following day, the field was searched by a counter-IED team and found numerous devices. Only then did Antelme realise that he had twice walked through a minefield.

Perhaps the most heartening aspect of Tor Shadey was that villagers had approached the British to warn them that five IEDs had been laid around the Green 6 junction, the site of the new base. One of the IEDs was a low-metal-content device that could easily have killed a soldier. In the village, a small IED factory was found with four devices, multiple RPG warheads, and a large cache of drugs. Bedding had been left there and it seemed the Taliban had fled in haste. Walkie-talkie messages indicated that Haji Talib Aka had only just managed to escape. The Taliban commander could not, however, be lucky every time. At 9:52 a.m. on October 1, as the Welsh Guards were preparing to leave Helmand, "Titusville" and a deputy were riding a motorbike along a remote dirt track when two Apache helicopters swooped, firing 230 rounds from their 30 mm cannons. "Other agencies found out where he was and killed him," said Antelme with a grin when he heard the news.

PB Shamal Storrai and the new CP Haji Alem soon became significant successes for the Battle Group, both in terms of the solid defensive line it helped to form and the two centers of population it influenced. Central to the success of the two bases were three snipers. The Rifles were created in 2007 as a result of an amalgamation that created a five-battalion super-regiment from the Royal Green Jackets Light Infantry, Devonshire and Dorset Light Infantry, and Royal Gloucestershire, Berkshire, and Wiltshire Light Infantry. The new regiment's fourth battalion—4 Rifles—was the former 2nd Battalion Royal Green Jackets. During the Peninsular War from 1808 to 1814, the 95th Rifles, the forerunners of the Green Jackets, had been among the first British soldiers to wear green uniforms instead of the traditional red, using Baker rifles to pick off advancing French troops at long range. The 95th Rifles was the regiment of Richard Sharpe, the fictional Napoleonic soldier in Bernard Cornwell's novels that were later made into a popular television series. Thus began the long tradition of marksmanship in the Green Jackets, which continued into the twenty-first century with a premium put on developing snipers and taking part in shooting competitions across the world.

The two snipers who were to be based at PB Shamal Storrai were regulars in these competitions and both had distinguished themselves in Iraq. Sergeant Tom Potter had notched up seven confirmed kills in Basra in 2007 to 2008 while Rifleman Mark Osmond's total was twenty-three. Both qualified as snipers in 2004 and were members of the Green Jackets team that won the 2006 British Army Sniper Championships at Bisley. Osmond was mentioned in dispatches for being "cool-headed, decisive and self-assured in exceptional circumstances" and his "selfless commitment, bravery, initiative and outstanding professionalism." In the first three-quarters of their four-month tour, Potter, aged thirty, killed twelve insurgents and Osmond, aged twenty-five, seven. Their arrival at Shamal Storrai marked the start of an astonishing episode in the history of British Army sniping when they achieved seventy-five confirmed kills in just forty days, with forty-four attributed to Osmond and thirty-one to Potter. Each kill was chalked up as a little stick man on the beam above the firing position in their camouflaged sangar beside the base gate—a stick man with no head denoting a target killed with a shot to the skull.

Osmond was an engaging, fast-talking enthusiast, eager to display his encyclopedic knowledge of every specification and capability of his equipment. He had stubbornly remained a rifleman because he feared that being promoted might lead to his being taken away from sniping, a job he loved and lived for.

Potter, who was promoted from corporal during the tour, was more laid back, projecting a calm professionalism and quiet confidence in the value of what he did. His favorite quotation was one attributed to George Orwell: "People sleep peaceably in their beds at night only because rough men stand ready to do violence on their behalf."[2]

Osmond killed three Taliban during Operation Tor Shadey before PB Shamal Storrai was established. On August 18, Potter shot a Taliban fighter who had just wounded an Afghan policeman with a bullet that passed through the officer's abdomen and both his arms. The fighter was brought to the gate of the base in a wheelbarrow pushed by an old man who kept saying: "My son! My son!" Later, while asking for compensation, he forgot his original story and started saying the fighter was his cousin. Potter watched the man he had shot die from the fist-sized hole in his chest. It was a difficult as well as a gruesome moment. Gidlow-Jackson was there listening to the old man's protestations that the fighter was an innocent civilian. The R Company interpreter, listening in to the Taliban walkie-talkie messages, was laughing and pointing to the dying man, saying: "Talib! Talib!" Osmond remembers feeling sick and watching Potter turn pale as the fighter died. "But the OC [Gidlow-Jackson] was very cool during the whole event, telling Tom he trusted his judgement and reassuring him that there was no problem."

Three days later, Potter and Osmond killed eight within the space of two hours. Most of the kills were at a range of 1,200 meters using the 7.62 mm L96 sniper rifle. "A bloke would come out, get in the fire position, look up this area and see what's going on, so we'll hit him," explained Potter, speaking on September 24 just before leaving PB Shamal Storrai. "Then another one will come out, his mate will be on the floor and he'll be looking around thinking: 'Where the f--- did that come from?' and he'd turn round and look down the road and we'd hit him and they'd just be piling up then." The bodies would be dragged away and other fighters sent in to take their places. Then the whole thing would happen again "once we've killed all their commanders, all their junior ranks, everybody, a new group comes in," Potter added. "There's no brief or changeover and the new lot make all the same mistakes."

The snipers used suppressors, reducing the sound of the muzzle blast. Although a ballistic crack could be heard, it was almost impossible to work out where the shot was coming from. With the bullet traveling at three times the speed of sound, a victim was unlikely to hear anything before he died. Walkie-talkie messages revealed that the Taliban thought they were being hit from helicopters. The extraordinary thing was that it took the Taliban a month to begin to realize what was killing so many of them. Up until then, fighters kept queuing up at the same firing points only to be killed one by one.

The pair reckoned that within two weeks they had killed the first group of thirty to forty Taliban. At Battle Group headquarters, the ops room watchkeepers were tiring of having to make so many entries recording the snipers' kills. One day when Osmond was in action, the watchkeeper wrote down: "Have not closed this event sooner as the sniper is on fire at the mo and knowing him he would have got about 5 more to his tally. Request to stay open just in case more wander over his arcs of fire."

The biggest haul on a single day at PB Shamal Storrai was nine. "I wasn't comfortable with it at first," said Osmond, also speaking on September 24, just after claiming the last two kills of his tour. "If you've got enemy, I'm going to engage enemy, but once you start getting nine a day figures and stuff you start wondering is it really necessary? This place was a ghost town in terms of civilians talking to us. We thought for a while: 'Is it really worth it, all these people we're hitting, they're just getting replaced.'" What persuaded Osmond that it was necessary was not the knowledge that a dead Taliban could not kill a British soldier, but the reaction of the locals in Gorup-e Shesh Kalay. "We had people coming up afterwards, not scared to talk to us," he said. "They had a feeling that they were being protected." Soon, villagers were content to visit the base and begin engaging in reconstruction projects. Not only were the Taliban no longer in the village, but the presence of snipers had pushed them 1,200 meters to the south. The longest-range shot taken was when Potter killed an insurgent at 1,430 meters away using a .338 (8.59 mm) L115 A1 long-range rifle and a .338 Lapua Magnum cartridge.

But the most celebrated shot of their tour was by Osmond at a range of just 196 meters. Previously, Osmond had seen a man on a motorcycle and called on him to halt. The man looked up at him but carried on. As he drove away, Osmond could see an AK-47 wrapped up in a prayer mat on the back of the motorcycle. Osmond picked up his 9 mm Sig Sauer pistol and fired a dozen shots at him, hitting him in the shoulder from thirty meters but failing to stop him. The Afghan police had also opened fire and missed. "God was on his side that day," said Osmond. The doctor in the village later reported that he had been forced to treat a bullet wound to the shoulder of a Taliban commander, who had then refused to pay him.

On September 12, the man appeared again, this time with a passenger riding pillion. The man was carrying an Icom walkie-talkie—a sign of hostile intent under the rules of engagement—and a British patrol was out in the village. As they drove off, Osmond fired warning shots with his pistol and then picked up his L96, the same weapon—serial number 0166—he had used in Iraq and on the butt of which he had written, "I love u 0166." When they failed to stop, Osmond took aim and fired a single shot. The bike tumbled, and both men fell onto the road and lay there motionless. When the British patrol returned, they checked the men and confirmed they were both dead, with large holes through their heads. The 7.62 mm bullet Osmond had fired had passed through the heads of both men. He had achieved the rare feat of "one shot, two kills" known in the sniping business as "a Quigley." The term comes from the 1990 film *Quigley Down Under* in which the hero, played by Tom Selleck, uses an old Sharps rifle to devastating effect. "We thought the reaction would be quite negative from the locals, but it wasn't," said Osmond. "They came to ask permission to collect the bodies and as they took them away they spat on them and hit them with their shoes."

Potter and Osmond's working day would begin around 7:00 a.m. and end a dozen or so hours later at last light. They each worked on a different weapon unless the targets were at a range of greater than 1,200 meters, when one would go on a 10–20 × 40 Leupold spotting scope and the other on the .338 weapon. An integral part of their team was Mohammed, the base interpreter, who hailed from Kabul. Mohammed monitored the Taliban walkie-talkie frequencies, relaying what the insurgents were saying about their next move and estimating their distance by the strength of the signal. The snipers would tend to aim at an insurgent's head up to about nine hundred meters and at the chest over longer ranges. Often, Potter would take one side of a compound and Osmond the other. Any insurgent moving from one side to the other was liable to be shot by the second sniper if the first had not already got him. Each used the scopes on the rifles to spot for the other man, identifying targets with nicknames to do with their appearance. A fighter wearing light blue was dubbed "the Virgin Mary," and one clad in what looked like sackcloth was referred to as "Hesco man," after the color of the base barriers. Both the Virgin Mary and Hesco man were killed. Others were given a nickname because of their activities, like "Hashish man," a Taliban who doubled up as a drug dealer. Occasionally, insurgents got posthumous monikers. If one target presented himself, both snipers aimed at him simultaneously in a coordinated shoot. "Everybody you hit they drop in a different way," said Potter. "We did a co-ord shoot on to the one bloke and he just looked like he just fell through a trap door. So we called him Trapdoor Man."

Both men enjoyed what they did but did not glory in the death they brought and strictly observed rules of engagement about hostile intent. Sometimes, they decided not to take a shot even though an insurgent was carrying a weapon, judging that he did not pose an imminent threat if simply traversing an area at long range. Gidlow-Jackson, their company commander, says that Potter and Osmond are the "epitome of the thinking riflemen" that the Rifles work so hard to produce. "They were battle-hardened before they came to Helmand, they know the consequences of what they're doing and they are very measured men. They are both highly dedicated to the art of sniping. They're both quiet, softly spoken, utterly charming, two of the nicest men in the company, if the most dangerous."

Down at the Haji Alem fort, before the CP moved up to Green 5, Corporal Chris Fitzgerald, a sniper for nine years and also part of the army championship team in 2006, had been having a similarly devastating effect. Five of Fitzgerald's kills came at a distance of more than a mile in the same incident, using a .338 L115A3 rifle. Four of these were in the space of less than a minute. The first kill was from 1,764 meters. The platoon commander and platoon sergeant were out on the ground to the north of Haji Alem, each with a section. Fitzgerald was up in one of the sangars lying in wait for the Taliban to appear. "I had my magazines laid out, my ammunition ready, a round up the spout and my spotter beside me," he remembers. Also in the sangar were two Forward Air Controllers from the U.S. Marine Corps, members of ANGLICO (Air Naval Gunfire Liaison Company), who had been lent to 4 Rifles. Two others were out with the patrol. In the sangar, the marines had a Toughbook laptop that was downloading information from a U.S. drone overhead.

About forty minutes into the patrol, chatter over the Taliban walkie-talkie frequencies indicated they had been seen. Beyond a range of 1,500 meters, vision through the scope on the .338 became distorted with the heat haze, so Fitzgerald was relying on his spotter using a Leupold x 40 scope to guide him. The marines gave him positions beamed down from the drone. Soon, Fitzgerald could see a group of men. One stood out. He had a brown *dishdasha* on and appeared to be talking through a Bluetooth device. "His beard wasn't long enough to cover it up," remembers Fitzgerald. "He was surveillance aware but he didn't realise the capabilities we had." No weapon had been seen, so Fitzgerald was initially denied permission to fire. A message then came over the walkie-talkies that "bananas" were about to be used—Taliban code for RPGs. Seconds later, Fitzgerald saw two men with weapons, the first with an RPG and the second with an RPK, the Kalashnikov machine gun. Within 40 seconds, he had clearance to fire. "We didn't really have data beyond 1,000 metres so it was pretty much working off the cuff. The suppressor was bringing up the elevation, I had a 19 mph wind and I was shooting over compounds, which also affected the wind. There was a lot of luck in it."

It took Fitzgerald nine shots to hit the insurgent with the RPG. The suppressor meant he did not hear any of them, except perhaps the one that killed him. "He just slumped straight down as if the life had been dragged out of him," says Fitzgerald. "It was like a computer game. Then I moved on to the next one." In less than a minute, guided by his spotter, Fitzgerald killed the man with the RPK, two other Taliban carrying AK-47s, and finally the Bluetooth man, who had also picked up a weapon. The U.S. Marines called in a Pedro Black Hawk that was in the area to recover the bodies, which were taken to Bastion. Each one had been killed with a single bullet to the torso, and DNA analysis revealed the Bluetooth man to have been a junior Taliban commander.

Fitzgerald's sniping had the effect of pushing out the enemy front line around CP Haji Alem from thirty meters to two thousand meters—the range of the .338. Previously, the Welsh Guards at Haji Alem had only been using an L96 sniper rifle, with a maximum range of 1,100 meters. "The Welsh Guards were chinned when we arrived," says Fitzgerald. "Their boss had been taken out and they just wanted to get out of the place. Haji Alem was just brilliant. It was a sniper's paradise. The arcs were great and it was elevated." During his Helmand tour, Fitzgerald wore a baseball cap while he was sniping except on the occasions he went out with a patrol. It was the same baseball cap he had worn in Iraq, where he had achieved seven confirmed kills. On it was the Ace of Spades death card along with a skull and crossbones.

In four months at Haji Alem, Fitzgerald registered thirty-seven confirmed kills. At Gorup-e Shesh Kalay and elsewhere before PB Shamal Storrai was set up, Osmond chalked up fifty-one and Potter forty-three. The 131 killed by the three snipers accounted for over 70 percent of the enemy fatalities achieved by 4 Rifles during their whole tour. It took a unique blend of skill, patience, and courage to make the split-second decision as to whether someone should live or die and observe up close the often-horrific effect of having opted to pull the trigger.

Antelme was a keen proponent of the use of snipers. He had cut his teeth as a platoon commander in South Armagh in 1997 when the British Army was being terrorized by IRA snipers. In Helmand, the sniper proved to be the ideal counter-insurgency weapon because it minimized the risk of collateral damage and scarcely interrupted the rhythms of normal life. "You're killing exactly the person that you want to kill, which is completely in line with McChrystal's direction," says Antelme. "You're involved in a war where you're trying to win people over, and the more precise you can be in taking out the enemy, the more likely you are to achieve your mission."

Lance Corporal Tom Lawrence, who had grown up in Newport a couple of streets away from Regimental Sergeant Major Mike Monaghan, was one of the Prince of Wales's Company snipers. Ginger-haired with freckles, Lawrence was softly spoken and earnest but had shown strong leadership qualities as a section commander. Until Helmand, he had never fired a shot at a human. Lawrence had already notched up four confirmed kills at Chah-e Anjir with his .338. The first was a Taliban fighter who was laying an IED in the middle of Route Dorset when he was hit in the side and killed instantly by a bullet fired by Lawrence from 750 meters away. Lawrence's second kill was a gruesome one, even for a sniper. As he lay in wait, Lawrence spotted a Taliban fighter with a big black beard, wearing a chest rig full of magazines and carrying an AK-47. He was creeping through the undergrowth and observing the checkpoint from an estimated 450 meters away. Lawrence aimed at the fighter's chest but had misjudged the distance. In fact, he was about 390 meters away, so the shot went high. Lawrence saw the bullet hit the fighter in the face, causing a fine red mist as the top of his head was sliced off. Guardsman Chris Morgan 18, from Aberdare, viewed everything through his rifle sight. "Morgan was shaking like a leaf," recalls Lawrence. "He couldn't believe what he was seeing. I didn't mean to hit him in the head. That was just the way it happened. Some of the officers spoke to me after I'd had a few kills and asked me how I felt about it. I genuinely feel fine. If the Taliban were in my shoes, they would have done exactly the same."

As well as killing people, the snipers observed the local pattern of life, which was vital to build intelligence picture and assess civil assistance needs. They also passed on target information for air strikes. Most critically, they kept the enemy at bay, pushing the Taliban farther away from the bases and the settlements of Noor Mohammed Khan Kalay and Gorup-e Shesh Kalay. This made the local population feel safer and gave 4 Rifles the breathing space to engage them. At CP Haji Alem, the Taliban initially surrounded the base and were operating from just a hundred meters away. By the time the base was moved, they seldom came within 1,500 meters. B Company had an additional platoon compared with their predecessors, 2 Company, and that made a major difference in having the forces to pacify Khowshaal Kalay and Noor Mohammed Khan Kalay. "They brought CP Haji Alem under control by the sniper working really, really patiently and slowly, psychologically bringing the place under control," says Lieutenant Colonel Rupert Jones, commanding officer of 4 Rifles. "Ultimately what you want your sniper to do is first disrupt the attacks. You also want him to deter the attacks so it quietens [sic] down. That is what started happening at CP Haji Alem. The interesting thing over at Shamal Storrai is it was disrupting the attacks on Gorup-e Shesh Kalay, but what it wasn't doing was deterring further attacks. That, we think, is because you had transient fighters coming through."

To the west of Gorup-e Shesh Kalay and CP Haji Alem, 4 Rifles were suffering heavy casualties, particularly from IEDs. In three months, B Company had one man killed while four lost both their legs in explosions. Rifleman Daniel Hume was killed on July 9 when he stepped on what was believed to be a low-metal-content IED. The incident report echoed Thorneloe's plaintive calls a month before for new ███████████████████████████. "The key lesson is that some devices will not be detected with the current C-IED kit in service," the report concluded. "There is an urgent need for a C-IED system that ████████████████████ not one based solely on ████████████."

The first double amputee in the Welsh Guards Battle Group was Captain Harry Parker, Harman's successor as influence officer at CP Silab and the son of Lieutenant General Sir Nick Parker, soon to become McChrystal's deputy in Kabul. Captain Parker, a talented painter, had attended Radley, the same school as Thorneloe. He was at the head of a patrol returning to

PB Silab on July 18 when he took a step back from the cleared route for the Vallon man to pass him and stood on an IED. His left leg was blown off and his right badly mangled.

The deaths of Birchall and Thorneloe had prompted a reassessment of the wisdom of having commanders at the front, given the high IED threat. The Parker incident report sent by 4 Rifles to brigade concluded: "Commanders must not lead the patrols, specifically the clearance of routes. The commanders are best suited to controlling any potential casualty situation, of which the lead man is most vulnerable." General Parker and his wife Beccy were on holiday in France when they received a call from General Sir David Richards, commander in chief of Land Forces. Apart from the rank of the informing officer, General Parker's experience was similar to that of any father. "It was pretty bad at that stage, they didn't know if Harry would survive or not," he later recalled.[3] "We just crossed our fingers and that's all you can do. Just sit and hope you'll see your son alive again and stay as calm as possible."

Four days later, as Captain Parker still battled in vain to keep his right leg, Rifleman Daniel Shaw, only eighteen, stepped on an IED. He was Barmaing a helicopter landing site for a Chinook flying supplies into Paraang. The Chinook had been due to land inside the base, but at the last moment the pilot refused to, saying there was not enough room. A Barma team was hastily assembled, and in the confusion Shaw strayed from the cleared area and lost both his legs. Shaw knew he had lost his left leg, but when he woke up in Selly Oak to find out his right was gone as well, he shouted at the nurses to fetch his limb. When they said this wasn't possible, he asked for the ashes. The next day, he decided he needed to accept what had happened. "Right, my legs are gone, there's no point in moaning about it," he said to himself.[4]

On the night of August 3, Lieutenant Ed Lycett, the platoon commander at Paraang, held a quiz night for his men. The prize for the soldier who got Lycett's question right was that the lieutenant would do a day and a night "stag" (duty) for him. "In which James Bond film does James Bond cry?" Lycett asked. Rifleman Sam Walpole immediately knew the correct answer: *On Her Majesty's Secret Service*. The next day, Lycett did Walpole's stag in the sangar before the platoon went out on a night patrol. Walpole was the fourth man in the line of soldiers when he set off an IED. He lost both his legs but remained conscious and lucid. As he was being carried on a stretcher to the helicopter, he grabbed another soldier and said: "F---ing make sure boss does my stag!" On August 13, Rifleman Tyler Christopher, twenty-five, was the tenth man walking along a lane cleared by a Vallon at the front. Once again, it appeared he stepped on a low-metal-content device.

In three months at CP Paraang, fourteen of Lycett's platoon of thirty men were wounded, eight by IEDs, five by grenades, and one, a sniper, by a bullet. Five were wounded on a single day in late September. The first was Rifleman Thomas Sobolewski, who became one of the only soldiers in Helmand to step on and detonate an IED but not lose any limbs. But Sobolewski's limbs were not the first thing on his mind as he lay on the ground afraid to look at his injuries after the explosion. When Lycett reached him, he asked: "Do I still have my cock?"[5] After Sobolewski, his genitals intact, was evacuated, the patrol continued, and three more soldiers were wounded by another IED, next to a footbridge. Lycett had to get the injured back across the footbridge to where the helicopter would land. As the platoon prepared to withdraw, a grenade was thrown over a compound wall, wounding a fourth soldier. Lycett grabbed Rifleman Evans and said: "This is really important. We can't get out of here unless the bridge is cleared. It's your job but I'm going with you." Evans picked up the Vallon and walked forward with Lycett behind him with one arm on his shoulder.

Low metal content IEDs continued to take their toll on vehicles. On August 23, the Estonians were tasked to clear a route from Blue 2 to Blue 10 ahead of a resupply convoy coming in from Camp Bastion. The road was Barmaed and one IED found, but a second detonated underneath a Pasi armored personnel carrier on the cleared route, ripping it apart. Master Sergeant Eerik Salmus was killed instantly while Sergeant Raivis Kang was severely injured and died on the Chinook medivac helicopter. Four others were wounded. Salmus and Kang were from the same section of the platoon that had been led by Master Sergeant Allain Tikko, killed by an RPG in June. Of Tikko's ten-man section, nine were killed or wounded during the tour, and two battle casualty replacements were also wounded. The only member of the section to emerge unscathed was Sergeant Ranno Pettai. "Tikko was my best friend and we were all very close," said Pettai as he was about to return home. "People tell me I'm the luckiest man in Afghanistan, but I don't feel lucky." There were only so many different routes a major resupply convoy could take, and the Taliban, calculating that another was due, had put in IEDs to stop it. After the incident, Antelme agreed to lend the Estonians some Mastiffs, whose heavier armor would provide them much greater protection against IEDs. In August 2010, the body of Sergeant Aare Viirmaa, the member of Tikko's section who had lost both his legs to an IED two months before Salmus and Kang were killed, was found at his home in Estonia. The local prosecutor treated the case as a suicide.

At the shura held in Gorup-e Shesh Kalay on August 9, the day PB Shamal Storrai was established, District Governor Habibullah Khan had preached the benefits of the new base. "Ask everyone to come back to the village, it is safe now," he said. "You have elections coming up in a few days' time, and you must vote. This battle has been fought so that you have the right to vote. Do not throw it away."[6] The two operations conducted by Antelme had indeed made the Nad-e Ali district safer just before the August 20 presidential elections, which were being hyped in Britain and the United States as a potential turning point for Afghanistan. Come voting day, no significant attacks were mounted from south of the new de facto boundary running from Paraang in the west, through Green 5 to Gorup-e Shesh Kalay in the east. Whether the election itself would improve the situation in Helmand was a different matter.

19

Dragon Punch

All warfare is based on deception.

Sun Tzu, The Art of War, *sixth century BC*

In wartime, truth is so precious that she should always be attended by a bodyguard of lies.

Winston Churchill to Joseph Stalin, 1943

E lection day dawned in Chah-e Anjir with the Welsh Guards planning to remain in the background and let the Afghan police and army take the lead. Major Giles Harris wanted to avoid engaging the Taliban if at all possible for fear of scaring away voters. He gave strict instructions for fire to be held unless it was absolutely vital to save life. The Afghan presidential election was an international news story and back in Britain was being portrayed as the reason for Operation Panther's Claw. Any mistake by British forces could be of strategic significance, and enormous store was being set on whether the people of Helmand would want to vote and would feel safe enough to do so. The polling station, one of thirteen in Nad-e Ali district, would be at the school in Chah-e Anjir, where a joint Welsh Guards and

Afghan police checkpoint had already been established. Throughout August 20, the plan was for the Welsh Guards to lurk out of sight behind the school so that voting would be seen as an Afghan affair. According to a Brigade document about the "messaging" objectives for Operation Qalbe Palang (Pashto for Panther's Heart), the aim was to achieve a "perception that the elections were legitimate and that security was provided by the Afghan National Security Forces."

The Taliban had different ideas. Their plan was to attack British and Afghan forces patrolling around the town, fixing them into position so that the polling station could be besieged and forced to close. In addition, the Taliban wanted to set up illegal vehicle checkpoints on roads into the town and to turn voters back. The first shots were fired by the Taliban at 8:12 a.m., and within the hour the town had turned into a battleground. There were simultaneous attacks on the school, Five Tanks, and Yellow 12 checkpoints. Giles Harris had no other option but to fight back. The only way he could prevent voters fleeing en masse, he decided, was to let them know what was going on and to keep his fingers crossed they would believe that the Welsh Guards rather than the Taliban could win the day.

Color Sergeant Neil Rowley, a Parachute Regiment reservist mentoring the Afghan police, was at the School checkpoint and using the radio callsign One Zero Hotel. Harris called for GMLRS rockets—which the Taliban referred to as the "Big Monster" on their Icom walkie-talkies—to be launched at the compounds being used by the enemy. "One Zero Hotel, this is One Zero Alpha," Harris told Rowley. "We are going to have GMLRS rounds in the air shortly and I want you to give everyone in the polling station the following message." Rowley listened to Harris outline what he wanted the people of Chah-e Anjir to be told. "This is One Zero Hotel, Roger," the color sergeant replied, and then ordered Hamid, the company's main interpreter, onto the roof of the school with the Sound Commander public address system. Minutes later, Harris radioed: "OK, rounds in the air. Tell them now!" Over Sound Commander, Hamid announced in Pashto: "You are about to hear some very loud bangs. That is the sound of the Taliban dying. They are trying to stop you from voting." Harris heard Hamid's voice in the distance just before a series of huge explosions rocked the town as the GMLRS rockets rained down on the Taliban. The company commander's head filled with images of Afghans screaming and running away from the polling station, and he began to wonder if he had done the right thing. "One Zero Hotel, this is

One Zero Alpha," Harris said, with trepidation. "What's going on?" Rowley paused and it was difficult to hear him above the hubbub. "They're dancing, sir, they're cheering," he reported. "They're loving it!" The Taliban gunfire had stopped, and at the polling station Afghans were celebrating the successful GMLRS strikes and waving their ink-stained fingers in the air to show that they had voted.

On election day, Harris watched live-streaming video from a Predator drone looking down on Chah-e Anjir that showed a Taliban checkpoint on the main road just to the south of the town. Whenever a vehicle came along, men would walk out from the trees, stop it, and talk to the driver, who would then turn around and drive back. Harris was getting reports back that the drivers were being told their hands would be chopped off if they voted. There were about ten Taliban, some of them with AK-47s, brazenly preventing Afghans from voting. Some of them were armed, and there were no civilians nearby apart from the vehicles that arrived periodically. It was an ideal opportunity to kill large numbers of enemy with a Hellfire missile from the Predator. Antelme, viewing the same Predator feed at Battle Group headquarters in FOB Shawqat, agreed. But it was not his call—a missile strike against men who offered no immediate threat had to be authorized by the brigade. The answer came back: permission denied. In the Prince of Wales's Company ops room there was frustration and disbelief. The brigade's logic was that no troops were under threat and there was no cast-iron guarantee against civilian casualties. Harris argued back that the reason for troops being out that day was to enable the people to vote, and these Taliban were stopping them. He rejected a Brigade proposal to send a patrol out there to attract fire so the missile strike could be authorized; it would mean putting his men's lives at additional risk just to manipulate the rules of engagement.

Time was running out if Harris was to stop the Taliban turning away perhaps hundreds of voters. He called for a sniper, and Lawrence was sent to the checkpoint at Yellow 12 with his .338. Lying on the ground with the barrel of his weapon pointing down the road, Lawrence watched the Taliban stopping vehicles. He could see men using Icom walkie-talkies but had been ordered not to open fire unless there was a weapon.

The Taliban seemed to have an almost instinctive feel for the British rules of engagement, knowing when they could flaunt their presence without being shot. Eventually, however, one Taliban fighter got complacent, and Lawrence saw him step out onto the road with an AK-47 slung over his shoulder and hold his hand up as a minivan approached. Lawrence placed the crosshairs of his scope onto the center of the fighter's back and pulled the trigger. The bullet hit exactly where he'd aimed, going straight through his target's body and killing him. It then carried on straight, hit the engine of the minibus, and shattered into several fragments, one of which hit a passenger in the leg. The remaining Taliban staging the illegal checkpoint scattered, and the minibus drove up to the Afghan police checkpoint with the wounded passenger. Fortunately, it turned out that the wounded man was a suspected Taliban fighter from Pakistan rather than an innocent civilian trying to vote. He was taken to PB Shahzad, his leg treated, and he survived. There were no more Taliban checkpoints that day.

There were thirty-one Taliban attacks in Chah-e Anjir on election day, and virtually every time the British responded, the locals were warned by the Welsh Guards of what was about to happen. An impressive total of 2,297 people voted in Chah-e Anjir, and across the brigade area all 107 polling stations remained open and counting was completed smoothly. Two British soldiers died in separate IED explosions in the Wishtan area of Sangin, but seventy-eight Taliban were killed. Militarily, election day in Helmand was a significant success for the Battle Group and the brigade. Beyond Chah-e Anjir, however, the numbers of voters were small—321 in Luy Bagh, 213 in Zarghun Kalay, and just 1 in Shin Kalay. There were 1,307 votes supposedly cast in the Nad-e Ali town, but the Welsh Guards witnessed widespread fraud and the genuine number was closer to five hundred. In one Nad-e Ali polling station, there was an "independent observer" wearing a Karzai baseball cap who stuffed bundles of votes into the Karzai pile. When this was mentioned to the local police chief, he responded: "This is an Afghan election. What did you expect?" Setting aside the estimated 800 fraudulent votes in the town of Nad-e Ali, fewer than 3,400 people voted across the Battle Group area out of a total of some 50,000 eligible voters. In Babaji, just 150 people voted, prompting the British press to ask whether fifteen votes for each dead soldier during Panther's Claw was worth it.

For the Welsh Guards, the election was a classic case of a tactical victory accompanied by a larger strategic defeat. The Taliban attempts to disrupt the election and kill British troops and Afghan forces came to naught. Routes and polling stations remained open, and Afghan forces were seen to take the lead. At FOB Shawqat, there was a joint operations center in which the

Afghan army and police commanders sat side by side manning radios and directing their men. Given that their respective forces had been murdering each other a few hundred yards away just three months earlier, this was a signal achievement. But Antelme described to brigade how "a potent cocktail of fear and apathy" kept voters at home and there was "clear evidence of vote rigging." Up near Luy Bagh, 2 Company were told by locals that the Taliban had used loudspeakers on the mosques to tell everyone that the roads were blocked by IEDs and that anyone found to have voted would be beheaded. The Taliban's Quetta shura had issued what Brigade intelligence officers described as "clear direction" for carrying out a systematic and largely uniform campaign of intimidation across Helmand. Most Afghans were unconvinced that British forces were there to stay and therefore judged that it was safer to stay at home rather than choose a side.

The British had consistently underestimated how decentralized Helmand was and the unpopularity of the Kabul government. For many Helmandis, the government was an institutionalized network of corruption and warlordism that exploited the people rather than helped them. "It doesn't take a lot of intimidation to stop people voting," reflects Antelme. "If you don't really believe in the government anyway and you don't know whether it's going to do you any good and someone comes and knocks on your door and says: 'If you vote, I'm going to chop all your fingers off,' then you are probably going to say: 'OK, maybe I'll stay indoors that day,' because it isn't really going to affect your life." On August 28, the brigade reported that turnout "was lower than expected and outside the political classes there does not appear to be any great appetite for engagement with the Elections." It concluded: "It is likely that a combination of INS [insurgent] intimidation and underlying doubts about the benefits of voting led to the limited participation, particularly in outlying areas."

Nationally, the presidential election came to be viewed by the international community as an unmitigated disaster. Turnout was about 30 percent overall and much less in the Pashtun south. Karzai eventually emerged as the winner of a new five-year term with just under 55 percent of the vote, well ahead of his nearest rival Abdullah Abdullah, who secured 27 percent. Ambassador Peter Galbraith, an American who resigned in disgust as deputy special representative of the United Nations in Afghanistan, charged in the *Washington Post* that the election was a "foreseeable train wreck" and estimated that as many as 30 percent of Karzai's votes were fraudulent. He concluded: "The fraud has handed the Taliban its greatest strategic victory in eight years of fighting the United States and its Afghan partners."

What the Welsh Guards had achieved in Chah-e Anjir, however, was a reason for the British to take heart. The approach taken by Giles Harris and his Prince of Wales's Company provided an inspirational example of how counterinsurgency principles could be adapted to a practical situation. Chah-e Anjir was the largest town in the Nad-e Ali district and sat at the southern edge of the CAT on a strategic crossroads next to the base of the Shamalan Canal. Thorneloe and Giles Harris had calculated that Chah-e Anjir was ripe for "tipping" towards the British because of the town's experience of previous eras when it had played host to Americans, Russians, and the Taliban. Whereas many Helmandis were waiting to see which force prevailed, those in Chah-e Anjir were used to choosing sides. One of the legacies of the Americans who ran the Helmand and Arghandab Construction Unit headquarters at Chah-e Anjir was an educated population and skilled workforce, including a number who spoke English.

Giles Harris had only three platoons and had to man two checkpoints on the Shamalan Canal. As with almost everything the British did in Helmand, on paper he had nowhere near enough troops for the job. He did, however, have the advantage of surprise and a temporary power vacuum in Chah-e Anjir while the Taliban, fearing the CAT itself was under threat, were preoccupied with fighting the Welsh Guards on the Shamalan. There was no dominant tribe in Chah-e Anjir, which made a direct appeal to the people more straightforward.

Giles Harris soon made a virtue of necessity. He did not have enough British troops so he co-opted the Afghan police and army, working with them as partners rather than mentors. This was a key distinction that later became NATO policy throughout Afghanistan: partnering meant doing what the Afghans did and vice versa rather than mentoring, which all too often became either shepherding or accepting without question the Afghan plan and simply helping them to carry it out.

From Harris's point of view, partnering entailed making the Afghan forces part of the overall plan. He combined his Welsh Guards with the Afghan army and police into one Company group, in which each element had its own task but under the direction of a joint plan run from a joint ops room in Shahzad. The Company had no dedicated British trainers for the Afghans, so Harris created small teams of leaders to conduct joint patrols. This meant that the Afghans could play to their strengths of patrolling in the town and engaging with the people while the Welsh Guards played to theirs of striking the Taliban and holding the ring of steel around Chah-e Anjir. The composition of each patrol was determined by the place on the spectrum where it was intended to operate. This would not have been possible if the Afghans had been outside Harris's chain of command and under the tutelage of a dedicated Operational Mentoring and Liaison Team or OMLT.

The Welsh Guards were fortunate that Harris's time in Iraq was a perfect preparation for this. Back in 2004, he had been down in the dumps because he had missed out on early promotion to major and was not being sent to staff college. Suddenly, he had no job to do. Then, in classic army fashion, they told the captain who they had decided was not ready for promotion that he was going to be made acting major and given command of 2 Company of the Welsh Guards in Basra, southern Iraq. Harris's job was to develop the Basra police force. After a very successful tour, he was awarded the MBE. Within months, police stations in Basra were being blown up by the British Army and officers sacked after it became clear that the force had been heavily infiltrated by Shia militias. The Welsh Guards joke was that Harris and 2 Company had done rather too good a job of arming and training the bad guys.

In Chah-e Anjir, Harris's first task was to persuade the locals that the British would remain after Panther's Claw and the elections. After that, he had to show that he had the cash and resources to make their lives better. Above all, he had to provide security, without which nothing else mattered. On the evening the Prince of Wales's Company arrived, he sent out Afghan troops into the bazaar to tell villagers the Welsh Guards meant business. Work on a checkpoint at the new PB Shahzad—an early proposal to call it PB Thorneloe was dropped—began immediately, and a sign went up outside the bazaar saying: "We are here to stay." Harris was aware that it needed more than the word of a young foreign army officer, of whom they had seen many over the years, and that he had to offer something tangible straight away. His stabilization team identified Chah-e Anjir school, closed since the headmaster had been assassinated four years earlier, as a key project to win over the town. It was one of the key areas of the town to be protected by the ring of steel, not least because it was to be used as an election polling center in August months later. It was decided that if voting could be conducted there safely then the townspeople would see the reopening of the school as the next step.

Intimidation was still a problem in the town and locals were reluctant to attend shuras held by the Welsh Guards to try to initiate projects. Harris therefore decided to use Wali Mohammed as a foreman to employ locals to come into the HACU headquarters to clear undergrowth and remove debris from the buildings. It was a calculated risk to allow Afghans onto the fledgling base, but he needed to prove that he had deep pockets and money could be earned. The toughest task of all was to persuade people he could achieve security. He called an early shura and positioned each of his platoons close to known Taliban firing points. Rather than providing a deterrent, he realized later that he had stirred a hornet's nest. "We've come to Chah-e Anjir to make this place secure and bring stability," Harris told the local elders as a series of firefights erupted outside. The shoulders of the old men began to shake, and Harris realized they were stifling giggles. It was not quite the reaction to his solemn pledge he had hoped for, and sitting in a shura while his men were in a firefight with the Taliban about two hundred meters away was not the easiest circumstance for coming up with the right response. He was saved by Jim Haggerty, the stability advisor, who said, thinking quickly: "When I first came to Nad-e Ali DC, this is what it was like. Now it is safe."

Harris decided that if he allowed himself to be constrained by traditional doctrine and the army's straitjacket of "SOPs"—Standard Operating Procedures—the result would be stalemate at best. If he had guarded PB Shahzad with his own men with a conventional QRF standing by at all times, he would have virtually no forces to use in the town and beyond. The burden placed on Harris for logistical moves meant the company's Mastiffs were often called away while the FSG had to keep overwatch on the canal to prevent IEDs being laid there.

The psychological battle to win the consent of the people of Chah-e Anjir had to be combined with mind games to outwit and unsettle the Taliban. Deception was central to his every move. Essentially, he had to trick the Taliban into believing he was much more powerful than he really was. Harris drew on his experience in South Armagh in 1997 when IRA "Sniper at Work" signs decorated telegraph poles and the fear of being felled by a single .50 calibre bullet was so great that it was hard to persuade soldiers to go out on patrol. The two IRA sniper teams killed only nine soldiers and policemen over the course of nearly five years and missed their quarry more often than they hit it. Their power lay in the psychological effect they were able to exert on the thousands of troops and policemen who patrolled in South Armagh during that period.

Harris wanted to do a little of the same with the Taliban. There were only two snipers in the company, Lawrence and Lance Sergeant Waisale Soko, a Fijian, but soldiers dressed up in ghillie suits left with a patrol through the town and then returned with another patrol via a different route. A message broadcast by Sound Commander then warned: "Everyone out farming should be aware we have a sniper at work. So when you are out, let us know that you're farmers." At night, the Welsh Guards crept over to a compound regularly used as a Taliban firing point and spray-painted circles on the front of it. When the sun rose, Harris was mortified to see that the Welsh Guards had drawn smiley faces in the circles—it looked like juvenile graffiti. He sent the men back to scratch the faces off. Later that day, the two snipers fired groupings of rounds into the center of each circle, and the message was broadcast: "You may have noticed we have snipers here. They're the best snipers in the world with the best weapon there is. We just thought we would let you know."

In Chah-e Anjir, Taliban night letters were pasted during the hours of darkness onto the walls of the mosque. Those working with the "Christian invaders" were threatened with death; anyone whose fingers were stained with indelible ink, signifying they had voted, was liable to have them chopped off. Harris decided to respond with his own night letters, just as Lieutenant Owen James had done around CP Paraang. "You come near this place again and you will all die" was the first night letter Harris left. Before long, a dialogue with the enemy had developed. One night, Harris's men left a message at a compound warning: "Next time you fire from here, you are going to get it." The following day, the Taliban fired from the compound and were hit with GMLRS rockets. Afterwards, they reported on Icom that two fighters had been killed by "the big monster." That night, Harris arranged for another letter to be left at the compound, gloating: "We told you and you were stupid and you ignored us. If you fire from here again, the big monster will return and kill more of you."

One night, Harris and his men patrolled a kilometer up Route Dorset, right into Taliban-controlled territory that had been used to mount attacks three or four times a day from close range. On each compound, the Welsh Guards left night letters saying: "We've searched this place"; "We can move wherever we like"; and "This is our ground, not yours." As well as the night letters, they left Cyalume light sticks everywhere they walked—blue ones on Route Dorset and red ones on all the paths to the compounds. Harris had originally planned to use them as temporary markers for potential IEDs identified by the Barma men, but he soon found that there were IEDs everywhere, and he decided to leave the Cyalumes—usual tactics would be to leave no signs on the ground at all—to create a visual statement that the Welsh Guards had been there. He knew that the road would have to be cleared of IEDs eventually, but in the meantime he wanted the Taliban to feel it had been penetrated by the Welsh Guards and therefore to concentrate on defending it rather than pushing further into the town.

"What I wanted was a visual impact," recalls Harris. "We basically recreated Heathrow Terminal 2 down that road. For the following weeks, snipers were dropping people down that road, Javelins were blowing up IED teams and we were broadcasting Sound Commander reminding them of the message." After that, the attacks from Route Dorset dwindled to one or two a week. "That was one night's work with a bit of imagination, a bit of mind games, a bit of cheekiness, and trying to get them to be psyched out by us rather than get us psyched out by them."

Harris was initially keen to expand his area. Antelme, however, was wary of falling into the usual British trap of overextending limited resources and leaving gaps for the Taliban to exploit. He vetoed the idea of moving into the neighboring village of Abd-ol Vahid Kalay in the CAT. Looking back, Harris concedes that Antelme was right. It took some imagination to divide his men up so that he had enough forces to deal with Chah-e Anjir and his checkpoints on the Shamalan Canal. Rather than patrolling with multiples of a dozen men, Harris broke the platoons down into sections of eight, giving him more options to outflank and deceive the Taliban. Instead of using Mastiffs to conduct resupplies, he used quad bikes going across country or even soldiers with supplies strapped to their backs. Soldiers from the stores or clerk staff were sent out to bases so that infantrymen could go out on offensive operations. Back at PB Shahzad, there was often only one Welsh Guardsman providing protection on the roof; all the other defenses were manned by Afghan police and army. Before the base was fortified, everyone in the ops room would work with a 9 mm pistol beside them on the desk—and many slept with one under their pillow.

At shuras, the elders highlighted five wishes, in order of priority: security, education, roads, electricity, and a health clinic. The first one was at the center of everything Harris did. For the other four, he drew up plans to create the conditions so that Battle Group and brigade assets could be brought in to achieve them. Every patrol that went out had a defined purpose and a desired effect on the local population or the enemy—and quite frequently both. Harris resisted GDAs, Ground Dominating Area patrols, or "advances to ambush" on the grounds that they achieved little, undermined stability, and exposed soldiers to unnecessary danger. "No GDAs" became a battle cry in the ops room.

The term "influence" had become part of British Army doctrine, but most units saw it as covering building projects and holding shuras—"soft" effects entirely separate from war fighting. Sometimes "influence operations" amounted to little more than the distribution of propaganda leaflets to counter the Taliban's night letters. In one especially tragic incident just outside the Welsh Guards area of operations, an RAF C-130 dropped a box of leaflets over Mukhtar refugee camp at 2:55 a.m. on June 27. It failed to open correctly and hit Maryam Tahir, aged five, causing devastating injuries to her pelvis and abdomen. She was operated on at Bost Hospital but died several days after the accident. Mohammed Tahir, her father, complained personally to General Mohammed Naim Khan, the head of the National Directorate of Security (NDS), the Afghan intelligence service. MI6's liaison officer in Helmand happened to be meeting Khan when Tahir arrived, brandishing British leaflets and the box that had killed his daughter. A British official later remarked that this was the last time the RAF used the "throwing-bits-of-paper-at-illiterate-farmers method of winning a counter-insurgency."

Harris viewed influence as an integral component of everything he did. On occasion, this resulted in his men almost literally fighting with one hand and talking to the people with the other, as happened on election day. This was the essence of what was being termed "hybrid warfare" by military strategists. In Basra, the British had all too often shied away from attacking insurgents for fear of destabilizing the city. But Harris concluded that in Afghanistan the so-called "non-kinetic"—peaceful—aspects of soldiering were bolstered rather than undermined by killing the enemy when required. In an essay for the *Infantryman*, an internal army journal, about Chah-e Anjir, Harris wrote that "despite all our humane and academic wishes for the non-kinetic fight, the key to success at the tactical level ... was the ability to wield credible power over the enemy such that they were intimidated and those we were trying to support or protect were encouraged." This equation, he noted, "necessarily required significant violence at times which, if properly balanced with honest engagement with the population, was a positive force."

During their three months in Chah-e Anjir, the Prince of Wales's Company reopened the school and bazaar, brought in Governor Habibullah Khan for shuras, built bridges, repaired roads, and enabled an election to be held. In the same period of ninety days, there were 140 engagements with the Taliban, all within five hundred meters of the town center and most within two hundred meters. The Prince of Wales's Company killed an estimated fifty-seven Taliban in and around Chah-e Anjir.

Although he presided over this complex intermingling of killing, intimidating, and expelling the enemy while extending a warm embrace to the locals, Harris worked hard at maintaining a public "bad cop" status. The message to the townspeople, he explains, was: "I'm a young man but I'm also a soldier and what I know best is killing bad guys. I love doing that and I'll continue to do it but I know that's not the long-term answer. So let me introduce you to this guy, who is your friend and is going to help you." He would then bring in Warrant Officer (Two) Chris Davis of the Royal Electrical and Mechanical Engineers, who was the company stabilization adviser. "They don't want to see just a good cop," says Harris. "They want me to be a nasty big bastard who's going to kill the bad guys because it makes them feel safe. But I also bring with me guys that can talk to their government, guys that can get contracts sorted out. The fact that I'm a lover not a fighter, they don't need to know that."

The villagers of Abd-ol Vahid Kalay, outside the "ring of steel," were clamoring to be included, and there was an influx of families returning to Chah-e Anjir and refugees turning up in the hope of getting work and living securely. An initial population of about 1,600 at the end of June became nearly 4,000 by the end of September. The Welsh Guards' plan was for the Chah-e Anjir ink spot to spread outwards into the CAT once more forces were available. In the meantime, Harris decided he needed to let those beyond his reach know that they had not been abandoned. He wanted his message also to keep the Taliban guessing what the Welsh Guards would do next. "Every time you talk to an Afghan you have to put something in there for the Taliban, because you know that they'll tell someone," explains Harris. "You tell all the punchy truths and all the weak truths you leave out. So the fact that we can't come up because we haven't got many men, we don't mention to them.

Instead, I say: 'I'm not coming up there yet because I've got other Taliban to kill but it's going to happen soon.'"

Operation Punch Ddraig 10—"Dragon Punch" in Welsh—was designed to deliver this dual message by visiting just one family in a compound in Abd-ol Vahid Kalay. Every plan Harris drew up involved an element of deception. This time, he put a platoon out to the east of the village to draw the Taliban away and then advanced directly to the compound with a dozen Welsh Guardsmen accompanying members of the Afghan Tiger Team and Afghan police. As they got to the compound, Lieutenant Chris Fenton virtually bumped into Abdullah Mahmoud, the top Taliban commander in the village. He was carrying an Icom walkie-talkie, so it was within the rules of engagement to shoot him dead. The encounter was such a surprise, however, that both men froze. It was like the moment in the Quentin Tarantino film *Pulp Fiction* when Butch Coolidge, played by Bruce Willis, stops at an intersection and is spotted by the gangster kingpin Marsellus Wallace, who wants to kill him and just happens to be crossing the road. Before Fenton could raise his rifle, Mahmoud had fled. Within a minute, the Taliban opened fire, and the Welsh Guards took refuge next to the compound wall. Lance Corporal Jack Ritchie, a Scots Guardsman who had volunteered to serve with the Welsh Guards for the tour, was at the corner of the wall, laying down machine gun fire.

"Where are the f---ing police?" said Harris, flat on the ground as bullets hit the wall. The Tiger Team were fighting alongside the Welsh Guards but the four policemen on the operation had disappeared. "They're hiding," replied Captain Duncan Campbell, pointing to the compound. "Right!" said Harris, who got up and strode into the compound along with Campbell and an army sergeant who spoke basic Pashto and was acting as cultural advisor. The policemen were cowering in a corner and smoking opium.

The normally low-key Harris was almost spluttering with outrage. "Translate this," he ordered the sergeant. After a lengthy and colorful outburst from the major on the merits of fighting rather than smoking drugs, the sergeant looked at him and said apologetically: "Sir, I'm afraid I don't know how to translate that." Harris grabbed one of the policemen and pulled him along the ground. "Chris, I need rapid fire now," he shouted to Fenton. "You and Ritchie, get the rounds down." Under the covering fire, Harris dragged the policeman all the way up to Ritchie. He looked back and saw the two other policemen following slowly, their heads so low they were almost crawling and their rifles raised above their heads. An image of meerkats, a type of African mongoose, flashed into his mind. A third was still hiding behind an oil drum. Once two of the policemen were in position, Harris lifted their rifles to their shoulders and told them to fire—which they did.

Back in the compound, Warrant Officer Davis spoke to the family the Welsh Guards had come to visit. "We are sorry there is fighting around our home," the father said. "We want you to come and help us but there is nothing we can do. The enemy is here and they are a nuisance." Harris told them what he was to tell the elders of Abd-ol Vahid Kalay when they came to see him several days later and begged him to extend the ring of security to their village. "If I keep coming into your village every day," he said, "I'm going to turn it into a battlefield. I cannot come over and stay yet because I still have work to do in Chah-e Anjir. But it will happen. We will come to Abd-ol Vahid Kalay soon." With that, Harris and his men pulled back to the Five Tanks checkpoint just outside PB Shahzad. As they did so, they heard the Taliban debating whether to evacuate one of their wounded, fearing they would be shot if they did. Harris ordered the translator Hamid onto the roof to relay a message in Pashto over Sound Commander: "Abdullah Mahmoud, we saw you and know who you are. Next time, we will kill you. You can collect your wounded man now because I need to go back for breakfast. If I had not forgotten to eat before I came out, we would have killed you all today." Harris stifled a smile as he watched the four policemen dancing and regaling fellow officers with tales of their bravery and the Taliban they had killed.

On August 6, Harris launched an operation to prevent Taliban gunfire reaching Chah-e Anjir bazaar. When the Welsh Guards had arrived in late June, only three shops in the bazaar had been doing business and then only for part of the day. Six weeks later the bazaar was bustling, but a single firefight resulting in locals being killed while out shopping could change all that. The School checkpoint was six hundred meters from the town center. Harris had originally wanted to push the Taliban 1.5 kilometers up Route Dorset and then move back and establish a new checkpoint at around the eight-hundred-meter point. The Welsh Guards had been repeatedly probing north, and it was a near-certainty that the Taliban were expecting them and had laid IEDs in the road. The operation had been delayed because no counter-IED team was available, giving the Taliban more time to prepare. The teams were in constant demand and working around the clock—after helicopters, no resource was scarcer or more valuable for British forces in Helmand.

Harris, concerned about the IED threat and wary of building a new checkpoint that would leave gaps for the Taliban to infiltrate behind, decided he would settle for a six-hundred-meter advance.

Sergeant Michael Parry 19, from Pwllheli in North Wales, led fifteen men from 1 Platoon up the western side of Route Dorset, where they had to clear seven compounds. They had gone 230 meters when they reached the first compound. The path leading down the eastern side of it was narrow, allowing room for only one Barma man. Guardsman Simon Price of Brynmawr, a twenty-eight-year-old rejoin who was considered the most proficient Vallon operator in the platoon, went first. Behind him was Ritchie, the Scots Guard, as cover man, Parry 19, and Lawrence, the sniper. Guardsman Tom Greenan was on top of a folding ladder, peering into the compound to check it was empty. At 11:19 a.m., Price moved off, sweeping the ground with his Vallon. Ritchie, behind him, had gone a few steps when he stepped on an IED. Greenan saw a cloud of dust and a boot fly into the air. Ritchie was lifted up by the blast and landed on his backside on the ground. He looked beside him and saw his left foot and half his shin lying on the path, cut clean off by the explosion. Then the pain kicked in. "Sergeant Parry, I need help," he shouted. Lance Corporal Channing Day, from Comber, Northern Ireland, and one of several female medics attached to the Welsh Guards, ran forward, put on a tourniquet, and patched up Ritchie's left arm, which had been ripped open by shrapnel. The Taliban had flooded the field behind them to block off the route back to the School checkpoint.

Parry 19 now had to organize a difficult extraction. Lieutenant Dave Harris and his 2 Platoon had been positioned further north for just this kind of eventuality. Giles Harris ordered him to advance towards suspected hostile positions and fire shots into the compound walls to distract Taliban who might otherwise have headed south to ambush the men carrying Ritchie back. "Upon firing warning shots, we were immediately smashed from multiple firing points," Dave Harris wrote in his diary. "It was the closest I have come to getting hit out here so far. Rounds were literally whizzing past my head and crashing into the ground in front of me. I remember turning towards the platoon and seeing LCpl Danso [a Ghanaian medic] a few metres away, hugging the ground. As I caught his eye, he just mouthed: 'F---!'"

Meanwhile, the Welsh Guards at the School checkpoint poured machine gun fire into the known Taliban compounds. Ritchie, well over six feet tall, kept slipping off the stretcher, so it was discarded, and he was put on the ladder instead. "It's really sore," said Ritchie, with remarkable understatement. Already on his second tour of Helmand, Ritchie had a natural authority and was one of the most impressive junior NCOs the Welsh Guards had seen. Now, there was no doubting his toughness either. As the men on the stretcher struggled back through knee-high mud and waist-high water, Greenan began singing: "I can ride my bike with no handlebars. No handlebars. No handlebars. Look at me, look at me, hands in the air like it's good to be alive." Ritchie groaned and smiled. He detested the Flobots song and was always telling Greenan to stop playing it. Within forty minutes, he was in the operating theater at Camp Bastion.

Once the Pedro Black Hawks had departed, Harris called Parry 19 over. His men were exhausted. Some were angry, some had their heads in their hands; a handful were saying they would not go back out. "You've got half an hour to sort your boys and then forward we go," Harris told Parry 19. "You need to tell them the operation continues and that's the way it is." Parry 19 knew it was going to be one of the hardest things he'd had to do in his ten-year career. "The boys are on their chinstraps, sir," he said. "But I know why you're doing this and I'll talk to them." Parry 19 gathered his men together. "If we don't go out there and continue the mission then Jack will have lost his leg for nothing," he told them. Harris watched as the men listened intently to their sergeant, their heads bowed. When Parry 19 had finished, Lawrence, his deputy, reinforced the message: "Come on boys, let's do it for Jack." Finally, Harris walked across to the men. "If we bugger off now, what's the point in coming out to Helmand at all?" he said. "We need to do this." When the thirty minutes were up, all fourteen men put their body armor back on and headed back up Route Dorset with Lawrence as lead Barma man and Parry 19 and Harris behind him.

Within a meter of their search of the road, the counter-IED team detected a device. Along the western side of the compound where Ritchie had lost his leg, they found another four pressure-pad IEDs. The Apache brought in to cover the extraction of Ritchie had swooped over the compounds and reported no people inside, so the Welsh Guards could leave the buildings alone. They were there to provide cover for the counter-IED team so they could clear the road. But progress, as ever in Helmand, was at a snail's pace. The counter-IED men, commanded by a color sergeant, were proceeding inch by inch and darkness was approaching. When they heard small-arms fire in the distance, they stopped and said it was not safe to continue. Harris was furious. He had two platoons spread out across either side of Route Dorset covering all the known Taliban firing points. The counter-IED team was safe. There was a stand-up row in a cornfield as Harris told the color sergeant: "I know where the enemy are. I know how they operate. I'm securing the area. You just worry about clearing the road." But the color sergeant would not budge. His superiors at Camp Bastion backed him up, and there was nothing Harris could do.

Only about a hundred meters of ground had been gained, but Harris had to stop there and build the new checkpoint. It would be further forward than the previous checkpoint on the road beside the school, and higher too. This was "workable if not perfect," Antelme reported to brigade. "They [the counter-IED team] didn't get as far as where Jack had his leg blown off," says Lawrence. "We were a bit disgruntled about it really because he had lost his leg pushing up there when we didn't even need to go that far." When Harris visited Ritchie in Selly Oak Hospital during his R&R, the young lance corporal was happy that there was a new checkpoint. He'd been out there providing protection for the counter-IED team, they had advanced, albeit a short distance, and Chah-e Anjir was a slightly safer place because of it; that was good enough for him.

For the next two months, the Welsh Guards stared out at Route Dorset and the counter-IED team's markers indicating where IEDs were buried. Somewhere out there was Ritchie's leg, which had never been recovered. "It's not much use to me now," says Ritchie. "Not even sentimental value. I'm gutted about my boot though. I can't use the heavy-duty boots they issue so I'd bought my own. I reckon the left one was still in pretty good nick."

British troops in Helmand often bought items of kit with their own money. "Dane [Elson] spent a fortune buying stuff, £900 before going to Afghan," says Debra Morris, his mother. "He was always complaining about issue stuff. He bought his own boots because they were substandard, that was over £100. A cold weather jacket, that was £160. Our lads have got nothing really. Compared to the Americans, they're the poor relations." Snipers found that the issue binoculars were too heavy and instead opted to buy Steiner binoculars from Germany. In earlier tours, some had bought their own helmets because the standard-issue helmets hampered their taking an accurate shot. By the end of the Welsh Guards tour, however, snipers were being issued with American MICH TC-2000 Special Forces helmets, originally developed for U.S. Special Forces, which did not need to be removed before firing.

Major Andrew Speed, the Battle Group second in command, maintains that guardsmen bought their own items "because they wanted the latest Gucci kit, not because the issue kit was inadequate." Fitzgerald, the 4 Rifles sniper, says that getting new kit via the internet was about wanting "something a little bit different, a little bit of swagger, a little bit ally."

Maps were a constant problem in Helmand. The 1:50,000 scale omitted some important place names while including others never used by locals. Before arriving in Afghanistan, the Welsh Guards received large numbers of maps of other areas, while maps showing compound numbers were often not available.

Compared with the British Army's past, the situation with personal kit was hardly a crisis. On Christmas Day 1915, Second Lieutenant Arthur Gibbs of the Welsh Guards wrote to his mother from the western front: "I haven't got any wire cutters and think I ought to have some: will you ask Dada to get me some: they must be strong ones." On January 6, 1916, he told her in another letter that his army issue personal weapon was not up to scratch: "The Service revolver is rather big, and you can't carry more than one of them around. You want something handy after you have fired the 6 rounds from your revolver. It should be small enough to put in your pocket, as there are such a lot of things to put on your belt already. Could you get one?"

Central to Harris's approach in Chah-e Anjir was "courageous restraint" and Antelme's interpretation of McChrystal's directive to avoid civilian casualties at almost any cost. In practice, this meant letting insurgents live if there was even a 1 percent chance of killing a civilian. The day after Ritchie lost his leg, Parry 19 radioed to the ops room asking for permission to fire a Javelin at a group of men digging on Route Dorset. There was a tense conversation as Harris denied permission because no component parts of a device could be seen. Harris remembered the 2 Company incident when the farmer Zahir Khan was killed at Green 5. It was hard to imagine the diggers were anything other than an IED team, but Harris would not authorize an attack unless he was certain.

Courageous restraint also involved using the minimum firepower needed to kill the enemy, rather than overwhelming force. Major John Oldroyd, the battery commander, built a culture within the Battle Group that put a premium on Fire Support Teams dropping as little ordnance as possible. Surveillance was so sophisticated that individual firing points in compounds could be identified and eliminated. There was no need, as had happened under previous British brigades, for a compound to be destroyed with a five-hundred-pound bomb unless lives were at stake and all else had failed. There was increasing evidence that the Taliban, knowing the propaganda value of civilians being killed, were using locals as human shields.

For the Prince of Wales's Company, Compound 3, to the northwest of the Five Tanks checkpoint and repeatedly used as a Taliban firing point, was an example of tactical patience. "We started off by suppressing with .50 cal machine guns for a couple of weeks, which managed to calm them down," says Captain Duncan Campbell, the FST commander. "Then when they were still suppressing us, we had Apache come in and Hellfire the compound. That stopped the contact. Five insurgents were killed but they then persisted again. We then used GMLRS, choosing different fuse settings to minimise collateral damage while having maximum effect on the insurgent. It continued and only then did we end up dropping a 500-pound bomb." A year or two earlier, a five-hundred-pound bomb would probably have been dropped at the first opportunity.

Even when all possible escalation measures were taken, however, there were still tragedies. On September 30, a patrol from B Company of 4 Rifles was pinned down near PB Silab and unable to withdraw. A Belgian F-16 Fighting Falcon jet identified the corner of a compound, previously unoccupied, where the fire was coming from and dropped a five-hundred-pound GBU-12 bomb on it. Shortly after the patrol returned safely, a tractor and car arrived at PB Silab loaded with body parts. Seven Afghans, six of them children, had been killed by the bomb, along with four insurgents. "It was tactically convenient for us to say that someone up there had dropped something rather than we on the ground had orchestrated it," says Major Neil Bellamy, who commanded B Company. "We found medical assistance and made sure that the compensation system went through as speedily as possible. Then we had our own influence campaign to highlight the fact that we wouldn't kill ten Taliban if it meant risking one local national." He conceded, however, that the deaths were "devastating for the family" and deeply regrettable. "We were incredibly careful, but I'd be lying if I said that it's a benign environment where you can be sterile with the use of force."

Civilian casualties had a profound effect on many of the soldiers who caused them. Giles Harris was haunted by the four caused during the actions of his Prince of Wales's Company. One was killed by a ricochet fired by a round from an Apache helicopter and one by a shot from the Afghan army.

Just two were killed directly by Harris's company. The first had been the elderly farmer Gul Mohammed back in May and the second four months later. On September 15 at Chah-e Anjir, Guardsmen Steven Parry 26 and Liam Thomas 01 were out on patrol close to the new Compound 24 checkpoint. There had been intelligence reports of heavy Taliban activity and they had just been engaged in a firefight in which Parry 26 had fired 150 rounds from his GPMG. The two guardsmen spotted two men walking across a maize field, visible only from the waist up. Parry 26 shouted *"Drezh"*— Pashto for "stop"—and fired two bursts of warning shots, aiming four meters over their heads, but the youths kept on walking towards them. Parry 26 had no warning flares with him and so fired a third burst. "Again I aimed approx 4–5 metres above them," he said in a subsequent witness statement. "I honestly believe they were not in my sights. I fired 2–3 rounds and I saw them both squat down in the field at the same time, at this point they were out of sight." Mohammed Nasm had been killed instantly by a bullet that entered by his mouth and exited behind an ear. He and his brother Sher, both teenagers, had been collecting wheat and watermelon for the family meal to celebrate the end of Ramadan. There was a military investigation into the incident, but Parry 26 was exonerated. "He was doing it with the right intent and the rules of engagement are there to give these guys guidance," says Harris. "He shouted and he fired and there was no response. The problem is, the GPMG is quite an unwieldy weapon. Parry 26 was extremely upset by it. Guardsmen have to make decisions like this every day for five months."

The hardest of all for Harris was the death of a six-year-old boy on September 21. Again, the incident took place near the Compound 24 checkpoint. During a firefight, a stray bullet from an Afghan army soldier struck the boy, dressed in his best Eid robe, who had been sent out to bring in the goats so that the animals would not be harmed in the firefight. The bullet had hit him in the back and exited through his chest. His mother found him and cradled him for twenty minutes before he died. Harris asked to view the body to establish whether it was small arms or a 30 mm round from a French Mirage that had killed him. He dreaded seeing the horrific injuries 30 mm fire would have caused, but he needed to know if it was the strafe he had called for or Afghan army fire that had killed the child. As soon as he saw the wounds, Harris was in no doubt that it was a bullet, confirming that the Afghan army had killed him. "He was just a little nipper like all the smiling kids in the bazaar," says Harris. "But there he was on a stretcher with a gunshot wound. We killed so many bad guys in Chah-e Anjir and a clean slate in terms of civilians would have been great, but I just don't think it was possible. It's easy to become blasé about it because they're Afghans and they have a hard life. But the civilian casualties I found really, really tough. The rest of it comes with the rations."

20

Time and the Clock

*We must frankly recognise that the hands of the clock of history are
set at different hours in different parts of the world.*

Henry Byroade, *U.S. Assistant Secretary of State for
Near Eastern Affairs, November 1953*

You have the clocks but we have the time.

Taliban commander, *November 2006*

A lmost as soon as the Welsh Guards had occupied Route Cornwall and
secured the crossing points along the Shamalan Canal, it became clear
that remaining there long-term was not feasible. By the end of July,
Chalmers had concluded that the Welsh Guardsmen at XP-7 and XP-9 were
achieving little, despite the dangers they were facing. Far from the block on
the canal being a "seal," the Taliban were wading across it almost at will and
enjoying near freedom of movement away from the checkpoints themselves.

The brigade staff who had drawn up the Panther's Claw plan, which had
envisaged semi-permanent bases on Route Cornwall, wanted the Welsh
Guards to stay. There was concern at the MoD and even Downing Street
about how a withdrawal from the Shamalan might be portrayed by the

media, not least because of Thorneloe's death. Chalmers, however, argued just as forcefully as Thorneloe, though perhaps with slightly more tact, that the brigade should not ask him to do something without providing him with the manpower to do it. "Given our force density, I just can't bring the key principle of defence to bear—depth," he reported on July 31. The Taliban, he argued, had found the gaps between the fixed Welsh Guards positions, and more troops would die in an attempt to continue to hold ground of dubious value. "They have identified our weakness and are now exploiting it. We will do what we can to mitigate the threat, but I sense holding the canal will continue to be attritional (2 MASTIFFS this week, 1 KIA and a JACKAL last week)."

Chalmers was worried that locals along the Shamalan were beginning to get used to the presence of troops. Harman was holding regular shuras and doing his best to help the Afghans. "I am also concerned that we are starting to build strong relationships with the farmers along the Canal—the result of lots of good low-level initiative," Chalmers wrote in his July 31 report. "We have not told them that we are staying but they are beginning to trust us— they will miss us when we go." The clinching argument was that the road would be a death trap in the winter with the near-certainty that Mastiffs would roll into the canal.

The checkpoints by the canal were isolated, fixed positions that were vulnerable to Taliban attack and had relatively little population to influence. At XP-9, where Brackpool had been killed, Sergeant Matthew Davies 96, commanding the base, would go out on patrol with eight men, leaving just four defending the compound. Gradually, the Taliban crept closer and closer and were regularly firing at the base from twenty meters away. Attacks took place at least once and often three times a day. The tension ratcheted up each day even as the heat of the summer began to subside.

"There were a few boys losing it up there," says Lance Corporal Watkin-Bennett, one of Davies 96's men at XP-9. "They were going quiet and when there was a slight explosion they'd throw themselves to the ground. Then there was panicking about going out and crying." When Lance Sergeant Soko slapped his arm because a fly landed on it, soldiers flinched as if it was the crack of a bullet. There were attempts to break the tension and monotony by building a makeshift gym using ammunition boxes and pooling all the ration packs to create an exotic concoction to be shared around a hexamine stove at night.

The southwest corner of the compound was most vulnerable because there was no lookout position there and buildings were nearby. Davies 96 directed his men to use the small latrine room on that corner as a firing position. The room jutted out, giving views on three sides to fire out through the slits in the walls. Its floor was raised up over a stream that ran underneath. The enemy had been watching and spotted an opportunity. When the Taliban attacked on the morning of August 26, Lance Sergeant Bjegovic went into the room and fired two magazines of rounds from his SA-80 before being replaced there by Guardsman Ian Hay, from Abergele in North Wales. Hay had fired just two shots when the room exploded, the floor crumbled beneath him, and the external wall collapsed. "I'm burning! Help me! I'm burning!" he screamed as he was dragged out and the Taliban opened fire. The Taliban had apparently slipped in at night to insert an IED underneath the latrine room. If they had followed up the explosion by running through the rubble to storm the base, there could well have been a dozen dead Welsh Guardsmen.

Hay received serious burns down his right side but made a full recovery. The incident made his mind up to leave the army. "I joined the Guards because of the ceremonial duties," he says. "That day was a life changer for me. It taught me not to regret any day and to live each one as if it's my last." XP-9 was a pressure cooker, and it got worse as the weeks went on.

At XP-7, Leon Peek continued to lead his men into action as he had done virtually every day for more than four months. Peek found the Taliban there to be more skilled and tenacious than those at CP Haji Alem, probably because of the influence of foreign fighters. One time, he was pinned down in a ditch under PKM machine gun fire that was so intense it was slicing off the branches above him and they were then falling onto his head. He listened over the radio as an American F-16 prepared to drop bombs on the Taliban positions. "I can see nine men," the pilot said. "Preparing to engage." Peek thought: "F---! There's 10 of us here. I hope he's not miscounted by one and he's going to drop it on us." He felt a rush of relief when the bomb was dropped on a Taliban firing point, killing all nine insurgents. But the lull was short-lived. Less than fifty meters away, Peek and his men were attacked again by PKM fire.

Back at the checkpoint, Major Ben Ramsay, acting company commander, told Peek: "I've never seen guys follow a man like they follow you. They were stood there and they knew they were going to get hit but they trusted you to bring them back." Peek replied: "Sir, I don't want to be funny but those are my f---ing boys."

The next day, however, Peek reached his limit. He hadn't been able to sleep for several nights, and when out on patrol he saw a group of Afghan men. It was a scenario he had encountered dozens of times before: there were no weapons visible, but he was certain they were Taliban. Peek knew the rules of engagement, and for months he had been as disciplined in firing his rifle as any Welsh Guardsman. "I just fired a shot at them and walked towards them," he remembers. "I thought I'd take the fight to them." Afterwards, Sergeant Dean Morgan 10 came over and sat down beside him. "You need to get out," he told Peek. "You're f---ed." As soon as Peek heard the words, he knew the sergeant was right and burst into tears. The next day, Peek was driven back to Camp Bastion for psychological assessment and given a job helping out with training troops arriving in Helmand for the first time. "I didn't want to go because I was worried about my men being still out on the ground," he says. "After five months, I felt they were like my kids." At Bastion, Peek was prescribed with Temazepam to help him sleep. "They was just drugging me," he says. "It was like being jammed full of morphine. I lied to them about how I was feeling because I wanted to finish the tour and not get sent back to the UK."

When 2 Company reached the top of the canal, Harman and others had questioned what the point of Operation Panther's Claw had been. They had expected Luy Mandah, formerly a bustling village with a bazaar at a key intersection where the Shamalan and Nahr-e Bughra canals met, to be full of Afghans welcoming them. "There was nothing there," recalls Harman. "It was surreal. We thought we were going to liberate Luy Mandah, like at the end of a Second World War film. But by the time we got there, there was nobody to liberate. The boys were like: 'All that, for what?' The people had gone and the bazaar was empty." Although the Taliban drug trading had ceased, so too had all other commercial activity, and the locals, probably threatened by the insurgents, had fled. The area around PB Wahid was an IED minefield. Shuras were held and efforts were made by Bettinson to lure the population to return, but it soon became clear they would not.

Tim Radford concedes that there had turned out to be a gap between how things appeared on aerial photographs and the ground-level facts, just as Thorneloe had feared before Panther's Claw began. "The Welsh Guards had moved into unknown territory, and sometimes it is a balancing act between what can be seen from the air and the reality on the ground," Radford says. After the dismantling of XP-7 and XP-9 only XP-1 at Luy Mandah, XP-13 and XP-11 would be left, each of which was a crossing point where vehicles could drive over the canal. XP-13 and XP-11 would be manned by the Afghan army. Radford contends that the Welsh Guards block had created the temporary psychological effect of a seal on the canal and that was a crucial factor in the success of Panther's Claw. The Light Dragoons, however, had not reached the Shamalan Canal in their push across Babaji from the east, as the operational plan had initially envisaged. Instead, they had stopped two-thirds of the way across Ops Box Tennyson. This left an area still infested with Taliban that became known as the "Babaji Pear." As they prepared to withdraw from the Shamalan, some Welsh Guardsmen remained skeptical about Panther's Claw and the need to have been there in the first place (see map of Shamalan Canal and CAT in Appendix).

On August 31, the pullout from the canal began. Lieutenant Owen James had temporarily taken command of 7 Platoon, now without Peek, and had spent two months at XP-7, which he describes as being "like the Alamo." Virtually no locals remained nearby, and it was not unusual for only six or seven people a day to cross the canal there. Patrols were attacked every time they went out. Vines grew around most of the compounds in the locality, so a favorite respite during a firefight was to eat fresh grapes. Troops from 3 Scots (the Black Watch) were lent to Antelme to provide flank protection on Route Dorset, to the west of the canal, as the Royal Engineers tore down all the fortifications they had built two months earlier. Mastiffs had made eight shuttle runs up to PB Wahid and were returning for the final run when the Taliban attacked with RPGs. James and Sergeant Morgan 10 were standing three meters apart when an RPG sailed between them, so close they could feel the heat on their faces, and destroyed a little shack the base interpreter had used. "Right, I think we'd better get into the vehicles and get out of here," said James nonchalantly, prompting everyone to sprint to the Mastiffs.

Earlier that day, about six hundred meters to the west, a group of Black Watch were on a compound roof when an RPG landed amongst them, killing Sergeant Stuart Millar and Private Kevin Elliott and wounding three others. It was a lucky shot by the Taliban and an unfortunate end to the experience of the Welsh Guards on the Shamalan, where Thorneloe and five others had been killed and more than a dozen vehicles blown up by IEDs. Antelme felt terrible that the Black Watch had lost two men supporting the Welsh Guards.

When he linked up with Major Matt Munro, their company commander, he offered his profound condolences and presented him with a box of one hundred Cohiba cigars from Cuba he had carried to the front to give to 2 Company. Back in Camp Bastion, the exhausted Scotsmen smoked them together in memory of their dead comrades.

Antelme tried to brush aside any feeling that the Welsh Guards were giving up the ground that Thorneloe had died for. "It's a great mistake to get emotionally attached to bits of ground, because otherwise you'll never make any decisions," he says. "The ground changes and it's about people, not ground." The soldiers had mixed feelings about leaving the canal. "It was good to get off there," says Sergeant Davies 96. "But there was also a sense of: "We've just lost guys, we fought for this for the last two and a half months and now we're giving it back to the Taliban." Part of us wanted to stay there but then part of us wanted to go. We were just spread out too much. We took on more ground than we could handle."

In Babaji, to the west of the Shamalan Canal, the Welsh Guards' FSG-3 had helped establish PB Falcon Laws with their Light Dragoon Battle Group. The temporary base was named after Lance Corporal Elson (his middle name had been Falcon) and Private Laws, who had been killed ten weeks earlier at the start of Panther's Claw. On September 16, Guardsman Lee Skates, a mortarman from Gelli in South Wales, was on sentry duty, sitting with a GPMG in a Land Rover that had no windscreen. The vehicle was parked in a gap in the outer wall, where an explosive charge had been used to breach the compound before assaulting it. Skates had just taken over in the Land Rover and had barely settled into the driving seat when the face of a youth wearing a light beard, a white dishdasha, and a manic grin popped up at the passenger-side window.

"Salam alaikum, motherf---er," the youth said, combining the Arabic greeting "Peace be with you" with an insult from the American ghetto, and threw a hand grenade into the vehicle. The grenade hit Skates in the face, bounced off, went through where the windscreen would have been, and landed on the bonnet. "Oh for f---'s sake," said Skates in what could well have been his last words. He flung himself beneath the dashboard and waited for the blast. The grenade exploded, blowing a hole in the bonnet and concussing Skates but leaving him otherwise uninjured.

Inside the base, Guardsman Gareth Scaife, brought up in Wolverhampton but from a Welsh family with a tradition of service in the Welsh Guards, saw a figure running towards him from the gap in the wall. At first, he thought it was a teenager who had somehow got into the base as a prank. Scaife, also a mortarman, started running towards him, preparing to rugby-tackle him. As he did so, he looked at the youth's face—he was no more than twenty and looked petrified. Scaife saw him reach down and pull out a wire attached to a black belt around his waist and realized he was a suicide bomber. As the guardsman turned away, the device detonated, sending shrapnel into Scaife's ankle, knee, and all the way up his left side. He was spattered with blood and shards of flesh.

Sergeant Gareth Evans 62, from Flint in North Wales, came running over to see Skates wandering around in shock and Scaife writhing on the ground. As he bent down to tend to Scaife, the young guardsman looked up at him and said: "I've lost my legs." Evans 62 was puzzled. "You f---ing haven't, mate," he said. Scaife insisted he had, pointing to a pair of feet lying ten meters away. Evans 62 suppressed a laugh and told Scaife he was going to be OK. The feet had belonged to the suicide bomber.

It was the first time the Welsh Guards had experienced a suicide attack, despite numerous intelligence warnings they were likely. This time, there had been no warning. The bomber, believed to have been from Pakistan, had taken his flip-flops off and left them next to the base wall before creeping up beside the Land Rover. He had used a British Army grenade taken from the rucksack of Private Gavin Elliott of 2 Mercians, left behind after he was shot dead in Babaji on September 3. "This fellow must have watched too many *Die Hard* movies," says Scaife, reflecting on the Taliban fighter's final words on earth. "He wasn't a very good suicide bomber because he killed himself and no one else. I doubt there were any virgins waiting for him afterwards."

Details of the incident, close to the end of a grueling tour that had seen more than its share of death and mayhem, buoyed the spirits of the Welsh Guards and spread like wildfire. It seemed to back up Antelme's observation that for all the horror and hardship it brings, "war is essentially an amusing activity."

War could also be exhilarating. Watkin-Bennett, from 2 Platoon, missed the excitement of combat when he returned to the United Kingdom. "I want to get back out there and do it again," he says. "As soon as I came back I went skydiving in America. I did three hours' training, went to 16,000 feet and just threw myself out of the plane. I didn't get as big a buzz as I did getting shot at back in Afghan." Watkin-Bennett had submitted his notice to leave the army, a decision he regretted, but got a job as a security contractor with Aegis and went straight out to Iraq.

Guardsman Richard Guest, a Recce Platoon sniper from Bangor in North Wales, also came to miss Helmand. "If I have a moaning phone call, the bath's leaking, the cat's getting on my nerves, you do find yourself wanting to go back," he says. "It's very simple over there—where's my next box of fags coming from, who's going back to Bastion? I've always had fast cars, taking those up to 150, 160 mph on the motorway on a Friday night, but it still isn't the adrenalin rush you get from fighting." Another guardsman said his experience of taking cocaine before he joined the army did not compare with the high of taking aim at a Taliban fighter and watching him die through a night sight. "Guys often don't tell their wives and girlfriends that they enjoy this stuff," says Antelme. "It's exciting. It's almost a dark secret."

As the end of the tour approached, however, the pressure became too much for some. Guardsman Daron Davies 93, a qualified sharpshooter from Caernarfon, was on lookout duty from 8:00 a.m. on September 4 in the new School checkpoint at Chah-e Anjir looking out over Route Dorset. Manpower was short, so single sentries were being used during the daytime. The previous day, there had been accurate Taliban fire onto the checkpoint that had perforated the mosquito net above Davies 93's head, but he had appeared to laugh the incident off afterwards. Davies 93 was a soldier of great promise, named as guardsman of the year in 2009 and due to go on a lance corporals' promotion course. In late July, he had been riding top cover in a Mastiff en route to Camp Bastion to go on R&R when the vehicle hit an IED, and he was thrown out, breaking his arm. He had returned to Helmand but was employed mainly on light duties because of his medical condition. At 8:07 a.m., Guardsman Sean Williams 63, from Mochdre in South Wales, who had just handed over his duty to Davies 93, heard a muffled shot and ran back towards the checkpoint. Davies 93 was lying on the ground clutching his left thigh where a bullet had passed right through. As the Welsh Guardsmen began shooting at the known Taliban firing points, Davies 93 said: "No, no. Don't fire! Don't fire!" It seemed odd, but those treating Davies 93 put it down to the trauma of being shot. Almost immediately, rumors began to circulate that the incident was suspicious, and two days later Davies 93, being treated in Camp Bastion, admitted that he had shot himself to get away from the front line.

The self-inflicted gunshot wound is a staple of war. Earlier in the tour, a guardsman from 2 Company had shot himself in the foot and then gone AWOL when he returned to Britain. Another AWOL case had feigned a broken ankle to get back home and then disappeared. Perhaps surprisingly, there was almost universal sympathy for Davies 93. "He was a really good bloke and it was a desperate thing for anyone to do that to themselves," says Giles Harris. "He must have been in a rough old state." Corporal Jimmy Martin, who spent many hours on duty at the same checkpoint, says: "When you're on stag at 2 am and it's pitch-black and you can hear noises, you have a little wander in your mind and you think all sorts of crazy stuff." Others spoke of a feeling of impending doom when the sun rose as they stared at compounds in the distance wondering if a Taliban sniper was watching. Antelme opted to discharge Davies 93 from the army.

In the final weeks, there was an increasing number of non-battle injuries that were questionable. Lieutenant Charles Fraser-Sampson found that men in his Barma teams were dropping out. "Having done it so many times and having seen what IEDs did, people were starting to come out with excuses why they couldn't do it. I had a couple of guys that went back to Bastion with hearing problems, but you could never say anything to them because they had been caught in an IED blast. You couldn't say: 'You're bluffing' because for all you knew maybe they did have hearing problems." Cases of battle shock being treated at Camp Bastion were listed as "genuine" or "questionable." After the May incident in which three Afghan soldiers were shot dead and two wounded in Nad-e Ali town by the Afghan police, four guardsmen who had treated them were flown back to Britain for blood tests. "After that, it was identified as a possible way out," says Major Giles Harris. "One guardsman was blown into a ditch by an RPG, picked himself up and was absolutely fine but said he had pricked his finger on a needle. He was in Britain for a month and a half for blood tests. Then he came back and broke his knuckles or something boxing in Bastion." Antelme relied on the trusty instincts of Regimental Sergeant Major Monaghan to assess who was "at it" and who was genuine.

There were a few instances of difficulties in getting individual Welsh Guardsmen to fight. Second Lieutenant Charlie Maltby, fresh out of Sandhurst, had just taken over 2 Platoon from Dave Harris when Watkin-Bennett shot and wounded a Taliban fighter close to the Compound 24 base. Giles Harris ordered Maltby to get men out and retrieve the injured insurgent.

Harris was conscious that his company's understanding of the enemy was thin; capturing an insurgent would have been a major intelligence opportunity. Maltby gathered a small team together, but one of his most trusted and experienced guardsmen refused to leave the compound because the patrol's ECM (electronic jamming) equipment had failed to work and the Taliban were fifty meters away. The nervousness of the guardsmen was heightened because earlier that day Parry 26 had accidentally killed the teenager Mohammed Nasm with a badly aimed warning burst. "We just didn't feel safe anymore," says Watkin-Bennett. "Equipment was failing and we weren't allowed air support because locals were complaining that civilians were getting killed by it. We were short-manned and going out that day with Taliban and pissed-off locals and broken kit just didn't seem right." With the minutes ticking away, Harris ordered the patrol to go out regardless, judging that a radio-controlled IED was unlikely in that area and detailing an alternative route that would lessen the risk still further. But the guardsman still would not budge. Maltby was facing a difficult leadership challenge. His battle-weary platoon had just returned from the pressure-cooker of XP-9, one of the most isolated positions on the Shamalan. The men were increasingly questioning the value of moving beyond the immediate vicinity of their new PB. In the end, a patrol carrying ECM equipment and already out on the ground was diverted to the area, but this took thirty minutes. By the time it arrived there were just drag marks in the dust where the wounded Taliban had been.

An apoplectic Giles Harris took Company Sergeant Major Jones 27 down to Compound 24 to find out from Maltby and the senior NCOs what was happening. Harris says: "The message I got was: 'We're just threaders. At the start of the tour, we would never go out with less than a platoon. Now you're asking us to go out with eight men and no ECM.'" It was getting to that stage of the tour where it was really one-to-one corralling. This guardsman's pool of courage was just dry. He was very remorseful about it." Harris decided not to discipline the guardsman. He concedes that he pushed his men very hard and often would not take no for an answer. In this respect, he was similar to Thorneloe, who had never seen command as a popularity contest but won respect for his determination to do things properly. There was some pushback from his men, particularly Dave Harris, who had argued that much too much was being asked of 2 Platoon. Watkin-Bennett says: "We agreed to go out in the end but the lads were tired after seeing mates get shot and killed and being made to do things that didn't seem as if they needed to be done just made them start to lose their heads."

Giles Harris says he was conscious that he was not spending as much time on the ground as his men. The difficulty of moving between positions and the complexity of the counterinsurgency battle he was directing from PB Shahzad meant he could not be forward as often as he wanted.

There was a serious wobble within the Prince of Wales's Company right at the end of the tour when news came through that they might have to remain in Helmand a fortnight longer than planned. Harris had been driving his men to the finishing line only for the finishing line to be shifted a few hundred meters farther away. "I feared that I had got it badly wrong by driving the guys too hard," Harris recalls. "There was a danger of a serious drop in battle discipline if they had to fight for another two weeks. It could have had a disastrous effect on the campaign in Chah-e Anjir and at the cost of the men themselves. It was pretty knife-edge stuff in those last few weeks, with a hundred-odd brave men at the end of their tether." Watkin-Bennett says: "It was a good job the tour ended when it did."

Two NCOs, who had been stalwarts throughout, were moved back to Camp Bastion early because they had become too jumpy. Giles Harris's dilemma was one that faced many commanders in Helmand. He had been taught to lead from the front, but in a counterinsurgency battle he had to keep close control over the overall plan. In Chah-e Anjir, he was not sharing the personal risks his men were taking and fretted that he was losing touch with his men holed up in remote outposts.

The top of the canal, where 2 Company remained at Luy Mandah and XP-1, was exposed and dangerous. Shortly after PB Wahid had been set up, Guardsman Richard Hill, Fraser-Sampson's driver, and Guardsman Matthew Malley were cleaning their Mastiff and Ridgeback vehicles. They had just returned from a 36-hour operation in which they had provided overwatch for a counter-IED team, codenamed "Brimstone," on Route Cornwall beside the Shamalan. A Chinook came in to pick up the Brimstone team, who were running out one by one from behind a barrier into the helicopter when it came under accurate fire. Bullets smashed into the cockpit, and the pilot immediately lifted off. As he did so, two of the IED team were thrown off the back of the Chinook. One fell two meters, injuring his back. The other fell five meters, smashing her teeth and breaking several bones, leaving her jagged femur sticking out of her leg. The rear gunner, attached to the helicopter by a safety cable, was dangling in the air before being pulled in. Hill and Malley, who were not wearing body armor or helmets, jumped into their vehicles and drove down to the two injured, parking next to them and jumping into top cover positions to fire back at the Taliban positions.

During a night operation on September 12, Captain Tom Spencer-Smith was leading his Recce Platoon down an alleyway in Luy Mandah Kalay, which 2 Company was clearing. He was the fifth man in the patrol and in front of him was Ahmed Popal, the interpreter. Just before the patrol, Sergeant Steve Peters had been speaking to Popal, who was excited about going back to Kabul on leave to see his family. "I can't wait for this to be over because I'm going back to Bastion today and then I'll be flying home." At 4:04 a.m. Spencer-Smith was scanning from side to side when he noticed that Popal was stepping slightly to the side of the route cleared by the Barma team. He turned to tell him to keep to the center of the path just as Popal stepped on an IED. Amid the dust and the screaming, Peters grabbed a Vallon and shouted: "Everyone shut up and everyone stand still." It was pitch-black, and as he edged towards the crater he was sure that Spencer-Smith was dead. He patted the ground and touched pieces of flesh and limbs before finding a torso. It was only when he felt the beard on the wounded man's face that he realized it was Popal. Peters turned a torch on. "What I saw was something a human being isn't supposed to see," he remembers. "From the bottom of his belly, everything was gone. It was ragged and flesh was hanging down." As well as his legs, the blast had taken off his right arm. All that was left of his left hand was the little finger, attached to the elbow by skin and muscle. He was still alive and was reciting what sounded like a verse of the Koran. Peters gave Popal morphine, but it was obvious he had only minutes to live.

Close to PB Wahid, Company Sergeant Major Martin Topps heard the explosion as he and Bettinson crossed a *wadi* heading for Luy Mandah Kalay. More than ten minutes later, he still had not heard Spencer-Smith on the radio. "Sir, I think it might be Captain Spencer-Smith," he told Bettinson. "F---," the major replied. Shortly afterwards, Spencer-Smith reported on the radio that the interpreter was a triple amputee and gave his own zap number as a second casualty. By the time Spencer-Smith arrived back at Wahid, Popal was dead. "Right, Company Sergeant Major," the captain said. "I've got a callsign out there and they're clearing the route."

Topps finished listening to the situation report and asked: "What about you, sir?" Spencer-Smith replied: "My f---ing shoulder's killing me, I think I dislocated it or something, my head is thumping, and I think I've got shrapnel in my helmet." Topps turned on a torch. Blood was pouring out of Spencer-Smith's ear. It was clear he would have to be evacuated. Spencer-Smith told Topps where his weapon sights and specialist equipment were. "When you pack my kit, can you make sure that all my personal mail, my books and everything get sent home. All the food parcels and everything I have under the bed, just dish that out to the Recce Platoon."

With that, Spencer-Smith turned and walked the four hundred meters to the MERT Chinook that had arrived. Within forty-five minutes, he was unconscious and being operated on in Camp Bastion. It turned out that Spencer-Smith had been hit in the neck by a piece of shrapnel the size of an AA battery. It had traveled down, just missed his lung, broken his collarbone, and was sitting on top of the subclavian artery, the severing of which had caused Lieutenant Mark Evison to bleed to death back in May. In Helmand, a few millimeters were the difference between life and death.

Antelme's priority for the final month of the tour was to rationalize the network of bases within Battle Group (Center South) and make the best use of his limited manpower in preparation for the arrival of the Grenadier Guards. Lieutenant Colonel Roly Walker, commanding the Grenadiers, was a kindred spirit. He and Antelme had fought alongside each other twice in Iraq, and the two men were firm friends. The biggest problem the Welsh Guards had, Antelme concluded, was that the Battle Group had been unable to dominate the lines of communication between its scattered locations. At one stage, there were seventeen British bases plus others manned by the Afghan army and police. It looked good on a map or a PowerPoint slide, but Antelme realized that his troops were only dominating the areas immediately around their bases. The lines of communication for the Welsh Guards were by now mainly external: to get from A to B, the route was usually via C in the Dasht-e Margo Desert. In a counterinsurgency campaign, this was a prescription for defeat.

In terms of the most important population centers, Chah-e Anjir, the Nad-e Ali town, and Luy Bagh were viewed as secure. But almost every other significant village—Showal and Naqelabad Kalay in the CAT, Chah-e Mirza, Shin Kalay, Noor Mohammed Khan Kalay, Kowashal Kalay, Gorup-e Shesh Kalay, and Zarghun Kalay—was under complete or partial Taliban control, along with the routes between them.

The problem of dispersed, isolated patrol bases was exacerbated by the size and locations of the Afghan forces. Most of the Afghan army troops were operating around Nad-e Ali town. Beyond them were the Afghan police. It should have been the other way around, though the fact that many police were regarded as corrupt and predatory by locals was a complicating factor.

Rather than training Afghan forces being an integral part of the way each battle group operated, the function had been hived off to Lieutenant Colonel Simon Banton's OMLT group. Antelme had no command relationship with the Afghan army kandak operating in his area or with Jim Haggerty, a former lieutenant colonel in the Intelligence Corps who worked as the Nad-e Ali stabilization advisor. When the Welsh Guards left Helmand, there were more British troops in Battle Group (Center South) than Afghan army and police—a situation that pointed towards eventual strategic failure. The shortage of Afghan forces had been a major problem across the brigade, which had only 7 percent of the Afghan army in the county despite experiencing 35 percent of Taliban activity. The brigade's persistent entreaties on this issue eventually bore fruit when another Afghan army brigade was sent to Helmand in March 2010.

Having cut his teeth as a platoon commander in South Armagh, Antelme was astonished by the poor intelligence picture in Helmand and the paucity of surveillance resources. His mantra after arriving had been "personalise the fight." Rather than talking about "the insurgents" or "the Taliban," he wanted to identify specific groupings and have the names and photographs of their leaders. In Northern Ireland, soldiers had carried montages of IRA and loyalist paramilitary suspects with them on patrol. "In Malaya, you knew who the key Chinese CT [Communist Terrorists] were and in Ireland we had a really good idea," he said as he prepared to hand over to Walker. "Out here it's a bit more opaque and difficult, but it's something you must really struggle to do because as Sun Tzu said, if you understand your enemy in a fight you will never be defeated." Antelme agitated for "field human intelligence teams" to be allocated to him. These were small groups of soldiers who spoke Pashto and could develop networks of informants and even negotiate defections from the Taliban. Perhaps drawing inspiration from the exploits of his ancestor France Antelme, he proposed the formation of an Afghan SOE to work behind enemy lines carrying out sabotage and assassinations.

One night, Antelme had been sitting waiting for yet another IED to be removed from the exact place where the bomb-disposal officer Captain Dan

Shepherd had been blown up a month earlier. He recalled that when he was commander of the Romeo 2-1 watchtower in South Armagh there had been motion sensors that would alert cameras to any movement at key locations. A dozen years on, there was nothing like that in Helmand. His experience had taught him that surveillance was key, and he discussed with Walker a plan for installing a network of "Revivor" observation balloons, watchtowers and Super Nikon cameras across the area.

Having worked with General McChrystal in Iraq, Antelme was well acquainted with how the use of technology could create a faster, flatter command structure. He was bemused to find that now he had to conduct battle-group conferences in the evenings huddled around a VHF radio that had to be held to a telephone handset, sometimes with the aid of Sellotape. This meant, he felt, that his companies were rather blinkered and inward-looking, a criticism that could also be leveled at battle groups and the brigade. Antelme was perplexed by the primitiveness of the communications systems and the fact that there were no British video teleconferencing facilities in Helmand. The poor communications meant—as Thorneloe had also concluded—that it was even more essential than normal for the commanding officer to get out on the ground to visit his men. This, however, was time-consuming and dangerous because of the IED-infested roads and the lack of helicopters.

Antelme felt that in the debate about the shortage of resupply helicopters, what was being missed was that helicopters were not being used for offensive operations either. During his three months in Helmand, helicopters had been used to deliver troops on patrol only once, when the Black Watch were landed in Luy Mandah at the start of Panther's Claw. "I don't buy into the whole "they'd just shoot them down" bollocks," says Antelme, who had extensive experience in helicopter operations in Iraq. "They'll try, but you just have to land them in the right place and be clever about where you go. Helicopters would make an enormous difference. You could drop people on patrol and pick people up. You could make the enemy feel less comfortable behind their lines." He cited the Rhodesian Fire Force concept, in which helicopters rapidly inserted elite troops to surround and destroy the enemy. "Helicopters are pretty damn useful, and the more you have, the more flexibility you have for the type of operations you can do. So do I think we could do with more? Absolutely."

The Welsh Guards had taken over an area of operations previously held by a company and had seen the Battle Group and its territory double in size over the course of five months. The ratio of counter-insurgents to population laid down by General David Petraeus was 1:40. Walker, the Grenadiers' commanding officer, calculated that with a 1,300-strong Battle Group plus Afghan forces (including many inadequate police) he was closer to 1:60. During Walker's time, the Battle Group was to swell to two thousand troops. Antelme had proposed establishing a bridge into the Dasht-e Margo Desert across the Nahr-e Bughra Canal at the Blue 22 crossing point west of Shin Kalay. Soon there was a tarmacked road that ran from Blue 22 east through Shin Kalay, Nad-e Ali town, Luy Bagh, and across the Bolan Desert to Lashkar Gah. Resupplies that had taken the Welsh Guards several days could happen in hours for the Grenadiers.

Early in the Grenadiers' tour, five men, including Regimental Sergeant Major Darren Chant, were shot dead and six wounded by a rogue policeman at a new Afghan police base at Blue 25, just east of Shin Kalay. This prompted a wholesale clearing out of the Afghan police, including all the commanders, in Nad-e Ali down from 150 to just 30. More police were brought in, along with eighty additional Afghan soldiers.

Mark Sedwill, the British ambassador to Afghanistan when the Welsh Guards were in Helmand and later the senior civilian NATO representative in the country, views Panther's Claw as "the last of the old-style operations" by the British. The ratio of NATO to Afghan forces was close to 10:1 during Panther's Claw and 2:1 in Operation Moshtarak in February 2010. "Moshtarak was almost over-resourced," he says. "There was lots of flexibility and surplus within the resources available and therefore plenty to deal with setbacks. If you look at Panther's Claw, we had barely enough and we couldn't, as in Moshtarak, go everywhere at once. And that wasn't just numbers of forces. With the US Marines, it was also the sheer number of helicopters."

Some diplomats were critical of the pattern of six-month brigade tours that led to a predictable cycle of operations. "I have seen seven brigadiers in Helmand now," said Sir Sherard Cowper-Coles after the Welsh Guards had left Helmand. "And each one comes in, each one has a series of seminars before he arrives, has his study days, reads the books on counter-insurgency. Each one arrives saying he is going to do the comprehensive approach, he is not going to do kinetic. Each one does one kinetic operation." He had seen this yet again, he said, in 2009. "Tim Radford came from a different background from everyone else. He was very quiet and thoughtful. A very good man. A very bright man. But I saw the same syndrome. I remember saying to him: 'Don't tire yourself, pace yourself. Every previous brigadier has done one big kinetic operation. Just consolidate, that is what counter-insurgency is about.' But sure enough, there was one big kinetic operation and a lot of casualties, which really worried ministers."

During Panther's Claw, the Taliban's proficiency with IEDs meant movement by the Light Dragoons Battle Group across Babaji was a slow grind. For Moshtarak, the number of helicopters available to insert troops meant that momentum was built up much more quickly. "We had virtually every helicopter in the whole of Afghanistan available to us," says Brigadier James Cowan, who took over from Radford and commanded 11th Light Brigade during Moshtarak in February 2010. "We weren't having to fight our way across a line of departure. We were inserted across enemy lines by air into clearly defined places." For Panther's Claw, Radford had received negligible support from above—especially in terms of the delivery of the promised Afghan army troops. Moshtarak, in contrast, was a divisional operation commanded by Major General Nick Carter, the new head of Regional Command (South). This made it possible to win the full backing of President Karzai, as well as Gordon Brown and the British government. Whereas the Welsh Guards had been starved of resources, Roly Walker found that he was getting most of what he wanted.

The limitations of Panther's Claw meant that during Moshtarak once again British forces had to return to fight for ground that had supposedly already been won. "We were blocking Marjah but also re-clearing, re-securing some of the areas in the Babaji area that we had cleared the previous summer," says Sedwill. "The insurgents had been able to re-infiltrate." Cowan's BRF went back up on the Shamalan Canal, now referred to by the army as "Canal 31," its original designation when completed in the 1950s and free of any obvious association with the death of Rupert Thorneloe. Rather than risk a repeat of the slow advance along Route Cornwall by the Welsh Guards, the BRF was inserted by helicopter as a preparation for the clearance of the CAT by the Royal Welsh, part of the Operation Moshtarak. This time Route Dorset, up which Giles Harris had so painstakingly advanced just a hundred meters, was cleared and a new patrol base established just west of where Thorneloe had been killed.

There was relatively little enemy resistance in the CAT, and the white Taliban flag that had flown from the crane in Showal for several years was cut down by an Afghan soldier. Shortly afterwards, General Stanley McChrystal and Governor Mangal arrived to hail the clearance as a significant victory. The CAT, the Shamalan Canal, and Chah-e Anjir, which continued to prosper, became part of a new Royal Welsh Battle Group area.

Walker had already pulled the Grenadiers out of Luy Mandah, replacing them with an Estonian company. He was skeptical of Luy Mandah's tactical value, in counterinsurgency terms, and of the decision to capture it with an air assault during Panther's Claw on June 29, when some fifty Taliban were killed in two days of hard fighting. "Luy Mandah was a hiding to nothing in the manner in which it had been cleared by Regional Battle Group (South) [the Black Watch] and the way the Taliban had IEDed the place up, so that even if the people wanted to go back they were never going to," he says. The U.S. Marines swept into Marjah, cleared it, and took control. It was apparent, however, that the Taliban would not relinquish the town easily, and a long, low-intensity battle would follow.

Within a year of the Welsh Guards departing, there were twenty thousand U.S. Marines in Helmand, twice the number of British troops. The British had handed over the old platoon house locations of Musa Qala, Sangin, Now Zad, and Kajaki to the Americans. Now, British forces were concentrating on the old Welsh Guards area of operations and Babaji, cleared by the Light Dragoons during Panther's Claw. It was a return to the old Afghan Development Zone concept, first put forward by General Sir David Richards, who had replaced Jock Stirrup (who agreed to retire early after discussion with the new Conservative government) as chief of the Defence staff. In many respects, this consolidation of British forces in heavily populated central Helmand vindicated Brigadier Tim Radford and his predecessor, Gordon Messenger, who had made the area their main priority and massed forces there.

Radford's brigade had fought for six weeks during Panther's Claw to link up Lashkar Gah to Gereshk by driving most of the Taliban from Babaji. The brigadier describes the "incredible courage and resilience" of the Welsh Guards on the Shamalan Canal as giving the Light Dragoons and the Danes to their east the opportunity to gain footholds in the crucial population areas of Spin Masjid and Babaji. The Light Dragoons established four patrol bases in the Babaji area, and, although small numbers of Taliban remained, Afghan governance, which had been absent for years, began to grow. Once the Light Dragoons had cleared through Babaji, "hot stabilization" teams came in to set up schools and clinics. In all, eighty-five stabilization projects were completed and 3,500 farmers applied for wheat seed to grow instead of opium poppy in 2010. The old Babaji road, crossing the area from east to west via the four patrol bases, was tarmacked and renamed Route Trident. In July 2009, it had taken a two-day fighting patrol to get across; a year later, the journey lasted eighteen minutes in a car.

At the same time, SAS and SBS units in Helmand were killing an increasing number of Taliban. "The prodigious effect of Special Forces activity on networks is something that it's just impossible is not registering on the insurgents," says Major General Richard Barrons, a British officer serving in NATO headquarters in Kabul, referring to Special Forces across ISAF. This was all part of what he described as showing the Taliban that "there is absolutely nothing happening that would take the foot off the neck of the terrorists." In November 2009, Gordon Brown revealed to Parliament that there were about five hundred British troops from Special Forces. In September 2010, it was reported that least 65 of 240 Taliban leaders on the "kill or capture" list had been accounted for by Task Force 42, the codename for UK Special Forces in Afghanistan. Among the dead was Qari Hazrat, codenamed Objective Commando Flood. He was the Taliban leader who had controlled many of the fighters who battled the Welsh Guards on the Shamalan Canal. The man most likely to have commanded those who planted the IED that killed Rupert Thorneloe, he was killed in an airstrike in August 2010 after long being on the Task Force 42 hit list.

Skeptics said that there was an almost infinite supply of Taliban, or men who would fight under that banner. Helmandis, moreover, would accept handouts of development aid and that did not mean they were supporters of "GIRoA," to use the acronym for the Government of the Islamic Republic of Afghanistan that had become a military buzzword. The inherent contradiction of pushing the notion of GIRoA—the central government in Kabul—amongst people who resented distant authority had never been resolved. Others argued that the land cleared during Panther's Claw had simply displaced Taliban elsewhere, just as the clearing of Nawa had moved fighters to Marjah and the clearing of Marjah had moved fighters to Sangin and Kandahar.

Within nine months of the Welsh Guards leaving Helmand, Antelme's mentor Stanley McChrystal, whom he described as "an exceptional man and the best commander I have worked for by some margin," had been fired. President Barack Obama dispensed with his services in June 2010, a year after he had arrived in Kabul, following some impolitic remarks by the general and his staff to a *Rolling Stone* magazine reporter. David Cameron's Conservatives announced that British forces would have concluded combat operations in Helmand by 2015 and could begin withdrawing from the province in 2011. Obama had set a deadline of American troops beginning to leave Afghanistan from July 2011, but that was eclipsed by a NATO agreement at Lisbon in November 2010 that the country be handed over to Afghan security forces by the end of 2014.

What had been achieved in the Nad-e Ali district showed that resources, the right number of troops, and time could ultimately deliver success. With American help, the British had, after four years, largely solved the first two issues. Time, however, was another matter, and it was unclear if even the Americans had invested enough forces. "Patience and scale are the two big questions," said Antelme as he prepared to fly back to Britain at the end of the tour. "We know it can work. The theory is correct and the way we are going about it now is, I think, correct. It's whether people are prepared to wait until it spreads. It's whether, if you're not prepared to wait, you can put in such a big influx that you can make a difference more quickly. And, once you've done all that, it's how long you're prepared to stick around until the Afghans are ready to take it on themselves."

Looking back, Antelme wondered whether the army's eagerness back in 2005 to say: "Yeah, Helmand, we can do that" without considering the worst-case scenario and what could be done with the resources available had been a flaw from the start. "Promise less, deliver more, is the way to do business. In a way that's what the Australians do brilliantly. They've got all the influence in the world and they just say: 'Well, we're not going to give you a lot but what we'll do, we'll give you 100 percent.' If we'd taken that approach and we'd turned Lashkar Gah into the land of milk and honey, then we could have said: 'OK, we've done that, let's do the next bit.' But if you scoop the whole thing up because of national prestige and you haven't thought it through properly then you're heading for trouble."

Captain John Bethell, the Battle Group Intelligence Officer, was sharply critical of British strategy in an article in the internal magazine *British Army*

Review that created waves when it was published in 2010. Intelligence, he wrote, was "under-resourced in every significant way, uncoordinated and amateurish at best" and a bigger problem than lack of helicopters or other equipment because "inadequate thinking is not so easily overcome." The British, he argued, had forgotten the lessons of Malaya and Northern Ireland, proving themselves "inexperienced amateurs at the business of designing and executing an effective counter-insurgency campaign." Four years into the war in Helmand, "ground-holding forces are still grappling with the basics of engagement with the local population" and understanding of the "low, flat and local" nature of the insurgency remains extremely limited. Within the Welsh Guards Battle Group, he stated, "while we crossed off the objectives on our campaign plan and increased the security bubble around the District Centre (DC), it was sometimes difficult to be sure we were making overall progress … [in Helmand] competent planning was much easier to find than coherent strategy." Panther's Claw, he contended, had "secured significant new areas of ground and a large population, but was unable to isolate, fix and destroy the insurgents to the extent which some had hoped."

At the highest levels of the British armed forces, there was frank acknowledgement that the Helmand mission had been badly mismanaged at the beginning. "We did get it wrong," said General Sir David Richards, just about to become chief of the Defence staff, at a dinner for the Mark Evison Foundation in September 2010. "Never at the tactical level. Never did our young officers and soldiers let us down. We got it wrong at the higher level. We were never resourced properly for the operation that we found ourselves in." The problem, he added, "is that today we're playing catch-up even now."

The Taliban remained confident that they were winning, if only because Western patience was limited and the killing of British and American troops was having a strategic effect. With a Taliban safe haven in Pakistan, NATO forces would always be fighting an elusive enemy. "The Welsh Guards commander was killed by our men," Maulavi Abdul Aziz Hamdard, a Taliban commander in the Nad-e Ali district, told the author in an interview conducted through an intermediary. "This was a great achievement. When the British want to do something, then they give their operations different names. But these big operations with their grand names have not been successful. If they take a building in a district, it doesn't mean that they took control of that district. They may take over the centre of a village but the edges and the fields are ours."

Standing before the Prince of Wales's Company at Chah-e Anjir, Antelme told his men that they had been "on the front line of the battle between good and evil" in Helmand. "Whatever anyone ever says to you for the rest of your lives, you have done something over the last five months which should make you feel ten feet tall. So it is something you will think about over the years. And when you are old guys and your grandchildren are running around your knees, you should think about what you have done over the last few months. I've seen a lot of stuff in my time, but I've never seen anything as spectacular as the changes you've made in this place." He had been very proud to lead them. "So thank you very much, from me as Commanding Officer of the Welsh Guards. And the nation that you represent should be f---ing proud of all your achievements."

During their five months in Helmand, the Welsh Guards and attached units lost sixteen men across Battle Group (Center South) and two guardsmen who were serving with other battle groups. Twenty-three Welsh Guardsmen were wounded in action. The Battle Group had discovered 297 IEDs in addition to the 96 that exploded. In all, troops from the Battle Group were attacked by the Taliban on 1,463 occasions, more than three times the number of any other battle group in Helmand. No one believed body counts had anything more than tangential relevance to a counterinsurgency campaign, but on the plus side of the ledger, an estimated 438 Taliban were killed by the Battle Group out of some 3,100 by the brigade. In addition, 3 Company in Sangin registered sixty-four confirmed kills.

In 2009, U.S. Marines would gently prod the British that the term "Task Force Helmand" was a misnomer—it should have been "Task Force Part of Helmand." By the end of 2010, that was incontestable. There were about 30,000 troops in Helmand, including 9,500 British fighting alongside 20,000 U.S. Marines. The total American force was 98,000, approaching the 110,000 Russians in Afghanistan that had not been enough to stave off defeat for the Soviet Union. It had long been a British conceit that their troops were innately superior to Americans, who relied far too much on brute force and technology. A 1947 Welsh Guards recruiting booklet stated that the British soldier's "good nature and his ever readiness to see "the funny" side of things as well as his "gifts of Nature, and Breed" set him apart." This meant that ultimately "there can only be one result, the reasonable men in the parties 'causing' the bother sooner or later come to realize that 'The British Way' will be the best way of solving their particular trouble."

American commanders felt that something of that mentality still lingered over a half-century later. In 2006, the British government had sent in little more than three thousand troops, of which barely seven hundred formed the fighting force. Four years later, the thinly resourced parochialism that had characterized the initial British approach to dealing with "Helmandshire" was in the past. Taming the province would ultimately become the job of the Americans.

From his unique vantage point working with the U.S. Marines, Major Rob Gallimore could only marvel at the resources at their disposal. During Operation Khanjar, the American clearance of Nawa and Garmsir, 2,500 U.S. Marines were inserted in eighty-nine helicopters to take control of one hundred square kilometers of the Green Zone in two days. "It was remarkable what sheer numbers of men could do to your attitude," Gallimore told the Welsh Guards at a battalion briefing back in Aldershot. "Every TIC [Troops in Contact] we had, there was a 60-man Quick Reaction Force sat in the PB with vehicles, waiting to go. There was a real forward momentum." The comparison with what was available on the day that Lieutenant Mark Evison was mortally wounded was unspoken but hung in the air. "They had the sheer manpower to picket routes," Gallimore said, explaining that as the Welsh Guards were strung out along the Shamalan Canal the U.S. Marines could flood an area with men. "If a route was high-threat and being hit a lot, they would just take 40 marines and sit them out there. They could do that for months."

To counter the IED threat, the U.S. Marines used a Ground Based Operational Surveillance System (GBOSS) which allowed up to twenty-five identified areas of threat to be photographed every two seconds. This was backed up by an incredible array of artillery, guided missiles, helicopters, drones, and jets. Rather than hitting IEDs or even exploding them in place, the Americans could usually kill the Taliban IED layers within minutes of them starting to dig in an IED. Military lawyers embedded with companies waited in place to authorize strikes. Once an IED team had been killed, the U.S. Marines would broadcast on Taliban radio frequencies: "Your friends will not be returning from their skulduggery because they have been killed by our magic. We suggest you lay down your arms." The ready availability of large numbers of helicopters meant that troops could be dropped away from the roads and resupplied by air. Most of the casualties suffered by the U.S. Marines Gallimore was fighting with came from gunshot wounds rather than IEDs.

When IEDs were discovered, the British approach was to isolate the device and use a specialist team to defuse it, a painstaking process that could take three hours per IED. The American approach was to blow them up in place as fast as possible. Gallimore and others operating with the U.S. Marines found themselves abandoning British caution. On one occasion, Gallimore was with Lieutenant Colonel Gus Fair, commanding officer of the Light Dragoons, when they were ambushed and forced into a ditch by crops set alight behind them. In the ditch, Fair found a length of fishing wire that he quickly concluded was likely to be a command wire for an IED. Rather than waiting for an IED specialist to examine it, Fair took out his knife and cut the wire. A few seconds later, the interpreter relayed that a Taliban fighter reporting on his walkie-talkie had said: "I am pressing it and they are in the place but nothing is happening."

Gallimore freely admitted that the "contagion of USMC positivism" had overcome his natural British cynicism. He was awed by what he described as the "American ability to innovate and adapt," a reflection, he felt, of "a young, bright and confident nation rather than a demonstration of Churchill's maxim that Americans will eventually get the right answer after exhausting all the other possibilities."

Captain Richard Sheehan, the Apache pilot, feels that the lack of resources to counter IEDs and overstretched manpower mean that the British fought fundamentally differently from US troops. "The Americans take fire, return fire and fight through," he says. "But because of the IED threat and how slow the movement was, we became so fixed it was take fire, take cover, take casualty, extract casualty, go home. We didn't really ever exploit through the Taliban firing points."

Unlike the U.S. Army, the U.S. Marines lived on bases that were deliberately Spartan to reinforce the philosophy that troops should be happiest out on patrol and living out of their rucksacks. At FOB Delhi, the U.S. Marines and X Company found themselves sharing toilet facilities with the Afghan army. The latrines were disgusting, filled with flies and the stench of excrement in the scorching heat. Despite his new love for all things American, Gallimore found himself swelling with patriotic pride at the stoicism and inventiveness of one of his guardsmen. Masturbation, like eating and defecating, is a habitual if sometimes infrequent activity of the young infantryman. One day, Gallimore was standing talking to a sergeant major when he saw a guardsman heading to the latrines carrying a gas mask and a laptop that was doubtless loaded with pornographic photographs. "That," said Gallimore admiringly, "is true bravery."

As the Welsh Guards arrived back at RAF Brize Norton, Antelme paid tribute to his "indefatigable warriors of Wales" who had renovated mosques, rebuilt roads and schools, and supplied water to villages. "All this starts to turn the people away from the repression of the Taliban and towards the possibility of a brighter future. These gains have been bought with the sweat and blood of Welsh Guardsmen, their brothers-in-arms from across the British Army, our American cousins, Estonians attached to the Guards and Afghans of great spirit and courage." The Welsh Guardsmen of 2009, he contended, were every bit as heroic as their forebears. "The threads of Agincourt, Rorke's Drift and Monte Piccolo remain unbroken; Welshmen shining amongst their comrades in the defence of the nation."

Back in Aldershot, Antelme addressed the whole battalion and was slightly less poetic. British soldiers did not have the advantages their American counterparts enjoyed, he said. "They do have all the kit. They do have all the resources. They're part of a superpower that is geared for war. We're part of a small country that isn't sure whether we should be at war or not and you're the guys who have been thrust forward into the front line."

Something new—or perhaps something old, resurrected—stirred among the British public in 2009. Aging veterans of previous wars stood to bear silent witness in Wootton Bassett as coffins draped in the Union Flag were driven past in hearses. Those who hadn't worn uniform since National Service ended, almost fifty years before, felt pangs of pride and tried to comprehend, but struggled because—thankfully—few had ever fought or had to kill. Public support for the war, close to 50 percent even at the height of Panther's Claw, had slipped to just over 30 percent a year later. Backing for the troops was higher, but most ordinary Britons barely paused to think about the soldiers in Afghanistan. Many of those who did pitied them. Much of the press coverage of "Hell-manned"—as the BBC pronunciation unit ruled it—had a cloying, maudlin quality. The Welsh Guards preferred to regard what they had done with pride rather than sadness or regret. Memorial services were held and comrades remembered privately, but the life of the regiment continued as its centenary approached. Although a portrait of Lieutenant Colonel Rupert Thorneloe was commissioned by the officers' mess, other memorials were resisted; there was no desire to turn the barracks into a mausoleum. After all, the Welsh Guards were due back in Helmand in 2012.

Epilogue

Only the dead have seen the end of war.

Attributed to Plato by General Douglas MacArthur

We fight. We try not to be killed, but sometimes we are. That's all.

Erich Maria Remarque, All Quiet on the Western Front *(1929)*

On New Year's Eve 2011, Lance Sergeant Dan Collins packed up his belongings and left his girlfriend's house. He was dressed in an old camouflage uniform and a bandanna he had worn in Helmand. His destination was woodland near a remote quarry in the Preseli mountains in Pembrokeshire where he had camped out as a child. After parking his Ford Escort, he laid out photos from Afghanistan on the dashboard, including one of him with Lance Dane Elson on the eve of Operation Panther's Claw, and walked more than a mile to set up a bivouac shelter.

The next morning, as the New Year dawned, he recorded a video on his iPhone. With tears streaming down his face and the sound of rain in the background, he said: "Hey Mum, just a video, just to say I'm sorry, OK? Ever since I've come back from hell, I've turned into a horrible person and I don't like who I am any more. This is why I'm doing what I'm doing, OK? I know it's selfish but it's what I want and what I need. I can't live like this any more. One thing I'd like to ask is could I have a full military funeral if that's possible? That's how I'd like to go."

He dialled 999, giving the operator his name, rank and service number. "I got shot twice in Afghanistan and I got blown up twice," he explained. "I lost a lot of friends and I should have died out there and now is my time. There'll be a body up on the Preseli mountains and it's me." He had already pulled out pieces of slate from a rugged wall, constructing a stack of stones much like a cairn used by the Celts in ancient times to memorialize their dead. He climbed onto the stones, placed his head inside a noose he'd made from a blue nylon rope tied to the branch of a pine tree, and jumped. He was 29.

Collins's family had noticed a change in him as soon as he returned. "He was dead behind the eyes when he came back," said his mother Deanna. In one recurrent nightmare, he kept seeing the face of the mortally wounded Lance Corporal David "Duke" Dennis. Elson's death continued to haunt him. His girlfriend Vicky would be woken up by his shouting "Medic!" "Man down!" or "Dane!" in his sleep. One day, Deana cooked him a lamb dinner. "He loved his roast dinners and my gravy," she said. "We were sitting there eating it and then he just threw the plate across the floor and he said, 'Mum, it's burning flesh.' He sat in the corner of the kitchen rocking like a baby."

By the time of Collins's suicide in 2012, Darren Booker, from the Prince of Wales's Company, was out of the Army and had not left his house in Llantwit Major for almost a year. "I'd just be on my own upstairs," he said. "Just like a zombie walking around. I was just going to hang myself." He was afraid of going out in case there were IEDs buried beneath the pavement or Taliban snipers in the trees. He remembered being trapped on a riverbed with the Taliban "following us everywhere" but never showing themselves: "I just stopped shooting, thinking it's pointless, you can't even see them. I just resigned myself. I thought I was gone." He was also disturbed by the fact that he had killed people. He had fired a Javelin at a three-man Taliban team laying an IED and had then seen the carnage through a thermal-imaging scope: "There were body parts just everywhere. Just makes me think I've taken somebody's dad away."

Booker sought treatment and slowly began to rebuild a normal life with his partner and three children. Others found there was no way to continue. In August 2011, Robert Gordon, a former trooper in the Queen's Royal Hussars, was found grievously injured at the foot of the flats in Oldbury, West Midlands, where he had lived on the eighth floor. Gordon, 25, had been with Marine Jason Mackie when Mackie was killed after a massive IED blew up his Viking in June 2009. Gordon never regained consciousness after he was found in Oldbury, and died in the hospital six weeks later. Although it would never be known whether he had jumped or fallen from his balcony, his girlfriend told an inquest he had seemed distressed that morning and "looking back it sounded like a cry for help."

Three months later, Daron Davies 93, the guardsman who had shot himself in the thigh at Chah-e-Anjir to get away from the front line and was subsequently thrown out of the Army, hanged himself in his rented home near Caernarfon. No details of his service in Afghanistan were offered at the inquest and the coroner said that his state of mind could have altered by cocaine or anti-depressants. Warrant Officer (Class Two) Terry Conley, who had worked with Thorneloe as a watchkeeper in the battle group operations room, shot himself dead at his barracks in Chilwell in May 2012. There was no mention of Helmand at the inquest, which focused on his marital difficulties. Sergeant Aare Viirmaa of the Estonian Army, who had lost both his legs when he stepped on an IED in a compound doorway north of PB Silab, also shot himself dead.

The Ministry of Defence had no system for tracking veterans so there was no complete record of how many former soldiers who served in the Welsh Guards Battle Group had taken their own lives or were suffering from PTSD.

John Williams "65 was 54" was one of the three Falklands veterans who served with the Welsh Guards in Helmand and the oldest man in the battle group. He adored the regiment and had meticulously recorded every detail of the tour in his diary. The high point for him was when he launched mortars at Taliban positions. "Not in my wildest dreams ... 10 mortar rounds fired at the enemy. Slept well last night," he wrote on June 5. On the day Thorneloe died, he recorded a well-known prayer: "God give me the strength to accept the things I cannot change." On August 20, he saw the body of a child, her legs missing, brought into Shawqat after she was hit by a Taliban rocket. "When I was returning from a sangar I saw the little girl (about 9) on a stretcher. But I didn't know she was dead."

On his return, Williams—who had noted "End of Adventure" and a smiley face on the last page of his diary—began to drink heavily. His wife Margaret would find him sitting on the floor and weeping about the little girl, saying: "She's gone. We tried to save her." For the first time in more than 27 years, he had flashbacks from the Falklands. In one, he'd be on board the *Sir Galahad* in the darkness and stumble on a Welsh Guardsman curled in a corner and grinning at him. "But he wasn't grinning—all his lips had gone," Margaret recalled.

He had nightmares about Thorneloe, who had persuaded him at a Welsh Guards dinner to go to Helmand. "Sometimes he would dream he was actually there with him—he hadn't been, of course—and saw him die," Margaret said. "Colonel Thorneloe was saying, 'Help me, help me,' but John couldn't help him." Eventually, Williams was drinking up to seven bottles of red wine a day. In mid-2012, he was admitted to hospital suffering from cirrhosis of the liver; his weight had dropped to just seven stone (about 98 lbs). He died three months later. "I never regretted him going out to Afghanistan," said Margaret. "He loved it. But he should never have died like that. He wished he'd died in battle. He was a soldier through and through."

PTSD seemed to affect more NCOs than guardsmen. In Helmand, they were the ones holding everyone else together and they were often heavily involved in treating casualties. One NCO tried to kill himself shortly after getting back but was saved when his wife found him hanging in the kitchen and cut the rope. Officers were not spared either. One young officer broke down when he went out to lunch in the West End with an Army contemporary. "I had a friend who died when he shouldn't have and I saw a soldier bleed to death in front of me," he explained to his lunch companion.

It was ever thus. After the Falklands War there were scores of Welsh Guardsmen who suffered from severe post-traumatic stress and a significant number of suicides. Sometimes it could take decades for the inner darkness to prevail. In 1963, the pajama-clad body of Brigadier James Windsor Lewis, Major Dai Bevan's grandfather, was found in the bedroom of his mother's Mayfair flat.

Beside him was the revolver he had used to shoot himself in the head. Outside his door was a note to his sister marked "Urgent." A steeplechase rider who had taken part in the Grand National, an escapee from a German prisoner of war camp and a war hero with two DSOs and an MC to his name, Windsor Lewis had been seeing a psychiatrist for years.

Right from the outset, the return home had been hardest for those who had been in the thick of the fighting. In Cyprus, where the Welsh Guards spent two days of "decompression" before landing in Britain, they were able to drink for the first time in months. One of the snipers was found sitting alone talking to a bush about the guilt he felt for missing a Taliban fighter when the bullet he fired should have killed him.

In February 2010, a group from the Prince of Wales's Company travelled to Lanzarote in the Canary Islands on an Army-funded windsurfing trip. A punch-up in an Argentine steak restaurant led to six soldiers being arrested and spending four months in jail. Tom Lawrence, the sniper, Craig Jones 23, who had gone into battle shock when Private John Brackpool was hit, and Steven Parry 26, who had accidentally killed the civilian near Compound 24, were among those who pleaded guilty to criminal damage and assault. They escaped prison sentences and were allowed to remain in the Army.

Leon Peek sought psychiatric help. "It wasn't until I came home that I realised I needed help because I was proper f---ed. I was told I had a serious case of PTSD," he said. "It was complicated because it went from childhood to Iraq to Afghanistan and now it's all come into one."

Rather than being welcomed home in Tonyrefail, he found himself being taunted in pubs. As a Welsh Guards NCO who drove a red Vauxhall Tigra with the personalised number plate "1WG P3EKS," Peek inspired envy among some locals. "They'd say: 'Look, action man's coming in,'" Peek said. "I was talking to a boy I'd known for years. He shakes my hand and the next thing is he puts one on my chin, punches me. Then my Mum hit him. They don't like soldiers because they're all gear heads. They look at a soldier who's fit and robust and they think you're looking down at them. They want to fight you because it's a challenge."

Peek was disciplined for punching a former guardsman who was mouthing off in the sergeants' mess after a long drinking session. When he went to a dinner to pick up the Hampshire Hero of the Year Award, which he won jointly with Lance Corporal Geraint Hillard, he dropped the glass trophy, which shattered on the floor as hundreds of guests watched.

Peek's wife Karly was expecting their first baby and his family urged him to stop drinking. "He's got to learn to forget it now," said his grandmother, Jean Button. "He's home every weekend and he should be working hard on his own house instead of drinking. I know he's gone through it but he's got to start growing out of it and think about the future." His grandfather Clive Button told him: "You're supposed to be a sergeant in the Welsh Guards but you're not acting like one. Put it behind you." During his session with the Army nurse psychologist, Peek was told to recount an incident in Helmand and then imagine a safe place. His safe place was lying on a beach. "I'm getting better," he said. "It's slow but I'll be all right."

Back home, the lack of interest in the Afghan war disgusted Peek. "If I went into a shop and said: 'Do you know Tobie Fasfous or Mark Evison or Dane Elson,' would they know?" he asked. "The civilian population don't understand what the f--- we are doing out there. If I got killed, they'd go: 'Poor f---er. Dead.' The next day, they wouldn't care." Gesturing across Tonyrefail, he said: "I don't fight for none of these f---ers. I fight for my mates." Since he returned from Afghanistan, Peek's younger brothers Christopher and Jonathan had joined the Welsh Guards. "The Peek brothers are known as being f---ing hard boys around here," he said. "That's what the Army needs."

At times in Afghanistan, Peek had thought he had been doing some good but he said he no longer believed that. "We achieved the square root of f---ing jack shit out there." Yet another drunken fight led to him being reduced in rank to lance corporal and in 2012 he was medically discharged from the Army on the grounds of his PTSD.

For most of the severely injured, just being alive was a plus. Guardsman Joe Penlington's Facebook information stated: "im joe. i gt blowen up nd survived!!!" Nearly two years after he had been blown up in Thorneloe's Viking, Penlington's left leg was amputated. "No point in carrying dead weight," he reasoned. Lance Corporal Geraint Hillard, severely wounded when his Jackal was blown up, took the same decision and opted to have his right leg taken off. Drummer Dale Leach, who lost his left leg in the same incident, and his fiancée Alex, the mother of his two children, won a £16,000 wedding competition complete with honeymoon in Paris. But the couple broke up and Leach began dating Dane Elson's stepsister Becky. With £50,000 of his compensation money, Leach bought a white BMW M3 with a number plate of "NO 1O LEG." Within months, he had crashed it and written off the vehicle.

The marriage of Guardsman Caswell, who had contemplated killing himself at XP-7 days before his wife gave birth to their son Charlie, foundered when he returned to Aldershot. He decided to leave the Army, hoping to become a forklift truck driver. "I'm not going out there as a sandbag again," he said in 2010. "800 quid a month I was pulling home. Shitting in a bucket for four months? You get better wages in f---ing Tesco." He also had doubts about what was being achieved in Helmand. "Is it worth it? Probably not. None of the Afghans would think twice about picking up an AK and just shooting at you. The question is: who is playing who? Are we playing the

Taliban? Are the Taliban playing us? Or are the local population playing both?"

In April 2011, Caswell went AWOL just before he was due to be on parade for Prince William's wedding to Kate Middleton. Three years later, he had not been tracked down by the Army. He had reconciled with his wife and had no contact with anyone from the Welsh Guards. "I'm still f---ed now," he said. "I can't go to the doctor because the Army has my medical documents. One night I tried to strangle my wife in my sleep. I've given up the booze and the cocaine but I still have the nightmares. It's always the same one, the day with Mark Evison. Sometimes it flips from there to Panther's Claw."

Caswell's anguish was exacerbated by learning that Evison had probably been killed by friendly fire. A Ministry of Defence report by a firearm and tool mark examiner had determined that the bullet that killed Evison was a 7.62 x 51 mm round—commonly known as a 7.62 NATO—of the type fired by a GPMG. While there was the remote possibility that the Taliban had been firing a weapon captured from the British, the strong likelihood was that he had been hit by GPMG rounds fired from CP Haji Alem. The fort was directly opposite compound 1 whereas the Taliban positions were at a more oblique angle to the doorway where Evison had been shot. "F---ing hell, no," said Caswell. "It couldn't have been, could it? It never even occurred to me. I was content in the knowledge that some smelly f---ing raghead took him out. That's too much."

There were two GPMG gunners firing from the fort. The gunner in sangar 1, to the northwest, was aiming at compounds 4 and 6, just to the north of compound 1, where Evison was. His radio was not working so he was reliant on directions being shouted up to him from below. During the engagement, he fired about 7,000 rounds, using three separate GPMGs and abandoning them when the barrels overheated. With less than 100 meters between compounds 4 and 1, it would have taken a tiny miscalculation for the wrong compound to have been hit. The other GPMG gunner was in sangar 2, on the south-west corner and his fire was concentrated on compounds 17, 19, and 22 to the south.

In another demonstration of the inadequacy of the inquest process, the possibility that friendly fire had killed Evison was not even considered, even though the MoD report that identified the bullet was available. The GPMG gunner from sangar 1 was not called to testify.

For Caswell, the prospect that Evison might well have been killed by one of his own men underlined the futility of Helmand. His beloved platoon commander, whose grave he still visited each year, had been leading a patrol that had no discernible purpose from a base that was in the wrong place. The radios did not work, medical equipment was inadequate and the helicopter had taken over an hour to arrive. After CP Haji Alem was evacuated, it was bombed by NATO forces to prevent it being used by the Taliban, its ruins left as a monument to military folly.

A number of Welsh Guardsmen married on their return, and within a year many babies had been born. Corporal Jimmy Martin called his new son Dane. The first birth after the Welsh Guards got back was Tomas, son of Guardsman Simeon Howells, the Javelin operator attached to the Prince of Wales's Company. Before he left for Helmand, Howells had written one letter to his fiancée Kirsty and another to his unborn child to be opened when he or she was old enough to understand. "I wrote that I was doing what I felt was right at the time and that I committed myself to doing a job. I said: 'I'm not going to be able to watch you grow up, look after your mother' and that sort of stuff." He had given the letters to a friend and immediately retrieved them. Sitting in his back garden in Dinas Powys in South Wales, he drank shots of Jägermeister, smoked a big Cuban cigar and opened the letters.

After reading the letters, he set fire to them, watching them burn as tears streamed down his face. Two weeks later, he had the words "*Nac Ofna ond Gwarth*"—Welsh for "Fear Nothing But Disgrace," the Support Company motto—tattooed on his arm.

In April 2011, Sean Birchall's widow Jo walked down the aisle of a Suffolk church to marry Major Ed Mellish of the Welsh Guards. It was Mellish who had first introduced Jo and Sean. When Sean was killed, he helped the Welsh Guards track down Jo, who was with her parents in Essex. Eerily, when Mellish had arrived in Lashkar Gah in September 2009 for a tour with the new brigade, he was allocated Sean Birchall's bunk space. With Jo unable to face her new husband being deployed to Helmand with the Welsh Guards in 2012, Mellish gave up a promising Army career and took a job in the city. A memorial fund ensured that Mellish's new stepson Charlie Birchall would attend Wellington College, giving him the public school education his late father had so self-consciously lacked.

* * *

Inside a marquee on a balmy April evening in the ante-bellum town of Beaufort, South Carolina, several toasts were being offered. The father of the bride paid tribute to the descendants of the Welshmen who fought at Agincourt. These twenty-first century Welshmen, he announced with pride, had gone into battle in Afghanistan under the command of his new son-in-law.

Next, James Grimsley, a Beaufort lawyer and former US Army paratrooper who served in Vietnam, turned to those who had gathered from both sides of the Atlantic to celebrate his daughter's marriage. "Among you right now is a cadre of some of the most decorated officers in the British Army," he said. "They won't tell you this, but they are here. They are at the tip of the spear along with American forces and they have done some extraordinary things."

The Antelme-Grimsley union in 2010 had been formed indirectly as a result of the turmoil that enveloped Central Asia and the Middle East. Many in the marquee had recently returned from wars and others would soon be departing to fight once again.

There was no mention of those whose return had been in flag-draped coffins, for this was an occasion for joy, not mourning. But the much-anticipated Antelme wedding, another sign of lives moving on, could not but remind some of the guests of other lives that had been ended in a moment.

"I firmly believe that if Colonel Rupert had lived my DSO would be sitting on his chest," Giles Harris had said earlier that day, sitting on the veranda of a nineteenth-century inn surrounded by oaks draped with Spanish moss. The former commander of the Prince of Wales's Company had recently married his fiancée Alice. He was about to take up a prestigious post in the MoD and the couple were soon to be expecting twins. Harris was referring to the decoration he had been awarded in the previous month's list of honours, in which there had been no medal for Thorneloe.

The DSO is awarded to commanders "for distinguished services during active operations against the enemy." Of Thorneloe's fellow battle group commanders, two received DSOs and the other three OBEs. Tim Radford was awarded a DSO and Doug Chalmers an OBE. The question of what Thorneloe should receive had been a delicate one.

Under existing rules, OBEs could not be awarded posthumously and DSOs only if the citation had been written before death. Lieutenant Colonel Kingsley Foster of the Royal Northumberland Fusiliers was awarded a posthumous DSO but this had been recommended by his brigadier two months before he was killed in April 1951. In the end, Thorneloe was given only a Queen's Commendation for Valuable Service (QCVS). Although there were several gallantry awards for members of the Welsh Guards Battle Group, to Harris's discomfort his DSO was the only medal won by a Welsh Guardsman. The rules for the award of posthumous decorations seemed perverse. No one would suggest that a soldier should be given a bravery award because he had been killed, but to be denied one for that reason was surely unjust. Before the tour, Thorneloe, discussing the demands of the Brigade and the shortage of resources, had told Major Rob Gallimore: "I'm not in this for a medal." But there was dismay within the Welsh Guards that their Commanding Officer, who had shown outstanding moral as well as physical courage, was not recognised.

In Helmand, the Welsh Guards had become the first British battalion to lose a commanding officer, company commander and platoon commander in action since the Royal Northumberland Fusiliers in 1951 during the Korean War.[1] Reflecting on this grim milestone, General McChrystal said that it showed that in the British Army "leaders are forward and leaders are doing the kinds of things that accept risk."

On the morning of the Antelme wedding, Gallimore woke up with a bad hangover and two new tattoos on his right shoulder—the Roman numeral X, for X Company, and an eagle, anchor, and emblem with "USMC" below it. The United States Marine Corps recruiting depot at Parris Island was just a few miles away, so it had not been hard to find a tattooist who would oblige. There was something of a tradition in the Welsh Guards of officers having tattoos. After the Iraq tour in 2005, Gallimore, Antelme and Bevan had been among a group who went to the "Rebel Rebel" tattoo parlour in Cardiff city center. They arrived armed with a photocopy of the Welsh Guards badge and emerged with leeks etched on their left shoulders. When his father expressed dismay about his son's body art, Bevan's mother, the honorary captain of X Company, pointed out that her father Brigadier James Windsor Lewis had been heavily tattooed. Windsor Lewis had sported the Eton crest and motto "Floreat Etona" (Let Eton Flourish) on his left forearm and the Welsh Guards leek on his right. When he first returned to Britain, Gallimore was resolutely behind the war in Afghanistan, though he felt that only the Americans were truly serious about it. He also resented the way the media pitied the soldiers. "I don't want your f---ing sympathy," he thundered over pre-dinner gin and tonics at the Cavalry and Guards Club in London. "If you'd stopped me as I got on that plane at Brize Norton and said there's a 90 percent chance of losing a limb or dying, I'd still have got on. I feel sorry for the guys on the Somme. Most of them didn't want to be there. We volunteered for this." The average Briton's view of the troops, he lamented, was summed up by the symbol chosen by the forces charity Help for Heroes. "I do not want a teddy bear representing us," he raged. "We're warriors, not f---ing teddy bears—that's pity, not pride. If you're proud of your armed forces, f---ing brilliant, bring it on, buy me a beer. But I don't want your pity."

His certainty about the nobility of soldiering was blunted two months before the South Carolina wedding when he was chosen as a casualty notification officer, the man who would inform the mother of a Coldstream Guards platoon commander that her son was dead. She screamed before he opened his mouth. Later, he excused himself and sat in her lavatory weeping. That night, Gallimore stood over his son's cot and silently begged him never to become a soldier. At the same time, he resolved that he would be remembered as a soldier by his children. He was overwhelmed by the sadness the war in Afghanistan had brought and began to question whether Britain should have been involved at all. Gallimore drank heavily that night, as he did on many nights.

Since leaving Helmand, Gallimore, like many Welsh Guardsmen, had struggled to readjust to normal life. A few weeks earlier, he had resigned from the Army, telling Antelme his heart was no longer in the career he had once considered a calling. Three months after the Antelme wedding, Gallimore was commanding 3 Company on a training exercise in the Falkland Islands when his carousing once again got the better of him.

Following a drinking session, he stripped naked and led a conga of Welsh Guardsmen through a room where a mess dinner was being held. The Air Commodore commanding the British garrison was not amused and ordered that he be flown home in disgrace. Gallimore was bored and frustrated by peacetime command and needed help dealing with his demons. It was a relief when Antelme agreed that he could relinquish command of 3 Company early and see out the rest of his Army time in a staff job outside the battalion before becoming a history teacher at an independent school in Berkshire.

The incident near Green 1 that had cost Leach and Hillard their legs was just one of the things that continued to haunt Terry Harman. When he first returned to Aldershot, he refused to eat in the officers' mess because Lieutenant Piers Lowry—whose name he would not utter—was dining there. Occasionally, he would see Leach in South Wales. "When I see him, it hurts. I know the circumstances and I'm reliving that moment. It shouldn't have happened." Harman told his wife and children very little about what he had done in Helmand and said he had spent most of his time in Camp Bastion. But when a young guards-man told his wife Ceri that her husband had been "a legend" at Paraang and on the Shamalan Canal, he knew he would have to tell his family the full truth. "I've sat down since and I told them how Mark was shot in the shoulder and got killed. I told them how the Commanding Officer got blown up and I've spoken a bit about unloading the vehicle and what happened afterwards." Telling his sons about how he had dealt with the body parts of Thorneloe and Trooper Hammond was the toughest task of all. "But with God's grace and a bit of strength, I think it was the right, Christian thing to do. It hurts and I still smell flesh now. I've told the boys about it because I think it's important for them to know. And if I did break down, at least they'd understand."

In 2014, Lieutenant Colonel Giles Harris DSO MBE became commanding officer of the Welsh Guards. By this time, Antelme had opted to leave the army for the second time, this time for good, and was working for an oil company in Kenya. Alex Corbet Burcher, who had taken over command of IX Company when Sean Birchall was killed, left to become an actor. One of his early roles was in the movie *Zero Dark Thirty* as a US Navy SEAL in the mission to kill Osama bin Laden

Churchill once said that a medal glitters but it also casts a shadow. Just as with his MBE from Iraq, Harris reflected on his DSO from Helmand and wondered whether he had earned it. As well as being a tribute to Thorneloe, Harris reasoned, the award was for the Prince of Wales's Company, whose achievements in Chah-e Anjir were being cited across the Army as a model of counterinsurgency operations. Yet what happened in Chah-e Anjir, he specu-lated, might prove transitory. "The British are very good at whipping ourselves up into a sense of achievement," he reflected in Helmand near the end of the tour. "We almost have to, to make it bearable. You can't do something like this and analyse it all the way through and think: 'Actually we got that wrong.' You just can't. It takes so much emotional investment. I'm not saying we lie to our-selves but there's an element of telling yourself that it's all right and it's going well, just to keep going."

Whether a place like Chah-e Anjir could have a strategic effect on the future of Afghanistan was questionable. "There's a slight arrogance perhaps born of past campaigns, that a young British officer can somehow change the world. Really, you've just got to satisfy yourself that you've had this little bit of Afghan-istan and you've made it a better place. There are so many bigger forces interact-ing above you." Making progress even in many places, moreover, did not mean overall success in Afghanistan. Numbers of new schools, shuras held with village elders and trained Afghan soldiers would not mean the war was won. As Brigadier Gordon Messenger, Radford's predecessor, had commented in June 2009: "You can produce a whole series of facts that demonstrate progress, but demonstrating progress is not the same as measuring success."

Sir Sherard Cowper-Coles, the former British ambassador to Afghanistan, said that a legitimate criticism of politicians and diplomats was that "we've been slow to develop a really credible political strategy that connects with the realities of Afghanistan."

Without this, no amount of progress locally would guarantee strategic success. "No one questions the need for the selective intelligent application of military force. But it needs to be connected to a realistic political strategy. And delivering development aid is secondary. What the Pashtun populations in Afghanistan want to know is who is going to be in charge of their village or their valley five months or five years from now. And they will back the winner."

He was withering about the Army for its eagerness to go to Helmand in 2006 and the subsequent briefing against the Government by senior officers over resources. "Militaries produce a lobby," he said. "They always say they want more and they always say they can do it. In many ways, Afghanistan has been hugely good for the British Army, billions of pounds' worth of new equipment and a new public respect in Britain. A serious war, the first time in a generation. Great prestige for the generals."

The Welsh Guards returned to Helmand in 2012. Four were killed, all of them shot by Afghan police officers they were helping to train. As the NATO combat mission in Afghanistan at the end of 2014 approached, one British official recalled an exchange in 2010 between Governor Gulab Mangal of Helmand and David Miliband, the British foreign secretary. When Miliband asked Mangal how long the British and American legacy would last in Helmand, the governor replied: "Forty-eight hours. After that, anyone in the Afghan government will either have fled or be hanging from the nearest tree."

The Thorneloe family, like all the families of the fallen, was left with a deep void in their lives. After the Welsh Guards memorial service, John Thorneloe spoke to a local mayor whose son had been killed in Northern Ireland. "How long does it take to recover?" he asked the mayor. "You never will," he replied. Time did blunt the grief. "I'm much more at ease when I'm talking about him," said Major Thorneloe, speaking six months after his son's death. "But I just never stop thinking about him. Wherever I go, I see him. I walk the dogs for about an hour a day in Kirtlington Park and that's where he used to take his ponies to play polo. I see him. When I want the back door of my car open, I have to click twice. And every time I do that, I remember him because I didn't know how to do it and he said: 'Oh, you've got to click twice.' All those things."

Sally Thorneloe moved to Wiltshire, as she and her late husband had planned. Corporal Kevin Williams came to visit her and she felt comforted that "the last voice that touched Rupert's ears" would have been kind and reassuring. "I hope, I pray that it would have calmed Rupe in that last moment. I'm very pleased that it was him." Every night, Hannah would say her prayers as part of her way of talking to her father. "Daddy, I had a good day, I hope you had a good day too," she would say. When she was given a bicycle, she asked whether her father had one too, because if so perhaps they could cycle and meet together somewhere. The trampoline in the garden, donated by the Welsh Guards welfare fund, was a way of getting closer to her father up in Heaven. One day, Hannah said she wished she had a long ladder so she could climb up and meet him. Sally Thorneloe decided it was best for her daughters to be able to talk about what happened to their father. "He died because the baddies put bombs underneath the roads," she would say. "Daddy was trying to help people and the baddies didn't want him there." John Thorneloe publicly criticised Gordon Brown's government for failing to resource the war in Afghanistan properly. Sally Thorneloe was less outspoken but also had her views. "If you are going to send an army to war, the government of the day should ensure that they are properly equipped," she says. "You can't, and you shouldn't, cut corners. It doesn't work and we've seen the results."

Terry Harman did not break down and he brushed aside suggestions that he see a military psychiatrist. "The shell that is the human being is fragile," he said. "It's a bit fractured. We crossed the line of humanity. It's difficult to fire a round knowing you'll kill somebody. It's also difficult to have to sit there and take incoming rounds. I get irritated and agitated by some things. But I'll be all right."

Nine months after he returned from Helmand, Harman resigned from the Army to take a job in the United Arab Emirates as the leader of a youth development programme. He had been promoted to major but the job of Regimental Quartermaster would not be his, so it was time to go. It was not how he had expected his career to end, but he insisted he had no regrets. "I joined as a happy guardsman and I left as a happy guardsman," he said. Hanging his uniform up for the last time, he knew he would never forget what had happened in Helmand but felt confident that in time he could be at peace with it. He was proud of his regiment and of his 24 years as a Welsh Guardsman. "It's finished," he whispered to himself. "Let it be."

Whether a Falklands veteran or a teenager born after the Gulf War of 1991 who had to wait to turn 18 before being sent to Helmand, no man came back the same. Some left limbs there; all lost friends, comrades and at least one commander. Some have already lost their minds, and the will to live, to the horror of that place and time. Death was a fear, a companion and, for the unlucky few, an outcome. For them, what happened in Helmand is over. For the rest, it will remain.

Appendix

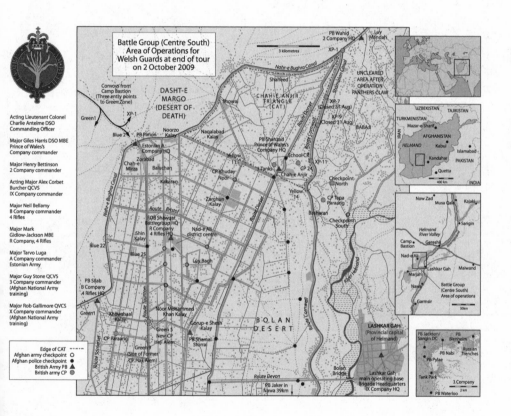

Acting Lieutenant Colonel
Charlie Antelme DSO
Commanding Officer

Major Giles Harris DSO MBE
Prince of Wales's
Company commander

Major Henry Bettinson
2 Company commander

Acting Major Alex Corbet
Burcher QCVS
IX Company commander

Major Neil Bellamy
B Company commander
4 Rifles

Major Mark
Gidlow-Jackson MBE
R Company, 4 Rifles

Major Tarvo Luga
A Company commander
Estonian Army

Major Guy Stone QCVS
3 Company commander
(Afghan National Army
training)

Major Rob Gallimore QVCS
X Company commander
(Afghan National Army
training)

Battle Group (Centre South)
Area of Operations for
Welsh Guards at end of tour
on 2 October 2009

Edge of CAT
Afghan army checkpoint
Afghan police checkpoint
British Army PB
British army CP

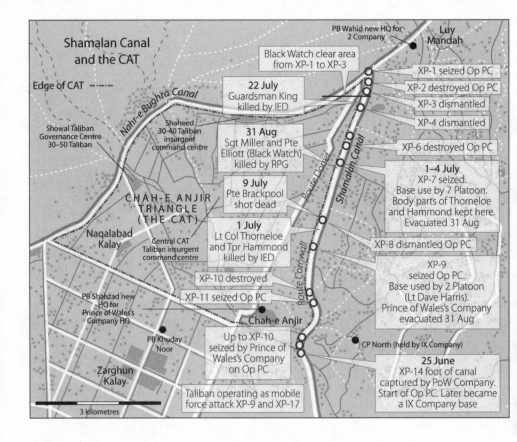

Shamalan Canal and the CAT

Edge of CAT

Nahr-e Bughra Canal

Showal Taliban Governance Centre 30–50 Taliban

Shaheed 30-40 Taliban insurgent command centre

CHAH-E ANJIR TRIANGLE (THE CAT)

Naqalabad Kalay

Central CAT Taliban insurgent command centre

PB Shahzad new HQ for Prince of Wales's Company HQ

PB Khuday Noor

Zarghun Kalay

3 kilometres

PB Wahid new HQ for 2 Company

Luy Mandah

Black Watch clear area from XP-1 to XP-3

22 July
Guardsman King killed by IED

31 Aug
Sgt Miller and Pte Elliott (Black Watch) killed by RPG

9 July
Pte Brackpool shot dead

1 July
Lt Col Thorneloe and Tpr Hammond killed by IED

XP-10 destroyed

XP-11 seized Op PC

Chah-e Anjir

Up to XP-10 seized by Prince of Wales's Company on Op PC

Taliban operating as mobile force attack XP-9 and XP-17

XP-1 seized Op PC

XP-2 destroyed Op PC

XP-3 dismantled

XP-4 dismantled

XP-6 destroyed Op PC

1–4 July
XP-7 seized.
Base use by 7 Platoon.
Body parts of Thorneloe and Hammond kept here.
Evacuated 31 Aug

XP-8 dismantled Op PC

XP-9
seized Op PC.
Base used by 2 Platoon (Lt Dave Harris).
Prince of Wales's Company evacuated 31 Aug

CP North (held by IX Company)

25 June
XP-14 foot of canal captured by PoW Company. Start of Op PC. Later became a IX Company base

Route Dorset

Shamalan Canal

Route Cornwall

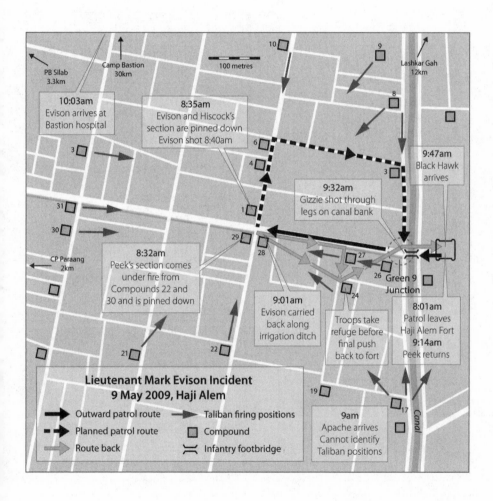

Lieutenant Mark Evison Incident
9 May 2009, Haji Alem

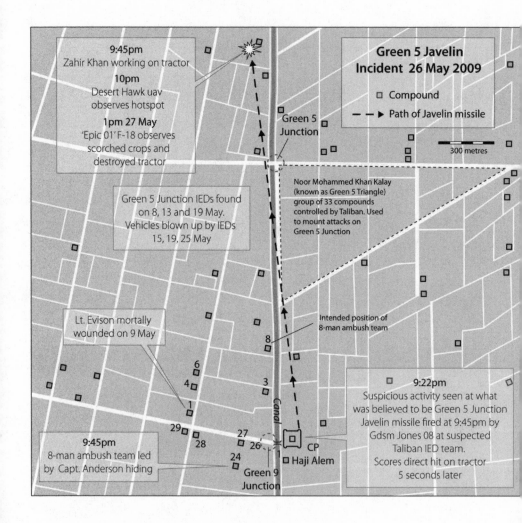

9:45pm
Zahir Khan working on tractor
10pm
Desert Hawk uav
observes hotspot
1pm 27 May
'Epic 01' F-18 observes
scorched crops and
destroyed tractor

**Green 5 Javelin
Incident 26 May 2009**

□ Compound
— — ▶ Path of Javelin missile

300 metres

Green 5
Junction

Noor Mohammed Khan Kalay
(known as Green 5 Triangle)
group of 33 compounds
controlled by Taliban. Used
to mount attacks on
Green 5 Junction

Green 5 Junction IEDs found
on 8, 13 and 19 May.
Vehicles blown up by IEDs
15, 19, 25 May

Lt. Evison mortally
wounded on 9 May

Intended position of
8-man ambush team

8

6
4

3

1

Canal

29
28

27
26
24

CP
Haji Alem

9:22pm
Suspicious activity seen at what
was believed to be Green 5 Junction
Javelin missile fired at 9:45pm by
Gdsm Jones 08 at suspected
Taliban IED team.
Scores direct hit on tractor
5 seconds later

9:45pm
8-man ambush team led
by Capt. Anderson hiding

Green 9
Junction

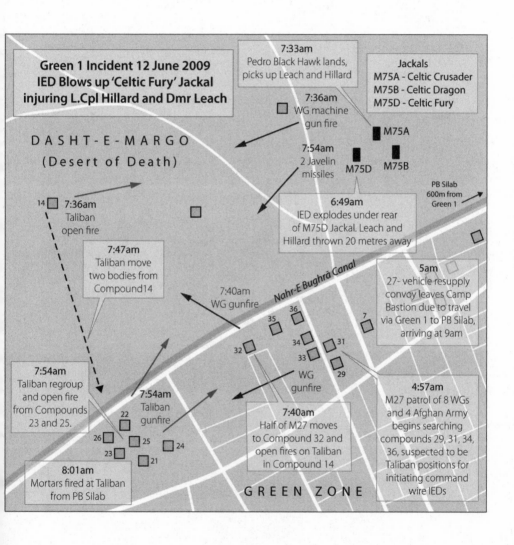

Green 1 Incident 12 June 2009
IED Blows up 'Celtic Fury' Jackal
injuring L.Cpl Hillard and Dmr Leach

7:33am
Pedro Black Hawk lands,
picks up Leach and Hillard

Jackals
M75A - Celtic Crusader
M75B - Celtic Dragon
M75D - Celtic Fury

7:36am
WG machine
gun fire

M75A

7:54am
2 Javelin
missiles

M75D   M75B

D A S H T - E - M A R G O
(Desert of Death)

PB Silab
600m from
Green 1

14 **7:36am**
Taliban
open fire

6:49am
IED explodes under rear
of M75D Jackal. Leach and
Hillard thrown 20 metres away

7:47am
Taliban move
two bodies from
Compound14

7:40am
WG gunfire

Nahr-E Bughra Canal

5am
27- vehicle resupply
convoy leaves Camp
Bastion due to travel
via Green 1 to PB Silab,
arriving at 9am

35 36

32

34 31

33 29

WG
gunfire

7:54am
Taliban regroup
and open fire
from Compounds
23 and 25.

22

7:54am
Taliban
gunfire

4:57am
M27 patrol of 8 WGs
and 4 Afghan Army
begins searching
compounds 29, 31, 34,
36, suspected to be
Taliban positions for
initiating command
wire IEDs

26

25 24

7:40am
Half of M27 moves
to Compound 32 and
open fires on Taliban
in Compound 14

23 21

8:01am
Mortars fired at Taliban
from PB Silab

G R E E N   Z O N E

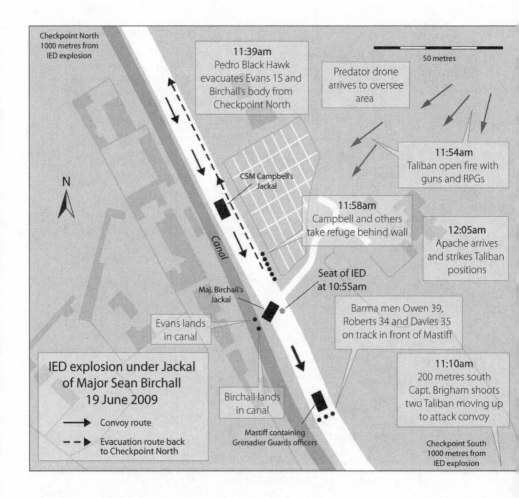

Checkpoint North
1000 metres from
IED explosion

50 metres

11:39am
Pedro Black Hawk
evacuates Evans 15 and
Birchall's body from
Checkpoint North

Predator drone
arrives to oversee
area

11:54am
Taliban open fire with
guns and RPGs

N

CSM Campbell's
Jackal

11:58am
Campbell and others
take refuge behind wall

12:05am
Apache arrives
and strikes Taliban
positions

Canal

Seat of IED
at 10:55am

Maj. Birchall's
Jackal

Barma men Owen 39,
Roberts 34 and Davies 35
on track in front of Mastiff

Evans lands
in canal

11:10am
200 metres south
Capt. Brigham shoots
two Taliban moving up
to attack convoy

**IED explosion under Jackal
of Major Sean Birchall
19 June 2009**

Birchall lands
in canal

→ Convoy route

- - ▶ Evacuation route back
to Checkpoint North

Mastiff containing
Grenadier Guards officers

Checkpoint South
1000 metres from
IED explosion

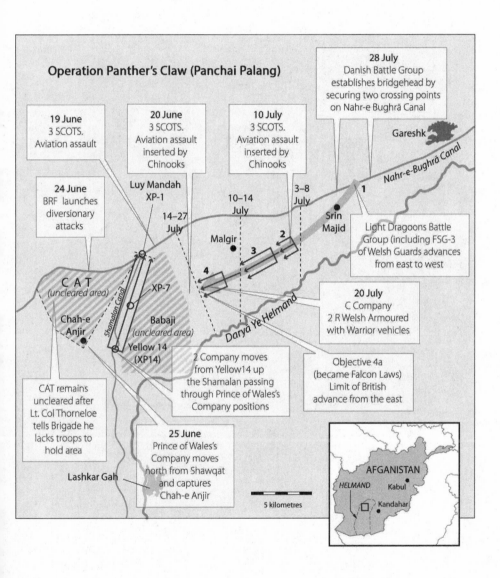

Operation Panther's Claw (Panchai Palang)

28 July
Danish Battle Group establishes bridgehead by securing two crossing points on Nahr-e Bughrā Canal

19 June
3 SCOTS.
Aviation assault

20 June
3 SCOTS.
Aviation assault inserted by Chinooks

10 July
3 SCOTS.
Aviation assault inserted by Chinooks

Gareshk

Nahr-e-Bughrā Canal

24 June
BRF launches diversionary attacks

Luy Mandah
XP-1

14–27 July

3–8 July

10–14 July

1

Srin Majid

Light Dragoons Battle Group (including FSG-3 of Welsh Guards advances from east to west

C A T
(uncleared area)

XP-7

Malgir

2

3

4

Chah-e Anjir

Shamalan Canal

Babaji
(uncleared area)

Darya Ye Helmand

20 July
C Company
2 R Welsh Armoured with Warrior vehicles

Yellow 14
(XP14)

2 Company moves from Yellow14 up the Shamalan passing through Prince of Wales's Company positions

Objective 4a
(became Falcon Laws)
Limit of British advance from the east

CAT remains uncleared after Lt. Col Thorneloe tells Brigade he lacks troops to hold area

25 June
Prince of Wales's Company moves north from Shawqat and captures Chah-e Anjir

Lashkar Gah

5 kilometres

AFGANISTAN

HELMAND   Kabul

Kandahar

List of Key Personnel

N ote: All abbreviations are explained in the Glossary. Ages of personnel are at the start of the tour on April 24, 2009. List includes all those who served in or were attached to the Welsh Guards Battle Group Headquarters, Prince of Wales's Company, 2 Company, 3 Company, IX Company, and X Company. All information has been provided by the Welsh Guards.

HEADQUARTERS COMPANY

Motto: "Ofna Dduw, Anrhydedda'r Benin" ("Fear God, Honor the King")

Lt. Col. Rupert Thorneloe MBE (KIA. QCVS). Commanding Officer. Age 39. Took command of the Welsh Guards in October 2008 and planned meticulously for the Helmand tour. The expansion of BG (CS) almost doubled the men under his command to more than 1,300.

Lt. Col. Doug Chalmers MBE (2PWRR. OBE). Commanding Officer. Age 43. As commanding officer of 2PWRR, he handed over BG (CS) to Thorneloe at the end of April 2009. The two men had similarly nuanced approaches to counterinsurgency, and Chalmers stepped into the breach on July 3, 2009, just after Thorneloe was killed. Awarded the OBE and since promoted to brigadier.

A/Lt. Col. Charlie Antelme DSO. Commanding Officer. Age 39. A former 3 Company commander who later served with Gen Stanley McChrystal in Iraq, Antelme won the DSO in 2008 for leadership under fire in Iraq. Although only a major when Thorneloe was killed, he was plucked from his anti-terrorism job at the MoD, promoted to lieutenant colonel and sent to Helmand. Left the army and now works for an oil company in Kenya.

Maj. Andrew Speed MBE (SG). Battle Group Second in Command. Age 40. Took over IX Company when Major Sean Birchall was killed and then briefly commanded the Welsh Guards and the Battle Group after Thorneloe's death. Since promoted to lieutenant colonel.

Maj. Martyn Miles MBE. Battle Group Logistics Officer. Age 48. Rose through the ranks after joining as a guardsman in 1977. A Falklands veteran who was slightly wounded when the *Sir Galahad* was hit by Argentine bombs. Since retired.

Maj. Mark Jenkins. Brigade Liaison Officer. Age 42. Based at Brigade headquarters in Lashkar Gah. A confidant of Thorneloe and close to Brigadier Tim Radford. Had left Welsh Guards in 2001 after a series of high profile appointments to become a schoolmaster. Rejoined army for the tour. Left early to take up post with Jordanian royal family.

Maj. Nicky Mott. Quartermaster. Age 46. One of the legendary Mott brothers, each of whom became a regimental sergeant major. A Falklands veteran, Nicky Mott was in charge of keeping isolated bases supplied, sending dangerous convoys along IED-strewn roads. Awarded MBE in 2011.

Maj. Ben Ramsay. Plans Officer. Age 36. Former Prince of Wales's Company commander who joined the tour late after Thorneloe decided he needed another senior major. Distinguished himself in charge of 2 Company when Bettinson was on leave. Later became battalion second-in-command.

Maj. John Oldroyd (RA. QCVS). Battery Commander. Age 38. Royal Artillery officer. In charge of coordinating all forms of fire support and implementing "courageous restraint" directive from Gen McChrystal. Third in command of Battle Group under Speed. Awarded QCVS.

Capt. James Aldridge. Adjutant. Age 29.

Capt. John Bethell. Intelligence Officer. Age 29

Capt. Alex Bourne. Estonian Liaison Officer. Age 24.

Capt. James Jeffrey. (QRL). Tactical air controller. Age 30.

Capt. Ed Launders. Operations Officer. Age 30. Promoted major in July.

Capt. Deiniol Morgan. Chaplain. Age 39.

Capt. Naim Moukarzel. Signals Officer and Battle Captain. Age 26.

WO1 Michael Monaghan. Regimental Sergeant Major. Senior NCO in Welsh Guards. Age 39.

WO2 Dorian Thomas 53. Regimental Quarter Master Sergeant. Age 41. Planned UK funerals before flying to Helmand in August.

WO2 John Williams 65 was 54. Ops room watchkeeper. Age 52. Falklands veteran and temporary rejoin after leaving army in 2000. Led resupply convoys and fired mortars. Suffered from PTSD. Died in 2012.

CSgt. Dai Matthews. Mastiff Group Commander. Age 42. Temporary rejoin.

PRINCE OF WALES'S COMPANY

Motto: "Y Ddraig Goch ddyry cychwyn" ("The Red Dragon gives the lead")

COMPANY HEADQUARTERS

Maj. Giles Harris MBE (DSO). Company Commander. Age 35. Previously commanded 2 Company in Iraq and was awarded MBE. Viewed as a rising star by Thorneloe and Antelme. Awarded DSO. Later joined MoD before being promoted to lieutenant colonel and sent to United States in an exchange post. Appointed Commanding Office of Welsh Guards in 2014.

1 PLATOON

Lt. Chris Fenton (MID). Platoon Commander. Age 25. Based at PB Argyll, CP Khuday Noor and PB Shahzad, where he led joint UK–Afghan patrols. Awarded MID. Now commands Recce Platoon.

Sgt. **Michael Parry 19** (MID). Platoon Sergeant. Age 33. Coordinated casevac of LCpl Ritchie after IED strike. Awarded MID.

2 PLATOON

Lt. Dave Harris. Platoon Commander. Age 29. Based at PB Pimon and XP-9. Close friend of Lt Mark Evison. Now works for Morgan Stanley.

Sgt. **Matthew Parry 700.** Platoon Sergeant. Age 32. Experienced "dead man's click" in Zorabad. Led taking of XP-9 on Shamalan Canal.

2 COMPANY

Motto: "Gwyr Ynys y Cedyrn" ("The Men of the Island of the Mighty")

COMPANY HEADQUARTERS

Maj. Henry Bettinson. Company Commander in PB Silab and then in the vanguard of the push up the Shamalan Canal during Panther's Claw before PB Wahid was established. Age 35. Now in charge of pre-deployment training for units going to Helmand.

Capt. Terry Harman. Influence Officer. Age 46. Native Welsh speaker who joined army in 1983 and rose through the ranks to become Regimental Sergeant Major during the Iraq tour of 2004–05. Sent to PB Silab by Thorneloe to help 2 Company begin engaging with Afghans. Earned nickname "Old Man of Paraang" and saw intensive action on Shamalan Canal. Took custody of body parts of Thorneloe and Trooper Josh Hammond for three days at XP-7. Left army in 2010 to work in Abu Dhabi.

4 PLATOON

Lt. Charles Fraser-Sampson (QCB). Platoon commander, initially based at PB Tanda. Age 25. Once Tanda was closed, he took charge of 2 Company's Mastiff Group and survived five IED blasts along with his driver, Guardsman Richard Hill. Awarded QCB. Became an equerry to the Prince of Wales before leaving the army.

Sgt. Dean Morgan 10. Platoon Sergeant. Age 29. Qualified sniper who later became platoon sergeant of 7 Platoon. Saw intense action on Shamalan Canal and told LSgt. Leon Peek that he needed to seek help for PTSD. Killed Taliban fighter during battle after death of Cpl. Lee Scott on July 10.

6 PLATOON

Lt. Owen James. Platoon commander. Age 23. Oxford graduate identified as future adjutant with fine career ahead of him. Originally commander of FSG-2, he was transferred to 6 Platoon once requirement to man two extra bases became known. Later commanded 7 Platoon. Decided to leave the army with plans to go to business school.

7 PLATOON

Lt. Mark Evison (KIA). Platoon commander. Age 26. Viewed by some as the top platoon commander in the Welsh Guards. Planned to take SAS selection course. Mortally wounded on May 9 and died at Selly Oak Hospital three days later.

LSgt. Leon Peek (JCC). Acting platoon sergeant. Age 23. From a tough, impoverished background and often in trouble with Welsh police, Peek proved himself in combat. Found himself in command of 7 Platoon after Evison was wounded. Taken to Camp Bastion after he began showing PTSD symptoms at XP-7. Recommended for MC but only awarded JCC. PTSD treatment continues. Daughter Taryn born in 2010. Discharged from army in 2010.

RECCE PLATOON

Capt. Tom Spencer-Smith (WIA). Platoon Commander. Age 29. One of the few officers qualified as a sniper, Spencer-Smith had already completed one Helmand tour. Involved in rescuing his men from the Shamalan Canal when their Viking rolled into the water on July 29. Wounded in shoulder when IED exploded, killing interpreter, on September 12. Became operations officer after tour.

LSgt. Steve Young (WIA). Promoted to sergeant by Thorneloe at start of tour. Age 27. Took over as 7 Platoon sergeant after Lt Evison was mortally wounded. Escaped from submerged Viking in Shamalan Canal on June 29 but fractured his back when his Mastiff was hit by an IED on August 3. Initially told he might never walk again. Recovered well and took part in North Pole trek with Prince William in 2011.

IX COMPANY

Motto: "A fynno Barch bid Gadarn" ("Let him be Strong who would be Respected")

COMPANY HEADQUARTERS

Maj. Sean Birchall (KIA). Company Commander. Age 34. Pushed Thorneloe hard for Helmand slot after missing out on Iraq in 2004–5. Proved an inspirational commander on Op Zafar at end of April and moulded IX Company into a fighting unit. Thorneloe had plans to give him a challenging new role during Panther's Claw but he was killed by an IED on 19 June.

Capt. Alex Corbet Burcher (QCVS). Commander TF Nawa. Age 29. Promoted to Acting Major when he became IX Company commander after Birchall was killed. With a tour training Afghan army soldiers under his belt, Thorneloe viewed him as a promising prospect. Commanded tiny band of Welsh Guards and others at PB Jaker in Nawa until US Marines took over in June. Awarded QCVS. Left the army and became an actor.

WO2 Andrew Campbell. Company Sergeant Major. Age 37. Welsh Guards rugby coach who leapt at chance to work with Birchall and knock IX Company into shape. Formed very close bond with him and was on the scene when he was killed. Commissioned as a Welsh Guards officer in 2014.

SUPPORT COMPANY

Motto: "Nac Ofna ond Gwarth" ("Fear Nothing but Disgrace")

FIRE SUPPORT GROUP 3 (FSG-3)

Operated in Garmsir and Babaji as part of Light Dragoons Battle Group.

Capt. Phil Durham. FSG commander. Age 28. Durham's FSG-3 was engaged in some of the hardest fighting of Panther's Claw. When Major Stuart Hill, commanding A Company, 2 Mercians, was seriously wounded, Durham briefly took over as company commander.

LSgt. Dan Collins. Survived being shot twice—one bullet hit his body armour, another grazed his leg—and two IED blasts. Age 29. A close friend of LCpl. Elson, he was there when he died and also tended to the dying LCpl. Duke Dennis, who had lost three limbs. Suffered from PTSD and committed suicide in January 2012.

MORTAR PLATOON

Dispersed throughout Brigade area, including FOB Price (Garmsir), PB Jaker, FOB Keenan (Gereshk Valley), Babaji, PB Silab, and PB Wahid.

WO2 Lee Scholes. Company Sergeant Major of Support Company. Age 40. Mortars specialist initially stationed at PB Jaker as part of TF Nawa. Later commanded 7 Platoon. After tour, became Drill Sergeant of the Welsh Guards.

3 COMPANY

Motto: "Fy Nuw, Fy Ngwlad, Fy Mrenin" ("My God, My Land, My King")

Training Afghan army (OMLT) as part of 2 Mercians Battle Group, operated in Sangin under 2 Rifles Battle Group.

Maj. Guy Stone (QCVS). Company Commander. Age 36. Disappointed that his company was broken up after he lost out to Bettinson's 2 Company in a contest as to who would remain with the Welsh Guards Battle Group. But Stone embraced with aplomb his task of training the Afghan army in the killing fields of Sangin. Awarded QCVS. Brought all his men back alive.

X COMPANY

Motto: "Heb ddial ni Ddychwelaf" ("I will not return Unavenged")

Training Afghan army (OMLT) as part of 2 Mercians Battle Group. Operated in Nawa under Light Dragoons Battle Group and in Garmsir under US Marines.

Maj. Rob Gallimore (QCVS). Company commander. Age 34. Thorneloe created this unusual role for Gallimore who, like Birchall, was anxious not to miss out on the Helmand tour. Gallimore reveled in fighting alongside the U.S. Marines. Struggled to readjust to life back in UK. Sent back from Falklands after drinking escapade and stood down as 3 Company commander. Resigned from army with plans to write a book and become a teacher.

KEY WELSH GUARDS FIGURES IN BRITAIN

Prince Charles. Colonel of the Regiment

Col. Sandy Malcolm. Regimental Lieutenant Colonel

Col. (Ret.) Tom Bonas. Regimental Adjutant

Maj. Dai Bevan. Rear Party Commander

Capt. Darren Pridmore. Welfare Officer

CSgt. Jiffy Myers (MBE). Welfare Color Sergeant (awarded MBE in 2011)

A full list of personnel in the Welsh Guards Battle Group can be found at www.tobyharnden.com/personnel.

Chronology

2001

September 11
Al Qaeda launches 9/11 attacks on New York and Washington.
October 7
United States begins air strikes against al Qaeda and Taliban targets in Afghanistan. British troops from the SAS take part in the subsequent invasion.

2002

April 9
First British soldier killed in Afghanistan.

2006

January 27

John Reid, Defence secretary, tells Parliament that United Kingdom will take over from Americans in Helmand with initial force of 3,300 troops, joining 1,100 others already elsewhere in Afghanistan.

April 23

Reid visits Helmand as British campaign against the Taliban begins and says UK forces would be "perfectly happy to leave in three years' time without firing one shot."

July 10

Des Browne, Defence secretary, announces increase in British troops in Afghanistan to 5,500.

2007

February 1

Announcement British troops in Afghanistan to increase to 6,300.

July 20

Announcement British troops in Afghanistan to increase to 7,800.

September 10

Prime Minister Gordon Brown visits Afghanistan for the first time. Lt. Col. Rupert Thorneloe accompanies him along with Browne.

2008

June 16

Announcement British troops in Afghanistan to increase to 8,030.

June 17

British death toll in Afghanistan reaches 100.

October 11

Nearly 300 Taliban mount unsuccessful assault on Lashkar Gah.

October 28

Lt. Col. Rupert Thorneloe assumes command of Welsh Guards.

December 15

Announcement British troops in Afghanistan to increase to 8,300.

2009

April 11

IX Company takes over from J Company, Royal Marines in Lashkar Gah.

April 19

Thorneloe arrives in Afghanistan.

April 24

Welsh Guards take over Battle Group (Center South) from 2 PWRR.

April 27

Operation Zafar (clearance of Basharan) begins.

April 28

LSgt. Tobie Fasfous killed by IED while on foot.

April 29

Announcement 700 extra troops will be sent to Helmand to assist in the August presidential election. Soldiers from 4 Rifles are chosen.

May 2

Operation Zafar ends. Checkpoint North and Checkpoint South established. Objective Worcester becomes CP Tapa Paraang.

May 9

Lt. Mark Evison shot and mortally wounded.

May 11

Firing of Gen. David McKiernan, ISAF commander, and announcement his replacement will be Gen. Stanley McChrystal.

May 12

Lt. Evison dies of wounds; three Afghan army soldiers killed and two wounded after being shot by Afghan police during altercation in the Nad-e Ali town.

May 14

Marine Jason Mackie killed when his Viking hits IED.

May 15

Lt. Col. Rupert Thorneloe stranded after daisy-chain IED at Green 5.

May 22

LCpl. Rob Richards (Royal Marines) mortally wounded when his Viking hits IED.

May 24

Operation Tor Kali (closure of PB Tanda).

May 26

Zahir Khan, Afghan farmer, killed by Javelin at Green 5.

May 27

LCpl. Rob Richards dies of his wounds.

May 29

LCpl. Gareth Davies 16 shot and wounded.

June 1

Prince of Wales's Company operation to establish CP Khuday Noor begins.

June 2

Thorneloe conducts Operation Barma for the first time.

June 4

Sgt. Aare Viirmaa (Estonian army) loses both legs when he steps on IED; operation to establish CP Khuday Noor ends.

June 12

Dmr. Dale Leach and LCpl. Geraint Hillard seriously wounded in their Jackal near Green 1.

June 15

Gen. Stanley McChrystal takes command of ISAF in Kabul; **MSgt. Allain Tikko**, Estonian army, killed by RPG while on foot.

June 19

Maj. Sean Birchall killed when his Jackal hits an IED; LCpl. Jamie Evans 15 wounded.

June 20

Operation Panther's Claw (Panchai Palang) begins.

June 21

R Company, 4 Rifles takes over PB Argyll in Nad-e Ali from the Prince of Wales's Company.

June 22

Handover of PB Jaker in Nawa to US Marines.

June 23

B Company, 4 Rifles takes over PB Silab from 2 Company.

June 25

D-Day for Welsh Guards in Panther's Claw as they move to base of Shamalan Canal; Acting Maj. Alex Corbet Burcher assumes command of IX Company; LSgt. Gethyn Rowlands 39 shot and wounded in Sangin.

June 29
Viking falls into Shamalan Canal; Lt. Piers Lowry shot and wounded.
July 1
Lt. Col. Rupert Thorneloe and **Tpr. Josh Hammond** (2 RTR) killed when IED hits their Viking; Gdsm. Joe Penlington very seriously wounded.
July 2
Newly arrived U.S. Marine forces launch Operation Khanjar to clear the lower River Helmand Valley, including Nawa and Garmsir; X Company takes part.
July 3
Lt. Col. Doug Chalmers arrives in Helmand to take over Welsh Guards Battle Group.
July 4
Pte. Robbie Laws (2 Mercians) killed when RPG hits his Spartan and **LCpl. David Dennis** (Light Dragoons) killed by IED while on foot during Operation Panther's Claw.
July 5
LCpl. Dane Elson killed by IED while on foot.
July 6
Repatriation of Lt. Col. Thorneloe and Tpr. Hammond.
July 8
Lt. Col. Charlie Antelme selected as new commanding officer of Welsh Guards; funeral of Maj. Sean Birchall; Welsh Guards officer visits advisor to David Cameron, opposition leader, in House of Commons.
July 9
Pte. John Brackpool shot and killed; **Rfn. Daniel Hume** (4 Rifles) killed when he steps on IED.
July 10
Cpl. Lee Scott (2 RTR) killed when IED hits his Viking.
July 15
Cameron confronts Brown during Prime Minister's Questions over lack of helicopters in Helmand.
July 16
Funeral of Lt. Col. Rupert Thorneloe.
July 19
Captain Harry Parker (4 Rifles) loses both legs when he steps on IED.

July 22

Lt. Col. Antelme arrives at FOB Shawqat. **Gdsm. Christopher King** (Coldstream Guards) killed by IED while Barmaing. **Capt. Dan Shepherd** (Royal Logistic Corps) killed while trying to defuse IED.

July 23

Funeral of Pte. John Brackpool.

July 26

Rfn. Daniel Shaw (4 Rifles) loses both legs when he steps on IED.

July 31

Operation Panther's Claw finishes.

August 7–10

Move of CP Haji Alem from Green 9 to Green 5.

August 10

LCpl. Jack Ritchie loses foot when he steps on IED. Part of leg later amputated.

August 11

Rfn. Sam Walpole (4 Rifles) loses both legs when he steps on IED.

August 13

LCpl. Tyler Christopher (4 Rifles) loses both legs when he steps on IED.

August 15

British death toll in Helmand reaches 200.

August 15–17

Operation Tor Shadey (clearance of Gorup-e Shesh Kalay and establishment of CP Shamal Storrai) begins.

August 20

Afghan presidential elections.

August 23

MSgt. Eerik Salmus and **Sgt. Raivis Kang** (Estonian army) killed when IED hits their Pasi.

August 31

Withdrawal from XP-7 and XP-9 on the Shamalan Canal; **Sgt. Stuart Millar** and **Pte. Kevin Elliott** (3 Scots) killed on compound roof by RPG.

September 12

Capt. Tom Spencer-Smith wounded and interpreter Ahmed Popal killed when Popal steps on IED; Rfn. Mark Osmond kills two Taliban insurgents with a single bullet fired with his L96 rifle from PB Shamal Storrai.

September 16

Guardsmen Lee Skates and Gareth Scaife slightly injured in suicide-bomb attack at PB Falcon Laws.

October 1

Haji Talib Aka, a Taliban leader codenamed "Objective Titusville," is killed by an Apache helicopter.

October 3

Welsh Guards hand over Battle Group (Center South) to Grenadier Guards.

October 14

Gordon Brown announces increase in British troops in Afghanistan to 9,500.

December 1

President Barack Obama's West Point speech in which he announces a surge of 30,000 American troops in Afghanistan, bringing the total U.S. force to almost 100,000. At the same time, he states that troops will begin to pull out from July 2011.

2010

February 13

Operation Moshtarak launched by American, British, and Afghan forces, the biggest operation since Panther's Claw. Marjah and the CAT are cleared.

June 21

British death toll in Helmand reaches 300.

June 23

Gen. Stanley McChrystal relieved of his duties as ISAF commander in Afghanistan and replaced by Gen. David Petraeus.

August 29

Qari Hazrat, Task Force 42's "Objective Commando Flood," killed by coalition air strike. He was believed to be in command of the Taliban fighters who laid the IED beside the Shamalan Canal that killed Lt. Col. Thorneloe and Tpr. Hammond.

Glossary

2IC: Second in command.

3 Yorks: 3rd Battalion, Yorkshire Regiment.

4 PARA: 4th Battalion, Parachute Regiment.

adjutant: A senior captain who is the personal staff officer for the commanding officer and is in overall charge of organization, personnel matters, and discipline. In 2009, Captain James Aldridge was the adjutant of the Welsh Guards, a post once held by Rupert Thorneloe and Giles Harris.

AGC: Adjutant General's Corps.

AH: Attack helicopter. In Helmand this is the Apache, used by British and American forces. Armed with rockets, Hellfire missiles, and a 30 mm cannon.

AK-47: The *Avtomat Kalashnikova*, or Automatic Kalashnikov, rifle developed by the Soviets in 1947. The world's most popular assault rifle and the weapon of choice for most Taliban fighters in Helmand.

ANA: Afghan National Army.

ANP: Afghan National Police.

AO: Area of operations. Defined area for which a brigade, battalion, or company is responsible.

Apache: *See* AH.

Barma: Operation Barma is the army name given to the procedure for searching the ground for IEDs using visual checks for ground sign and Vallon metal detectors. Carried out on foot, often walking in front of a vehicle. Hence, the verb "to Barma."

battalion: Unit commanded by a lieutenant colonel and comprising three rifle companies and about 700 men. The Welsh Guards is a single-battalion regiment.

battle group: Based around a battalion bolstered by additional sub-units, a battle group is formed for an operational tour. Can comprise more than 1,500 men.

bergen: Standard-issue military rucksack (also known as a daysack).

bivouac sack: Lightweight waterproof shelter originally used by climbers.

Black Hawk: U.S. Army's UH-60, a four-bladed, twin-engine, medium-lift utility helicopter. Used in Helmand for casevac.

Bowman: The army's principal radio system since 2005. Supposed to revolutionize command and control, it proved to be cumbersome and unreliable and performed poorly in Helmand.

BRF: Brigade Reconnaissance Force.

brigade: Military grouping made up of a number of battalions or battle groups, commanded by a brigadier, and comprising between 4,000 and 10,000 troops. The Welsh Guards Battle Group was part of 19 Light Brigade, commanded by Brigadier Tim Radford.

C-17: A large military transport plane operated by the RAF and also known as the Globemaster. Used for the repatriation of bodies from Helmand.

C2: Command and control.

callsign: An independent unit with its own radio callsign made up of letters and digits. For instance, M12A was Alpha section of 2 Platoon of the Prince of Wales's Company. A guardsman would refer to his section as "my callsign."

casevac: Casualty evacuation.

CAT: Chah-e Anjir triangle. Taliban-controlled area that included the villages of Showal, Naqalabad, Abd-ol Vahid Kalay, and Shaheed.

CDS: Chief of the Defence Staff. Uniformed head of the British armed service. Air Marshal Sir Jock Stirrup in 2009.

CG: Coldstream Guards.

CGC: Conspicuous Gallantry Cross.

CGS: Chief of the General Staff. Uniformed head of the British army. General Sir Richard Dannatt until July 2009, when he was succeeded by General Sir David Richards.

CHES: Cheshire Regiment.

Chinook: CH-47 twin-rotored medium-lift helicopter used for troop movement, casevac, and logistics.

CLP: Combat logistics patrol—a resupply convoy.

CLU: Command launch unit, used to acquire targets and initiate Javelin missiles. Also used for surveillance.

COIN: Counterinsurgency.

company: A rifle company usually consists of about 100 men and is broken down into three platoons and a headquarters element. Commanded by a major.

company quartermaster sergeant: Color sergeant who is in charge of all the stores for a company.

compound: A low mud building used in Afghanistan to house extended families. Usually square with a large open area in the center and rooms around the perimeter.

contact: Term for being engaged in action against the enemy.

CP: Checkpoint. Smaller than a patrol base (PB).

CVRT: Combat vehicle reconnaissance (tracked). Tracked light-armored reconnaissance vehicle. British forces in Afghanistan use Scimitar and Spartan CVRTs.

Dasht-e Margo: Desert of Death. The large desert to the northwest of Green Zone where the Welsh Guards were operating. Contains Camp Bastion.

DC: District center. The centre of administration, police, etc. within the main town in an Afghan district, e.g. Nad-e Ali DC.

Desert Hawk: Small hand-launched UAV used as a tactical surveillance system.

dicker: Northern Ireland term for IRA sympathizer who would watch and report the movements of the British security forces. Now used to refer to locals who pass similar information to the Taliban. A "dicking screen" is an organized system of human surveillance used by the enemy in which dickers are used en masse.

division: Large military unit at the level above a brigade comprising between 10,000 and 30,000 troops. Commanded by a two-star officer. In Helmand, British forces were part of the Regional Command (South) division commanded by Maj. Gen. Mart de Kruif of the Dutch army.

DSO: Distinguished Service Order.

ECM: Electronic counter-measures. Manpack or vehicle-mounted equipment designed to prevent the detonation of remote-controlled bombs and IEDs by jamming radio frequencies.

EF: Enemy forces.

F-15: U.S. Air Force fighter jet.

FLET: Forward line of enemy troops.

FOB: Forward Operating Base.

Foden: A heavy-duty army truck. Also known as DROPS (Demountable Rack Offload and Pickup System) truck.

FoM: Freedom of Movement.

foot guards: Infantry regiments of the Household Division. In order of precedence they are the Grenadier Guards, Coldstream Guards, Scots Guards, Irish Guards, and Welsh Guards.

forage cap: Peaked cap used for parade and dress occasions. Placed on coffin at funerals.

FSG: Fire support group. Equipped with a mixture of heavy weapons such as Javelin, GMG, GPMG, FSGs are platoon-sized and attached temporarily to rifle companies. Usually they operate in Jackals. For the Welsh Guards tour, FSG-1 was attached to the Prince of Wales's Company and FSG-2 to 2 Company. FSG-3 was attached to B Company of 2 Mercians.

FST: Fire support team. Responsible for coordinating mortar, artillery, and air support. Each company had an FST from the Royal Artillery attached.

GDA: Ground dominating area. Used to describe a route patrol.

Ghillie suit: Camouflage clothing used by a sniper for concealment. Comes from the word *gille*, Gaelic for "servant." Originally developed by

Scottish gamekeepers and worn by retainers assisting them during hunting expeditions.

GIRoA: Government of the Islamic Republic of Afghanistan. The Afghan central government based in Kabul and led by President Hamid Karzai.

GMG: Grenade machine gun. A belt-fed grenade launcher that fires 40 mm grenades up to a range of 2,000 meters. Normally mounted on a vehicle or in a sangar.

GMLRS: Guided Multiple-Launch Rocket System. A battlefield artillery rocket system that fires high-explosive grenades in batches of 6 or 12 from mobile launch vehicles. Based at Camp Bastion in Helmand, GMLRS is used against personnel and has a range of more than 70 km. With an inertial guidance system coupled with a Global Positioning Satellite (GPS) system, GMLRS is highly accurate and creates minimal collateral damage.

GPMG: General-purpose machine gun. A 7.62 mm belt-fed machine gun. When used with bipod legs it can hit targets up to a range of 800 meters. Each section is equipped with one GPMG.

GPR: Ground Penetrating Radar. Radar system used to detect buried objects that would be missed by a metal detector. In 2009, American and other NATO forces had GPR devices to combat landmines and low-metal-content IEDs.

Green Zone: Lush fertile area in the Helmand River Valley created by extensive irrigation system. Not to be confused with the Green Zone in Baghdad, the fortified area protecting American forces and their allies.

guardsmen: Collective name for soldiers in a Guards regiment.

HACU: Helmand and Arghandab Construction Unit.

Hellfire: AGM-114 laser-guided air-to-surface missile used by British and American forces. Name comes from HELicopter-Launched FIRE-and-forget.

Herrick: Operation Herrick is the codename given by the MoD to military activities in Afghanistan. A suffix is added for each six-month tour. The Welsh Guards were in Helmand during Herrick 10.

Hesco: A large collapsible container made of wire mesh and lined with hardy felt. Delivered in a flat pack and then filled with soil or sand. Used to protect bases from blast and bullets.

HLS: Helicopter landing site. Any area of ground where a helicopter can land. If not a permanent HLS, the ground is usually cleared and Barmaed by troops to ensure there are no obstructions or IEDs.

HMG: Heavy machine gun.

Icom: Walkie-talkie system used by Taliban and monitored by an Icom scanner.

IED: Improvised explosive device.

IG: Irish Guards.

INS: Insurgents.

IRT: Immediate Response Team. Medical unit in a casevac helicopter.

ISAF: NATO's International Security Assistance Force.

Jackal: Highly mobile desert patrol vehicle originally designed for Special Forces. Used for reconnaissance, rapid assault and fire support, and convoy protection. Very vulnerable to IEDs. Armed with GPMG, HMG, or GMG.

Jam Boys: Slang for the Prince of Wales's Company.

Javelin: 127 mm anti-tank missile guided by an imaging infrared seeker and fired in conjunction with the CLU. Maximum range of 2,500 meters.

JCC: Joint Commander's Commendation

JHF(A): Joint Helicopter Force (Afghanistan). Based at Kandahar air base and in charge of all British aircraft in RC (South) divisional area.

JTAC: Joint tactical air controller: a member of the FST, responsible for coordinating air power in support of troops on the ground.

kandak: Afghan army battalion of about 500 men.

KIA: Killed in Action.

kinetic: American term, now common in British military parlance, that means an action involving military force.

kinforming: Informing the next of kin of a death or injury.

lance sergeant: The Guards rank that is equivalent to corporal. Wears three stripes and is a member of the sergeants' mess.

Little Iron Men: Slang for 3 Company of the Welsh Guards.

LMG: Light machine gun.

Lynx: Multi-purpose military helicopter.

madrassa: Arabic word for school, used to refer to a place of religious learning, nowadays often linked to Islamic fundamentalism.

Main Effort: The part of the battlefield or operation or the unit that a commander designates as his top priority or main focus to fulfill the mission. Battle Group (Center South) was 19 Brigade's Main Effort, though during Operation Panther's Claw the Main Effort became the Light Dragoons Battle Group.

Mastiff: A heavily armoured wheeled vehicle used for road patrols and convoys. Based on the American 6x6 Cougar. Carries six troops plus two crew. Armed with a machine gun, 50 mm cannon, or 40 mm automatic grenade launcher. Heavily protected against IEDs (no soldier was killed in one in 2009) but heavy and difficult to maneuver. Arrived in Helmand in 2009.

MC: Military Cross.

medevac: Medical evacuation.

MERT: Medical emergency response team. Often used as a shorthand term for the Chinook casevac helicopter.

MFC: Mortar fire controller. A member of the FST responsible for calling in mortar fire for a company group or other military unit.

MID: Mentioned in Dispatches.

Minimize: Operation Minimize was the turning off of all telephones and internet connections once a serious casualty was sustained so that the news would not be relayed back to Britain before families could be informed. Patrol Minimize was a direction that no routine patrols should take place.

MoD: Ministry of Defence.

mortar: Portable muzzle-loading cannon used to fire shells at low velocities, short ranges, and high trajectories. Able to engage targets not in line of sight.

NCO: Non-commissioned officer. Any soldier holding a rank between lance corporal and warrant officer (Class One).

nine-liner: A nine-point format for passing categories of operational information up the chain of command by radio. There are different nine-liners for casevac and close air support requests.

O Group: Orders Group. The individuals that make up the command group and key specialists in a military unit. Also used to refer to the process of a commander delivering orders to his O Group.

OMLT: Operational mentoring and liaison team. A team of soldiers attached to the ANA for training purposes.

Pashtun: Those who speak the Pashto language and follow the code practice of Pashtunwali. Known as "Pathans" by the British in the nineteenth century. Vast majority of Pashtuns live in the area stretching from southeastern Afghanistan to northwestern Pakistan. The Taliban is overwhelmingly Pashtun, as are more than 90 percent of those living in Helmand.

PB: Patrol base. Bigger than a CP, smaller than an FOB.

Pedro: Codename for American Black Hawk helicopter in medevac role.

PJHQ: Permanent Joint Headquarters. Operational headquarters for British armed forces. At Northwood, Middlesex.

PKM: Literally "Kalashnikov's machine gun modernized," an updated version of the *Pulemyot Kalashnikova* (PK). A 7.62 mm Soviet-designed machine gun that entered service in 1969 and is used by the Taliban in Helmand.

platoon: A group of about 30 soldiers with a lieutenant or second lieutenant in command. A sergeant normally acts as second in command. The platoon has a small headquarters element and is subdivided into three sections.

Predator: *See* UAV.

PRR: Personal role radio. Every man carries an insecure PRR operating on a platoon channel.

PTSD: Post-Traumatic Stress Disorder.

PWRR: Princess of Wales's Royal Regiment.

QBO: Quick battle orders. Rapid verbal orders by a commander to his men, giving only essential information, before launching an operation, e.g., an attack, when time is short. Often used when in contact or at close quarters with the enemy and there is no time for longer, more detailed orders.

QCVS: Queen's Commendation for Valuable Service. Recognition of excellence below that meriting a medal. Shown by an oak leaf placed on the campaign medal ribbon.

QRF: Quick Reaction Force.

QRL: Queen's Royal Lancers.

RA: Royal Artillery.

RAEC: Royal Army Education Corps.

RAMC: Royal Army Medical Corps.

RAPTC: Royal Army Physical Training Corps.

RCIED: Radio-controlled improvised explosive device.

RCS: Royal Corps of Signals.

RE: Royal Engineers.

Recce Platoon: Reconnaissance Platoon.

regimental adjutant: Retired officer who works full time at Regimental Headquarters in Wellington Barracks, London, as the lead person on all non-operational matters. Officer recruiting, fundraising, and links to retired officers are among his duties. In 2009, post occupied by Colonel Tom Bonas.

regimental colonel: An honorary appointment held by a serving officer originally from the Welsh Guards who holds another, full-time post. Advises the commanding officer on operational and command matters and represents the regiment within the army. Colonel Sandy Malcolm held the post in 2009.

regimental quartermaster sergeant: Warrant officer (Class Two) who is the senior NCO in the battalion in charge of stores and logistics and assists the quartermaster. During the Welsh Guards' tour, this was WO2 Dorian Thomas 53.

REME: Royal Electrical and Mechanical Engineers.

Ridgeback: The British version of the American Cougar 4 × 4 armored vehicle. Arrived in service in Helmand early on in the Welsh Guards' tour. Similar to the Mastiff but smaller, it offered formidable protection against IEDs.

ROE: Rules of engagement.

RPG: Rocket-propelled grenade. In Afghanistan this normally refers to the Russian-designed RPG-7, which is shoulder-launched and used to fire a warhead at distances of about 20 meters. Warheads explode on impact or self-destruct between 800 and 900 meters, causing them to "air burst."

RPK: The *Ruchnoy Pulemyot Kalashnikova,* or "Kalashnikov's hand-held machine gun." A 7.62 mm weapon of Soviet design that dates back to the 1950s and was used by the Taliban in Helmand.

R&R: Rest and recuperation.

SA-80: Standard British Army 5.56 mm assault rifle.

sangar: A watchtower. Term originated in the North-West Frontier of Imperial India. In Afghanistan, normally made from sandbags and Hesco.

SAS: Special Air Service.

SBS: Special Boat Service.

Scimitar: Type of CVRT. Fitted with a 30 mm cannon and 7.62 mm machine gun.

section: Subdivision of a platoon consisting of 8 men. Usually headed by a lance sergeant with a lance corporal as second in command.

SG: Scots Guards.

shura: Gathering of tribal or village elders to discuss matters of collective importance.

Sound Commander: A small but powerful amplifier with a microphone that can be carried in a rucksack and used to communicate messages to the locals.

Spartan: Type of CVRT.

SRR: Special Reconnaissance Regiment.

stabad: Stability advisor.

stag: Sentry duty, as in to be "on stag."

Sunray: Codename for a commander.

Tankies: Soldiers from the Royal Tank Regiment.

terp: Slang for interpreter.

TIC: Troops in contact. A term used to describe forces under fire or exchanging fire with the enemy.

top cover: Position in a vehicle in which a soldier stands with his upper body and head protruding so that he can aim a weapon and view the surrounding area.

tracer: Ammunition fitted with a small pyrotechnic charge that ignites upon firing, burning brightly so that the projectile is visible to the naked eye. This enables the firer to follow the bullet and adjust his aim.

TRiM: Trauma and risk management—system of counseling to deal with combat stress.

UAV: Unmanned air vehicle or drone. A pilotless aircraft remotely controlled from the ground. Can be fitted with cameras and other sensors and with weapons. Those used in Helmand include Predator A, Predator B (Reaper), Hermes 450, Desert Hawk, or Raven.

UGL: Underslung grenade-launcher. A 40 mm grenade launcher that can be fitted to the SA-80 rifle. Can fire a high-explosive grenade up to 350 meters.

Ugly: Codename for Apache helicopter.

Vallon: German metal detector used for Barmaing.

Viking: An armoored tracked articulated vehicle, crewed by the Royal Marines or Royal Tank Regiment with room for up to 10 infantrymen in the separate front and rear cabs. Flat-bottomed and highly vulnerable to IEDs. Bar armor was added to the sides in Helmand. Once the IED threat increased, the front and then rear cabs were fitted with extra armor underneath.

WIA: Wounded in Action.

WMIK: Weapons mount installation kit. Pronounced "Wimik." A Land Rover fitted with a 0.50 cal. or GMG on the back and GPMG in the commander's position.

XP: Crossing point.

Acknowledgments

first learned of the death of Lieutenant Colonel Rupert Thorneloe when I logged onto my laptop in a hotel in Dubuque, Iowa, on July 2, 2009, during a stop on a reporting journey down the Mississippi. As was the case with all those who knew Rupert, the news hit me like a kick in the stomach. More than a decade earlier in Northern Ireland, Rupert had become a friend when he was a captain working as an intelligence liaison officer with 3 Brigade. He made a significant contribution to the research for my first book *Bandit Country: The IRA and South Armagh*, though he was too discreet ever to allow me to acknowledge his help. Still stunned by what had happened to Rupert, that night I wrote to his parents, with whom I had once stayed at their farm in Kirtlington, to express my profound sorrow.

Over the next fortnight I found myself having a number of conversations with people who were mutual friends of Rupert. These included Brigadier Ben Bathurst, a former commanding officer of the Welsh Guards, and Harry Wynne-Williams, whom I had first met in 2004 in Iraq, when he was a Welsh Guards captain. From these conversations and others, the germ of an idea began to emerge as people impressed on me that the story of Rupert Thorneloe and his men was one that should be told. During that same Iraq visit in 2004, I had gone out on patrol with Charlie Antelme, then a major and clearly destined for great things, and we had subsequently met in London. His appointment to succeed Rupert as commanding officer of the Welsh Guards in Helmand underlined that this was a book that needed to be written. Eventually, I was persuaded that, despite all the practical difficulties, I might be the person to do it.

To turn this notion into a reality, I needed a lot of help. Once Ben Bathurst had set the ball rolling, Paula Edwards at the MoD and her boss Colonel Andrew Jackson were instrumental in smoothing the path through the bureaucracy and ensuring that an MoD contract was drawn up in quick time. Colonel Sandy Malcolm, regimental lieutenant colonel, and Colonel Tom Bonas, regimental adjutant, embraced the proposal with great enthusiasm, which endured. Most notably, Lieutenant Colonel Charlie Antelme, with a war to fight, not only welcomed me to FOB Shawqat, but gave me unfettered access to his battalion. As I embedded with the Welsh Guards and traveled to Lashkar Gah, Chah-e Anjir, PB Pimon, Checkpoint North, Yellow 14, PB Shamal Storrai, PB Wahid, and Camp Bastion, I was met with unfailing courtesy and openness from Welsh Guardsmen and others in the Battle Group and brigade eager to tell me of their experiences. This cooperation continued back in Aldershot during my many visits there. Families in Wales and elsewhere were equally accommodating throughout my research. The frankness, cooperative spirit, and good humor of Welsh Guardsmen right through the rank structure is a tribute to the battalion. The dignity and kindness towards me from those who lost loved ones in Helmand was humbling. I acknowledge permission from Margaret Evison and the Mark Evison Foundation (www.markevisonfoundation.org) to publish extracts from Lieutenant Mark Evison's diaries in return for a donation. A substantial proportion of the proceeds of this book will be given to the Welsh Guards Afghanistan Appeal. I am grateful to Andrew Motion for kind permission to quote from his poem "Home Front," published in the collection *Laurels and Donkeys* (Clutag, 2010).

I would like to thank my superb agent Julian Alexander of Lucas, Alexander, Whitley for his skill at securing the deal with Quercus and his patience in having me on his books for six years before I began to produce. His enthusiasm, encouragement, and judicious advice have been invaluable. Quercus have been the ideal publishers, taking the time and trouble to consider every detail, always taking my views into account, and backing me all the way. Richard Milner, publishing director for nonfiction, has been a considerate, skilled, and hugely supportive editor. A big thank you also to Joshua Ireland for his stalwart assistance throughout, designer Patrick Carpenter for a wonderful book jacket, and to Mark Smith, David North, Caroline Proud, and the rest of the Quercus team. Martin Soames, Robin Fry, and Campbell Dyer provided thorough, perceptive, and very quick legal advice. After printing, I found myself on a second embed—within the Quercus senior management team. I could not wish for better comrades to be with in the trenches. Thanks to Steve Cox for skillful copyediting and to William Donohoe for fine maps. Sonja Hall at the MoD coordinated a complex review process that was extremely challenging for all concerned. The tact and calmness with which she handled all the obstacles and her sensible guidance and advice to me throughout were instrumental in getting the book published despite very serious obstacles. On the publicity side, the irrepressible Digby Halsby of Flint Public Relations kept me very busy.

Those who have helped me in different ways include Andrew Marshall, Michael McDowell, Nick Lockwood, Jens Dakin, Patrick Wilson, Alex Spillius, Rachel Ray, Michele Walk, Andrea Viola, Sam Ryan, Robert Fraser, John Mayhead, Ben Farmer, Wahid Frogh, Naiem Naiemullah, Chris Perrin, David Archer, Gavin Fuller at the *Telegraph*'s library, the BBC's Sima Kotecha, Patrick Chisholm of Accentance, Veronica Hale, Phelim McAleer, Liza Meckler, Mike Smith, Conor Hanna, my brother, William Harnden, and my parents, Keith and Valerie Harnden. Thanks to Martin Browne, Mike Cummins, Mike Wakely, and Nick Farr at welshguardsreunited.co.uk. Jacqui Bennett, Phil Leese, Angeleen Whyte, Mary Jo Bishop, and Sarah Strickland braved Welsh accents, the sound of rumbling Mastiffs, and lots of swearing to transcribe interviews. Jennifer Ryan worked wonders in knocking the text into shape, relegating historical material to endnotes, and banishing Humpty Dumpty.

Michael Gates was an outstanding researcher and general factotum in Washington, helping out with transcription, baroque theories about just what was happening in 2 Company, and keeping me organized. Edward Malnick, a very talented young journalist, was my researcher on the other side of the Pond, burrowing away in the Welsh Guards regimental archives and the Imperial War Museum in London. He helped bring an extra dimension to the book. My mother-in-law Linda Bosse kindly allowed me to use her serene lakeside cabin at Deep Creek, Maryland, where I did most of my writing. My dog Finn was a faithful companion during the creation of *Dead Men Risen*, just as he was with *Bandit Country*; I always knew he had another book in him.

At the *Daily Telegraph*, my professional home for more than sixteen years, I owe a debt of gratitude to Adrian Michaels and everyone on his foreign desk team for their support. I greatly appreciate the patience of Tony Gallagher, Ian MacGregor, and Ben Brogan in putting up with the prolonged absences of their U.S. editor in Afghanistan and Wales.

Bringing up two children under four is a challenge at the best of times. My wife Cheryl has managed to do it with a constantly distracted, perennially preoccupied, and often absent husband. She is a wonderful mother and wife, and I cannot thank her enough for everything. Tessa, three, gamely developed a keen interest in soldiers and "ghanistan," while Miles, two, frequently tested my skills of concentration by attempting to climb on my head while I was typing. Cheryl, Tessa, and Miles—I love you, and you mean everything to me.

Further information about this book and my other work can be found at www.tobyharnden.com. I welcome communication about this book and can be contacted via my website.

Notes

CHAPTER 1: CYMRU AM BYTH

1. Quoted in Trevor Royle, *Anatomy of a Regiment: Ceremony & Soldiering in the Welsh Guards* (London: Michael Joseph, 1990), 60.
2. Their new title of "The Royal Regiment of Guards" gave them the status of Household Troops, making them the senior regiment of the Foot Guards and the first in precedence. The Scots and Coldstream Guards dispute the primacy of the Grenadiers to this day—the motto of the Coldstream is *"Nulli Secundus"*—"Second to None."
3. On March 25, the *Times* reported an announcement by King George V: "That the badge of the Welsh Guards shall be the Leek, that the Dragon shall be emblazoned on the King's Colour; that the motto shall

be '*Cymru am Byth*' ('Wales for Ever')." The leek was the natural choice for the regiment's emblem. In Shakespeare's *Henry V*, the Welsh captain Fluellen (Llewelyn) reminds the king after the Battle of Agincourt, fought in 1415, that "the Welshmen did good service in a garden where leeks did grow, wearing leeks in their Monmouth caps" as a way of distinguishing them from the Saxon enemy. The king responds that he sports a leek on St. David's Day: "I wear it for a memorable honour; for I am Welsh, you know, good countryman." The legend of the leek field is traced back to Cadwalladr, King of Gwynedd, and the Battle of Hatfield Chase in 633, or even to St. David himself a century earlier. The origin of the red dragon symbol is lost in the mists of time and could date back to the period when the Romans left Britain in the sixth century. It featured on the battle standard of Cadwalladr and that of Henry Tudor at the Battle of Bosworth Field in 1485 during the War of the Roses. There were other details that had to be worked out for the new regiment, which was to have a 1st Battalion on active service and a 2nd Battalion in reserve, as it prepared for war. It was decided that the plume on the bearskins of the Welsh Guards should be white, green, and white and worn on the left side. This was to differentiate them from the Grenadiers, with a white plume on the left side; the Coldstream, with a red plume on the right side; the Scots Guards, with no plume; and the Irish Guards, with a blue plume on the right side. In the Guards, even the arrangement of tunic buttons has prescribed differences between regiments. To reflect the order of precedence within the Foot Guards, the buttons of the Grenadiers are spaced singly; the Coldstream in pairs; the Scots Guards in threes; the Irish Guards in fours; and Welsh Guards in fives.

4. Royle, *Anatomy of a* Regiment, 56.

5. Alexander Stanier, *Sammy's Wars* (n.p.: privately published, 1998).

6. L. F. Ellis, *Welsh Guards at War* (Aldershot: Gale & Polden, 1946), 40.

7. Dan O'Neill, "Luck and Good Weather Turned the Fortunes of War," *South Wales Echo* (June 1, 2010).

8. At Dunkirk, Lieutenant John Buckland, the 1st Battalion quartermaster, managed to acquire two huge containers of hot tea from General Lord Gort's headquarters. He waded into the English Channel handing

out mess tins to Welsh Guardsmen as they waited patiently to embark on boats so they could warm themselves on the way home.

9. Imperial War Museum collection 3922 84/19/1.

CHAPTER 2: GREEN ZONE

1. Quoted in David Loyn, *In Afghanistan: Two Hundred Years of British, Russian and American Occupation* (New York: Palgrave MacMillan, 2009), 68.

2. Percy Sykes, *A History of Afghanistan*, vol. 1 (New Delhi, Munshiram Manoharlal, 2002), 64.

3. Stephen Grey, *Operation Snakebite: The Explosive True Story of an Afghan Desert Siege* (London: Viking, 2009), 18.

4. Loyn, *In Afghanistan*, 97.

5. Grey, *Operation Snakebite*, 19.

6. Peter Hopkirk, *The Great Game: The Struggle for Empire in Central Asia* (New York: Kodansha America, 1994), 399.

7. Sykes, *A History of* Afghanistan, vol. 2, 145.

8. Arnold Fletcher, *Afghanistan: Highway of Conquest* (New York: Cornell University Press, 1965), 13.

9. This section draws extensively on the excellent "From New Deal to New Frontier in Afghanistan: Modernization in a Buffer State." Nick Cullather, "From New Deal to New Frontier in Afghanistan: Modernization in a Buffer State," Project on the Cold War as Global Conflict, International Center for Advanced Studies at New York University, August 2002.

10. Cynthia Clapp-Wincek, "A.T.D. Evaluation Special Study No. 18," Helmand Valley project in Afghanistan, December 1983, xi.

11. Ira Stevens and K. Tarzai, *Afghanistan: Economics of Agricultural Production in Helmand Valley* (Washington, D.C.: Agency for International Development, Department of State), 1965.

12. Ali Ahmad Jalali and Lester W. Grau, *Afghan Guerrilla Warfare: In the Words of the Mujahideen Fighters* (Minneapolis: Zenith Press, 2001), 139–41.

13. *Op Herrick 10 Operational Guide*, 9-1–9-3.

14. Gretchen Peters, *Seeds of Terror: How Heroin is Bankrolling the Taliban and Al Qaeda* (New York: Thomas Dunne, 2009), 4–5.

CHAPTER 3: WHITEHALL WARRIOR

1.   Windsor Lewis escaped from a hospital at Liège in July 1940 and arrived back in Britain five months later after reputedly spending some weeks staying with friends on the French Riviera. He subsequently took command of the 2nd Battalion. In September 1944, he led the troops who liberated Brussels, noting that he had passed through the Belgian capital four years earlier. "On that occasion I had entered the city from the east in a tram. Today I entered it from the west in a tank."

CHAPTER 4: FIGHTING SEASON

1.   Mark Smalley, "Colour Barred?," BBC, September 11, 2006.
2.   Quoted in Emma Elms, "The Loved Ones Left Behind," *Daily Express*, November 9, 2009.

CHAPTER 5: THE AFGHAN FACTOR

1.   The first company commander of IX Company, known in the Second World War as One Company, 2nd Battalion, was Captain Cyril Heber-Percy, who said after helping evacuate the Dutch royal family in May 1940: "War is more exciting than fox hunting." The following month, his company headquarters came under fire, and it was noticed that there was a spy signaling to the Germans from a church tower. When small-arms fire failed to dislodge him, Heber-Percy turned an anti-tank gun on the tower, destroying it and killing the spy. Four years later, Heber-Percy was a lieutenant colonel commanding the 1st Battalion at Montchamp. He was at the forefront of an attack on German tanks when he was shot and wounded by a sniper dressed in civilian clothes and firing from a church tower. "That was his last shot, but he had wounded a very important person, and needless to say justifiable retribution was dealt to this sniper," Company Sergeant Major Edward Edwards 14 later recalled. Other officers of the original IX Company formed in 1939 included Lieutenant Baron John de Rutzen, a poet who was killed in Italy in 1944, and Second Lieutenant Nigel Fisher, later a Conservative MP.
2.   Mark Thompson and Aryn Baker, "A New General, and a New War, in Afghanistan," *Time*, July 10, 2009.

CHAPTER 6: BARMA INSHALLAH

1. The main force at Rorke's Drift was drawn from the 24th Regiment of Foot, which later became the South Wales Borderers. Only thirty-two of those who fought were Welshmen, but the 1964 film *Zulu* cemented the popular myth of the battle as a Welsh victory. In one scene, two Welshmen called Jones address each other as "Seven One Six" and "Five Nine Three"—the last three digits of their service numbers. When Corporal Scheiss, of the Natal National Contingent, asks them whether they have names instead of numbers, Jones 593 replied: "This is a Welsh regiment, man—though there are some foreigners from England in it, mind. I am Jones from Builth Cynwyd. He is Jones from Builth Wells. There are four more Joneses in C Company. Confusing, isn't it, Dutchy?"

2. Gallimore might have consoled himself that previous Welsh Guards officers had turned a blind eye to the killing of prisoners or had even ordered executions themselves. In France in 1940, members of the 2nd Battalion caught a priest with a Bible in his cassock with lots of notes in it that were assessed by the intelligence officer as information of use to the Germans. Decades later, Lieutenant Colonel Alexander Stanier, commanding the 2nd Battalion, recalled: "I believe the troops threw him into the drain. I should think he was drowned. The sort of thing you don't ask about." On the jetty at Boulogne, Major James Windsor Lewis, father of the Gallimore-appointed honorary captain of X Company in 2009, was a company commander in the 2nd Battalion when a fifth-columnist who had been shooting Welsh Guardsmen was apprehended. Guardsman Sydney Pritchard of Aberdare wrote in his 2007 memoir that "Major Lewis gave the order to execute him and throw him into the sea."

3. Emma Elms, "The Loved Ones Left Behind," *Daily Express*, November 9, 2009.

CHAPTER 7: FLASHMAN'S FORT

1. Peek was airing the sentiments of many a determined infantryman before him. At Mortaldje in July 1916, Second Lieutenant James Dudley Ward recounted in his diary how Corporal J. Harris of Newport and Private William Jones 89 of Port Talbot had pursued three fleeing Germans. They captured two, and Harris bayoneted one to death. Ward

then witnessed Harris and Jones "having an argument over two wretched Huns, who were screaming and crouching by them, with their hands up and yelling 'Mercy' in a hysterical panting way." Jones 89 was shouting: "You killed one. Why shouldn't I have one too?" Harris had grabbed Jones 89 and was "explaining in forcible miner language" that the Germans should be taken back as prisoners and he was not to bayonet them. Dudley Ward intervened, saving the two Germans. Afterwards, the young officer found Jones advancing alone up the trench towards the enemy line "looking for more Germans ... he was plodding along in a crouching attitude, and his bayonet flashing about in front of him." Jones 89 was awarded the Military Medal for his actions that day. Two months later, he died of wounds sustained at the Somme.

CHAPTER 9: MYSTERY JUNCTION

1. Quoted in Walter Laqueur, *Guerrilla: A Historical and Critical Study* (Boston: Little, Brown, 1976), 40–41.

2. Harman's actions at Haji Alem had echoes of those of Major Hugh Lister, a Welsh Guards officer who was killed by machine gun fire outside Hechtel in Belgium in 1944. Lister was a Church of England clergyman who decided to join the army as a regular officer rather than as a chaplain because he believed he could help his men more that way. He had also been fascinated with the idea of being a soldier since reading as a child *The Life of Lord Roberts* by Sir George Forrest, a biography of the victor of the Battle of Kandahar in 1880. A trade union organizer in the East End of London, Lister had unusually left-wing views for a Guards officer. He caused a stir at Wormwood Scrubs when he arrived there in full uniform to visit a friend who was a conscientious objector. Lister became an accomplished officer and rose to command the 1st Battalion's Support Company. Lieutenant Robert Mosse, one of his platoon commanders, wrote that Lister had a theory of "testing fire" that "if he just walked up the road then the enemy would be so astounded that anybody shooting at him would miss with their first shots, which would enable him to get clear and us to identify the enemy position." It was common for Lister to walk out into the open with a near-certainty of being attacked. "Nobody else would dare to do it. Hugh would say, 'Well let's see if there are any enemy here.' We'd all be

peering around the corner, looking over the wall or something. He'd walk right up the middle while we were sweating back there watching him."

3.   During the First World War, eight men from Treherbert served in the Welsh Guards, one of whom was killed and four of whom, including Guardsman Dai Jones 92, a Welsh rugby international and miner, were wounded. Men from Treherbert also served in the Welsh Guards during the Second World War. Among them was Guardsman William "Wacky" Jones 43, killed near Dunkirk in 1940. In his memoirs, Guardsman Bill Williams 36 remembered: "Poor Wack, he was from Treherbert, dead as mutton, shot through the neck. I lifted him, took his bandolier and the blood spurted through the open wound in his neck and drenched my own uniform. I propped him up as decently as I could and left him in the bottom of the trench." Treherbert's links with the Welsh Guards and its wars are not unusual. War memorials show a similar pattern in numerous villages across Wales.

CHAPTER 13: ON THE CANAL

1.   Arnold Fletcher, *Afghanistan: Highway of Conquest* (New York: Cornell University Press, 1965), 9.

CHAPTER 14: TOP COVER

1.   Reverence for the remains of a dead comrade, no matter how gruesome the situation, is universal among soldiers. In France in 1940, Guardsman Bill Williams 36 witnessed Guardsman Robert Jones 10, from Cardiff, get killed by a German tank shell and heavy machine gun. He later recalled in his memoir: "When the dust settled I crawled over, gathered his torn limbs into a respectable pile and placed his steel helmet over his sightless blue eyes."

2.   Blair was educated at Radley, as was Thorneloe.

CHAPTER 15: REGRET TO INFORM

1.   Sandy Malcolm's family was steeped in Welsh Guards tradition. Billy Malcolm, his grandfather, commanded all three battalions of the Welsh Guards at different times and spent five years as a POW in Germany after being captured at Dunkirk in 1940. James Malcolm, his father, commanded the Welsh Guards from 1969 to 1971 and later became

regimental lieutenant colonel. The Malcolms had the unique distinction of having had three generations command the Welsh Guards at the Trooping of the Color.

2. In the past, the Welsh Guards had certainly been welcoming of those with an artistic temperament. In October 1939, Rex Whistler, an accomplished painter, had followed up an interview with the regimental colonel of the Welsh Guards with a letter decorated by sketches, including one of a skull in a German helmet, in which he made a successful plea to be accepted. "I do naturally realise that drawing or painting can be of very little use at such a time as this but I had faintly hoped that there might be occasion—just now and then—in which I would be of more use than the man who couldn't draw at all," he wrote. While waiting for the Normandy invasion, Lieutenant Rex Whistler commissioned his village blacksmith to make a metal container to fix on his Cromwell tank turret to carry his paints and brushes. He also painted a phoenix on the canvas muzzle of another tank. On July 18, 1944, Whistler died instantly when he was hit by a mortar-bomb fragment after he had dismounted from his Cromwell to untangle some telephone wire at Emiéville. A copy of Whistler's letter to the regimental colonel hung in the Welsh Guards officers' mess in 2009.

3. In October 1917, the Reverend Miles Staveley Oldham, attached to the Welsh Guards on the western front, wrote to Second Lieutenant Christopher Tennant's mother, whose son had been buried in a row along with seven fellow Welsh Guardsmen. Each grave was marked by a simple wooden cross, and Oldham wrote: "I think it is one of the good points out here that officers and men are treated exactly alike when it comes to their last earthly incident."

4. In a letter to the father of Captain David Elliot, killed on Monte Cerasola in Italy in 1944, Lieutenant Colonel Albert Bankier, commanding the 3rd Battalion, Welsh Guards, wrote: "He was buried on the mountain and at some later date will be buried with all Welsh Guardsmen in a cemetery which we shall create. Personally I would much rather be left on the mountain; it is a lovely place except for this bloody war." Captain Elliot now rests in Cassino Cemetery.

CHAPTER 16: MEN OF HARLECH

1. This version, taken from the 1964 film *Zulu*, was sung at all the funerals of Welsh Guardsmen killed in Afghanistan in 2009.

2. In addition to that of Rupert Thorneloe MBE, in 2010 the Commanding Officers Memorial in the chapel at Sandhurst contained the names of seven lieutenant colonels killed on active service while leading their battalions: Geoffrey Hildebrand DSO, 12th Anti Tank Regiment, Royal Artillery, killed at Pardes Hanna, Palestine, April 6, 1948; Kingsley Foster DSO OBE, 1st Battalion, Royal Northumberland Fusiliers, killed at the Battle of the Imjin River, April 25, 1951; Alan Forestier-Walker MBE, 1st Battalion, 7th Gurkha Rifles, killed at Negri Sembilan, Malaya, February 3, 1954; Ian Corden-Lloyd OBE MC, 2nd Battalion, Royal Green Jackets, killed near Jonesborough, Co Armagh, Northern Ireland, February 17, 1978; David Blair, 1st Battalion, Queen's Own Highlanders, killed at Warrenpoint, Co Down, Northern Ireland, August 27, 1979; Herbert Jones VC, 2nd Battalion, the Parachute Regiment, killed at the Battle of Goose Green, Falkland Islands, May 28, 1982.

3. Music and song has long been a tradition in the Welsh Guards, just as it has been in Wales. After the attack on Gouzeaucourt Ridge in December 1917, the Welsh Guards, who had sustained 278 casualties, sang: "In the sweet bye and bye, We shall meet on that beautiful shore." An officer who heard them remembered: "To those listening silently, the song was a triumphal tribute to the indomitable spirit of the Welshmen ... in song, these men were showing yet again in their traditional manner that Welshmen are a people whom no terrible power can still for long." During the evacuation from Dunkirk in May 1940, David Lewis, from Caersws, later to become acting company sergeant major of the Prince of Wales's Company, could see burning petrol and ammunition dumps behind him and the roads ablaze as shells landed. "It was like a nightmare from Dante's Inferno," he recalled. "Here were troops sheltering in the sand dunes, bombed almost continuously. Suddenly, incredibly, the sound of singing—*She was only a bird in a gilded cage*—one of the company's favourite songs." Alistair Ritchie, a Scots Guardsman and friend of Thorneloe's father, remembered the Welsh Guardsmen

teaching him how to sing "Land of My Fathers," the Welsh national anthem, in Normandy in 1944.

4.   Richard Pendlebury and Jamie Wiseman, "Shattered in the Shadow of Death," *Daily Mail*, July 4, 2009.

5.   The returning of a dead man's effects had always been carried out punctiliously. On September 5, 1917 Captain Arthur Gibbs of the Welsh Guards wrote to Second Lieutenant Tennant's mother: "I am sending home in a registered parcel his small belongings which were on him. Wrist watch, identity disc, pen, diary, flask, pipe, map, compass, cigarette case, whistle, writing pad." On April 18, 1974, the parents of Guardsman David Roberts 04, from Holywell in North Wales, received his possessions. He had been killed by a radio-controlled IED placed in a beer keg in Crossmaglen in South Armagh. The items included an electric iron, set of darts, Soldier's Testament, tobacco pouch, pipe, bar of Lifebuoy soap, eight Player's No. 6 cigarette coupons, and a Tartan holdall.

CHAPTER 17: BATTLE SHOCK

1.   "Hero Soldier's Heartbreaking Last Letters Home Days before his Death," *Sunday People*, August 2, 2009.

2.   Contemporary accounts of battle tend to portray every soldier as a hero. But this has been no truer in Helmand than in any other war. At San Marco in Italy in 1944, Lieutenant Philip Brutton of the 3rd Battalion, Welsh Guards, was leading an attack against the Germans when a corporal in charge of a section suddenly asked him who should look after the body of a guardsman who had just been killed. Brutton viewed the timing of the question as tantamount to refusing to go forward in the face of the enemy, a capital offense. "It was, therefore, not the Germans who nearly killed the corporal but his platoon commander," Brutton recalled in his 1992 memoir. "My Tommy gun was slung over my right shoulder, naturally cocked and fully loaded. I brought it up slightly to shoot him on the spot. He saw the movement and froze. I then thought better of it."

3.   Desertion and battle shock among soldiers are seldom talked about but are an inevitable part of every war. In 1945, Lieutenant Philip Brutton experienced instances of each on consecutive days while serving in Italy with the 3rd Battalion of the Welsh Guards. In his diary entry for

February 7, he recorded: "Guardsman S … deserts to enemy. Probably temporarily insane." The guardsman had jumped out of his slit trench and run, unarmed, towards the German lines. Lieutenant Colonel Jocelyn Gurney ordered his brigade's artillery, mortars, and machine guns to open fire on the point at which the guardsman was likely to cross the lines. Brutton listened in on his radio as Gurney shouted: "Kill him! Kill him! Kill him!" The guardsman, however, managed to double back and evade death and capture. Guardsman S was eventually picked up by the Military Police in Rome, and it transpired that he had fled because he had been threatened by his comrades after being accused of stealing their kit. On February 8, Brutton was sitting in his slit trench with his sergeant when "Corporal P" requested leave to speak to him— an approach that Brutton noted "was considerably formal, given the circumstances, even for the Brigade of Guards." The corporal was standing to attention above the trench and in considerable danger from enemy fire. When Brutton got up, the corporal saluted him and said: "My nerves have gone, Sir. I ask leave to report to the Medical Officer." Brutton granted him permission, and Corporal P saluted again, turned smartly to his right, and marched off.

CHAPTER 18: ONE SHOT, TWO KILLS

1. Quoted in Stanley Karnow, *Vietnam: A History* (New York: Viking, 1991).

2. According to Michael Shelden, Orwell's biographer, the accurate quotation from Orwell is from an essay on Rudyard Kipling published in *Horizon* magazine in 1942: "He sees clearly that men can only be highly civilised while other men, inevitably less civilised, are there to guard and feed them."

3. Paul McNamara, "Britain's Top Soldier in Afghanistan Tells of his Family's Nightmare," *News of the World*, November 15, 2009.

4. Miles Amoore,"Blood, Bombs and Boys' Talk" *Sunday Times*, December 13, 2009.

5. In 2010, BCB International, a Cardiff-based firm, began to manufacture Kevlar-lined "Blast Boxers" to help assuage such fears.

6. Kim Sengupta, "In the Field with the Troops in Helmand," *Independent*, August 18, 2009.

EPILOGUE

1. In addition to Lieutenant Colonel Foster, killed on April 25, 1951, Major Colin Milward, commanding S Company, and Lieutenant Gerald Fitz-Gibbon, commanding the Assault Pioneer Platoon, were killed at Kan-dong on January 3, 1951.

Bibliography

AFGHANISTAN

Barthorp, Michael. *Afghan Wars and the North-West Frontier, 1839–1947.* London: Cassell, 1982.

Bellew, H. W. *The Races of Afghanistan: Being a Brief Account of the Principal Nations Inhabiting that Country.* Calcutta: Thacker, Spink, 1880.

Berntsen, Gary, and Ralph Pezzullo. *Jawbreaker: The Attack on Bin Laden and Al-Qaeda.* New York: Crown, 2005.

Caroe, Olaf. *The Pathans.* London: Oxford University Press, 1958.

Chayes, Sarah. *The Punishment of Virtue: Inside Afghanistan after the Taliban.* New York: Penguin Press, 2006.

Coll, Steve. *Ghost Wars.* New York: Penguin Press, 1984.

Crile, George. *Charlie Wilson's War: The Extraordinary Story of the Largest Covert Operation in History.* New York: Atlantic Monthly Press, 2003.

Dorn, Bernhard. *The History of the Afghans.* Lahore: Vanguard Books, 1999.

Dupree, Louis. *Afghanistan.* Princeton, NJ: Princeton University Press, 1980.

Dupree, Nancy Hatch. *An Historical Guide to Afghanistan.* Kabul: Afghan Tourist Organization, 1977.

Ewans, Martin. *Afghanistan: A Short History of Its People and Politics.* New York: Perennial, 2001.

Feifer, Gregory. *The Great Gamble: The Soviet War in Afghanistan.* New York: HarperCollins, 2009.

Fergusson, James. *Taliban: The True Story of the World's Most Feared Guerrilla Fighters.* London: Bantam Press, 2010.

Fletcher, Arnold. *Afghanistan: Highway of Conquest.* New York: Cornell University Press, 1965.

Fraser-Tytler, W. K. *Afghanistan.* London: Oxford University Press, 1950.

Giustozzi, Antonio. *Decoding the New Taliban: Insights from the Afghan Field.* New York: Columbia University Press, 2009.

———. *Empires of Mud: Wars and Warlords in Afghanistan.* New York: Columbia University Press, 2009.

———. *Koran, Kalashnikov and Laptop: The Neo-Taliban Insurgency in Afghanistan.* New York: Columbia University Press, 2008.

Griffiths, John C. *Afghanistan.* New York: Praeger, 1967.

Hafvenstein, Joel. *Opium Season: A Year on the Afghan Frontier.* Guilford, CT: Lyons Press, 2007.

Hodgskin, Captain Edward. Untitled and unpublished draft account of 2nd Royal Tank Regiment tour in Helmand 2009. N.p.

Hopkirk, Peter. *The Great Game: The Struggle for Empire in Central Asia.* New York: Kodansha America, 1994.

Isby, David. *Afghanistan: Graveyard of Empires: A New History of the Borderlands.* New York: Pegasus, 2010.

Jalali, Ali Ahmad, and Lester W. Grau. *Afghan Guerrilla Warfare: In the Words of the Mujahideen Fighters.* Minneapolis: Zenith Press, 2001.

Jones, Paul S. *Afghanistan Venture.* San Antonio, TX: Naylor, 1956.

Jones, Seth. *In the Graveyard of Empires: America's War in Afghanistan.* New York: Norton, 2009.

Junger, Sebastian. *War.* New York: Twelve, 2010.

Kakar, Hassan M. *A Political and Diplomatic History of Afghanistan, 1863–1901.* Leiden: Brill, 2006.

Macrory, Patrick. *Signal Catastrophe: The Story of the Disastrous Retreat from Kabul, 1842.* London: Hodder & Stoughton, 1966.

Michener, James A. *Caravans.* New York: Random House, 1963.

O'Ballance, Edgar. *Afghan Wars: Battles in a Hostile Land, 1839 to the Present.* London: Oxford University Press, 2003.

Omrani, Bijan, Matthew Leeming, and Elizabeth Chatwin. *Afghanistan: A Companion and Guide.* New York: Odyssey, 2005.

Peters, Gretchen. *Seeds of Terror: How Heroin is Bankrolling the Taliban and Al Qaeda.* New York: Thomas Dunne, 2009.

Rashid, Ahmed. *Taliban.* New Haven, CT: Yale University Press, 2000.

Schultheis, Rob. *Night Letters: Inside Wartime Afghanistan.* New York: Orion Books, 1992.

Stephens, Ian. *Horned Moon: An Account of a Journey through Pakistan, Kashmir and Afghanistan.* London: Chatto & Windus, 1953.

Stevens, Ira, and K. Tarzai. *Afghanistan: Economics of Agricultural Production in Helmand Valley.* Washington, D.C.: Agency for International Development, Department of State, 1965.

Stewart, Rory. *The Places in Between.* London: Picador, 2004.

Sykes, Percy. *A History of Afghanistan,* vols. 1 and 2. New Delhi, Munshiram Manoharlal, 2002.

Toynbee, Arnold J. *Between Oxus and Jumna: A Journey in India, Pakistan and Afghanistan.* London: Oxford University Press, 1961.

Zaeef, Abdul Salam. *My Life with the Taliban.* London: Hurst, 2010.

ARTICLES

Bethell, John. "Accidental Counterinsurgents: Nad E Ali, Hybrid Warfare and the Future of the British Army." *British Army Review* (Summer 2010).

Betz, David, and Anthony Cormack. "Iraq, Afghanistan and British Strategy." *Orbis* (Spring 2009).

Crawshaw, Michael. "Running a Country: The British Colonial Experience and Its Relevance to Present Day Concerns." *Shrivenham Papers* (April 2007).

Cullather, Nick. "From New Deal to New Frontier in Afghanistan: Modernization in a Buffer State." Project on the Cold War as Global Conflict, International Center for Advanced Studies at New York University, August 2002.

Dressler, Jeffrey A. "Securing Helmand: Understanding and Responding to the Enemy." Institute for the Study of War (September 2009).

Farrell, Theo. "Appraising Moshtarak: The Campaign in Nad-e-Ali District, Helmand." Royal United Services Institute, June 2010.

Farrell, Theo, and Stuart Gordon. "COIN Machine: The British Military in Afghanistan." *RUSI Journal* (June 2009).

Flynn, Mike. "Fixing Intel: A Blueprint for Making Intelligence Relevant in Afghanistan." Center for a New American Security, January 2010.

Galbraith, Peter W. "What I Saw at the Afghan Election." *Washington Post*, October 4, 2009.

Gallimore, Robert. "'No Better Friend No Worse Enemy': X Company, 1st Battalion Welsh Guards Fighting with Afghans and United States Marines." *Guards Magazine* (Spring 2010).

Gibbs, Philip. "Veil Lifted from the Record of War's Agony." *New York Times*, April 6, 1919.

Gidlow-Jackson, Mark. "Reaction to Contact at the Tactical Level: Firepower v. Manoeuvre." *Infantryman*, 2010.

Harris, Giles. "Fighting the COIN Battle at Company Level." *Infantryman*, 2010.

Hein, David. "Hugh Lister (1901–44): A Modern Saint?," *Theology* 103 (2000).

Holloway, Adam. "In Blood Stepp'd So Far? Towards Realism in Afghanistan." Center for Policy Studies, October 2009.

Johnson, Thomas H. "The Taliban Insurgency and an Analysis of *Shabnamah* (Night Letters)." *Small Wars and Insurgencies*, September 2007.

King, Anthony. "Understanding the Helmand Campaign: British Military Operations in Afghanistan." *International Affairs* 86, no. 2 (2010).

Launders, Ed. "Battle Group Operations in Afghanistan: An Operations Officer's Perspective." *The Infantryman*, 2010

Marston, Daniel. "British Operations in Helmand Afghanistan." *Small Wars Journal* (September 2008).

Rigden, I. A. "The British Approach to Counter-Insurgency: Myths, Realities, and Strategic Challenges." U.S. Army War College, Carlisle, Pennsylvania, March 2008.

Scott, Richard B. "Tribal & Ethnic Groups in the Helmand Valley." *Asia Society* (Spring 1980).

Xinhua General News Service. "Afghan Moslem Guerrillas Seize Government Fort." October 23, 1981.

BRITISH ARMY IN HELMAND

Allan, Alexander. *Afghanistan: A Tour of Duty*. London: Third Millennium, 2009.

Beattie, Doug. *Task Force Helmand: A Soldier's Story of Life, Death and Combat on the Afghan Front Line*. London: Simon & Schuster, 2009.

Bishop, Patrick. *3 PARA: Afghanistan, Summer 2006*. London: HarperPress, 2007.

———. *Ground Truth: 3 PARA Return to Afghanistan*. London: Harper-Press, 2009.

Docherty, Leo. *Desert of Death: A Soldier's Journey from Iraq to Afghanistan*. London: Faber & Faber, 2007.

Doherty, Richard. *Helmand Mission: With the Royal Irish Battlegroup in Afghanistan, 2008*. Barnsley: Pen and Sword, 2009.

Fergusson, James. *A Million Bullets: The Real Story of the British Army in Afghanistan*. London: Bantam Press, 2008.

Grey, Stephen. *Operation Snakebite: The Explosive True Story of an Afghan Desert Siege*. London: Viking, 2009.

Hennessey, Patrick. *Junior Officers' Reading Club: Killing Time and Fighting Wars*. London: Allen Lane, 2009.

Kemp, Richard, and Chris Hughes. *Attack State Red*. London: Michael Joseph, 2009.

Kiley, Sam. *Desperate Glory: At War in Helmand with Britain's 16 Air Assault Brigade*. London: Bloomsbury, 2009.

Loyn, David. *In Afghanistan: Two Hundred Years of British, Russian and American Occupation*. New York: Palgrave MacMillan, 2009.

Macy, Ed. *Apache: The Man. The Machine. The Mission. The Blazing True Story from the Heart of Afghanistan*. London: Harper Press, 2008.

Ryan, Mike. *Battlefield Afghanistan*. Stroud, Gloucestershire: Spellmount, 2007.

———. *Frontline Afghanistan*. Stroud, Gloucestershire: Spellmount, 2010.

Scott, Jake. *Blood Clot: In Combat with the Patrols Platoon, 3 Para, Afghanistan 2006*. Solihull: Helion, 2008.

Southby-Tailyour, Ewen. *3 Commando Brigade*. London: Ebury Press, 2008.

Tootal, Stuart. *Danger Close: Commanding 3 Para in Afghanistan*. London: John Murray, 2009.

Wilson, Robert. *Helmand*. London: Jonathan Cape, 2008.

FOOT GUARDS

Arkwright, Alexander Gore, Earl of Gowrie. *Welsh Guards: A Call to You*. Bournemouth: Henbest Publicity Service, 1947.

Bathurst, B. J. *Welsh Guards*. Regimental publication, 2005.

Briant, Keith. *Fighting with the Guards*. Bungay, Suffolk: Richard Clay, 1958.

Brutton, Philip. *Ensign in Italy: A Platoon Commander's Story*. London: Leo Cooper, 1992.

Dudley Ward, C. H. *History of the Welsh Guards*. John Murray, London, 1920.

———. *The Welsh Regiment of Footguards*. London: John Murray, 1936.

Dunstan, Simon. *The Guards: Britain's Household Division*. London: Windrow & Greene, 1996.

Ellis, L. F. *Welsh Guards, 1915–1965: An Informal Account of the Fifty Years*. Devonport: Hiorns & Miller, 1965.

———. *Welsh Guards at War*. Aldershot: Gale & Polden, 1946.

Headlam, Cuthbert. *History of the Guards Division in the Great War, 1915–1918*, vols. 1 and 2. London: John Murray, 1924.

Kipling, Rudyard. *The Irish Guards in the Great War*, vols. 1 and 2. London: Macmillan, 1923.

Lodge, Oliver. *Christopher: A Study in Personality*. New York: George H. Doran, 1919.

Paget, Julian. *The Story of the Guards*. San Rafael, CA: Presidio Press, 1977.

Pritchard, Sydney. *Life in the Welsh Guards, 1939–46*. Talybont: Y Lolfa Cyf, 2007.

Rettallack, John. *The Welsh Guards*. Frederick Warne, London, 1981.

Royle, Trevor. *Anatomy of a Regiment: Ceremony & Soldiering in the Welsh Guards*. London: Michael Joseph, 1990.

Spencer-Smith, Jenny. *Rex Whistler's War, 1939–July 1944: Artist into Tank Commander*. Chelsea: National Army Museum, 1994.

Stanier, Alexander. *Sammy's Wars*. N.p.: privately published, 1998.

Uloth, Rupert, ed. *Excellence in Action: A Portrait of the Guards*. London: Third Millennium, 2008.

Weston, Simon. *Walking Tall: An Autobiography*. London: Bloomsbury, 1989.

Whistler, Laurence. *Laughter and the Urn: The Life of Rex Whistler*. London: Weidenfeld & Nicolson, 1985.

Williams, Arfon. *In the Tin*. N.p.: privately published, 2005.

Williams, Bill. *Tough at the Bottom, 1939–1946*. Memoir N.p.: privately published.

GENERAL

Antelme, Felix. *In Retrospect: The Story of a Family*. N.p.: privately published, 2004.

Arkinstall, Michael. *Seeking the Red Dragon*. N.p.: privately published, 2007.

Cameron, Alice Mackenzie. *In Pursuit of Justice: The Story of Hugh Lister and His Friends in Hackney Wick*. London: S. C. M. Press, 1946.

Morris, Jan. *The Matter of Wales: Epic Views of a Small Country*. London: Oxford University Press, 1984.

Sasek, Miroslav. *This Is London*. New York: Universe, 1959.

MILITARY

Baker, Mark. *Nam: The Vietnam War in the Words of the Men and Women Who Fought There*. New York: William Morrow, 1981.

Barbusse, Henri. *Under Fire*. Translation. London: J. M. Dent & Sons, 1926.

Bausch, Richard. *Peace: A Novel*. New York: Knopf, 2008.

Beevor, Antony. *D-Day: The Battle for Normandy*. New York: Viking, 2009.

Bentley, James, ed. *Some Corner of a Foreign Field: Poetry of the Great War*. London: Little, Brown, 1992.

Bourne, Peter G., ed. *The Psychology and Physiology of Stress: With Reference to Special Studies of the Vietnam War*. New York: Academic Press, 1969.

Bowden, Mark. *Black Hawk Down: A Story of Modern War*. New York: Atlantic Monthly Press, 1999.

Buck, Rinker. *Shane Comes Home*. New York: William Morrow, 2005.

Burke, Gregory. *The National Theatre of Scotland's Black Watch*. London: Faber & Faber, 2007.

Caputo, Philip. *A Rumor of War*. New York: Holt, Rinehart & Winston, 1977.

Churchill, Winston. *The Second World War: The Hinge of Fate*, vol. 4. London; Cassell, 1951.

———. *The Story of the Malakand Field Force*. London: Longmans, Green, 1898.

Clayton, Anthony. *The British Officer*. Harlow: Pearson, 2006.

Daglish, Ian. *Over the Battlefield: Operation Epsom*. Barnsley: Pen and Sword, 2007.

Dannatt, Richard. *Leading from the Front*. London: Bantam Press, 2010.

Dixon, Norman F. *On the Psychology of Military Incompetence*. London: Jonathan Cape, 1976.

Dyer, Gwynne. *War: The Lethal Custom*. Carroll & Graf, New York, 2004.

Eddy, Paul, and Magnus Linklater, with Peter Gillman. *War in the Falklands: The Full Story*. New York: Harper & Row, 1982.

Ellis, John. *The Sharp End: The Fighting Man in World War II*. New York: Scribner, 1980.

Finkel, David. *The Good Soldiers*. New York: Sarah Crichton, 2009.

Fitton, Robert A, ed. *Leadership: Quotations from the Military Tradition*. Boulder, CO: Westview Press, 1990.

Fussell, Paul. *The Great War and Modern Memory*. London: Oxford University Press, 1975.

Gibbs, Philip. *Now It Can Be Told*. New York: Harper & Brothers, 1920.

Goldman, Peter, and Tony Fuller. *Charlie Company: What Vietnam Did to Us*. New York: William Morrow, 1983.

Graves, Robert. *Goodbye to All That*. London: Cassell, 1929.

Grinker, Roy R., and John P. Spiegel. *Men under Stress*. Philadelphia: Blakiston, 1945.

Harnden, Toby. *Bandit Country: The IRA and South Armagh*. London: Hodder & Stoughton, 1999.

Hastings, Max. *The Korean War*. New York: Simon & Schuster, 1987.

Hastings, Max, and Simon Jenkins. *The Battle for the Falklands*. London: Michael Joseph, 1983.

Hedges, Chris. *War Is a Force That Gives Us Meaning*. New York: Public Affairs, 2002.

Herr, Michael. *Dispatches*. New York: Alfred Knopf, 1977.

Holden, Wendy. *Shell Shock: The Psychological Impact of War*. London: Channel Four Books, 1998.

Holmes, Richard. *Acts of War: The Behavior of Men in Battle*. New York: Free Press, 1985.

———. *Dusty Warriors: Modern Soldiers at War*. London: HarperPress, 2006.

Jolly, Rick. *Red and Green Life Machine: Diary of the Falklands Field Hospital*. London: Century, 1983.

Jones, Edgar, and Simon Wessely. *Shell Shock to PTSD: Military Psychiatry from 1900 to the Gulf War*. Hove, East Sussex: Psychology Press, 2005.

Karnow, Stanley. *Vietnam: A History*. New York: Viking, 1991.

Keane, Fergal. *Road of Bones: The Siege of Kohima, 1944*. London: HarperPress, 2010.

Kilcullen, David. *The Accidental Guerrilla: Fighting Small Wars in the Midst of a Big One*. New York: Oxford University Press, 2009.

Knightley, Phillip. *The First Casualty—From the Crimea to Vietnam: The War Correspondent as Hero, Propagandist and Myth Maker*. New York: Harcourt, Brace, Jovanovich, 1975.

Laqueur, Walter. *Guerrilla: A Historical and Critical Study*. Boston: Little, Brown, 1976.

Mailer, Norman. *The Naked and the Dead*. New York: Holt, Rinehart and Winston, 1948.

Marshall, S. L. A. *The Soldier's Load and the Mobility of a Nation*. Quantico, VA: Marine Corps Association, 1950.

Marston, Daniel, and Carter Malkasian, eds. *Counterinsurgency in Modern Warfare*. Oxford: Osprey, 2008.

McGowan, Robert, and Jeremy Hands. *Don't Cry For Me, Sergeant-Major*. London: Futura, 1983.

McNally, Tony. *Watching Men Burn: A Soldier's Story*. London, Monday Books, 2007.

Miller, David. *Commanding Officers*. London: John Murray, 2001.

Moore, Harold G., and Joseph L. Galloway. *We Were Soldiers Once ... and Young: Ia Drang—the Battle That Changed the War in Vietnam*. New York: Random House, 1992.

Moore, Michael. *Battalion at War: Singapore 1942*. Norwich: Gliddon Books, 1988.

Moyar, Mark, ed. *A Question of Command: Counterinsurgency from the Civil War to Iraq*. New Haven, CT: Yale University Press, 2009.

Norman, Michael. *These Good Men: Friendships Forged from War.* New York: Crown, 1985.

O'Brien, Tim. *If I Die in a Combat Zone: A Memoir of Vietnam.* Boston: Delacorte Press/Seymour Lawrence, 1973.

———. *The Things They Carried.* Boston: Houghton Mifflin, 1990.

Perrins, Anthony R. D. *"A Pretty Rough Do Altogether": The Fifth Fusiliers in Korea, 1950–1951.* AlnwickL Trustees of the Fusiliers Museum of Northumberland, 2004.

Pike, Hew. *From the Front Line: Family Letters and Diaries, 1900 to the Falklands and Afghanistan.* Barnsley: Pen and Sword, 2008.

Raddatz, Martha. *The Long Road Home: A Story of Family and War.* New York: Putnam, 2007.

Remarque, Erich Maria. *All Quiet on the Western Front.* London: Putnam's, 1929.

Roberts, Andrew. *Masters and Commanders: How Four Titans Won the War in the West, 1941–1945.* London: Allen Lane, 2008.

Royle, Trevor. *A Dictionary of Military Quotations.* London: Routledge, 1989.

Ryan, Cornelius. *A Bridge Too Far.* New York: Simon & Schuster, 1974.

Sebag-Montefiore, Hugh. *Dunkirk: Fight to the Last Man.* Cambridge, MA: Harvard University Press, 2006.

Sheehan, Neil. *A Bright Shining Lie.* London: Jonathan Cape, 1989.

Simkins, Peter. *Kitchener's Army: The Raising of the New Armies, 1914–1916.* Manchester: Manchester University Press, 1988.

Sledge, Michael. *Soldier Dead: How We Recover, Identify, Bury and Honor Our Military Fallen.* New York: Columbia University Press, 2005.

Southby-Tailyour, Ewen. *Reasons in Writing: A Commando's View of the Falklands War.* London: Leo Cooper, 1993.

Swofford, Anthony. *Jarhead: A Marine's Chronicle of the Gulf War and Other Battles.* New York: Scribner, 2003.

Tsouras, Peter G. *The Book of Military Quotations.* St. Paul, MN: Zenith Press, 2005.

Tuchman, Barbara. *The March of Folly: From Troy to Vietnam.* New York: Alfred Knopf, 1984.

Tupper, Benjamin. *Greetings from Afghanistan Send More Ammo: Dispatches from Taliban Country.* New York: Nal Caliber, 2010.

Urban, Mark. *Task Force Black: The Explosive True Story of the SAS and the Secret War in Iraq.* London: Little, Brown, 2010.

Wilsey, John. *H Jones VC: The Life and Death of an Unusual Hero.* London: Hutchinson, 2002.

Winter, J. M. *The Experience of World War One.* Oxford: Andromeda, 1988.

Index

M

S